Common Culture

Reading and Writing About American Popular Culture

SIXTH EDITION

Edited by

Michael Petracca
Madeleine Sorapure
University of California at Santa Barbara

Prentice Hall
Upper Saddle River   London   Singapore
Toronto   Tokyo   Sydney   Hong Kong   Mexico City

Editorial Director: Leah Jewell
Editor in Chief: Craig Campanella
Senior Acquisitions Editor: Brad Potthoff
Editorial Assistant: Gina Aloe
VP/Director of Marketing: Tim Stookesbury
Senior Marketing Manager: Sandra McGuire
Marketing Assistant: Jean-Pierre Dufresne
Assistant Managing Editor: Melissa Feimer
Text Permissions Specialist: Kathleen Karcher
Senior Operations Specialist: Sherry Lewis
Creative Director: Jayne Conte
Cover Designer: Bruce Kenselaar
Manager, Image Rights and Permissions: Zina Arabia

Manager, Visual Research: Beth Boyd-Brenzel
Manager, Cover Visual Research & Permissions: Karen Sanatar
Senior Image Permissions Coordinator: Cynthia Vincenti
Photo Researcher: Terri Stratford
Composition/Full-Service Project Management: GGS higher education resources, a division of PreMedia Global, Inc.
Printer/Binder: R.R. Donnelley & Sons Company
Cover Printer: R.R. Donnelley & Sons Company

This book was set in 10/12 Palatino.

Cover: Person in front of screen credit: Photos.com; hand holding cards: Photos.com; young woman relaxing: Photos.com; male breakdancing: Photos.com; MySpace Web site: Erik Freeland/Corbis

For permission to use copyrighted material, grateful acknowledgment is made to the copyright holders on pages 633–636, which are hereby made part of this copyright page.

Library of Congress Cataloging-in-Publication Data

Common culture : reading and writing about American popular culture / edited by Michael Petracca, Madeleine Sorapure.—6th ed.
   p. cm.
  Includes bibliographical references and index.
  ISBN 978-0-205-64577-0 (pbk.)
  1. Popular culture—United States. 2. United States—Social life and customs—1971-
3. United States—Civilization—1970- 4. Popular culture—Study and teaching—
United States. 5. United States—Social life and customs—1971—Study and teaching.
6. United States—Civilization—1970—Study and teaching. I. Petracca, Michael,
II. Sorapure, Madeleine.
  E169.Z83C65 2010
  306.0973—dc22

2008043741

10 9 8 7 6 5 4 3 2 1

Prentice Hall
is an imprint of

Student ISBN-13: 978-0-205-64577-0
ISBN-10:   0-205-64577-1
Exam ISBN-13: 978-0-205-64890-0
ISBN-10:   0-205-64890-8

www.pearsonhighered.com

For young Honeyware, who teaches
more writing in a day than I have in a lifetime.
—M.P.

For my daughter Sophia, from whom I will learn much
about popular culture (and much else) in the coming years.
—M.S.

Contents

5 Technology 357

6 Sports and Games 453

Preface

When we started teaching composition courses that examined television, pop music, movies, and other media-generated artifacts, we looked for a text that would cover a full range of topics in the field of popular culture from a variety of theoretical perspectives. We discovered that no satisfactory text existed, and therefore we began putting together assignments and reading materials to meet our needs. From this compilation *Common Culture* emerged.

The more we've taught writing courses based on popular culture, the more convinced we've become that such courses are especially appealing for students and effective in improving their critical thinking, reading, and writing skills. Students come into the writing classroom already immersed in the culture of Coldplay, YouTube, iPhone, and Wii. The advantage, then, is that we don't have to "sell" the subject matter of the course and can concentrate on the task at hand—namely, teaching students to think critically and to write clear and effective prose. Obviously, a course that panders to the lowest common denominator of students' taste would be a mindless, unproductive enterprise for all concerned. However, the underlying philosophy of a pop culture-based writing course is this: By reading, thinking, and writing about material they find inherently interesting, students develop their critical and analytical skills—skills which are, of course, crucial to their success in college.

Although students are already familiar with the many aspects of popular culture, few have directed sustained, critical thought to its influence or implications—that is, to what shopping malls might tell them about contemporary culture or to what they've actually learned from watching *South Park*. Because television shows, advertisements, and music videos, for example, are highly crafted artifacts, they are particularly susceptible to analysis; and because so much in contemporary culture is open to interpretation and controversy, students enjoy the opportunity to articulate and argue for their own interpretations of objects and institutions in the world around them.

Although popular culture is undeniably a sexy (or, at least, lively) subject, it has also, in the past two decades, become accepted as a legitimate object of academic discourse. While some may contend that it's frivolous to write a dissertation on *Buffy the Vampire Slayer*, most scholars recognize the importance of studying the artifacts and institutions of contemporary life. Popular culture is a rich field of study, drawing in researchers from a variety of disciplines. Because it is also a very inviting field of study for students, a textbook that addresses this subject in a comprehensive and challenging way will be especially appealing both to them and to their writing teachers.

Common Culture, Sixth Edition, contains an introductory chapter that walks students through one assignment—in this case, focusing on the Barbie doll—with step-by-step instruction in reading carefully and writing effectively. The chapters that follow open with a relevant and catchy cultural artifact (for example, a cartoon, an ad, an album cover) that leads into a reader-friendly, informative introduction; a selection of engaging essays on an issue of current interest in the field of pop culture; carefully constructed reading and discussion questions; and writing assignments after each reading and at the end of the chapter. This edition also contains sections on visual literacy and conducting research on popular culture, along with a selection of color and black and white images that students can analyze and enjoy.

Common Culture approaches the field of popular culture by dividing it into its constituent parts. The book contains chapters on advertising, television, music, technology, sports, and movies. Most of the chapters are divided into two parts: the first presents essays that address the topic generally, while the second offers essays that explore a specific aspect of the topic in depth. For example, in the chapter on advertising, the essays in the first group discuss theories and strategies of advertising, while later essays explore how gender is depicted in advertisements.

We've purposely chosen readings that are accessible and thought-provoking, while avoiding those that are excessively theoretical or jargon-ridden. The 44 readings in this book, 21 of which are new to the sixth edition, have the added advantage of serving as good models for students' own writing; they demonstrate a range of rhetorical approaches, such as exposition, analysis, and argumentation; and they offer varying levels of sophistication and difficulty in terms of content and style. Similarly, the suggested discussion and writing topics, including a "Thinking Rhetorically" prompt with each selection, move from relatively basic concerns to tasks that require a greater degree of critical skill. Because of this range, instructors using *Common Culture* can easily adapt the book to meet the specific needs of their students.

SUPPLEMENTARY MATERIAL FOR INSTRUCTORS AND STUDENTS

For more details on these supplements, available for college adoptions, please contact your Pearson representative.

Instructor's Manual

A comprehensive Instructor's Manual is available online and includes sample syllabi, teaching tips, and other information. Please contact your Pearson representative for access.

The NEW MyCompLab® Web Site

The new MyCompLab integrates the market-leading instruction, multimedia tutorials, and exercises for writing, grammar, and research that users have come to identify with the program with a new online composing space and new assessment tools. The result is a revolutionary application that offers a seamless and flexible teaching and learning environment built specifically for writers. Created after years of extensive research and in partnership with composition faculty and students across the country, the new MyCompLab provides help for writers in the context of their writing, with instructor and peer commenting functionality, proven tutorials and exercises for writing, grammar, and research, an e-portfolio, an assignment-builder, a bibliography tool, tutoring services, and a gradebook and course management organization created specifically for writing classes. Visit www.mycomplab http://www.mycomplab.com for more information.

ACKNOWLEDGMENTS

As California instructors and therefore participants in the growth-and-awareness movement, we'd like first to thank each other for never straying from the path of psychic goodwill and harmony, and then to thank the universe for raining beneficence and light upon this project. And while on the subject of beneficence and light, we'd like to thank our original editor, Nancy Perry, as well as Harriett Prentiss, who helped us with the second edition; Vivian Garcia, who patiently shepherded us through the third; and Karen Schultz, who worked with us on the fourth edition. We thank our current editorial team—Brad Potthoff,

Teri Stratford, Kathleen Karcher, Tracy Clough, and Kelly Keeler—for their expert assistance with this edition.

We also want to thank Muriel Zimmerman, Judith Kirscht, and Susan McLeod, former Directors of the Writing Program at UCSB, for lending moral and intellectual support to the project in its various editions. Thanks also to Larry Behrens and Sheridan Blau for lending their expertise in the area of textbook publishing. Madeleine would like to thank Bob Samuels for his many delightful contributions to the cause of *Common Culture*. Michael would like to rain appreciation upon Constance Ware for her proofreading efforts, along with her inspiring devotion to every television series available on DVD, especially *The West Wing*. Aaron Sorkin rocks, by the way, and John Spencer is sorely missed. In addition, we extend our thanks to the following reviewers: Adrielle Mitchell, Nazareth College of Rochester; Cara Blue-Adams, University of Arizona; Crystal Doss, Maple Woods Community College; Diane Goff, Lansing Community College; Holly Ryan, Duke University; Peter Dorman, Central Virginia Community College; Peyton Paxson, Middlesex Community College; Terry Spaise, University of California at Riverside.

Michael Petracca

Madeleine Sorapure

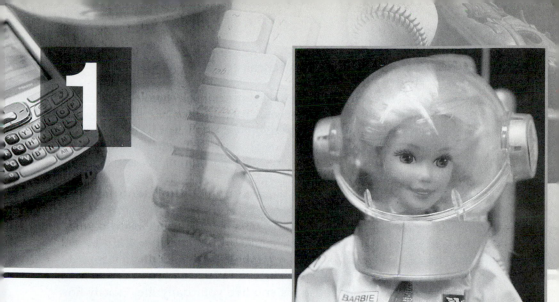

Reading and Writing About American Popular Culture

iPhone.
CSI.
Lucky Brand.
Caesar's Palace.
Tiger Woods.
MySpace.
The Daily Show.
The World Series of Poker.
The White Stripes.

If any of these names and phrases sound familiar—and it would be a great surprise if some didn't—it's because we spend our lives immersed in popular culture. There's no escaping it. Like hydrogen atoms and common cold viruses, pop culture is everywhere. You absorb it at home watching television, listening to the stereo, or reading a magazine or newspaper; passing billboards or listening to the radio on the street; chatting over coffee at work or having a burger with friends; going out to movies and dance clubs, health spas, fast-food restaurants, shopping malls and sports arenas; even noticing the graffiti that glares out at you on building facades and highway overpasses.

In fact, unless you're isolated in a mountaintop cave, you can hardly avoid the influence of popular culture. Television, radio, newspapers, and magazines shape your ideas and behavior; like family, friends, and school, pop culture is part of your learning environment, supplying ready-made images, ideas, and patterns of behavior that you draw from, consciously or unconsciously, as you live your daily life. Exactly how you learn and just what you learn may not be all that certain, but it is undeniable that popular culture is one of your most powerful teachers.

One reason to study popular culture is that by paying closer attention to this daily bombardment of information you can think more critically about how it affects you and others. You may start by asking relatively simple questions—"Do I really need my breath to be 'Mentos fresh and full of life'?"—and work your way to far more significant ones—"How can we keep young women from starving themselves in their desire to conform to the images they see in advertisements?" Analyzing pop culture with a critical eye allows you to begin to free yourself from the manipulation of the media; it is an important step toward living an examined life.

WHAT IS POPULAR CULTURE?

What do we mean by popular culture? The term may at first seem contradictory. *Popular,* in its broadest sense, means "of the people," while we often associate *culture* with refinement and intellectual superiority, "the best which has been thought and said," as Matthew Arnold put it. We might ask how culture, traditionally reserved for the elite, the educated, and the upper class, can simultaneously belong to the common mass of humanity.

One way to resolve this seeming dilemma is to think of culture in an anthropological sense, as the distinct practices, artifacts, institutions, customs, and values of a particular social group. This is the way, for instance, that we distinguish the culture of the United States in the early twenty-first century from the culture of our great grandparents or from that of societies in other times and places.

We can also define popular culture by distinguishing it from its counterparts: *high culture* and *folk culture.*

High culture consists of the artifacts traditionally considered worthy of study by university academics and other educated people: classical music by composers such as Beethoven and Brahms; "fine" art from the impressionists and expressionists; literature and philosophy written by the likes of Shakespeare and Sartre.

At the other end of the spectrum, folk culture refers to artifacts created by a specific community or ethnic group, usually a relatively isolated nontechnological society such as the pygmies of Africa's Ituri Forest or certain communities in our own Appalachian Mountains. While high culture is primarily preserved and studied in the academy, folk culture is generally transmitted through oral communication; both, however, place a high value on tradition, on artifacts produced in the past, and on the shared history of the community.

By contrast, popular culture encompasses the most immediate and contemporary elements in our lives—elements that are often subject to rapid changes in a highly technological world in which people are brought closer and closer by the ubiquitous mass media. Pop culture offers a common ground as the most visible and pervasive level of culture in a given society. If the Metropolitan Opera House represents high culture, then Madison Square Garden represents pop. If the carefully crafted knives used in Asian cooking rely on a folk tradition, then the Veg-O-Matic is their pop counterpart.

Several other terms help us establish a working definition of popular culture. *Mass culture* refers to information we receive through print and electronic media. While mass culture is often denigrated as juvenile or "low," it has to be treated as an important component of popular culture by virtue of the immense size of its audience. The terms *subculture* and *counterculture,* on the other hand, suggest a desire to resist the pressures, implied or explicit, to conform to a common culture. Subcultures are specific segments of society outside the core of dominant culture. Minority groups in the United States might be called subcultures, just as certain groups such as artists, homosexuals, lawyers, or teenagers can be thought of as having cultural markers distinct from the broader culture. A counterculture, on the other hand, is a group or movement that defines itself specifically as opposing or subverting the dominant culture. Hippies of the 1960s and punk rockers of the 1980s defined themselves as countercultural groups.

Although we may place ourselves in specific folk or high cultures, subcultures, or countercultures, we are still aware of and immersed in the broader popular culture simply by virtue of living in society. As Edward Jay Whetmore notes,[1] "Popular culture represents a common

3

---

[1]Whetmore, Edward Jay. *Mediamerica: Form, Content, and Consequence of Mass Communication.* Belmont, CA: Wadsworth, 1989.

denominator, something that cuts across most economic, social, and educational barriers." If the notion of culture reflects a certain degree of social stratification and differentiation, then popular culture represents the elements of everyday life, the artifacts and institutions shared by a society, and a body of common knowledge.

Another distinguishing characteristic of popular culture is its transitory nature. New images appear on our TV screens, replacing the popular images of years or seasons before; new phrases supersede former favorites in our popular lexicon; unknown entertainers become celebrities overnight, while others fade just as quickly from the spotlight. Beyoncé takes the place of Britney, who took the place of Madonna, who took the place of Gidget. *The Bachelor* replaces *A Change of Heart*, which replaced *Studs*, which replaced *Singled Out*, which took over from *The Dating Game*; the expression "Just do it!" was for the 1990s and 2000s what "Ring around the collar!" was for the 1970s.

Interestingly, if an icon of popular culture survives, it can often make the leap into high culture. For example, Wilkie Collins's nineteenth-century horror stories were read as avidly as Stephen King's novels are today. His works survive among today's elite audiences but are virtually unknown to most popular audiences. We might ask then, what of contemporary popular culture might survive beyond the immediate here and now and ultimately speak to future audiences at a higher, more specialized level?

What, then, is pop culture? Although it's notoriously difficult to define, some elements of a definition emerge from this discussion: pop culture is the shared knowledge and practices of a specific group at a specific time. Because of its commonality, pop culture both reflects and influences people's way of life; because it is linked to a specific time and place, pop culture is transitory, subject to change, and often an initiator of change.

WHY STUDY POPULAR CULTURE?

Though pop culture is increasingly accepted as a legitimate object of academic inquiry, educators still debate whether it should be studied. Some critics contend that it would be more valuable to study the products of high culture—Shakespeare rather than Spielberg, Eliot rather than Elvis. Their arguments often center on the issue of *quality*, as they assert that pop culture, transitory and often trendy, lacks the lasting value and strong artistic merit of high culture. Further, they argue that, because pop appeals to a mass audience rather than an educated elite, it is necessarily of low quality, no better than average. Although few critics of pop culture deny its pervasive influence, many argue that this influence should be considered negative, and they point to the violence and sexual explicitness of song lyrics, television programs, and movies, as well as to the triviality and downright foolishness of many popular trends. Pop culture debases us, these critics contend, turning us into passive recipients of low-quality goods, distracting us from higher pursuits.

It's important to note that very few proponents of pop culture—pop cultists, as Marshall Fishwick[2] calls them—take a wholesale, uncritical approach and approve all things popular. Many, for example, accept the argument that products with mass appeal are often qualitatively inferior to those intended for an educated, elite audience. However, pop cultists remind us that the gap between the two isn't always so wide; that the same basic activities of creation, refinement, and reception are involved in both popular and high culture; and that, as we've noted, the "popular" works of one era can become the "classics" of another.

Moreover, pop cultists argue for the validity of studying MTV, *The National Enquirer,* video games, and the Miss America Pageant because such mass phenomena serve as a kind of mirror in which we can discern much about ourselves. George Lipsitz,[3] for instance, suggests that "perhaps the most important facts about people have always been encoded within the ordinary and the commonplace." And as Ray Browne,[4] a noted scholar of pop culture, puts it, "Popular culture is a very important segment of our society. The contemporary scene is holding us up to ourselves to see; it can tell us who we are, what we are, and why."

We see reflected in pop culture certain standards and commonly held beliefs about beauty, success, love, or justice. We also see reflected there important social contradictions and conflicts—the tension between races, genders, or generations, for example. To find out about ourselves, then, we can turn to our own popular products and pastimes.

Another argument for studying popular culture focuses on the important influence it exerts on us. The media and other pop culture components are part of the fund of ideas and images that inform our daily activities, sometimes exerting a more compelling influence than family or friends, school or work. When we play sports, we mimic the gestures and movements of professional athletes; we learn to dance

---

[2]Browne, Ray B., and Marshall Fishwick. *Symbiosis: Popular Culture and Other Fields.* Bowling Green, OH: Bowling Green University Press, 1988.

[3]Lipsitz, George. *Time Passages: Collective Memory and American Popular Culture.* Minneapolis: University of Minnesota Press, 1990.

[4]Browne, Ray B., and Marshall Fishwick. *Symbiosis: Popular Culture and Other Fields.* Bowling Green, OH: Bowling Green University Press, 1988.

from the videos on MTV; we even name our children after popular television characters. More importantly, we discover role models; we learn lessons about villainy and heroism, love and relationships, acceptable and unacceptable behavior; we see interactions with people from other cultures. Even if popular culture is merely low-quality amusement or a means of escaping the demands of the "real" world, it delivers important messages that we may internalize and later act on—for better or for worse. We should examine and analyze pop culture, then, in order to assess—and sometimes resist—its influences.

The readings and assignments in *Common Culture* give you the chance to explore these issues and determine for yourself the role of popular culture in shaping society and in shaping you as an individual. The book includes chapters on important components of popular culture: advertising, television, music, technology, sports, and movies. You may already know quite a lot about some of these topics, and you may have relatively little interest in or exposure to others. Either way, as an engaged participant or a disinterested observer, you can bring your critical skills to bear on phenomena of the contemporary world. The readings and assignments encourage you to observe carefully, to question, and to construct and defend your own interpretations of some of the institutions and events, the beliefs and practices, the media and the messages in your everyday life.

Before beginning, we will look at methods of reading and writing that will help you participate fully and critically in reaching the goals of this book.

ACTIVE READING

We've discussed the importance of paying attention to the "common culture" that surrounds you in order to recognize its meanings and influences on your life. In this section, we present specific reading strategies that you can apply both to pop culture and to the essays in this book. Whether you're watching TV or reading an essay about TV, the habit of active, engaged interpretation will make the experience much more worthwhile. While you may have been encouraged to be an active reader of print material, the essays throughout this book also encourage you to be an active reader of the culture around you, including the images in which popular culture immerses you. We use the term *reading* here to apply both to texts and images, although in a later section we suggest specific strategies for reading and interpreting images.

There's a crucial difference between passively receiving and actively reading. Passively ingesting information requires very little effort or interest, and it gives very little in terms of reward or stimulation. Active reading demands more of your time, effort, and thought, but it is ultimately much more useful in helping you develop a better understanding of ideas.

Although reading a text or an image is generally a solitary activity, it helps to think of active reading as a discussion or dialogue with another person. You look and listen carefully; you compare what the person tells you to what you already know; you question statements that strike you as complicated, confusing, or incorrect; you identify ideas that are particularly interesting and important to you; you respond with ideas of your own. As a result of your active participation, you come away with new insights and a clearer sense of your own position. You may even be stimulated to seek out more information from other sources in order to clarify your thoughts.

When you read actively—whether printed texts or visual products of popular culture—you use very similar strategies, questioning and responding and speculating about what you're reading. You are no longer a disinterested bystander simply "listening in"; rather you are a participant who is energetically engaged with an author's ideas.

Strategies for Actively Reading a Text

Active reading involves a number of specific stages and strategies. In the **preparatory** stage you develop a general sense of what the essay will be about. In the **reading** stage, you begin the actual dialogue with the author by paying close attention to what he or she has written, identifying key points, responding to certain ideas, and asking questions. Next comes the **rereading** stage, in which you go back through the essay to get a clear and firm understanding of what you've read. Finally, in the **reviewing** stage, you take time to draw conclusions, evaluate the author's position, and develop your own responses; often you'll want to go back to the essay and read certain sections even more carefully or to turn to other sources to help you formulate your response. In the actual practice of active reading, these four stages circle back on one another as well as spiral outward, prompting you to do further reading and exploration.

As you see, actively reading a text is quite different from passively receiving or consuming information. By reading actively, you'll be able to clarify and develop your own ideas and your responses to the influences operating on you in your everyday life. You can become a more proficient and accomplished writer, increasing the range and precision of your vocabulary, using different options for constructing sentences and paragraphs, creating different stylistic effects, and, in general, improving your "feel" for written language.

An Active Reading Casebook: Three Selections
About Barbie

This section includes three reading selections—a poem and two essays about the Barbie doll—that demonstrate the strategies of active reading and suggest the kind of reading you'll be doing in later chapters. In the color insert at the center of the book, you will find two images of Barbie (p. CI-1) that you can interpret using strategies discussed in the "Reading Images" section.

We've chosen to begin with a look at Barbie because of her longevity, popularity, and cultural significance. Since her "birth" in 1959, Barbie has achieved celebrity status in United States culture and, indeed, worldwide. More than one billion Barbies have been sold in the last forty-five years, and Barbie products continue to bring in over a billion dollars every year for Mattel, Inc., her owner and America's biggest toy company. Placed head to toe, all of the Barbies and friends sold since 1959 would circle the earth three and a half times. Barbie lives in nearly every United States and Canadian household that includes children and in more than 140 other countries as well. In addition to her extensive accessories and her many friends (among them, her boyfriend, Ken, and her African American pal, Shani), Barbie has her own magazine and fan club and her own corps of press agents, advertising executives, and "personal secretaries" to answer her fan mail. Versace, Dolce & Gabbana, Vera Wang, Gucci, Yves St. Laurent, and Bill Blass have designed clothes especially for her; Tiffany created a sterling silver version of Barbie; and New York City's Fifth Avenue became "Barbie Boulevard" to mark her twenty-fifth birthday.

For three decades, girls (and curious little boys, as well) have been playing with and learning from Barbie, and thus she serves as an important force in conveying cultural values and attitudes. Barbie's influence is undeniable, but opinions vary as to the quality of that influence on the children who play with her and on the adults they become. Barbie's critics argue that her influence has been largely detrimental, that her improbable measurements (36-18-33), her even more improbable hair, and her inexhaustible supply of clothes and accessories help perpetuate an inappropriate model of women's interests and lives. However, defenders argue that her influence has been positive, at least in part. They point out that Barbie has recently had careers such as corporate executive, airline pilot, medical doctor, animal rights activist, and even presidential candidate, offering girls a chance to envision themselves being successful in the working world. Although Barbie's wedding dress is one of her most popular outfits, she's never officially married Ken (or G.I. Joe), and she remains a single, independent career woman, providing, some observers say, an alternative to the view that women's primary roles are as wives and mothers.

You can see that Barbie has served as a symbolic reference point for broader debates about femininity and masculinity, about beauty and success, about consumerism and lifestyle in our culture. Barbie is a good example of the way elements of popular culture can be interpreted in order to reveal some fundamental aspects of our society.

While reading this background information on Barbie, you may be thinking of your own experience as a child playing with Barbie or with other dolls and toys, and speculating about their formative influence on you. If so, you've begun to prepare for reading, by orienting yourself to the topic, by exploring your own ideas and experiences, and by thinking about the issues at hand.

Preparing to Read   Let's turn now to our first selection, a poem about Barbie written by Hilary Tham. All the readings in this book are accompanied by headnotes, which briefly explain what the reading is about and give some background information on the author. In this sense, headnotes are like the front and back covers of many books, providing an overview of what will follow and serving as the place to begin thinking about the topic. Here is the headnote for the poem "Barbie's Shoes":

> Our first selection is a poem by Hilary Tham. Tham was born in Kelang, Malaysia, and currently lives in Virginia with her husband and three daughters. She teaches creative writing in high schools and has published several books of poetry, including *No Gods Today, Paper Boats, Bad Names for Women,* and *Tigerbone Wine.*

You can get an idea of what to expect from the poem both by reading the headnote and by recalling what you know about poetry in general. The headnote tells you that Hilary Tham is originally from Malaysia and now lives in the United States. You might conclude from this information that Tham brings a dual perspective to the Barbie doll and other features of United States pop culture. The headnote also points out that Tham has three daughters and teaches high school students. Before you read the poem, then, you might speculate on how being a mother and a teacher would influence Tham's thoughts about the Barbie doll.

Reading and Annotating   In the reading stage, one of the most useful strategies you can use is *annotating* the text. When you annotate you use a pencil or pen to mark key words and phrases in the text and to write questions and responses in the margins. You underline words that you need to look up in a dictionary and phrases that you find particularly interesting, forceful, important, questionable, or confusing. You also record your reactions, thoughts, questions, and ideas in the margins. By annotating in this way, you keep track of what the author is saying and of what you're thinking as you read.

Here are one student's annotations of Tham's poem . . . but keep in mind that your annotations would probably identify different elements as particularly important.

_____

Barbie's Shoes
HILARY THAM

I'm down in the(basement)   *Why the basement?*
sorting Barbie's shoes.
   sequin pumps, satin courts,
   western boots, Reebok sneakers,   *Different shoes show*
   glass slippers, ice-skates, thongs.   *Barbie's many activities*
All will fit the dainty, forever arched
feet of any one Barbie: Sweet Spring
   Glitter-Eyed, Peaches and Cream,
   a Brazilian, Russian, Swiss, Hong Kong
   Hispanic or Mexican, Nigerian
   or Black Barbie. All are cast   *Barbies are different*
in the(same)mold,(same)rubbery,   *But also the same*
impossible embodiment of male fantasy
with carefully measured
   doses of melanin to make
    a Caucasian Barbie,
     Polynesian Barbie
     African-American Barbie.
Everyone knows that she is the(same)   *Barbie =*
Barbie and worthy of the American Dream   *American Dream*
House, the Corvette, opera gloves, a
hundred pairs of shoes to step into. If only
the differently colored men and women we know
could be like Barbie, always smiling, eyes
wide with admiration, even when we yank
off an arm with a hard-to-take-off dress.
Barbie's shoes, so easily lost, mismatched,   *simile: Barbie's shoes*
useless; they end up, like our prejudices,   *are like our prejudices—*
in the basement, forgotten as spiders   *forgotten, but still there,*
sticking webs in our darkest corners,   *in the basement, like*
we are amazed we have them still.   *spider webs.*

Rereading   After you read and annotate the poem, your task is to fully understand it and formulate your own response to it. Many students close the book after just the first reading without realizing that the next two stages, rereading and reviewing, are crucial to discovering the significance of what they have read.

In the rereading stage, you go back through the poem and the annotations in order to develop a good understanding of the writer's ideas. Then you begin to articulate those ideas—in your own words. Here's an example drawn from the earlier annotation of "Barbie Shoes."

> I'm really drawn to the simile in the last few lines: that Barbie's shoes are "like our prejudices, / in the basement, forgotten as spiders / sticking webs in our darkest corners, / we are amazed we have them still." Tham is saying that Barbie's shoes are more than just tiny plastic footwear. They represent prejudices which we think we've thrown away but in fact still have in our "basements" (our subconscious thoughts?). And by comparing these prejudices to spiders' webs "in our darkest corners," perhaps Tham is suggesting that our prejudices still "catch" things; they still operate in our lives even if we've forgotten them or don't see them.

With ideas like these as a starting point, you can go back through the entire poem and begin to formulate a response to other key ideas and phrases: the list of Barbie's shoes; the list of different nationalities and ethnicities of Barbie dolls; the idea that all Barbies are in some way the same; the suggestion that Barbie represents the American Dream. Rereading like this will surely provoke further questions about the poem. For instance, why does Tham make a point of mentioning the many different types of Barbies? In what ways are these differences only superficial and unrealistic? And what does Tham mean when she writes, "If only / the differently colored men and women we know / could be like Barbie, always smiling, even when we yank / off an arm . . . ."? You know that Tham is being ironic since we don't generally yank arms off other people, but what point is she making in this comparison, and how does it relate to her ideas about prejudice?

These kinds of questions lead you to reread the poem, clarifying your understanding and finding further meanings in it. After each essay in this book there are similar sorts of reading questions that will help you explore the ideas you've read about. We also encourage you to develop your own questions about what you read to focus your exploration on those points that you find most interesting, important, or controversial.

Reviewing　After rereading, questioning, and exploring the writer's ideas in detail, you should take time to summarize what you've learned. Here is a student's summary of her analysis of "Barbie's Shoes."

1. Tham suggests that Barbie's shoes are like prejudices (forgotten, seemingly lost, down in the basement, "useless" and "mismatched"); why can't we just throw them out? why are they still in the basement?

2. Why does Barbie have so many shoes?! Perhaps Tham is implying that we have an equal number of seemingly insignificant
prejudices, one for every occasion, even.

3. Tham points out that there are many different kinds of Barbie
dolls (Caucasian, Polynesian, African American) but all are "worthy of the American Dream House." In this sense Barbies are all
the same. So does Barbie influence us to overlook the real differences in women's lives? We're not dolls, after all, and although
we're all worthy of success and accomplishment, we don't all get
the same chances.

4. Tham describes Barbie as the "impossible embodiment of male
fantasy." How is this observation related to the rest of the poem?
Could she be saying that this fantasy is related to prejudice?

Such questions and tentative answers can help you begin to formulate your own interpretation of and complete response to what
you've read.

Reading Pop Cultural Criticism   In the previous discussion we
used Hilary Tham's poem as our example because poetry can pack so
much meaning into the space of relatively few words. In the chapters
that follow you'll be reading, not poems, but rather articles, essays, and
chapters of books, most of which fall into one of two categories. The
first we might call *pop cultural criticism* and includes the kind of pieces
written for general audiences of popular magazines and mass market
books. Typically these reflect a particular social perspective, whether
traditionalist or cutting edge, conservative or liberal, pro or anticapital-
ist, and often they are written in response to a particular issue or phenomenon reported in the media.

The following piece by John Leo is an example of pop cultural criticism. As you read, practice the strategies that we've discussed. Begin
by considering the headnote and what it suggests about Leo's perspective and purpose, then underline important passages in the essay and
jot down your thoughts, responses, and questions in the margins.

_____

The Indignation of Barbie
JOHN LEO

John Leo's "The Indignation of Barbie" was first published in U.S. News &
World Report *in 1992. Leo, a conservative journalist and social commentator,
writes about the controversy surrounding the talking Barbie doll produced by
Mattel in the early 1990s. Among Talking Barbie's repertoire of phrases was
"Math class is tough," viewed by some feminists and professional women as*

12

discouraging girls from pursuing the subject. Here, Leo imagines a dialogue with Barbie, in which the talking doll defends herself against charges that she's a "prefeminist bimbo."

Barbie will probably survive, but the truth is, she's in a lot of trouble. It seems that the new Teen Talk Barbie, the first talking Barbie in 20 years, has shocked many feminists with a loose-lipped comment about girls and math. Each $25 doll speaks four of 270 programmed one-liners. In one of those messages, Barbie says, "Math class is tough." This was a big error. She should have said, "Math is particularly easy if you're a girl, despite the heavy shackles of proven test bias and male patriarchal oppression." 1

Because of this lapse from correctness, the head of the American Association of University Women is severely peeved with Barbie, and you can no longer invite both of them to the same party. Other feminists and math teachers have weighed in with their own dudgeon. 2

Since this is Barbie's darkest hour, I placed a phone call out to Mattel, Inc. in California to see how the famous long-haired, long-legged forerunner of Ivana Trump was holding up. To my astonishment, they put me right through to Barbie herself. 3

"Barbie, it's me," I said. As the father of three girls, I have shopped for 35 to 40 Barbies over the years, including doctor Barbie, ballerina Barbie, television news reporter Barbie, African-American Barbie, animal-rights Barbie, and Barbie's shower, which takes two days to construct and makes the average father feel like a bumbling voyeur. So I figured that Barbie would know me. 4

Barbie spoke: "Do you want to go for a pizza? Let's go to the mall. Do you have a crush on anyone? Teaching kids is great. Computers make homework fun!" 5

In a flash I realized that Barbie was stonewalling. These were not spontaneous comments at all. They were just the prerecorded messages that she was forced to say, probably under pressure from those heartless, controlling patriarchs at Mattel. 6

Subtle rebuttal. At the same time, I began to appreciate Barbie's characteristic subtlety; by reminding me that she was recommending the educational use of computers to young girls, she was, in effect, stoutly rebutting the charge of antifeminist backlash among talking toys. I had to admit it was pretty effective. 7

So I pleaded with her to speak honestly and clear her name. I heard a telltale rustle of satin, and then she spoke. "You're the one who took three days to put my shower together. That was ugly." 8

"Two days," I said, gently correcting the world-famous plastic figurine. I asked her about the harsh words of Sharon Schuster, the awfully upset head of the AAUW. Schuster had said, "The message is a negative one for girls, telling them they can't do well in math, and that perpetuates a stereotype." 9

"That's a crock," Barbie replied. "Just because a course is tough or challenging doesn't mean my girls can't do it. Weren't your daughters a 10

13

little apprehensive about math?" I admitted that they were. "Well, how did they do?" "Top of the class," I replied brightly.

"Then tell Sharon Schuster to stop arguing with dolls and go get a 11
life." Her remark was an amazement. This was not roller-skating Barbie or perfume-wearing Barbie. It was the real thing: in-your-face tough-talking Barbie.

"The first time I open my mouth after 20 years, and what happens? 12
I get squelched by a bunch of women." At this point, I mentioned that my friend M. G. Lord, the syndicated columnist who is doing a book on Barbie, is firmly on her side. M. G. told me: "Math class *is* tough, but it doesn't mean you have to drop out and go to cosmetology school. These people are projecting a lot of fears onto Barbie."

Barbie was grateful. "Thank M. G. and tell her I look forward to 13
her biography of me. And tell her that if she ever fails in life, she can always become head of the AAUW." That remark may have been a trifle sharp, I said. "Well," said Barbie, "I'm just tired of taking all this guff from women's groups. They're scapegoating the wrong girl. I'll match feminist credentials with any of them. I worked my way up from candy striper to doctor. I was a stewardess in the '60s, and now I'm a pilot. Ken is one of my flight attendants. You can buy me as Olympic athlete, astronaut and executive."

Barbie was on a roll now. I was writing furiously to keep up. "This 14
summer they put out a presidential candidate Barbie, and two days later, Ross Perot withdrew. Figure it out," she said. "As far back as 1984, my ad slogan was, 'We girls can do anything.' I've done more than any other doll to turn girls into achievers, and still they treat me as a prefeminist bimbo. What's wrong with the women's movement?"

I knew enough not to touch that one. Besides, it's a very short col- 15
umn. But I was struck by her comment that Ken was now employed as a flight attendant. "Didn't he used to be a corporate executive?" I asked. "We're not voting for Bush again," she replied bitterly.

Then I heard a muffled side comment: "Ken! Be careful with those 16
dishes." I said I felt bad about Ken's comedown, but Barbie brought me back to reality: "Remember," she said, "he's only an accessory." This was tough to take, but the issue was settled. Barbie is indeed a feminist. Over to you, Sharon Schuster.

As you first read Leo's essay, his technique of personifying the doll as an "in-your-face tough-talking Barbie" is most striking and allows him to humorously present a talking Barbie who seemingly speaks up for herself. In rereading you can see even more clearly Leo's purpose: he uses Barbie's "voice" to offer his own defense of her influence and significance. Moreover, ultimately he is making fun of feminists "projecting a lot of fears onto Barbie," since she herself derisively asks, "What's wrong with the women's movement?" When Leo has Barbie "say" that she's "done more than any other doll to turn girls into achievers," it's clear that Leo himself agrees and feels that Barbie critics should lighten up.

As a reviewing activity, you might write down your thoughts about the following questions and discuss them with your group or class:

1. Do you agree that Barbie has "done more than any other doll to turn girls into achievers" (paragraph 14)?
2. Do you think Leo's use of humor contributes to the effect of his essay?
3. According to Leo, what is the relationship between Barbie and Ken? Do you agree with Leo's ideas?
4. If you could give speech to Barbie, what would you have her say?

Reading Academic Analysis   In addition to pop cultural criticism, this book provides essays on pop cultural phenomena written not for a general audience, but by academics primarily for other academics. Generally published in academic journals or in collections from scholarly presses, these essays often present the results of extensive research or provide a very close, detailed, and original analysis of the subject at hand. You might find them more difficult than the pieces of pop cultural criticism, but in many ways they are closer to the kind of writing that will be expected of you in many of your college courses.

Note that, while "objective" in tone, academic cultural analysis generally reflects a particular interpretive framework, which may be ideological (e.g., feminist or Marxist) or methodological (e.g., semiotic, structuralist, or quantitative) or some combination of the two. These frameworks will be discussed in more detail in the headnotes to individual readings.

The following excerpt from an essay by Marilyn Ferris Motz is an example of academic cultural analysis, written from a perspective that might be called "feminist–historical." As you read the headnote and the essay itself, apply the strategies we've discussed: familiarize yourself with Motz's view and with the topic as it's presented in the headnote; then read the essay carefully and make your own annotations in the text and in the margins.

"Seen Through Rose-Tinted Glasses:" The Barbie Doll in American Society
MARILYN FERRIS MOTZ

Originally published in a longer form in The Popular Culture Reader, *Marilyn Motz's "'Seen Through Rose-Tinted Glasses': The Barbie Doll in American Society," takes its title from a 1983 Barbie sticker album marketed by Mattel: "If you stay close to your friend Barbie, life will always be seen through rose-tinted glasses." In her essay, however, Motz suggests that Barbie has other messages for us and that the doll's influence is more problematic, especially for children. Pointing out that several generations of girls have learned cultural values and norms from playing with Barbie, Motz focuses on the fact that, although Barbie has changed through the years to keep up with changes in the "baby boom" generation, the doll and her accessories still convey an outdated image of women's circumstances and interests.*

A 1983 Barbie sticker album copyrighted by Mattel describes Barbie:

As beautiful as any model, she is also an excellent sportswoman. In fact, Barbie is   1
seen as a typical young lady of the twentieth century, who knows how to appreciate beautiful things and, at the same time, live life to the fullest. To most girls, she appears as the ideal elder sister who manages to do all those wonderful things that they can only dream of. With her fashionable wardrobe and constant journeys to exciting places all over the world, the adventures of Barbie offer a glimpse of what they might achieve one day. If Barbie has a message at all for us, it is to ignore the gloomy outlook of others and concentrate on all those carefree days of youth. Whatever lies in store will come sooner or later. If you stay close to your friend Barbie, life will always be seen through rose-tinted glasses.

Most owners of Barbie dolls are girls between the ages of three and   2
eleven years of age. A Mattel survey shows that by the late 1960s, the median age for Barbie doll play had dropped from age ten to age six (Rakstis 30). Younger children find it difficult to manipulate the relatively small dolls, although Mattel created "My First Barbie," that ostensibly was easier for young children to handle and dress. Although some boys admit to playing with Ken, or even Barbie, Barbie doll play seems to be confined largely to girls.

Like all small figures and models, Barbie, at 11 1/2 inches high, has   3
the appeal of the miniature. Most people are fascinated with objects recreated on a smaller scale, whether they are model airplanes, electric trains, dollhouse furnishings, or doll clothes. Miniatures give us a sense of control over our environment, a factor that is particularly important for children, to whom the real world is several sizes too large. In playing with a Barbie doll, a girl can control the action, can be omnipotent in a miniature world of her own creation.

When a girl plays with a baby doll, she becomes in her fantasy the   4
doll's mother. She talks directly to the doll, entering into the play as an actor in her own right. When playing with a Barbie doll, on the other hand, the girl usually "becomes" Barbie. She manipulates Barbie, Ken and the other dolls, speaking for them and moving them around a miniature environment in which she herself cannot participate. Through the Barbie doll, then, a preadolescent can engage in role-playing activities. She can imitate adult female behavior, dress and speech and can participate vicariously in dating and other social activities, thus allaying some of her anxieties by practicing the way she will act in various situations. In consultation with the friends with whom she plays, a girl can establish

the limits of acceptable behavior for a young woman and explore the possibilities and consequences of exceeding those limits.

The girl playing with a Barbie doll can envision herself with a 5
mature female body. "Growing-Up Skipper," first produced in 1975, grew taller and developed small breasts when her arms were rotated, focusing attention on the bodily changes associated with puberty. Of course, until the end of puberty, girls do not know the ultimate size and shape their bodies will assume, factors they realize will affect the way others will view and treat them. Perhaps Barbie dolls assuage girls' curiosity over the appearance of the adult female body, of which many have only limited knowledge, and allay anxiety over their own impending bodily development.

Through Barbie's interaction with Ken, girls also can explore their 6
anxieties about future relationships with men. Even the least attractive and least popular girl can achieve, by "becoming" Barbie, instant popularity in a fantasy world. No matter how clumsy or impoverished she is in real life, she can ride a horse or lounge by the side of the pool in a world undisturbed by the presence of parents or other authority figures. The creator of the Barbie doll, Ruth Handler, claims that "these dolls become an extension of the girls. Through the doll each child dreams of what she would like to be" (Zinsser, "Barbie" 73). If Barbie does enable a girl to dream "of what she would like to be," then what dreams and goals does the doll encourage? With this question, some of the negative aspects of the Barbie doll emerge.

17

The clothes and other objects in Barbie's world lead the girl play- 7
ing with Barbie to stress Barbie's leisure activities and emphasize the importance of physical appearance. The shape of the doll, its clothes and the focus on dating activities present sexual attractiveness as a key to popularity and therefore to happiness. Finally, Barbie is a consumer. She demands product after product, and the packaging and advertising imply that Barbie, as well as her owner, can be made happy if only she wears the right clothes and owns the right products. Barbie conveys the message that, as the saying goes, a woman can never be too rich or too thin. The Barbie doll did not create these attitudes. Nor will the doll insidiously instill these values in girls whose total upbringing emphasizes other factors. An individual girl can, of course, create with her own doll any sort of behavior and activities she chooses. Still, the products available for the doll tend to direct play along certain lines. Barbie represents an image, and a rather unflattering one, of American women. It is the extent to which this image fits our existing cultural expectations that explains the popularity of the Barbie doll....

As an icon, Barbie not only reflects traditional, outdated roles for 8
women; she and Ken also represent, in exaggerated form, characteristics of American society as a whole. Through playing with these dolls, children learn to act out in miniature the way they see adults behave in real life and in the media. The dolls themselves and the accessories provided for them direct this play, teaching children to consume and conform, to seek fun and popularity above all else.

Thorstein Veblen wrote in 1899 that America had become a nation 9 of "conspicuous consumers." We buy objects, he wrote, not because we need them but because we want others to know we can afford them. We want our consumption to be conspicuous or obvious to others. The more useless the object, the more it reflects the excess wealth the owner can afford to waste. In the days before designer labels, Veblen wrote that changing fashions represent an opportunity for the affluent to show that they can afford to waste money by disposing of usable clothing and replacing it with new, faddish styles that will in turn be discarded after a few years or even months of wear (Veblen 60–131).

Sociologist David Riesman wrote in 1950 that Americans have 10 become consumers whose social status is determined not only by what they can afford to buy but also by the degree to which their taste in objects of consumption conforms to that of their peers. Taste, in other words, becomes a matter of assessing the popularity of an item with others rather than judging on the basis of one's personal preference. Children, according to Riesman, undergo a process of "taste socialization," of learning to determine "with skill and sensitivity the probable tastes of the others" and then to adopt these tastes as their own. Riesman writes that "today the future occupation of all moppets is to be skilled consumers" (94, 96, 101). This skill lies not in selecting durable or useful products but in selecting popular, socially acceptable products that indicate the owner's conformity to standards of taste and knowledge of current fashion.

18

The Barbie doll teaches a child to conform to fashion in her con- 11 sumption. She learns that each activity requires appropriate attire and that outfits that may at first glance appear to be interchangeable are slightly different from one another. In the real world, what seems to be a vast array of merchandise actually is a large collection of similar products. The consumer must make marginal distinctions between nearly identical products, many of which have different status values. The child playing with a Barbie doll learns to detect these nuances. Barbie's clothes, for instance, come in three lines: a budget line, a medium-priced line, and a designer line. Consumption itself becomes an activity to be practiced. From 1959 to 1964, Mattel produced a "Suburban Shopper" outfit. In 1976 the "Fashion Plaza" appeared on the market. This store consisted of four departments connected by a moving escalator. As mass-produced clothing made fashion accessible to all classes of Americans, the Barbie doll was one of the means by which girls learned to make the subtle fashion distinctions that would guarantee the proper personal appearances.

Barbie must also keep pace with all the newest fashion and leisure 12 trends. Barbie's pony tail of 1959 gave way to a Jackie Kennedy style "Bubble-cut" in the early 1960s and to long straight hair in the 1970s. "Ken-A-Go-Go" of 1960s had a Beatle wig, guitar and microphone, while the "Now Look Ken" of the 1970s had shoulder-length hair and wore a leisure suit (Leavy 102). In the early 1970s, Ken grew a detachable beard. In 1971 Mattel provided Barbie and Ken with a motorized stage on which to dance in their fringed clothes, while Barbie's athletic activities, limited to skiing, skating, fishing, skydiving and tennis in the 1960s, expanded to include backpacking, jogging, bicycling, gymnastics and sailing in the 1970s. On the shelves in the early 1980s were Western outfits, designer jeans, and Rocker Barbie dressed in neon colors and playing an electric guitar. In 1991 Rollerblade Barbie was introduced.

Barbie clearly is, and always has been, a conspicuous consumer. 13 Aside from her lavish wardrobe, Barbie has several houses complete with furnishings, a Ferrari and a '57 Chevy. She has at various times owned a yacht and several other boats, as well as a painted van called the "Beach Bus." Through Barbie, families who cannot afford such luxury items in real life can compete in miniature. In her early years, Barbie owned a genuine mink coat. In the ultimate display of uselessness, Barbie's dog once owned a corduroy velvet jacket, net tutu, hat, sunglasses and earmuffs. Barbie's creators deny that Barbie's life is devoted to consumption. "These things shouldn't be thought of as possessions," according to Ruth Handler. "They are props that enable a child to get into play situations" (Zinsser 73). Whether possessions or props, however, the objects furnished with the Barbie doll help create play situations, and those situations focus on consumption and leisure.

A perusal of the shelves of Barbie paraphernalia in the Midwest 14 Toys "R" Us store reveals not a single item of clothing suitable for an executive office. Mattel did produce a doctor's outfit (1973) and astronaut suit (1965 and 1986) for Barbie, but the clothes failed to sell. According to Mattel's marketing manager, "We only kept the doctor's uniform in the line as long as we did because public relations begged us to give them something they could point to as progress" in avoiding stereotyped roles for women (Leavy 102). In the 1960s, Mattel produced "all the elegant accessories" for the patio including a telephone, television, radio, fashion magazines and a photograph of Barbie and Ken (Zinsser 72). The "Busy Barbie," created in 1972, had hands that could grasp objects and came equipped with a telephone, television, record player, "soda set" with two glasses and a travel case. Apparently Barbie kept busy only with leisure activities; she seems unable to grasp a book or a pen. When Barbie went to college in the 1970s, her "campus" consisted only of a dormitory room, soda shop (with phone booth), football stadium and drive-in movie (Zinsser 72). In the 1980s, Barbie traveled in her camper, rode her horse, played with her dog and cat, swam in her pool and lounged in her bubble bath (both with real water).

The Barbie doll of the 1980s presents a curiously mixed message. 15 The astronaut Barbie wore a pink space suit with puffed sleeves. The executive Barbie wore a hot pink suit and a broad-brimmed straw hat, and she carried a pink briefcase in which to keep her gold credit card. Lest girls think Barbie is all work and no play, the jacket could be removed, the pink and white spectator pumps replaced with high-heeled sandals, and the skirt reversed to form a spangled and frilly evening dress. Barbie may try her hand at high-status occupations, but her appearance does not suggest competence and professionalism. In a story

19

in *Barbie* magazine (Summer 1985) Barbie is a journalist reporting on lost treasure in the Yucatan. She spends her time "catching some rays" and listening to music, however, while her dog discovers the lost treasure. Barbie is appropriately rewarded with a guest spot on a television talk show! Although Barbie is shown in a professional occupation and even has her own computer, her success is attributed to good luck rather than her own (nonexistent) efforts. She reaps the rewards of success without having had to work for it; indeed, it is her passivity and pleasure-seeking (could we even say laziness) that allows her dog to discover the gold. Even at work, Barbie leads a life of leisure.

Veblen wrote that America, unlike Europe, lacked a hereditary   16
aristocracy of families that were able to live on the interest produced by inherited wealth. In America, Veblen wrote, even the wealthiest men were self-made capitalists who earned their own livings. Since these men were too busy to enjoy leisure and spend money themselves, they dele-gated these tasks to their wives and daughters. By supporting a wife and daughters who earned no money but spent lavishly, a man could prove his financial success to his neighbors. Therefore, according to Veblen, affluent women were forced into the role of consumers, establishing the social status of the family by the clothes and other items they bought and the leisure activities in which they engaged (Veblen 44–131).

Fashions of the time, such as long skirts, immobilized women,   17
making it difficult for them to perform physical labor, while ideals of beauty that included soft pale hands and faces precluded manual work or outdoor activities for upper-class women. To confer status, Veblen writes, clothing "should not only be expensive, but it should also make plain to all observers that the wearer is not engaged in any kind of pro-ductive employment." According to Veblen, "the dress of women goes even farther than that of men in the way of demonstrating the wearer's abstinence from productive labor." The high heel, he notes, "makes any, even the simplest and most necessary manual work extremely difficult," and thus is a constant reminder that the woman is "the economic depen-dent of the man—that, perhaps in a highly idealized sense, she still is the man's chattel" (Veblen 120–21, 129)....

Despite changes in the lives and expectations of real women, Barbie   18
remains essentially the woman described by Veblen in the 1890s, excluded from the world of work with its attendant sense of achievement, forced to live a life based on leisure activities, personal appearance, the accumula-tion of possessions and the search for popularity. While large numbers of women reject this role, Barbie embraces it. The Barbie doll serves as an icon that symbolically conveys to children and adults the measures of success in modern America: wealth, beauty, popularity and leisure.

Suggestions for Further Reading
Leavy, Jane. "Is There a Barbie Doll in Your Past?" *Ms.* Sept. 1979.
Riesman, David, Nathan Glazer, and Reual Denney. *The Lonely Crowd: A Study of the Changing American Character.* Garden City, NY: Doubleday Anchor, 1950.

Rakstis, Ted. "Debate in the Doll House." *Today's Health* Dec. 1970.

Veblen, Thorstein. *The Theory of the Leisure Class.* 1899. New York: Mentor, 1953.

Zinsser, William K. "Barbie Is a Million Dollar Doll." *Saturday Evening Post* 12 Dec. 1964: 72–73.

As you can see from Motz's essay, academic cultural analysis can present you with much information and many ideas to digest. A useful rereading activity is to go through the text and highlight its main points by writing a one- or two-page summary of it. Then in the reviewing stage, you can use your summary to draw your own conclusions and formulate your own responses to the writer's ideas. To do so with Motz's essay, you might use the following questions as starting points:

1. In what ways do you think fashion dolls like Barbie provide a different play experience for children than "baby dolls"? Do you think one type of doll is "healthier" or more appropriate than the other?
2. To what extent do you think Thorstein Veblen's comments on status and consumerism in American society (paragraph 9) still apply today? Do you agree with Motz that Barbie contributes to the promotion of "conspicuous consumption"?
3. If Motz is right that Barbie represents an outdated and potentially detrimental image of women's lives, why do you think the doll continues to sell more and more successfully every year?
4. To what extent do you think that the values represented by Barbie—"wealth, beauty, popularity and leisure" (18)—are still central to success in America?

21

Ultimately, your goal as a reader in this course will most likely be to prepare yourself to complete specific writing assignments. In the "Writing Process" section, we will present the process one writing student went through in composing an essay requested in the following assignment:

What do you see as the significance of the Barbie doll in contemporary American culture? How are your ideas related to those of Tham, Leo, and Motz in the selections presented here?

READING IMAGES

Before turning to this assignment, however, we will address strategies you can use to read images effectively. In many ways, the four-step process we just described for reading texts—Preparing to Read, Reading and Annotating, Rereading, and Reviewing—applies to images as well. There are some differences, though, as we discuss below.

Preparing to Read

With both text and image, it is wise to begin by getting an idea of what to expect, a first impression. Just as you read the headnote in order to get an introduction to an essay or poem, so too can you read the information that surrounds the image. Next to a painting in a museum, for instance, you'll often find information about the work: the name of the artist, the dates he or she lived, the date the work was completed, the media used in the work (oils, watercolor, paper, etc.), the dimensions of the work.

But outside of a museum, images are often presented to you without this kind of helpful, orienting information. In these instances, which are of course far more common in the world of popular culture, an important strategy to prepare yourself before diving in to interpret the image is to look at the context in which the image occurs. Is it an advertisement you're being asked to analyze? If so, what magazine is the ad in? What is the typical audience of this magazine? On what page of the magazine is the ad found (in the expensive beginning pages or in the more modestly priced pages toward the end of the magazine)? Is it a Web site you're interpreting? If so, who is the author of the site? Who is its audience? What is the purpose of the site? When was the site last updated?

These questions of context can orient you in the same way that headnotes can: they give you a general sense of what to expect. Moreover, knowing the context, and especially the audience and purpose of an image, can guide your subsequent interpretation by helping you determine why certain features are present or absent in the image.

Finally in the "Preparing to Read" stage, you should think about your initial impressions of the image you're analyzing. What key features do you notice immediately? What mood or feeling does the image evoke in you? What immediate response do you have to the image?

Let's turn to a specific example and begin with the "Preparing to Read" process. Take a look at the image of Barbie at the top of page CI-1. As you can see from the information included below the image, the photographer is Aaron Goodman and the caption for the image is "Barbie and Ken Branding." This information gets you started on your analysis of the image, particularly with the idea of "branding" mentioned in the caption. The fact that the image is created by a photographer indicates, in this instance, that it is a composite of many photographs that generate a not-quite realistic image of Barbie and Ken in New York City's Times Square.

As you think about determining the audience and purpose of this image, you might consider the fact that it doesn't seem to be officially sponsored or endorsed by Mattel, Inc., Barbie's creator. We can assume that the primary purpose of the information and images generated by

Mattel would be to promote its products. If you take a look at Barbie's official Web site (*http://barbie.everythinggirl.com/*), for example, you can assume that everything included there has the ultimate function of selling Barbie dolls to little girls and their parents. Aaron Goodman's image, by contrast, doesn't have this promotional purpose; rather, it is more likely to be driven by aesthetic goals or intended to deliver a critical interpretation of Barbie.

What's your first impression of this image? What strikes you as most immediately noticeable about it? We can put it in one word: brands! We count at least seventeen identifiable brand names and/or logos competing for space in this image. Let's move on now to the next step, in which you take a closer look at the details of the image and begin interpreting it.

Reading and Annotating

Unless you own the image that you're interpreting, it would probably be a good idea to refrain from annotating (that is, writing on it). You can get into some trouble doing this, particularly in places like the Metropolitan Museum of Art. Instead, annotating becomes a process of note-taking, and reading becomes a process of looking. Put simply, look at the image and take notes.

But that's putting it too simply. What should you look at in an image, and what sort of notes should you take?

One of the major differences between text and image is that a text generally presents information in a sequential and linear manner; there's usually no question about where you should begin reading and, having read one word, it's not usually difficult to decide what word you should read next. With images (and here we're speaking only of still images and not videos, commercials, or other kinds of sequenced images), everything is presented simultaneously so that you can begin and end where you choose and your eyes can follow different paths through the image. Having said that, though, it's also the case that images often try to draw your attention to a certain place, a focus point. This focus point is often relevant in understanding the key messages of the image.

What is the focus point of the Barbie image? For us, it's Barbie herself. It seems fairly obvious that Barbie would be the key element in an image with the caption "Barbie and Ken Branding," but what details in the image can we find to support this claim? Here's where the qualities of *arrangement* and *dimension* come into play. The arrangement (or placement) of elements in the image clearly draws our attention to Barbie. Although the center is the key focus point in many images, in this case Barbie's placement closest to the viewer makes us notice her first. Dimension (or proportion) also draws our attention to Barbie

23

because she is larger than any other object in the image. In fact, she's unnaturally large, as is Ken; it's difficult to imagine them cramming themselves into the taxicab that's right alongside them. So here again, evidence in the image supports a (fairly obvious) claim that the focus of the image is Barbie herself.

It's often helpful to imagine alternative arrangements and dimensions for images that you're analyzing in order to register the impact of the image as it is. For instance, what if the placement of Ken and Barbie were switched in this image? That would place Barbie in the center, but it would also make her significantly smaller than Ken, and perhaps would even suggest that she's tagging along after him or is subordinate to him. Envisioning this alternative, we can see all the more clearly that placement gives Barbie primary importance. In terms of dimension, what if Barbie and Ken were realistically sized? The taxi and car would become more important elements of the image, and the "Times Square" background might threaten to overwhelm them. As it is, Barbie and Ken are disproportionately large in order to draw attention to their significance in the image.

Continuing to look at the image and to take notes, we might next turn to the remarkable number of brand names and logos and try to determine why they're there and how they contribute to the meaning of the image. While the real Times Square certainly has many billboards and advertisements, a photograph of it wouldn't show so many legible, identifiable, and well-placed brand names. Clearly, Aaron Goodman created this composite photograph with brands and branding in mind. But what is the relation between Barbie and all of the other brands in the image? The *perspective* of the image suggests that Barbie and Ken are in the forefront of a world composed almost entirely of consumer goods. Perspective is often a helpful category to use in analyzing images. The perspective essentially situates the viewer, defining the relation of the viewer to the image: are you positioned above or below the objects in the image? Are you on the outside looking in (implying perhaps that you're excluded or don't belong)? In this case, the perspective asks you to see Barbie and Ken first, and then to see brand names and consumerism all around them. Carrying her Coke, her Gap bag, and her American Express Card, Barbie is clearly in her element.

Rereading

Having looked carefully at the image and taken notes on its focus, arrangement, dimension, and perspective, the next step is to articulate the ideas you've developed. Making statements about the image and writing down questions you have about it will compel you to look at it even more closely, clarifying your understanding and finding further meanings.

Based on the information discussed above, a general statement about the image might be that it promotes an idea of Barbie as a key player in an overwhelmingly consumerist world. Given the fact that many little girls play with Barbie, the image may be suggesting that Barbie initiates girls into this consumerist culture. Indeed, perhaps the image is implying that just as girls collect Barbie's clothes and accessories, grownups continue this collecting by buying other name brand products.

But some questions remain. For instance, what is the significance of the fact that the image evokes Times Square as its setting? What connotations does Times Square have for Barbie, for branding, and for consumerism? Concerning the *colors* and *contrasts* of elements in the image, why do red, white, and blue seem to be the predominant colors (along with yellow in the taxi and Kodak sign on the left side of the image)? How would the meaning of the image be changed if the colors were mostly browns, greens, or purples? Taken together with the Times Square reference, is the image suggesting a strong connection between Barbie, consumer brands, and the American lifestyle? Finally, the *medium* of the image can be an important component of its meaning. In this case, the composite photograph created by Goodman suggests both the realism of photography (which captures how people and places actually look) and the complete artificiality of this particular scene (with Barbie and Ken figured as real people walking in a distorted version of New York). In what ways might this interplay of reality and illusion be related to the meaning of the image?

Reviewing

So we've examined the image, taken notes, looked at the image again, asked questions, and formulated some ideas and some questions about it. In the final stage, take the time to summarize what you've learned. Perhaps you can do this in the form of a statement about what you think the image means, or perhaps it's more effective to write about what strategies the image uses to convey its messages. In either case, you'll be prepared if you're asked to write about the image or to include an analysis of it with an analysis of a text.

Before concluding this section and turning to the writing process, take a look at the second Barbie image we've selected at the bottom of page CI-1. Follow the same steps described above in reading this image:

1. Take a look at the explanatory information and decide on the context of the image. Who is its audience, and what is its purpose? Note your first impressions of the image.
2. Read the image by noting where your eyes are initially drawn; why is this focal point important to the message of the image?

Note other important features of the image: color, dimension, contrast, perspective, arrangement, shape, and medium. What reasons can you determine for the choices the artist made in these areas?

3. Write down a statement or two that you think explains the meaning of the image, along with any questions you still have about it. Examine it carefully to see what elements you have previously missed.

4. Summarize what you think are the messages and strategies of this image.

We think that one of the most enjoyable parts of studying popular culture is gaining expertise in interpreting the images that bombard us every day, from all angles, from many media. This composite photograph of Barbie gives us a lot to think about in terms of what the doll symbolizes for American culture.

At the end of the introductory chapter and scattered throughout *Common Culture*, you'll find more images upon which you can exercise your interpretative powers. They are drawn from magazines, posters, the Web, and other sources, and they comment on the themes of the chapters of this text: advertising, television, music, technology, sports, and movies. In a highly visual culture like ours, these images serve as "readings" that supplement and provide a different perspective on the more traditional reading materials in each chapter.

THE WRITING PROCESS

Frequently, when an instructor gives a writing assignment—for example, "Write an essay exploring the significance of the Barbie doll in contemporary American culture"—students experience a type of mini-panic: producing a focused, coherent, informative, and logically developed paper seems a monumental task. Some students may be overwhelmed by the many ideas swirling around in their heads, worrying they won't be able to put them into coherent order. Others may think they won't have enough to say about a given topic and complain, "How long does the paper have to be? How can I come up with four pages!"

However, there's really no reason to panic. Just as there are definable activities in the active process of reading, so the writing process can be broken down into four discrete stages: **prewriting, drafting, distancing,** and **revising.** Taking it a step at a time can make writing an essay a manageable and productive experience.

26

Prewriting

The first stage of the essay-writing process should be especially invigo-rating and stress-free since at this point you don't have to worry about making your prose grammatically sound, logically organized, or con-vincing to a reader. All you have to do is write whatever comes into your head regarding your topic so that you can discover the beginnings of ideas and phrasings that may be developed in the drafting stage and ultimately massaged into an acceptable form of academic writing.

Writers use a number of prewriting strategies to generate ideas and happy turns of phrase. Experiment with all of these to discover which of them "click" in terms of how you think and which help you most productively get your ideas down on paper. Most writers rely more heavily on one or two of these prewriting strategies, depending on their own styles and dispositions; it's a matter of individual preference. If you're a spontaneous, organic sort of person, for example, you might spend more time freewriting. On the other hand, if you have a more log-ical, mathematical mind, you might gravitate naturally to outlining and do very little freewriting. There's no right or wrong way to prewrite; it comes down to whatever works best for you. But what's best usually involves some combination of the three following techniques.

27

Freewriting   This prewriting strategy lets your mind wander, as minds will, while you record whatever occurs to you. Just write, write, write, with no judgment about the validity, usefulness, grammatical correctness, or literary merit of the words you're putting down. The only requirement is that you write nonstop, either on paper or a word processor, for a manageable period of time, say, fifteen minutes without a break.

Your freewriting can be open—that is, it can be pure, stream-of-consciousness writing in which you "stay in the present moment" and record every thought, sense impression, disturbing sound—or it can be focused on a specific topic, such as Barbie dolls. When freewriting in preparation for writing an essay, it's frequently helpful to keep in mind a central question, either one from your instructor's original topic assignment or one sparked by your own curiosity, so that your freewritten material will be useful when you start composing your actual essay. Here is a typical focused freewrite on the subject of Barbie dolls written by a student in response to the writing assignment quoted earlier:

> *Toys: what did you want as a child vs. what you were given? I don't know, but I wanted cars and ended up with Barbie Corvette. Brother got G.I. Joe, Tonka trucks, I got talking Barbie, Barbie playhouse, Corvette.*

B. served as model for ideal female figure, and now that ideal is depicted in magazines. I guess that represents a kind of perpetuation of this image: girls raised on Barbie ? cycle continues w/images in the media. The I = ideal image of women in America seems to be let's see: white, flawless, flat nose, wide eyes, that kind of thing. Whatever, it's clear that Barbie creates unreal expectations for women.

Yeah! her figure would be inhuman if a real person had it—they would probably die! If she puts on jogging shoes, Barbie stands sloped because she's designed for high heels . . . so it seems as though Barbie is clearly designed for display rather than real activity, let alone profession. Display.

literature (written stuff) on Barbie packages—she's not interested in doctoring nurse, etc.; just having money, cars, looking good, taking trips etc. Re: tech—women think computers are "fun." Re: math—women supposedly aren't good at it. Barbie reinforces these stereotypes—and lots more—in girls

Changes in society? discuss for concl.?

Clustering   Clustering is especially useful for discovering relationships between ideas, impressions, and facts. As a prewriting activity, it falls between freewriting and outlining in that it's usually more focused than freewriting but less logically structured than an outline.

To prewrite by clustering, begin by writing a word or central phrase down in the center of a clean sheet of paper. In the case of the Barbie doll assignment, for example, you would probably start by writing "Barbie" in the middle of the page, and then drawing a circle around it. Having written and circled this central word or phrase, you can then jot down relevant facts, concrete examples, interesting ideas, and so on. Cluster these around the circled word, like this:

Frequently, one or more of your random jottings will serve as a new central word—as a jumping-off point for a new cluster of ideas. Later on, when you're drafting, you can use these clustered "nodes" as the basis for supporting paragraphs in the body of your essay.

Outlining   If you have a rough idea of what the main points of your paper will be, outlining is an extremely useful prewriting technique in that it helps you plan the overall structure for your paper and often generates new ideas about your topic. There are several different types of outlines, most notably scratch, sentence, and topic outlines.

For a *scratch outline* you list your intended points in a very tentative order, one that may only reflect the fact that you don't yet know in what order you want to put your supporting ideas. A scratch outline might not even suggest which subordinating points are most important to developing your thesis. For this reason, scratch outlines are most useful early in the prewriting phase, as a means of generating ideas as well as beginning to organize your thoughts logically. In fact, if you have not yet arrived at a thesis for your paper, one may emerge in the process of listing all your main and subordinate points and then reviewing that list to discover which of those ideas is the most central and important.

As you think more about your essay and come up with new ideas and supporting evidence, you will almost certainly revise your scratch outline to make it more detailed and conventionally formatted with numbered and lettered headings and subheads. A *topic outline* presents items in key words or brief phrases, rather than sentences, and frequently features no indentation. A *sentence outline* is even more developed than a topic outline in that it describes the listed items in complete sentences, each of which is essentially a subtopic for a supporting paragraph. In fact, sentence outlines, when fully developed, can contain most of the supporting information you're going to present in your essay and can therefore be extremely useful tools during the prewriting process.

Developing her freewritten material about Barbie into an outline, our student writer sketched out the following:

I. *Introduction*
    A. *Discuss my own experience with toys while growing up: parents "let" me play with Tonka trucks, but they gave me a Barbie Corvette when I wanted a race car.*
    B. *Discuss social shaping of gender roles generally.*
    C. *Working Thesis: Significance of Barbie in American society is that although people say women have "come a long way" and that there are new expectations, this is not really true. If it were, Barbie, depicted as mere sexual, leisure seeking consumer, could not be accepted.*

II. *The media see that people—especially young ones—need role models, and man-ufacture products to fill the following needs.*
   A. *Childhood: Barbie.*
      1. *Barbie presents a totally unrealistic female body as a role model for young women.*
      2. *This role-modeling is crucial in young women's psychological development, because little girls role-play with Barbie, taking her actions as their own.*
   B. *Pre-teen: Models in Seventeen magazine.*
   C. *Teen: Vogue and Mademoiselle.*
   D. *Adult: Cosmopolitan, Victoria's Secret lingerie models, advertisements in mainstream magazines.*

III. *The popularity of Barbie depicts the entrenched nature of traditional female roles.*
   A. *The change toward women's equality is not something that is deemed beneficial by everyone, such as the religious ultra-right.*
   B. *People purchasing Barbie either:*
      1. *don't see the image that's being perpetuated; or*
      2. *respect those values and want to pass them on to their children.*
   C. *Significance in popular culture of Barbie is that she illustrates incon-sistencies between changing social roles (women and minorities) and the concepts we are teaching youngsters.*
   D. *Although the makers of Barbie make a superficial attempt at updating her, Barbie depicts traditional women absorbed in leisure, consump-tion, and beauty.*
      1. *Barbie completely reinforces old role expectations.*
      2. *Barbie in the '90s can have a career (she has some doctor outfits, I think), but she isn't ever functional in that career. The emphasis is still on leisure.*

IV. *The Racial Issue*
   A. *Barbie illustrates the assimilation of minorities; they lose part of their culture, because Americans are supposed to belong to the "same mold."*
   B. *In the '90s we say that we aren't prejudiced and that everyone should be accepted for who they are, but since the dominant culture is white, white men and women unconsciously (or in some cases consciously, I'm afraid) assume that others must take on white norms.*

V. *Conclusion*
   A. *Bring it back around to my childhood play time and the necessity for parents to think about the sorts of toys they are giving their children, so that they don't reinforce and perpetuate these old patterns.*

You'll discover that this outline, while detailed, doesn't contain some of the points raised in the final essay's supporting paragraphs and that it includes a good deal of material that was not used in the final essay. The reason for this discrepancy is simple and illustrates a key point for you to remember about the writing process. As this writer began her essay, she discovered new points that she thought relevant to her thesis. At the same time, she realized that some of her outlined points were tangential and digressive rather than helpful in supporting her main point. She therefore cut some of those points, even though she thought they were valid and interesting ideas. That's one of the most painful but absolutely necessary tasks of the writer: getting rid of material that took some work to create and seems interesting and well written. If cutting some of your previously written material makes the final result better, then it's worth the sacrifice!

Drafting

Having generated a good amount of prewritten material and perhaps developed it into a detailed outline, your next task is to transform that material into an actual essay. Before proceeding with the drafting of your essay, however, it's a good idea first to consider your audience—your instructor only? Your instructor *and* your classmates? An imaginary editor or publisher? A third-grade student? Consider, too, the point you want to make about your topic to that audience. Unlike freewriting, which is by its nature often rambling and disjointed, essays succeed to the degree that they focus on a specific point and develop that point with illustrations and examples.

Thesis and Thesis Statement   The main point, the central assertion of your essay, is called a *thesis*. It helps to have a clear sense of your thesis before writing a paper. However, keep in mind that this isn't always necessary: some people use writing as a discovery process and don't arrive at their thesis until they've completed a first draft. Generally, however, the process is easier if you have a thesis in mind—even one that's not yet fully formed or that's likely to change—before you begin drafting.

While the form of thesis statements may vary considerably, there are some qualities that separate effective thesis statements from vague or weak ones. First, your thesis statement should be inclusive but focused; that is, it should be broad enough to encompass your paper's main supporting ideas, but narrow enough to represent a concise explanation of your paper's main point that won't require you to write fifty pages to cover the topic adequately. Furthermore, you want your thesis statement to be a forceful assertion rather than a question or an ambiguous statement of purpose such as, "In this paper I am going to talk about Barbie dolls and their effect on society."

Much more effective, as you will see in the sample student paper that concludes this chapter, is a statement that takes a stand:

> This is certainly one of the more dangerous consequences of Barbie's popularity in our society: a seemingly innocent toy defines for

young girls the sorts of career choices, clothing, and relationships
that will be "proper" for them as grown-up women.

Notice how this statement gives an excellent sense of the thematic
direction the paper will take: clearly, it will examine the relationship
between Barbie dolls and gender-role identification in contemporary
America.

Opening Paragraphs   In most academic writing, you want to
arrive at your thesis statement as quickly as possible so that your reader
will have a clear sense of your essay's purpose from the start. Many readers expect to find a thesis statement at the end of the introduction—
generally, the final sentence of the first or second paragraph. Effective
introductions are often structured so as to lead up to the thesis statement:
they draw the reader in by opening with an interesting specific point or
question, a quotation, a brief anecdote, a controversial assertion—which
serves to introduce the topic generally; a general overview then leads up
to the specific statement of the thesis in the last sentence.

In the student essay on pages 43–45, for example, observe how the
writer begins with a personal reflection about Barbie. Her anecdote may
strike a familiar chord with readers and therefore draw them into the
topic. Having made the attempt to arouse her readers' interest in her
opening paragraph, the writer moves more pointedly into the general
topic, discussing briefly the possible social and psychological implications of her parents' gift choices. This discussion leads into her thesis
statement, a focused assertion that concludes her second paragraph.

Keep in mind that many writers wait until they have written a
first draft before they worry about an introduction. They simply lead
off with a tentative thesis statement, then go back later to look for effective ways to lead up to that statement.

Supporting Paragraphs   As you draft the body of your paper,
keep two main goals in mind. First, try to make sure that all your supporting paragraphs are aimed at developing your thesis so that you
maintain your focus and don't ramble off the topic. Second, work
toward presenting your supporting ideas in logical order and try to
provide smooth transitions between points.

The order in which you choose to present your ideas depends, in
large part, on your topic and purpose. When you are arguing for a particular position, you might begin with less important ideas and work
toward a final, crucial point. In this way you can build a case that you
"clinch" with your strongest piece of evidence. Other kinds of essays
call for different structures. For example, an essay tracing the history of
the Barbie doll and its effect on American culture would probably be

structured chronologically, from the introduction of the toy to its present-day incarnations, since that would be the most natural way to develop the discussion.

The student essay at the end of this chapter moves from a personal reflection on the topic of Barbie (paragraph 1); to a thesis statement that asserts the point of the paper (2); to a transitional paragraph moving from the writer's childhood experiences and a more general discussion of Barbie's role in reinforcing gender-role stereotypes in other young girls (3); to an overview of how sociologists and historians critique the Barbie phenomenon (4); to an examination of whether Barbie has changed in response to evolving attitudes regarding women in society (5–7), the heart of the writer's argument; to a conclusion that frames the essay by returning to the original, personal example (8). Each new discussion seems to flow naturally into the next because the writer uses a transitional phrase or parallel language to link the first sentence in each paragraph to the end of the preceding paragraph.

Evidence   Using evidence effectively is the critical task in composing body paragraphs, because your essay will be convincing only to the degree that you make your arguments credible. Evidence can take many forms, from facts and figures you collect from library research to experiences you learn about in conversations with friends. While library research isn't necessary for every paper, it helps to include at least some "hard" facts and figures gathered from outside sources—journals, newspapers, textbooks—even if you're not writing a full-blown research paper. Frequently, gathering your evidence doesn't require scrolling through computer screens in your school's library; it could be accomplished by watching the six o'clock newscast or while reading the paper over breakfast.

Quotations from secondary sources are another common way of developing and supporting a point in a paragraph. Using another person's spoken or written words will lend your arguments a note of authenticity, especially when your source is a recognized authority in the field about which you're writing. A few points to remember when using quotations:

1. Generally, don't begin or end a supporting paragraph with a quotation. Articulate your point *in your own words* in the first sentence or two of the paragraph; *then* provide the quotation as a way of supporting your point. After the quotation, you might include another focusing sentence or two that analyzes the quotation and suggests how it relates to your point.
2. Keep your quotations brief. Overly lengthy quotations can make a paper difficult to read. You've probably read texts that nearly

put you to sleep because of their overuse of quotations. As a general rule, quote source material only when the precise phrasing is necessary to support your abstract points. Be careful not to allow cited passages to overpower your own assertions.

3. Remember that all of your secondary material—whether quoted or paraphrased—needs to be accurately attributed. Make sure to mention the source's name and include other information (such as the publication date or page number) as required by your instructor.

While quotations, facts, and figures are the most common ways of developing your supporting paragraphs with evidence, you can also use your imagination to come up with other means of substantiating your points. Design a questionnaire, hand it out to your friends, and compile the resulting data as evidence. Interview a local authority on your topic, make notes about the conversation, and draw upon these as evidence. Finally, be your own authority: use your own powers of reasoning to come up with logical arguments that convince your readers of the validity of your assertions.

This body paragraph from the student essay on Barbie provides a good example of a writer using evidence to support her points:

> As Motz observes later in her article, Barbie has changed to adjust to the transforming attitudes of society over time. Both her facial expressions and wardrobe have undergone subtle alterations: "The newer Barbie has a more friendly, open expression, with a hint of a smile, and her lip and eye make-up is muted" (226), and in recent years Barbie's wardrobe has expanded to include some career clothing in addition to her massive volume of recreational attire. This transition appears to represent a conscious effort on the part of Barbie's manufacturers to integrate the concept of women as important members of the work force, with traditional ideals already depicted by Barbie.

The paragraph begins with an assertion of the general point that Barbie has changed in some ways over the years to reflect changes in societal attitudes toward women. This point is then supported with a quotation from an expert, and the page number of the original source is noted parenthetically. (Note that page references in this student essay are from the complete original essay by Motz, published in *The Popular Culture Reader*, not from the excerpt of the Motz essay earlier in this chapter.) The point is further developed with evidence presented in the writer's own words. The paragraph concludes with a final sentence that summarizes the main point of the evidence presented in the previous sentences, keeps the paragraph focused on the essay's thesis that

Barbie perpetuates gender stereotypes, and sets the reader up for a transition into the next subtopic.

Obviously, all supporting paragraphs won't take this exact form; essays would be deadly boring if every paragraph looked the same. You'll encounter body paragraphs in professional essays that begin with quotations or end with quotations, for example. Just keep in mind that you want to *support* whatever general point you're making, so each paragraph should include a measure of specific, concrete evidence. The more you practice writing, the more ways you'll discover to develop body paragraphs with illustrations, examples, and evidence.

Conclusions   You may have learned in high school English courses that an essay's conclusion should restate the main points made in the paper so that the reader is left with a concise summary that leaves no doubt as to the paper's intention. This was an excellent suggestion for high school students as it reinforced the notion of focusing an essay on a specific, concrete point. In college, however, you'll want to start developing a more sophisticated academic style. Conclusions to college-level essays should do more than merely repeat the paper's main points; they should leave the reader with something to think about.

Of course, what that *something* is depends on your topic, your audiences, and your purpose in writing. Sometimes it may be appropriate to move from an objective discussion of a topic to a more subjective reflection on it. For instance, in analyzing the social effects of Barbie dolls, you might end by reflecting on the doll's significance in your own life or by commenting ironically on feminist critics who in your view make too much of Barbie's influence. Other ways to conclude are providing a provocative quotation, offering a challenge for the future, asserting a forceful opinion, creating a striking image or memorable turn of phrase, or referring back to an image or idea in your introduction.

What you want to avoid is a bland and overly general conclusion along the lines of, "Thus, in conclusion, it would seem to this author that Barbie has had a great and wide-reaching impact on today's contemporary society." Note how the writer of the Barbie essay created a strong conclusion by first returning to the subject of her opening paragraph—her own childhood toys—and then leaving the reader with a relatively memorable final sentence offering a challenge for the future:

> Looking back at my childhood, I see my parents engaged in this same struggle. By surrounding me with toys that perpetuated both feminine and masculine roles, they achieved a kind of balance among the conflicting images in society. However, they also seemed to succumb to traditional social pressures by giving me that Barbie

35

Corvette, when all I wanted was a radio-controlled formula-one racer, like the one Emerson Fittipaldi drives. In a time when most parents agree that young girls should be encouraged to pursue their goals regardless of gender boundaries, their actions do not always reflect these ideals. Only when we demand that toys like Barbie no longer perpetuate stereotypes will this reform be complete.

Distancing

Distancing is the easiest part of the writing process because it involves doing nothing more than putting your first draft aside and giving yourself some emotional and intellectual distance from it. Pursue your daily activities, go to work or complete assignments for other classes, take a hike, throw a Frisbee, polish your shoes, do anything but read over your draft . . . ideally for a day or two.

The reason to take the time to distance yourself is simple: you've been working hard on your essay and therefore have a strong personal investment in it. To revise effectively, you need to be able to see your essay dispassionately, almost as though someone else had written it. Stepping away from it for a day or two gives you the opportunity to approach your essay as an editor who has no compunction about changing, reordering, or completely cutting passages that don't work.

Also, the process of distancing allows your mind to work on the essay subconsciously even while you're going about your other non-writing activities. Frequently, during this distancing period, you'll find yourself coming up with new ideas that you can use to supplement your thesis as you revise.

Finally, factoring the process of distancing into the writing process will help you avoid the dread disease of all students: procrastination. Since you have to allot yourself enough time to write a draft *and* let it sit for a couple of days, you'll avoid a last-minute scramble for ideas and supporting material, and you'll have time to do a thorough revision.

One note of warning: Don't get so distanced from your draft that you forget to come back to it. If you do forget, all your prewriting and drafting will have gone to waste.

Revising

Many professional writers believe that revision is the most important stage in the writing process. Writers view the revision stage as an opportunity to clarify their ideas, to rearrange text so that the logical flow of their work is enhanced, to add new phrases or delete ones that don't work, to modify their thesis and change editorial direction . . . or, in some extreme cases, to throw the whole thing out and start over!

Just as with prewriting and drafting, many students dread revision because all the different issues that need to be considered make it appear to be a forbidding task. Most find it helpful to have a clear set of criteria with which to approach their first drafts. Following is such a checklist of questions, addressing specific issues of content, organization, and stylistics/mechanics. If you find that your answer is "no" to any one of these questions, then you need to rework your essay for improvement in that specific area.

Revision Checklist

Introduction
✔ Does the paper begin in a way that draws the reader into the paper while introducing the topic?

✔ Does the introduction provide some general overview that leads up to the thesis?

✔ Does the introduction end with a focused, assertive thesis in the form of a statement (not a question)?

Supporting Paragraphs and Conclusion

✔ Do your supporting paragraphs relate back to your thesis, so that the paper has a clear focus?

✔ Do your body paragraphs connect logically, with smooth transitions between them?

✔ Do your supporting paragraphs have a good balance between general points and specific, concrete evidence?

✔ If you've used secondary sources for your evidence, do you attribute them adequately to avoid any suspicion of plagiarism?

✔ If you've used quotations extensively, have you made sure your quoted material doesn't overpower your own writing?

✔ Does your last paragraph give your readers something to think about rather than merely restate what you've already said elsewhere in the essay?

Style and Mechanics
✔ Have you chosen your words aptly and sometimes inventively, avoiding clichés and overused phrases?

✔ Have you varied your sentence lengths effectively, thus helping create a pleasing prose rhythm?

✔ Have you proofread carefully, to catch any grammatical problems or spelling errors?

Make the minor changes or major overhauls required in your first draft. Then type or print out a second draft, and read it *out loud* to yourself to catch any awkward or unnatural sounding passages, wordy sentences, grammatical glitches, and so on. Reading your prose out loud may seem weird—especially to your roommates who can't help overhearing—but doing so helps you gain some new perspective on the piece of writing you have been so close to, and frequently highlights minor, sentence-level problems that you might otherwise overlook.

Writing Research on Popular Culture

A research essay focusing on popular culture follows the same steps as those presented in the previous discussion of essay writing in general—with a significant addition: the research essay focuses on a central hypothesis or research question, and it includes outside sources. For that reason, you might envision a slightly different sequence of activities for your writing process, one that moves according to the following stages:

- *Topic Selection:* Spend some time thinking about an issue that you actually are interested in or want to know more about. Your teachers will sometimes give you relatively open-ended essay prompts, allowing you to select a research area with which you are familiar and/or interested. Even in those cases in which the teacher narrows the topic significantly—perhaps assigning an essay on the relationship between Barbie dolls and gender stereotyping, or between music lyrics and violence, for example—you still have a great deal of leeway in focusing the topic on elements of interest to you. In the music/violence example, you still have the freedom to select bands and lyrics you know well, and this will make your research much more well informed, while keeping the topic fresh and interesting to you.
- *Focus:* Narrow the topic as much as you can to ensure that your work will be thorough, focused, and well supported with evidence. In the Barbie example at the end of this chapter, the author focused on childhood psychological development as it is affected by stereotype-perpetuating toys such as Barbie. Likewise, in the music/violence example, you might narrow the focus by restricting your research to certain types of popular music, such as punk or hip-hop, or to music by artists of a certain gender or ethnic population. The less global you make your topic, the less you will

find yourself awash in volumes of disparate material as you develop your essay drafts.

- *Working Thesis:* Develop a preliminary research question or hypothesis related to your topic. This working thesis will undoubtedly go through several refinements as you begin researching your topic, but it helps greatly to organize your research material if you begin with a concrete point of view, even if you change it later on, as you find more information on the topic. In the student essay that follows, a research question might have been: do certain toys reinforce gender stereotyping in children? The working hypothesis would probably have supported the affirmative position. In the music/violence topic, a working thesis might be something such as: while many observers believe that lyrics in hip-hop music incite young people to violence, research demonstrates that there is no causal connection between listening to certain types of music and violent behavior. You would then proceed to the next step, to find material that supports (or disproves) this initial hypothesis.

- *Secondary Sources:* Find the most valuable materials written by other people on your chosen topic. As much as possible, include examples from a wide range of sources, including scholarly journals, books, popular literature (such as magazine and newspaper articles), and World Wide Web sites. Don't be daunted if you don't find materials from each of these source categories; in some cases, for example, a topic will be so new and fresh that there haven't been books written about it, and you may have to rely more on newspaper articles and Web sites.

- *Primary Sources:* If possible and applicable to your assignment, include some research conducted by yourself, such as interviews with professors who are experts on the topic you are examining, or even with friends and peers who can provide a "person-on-the-street" perspective to balance some of the more academic or journalistic perspectives found in your secondary sources.

- *Critical Reading:* To avoid becoming a passive receptor of someone else's obvious or popular conclusions, analyze your assembled source information to find its literal and implied meanings and to weigh the validity of the information it presents. At the same time, check the validity of your own previously held assumptions and beliefs; as much as possible, try to have an open mind about your topic, even if you have a working hypothesis you are developing. In the above-described working thesis on the relationship between music and violence, you may find material that disproves your original hypothesis, suggesting that there is in fact a relationship between listening to music and acting violently. You may then want to revise your thesis to reflect the material you have found, if you think that information is valid. Feel free to use or reject discovered information based on your critical analysis of it.

- *Documentation:* Finally, keep careful record of your sources so that you can attribute them accurately, using a bibliographic format appropriate to your research topic and approach. Keep in mind that any time you use source material to support your arguments in academic papers, it is necessary that you document that material. You accomplish this by using footnotes and/or parenthetical in-text citations in the body of your essay, along with bibliographies and/or Works Cited pages at the end of your essay. This academic convention accomplishes two purposes: first, it serves to acknowledge your having relied on ideas and/or actual phrases from outside source material; and second, it allows readers to explore a paper's topic further, should they find the issues raised thought-provoking and worthy of pursuit.

40

In academic settings, the major systems of documentation—namely, APA, MLA, and CSE—share certain key characteristics; that is, they all furnish readers with uniform information about quoted or paraphrased material from books, journals, newspapers, Web sites, and so forth. While it may seem strange for such a multiplicity of documenting styles to exist, there actually is a good reason why there is not one single documentation format for all academic disciplines: the different documentation styles support the unique needs and preferences of certain academic communities. Social scientists cite their sources by author and date because in the social sciences, broad articulations of concepts, refined through time, are paramount; APA format reflects this. By contrast, researchers working in humanities-related fields rely frequently on direct quotations; the MLA format therefore furnishes page numbers rather than dates.

If you have already selected a major, you will probably be writing most, if not all, of your essays for a certain discipline, such as English literature or psychology. While you will probably want to acquaint yourself to some degree with the basics of all the major citation formats, you will certainly want to learn, memorize, and practice with special diligence the documentation requirements of the area in which you will be majoring. All three of the above-mentioned professional organizations periodically issue revised guidelines for documentation, and if you want to be sure about the specific rules in your area of specialization, you might want to buy one of the following:

> *MLA Handbook for Writers of Research Papers* (6th edition, 2003)
>
> *Publication Manual of the American Psychological Association* (5th edition, 2001)
>
> *The CSE Manual for Authors, Editors, and Publishers* (7th edition, 2006)
>
> *The Chicago Manual of Style* (15th edition, 2003)

Furthermore, there are numerous handbooks available, such as the *Prentice Hall Guide to Research: Documentation*, 6th edition, which provide detailed information on documentation in all of the disciplines. In the absence of such books, the following section gives features of the two most popular documentation styles, the MLA and the APA.

Modern Language Association Documentation Format

- Within the body of the text, all sources are cited within parentheses (known in the academic world as "in-text parenthetical citations"), using the author's name and the number of the page from which the source was derived. You should include an in-text citation any time you use another writer's ideas or phrasings within the text of your own paper, either by direct quotation or by paraphrase.
- At the end of the paper, sources are listed alphabetically, on a page or pages with the heading "Works Cited." In the "Works Cited" section, list book-derived citations using the following information, in this order: the author's name exactly as it appears on the book's title page, last name first; the title of the book, underlined; the place of publication followed by a colon; the publisher, followed by a comma; and the date of publication. A typical MLA-formatted book listing will look like this:

> Berger, Arthur Asa. Television as an Instrument of Terror: Essays on Media, Popular Culture, and Everyday Life. New Brunswick, N.J.: Transaction Books, 1980.

A typical MLA journal or magazine citation will contain six pieces of information: the author, listed last name first; the article's title in quotation marks; the journal's title underlined; the volume number followed by the issue number; the date of publication; and the article's page numbers. A typical MLA-formatted journal listing will appear in this way:

> Auerbach, Jeffrey. "Art, advertising, and the legacy of empire."
> Journal of Popular Culture 35.4 (2002): 1–23.

For files acquired from the World Wide Web, give the author's name (if known), the full title of the work in quotation marks, the title of the complete work (if applicable) in italics, and the full HTTP address. For example:

> Brooke, Collin. "Perspective: Notes Toward the Remediation of Style." *Enculturation: Special Multi-journal Issue on Electronic Publication* 4.1 (Spring 2002)<http://enculturation.gmu.edu/4_1/style>.

American Psychological Association Documentation Format

• Within the body of the text, all sources are cited within parentheses, using the author's name, along with the year of publication. That latter bit of information—the publication date—is the important difference in parenthetical in-text citation format between the APA and MLA documentation styles. When directly quoting from a source, include the number of the page from which the quotation is taken.

• At the end of the paper, sources are listed alphabetically on a page or pages of reference materials. List book-derived citations using the following information, in order: the author's last name and initials for first name (and middle name if given), last name first; the year of publication in parentheses; the title of the book in italics with only the first word of the title capitalized; the place of publication followed by a colon; and the publisher, followed by a period. A typical APA-formatted book listing will look like this:

> Charyn, J. (1989). *Movieland: Hollywood and the great American dream culture*. New York: Putnam.

An APA-formatted journal or magazine citation will contain six pieces of information: the author's name; the date of publication; the article's title; the journal's title, italicized along with the volume number; and the article's page numbers. A typical APA-formatted journal listing will look like this:

> Banks, J. (1997). MTV and the globalization of popular culture.
> *Gazette, 59* (1), 43–44.

For electronic citations, give the author's name (if known), the date of publication or of the latest update, the full title of the work, and the title of the online journal in which the work appears (if applicable). Then start a sentence with the word "Retrieved," followed by the date on which the source was accessed and the source's URL or HTTP address. For example,

> Cole, S. K. (1999). I am the eye, you are my victim: The porno-graphic ideology of music video. *Enculturation Magazine.* Retrieved March 4, 2006, from http://enculturation.gmu. edu/2_2/cole/

Of course, there are many other sources—newspapers, interviews, videos, email conversations, just to name a few—that are omitted here for the sake of brevity, but that carry specific formatting requirements within the major documentation styles. You will undoubtedly want to refer to a handbook or a style sheet published by one of the national associations, should you be asked to write a more extensive research paper that includes the full range of source materials.

Sample Student Essay

The following essay demonstrates one way of approaching the assign-ment we presented earlier. As you read, note the essay's introductory paragraphs and thesis statement, the way body paragraphs are de-veloped with illustrations and examples, the way it concludes without simply restating the writer's points, the writer's effective use of words and sentence structure, the ways in which it incorporates source material into the developing arguments, and the correct MLA documentation format. While this is not, strictly speaking, a research essay as described above, it does incorporate source material in the ways discussed above.

_____

Role-Model Barbie: Now and Forever?
CAROLYN MUHLSTEIN

During my early childhood, my parents avoided placing gender bound-aries on my play time. My brother and I both had Tonka trucks, and these were driven by Barbie, Strawberry Shortcake, and GI Joe to my doll house, or to condos built with my brother's Erector Set. However, as I got older, the boundaries became more defined, and certain forms of play became "inappropriate." For example, I remember asking for a remote controlled car one Christmas, anticipating a powerful race car like the ones driven at De Anza Days, the local community fair. Christmas morn-ing waiting for me under the tree was a bright yellow Barbie Corvette. It seemed as though my parents had decided that if I had to have a remote controlled car, at least it could be a feminine Barbie one!

Although I was too young to realize it at the time, this gift repre- 2
sented a subtle shift in my parents' attitudes toward my gender-role
choices. Where before my folks seemed content to let me assume either
traditional "boy" or traditional "girl" roles in play, now they appeared to
be subtly directing me toward traditional female role-playing. This is certainly one of the more dangerous consequences of Barbie's popularity in
our society: a seemingly innocent toy defines for young girls the sorts of
career choices, clothing, and relationships that will be "proper" for them
as grown-up women.

Perhaps the Barbie Corvette was my parents' attempt to steer me 3
back toward more traditional feminine pursuits. Since her birth thirty-five
years ago, Barbie has been used by many parents to illustrate the "appropriate" role of a woman in society. During earlier decades, when women
were expected to remain at home, Barbie's lifestyle was extremely fitting.
Marilyn Ferris Motz writes that Barbie "represents so well the widespread
values of modern American society, devoting herself to the pursuit of
happiness through leisure and material goods . . . teaching them [female
children] the skills by which their future success will be measured" (212).
Barbie, then, serves as a symbol of the woman's traditional role in our
society, and she serves to reinforce those stereotypes in young girls.

Motz' opinion isn't an isolated one. In fact, the consensus among 4
sociologists, historians, and consumers is that Barbie represents a life of
lazy leisure and wealth. Her "forever arched feet" and face "always smiling, eyes wide with admiration" (Tham 180) allow for little more than
evenings on the town and strolls in the park. In addition, the accessories
Barbie is equipped with are almost all related to pursuits of mere pleasure. According to a Barbie sticker album created by Mattel:

Barbie is seen as a typical young lady of the twentieth century, who knows how to
appreciate beautiful things and, at the same time, live life to the fullest . . . with
her fashionable wardrobe and constant journeys to exciting places all over the
world, the adventures of Barbie offer a glimpse of what they [girls] might achieve
one day. (qtd. in Motz 218)

In this packaging "literature"—and in the countless other adver- 5
tisements and packaging materials that have emerged since Barbie's
invention some thirty years ago—the manufacturers exalt Barbie's materialism, her appreciation of "beautiful things," fine clothing, and expensive trips as positive personality traits: qualities which all normal,
healthy girls in this society should try to emulate, according to the traditional view.

As Motz observes later in her article, Barbie has changed to adjust 6
to the transforming attitudes of society over time. Both her facial expressions and wardrobe have undergone subtle alterations: "The newer
Barbie has a more friendly, open expression, with a hint of a smile, and
her lip and eye make-up is muted" (226), and in recent years Barbie's
wardrobe has expanded to include some career clothing in addition to
her massive volume of recreational attire. This transition appears to

represent a conscious effort on the part of Barbie's manufacturers to integrate the concept of women as important members of the work force, with traditional ideals already depicted by Barbie.

Unfortunately, a critical examination of today's Barbie doll reveals 7 that this so-called integration is actually a cynical, half-hearted attempt to satisfy the concerns of some people—especially those concerned with feminist issues. Sure, Barbie now has office attire, a doctor outfit, a nurse outfit, and a few other pieces of "career" clothing, but her image continues to center on leisure. As Motz observes, "Barbie may try her hand at high-status occupations, but her appearance does not suggest competence and professionalism" (230). Quite the opposite, in fact: there are few, and in some cases, no accessories with which a young girl might imagine a world of professional competence for Barbie. There are no Barbie hospitals and no Barbie doctor offices; instead, she has only mansions, boats, and fast cars. Furthermore, Barbie's arched feet make it impossible for her to stand in anything but heels, so a career as a doctor, an astronaut—or anything else that requires standing up for more than twenty minutes on a fashion runway—would be nearly impossible!

From these examples, it's clear that Barbie's manufacturers have 8 failed to reconcile the traditional image of women as sexual, leisure-seeking consumers with the view that women are assertive, career-oriented individuals, because their "revision" of the Barbie image is at best a token one. This failure to reconcile two opposing roles for Barbie parallels the same contradiction in contemporary society. By choice and necessity, women are in the work force in large numbers, seeking equal pay and equal opportunities with men; yet the more traditional voices in our culture continue to perpetuate stereotyped images of women. If we believe that we are at a transitional point in the evolution toward real equality for women, then Barbie exemplifies this transitional stage perfectly.

Looking back at my childhood, I see my parents engaged in this 9 same struggle. By surrounding me with toys that perpetuated both feminine and masculine roles, they achieved a kind of balance among the conflicting images in society. However, they also seemed to succumb to traditional social pressures by giving me that Barbie Corvette, when all I wanted was a radio-controlled formula-one racer, like the one Emerson Fittipaldi drives. In a time when most parents agree that young girls should be encouraged to pursue their goals regardless of gender boundaries, their actions do not always reflect these ideals. Only when we demand that toys like Barbie no longer perpetuate stereotypes will this reform be complete.

Works Cited

Motz, Marilyn Ferris. "Through Rose-Tinted Glasses." *Popular Culture: An Introductory Text.* Ed. Jack Trachbar and Kevin Lause. Bowling Green, OH: Bowling Green University Press, 1992.

Tham, Hilary. "Barbie's Shoes." *Mondo Barbie.* Ed. Lucinda Ebersole and Richard Peabody. New York: St. Martin's Press, 1993.

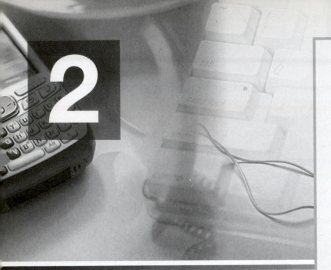

If you think it's cool, it is.

STYLE NO: 44108
ORIGINAL DESIGN: 1972
PRICE: Around $43 with Indiglo*

TIMEX*

Advertising

What you see above is a very simple advertisement for a Timex watch. A picture of the watch, a short statement, a tag with information about the watch and the familiar Timex slogan, some small print at the bottom: there doesn't seem to be much more to it than that. But appearances can be deceiving—and indeed, they often are in advertisements.

Let's take a closer look. The ad is centered on a simple statement: "If you think it's cool, it is." The longest word in the sentence is only five letters, reminding us of other familiar advertising slogans such as "Just do it" and "Coke is it." In addition to their quite basic vocabulary, these slogans share a certain quality of vagueness: the "it" in "Just do it," like the "it" in "Coke is it," are what semioticians might call "floating signifiers"; their meaning is open and flexible, determined substantially by the reader of the ad. The same can be said for the "it" in this Timex ad: does "it" refer only to the watch? If so, why doesn't the statement say, "If you think *this watch* is cool, it is"? Clearly, an all-encompassing word like "it" allows the statement to be about more than just the watch.

Even more interesting in this ad is the word "cool": what exactly is "cool"? It's a word that we all define differently, and Timex invites us here to take our own definition of "cool" and associate it with the watch. Whatever each of us thinks of as "cool," that's what this watch is. While vagueness usually leads to poor communication, you can see how it's used effectively here by the advertiser: "cool" tells us virtually nothing about the watch, but makes us feel good about it nonetheless. And of course, "cool" appeals to a certain audience: precisely the young, upscale, Generation X types who might be reading *Icon*, the glossy and expensive "thoughtstyle" magazine in which we found the ad. So, targeting a smaller audience, Timex can afford to be more specific than Coke can be when it claims to be "it." Still, the watch is "cool" rather than "groovy" (too old) or "rad" (too California-surfer). In that one word alone and in the way it's used, we can see the ad hard at work trying to make its product appealing to potential customers.

When we look at the entire sentence, we can also see a degree of complexity behind its seeming simplicity. Even if we accept that the word "it" refers only to the watch, the sentence invites two different interpretations:

1. "If you think this watch is cool, well, you're right, because it is."
2. "If you think this watch is cool, then it is (because you say it is)."

This is a fine difference, but an important one. The first way of reading the sentence suggests that the watch is naturally, essentially cool, and so the reader is to be congratulated on being perceptive enough to see coolness when he or she comes across it. In the second reading, the watch isn't naturally cool at all; it's the reader who decides that the watch is cool. Either way, the reader of the ad gets a compliment and perhaps an ego-boost: either he or she is cool enough to recognize a cool watch, or he or she has the power to determine coolness. The first option might appeal to a more insecure sort of reader, someone who fears that he or she can't distinguish cool from uncool. The second reading confirms the confidence of a more secure reader, someone who knows perfectly well what's cool and what isn't. In other words, the statement appeals simultaneously to both the "wanna-be cools" and the "already cools" who might be reading *Icon*.

Now you may think that we're reading too much into so simple an advertisement, especially considering the fact that we haven't gotten past the statement yet to consider other elements in the ad: all that white space, the strange information presented on the label (why do we need to know the date of the original design?), the Timex slogan at the bottom of the label. It's true that we're spending far more time interpreting this ad than most readers spend on it as they thumb through *Icon* looking for an interesting article to read. But we're not spending nearly as much time on the ad as its designers did. The fact is that nothing in this ad— or in any ad—is there by mistake; every detail is carefully chosen, every word carefully selected, every photograph carefully arranged. Advertisers know that readers usually spend only a few seconds glancing at ads as they page through a magazine; we drive quickly past billboards and use TV commercial minutes to grab food from the fridge. In those seconds that the advertisers have our attention, they need to make as strong a pitch as possible. All that we're doing with the Timex ad is speculating about each of the choices that the designers of the ad made in creating their pitch. In several writing and discussion assignments in this chapter, you'll be asked to do the same kind of analysis with ads that you select, and in readings in this chapter, you'll see more detailed and complete analyses of ads that can serve, along with this mini-analysis of the Timex ad, as models for your own interpretations.

Keep in mind, too, that advertising agencies spend a great deal of time and money trying to understand the complex psychodynamics of their target audiences and then tailoring ads to appeal to those audiences. Even their simplest and most seemingly direct advertisements still carry subtly powerful messages—about "coolness" as well as about appropriate modes of behavior, standards of beauty and success, gender roles, and a variety of other markers for normalcy and status. In tailoring ads to appeal both to basic human impulses and to more culturally conditioned attitudes, they also ultimately reinforce and even engender such impulses and attitudes. So although advertisements like the one above seem to be thoroughly innocuous and unimportant, the argument of many pop culture critics is that they have quite an influence—perhaps all the more so because we think they're so bland and harmless.

Several readings in this chapter explain in further detail the ways in which we can be manipulated by advertising. Jib Fowles, for example, points out a variety of strategies advertisements use to appeal to our emotions even though we may think we are making product choices using our intellect. The readings in the second section of the chapter look at how advertising works to manipulate our notions of masculinity and femininity. You'll probably find that many advertisements, especially the ones in gender-specific magazines like *GQ* and *Vogue,* attempt to sell products by connecting them, however tenuously, to idealized and highly desirable images of masculinity and femininity: put bluntly, it's "buy this cologne (perfume) and you'll be the man (woman) you've always dreamed of being." No one really believes that, of course . . . at least not consciously. But these kinds of ads must be working or else advertisers would find other, more effective strategies to make their products appealing to consumers.

Whatever your view of advertising, keep in mind as you read the following sections that everything in advertisements—from sexy models to simple black and white pictures of watches—exist solely for three well-calculated reasons: to sell, sell, and sell.

Approaches to Advertising

The Cult You're In

KALLE LASN

We begin this chapter on advertising with an intriguing, lyrical, but quite bleak piece by one of advertising's most interesting critics, Kalle Lasn. Lasn is one of the founders of Adbusters Media Foundation, which publishes Adbusters *magazine and coordinates such "culture jamming" campaigns as "TV Turn-Off Week," "Buy Nothing Day," and "Car Free Day" (http://www. adbusters.org). The selection reprinted here comes from Lasn's book* Culture Jam: The Uncooling of America.*

Through his book, magazine, Web site, and "culture jamming" campaigns, Lasn delivers a critique of contemporary consumer culture, focused in particular on advertising, the influence of mass media, and the power of large corporations. In Lasn's words, his movement is "about reclaiming democracy, returning this country to its citizens as citizens, not marketing targets or demographics. It's about being a skeptic and not letting advertising tell you what to think."

In the following article, Lasn describes a scenario in which advertising does tell us what to think, and even what to dream, exerting a profound and complete power over our lives as citizen-consumers. Whether this scenario is an accurate description of the present or a disturbing possibility for the future is for you to decide. **Before you read**, *consider the title of this article: "The Cult You're In." What effect does it have to be told in this title that you're in a cult? What do you already know about cults that might influence your reaction to the title?*

A beeping truck, backing up in the alley, jolts you out of a scary 1 dream—a mad midnight chase through a supermarket, ending with a savage beating at the hands of the Keebler elves. You sit up in a cold sweat, heart slamming in your chest. It was only a nightmare. Slowly, you reintegrate, remembering who and where you are. In your bed, in your little apartment, in the very town you grew up in.

It's a "This Is Your Life" moment—a time for mulling and stock- 2 taking. You are still here. Just a few miles from the place you had your first kiss, got your first job (drive-through window at Wendy's), bought your first car ('73 Ford Torino), went nuts with the Wild Turkey on prom night and pulled that all-nighter at Kinko's, photocopying transcripts to send to the big schools back East.

Those big dreams of youth didn't quite pan out. You didn't get into 3
Harvard, didn't get courted by the Bulls, didn't land a recording contract
with EMI (or anyone else), didn't make a million by age twenty-five.
And so you scaled down your hopes of embarrassing riches to reasonable expectations of adequate comfort—the modest condo downtown,
the Visa card, the Braun shaver, the one good Armani suit.

Even this more modest star proved out of reach. The state college 4
you graduated from left you with a $35,000 debt. The work you found
hardly dented it: dreadful eight-to-six days in the circulation department of a bad lifestyle magazine. You learned to swallow hard and just
do the job—until the cuts came and the junior people were cleared out
with a week's severance pay and sober no-look nods from middle management. You began paying the rent with Visa advances. You got call-
display to avoid the collection agency.

There remains only one thing no one has taken away, your only 5
real equity. And you intend to enjoy fully that Fiat rustmaster this weekend. You can't run from your problems, but you may as well drive. Road
Trip. Three days to forget it all. Three days of living like an animal (in the
best possible sense), alert to sights and sounds and smells: Howard Stern
on the morning radio, Slumber Lodge pools along the I-14. "You may
find yourself behind the wheel of a large automobile," sings David
Byrne from a tape labeled "Road Tunes One." The Fiat is, of course, only
large at heart. "You know what FIAT stands for?" Liv said when she first
saw it. "Fix It Again, Tony." You knew then that this was a girl you could
travel to the ends of the Earth with. Or at least to New York City.

The itinerary is set. You will order clam chowder from the Soup 6
Nazi, line up for standby Letterman tickets and wander around Times
Square (Now cleaner! Safer!) with one eye on the Jumbotron. It's a
place you've never been, though you live there in your mind. You will
jog in Battery Park and sip Guinness at Michael's Pub on Monday night
(Woody Allen's night), and you will dance with Liv in the Rainbow
Room on her birthday. Ah Liv, who when you first saw her spraying
Opium on her wrist at the cosmetics counter reminded you so much of
Cindy Crawford—though of late she's put on a few pounds and now
looks better when you close your eyes and imagine.

And so you'll drive. You'll fuel up with Ho Ho's and Pez and 7
Evian and magazines and batteries for your Discman, and then you'll
bury the pedal under your Converse All-Stars—like the ones Kurt
Cobain died in. Wayfarers on, needle climbing and the unspoken
understanding that you and Liv will conduct the conversation entirely
in movie catchphrases.

"Mrs. Nixon would like you to pass the Doritos." 8
"You just keep thinking, Butch. That's what you're good at." 9
"It's over, Rock. Nothing on Earth's gonna save you now." 10

It occurs to you that you can't remember the last time Liv was just Liv 11 and you were just you. You light up a Metro, a designer cigarette so obviously targeted at your demographic . . . which is why you steered clear of them until one day you smoked one to be ironic, and now you can't stop.

You'll come back home in a week. Or maybe you won't. Why 12 should you? What's there to come back *for*? On the other hand, why should you stay?

A long time ago, without even realizing it, just about all of us 13 were recruited into a cult. At some indeterminate moment, maybe when we were feeling particularly adrift or vulnerable, a cult member showed up and made a beautiful presentation. "I believe I have something to ease your pain." She made us feel welcome. We understood she was offering us something to give life meaning. She was wearing Nike sneakers and a Planet Hollywood cap.

Do you *feel* as if you're in a cult? Probably not. The atmosphere is 14 quite un-Moonielike. We're free to roam and recreate. No one seems to be forcing us to do anything we don't want to do. In fact, we feel privileged to be here. The rules don't seem oppressive. But make no mistake: There are rules.

By consensus, cult members speak a kind of corporate Esperanto: 15 words and ideas sucked up from TV and advertising. We wear uniforms—not white robes but, let's say, Tommy Hilfiger jackets or Airwalk sneakers (it depends on our particular subsect). We have been recruited into roles and behavior patterns *we did not consciously choose.*

Quite a few members ended up in the slacker camp. They're 16 bunked in spartan huts on the periphery, well away from the others. There's no mistaking cult slackers for "downshifters"—those folks who have *voluntarily* cashed out of their high-paying jobs and simplified their lives. Slackers are downshifters by necessity. They live frugally because they are poor. (Underemployed and often overeducated, they may never get out of the rent-and-loan-repayment cycle.)

There's really not much for the slackers to *do* from day to day. They 17 hang out, never asking, never telling, just offering intermittent wry observations. They are postpolitical, postreligious. They don't define themselves by who they vote for or pray to (these things are pretty much prescribed in the cult anyway). They set themselves apart in the only way cult members can: by what they choose to wear and drive and listen to. The only things to which they confidently ascribe value are things other people have already scouted, deemed worthy, and embraced.

Cult members aren't really citizens. The notions of citizenship 18 and nationhood make little sense in this world. We're not fathers and mothers and brothers: We're consumers. We care about sneakers, music, and Jeeps. The only *Life, Freedom, Wonder,* and *Joy* in our lives are the brands on our supermarket shelves.

Are we happy? Not really. Cults promise a kind of boundless con-   19
tentment—punctuated by moments of bliss—but never quite deliver
on that promise. They fill the void, but only with a different kind of
void. Disillusionment eventually sets in—or it would if we were
allowed to think much about it. Hence the first commandment of a cult:
Thou shalt not think. Free thinking will break the trance and introduce
competing perspectives. Which leads to doubt. Which leads to contem-
plation of the nearest exit.

How did all this happen in the first place? Why have we no memory   20
of it? When were we recruited?

The first solicitations began when we were very young. If you   21
close your eyes and think back, you may remember some of them.

You are four years old, tugging on your mother's sleeve in the   22
supermarket. There are products down here at eye level that she cannot
see. Cool products with cartoon faces on them. Toys familiar from
Saturday morning television. You want them. She keeps pushing her
cart. You cry. She doesn't understand.

You are eight. You have allowance money. You savor the buying   23
experience. A Coke here, a Snickers bar there. Each little fix means not
just getting what you want, but *power.* For a few moments *you* are the
center of attention. *You* call the shots. People smile and scurry around
serving you.

Michael Jordan goes up on your bedroom door. He is your first   24
hero, throwing a glow around the first brand in your life—Nike. You
wanna be like Mike.

Other heroes follow. Sometimes they contradict each other.   25
Michael Jackson drinks Pepsi but Michael Jordan drinks Coke. Who is
the false prophet? Your friends reinforce the brandhunting. Wearing
the same stuff and hearing the same music makes you a fraternity,
united in soul and form.

You watch TV. It's your sanctuary. You feel neither loneliness nor   26
solitude here.

You enter the rebel years. You strut the malls, brandishing a Dr.   27
Pepper can full of Scotch, which you drink right under the noses of the
surveillance guards. One day you act drunk and trick them into
"arresting" you—only this time it actually *is* soda in the can. You are
immensely pleased with yourself.

You go to college, invest in a Powerbook, ride a Vespa scooter,   28
don Doc Martens. In your town, a new sports complex and performing
arts center name themselves after a car manufacturer and a software
company. You have moved so far into the consumer maze that you can
smell the cheese.

After graduating you begin to make a little money, and it's quite   29
seductive. The more you have, the more you think about it.

You buy a house with three bathrooms. You park your BMW out- 30
side the double garage. When you grow depressed, you go shopping.

The cult rituals spread themselves evenly over the calendar: 31
Christmas, Super Bowl, Easter, pay-per-view boxing match, summer
Olympics, Mother's Day, Father's Day, Thanksgiving, Halloween. Each
has its own imperatives—stuff you have to buy, things you have to do.

You're a lifer now. You're locked and loaded. On the go, trying to 32
generate more income to buy more things and then, feeling dissatisfied
but not quite sure why, setting your sights on even greater income and
more acquisitions. When "consumer confidence is down," spending is
"stagnant," the "retail sector" is "hurting" and "stingy consumers are
giving stores the blues," you do your bit for the economy. You are a star.

Always, always you have been free to dream. The motivational 33
speakers you watched on late-night TV preached that even the most
sorry schleppers can achieve their goals if they visualize daily and stay
committed. *Think and grow rich.*

Dreams, by definition, are supposed to be unique and imaginative. 34
Yet the bulk of the population is dreaming the same dream. It's a dream of
wealth, power, fame, plenty of sex, and exciting recreational opportunities.

What does it mean when a whole culture dreams the same dream? 35

53

Examining the Text

1. What is the function of the story that opens this reading? What feelings does
the story evoke in you?

2. What is the effect of all of the products and brand names that Lasn includes
in this article?

3. How does Lasn define the term "cult"? How is his definition different from
(and similar to) the common usage of this word?

4. *Thinking rhetorically*: In this article, Lasn uses the rhetorical strategy of direct
address—that is, he uses the pronoun "you" and directly addresses readers of
the article. Why do you think Lasn uses this strategy? What effect does it have
on you as a reader? How does the strategy of direct address contribute to (or
detract from) Lasn's argument?

For Group Discussion

Discuss the characteristics of the cult that Lasn describes. Who are its members
(and nonmembers)? What are its rules? How are we initiated into this cult? What
are the cult's beliefs and rituals? How do we get ourselves out of this cult? After
discussing these questions, decide on the extent to which you're persuaded by
Lasn's argument that contemporary consumer culture is a kind of cult.

Writing Suggestion

Lasn ends his essay by asking, "What does it mean when a whole culture
dreams the same dream?" Try writing a response to this question. What are the

characteristics of this dream that Lasn claims are shared by the entire culture? Why is it a problem if everyone dreams the same dream? Alternately, you can take issue with the question itself, either by arguing that what it implies isn't true (in other words, that we each dream different dreams), or by arguing that it's perfectly acceptable if we all dream the same dream. Be sure to support any claims in your essay with specific evidence drawn from Lasn's argument as well as from your own experiences and observations.

You might consider using the black-and-white image above as one of the examples in your essay. This image, a poster for Adbuster's "Buy Nothing Day," graphically presents the problem Lasn discusses in "The Cult You're In," and it also points to a solution, of sorts. How might the image be used to bolster an argument either for or against Lasn's assertions?

Salespeak

ROY FOX

A colleague who shall remain nameless once suggested an intriguing way for teachers to supplement their generally meager salaries: we could have our classes sponsored. We live in an age where double plays in baseball are sponsored by Jiffy Lube, where pro football games include the "Taco Bell Halftime Report," and where our shirts, shorts, shoes, and even underwear are imprinted with product names and logos. Why shouldn't teachers take advantage of a little corporate sponsorship? After all, we've got a captive audience of a very desirable demographic group (that's you). For a few extra dollars, we could easily play an advertising jingle softly in the background before class

starts; we could say, "This class is brought to you by Snapple!" at the begin-
ning of class, and distribute free samples as students leave at the end of class.

If this scenario seems strange to you, you're about to read an even
stranger scenario described by Roy Fox. Fox places us in a school of the
future, in which students attend classes to learn how to be good consumers.
They are inundated by advertisements, marketing pitches, and product-
testing at school, where they watch commercially sponsored lessons on TV,
read corporate-produced instructional materials, and shop at the school's
"Commoditarium." But what's more surprising is Fox's assertion that this
scenario is closer to reality than we might think.

What Fox calls "Salespeak" is infiltrating all aspects of our lives, but
in this selection, he is most interested with the ways that advertising and
merchandising have established themselves in classrooms and schools across
the country, changing the content and purpose of education. Fox is a
Professor of Education at the University of Missouri at Columbia and the
author of Mediaspeak, *from which this selection was excerpted.*

Before you read, *reflect on your experience as a student in a variety*
of schools. Have you been exposed to advertising or merchandising in the
classrooms, hallways, or cafeterias of your schools, or at school-sponsored
events? Does this strike you as odd?

No profit whatsoever can possibly be made but at the expense of another.
—Michel de Montaigne, "Of Liars," 1580

WHAT IS SALESPEAK?

Salespeak is any type of message surrounding a transaction between   1
people. First, Salespeak is persuasive in nature. It can convince us to purchase products and services. It can also persuade us, directly and indirectly, to "buy into" political candidates, beliefs, ideologies, attitudes,
values, and lifestyles. Salespeak persuades by presenting us with facts,
where logic, language, and numbers dominate the message. More often,
though, it persuades by massaging us—entertaining and arousing us,
and changing our emotions with imagery, sound effects, and music.

Second, Salespeak can function as a type of entertainment or   2
escapism—as an end in itself, where we are more focused on the experiences surrounding consumerism (e.g., browsing through an L. L.
Bean catalog) than we are on actually purchasing something. Salespeak
occurs when messages are crafted so as to "hit" a specific, "targeted"
audience. Therefore, Salespeakers collect and analyze information
about their audiences to help them shape their messages.

Third, Salespeak usually employs a systematic approach in 3
targeting its audience. A theme for Boltz laundry detergent, such as, "It's
white as lightning!" might unify different types of messages communicated through different channels. The goal here is to create "overlapping
fields of experience" (Ray 1982), hitting us from several sides in different
ways, in short, to create an "environment" of persuasion. In this chapter,
Salespeak also includes any type of message about transactions between
people, such as a market report describing a specific group of consumers.

We live in a market-driven economy in which we consume more 4
than we produce. It's little wonder, then, that Salespeak flows constantly—from television, billboards, print ads, and blinking Internet
messages. Because Salespeak touches nearly every area of life, its infinite tones and painstakingly crafted imagery appear in an endless variety of forms. Salespeak ranges from the hard-sell radio pitch of the
local Ford dealer to the vague, soft, amorphous TV commercial that
merely wants you to know that the good folks at Exxon care.

Salespeak includes the envelope in your mailbox that states, "God's 5
Holy Spirit said, 'Someone connected with this address needs this help.' "
Salespeak ranges from the on-screen commercial loops playing on the
ATM machine while you wait for your cash, to the plugs for car washes
that appear on the screens affixed to the gas pump as you fill up your car.
Salespeak even shows up in slot machines designed to entice children
(Glionna 1999). These slots for tots now feature themes such as
Candyland, Monopoly, the Three Stooges, the Pink Panther, and South
Park. This is the gaming industry's attempt to promote a "family-friendly"
image, which will help ensure that future generations will support the
casino industry (Ruskin 1999). Salespeak also sprouts from the "product
information" about a new computer embedded within the instructions for
installing a software program, from the camera shot in a popular film that
lingers on a bag of Frito's corn chips, and from the large sign inside
Russia's Mir space station that states, "Even in Space . . . Pepsi is Changing
the Script." Salespeak is indeed the script, on earth as it is in heaven.

A DAY IN THE LIFE

At 6:03 A.M., Mrs. Anderson's voice comes over the intercom into her 6
teenaged daughter's bedroom. Mrs. Anderson asks, "Pepsi? It's time to
wake up, dear. Pehhhp-si . . . are you up and moving?"

Pepsi answers groggily, "Yeah . . . I'm up. Morning, Mom." As 7
Pepsi sits up in bed, she reaches over and hits the button on her old
pink Barbie alarm clock, which rests on her old American Girl traditional oak jewelry box. As both cherished items catch her eye, she
pauses and wistfully recalls those happy days of girlhood, rubbing her

hand over the *Little Mermaid* bedsheet. If only she hadn't given away her favorite purple My Little Pony to her best childhood friend, Microsoft McKenzie, who lives next door.

Just then her mother's voice calls her back to reality, "Good deal, sweetie. Let me know when you finish your shower. I just got your Gap sweatshirt out of the dryer, but I couldn't get that Gatorade stain out of your Tommy Hilfiger pants, so I'm washing them again." 8

Once upstairs, Pepsi sits down for a bowl of Cap'n Crunch cereal. She peels a banana, carefully pulling off a bright yellow sticker, which states, "ABC. Zero calories." She places the used sticker onto her McDonald's book cover. Pepsi's younger brother, Nike, dressed in his Babylon Five T-shirt, places a Star Trek notebook into his Star Wars book bag as he intently watches the Amoco morning newscast on the video wall. The network anchor tells about the latest corporate merger as he reads from his perch within the "N" of the giant MSNBC logo. Then Mrs. Anderson walks into the nutrition pod. 9

Mrs. Anderson: Hey, Peps, what's going on at school today?
Pepsi: Nothing much. Just gotta finish that dumb science experiment.
Mrs. Anderson: Which one is that?
Pepsi: That one called "Digging for Data." We learned about scientific inquiry stuff and how to deduce conclusions. We learned that American settlers were short because they didn't eat enough meat and stuff like that.
Mrs. Anderson: Oh, yes! That was one of my favorites when I was in school. Those National Livestock and Meat Board teaching kits are wonderful! I liked it even better than Campbell Soup's "Prego Thickness Experiment." How 'bout you?
Pepsi: I dunno. Everyone already knows that Prego spaghetti sauce is three times thicker and richer than Ragu's sauce.
Mrs. Anderson: Well, yes, of course they do. But that's not the only point. There are larger goals here, namely, your becoming the best high-volume consumer possible. Isn't that right, dear?
Pepsi: Yeah, I guess so.

Pepsi's school bus, equipped with the latest electronic wraparound billboard, mentions that the price of Chocolate Cheetah Crunch "is being sliced as you read this—down to $48.95 per ten-pounder!" Pepsi takes her seat and discusses this price reduction with her locker partner, Reebok Robinson. They engage in a lively conversation about which of them loves Cheetah Crunch more. Next, the screen on the back of the seat in front of them catches their attention: a large dancing lamb sings, "Be there! Tonight only! At the IBM Mall! All remaining Rickon collectibles must go! Pledge bidding only! Be there!" Even Reebok cannot contain a squeal. 10

57

At school, Pepsi watches Channel One, the National Truth   11
Channel, during her first three classes. The first news story documents
the precise steps in which Zestra, the new star of the Z-5 Lectradisk corporate communication spots, went about purchasing her new video
wall unit. Afterward, Pepsi and her peers receive biofeedback printouts
of their responses registered during this program via the reaction console on their desks. Next, the students use voice-print technology to
describe what they were feeling during the broadcast.

Then their teacher, Ms. Qualcomm, tells them to take a twenty-   12
minute recess at the Commoditarium before they return for Tech Lab,
where they will begin the unit "Product Scanning: Art or Science?" At
the Commoditarium, Pepsi purchases one bag of Kwizzee sticks, one
can of Channel One soda, and a One-der Bar, in addition to a pair of
Golden Arch earrings she can't live without. The accessories for the
earrings, which she also longs for, will have to wait.

Back at Tech Lab, Pepsi and her peers receive a half hour of AT&T   13
("Allotted Time & Testing," sponsored by AT&T, in which students are
free to explore their own interests on the God-Net). In the upper-left
corner of her computer screen, Pepsi watches what appears to be an
enlarged part of human anatomy, alternately shrinking and enlarging,
as one of her favorite new songs beats in sync. The olfactory port of her
computer emits a musky odor. In the background of this pulsating
image, sticks of lightning flare randomly against a deep blue sky. Pepsi
looks at them more closely and detects that each one contains three
small letters: A, T, and T. She smiles, points, and clicks on the window.

Immediately, this message forms on screen in large, puffy blue   14
letters: "A, T, & T Loves You." Then the message begins dissolving and
enlarging simultaneously, so that the background is now the same blue
as the message. Huge lips fill the screen. Pepsi is unsure whether they
are the lips of a man or woman. The lips slowly murmur, "You,
Pepsi . . . You're the one . . . Oh, yes . . . Nobody else. Just you."

Pepsi, mesmerized, half whispers to herself, "Me?" as the lips   15
fade at the same time that the blue background re-forms into the previous message, "A, T, & T Loves You." Pepsi clicks again. Three golden
books appear on screen. One is titled "A, T, & T's Pledge to You, Pepsi
Anderson." Another one is titled, "Making Love Rich," and the third is
titled, "Us . . . Forever." The lights of the Tech Lab dim, signaling students that it's time to begin their new unit. The lights slowly fade out
until the lab is nearly dark. Pepsi hears muffled patriotic music from
the opposite side of the room—a flute and drum, playing the tune of
"Yankee Doodle Dandy." From the far end of the ceiling, an image of
the traditional "fyfe and drum corps"—the three ragged soldiers in
Revolutionary Army garb—come marching across the screen; above
the U.S. flag flies a larger one, with a golden arch on it.

As the tattered trio exit via a slow dissolve on the opposite end of 16
the ceiling screen, the room goes completely dark. Pepsi twists her
head and limbers up, as her classmates do, almost in unison. Then, on
instinct, Pepsi and her peers look upward to the neon green and pink
Laser Note swirling above them: "To thine own self, be blue. And rak-
est thou joy into thine own taste sphere! Tru-Blu Vervo Dots: now half
price at Commoditarium!" A laser image of Shakespeare forms from
the dissolving lights. Next, the bard's face dissolves into blue Vervo
Dots. Pepsi, feeling vaguely tired and hungry, saves her place on screen
so she can return later to find out what's in the three golden books.
Before she exits, she is automatically transferred to another screen so
that she can input her biofeedback prints from the past half hour.

At home that night, Pepsi and her family gather in the Recipient 17
Well. To activate the video wall, Mrs. Anderson submits a forehead print
on the ConsumaScan. Before any audio can be heard, a Nike logo appears
on the screen for two minutes. Mrs. Anderson turns to her daughter.

> *Mrs. Anderson:* So, Peps, you were awfully quiet at dinner. Are
> you okay? Everything all right at school?
>
> *Pepsi:* Fine. I just get tired of learning all the time.
>
> *Mrs. Anderson (sighing):* Well, sweetie, I know. Things are so much
> different nowadays than when I was your age. You kids have to
> work harder in school because there are so many more prod-
> ucts and services to keep up with.
>
> *Pepsi:* Yeah, I guess so . . . .
>
> *Mrs. Anderson:* But you've also got many luxuries we never had.
> Why, when I was born, parents were completely ignorant about
> giving their children beautiful names. My family just called me
> "Jennifer." Ugh! Can you believe it?
>
> *Pepsi:* Oh, gag me, Mom! "Jennifer"?! You're kidding! How did
> you and Dad name me?
>
> *Mrs. Anderson:* Well, let's see . . . .We first fell in love with your
> name when Pepsico offered us a lifetime membership at the
> Nova Health Spa if we'd name you "Pepsi." I thought it was so
> refreshing—not to mention thirst quenching and tasty. Besides—
> it's your generation!
>
> *Pepsi:* And I'll always love you and Dad for bestowing me with
> eternal brandness . . .
>
> *Mrs. Anderson:* It's just because we love you, that's all. Growing
> up branded is a lot easier these days—especially after the
> Renaissance of 2008, just after you were born.
>
> *Pepsi:* What was that?
>
> *Mrs. Anderson:* You know—*life cells!* We got them a few years after
> the Second Great Brand Cleansing War.

59

Pepsi: But I thought we always had life cells, that we were just born with 'em . . . .

Mrs. Anderson: My gosh, no, girl! When I was your age we had to stay glued to National Public Radio to keep up with the latest fluctuations of the NASDAQ and high tech markets.

Pepsi: Jeez . . . I can't imagine life without life cells.

Mrs. Anderson: Me either—now! Back then, it all started with Moletronics and the first conversions of Wall Street datastreams into what they used to call "subcutaneous pseudo-neurons." But that's ancient history for you!

Pepsi: Mom?

Mrs. Anderson: Yes, dear?

Pepsi: Can we set aside some special family time, so we can talk about that relationship portfolio with AT&T?

Mrs. Anderson: Well, of course! Maybe during spring break at the cabin? That's not the kind of thing we ever want to slight.

At this moment, the video wall's audio activates. The Nike   18
swoosh logo forms into a running cheetah as a male voice-over states, "Nike Leopard-Tech Laser Runners. Be the Cheetah you were born free to be." Mrs. Anderson turns back to her daughter and asks, "Would you mind running to the Pantry Pod and seeing if there's any more of that Chocolate Cheetah Crunch left?" "Sure," says Pepsi, turning as she leaves the room, "*If* we can talk about those new shoes I need." . . .

IS PEPSI'S WORLD ALREADY HERE?

Yes. Most of what happens to Pepsi in this scenario is based on fact. A   19
few other parts are extensions or exaggerations of what already occurs in everyday life. Let's begin with a girl named Pepsi. In Pepsi's world of Salespeak, nearly every facet of life is somehow linked to sales. Pepsi, the girl, lives in a Pepsi world, where person, product, and hype have merged with everyday life.

Salespeak is all-powerful. As small children, as soon as we   20
become aware that a world exists outside of ourselves, we become a "targeted audience." From then on, we think in the voices of Salespeak. We hear them, we see them. We smell them, taste them, touch them, dream them, become them. Salespeak is often targeted at young people, the group marketers most prize because first, they spend "disposable" income, as well as influence how their parents spend money (see the following section, "Notes from the World of Salespeak"); second, people tend to establish loyalties to certain brands early in life; and third, young people are more likely to buy items on impulse. For these

reasons and more, Salespeak is most prevalent and vivid for children and young adults. Hence, most of this chapter focuses on the layers of Salespeak that surround these groups. The core issue is targeting kids in the first place, regardless of the product being sold.

What's in a Name?

At this writing, I've neither read nor heard of a human being legally named after a product or service (though I feel certain that he or she is out there). I have, though, heard that school administrators in Plymouth, Michigan, are considering auctioning off school names to the highest bidder. It's only a matter of time before kids attend "Taco Bell Middle School" or "Gap Kids Elementary School" (Labi 1999). Appropriating names—and hence identities—is essentially an act of aggression, of control over others' personal identity. Our practice of naming things for commercial purposes is not new. Consider San Diego's Qualcomm Stadium. Unlike St. Louis's Busch Stadium or Denver's Coors Field, the name Qualcomm has no connections to people or things already traditionally linked with baseball. In Pepsi's world, "AT&T" stood for "Allotted Time for Testing." To my knowledge, commercial or corporate names have yet to be used for identifying processes. However, they have been used to identify specific places where educational processes occur. 21

For example, the Derby, Kansas, school district named its elementary school resource center the GenerationNext Center. The district agreed to use the Pepsi slogan to name their new facility, as well as to serve only Pepsi products, in exchange for one million dollars (Perrin 1997, 1A). Even ice cream is now named so that it can advertise something else: the name of Ben and Jerry's butter almond ice cream is called "Dilbert's World: Totally Nuts" (Solomon 1998a). 22

Every time we see or read or hear a commercial name, an "impression" registers. Advertising profits depend on the type and number of impressions made by each ad message. Therefore, Pepsi Anderson and her friend, Microsoft McKenzie, are walking, breathing, random ad messages. (Similar important names) are now devised solely for purposes of advertising. Nothing more. Such names become ads. In earlier times and in other cultures, as well as our own, names were sacred: they communicated the essence of our identity, not just to others but to ourselves as well. To rob someone of her name was to appropriate her identity, to deny her existence. In *I Know Why the Caged Bird Sings*, Maya Angelou speaks of how demoralizing it was for African Americans to be "called out of name" by white people, who would refer to any African American male as "boy," "Tom," or "Uncle." 23

Similarly, several years ago, the rock musician and composer known as Prince changed his name to a purely graphic symbol. The 24

61

result, of course, was that nobody could even pronounce it! By default he became known as "The Artist Formerly Known as Prince." In an interview on MTV, this musician-composer explained that the public believed he was crazy because print and electronic media had proclaimed him so, over and over. He therefore changed his name to something unpronounceable to halt this labeling. It worked. In effect, this man regained control of his own life because he found a way to stop others from controlling it for him, as they were doing by writing about him in the media. This man understands the general semantics principle that the word is not the thing symbolized—that the map is not the territory . . . .

The long-term effects of replacing real names with commercial   25
labels (of important spaces, processes, and possibly even people) can benefit nobody except those doing the appropriating—those reaping revenue from increased sales. At the very least, this practice demonstrates, in concrete, definitive ways, that we value materialism and the act of selling above all else.

Celebrating Coke Day at the Carbonated Beverage Company

At century's end, the question is not, "Where and when does Salespeak   26
appear?" Rather, the real question is, "Where and when does Salespeak *not* appear?" Only in churches and other places of worship? (Not counting, of course, the church that advertised itself by proclaiming on its outside message board: "Come in for a faith lift.") Salespeak is more than a voice we hear and see: we also wear it, smell it, touch it, play with it. Ads on book covers, notebooks, backpacks, pencils, and pens are common. So are the girl Pepsi's Gap sweatshirt, Tommy Hilfiger pants, Barbie alarm clock, and *Little Mermaid* bedsheets. The bulletins that Pepsi and her classmates received about current sales are also authentic: PepsiCo has offered free beepers to teens, who are periodically contacted with updated ad messages.

Salespeak is seeping into the smallest crevices of American life.   27
As you fill your car with gas, you can now watch commercials on a small screen on the gas pump. As you wait for your transaction at the ATM machine, you can view commercials. As you wait in the switchback line at an amusement park, you can watch commercials on several screens. As you wait in your doctor's office, you can read about medicines to buy, as well as watch commercials for them. As you stand in line at Wal-Mart's customer service desk, you can watch ads for Wal-Mart on a huge screen before you. As you wait for the phone to ring when making a long-distance call, you'll hear a soft, musical tinkle, followed by a velvety voice that intones, "AT&T."

As your children board their school bus, you'll see ads wrapped 28
around it. When you pick up a bunch of bananas in the grocery store,
like our friend Pepsi in the earlier scenario, you may have to peel off
yellow stickers that state, "ABC. Zero calories." When you call a certain
school in Texas and don't get an answer, you'll hear this recorded message: "Welcome to the Grapevine-Colleyville Independent School
District, where we are proudly sponsored by the Dr. Pepper Bottling
Company of Texas" (Perrin 1997).

Salespeak also commonly appears under the guise of school "cur- 29
riculum"—from formal business–education partnerships, to free teacher
workshops provided to introduce new textbooks. Corporate-produced
"instructional materials" are sometimes thinly veiled sales pitches that
can distort the truth. The curriculum unit "Digging for Data," mentioned
earlier as part of Pepsi's school day, is actual material used in schools.

For another "learning experience," students were assigned to be 30
"quality control technicians" as they completed "The Carbonated
Beverage Company" unit, provided free to schools by PepsiCo. Students
taste-tested colas, analyzed cola samples, took video tours of the St.
Louis Pepsi plant, and visited a local Pepsi plant (Bingham 1998, 1A).
Ads have even appeared in math textbooks. *Mathematics: Applications
and Connections,* published by McGraw-Hill, and used in middle schools,
includes problems that are just as much about advertising as they are
arithmetic—salespeak masquerading as education. Here's a sample dec-
imal division problem: "Will is saving his allowance to buy a pair of Nike
shoes that cost $68.25. If Will earns $3.25 per week, how many weeks will
Will need to save?" Directly next to this problem is a full-color picture of
a pair of Nike shoes (Hays 1999). The 1999 edition of this book contains
the following problem: "The best-selling packaged cookie in the world is
the Oreo cookie. The diameter of the Oreo cookie is 1.75 inches. Express
the diameter of an Oreo cookie as a fraction in simplest form." It seems
no accident that "Oreo" is repeated three times in this brief message; repetition is an ancient device used in propaganda and advertising. More
insidious is the fact that such textbooks present the act of saving money
for Nike shoes as a *natural* state of affairs, a given in life. Requiring captive audiences of kids to interact with brand names in such mentally
active ways helps ensure product-identification and brand-name loyalty
during kids' future years as consumers.

Some schools slavishly serve their corporate sponsors. After 31
sealing a deal with Coca-Cola, a school in Georgia implemented an
official "Coke Day" devoted to celebrating Coca-Cola products. On
that day, Mike Cameron, a senior at the school, chose to exercise his
right to think by wearing a T-shirt bearing the Pepsi logo. He was
promptly suspended ("This School Is Brought to You By: Cola?
Sneakers?" 1998, 11A).

63

This intense focus on selling products to a captive audience of   32
students is illustrated by the following letter sent to District 11's school
principals in Colorado Springs, Colorado. The letter was written by the
district's executive director of "school leadership." In September 1997,
the district had signed an $8 million contract with Coca-Cola (Labi 1999).

Dear Principal:

Here we are in year two of the great Coke contract . . . .

First, the good news: This year's installment from Coke is "in the house,"
and checks will be cut for you to pick up in my office this week. Your share will
be the same as last year.

Elementary School	$3,000
Middle School	$15,000
High School	$25,000

Now the not-so-good news: we must sell 70,000 cases of product (including
juices, sodas, waters, etc.) at least once during the first three years of the contract. If we reach this goal, your school allotments will be guaranteed for the
next seven years.

The math on how to achieve this is really quite simple. Last year we had
32,439 students, 3,000 employees, and 176 days in the school year. If 35,439 staff
and students buy one Coke product every other day for a school year, we will
double the required quota.

Here is how we can do it:

1. Allow students to purchase and consume vended products throughout the day.
   If sodas are not allowed in classes, consider allowing juices, teas, and waters.
2. Locate machines where they are accessible to the students all day. Research
   shows that vender purchases are closely linked to availability. Location, location,
   location is the key. You may have as many machines as you can handle. Pueblo
   Central High tripled its volume of sales by placing vending machines on all three
   levels of the school. The Coke people surveyed the middle and high schools this
   summer and have suggestions on where to place additional machines.
3. A list of Coke products is enclosed to allow you to select from the entire
   menu of beverages. Let me know which products you want, and we will get
   them in. Please let me know if you need electrical outlets.
4. A calendar of promotional events is enclosed to help you advertise
   Coke products.

I know this is "just one more thing from downtown," but the long-term benefits are worth it.

Thanks for your help.

John Bushey
The Coke Dude
(Bushey 1998)

With visionary leaders such as "The Coke Dude" to inspire them, 33
students will be well-prepared to perpetuate a world ruled by
Salespeak. Of course, Pepsi (the girl), Mike (the actual student expelled
for wearing a Pepsi T-shirt), and their fellow students did not begin
encountering ads in high school. It begins much earlier . . . .

The National Truth Channel

Many other details of Pepsi's day are anchored in fact, not fiction. In 34
Pepsi's not-too-distant world, Channel One television has become the
"National Truth Channel." Today Channel One, owned by a private
corporation, beams daily commercials to more than 8 million American
kids attending middle schools and high schools. It therefore imposes
more uniformity on public school kids and their curriculum than the
federal government ever has. For all practical purposes, it has indeed
been our "national" channel for several years.

Although I made up the "Truth" part of "The National Truth 35
Channel," I want to note that it serves as Doublespeak nested within
Salespeak—a common occurrence in real life. For example, the term "corporate communication" (used in Pepsi's world, above, to refer to commercials) is a euphemism that the Benetton company actually used to
refer to its ads. And although laser ads have yet to appear on the ceilings
of classrooms, as they do in Pepsi's world, it is true that a few years ago, a
company wanted to launch into geosynchronous orbit a massive panel
that could be emblazoned with a gigantic corporate logo, visible for periods of time, over certain cities (Doheny-Farina 1999). Here, the promise of
reality far exceeds what happened in Pepsi's fictional classroom.

Also, remember that "news story" about Zestra, a star of "corporate 36
communication" spots that Pepsi watched on Channel One? More truth
than fiction here, too. Since 1989, Channel One has sometimes blurred the
lines between news, commercials, and public service announcements. In
one study (Fox 1996), many students mistook commercials for news programs or public service announcements, such as those that warn viewers
about drunk driving. The result was that students knew the product
being advertised and regarded it warmly because, as one student told me,
"They [the manufacturers and advertisers] are trying to do good. They
care about us."

In the worst case of such blurring that I observed during the two- 37
year period of this study, the students could hardly be faulted. Instead,
the Salespeak was highly deceptive (merging with Doublespeak). That
is, PepsiCo's series of ads called "It's Like This" were designed to look
very much like documentary news footage and public service
announcements. The actors spoke directly into the swinging, handheld
camera, as if they were being interviewed; the ads were filmed in black

65

and white, and the product's name was never spoken by any of the people in the commercial, although the rapid-fire editing included brief shots of the Pepsi logo, in color, on signs and on merchandise.

Just as in Pepsi's world, described earlier in this chapter, real-life 38 ads are often embedded within programs, as well as other commercials, products, instructions, and even "transitional spaces" between one media message and another. For example, when the girl Pepsi took a break from her "learning," she went to the school's Commoditarium, or mini-mall, to shop for items that had been advertised at school. Again, there is truth here. Although schools do not yet contain minimalls, they do contain stores and increasing numbers of strategically placed vending machines. A ninth-grade girl told me that after students viewed Channel One in the morning and watched commercials for M&Ms candies, her teacher allowed them to take a break. The student said she'd often walk down the hall and purchase M&Ms from the vending machine. In such schools, operant conditioning is alive and well. This is not the only way in which many schools are emulating shopping malls. My daughter's high school cafeteria is a "food court," complete with McDonald's and Pizza Hut.

By establishing itself in public schools, Channel One automati- 39 cally "delivers" a captive, well-defined audience to its advertisers, more than was ever possible before. "Know thy audience"—as specifically as possible—is the name of the advertising game. Marketers have become increasingly effective at obtaining all kinds of demographic and psychographic information on consumers. Channel One increasingly hones its messages based on the constant flow of demographic information it extracts from viewers, often under the guise of "clubs" and contests, which seek information on individuals, teams, classes, and entire schools ("Be a Channel One School"). Channel One's printed viewing and "curriculum" guides for teachers, as well as its Web site for students, also constantly solicit marketing information.

NOTES FROM THE WORLD OF SALESPEAK

More than anything else, dominant voices may be shaped by their 40 environment. Consider the following facts about the environment that generates Salespeak:

- *$150 billion:* Amount spent by American advertisers each year, a cost that is passed on to consumers in higher prices. Landay (1998) summarizes our relationship with advertisers: "We pay their ad bills, we provide their profits, and we pay for their total tax write-off on the ads they place."

- *12 billion and 3 million:* The number of display ads and broadcast ads that Americans are collectively exposed to each day (Landay 1998).
- *2:* The number of times that we pay for advertising. First, advertising costs are built into the product. We pay again in terms of the time, money, and attention spent when processing an ad message.
- *1,000:* The number of chocolate chips in each bag of Chips Ahoy! cookies. The cookie company sponsored a "contest" in which students tried to confirm this claim (Labi 1999, 44).
- *$11 billion:* The amount of money dedicated to market research throughout the world (*World Opinion* Web site, November 11, 1998).
- *"Gosh, I don't understand—there are so many brands":* This is what one marketing firm has its researchers say, after they go into stores and place themselves next to real shoppers, in an effort to elicit what consumers are thinking in an authentic context (from the May 30, 1997, issue of the *Wall Street Journal* [McLaren 1998]).
- *$66 billion:* The amount of money spent by kids and young adults (ages 4–19) in 1992 (Bowen 1995).
- *16 million:* Approximate number of American children who use the Internet (*Brill's Content,* December 1998, 140).
- *115.95:* The number of banner ads viewed per week by the average Web user (*World Opinion* Web site, November 11, 1998).
- *"Save water. It's precious":* Message on a Coca-Cola billboard in Zimbabwe, where, according to the August 25, 1997, issue of the *Wall Street Journal,* the soft drink has become the drink of choice (necessity?) because of a water shortage (McLaren 1998).
- *$204 billion:* The estimated amount of Web-based transactions in 2001, up from $10.4 billion in 1997 (Zona Research 1999 on the *World Opinion* Web site).
- *89:* Percentage of children's Web sites that collect users' personal information (*Brill's Content,* December 1998, 140).
- *23:* Percentage of children's Web sites that tell kids to ask their parents for permission before sending personal information. (*Brill's Content,* December 1998, 140).
- *$29 million:* Net income for Nielsen Media Research during the first six months of 1998. (*Brill's Content,* December 1998, 140).
- *$36 billion:* The amount of money spent by kids and young adults in 1992 (ages 4–19) that belonged to their parents (Bowen 1995).
- *$3.4 million:* The amount of money received by the Grapevine-Colleyville Texas School District for displaying a huge Dr. Pepper logo atop the school roof. This school is in the flight path of Dallas-Fort Worth International Airport (Perrin 1997).
- *$8 million:* The amount of money received by the Colorado Springs School District in Colorado from Coca-Cola for an exclusive ten-year service agreement (Perrin 1997).

- *"A tight, enduring connection to teens"*: What Larry Jabbonsky, a spokesman at Pepsi headquarters, said his company seeks (Perrin 1997).
- *9,000*: The number of items stocked in grocery stores in the 1970s (Will 1997).
- *30,000*: The number of items now stocked in grocery stores (Will 1997).
- *99*: The percentage of teens surveyed (N = 534 in four cities) who correctly identified the croaking frogs from a Budweiser television commercial (Horovitz and Wells 1997, 1A).
- *93*: The percentage of teens who reported that they liked the Budweiser frogs "very much" or "somewhat" (Horovitz and Wells 1997, 1A).
- *95 and 94*: The percentages of teens who know the Marlboro man and Joe Camel (Wells 1997, 1A).
- *Great Britain's white cliffs of Dover*: The backdrop for a laser-projected Adidas ad (Liu 1999).
- *$200 million*: The amount of money Miller Beer spends on advertising each year.
- *Time Warner*: A corporate empire that controls news and information in America. (There are fewer than twelve.) Time Warner owns large book publishers, cable TV franchises, home video firms, CNN and other large cable channels, and magazines such as *Time, Life, People, Sports Illustrated, Money, Fortune,* and *Entertainment Weekly* (Solomon 1999b).
- *$650 billion*: Annual sales of approximately 1,000 telemarketing companies, which employ 4 million Americans (Shenk 1999, 59).
- *350,000*: The number of classrooms that view two minutes of television commercials every day on Channel One ("Selling to School Kids" 1995).
- *154*: The number of Coca-Cola cans that students must find on a book cover and then color in, to reveal a hidden message ("Selling to School Kids" 1995).
- *50*: The percentage of increase in advertising expenditures during the past fifteen years (Bowen 1995).
- *560*: The daily number of ads targeted at the average American in 1971 (Shenk 1999, 59).
- *3,000*: The daily number of ads targeted at the average American in 1991 (Shenk 1999, 59).
- *Business Update*: An hourly segment broadcast on National Public Radio. Even though NPR is supposed to focus on "public broadcasting," it does not offer a *Labor Update*.
- *3.4 trillion*: The number of e-mail messages that crossed the Internet in the United States in 1998—a number expected to double by 2001 (McCafferty 1999).

- *80 percent:* The percentage of America's e-mail messages in 1998 that were mass-produced e-mailings, "most from corporations with something to sell" (McCafferty 1998).

It's hardly unusual for a free enterprise system to employ   41
Salespeak. Advertising is a necessary ingredient for informing consumers about the goods and services they need. This is true for much of America's history. A sign hung in a trading post at the beginning of the Oregon Trail, 150 years ago, stating, "Sugar, 2 cents per lb.," contains necessary information for specific readers who had definite goals. Today, though, America is quite different.

First, unlike even forty years ago, most of today's advertising   42
carries scant information about the product or service. Second, the more affluent America becomes, the fewer true "needs" we have. To make up for it, advertisers now focus not so much on what we truly need, but on what we may desire. Third, very few limits are placed upon advertising: we have little control over where it appears, who can see it (note how many of the previous items focus on young people), how often it appears, how messages are constructed, or how much money is budgeted for them (at the expense of, say, improving the product). The field of advertising itself is now a major industry. The Bureau of Labor Statistics reports that in 1995, more people died on the job in advertising than in car factories, electrical repair companies, and petroleum refining operations (*Advertising Age*, August 19, 1996). Because advertising has such free rein in America, it's become one of our most dominating voices, if not the most dominating voice.

69

REFERENCES

Bingham, Janet. 1998. "Today's Topic: Soft Drink Flavors." *Denver Post,* June 12: p. 1A.

Bowen, Wally. 1995. "Ads, Ads Everywhere! Are There Any Limits?" *New Citizen* 2, no. 2:1.

Doheny-Farina, Stephen. 1998. Personal correspondence (March 17).

————. 1996. *Harvesting Minds: How TV Commercials Control Kids.* Westport, CT. Praeger Press.

Glionna, John. 1999. "Slot Machine Designers Use Controversial Spin." *Los Angeles Times.* (October 25): p. 4A.

Hays, Constance L. 1999. "Math Books Salted with Brand Names Raises New Alarm." *New York Times,* March 21: p. 1A, 22A.

Horovitz, Bruce, & Melanie Wells. 1997. "Ads for Adult Vices Big Hit with Teens." *USA Today,* January 31–February 2: pp. 1A–2A.

Labi, Nadya. 1999. "Classrooms for Sale." *Time* (April 19).

Landy, Jerry M. 1998. "Speed-Up Victims, Unite." Posting to Cultural Environment Movement Listserv (March 10).

Liu, Eric. 1999. "Remember When Public Spaces Didn't Carry Brand Names?" *USA Today*, March 25: p. 15A.

McCaffetry, Dennis. 1999. "www.hate.comes to your home." *USA Weekend* (March 26–28).

———. 1998. "World View." *Stay Free!* (January): 4–5.

Perrin, Tom. 1997. "Pop Quiz: Who's Paying Schools Big Bucks to Advertise?" *Kansas City Star*, October 18: p. 1A.

Ray, Michael. 1982. *Advertising and Communication Management, x.* Englewood Cliffs, NJ: Prentice-Hall.

Ruskin, Gary. 1999. "Slot Machines for Children." Personal correspondence, coalition letter to Senator John McCain, Representative Thomas Bliley, et al. (November 19). Commercial Alert: http://www.essential.org/alert.

"Selling to School Kids." 1995. *Consumer Report* (May): 327–329.

———. 1999. "Why You Feel the Way You Do?" *INC.* (January): 56–70.

Solomon, Norman. 1998a. "When All the World's a Stage—For Cashing In." Posting to Cultural Environment Movement Listserv (April 20).

———. 1999b. "And Now . . . Another Episode of Media Jeopardy." Posting to Cultural Environment Listserv (February 18).

"This School Is Brought to You By: Cola? Sneakers?" 1998. *USA Today*, March 27: p. 11A.

Wells, Melanie. 1997a. "Absolut's Eye-Catching Ads Command Teens' Attention." *USA Today*, January 31–February 2: p. 5B.

Will, George. 1997. "Advertisers Are in the Business to 'Rent' Our Attention." *Columbia* (Missouri) *Daily Tribune*, July 9: p. 6A.

World Opinion, November 11, 1998. "Quick Facts." http://www.worldopinion.com/latenews.

Examining the Text

1. Which parts of Pepsi's story ("A Day in the Life") are based on fact, according to Fox? Which parts of the story are "extensions or exaggerations of what already occurs in everyday life"? Do you find any of these "extensions or exaggerations" unrealistic or difficult to believe?

2. According to Fox, what's wrong with naming a person or a place after a product? Do you think there are qualitative differences between giving a product's name to a person, to a baseball stadium, or to a school?

3. What is a euphemism? List some of the euphemisms that Fox mentions in this reading. What problems does Fox see with these euphemisms?

4. *Thinking rhetorically:* In this article, Fox juxtaposes the fictional, futuristic, and seemingly outrageous story of the girl Pepsi with paragraphs of exposition and argument based on research. Do you find one of these strategies more persuasive than the other? How do they work together to prove his points?

For Group Discussion

In this article, Fox shows that he is particularly concerned with Salespeak in educational settings. In your discussion group, make a list of all the examples Fox gives to show where Salespeak is found in schools. Add examples to this list based on your own experience with Salespeak in your grade school, high school, and college experience. As a group, discuss whether your experiences tend to confirm or contradict Fox's claims that Salespeak exerts an undue influence in education.

Writing Suggestion

The article ends with a list of statistics about advertising. Use some of these statistics as evidence in an essay in which you give your opinion of the influence of advertising on our society. Consider using quotations from the article. You can use these statistics and quotations to support a position in which you agree with Fox's argument, or you can construct your essay by arguing against Fox, reinterpreting the statistics he offers, and taking issue with statements that you quote from the article.

Advertising's Fifteen Basic Appeals

JIB FOWLES

In the following essay, Jib Fowles looks at how advertisements work by examining the emotional, subrational appeals that they employ. We are confronted daily by hundreds of ads, only a few of which actually attract our attention. These few do so, according to Fowles, through "something primary and primitive, an emotional appeal, that in effect is the thin edge of the wedge, trying to find its way into a mind." Drawing on research done by the psychologist Henry A. Murray, Fowles describes fifteen emotional appeals or wedges that advertisements exploit.

Underlying Fowles's psychological analysis of advertising is the assumption that advertisers try to circumvent the logical, cautious, skeptical powers we develop as consumers, to reach, instead, the "unfulfilled urges and motives swirling in the bottom half of [our] minds." In Fowles's view, consumers are well-advised to pay attention to these underlying appeals in order to avoid responding unthinkingly.

As you read, note which of Fowles's fifteen appeals seem most familiar to you. Do you recognize these appeals in ads you can recall? How have you responded?

EMOTIONAL APPEALS

The nature of effective advertisements was recognized full well by the 1
late media philosopher Marshall McLuhan. In his *Understanding Media,*
the first sentence of the section on advertising reads, "The continuous
pressure is to create ads more and more in the image of audience
motives and desires."

By giving form to people's deep-lying desires, and picturing 2
states of being that individuals privately yearn for, advertisers have the
best chance of arresting attention and affecting communication. And
that is the immediate goal of advertising: to tug at our psychological
shirt sleeves and slow us down long enough for a word or two about
whatever is being sold. We glance at a picture of a solitary rancher at
work, and "Marlboro" slips into our minds.

Advertisers (I'm using the term as a shorthand for both the prod- 3
ucts' manufacturers, who bring the ambition and money to the process,
and the advertising agencies, who supply the know-how) are ever more
compelled to invoke consumers' drives and longings; this is the "continuous pressure" McLuhan refers to. Over the past century, the American
marketplace has grown increasingly congested as more and more products have entered into the frenzied competition after the public's dollars.
The economies of other nations are quieter than ours since the volume of
goods being hawked does not so greatly exceed demand. In some
economies, consumer wares are scarce enough that no advertising at all is
necessary. But in the United States, we go to the other extreme. In order to
stay in business, an advertiser must strive to cut through the considerable
commercial hub-bub by any means available—including the emotional
appeals that some observers have held to be abhorrent and underhanded.

The use of subconscious appeals is a comment not only on condi- 4
tions among sellers. As time has gone by, buyers have become stoutly
resistant to advertisements. We live in a blizzard of these messages and
have learned to turn up our collars and ward off most of them. A study
done a few years ago at Harvard University's Graduate School of
Business Administration ventured that the average American is exposed
to some 500 ads daily from television, newspapers, magazines, radio, billboards, direct mail, and so on. If for no other reason than to preserve one's
sanity, a filter must be developed in every mind to lower the number of
ads a person is actually aware of—a number this particular study estimated at about seventy-five ads per day. (Of these, only twelve typically
produced a reaction—nine positive and three negative, on the average.)
To be among the few messages that do manage to gain access to minds,
advertisers must be strategic, perhaps even a little underhanded at times.

There are assumptions about personality underlying advertisers' 5
efforts to communicate via emotional appeals, and while these

assumptions have stood the test of time, they still deserve to be aired. Human beings, it is presumed, walk around with a variety of unfulfilled urges and motives swirling in the bottom half of their minds. Lusts, ambitions, tendernesses, vulnerabilities—they are constantly bubbling up, seeking resolution. These mental forces energize people, but they are too crude and irregular to be given excessive play in the real world. They must be capped with the competent, sensible behavior that permits individuals to get along well in society. However, this upper layer of mental activity, shot through with caution and rationality, is not receptive to advertising's pitches. Advertisers want to circumvent this shell of consciousness, if they can, and latch on to one of the lurching, subconscious drives.

In effect, advertisers over the years have blindly felt their way 6
around the underside of the American psyche, and, by trial and error, have discovered the softest points of entree, the places where their messages have the greatest likelihood of getting by consumers' defenses. As McLuhan says elsewhere, "Gouging away at the surface of public sales resistance, the ad men are constantly breaking through into the *Alice in Wonderland* territory behind the looking glass, which is the world of subrational impulses and appetites."

An advertisement communicates by making use of a specially 7
selected image (of a supine female, say, or a curly-haired child, or a celebrity) which is designed to stimulate "subrational impulses and desires" even when they are at ebb, even if they are unacknowledged by their possessor. Some few ads have their emotional appeal in the text, but for the greater number by far the appeal is contained in the artwork. This makes sense, since visual communication better suits more primal levels of the brain. If the viewer of an advertisement actually has the importuned motive, and if the appeal is sufficiently well fashioned to call it up, then the person can be hooked. The product in the ad may then appear to take on the semblance of gratification for the summoned motive. Many ads seem to be saying, "If you have this need, then this product will help satisfy it." It is a primitive equation, but not an ineffective one for selling.

Thus, most advertisements appearing in national media can be 8
understood as having two orders of content. The first is the appeal to deep-running drives in the minds of consumers. The second is information regarding the good[s] or service being sold: its name, its manufacturer, its picture, its packaging, its objective attributes, its functions. For example, the reader of a brassiere advertisement sees a partially undraped but blandly unperturbed woman standing in an otherwise commonplace public setting, and may experience certain sensations; the reader also sees the name "Maidenform," a particular brassiere style, and, in tiny print, words about the material, colors, price. Or, the viewer of a television commercial sees a demonstration with four small boxes labeled 650, 650, 650, and 800; something in the viewer's mind catches hold of

this, as trivial as thoughtful consideration might reveal it to be. The viewer is also exposed to the name "Anacin," its bottle, and its purpose.

Sometimes there is an apparently logical link between an ad's 9 emotional appeal and its product information. It does not violate common sense that Cadillac automobiles be photographed at country clubs, or that Japan Air Lines be associated with Orientalia. But there is no real need for the linkage to have a bit of reason behind it. Is there anything inherent to the connection between Salem cigarettes and mountains, Coke and a smile, Miller Beer and comradeship? The link being forged in minds between product and appeal is a pre-logical one.

People involved in the advertising industry do not necessarily 10 talk in the terms being used here. They are stationed at the sending end of this communications channel, and may think they are up to any number of things—Unique Selling Propositions, explosive copy-writing, the optimal use of demographics or psychographics, ideal media buys, high recall ratings, or whatever. But when attention shifts to the receiving end of the channel, and focuses on the instant of reception, then commentary becomes much more elemental: an advertising message contains something primary and primitive, an emotional appeal, that in effect is the thin end of the wedge, trying to find its way into a mind. Should this occur, the product information comes along behind.

When enough advertisements are examined in this light, it 11 becomes clear that the emotional appeals fall into several distinguishable categories, and that every ad is a variation on one of a limited number of basic appeals. While there may be several ways of classifying these appeals, one particular list of fifteen has proven to be especially valuable.

Advertisements can appeal to:

1. The need for sex
2. The need for affiliation
3. The need to nurture
4. The need for guidance
5. The need to aggress
6. The need to achieve
7. The need to dominate
8. The need for prominence
9. The need for attention
10. The need for autonomy
11. The need to escape
12. The need to feel safe
13. The need for aesthetic sensations
14. The need to satisfy curiosity
15. Physiological needs: food, drink, sleep, etc.

MURRAY'S LIST

Where does this list of advertising's fifteen basic appeals come from? 12
Several years ago, I was involved in a research project which was to
have as one segment an objective analysis of the changing appeals made
in post–World War II American advertising. A sample of magazine ads
would have their appeals coded into the categories of psychological
needs they seemed aimed at. For this content analysis to happen, a complete roster of human motives would have to be found.

The first thing that came to mind was Abraham Maslow's famous 13
four-part hierarchy of needs. But the briefest look at the range of
appeals made in advertising was enough to reveal that they are more
varied, and more profane, than Maslow had cared to account for. The
search led on to the work of psychologist Henry A. Murray, who
together with his colleagues at the Harvard Psychological Clinic has
constructed a full taxonomy of needs. As described in *Explorations in
Personality*, Murray's team had conducted a lengthy series of in-depth
interviews with a number of subjects in order to derive from scratch
what they felt to be the essential variables of personality. Forty-four
variables were distinguished by the Harvard group, of which twenty
were motives. The need for achievement ("to overcome obstacles and
obtain a high standard") was one, for instance; the need to defer was
another; the need to aggress was a third; and so forth.

Murray's list had served as the groundwork for a number of 14
subsequent projects. Perhaps the best-known of these was David
C. McClelland's extensive study of the need for achievement, reported
in his *The Achieving Society*. In the process of demonstrating that a
people's high need for achievement is predictive of later economic
growth, McClelland coded achievement imagery and references out of
a nation's folklore, songs, legends, and children's tales.

Following McClelland, I too wanted to cull the motivational 15
appeals from a culture's imaginative product—in this case, advertising.
To develop categories expressly for this purpose, I took Murray's twenty
motives and added to them others he had mentioned in passing in
Explorations in Personality but not included on the final list. The extended
list was tried out on a sample of advertisements, and motives which
never seemed to be invoked were dropped. I ended up with eighteen of
Murray's motives, into which 770 print ads were coded. The resulting distribution is included in the 1976 book *Mass Advertising as Social Forecast*.

Since that time, the list of appeals has undergone refinements as a 16
result of using it to analyze television commercials. A few more adjust-
ments stemmed from the efforts of students in my advertising classes
to decode appeals; tens of term papers surveying thousands of advertisements have caused some inconsistencies in the list to be hammered

out. Fundamentally, though, the list remains the creation of Henry Murray. In developing a comprehensive, parsimonious inventory of human motives, he pinpointed the subsurface mental forces that are the least quiescent and most susceptible to advertising's entreaties.

FIFTEEN APPEALS

1. *Need for sex.* Let's start with sex, because this is the appeal which seems to pop up first whenever the topic of advertising is raised. Whole books have been written about this one alone, to find a large audience of mildly titillated readers. Lately, due to campaigns to sell blue jeans, concern with sex in ads has redoubled. 17

The fascinating thing is not how much sex there is in advertising, but how little. Contrary to impressions, unambiguous sex is rare in these messages. Some of this surprising observation may be a matter of definition: the Jordache ads with the lithe, blouse-less female astride a similarly clad male is clearly an appeal to the audience's sexual drives, but the same cannot be said about Brooke Shields in the Calvin Klein commercials. Directed at young women and their credit-card carrying mothers, the image of Miss Shields instead invokes the need to be looked at. Buy Calvins and you'll be the center of much attention, just as Brooke is, the ads imply; they do not primarily inveigle their target audience's need for sexual intercourse. 18

In the content analysis reported in *Mass Advertising as Social Forecast,* only two percent of ads were found to pander to this motive. Even *Playboy* ads shy away from sexual appeals: a recent issue contained eighty-three full-page ads, and just four of them (or less than five percent) could be said to have sex on their minds. 19

The reason this appeal is so little used is that it is too blaring and tends to obliterate the product information. Nudity in advertising has the effect of reducing brand recall. The people who do remember the product may do so because they have been made indignant by the ad; this is not the response most advertisers seek. 20

To the extent that sexual imagery is used, it conventionally works better on men than women; typically a female figure is offered up to the male reader. A Black Velvet liquor advertisement displays an attractive woman wearing a tight black outfit, recumbent under the legend, "Feel the Velvet." The figure does not have to be horizontal, however, for the appeal to be present as National Airlines revealed in its "Fly me" campaign. Indeed, there does not even have to be a female in the ad; "Flick my Bic" was sufficient to convey the idea to many. 21

As a rule, though, advertisers have found sex to be a tricky appeal, to be used sparingly. Less controversial and equally fetching are the appeals to our need for affectionate human contact. 22

2. *Need for affiliation.* American mythology upholds autonomous 23
individuals, and social statistics suggest that people are ever more going
it alone in their lives, yet the high frequency of affiliative appeals in ads
belies this. Or maybe it does not: maybe all the images of companionship
are compensation for what Americans privately lack. In any case, the
need to associate with others is widely invoked in advertising and is
probably the most prevalent appeal. All sorts of goods and services are
sold by linking them to our unfulfilled desires to be in good company.

According to Henry Murray, the need for affiliation consists of 24
desires "to draw near and enjoyably cooperate or reciprocate with
another; to please and win affection of another; to adhere and remain
loyal to a friend." The manifestations of this motive can be segmented
into several different types of affiliation, beginning with romance.

Courtship may be swifter nowadays, but the desire for pair-bonding 25
is far from satiated. Ads reaching for this need commonly depict a
youngish male and female engrossed in each other. The head of the male is
usually higher than the female's, even at this late date; she may be sitting
or leaning while he is standing. They are not touching in the Smirnoff
vodka ads, but obviously there is an intimacy, sometimes frolicsome,
between them. The couple does touch for Martell Cognac when "The
moment was Martell." For Wind Song perfume they have touched, and
"Your Wind Song stays on his mind."

Depending on the audience, the pair does not absolutely have to 26
be young—just together. He gives her a DeBeers diamond, and there is
a tear in her laugh lines. She takes Geritol and preserves herself for
him. And numbers of consumers, wanting affection too, follow suit.

Warm family feelings are fanned in ads when another generation 27
is added to the pair. Hallmark Cards brings grandparents into the picture, and Johnson and Johnson Baby Powder has Dad, Mom, and baby,
all fresh from the bath, encircled in arms and emblazoned with "Share
the Feeling." A talc has been fused to familial love.

Friendship is yet another form of affiliation pursued by advertisers. 28
Two women confide and drink Maxwell House coffee together; two men
walk through the woods smoking Salem cigarettes. Miller Beer promises
that afternoon "Miller Time" will be staffed with three or four good buddies. Drink Dr. Pepper, as Mickey Rooney is coaxed to do, and join in
with all the other Peppers. Coca-Cola does not even need to portray the
friendliness; it has reduced this appeal to "a Coke and a smile."

The warmth can be toned down and disguised, but it is the same 29
affiliative need that is being fished for. The blonde has a direct gaze and
her friends are firm businessmen in appearance, but with a glass of Old
Bushmill you can sit down and fit right in. Or, for something more
upbeat, sing along with the Pontiac choirboys.

As well as presenting positive images, advertisers can play to the 30
need for affiliation in negative ways, by invoking the fear of rejection. If

77

we don't use Scope, we'll have the "Ugh! Morning Breath" that causes the male and female models to avert their faces. Unless we apply Ultra Brite or Close-Up to our teeth, it's good-bye romance. Our family will be cursed with "House-a-tosis" if we don't take care. Without Dr. Scholl's antiperspirant foot spray, the bowling team will keel over. There go all the guests when the supply of Dorito's nacho cheese chips is exhausted. Still more rejection if our shirts have ring-around-the-collar, if our car needs to be Midasized. But make a few purchases, and we are back in the bosom of human contact.

As self-directed as Americans pretend to be, in the last analysis we remain social animals, hungering for the positive, endorsing feelings that only those around us can supply. Advertisers respond, urging us to "Reach out and touch someone," in the hopes our monthly bills will rise. 31

3. *Need to nurture.* Akin to affiliative needs is the need to take care of small, defenseless creatures—children and pets, largely. Reciprocity is of less consequence here, though; it is the giving that counts. Murray uses synonyms like "to feed, help, support, console, protect, comfort, nurse, heal." A strong need it is, woven deep into our genetic fabric, for if it did not exist, we could not successfully raise up our replacements. When advertisers put forth the image of something diminutive and furry, something that elicits the word "cute" or "precious," then they are trying to trigger this motive. We listen to the childish voice singing the Oscar Mayer wiener song, and our next hotdog purchase is prescribed. Aren't those darling kittens something, and how did this Meow Mix get into our shopping cart? 32

This pitch is often directed at women, as Mother Nature's chief nurturers. "Make me some Kraft macaroni and cheese, please," says the elfin preschooler just in from the snowstorm, and mothers' hearts go out, and Kraft's sales go up. "We're cold, wet, and hungry," whine the husband and kids, and the little woman gets the Manwiches ready. A facsimile of this need can be hit without children or pets: the husband is ill and sleepless in the television commercial, and the wife grudgingly fetches the NyQuil. 33

But it is not women alone who can be touched by this appeal. The father nurses his son Eddie through adolescence while the John Deere lawn tractor survives the years. Another father counts pennies with his young son as the subject of New York Life Insurance comes up. And all over America are businessmen who don't know why they dial Qantas Airlines when they have to take a trans-Pacific trip; the koala bear knows. 34

4. *Need for guidance.* The opposite of the need to nurture is the need to be nurtured: to be protected, shielded, guided. We may be loath to admit it, but the child lingers on inside every adult—and a good thing it does, or we would not be instructable in our advancing years. Who wants a nation of nothing but flinty personalities? 35

Parent-like figures can successfully call up this need. Robert 36
Young recommends Sanka coffee, and since we have experienced him
for twenty-five years as television father and doctor, we take his word
for it. Florence Henderson as the expert mom knows a lot about the
advantages of Wesson oil.

The parent-ness of the spokesperson need not be so salient; some- 37
times pure authoritativeness is better. When Orson Welles scowls and
intones, "Paul Masson will sell no wine before its time," we may not
know exactly what he means, but we still take direction from him.
There is little maternal about Brenda Vaccaro when she speaks up for
Tampax, but there is a certainty to her that many accept.

A celebrity is not a necessity in making a pitch to the need for 38
guidance, since a fantasy figure can serve just as well. People accede to
the Green Giant, or Betty Crocker, or Mr. Goodwrench. Some advertisers
can get by with no figure at all: "When E.F. Hutton talks, people listen."

Often it is tradition or custom that advertisers point to and 39
consumers take guidance from. Bits and pieces of American history are
used to sell whiskeys like Old Crow, Southern Comfort, Jack Daniel's. We
conform to traditional male/female roles and age-old social norms when
we purchase Barclay cigarettes, which informs us *The pleasure is back.*

The product itself, if it has been around for a long time, can constitute 40
a tradition. All those old labels in the ad for Morton salt convince us that
we should continue to buy it. Kool-Aid says, "You loved it as a kid. You
trust it as a mother," hoping to get yet more consumers to go along.

Even when the product has no history at all, our need to conform to 41
tradition and to be guided are strong enough that they can be invoked
through bogus nostalgia and older actors. Country-Time lemonade sells
because consumers want to believe it has a past they can defer to.

So far the needs and the ways they can be invoked which have 42
been looked at are largely warm and affiliative; they stand in contrast
to the next set of needs, which are much more egoistic and assertive.

5. *Need to aggress.* The pressures of the real world create strong 43
retaliatory feelings in every functioning human being. Since these
impulses can come forth as bursts of anger and violence, their display
is normally tabooed. Existing as harbored energy, aggressive drives
present a large, tempting target for advertisers. It is not a target to be
aimed at thoughtlessly, though, for few manufacturers want their
products associated with destructive motives. There is always the danger that, as in the case of sex, if the appeal is too blatant, public opinion
will turn against what is being sold.

Jack-in-the-Box sought to abruptly alter its marketing by going 44
after older customers and forgetting the younger ones. Their television
commercials had a seventy-ish lady command, "Waste him," and the
Jack-in-the-Box clown exploded before our eyes. So did public reaction

until the commercials were toned down. Print ads for Club cocktails carried the faces of octogenarians under the headline, "Hit me with a Club"; response was contrary enough to bring the campaign to a stop.

Better disguised aggressive appeals are less likely to backfire: 45 Triumph cigarettes has models making a lewd gesture with their uplifted cigarettes, but the individuals are often laughing and usually in close company of others. When Exxon said, "There's a Tiger in your tank," the implausibility of it concealed the invocation of aggressive feelings.

Depicted arguments are a common way for advertisers to tap the 46 audience's needs to aggress. Don Rickles and Lynda Carter trade gibes, and consumers take sides as the name of Seven-Up is stitched on minds. The Parkay tub has a difference of opinion with the user; who can forget it, or who (or what) got the last word in?

6. *Need to achieve.* This is the drive that energizes people, causing 47 them to strive in their lives and careers. According to Murray, the need for achievement is signalled by the desires "to accomplish something difficult. To overcome obstacles and attain a high standard. To excel one's self. To rival and surpass others." A prominent American trait, it is one that advertisers like to hook on to because it identifies their product with winning and success.

The Cutty Sark ad does not disclose that Ted Turner failed at his 48 latest attempt at yachting's America Cup; here he is represented as a champion on the water as well as off in his television enterprises. If we drink this whiskey, we will be victorious alongside Turner. We can also succeed with O.J. Simpson by renting Hertz cars, or with Reggie Jackson by bringing home some Panasonic equipment. Cathy Rigby and Stayfree Maxipads will put people out front.

Sports heroes are the most convenient means to snare consumers' 49 needs to achieve, but they are not the only one. Role models can be established, ones which invite emulation, as with the profiles put forth by Dewar's scotch. Successful, tweedy individuals relate they have "graduated to the flavor of Myer's rum." Or the advertiser can establish a prize: two neighbors play one-on-one basketball for a Michelob beer in a television commercial, while in a print ad a bottle of Johnnie Walker Black Label has been gilded like a trophy.

Any product that advertises itself in superlatives—the best, the 50 first, the finest—is trying to make contact with our needs to succeed. For many consumers, sales and bargains belong in this category of appeals, too; the person who manages to buy something at fifty percent off is seizing an opportunity and coming out ahead of others.

7. *Need to dominate.* This fundamental need is the craving to be 51 powerful—perhaps omnipotent, as in the Xerox ad where Brother Dominic exhibits heavenly powers and creates miraculous copies. Most of us will settle for being just a regular potentate, though. We

drink Budweiser because it is the King of Beers, and here comes the powerful Clydesdales to prove it. A taste of Wolfschmidt vodka and "The spirit of the Czar lives on."

The need to dominate and control one's environment is often 52 thought of as being masculine, but as close students of human nature advertisers know, it is not so circumscribed. Women's aspirations for control are suggested in the campaign theme, "I like my men in English Leather, or nothing at all." The females in the Chanel No. 19 ads are "outspoken" and wrestle their men around.

Male and female, what we long for is clout; what we get in its 53 place is Mastercard.

8. *Need for prominence.* Here comes the need to be admired and 54 respected, to enjoy prestige and high social status. These times, it appears, are not so egalitarian after all. Many ads picture the trappings of high position; the Oldsmobile stands before a manorial doorway, the Volvo is parked beside a steeplechase. A book-lined study is the setting for Dewar's 12, and Lenox China is displayed in a dining room chock full of antiques.

Beefeater gin represents itself as "The Crown Jewel of England" 55 and uses no illustrations of jewels or things British, for the words are sufficient indicators of distinction. Buy that gin and you will rise up the prestige hierarchy, or achieve the same effect on yourself with Seagram's 7 Crown, which ambiguously describes itself as "classy."

81

Being respected does not have to entail the usual accoutrements 56 of wealth: "Do you know who I am?" the commercials ask, and we learn that the prominent person is not so prominent without his American Express card.

9. *Need for attention.* The previous need involved being *looked up to,* 57 while this is the need to be *looked at.* The desire to exhibit ourselves in such a way as to make others look at us is a primitive, insuppressible instinct. The clothing and cosmetic industries exist just to serve this need, and this is the way they pitch their wares. Some of this effort is aimed at males, as the ads for Hathaway shirts and Jockey underclothes. But the greater bulk of such appeals is targeted singlemindedly at women.

To come back to Brooke Shields: this is where she fits into 58 American marketing. If I buy Calvin Klein jeans, consumers infer, I'll be the object of fascination. The desire for exhibition has been most strikingly played to in a print campaign of many years' duration, that of Maidenform lingerie. The woman exposes herself, and sales surge. "Gentlemen prefer Hanes" the ads dissemble, and women who want eyes upon them know what they should do. Peggy Fleming flutters her legs for L'eggs, encouraging females who want to be the star in their own lives to purchase this product.

The same appeal works for cosmetics and lotions. For years, the lit- 59 tle girl with the exposed backside sold gobs of Coppertone, but now the company has picked up the pace a little: as a female, you are supposed to "Flash 'em a Coppertone tan." Food can be sold the same way, especially to the diet-conscious; Angie Dickinson poses for California avocados and says, "Would this body lie to you?" Our eyes are too fixed on her for us to think to ask if she got that way by eating mounds of guacamole.

10. *Need for autonomy.* There are several ways to sell credit card ser- 60
vices, as has been noted: Mastercard appeals to the need to dominate, and American Express to the need for prominence. When Visa claims, "You can have it the way you want it," yet another primary motive is being beckoned forward—the need to endorse the self. The focus here is upon the independence and integrity of the individual; this need is the antithesis of the need for guidance and is unlike any of the social needs. "If running with the herd isn't your style, try ours," says Rotan-Mosle, and many Americans feel they have finally found the right brokerage firm.

The photo is of a red-coated Mountie on his horse, posed on a 61
snow-covered ledge; the copy reads, "Windsor—One Canadian stands alone." This epitome of the solitary and proud individual may work best with male customers, as may Winston's man in the red cap. But one-figure advertisements also strike the strong need for autonomy among American women. As Shelly Hack strides for Charlie perfume, females respond to her obvious pride and flair; she is her own person. The Virginia Slims tale is of people who have come a long way from subservience to independence. Cachet perfume feels it does not need a solo figure to work this appeal, and uses three different faces in its ads; it insists, though, "It's different on every woman who wears it."

Like many psychological needs, this one can also be appealed to in 62
a negative fashion, by invoking the loss of independence or self-regard. Guilt and regrets can be stimulated: "Gee, I could have had a V-8." Next time, get one and be good to yourself.

11. *Need to escape.* An appeal to the need for autonomy often co- 63
occurs with one for the need to escape, since the desire to duck out of our social obligations, to seek rest or adventure, frequently takes the form of one-person flight. The dashing image of a pilot, in fact, is a standard way of quickening this need to get away from it all.

Freedom is the pitch here, the freedom that every individual 64
yearns for whenever life becomes too oppressive. Many advertisers like appealing to the need for escape because the sensation of pleasure often accompanies escape, and what nicer emotional nimbus could there be for a product? "You deserve a break today," says McDonald's, and Stouffer's frozen foods chime in, "Set yourself free."

For decades men have imaginatively bonded themselves to the 65
Marlboro cowboy who dwells untarnished and unencumbered in Marlboro Country some distance from modern life; smokers' aching needs for autonomy and escape are personified by that cowpoke. Many

women can identify with the lady ambling through the woods behind the words, "Benson and Hedges and mornings and me."

But escape does not have to be solitary. Other Benson and Hedges ads, part of the same campaign, contain two strolling figures. In Salem cigarette advertisements, it can be several people who escape together into the mountaintops. A commercial for Levi's pictured a cloudbank above a city through which ran a whole chain of young people. 66

There are varieties of escape, some wistful like the Boeing "Someday" campaign of dream vacations, some kinetic like the play and parties in soft drink ads. But in every instance, the consumer exposed to the advertisement is invited to momentarily depart his everyday life for a more carefree experience, preferably with the product in hand. 67

12. *Need to feel safe.* Nobody in their right mind wants to be intimidated, menaced, battered, poisoned. We naturally want to do whatever it takes to stave off threats to our well-being, and to our families'. It is the instinct of self-preservation that makes us responsive to the ad of the St. Bernard with the keg of Chivas Regal. We pay attention to the stern talk of Karl Malden and the plight of the vacationing couples who have lost all their funds in the American Express travelers cheques commercials. We want the omnipresent stag from Hartford Insurance to watch over us too. 68

In the interest of keeping failure and calamity from our lives, we like to see the durability of products demonstrated. Can we ever forget that Timex takes a licking and keeps on ticking? When the American Tourister suitcase bounces all over the highway and the egg inside doesn't break, the need to feel safe has been adroitly plucked. 69   **83**

We take precautions to diminish future threats. We buy Volkswagen Rabbits for the extraordinary mileage, and MONY insurance policies to avoid the tragedies depicted in their black-and-white ads of widows and orphans. 70

We are careful about our health. We consume Mazola margarine because it has "corn goodness" backed by the natural food traditions of the American Indians. In the medicine cabinet is Alka-Seltzer, the "home remedy"; having it, we are snug in our little cottage. 71

We want to be safe and secure; buy these products, advertisers are saying, and you'll be safer than you are without them. 72

13. *Need for aesthetic sensations.* There is an undeniable aesthetic component to virtually every ad run in the national media: the photography or filming or drawing is near-perfect, the type style is well chosen, the layout could scarcely be improved upon. Advertisers know there is little chance of good communication occurring if an ad is not visually pleasing. Consumers may not be aware of the extent of their own sensitivity to artwork, but it is undeniably large. 73

Sometimes the aesthetic element is expanded and made into an ad's primary appeal. Charles Jordan shoes may or may not appear in the 74 accompanying avant-garde photographs; Kohler plumbing fixtures catch attention through the high style of their desert settings. Beneath the slightly out of focus photograph, languid and sensuous in tone, General Electric feels called upon to explain, "This is an ad for the hair dryer."

This appeal is not limited to female consumers: J&B scotch says 75 "It whispers" and shows a bucolic scene of lake and castle.

14. *Need to satisfy curiosity.* It may seem odd to list a need for 76 information among basic motives, but this need can be as primal and compelling as any of the others. Human beings are curious by nature, interested in the world around them, and intrigued by tidbits of knowledge and new developments. Trivia, percentages, observations counter to conventional wisdom—these items all help sell products. Any advertisement in a question-and-answer format is strumming this need.

A dog groomer has a question about long distance rates, and Bell 77 Telephone has a chart with all the figures. An ad for Porsche 911 is replete with diagrams and schematics, numbers and arrows. Lo and behold, Anacin pills have 150 more milligrams than its competitors; should we wonder if this is better or worse for us?

15. *Physiological needs.* To the extent that sex is solely a biological 78 need, we are now coming around full circle, back toward the start of the list. In this final category are clustered appeals to sleeping, eating, drinking. The art of photographing food and drink is so advanced, sometimes these temptations are wondrously caught in the camera's lens: the crab meat in the Red Lobster restaurant ads can start us salivating, the Quarterpounder can almost be smelled, the liquor in the glass glows invitingly. Imbibe, these ads scream.

STYLES

Some common ingredients of advertisements were not singled out for 79 separate mention in the list of fifteen because they are not appeals in and of themselves. They are stylistic features, influencing the way a basic appeal is presented. The use of humor is one, and the use of celebrities is another. A third is time imagery, past and future, which goes to several purposes.

For all of its employment in advertising, humor can be treacherous, 80 because it can get out of hand and smother the product information. Supposedly, this is what Alka-Seltzer discovered with its comic commercials of the late sixties; "I can't believe I ate the whole thing," the sad-faced husband lamented, and the audience cackled so much it forgot the antacid. Or, did not take it seriously.

But used carefully, humor can punctuate some of the softer 81 appeals and soften some of the harsher ones. When Emma says to the

84

Fruit-of-the-Loom fruits, "Hi, cuties. Whatcha doing in my laundry basket?" we smile as our curiosity is assuaged along with hers. Bill Cosby gets consumers tickled about the children in his Jell-O commercials, and strokes the need to nurture.

An insurance company wants to invoke the need to feel safe, but does not want to leave readers with an unpleasant aftertaste; cartoonist Rowland Wilson creates an avalanche about to crush a gentleman who is saying to another, "My insurance company? New England Life, of course. Why?" The same tactic of humor undercutting threat is used in the cartoon commercials for Safeco when the Pink Panther wanders from one disaster to another. Often humor masks aggression: comedian Bob Hope in the outfit of a boxer promises to knock out the knock-knocks with Texaco; Rodney Dangerfield, who "can't get no respect," invites aggression as the comic relief in Miller Lite commercials.

Roughly fifteen percent of all advertisements incorporate a celebrity, almost always from the fields of entertainment or sports. The approach can also prove troublesome for advertisers, for celebrities are human beings too, and fully capable of the most remarkable behavior. If anything distasteful about them emerges, it is likely to reflect on the product. The advertisers making use of Anita Bryant and Billy Jean King suffered several anxious moments. An untimely death can also react poorly on a product. But advertisers are willing to take risks because celebrities can be such a good link between producers and consumers, performing the social role of introducer.

There are several psychological needs these middlemen can play upon. Let's take the product class of cameras and see how different celebrities can hit different needs. The need for guidance can be invoked by Michael Landon, who plays such a wonderful dad on "Little House on the Prairie"; when he says to buy Kodak equipment, many people listen. James Garner for Polaroid cameras is put in a similar authoritative role, so defined by a mocking spouse. The need to achieve is summoned up by Tracy Austin and other tennis stars for Canon AE-1; the advertiser first makes sure we see these athletes playing to win. When Cheryl Tiegs speaks up for Olympus cameras, it is the need for attention that is being targeted.

The past and future, being outside our grasp, are exploited by advertisers as locales for the projection of needs. History can offer up heroes (and call up the need to achieve) or traditions (need for guidance) as well as art objects (need for aesthetic sensations). Nostalgia is a kindly version of personal history and is deployed by advertisers to rouse needs for affiliation and for guidance; the need to escape can come in here, too. The same need to escape is sometimes the point of futuristic appeals, but picturing the avant-garde can also be a way to get at the need to achieve.

85

ANALYZING ADVERTISEMENTS

When analyzing ads yourself for their emotional appeals, it takes a bit   86
of practice to learn to ignore the product information (as well as one's
own experience and feelings about the product). But that skill comes
soon enough, as does the ability to quickly sort out from all the non-
product aspects of an ad the chief element which is the most striking,
the most likely to snag attention first and penetrate brains farthest. The
key to the appeal, this element usually presents itself centrally and for-
wardly to the reader or viewer.

Another clue: the viewing angle which the audience has on the   87
ad's subjects is informative. If the subjects are photographed or filmed
from below and thus are looking down at you much as the Green Giant
does, then the need to be guided is a good candidate for the ad's emotional appeal. If, on the other hand, the subjects are shot from above
and appear deferential, as is often the case with children or female
models, then other needs are being appealed to.

To figure out an ad's emotional appeal, it is wise to know (or have   88
a good hunch about) who the targeted consumers are; this can often be
inferred from the magazine or television show it appears in. This piece
of information is a great help in determining the appeal and in deciding between two different interpretations. For example, if an ad features a partially undressed female, this would typically signal one
appeal for readers of *Penthouse* (need for sex) and another for readers of
Cosmopolitan (need for attention).

It would be convenient if every ad made just one appeal, were   89
aimed at just one need. Unfortunately, things are often not that simple. A
cigarette ad with a couple at the edge of a polo field is trying to hit both
the need for affiliation and the need for prominence; depending on the
attitude of the male, dominance could also be an ingredient in this. An ad
for Chimere perfume incorporates two photos: in the top one, the lady is
being commanding at a business luncheon (need to dominate), but in the
lower one she is being bussed (need for affiliation). Better ads, however,
seem to avoid being too diffused; in the study of post–World War II
advertising described earlier, appeals grew more focused as the decades
passed. As a rule of thumb, about sixty percent have two conspicuous
appeals; the last twenty percent have three or more. Rather than looking
for the greatest number of appeals, decoding ads is most productive
when the loudest one or two appeals are discerned, since those are the
appeals with the best chance of grabbing people's attention.

Finally, analyzing ads does not have to be a solo activity and   90
probably should not be. The greater number of people there are
involved, the better chance there is of transcending individual biases
and discerning the essential emotional lure built into an advertisement.

DO THEY OR DON'T THEY?

Do the emotional appeals made in advertisements add up to the sinister manipulation of consumers?

It is clear that these ads work. Attention is caught, communication 91 occurs between producers and consumers, and sales result. It turns out to be difficult to detail the exact relationship between a specific ad and a specific purchase, or even between a campaign and subsequent sales figures, because advertising is only one of a host of influences upon consumption. Yet no one is fooled by this lack of perfect proof; everyone knows that advertising sells. If this were not the case, then tight-fisted American businesses would not spend a total of fifty billion dollars annually on these messages.

But before anyone despairs that advertisers have our number to 92 the extent that they can marshal us at will and march us like automatons to the check-out counters, we should recall the resiliency and obduracy of the American consumer. Advertisers may have uncovered the softest spots in minds, but that does not mean they have found truly gaping apertures. There is no evidence that advertising can get people to do things contrary to their self-interests. Despite all the finesse of advertisements, and all the subtle emotional tugs, the public resists the vast majority of the petitions. According to the marketing division of the A.C. Nielsen Company, a whopping seventy-five percent of all new products die within a year in the marketplace, the victims of consumer disinterest which no amount of advertising could overcome. The appeals in advertising may be the most captivating there are to be had, but they are not enough to entrap the wiley consumer.

The key to understanding the discrepancy between, on the one 93 hand, the fact that advertising truly works, and, on the other, the fact that it hardly works, is to take into account the enormous numbers of people exposed to an ad. Modern-day communications permit an ad to be displayed to millions upon millions of individuals; if the smallest fraction of that audience can be moved to buy the product, then the ad has been successful. When one percent of the people exposed to a television advertising campaign reach for their wallets, that could be one million sales, which may be enough to keep the product in production and the advertisements coming.

In arriving at an evenhanded judgment about advertisements and 94 their emotional appeals, it is good to keep in mind that many of the purchases which might be credited to these ads are experienced as genuinely gratifying to the consumer. We sincerely like the goods or service we have bought, and we may even like some of the emotional drapery that an ad suggests comes with it. It has sometimes been noted that the most avid students of advertisements are the people who have just bought the

87

product; they want to steep themselves in the associated imagery. This may be the reason that Americans, when polled, are not negative about advertising and do not disclose any sense of being misused. The volume of advertising may be an irritant, but the product information as well as the imaginative material in ads are partial compensation.

A productive understanding is that advertising messages involve costs and benefits at both ends of the communications channel. For those few ads which do make contact, the consumer surrenders a moment of time, has the lower brain curried, and receives notice of a product; the advertiser has given up money and has increased the chance of sales. In this sort of communications activity, neither party can be said to be the loser.

95

Examining the Text

1. Fowles's claim in this essay is that advertisers try to tap into basic human needs and emotions, rather than consumers' intellect. How does he go about proving this claim? What examples or other proof strike you as particularly persuasive? Where do you see weaknesses in Fowles's argument?

2. What do advertisers assume about the personality of the consumer, according to Fowles? How do these assumptions contribute to the way they sell products? Do you think that these assumptions about personality are correct? Why or why not?

3. Fowles's list of advertising's fifteen basic appeals is, as he explains, derived from Henry Murray's inventory of human motives. Which of these motives strike you as the most significant or powerful? What other motives would you add to the list?

4. *Thinking rhetorically:* What do you think is Fowles's ultimate purpose in writing this article? Who is he targeting as the audience for his arguments, and what do you think he intends this audience to do or to think after reading the article? What, if any, real world effects do you imagine Fowles wants to achieve by writing this article?

For Group Discussion

In his discussion of the way advertising uses "the need for sex" and "the need to aggress," Fowles debunks the persistent complaints about the use of sex and violence in the mass media. What current examples support Fowles's point? Discuss your responses to his explanations.

Writing Suggestion

Working with Fowles's list of the fifteen appeals of advertising, survey a recent magazine, looking at all the ads and categorizing them based on their predominant appeal. In an essay, describe what your results tell you about the magazine and its readership. Based on your survey, would you amend Fowles's list? What additions or deletions would you make?

How Advertising Informs to Our Benefit

JOHN E. CALFEE

This article, adapted from John E. Calfee's book Fear of Persuasion: A New Perspective on Advertising and Regulation, *provides a different view of the effect of advertising on our society. Calfee, a former Federal Trade Commission economist and a resident scholar at the American Enterprise Institute, argues that advertising actually provides many benefits to consumers. Calfee relates several specific cases in which advertisements spread important health information to people who might not have learned about it otherwise. Because advertisers have huge budgets and can reach into virtually every home through television, newspapers, billboards, and radio campaigns, advertisements have the potential to spread information in a way that government-sponsored public service initiatives cannot.*

Calfee also diverges from previous articles in this chapter by suggesting that regulations on advertising are unnecessary and counterproductive. Indeed, Calfee argues that advertising is, to a large extent, self-regulating. Free-market competition compels companies to be truthful, or else competitors will challenge their claims, resulting in negative publicity.

As you read this article, *consider your own feelings about advertising: do you think it's a destructive force in our society or a valuable tool for disseminating information? Given the power and reach of advertising, how can it be used as a positive information resource?*

89

———————

A great truth about advertising is that it is a tool for communicating information and shaping markets. It is one of the forces that compel sellers to cater to the desires of consumers. Almost everyone knows this because consumers use advertising every day, and they miss advertising when they cannot get it. This fact does not keep politicians and opinion leaders from routinely dismissing the value of advertising. But the truth is that people find advertising very useful indeed.

Of course, advertising primarily seeks to persuade, and everyone knows this, too. The typical ad tries to induce a consumer to do one particular thing—usually, buy a product—instead of a thousand other things. There is nothing obscure about this purpose or what it means for buyers. Decades of data and centuries of intuition reveal that all consumers everywhere are deeply suspicious of what advertisers say and why they say it. This skepticism is in fact the driving force that makes advertising so effective. The persuasive purpose of advertising and the ticism with which it is met are two sides of a single process. ..suasion and skepticism work in tandem so advertising can do its job in competitive markets. Hence, ads represent the seller's self interest, consumers know this, and sellers know that consumers know it.

By understanding this process more fully, we can sort out much of the popular confusion surrounding advertising and how it benefits consumers.   3

HOW USEFUL IS ADVERTISING?

Just how useful is the connection between advertising and information? At first blush, the process sounds rather limited. Volvo ads tell consumers that Volvos have side-impact air bags, people learn a little about the importance of air bags, and Volvo sells a few more cars. This seems to help hardly anyone except Volvo and its customers.   4

But advertising does much more. It routinely provides immense amounts of information that benefits primarily parties other than the advertiser. This may sound odd, but it is a logical result of market forces and the nature of information itself.   5

The ability to use information to sell products is an incentive to create new information through research. Whether the topic is nutrition, safety, or more mundane matters like how to measure amplifier power, the necessity of achieving credibility with consumers and critics requires much of this research to be placed in the public domain, and that it rest upon some academic credentials. That kind of research typically produces results that apply to more than just the brands sold by the firm sponsoring the research. The lack of property rights to such "pure" information ensures that this extra information is available at no charge. Both consumers and competitors may borrow the new information for their own purposes.   6

Advertising also elicits additional information from other sources. Claims that are striking, original, forceful or even merely obnoxious will generate news stories about the claims, the controversies they cause, the reactions of competitors (A price war? A splurge of comparison ads?), the reactions of consumers, and the remarks of governments and independent authorities.   7

Probably the most concrete, pervasive, and persistent example of competitive advertising that works for the public good is price advertising. Its effect is invariably to heighten competition and reduce prices, even the prices of firms that assiduously avoid mentioning prices in their own advertising.   8

There is another area where the public benefits of advertising are less obvious but equally important. The unremitting nature of consumer   9 interest in health, and the eagerness of sellers to cater to consumer desires, guarantee that advertising related to health will provide a store-house of telling observations on the ways in which the benefits of adver-tising extend beyond the interests of advertisers to include the interests of the public at large.

A CASCADE OF INFORMATION

Here is probably the best documented example of why advertising is 10 necessary for consumer welfare. In the 1970s, public health experts described compelling evidence that people who eat more fiber are less likely to get cancer, especially cancer of the colon, which happens to be the second leading cause of deaths from cancer in the United States. By 1979, the U.S. Surgeon General was recommending that people eat more fiber in order to prevent cancer.

Consumers appeared to take little notice of these recommenda- 11 tions, however. The National Cancer Institute decided that more action was needed. NCI's cancer prevention division undertook to communi-cate the new information about fiber and cancer to the general public. Their goal was to change consumer diets and reduce the risk of cancer, but they had little hope of success given the tiny advertising budgets of federal agencies like NCI.

Their prospects unexpectedly brightened in 1984. NCI received a 12 call from the Kellogg Corporation, whose All-Bran cereal held a com-manding market share of the high-fiber segment. Kellogg proposed to use All-Bran advertising as a vehicle for NCI's public service messages. NCI thought that was an excellent idea. Soon, an agreement was reached in which NCI would review Kellogg's ads and labels for accu-racy and value before Kellogg began running their fiber–cancer ads.

The new Kellogg All-Bran campaign opened in October 1984. A 13 typical ad began with the headline, "At last some news about cancer you can live with." The ad continued: "The National Cancer Institute believes a high-fiber, low-fat diet may reduce your risk of some kinds of cancer . . . . That's why one of their strongest recommendations is to eat high-fiber foods. If you compare, you'll find Kellogg's All-Bran has nine grams of fiber per serving. No other cereal has more. So start your day with a bowl of Kellogg's All-Bran or mix it with your regular cereal."

The campaign quickly achieved two things. One was to create a 14 regulatory crisis between two agencies. The Food and Drug Administration thought that if a food was advertised as a way to pre-vent cancer, it was being marketed as a drug. Then the FDA's regula-tions for drug labeling would kick in. The food would be reclassified as a drug and would be removed from the market until the seller either stopped making the health claims or put the product through the clinical testing necessary to obtain formal approval as a drug.

But food advertising is regulated by the Federal Trade Commission, 15 not the FDA. The FTC thought Kellogg's ads were nondeceptive and were therefore perfectly legal. In fact, it thought the ads should be encouraged. The Director of the FTC's Bureau of Consumer Protection declared that "the [Kellogg] ad has presented important public health recommendations in an accurate, useful, and substantiated way. It informs the members of the public that there is a body of data suggesting certain relationships between cancer and diet that they may find important." The FTC won this political battle, and the ads continued.

The second instant effect of the All-Bran campaign was to unleash 16 a flood of health claims. Vegetable oil manufacturers advertised that cholesterol was associated with coronary heart disease, and that vegetable oil does not contain cholesterol. Margarine ads did the same, and added that vitamin A is essential for good vision. Ads for calcium products (such as certain antacids) provided vivid demonstrations of the effects of osteoporosis (which weakens bones in old age), and recounted the advice of experts to increase dietary calcium as a way to prevent osteoporosis. Kellogg's competitors joined in citing the National Cancer Institute dietary recommendations.

Nor did things stop there. In the face of consumer demand for bet- 17 ter and fuller information, health claims quickly evolved from a blunt tool to a surprisingly refined mechanism. Cereals were advertised as high in fiber and low in sugar or fat or sodium. Ads for an upscale brand of bread noted: "Well, most high-fiber bran cereals may be high in fiber, but often only one kind: insoluble. It's this kind of fiber that helps promote regularity. But there's also a kind of fiber known as soluble, which most high-fiber bran cereals have in very small amounts, if at all. Yet diets high in this kind of fiber may actually lower your serum cholesterol, a risk factor for some heart diseases." Cereal boxes became convenient sources for a summary of what made for a good diet.

INCREASED INDEPENDENT INFORMATION

The ads also brought powerful secondary effects. These may have been 18 even more useful than the information that actually appeared in the ads themselves.

One effect was an increase in media coverage of diet and health. 19 *Consumer Reports,* a venerable and hugely influential magazine that carries no advertising, revamped its reports on cereals to emphasize fiber and other ingredients (rather than testing the foods to see how well they did at providing a complete diet for laboratory rats). The health-claims phenomenon generated its own press coverage, with articles like "What Has All-Bran Wrought?" and "The Fiber Furor." These stories recounted the ads and the scientific information that prompted the ads; and articles on food and health proliferated. Anyone who lived through these years in the United States can probably remember the unending media attention to health claims and to diet and health generally.

Much of the information on diet and health was new. This was no   20
coincidence. Firms were sponsoring research on their products in the hope of finding results that could provide a basis for persuasive advertising claims. Oat bran manufacturers, for example, funded research on the impact of soluble fiber on blood cholesterol. When the results came out "wrong," as they did in a 1990 study published with great fanfare in *The New England Journal of Medicine*, the headline in *Advertising Age* was "Oat Bran Popularity Hitting the Skids," and it did indeed tumble. The manufacturers kept at the research, however, and eventually the best research supported the efficacy of oat bran in reducing cholesterol (even to the satisfaction of the FDA). Thus did pure advertising claims spill over to benefit the information environment at large.

The shift to higher fiber cereals encompassed brands that had   21
never undertaken the effort necessary to construct believable ads about fiber and disease. Two consumer researchers at the FDA reviewed these data and concluded they were "consistent with the successful educational impact of the Kellogg diet and health campaign: consumers seemed to be making an apparently thoughtful discrimination between high- and low-fiber cereals," and that the increased market shares for high-fiber non-advertised products represented "the clearest evidence of a successful consumer education campaign."

Perhaps most dramatic were the changes in consumer awareness   22
of diet and health. An FTC analysis of government surveys showed that when consumers were asked about how they could prevent cancer through their diet, the percentage who mentioned fiber increased from 4% before the 1979 Surgeon General's report to 8.5% in 1984 (after the report but before the All-Bran campaign) to 32% in 1986 after a year and a half or so of health claims (the figure in 1988 was 28%). By far the greatest increases in awareness were among women (who do most of the grocery shopping) and the less educated: up from 0% for women without a high school education in 1984 to 31% for the same group in 1986. For women with incomes of less than $15,000, the increase was from 6% to 28%.

The health-claims advertising phenomenon achieved what years   23
of effort by government agencies had failed to achieve. With its mastery of the art of brevity, its ability to command attention, and its use of television, brand advertising touched precisely the people the public

93

health community was most desperate to reach. The health claims expanded consumer information along a broad front. The benefits clearly extended far beyond the interests of the relatively few manufacturers who made vigorous use of health claims in advertising.

A PERVASIVE PHENOMENON

Health claims for foods are only one example, however, of a pervasive 24 phenomenon—the use of advertising to provide essential health information with benefits extending beyond the interests of the advertisers themselves.

Advertising for soap and detergents, for example, once improved 25 private hygiene and therefore, public health (hygiene being one of the underappreciated triumphs in twentieth century public health). Toothpaste advertising helped to do the same for teeth. When mass advertising for toothpaste and tooth powder began early in this century, tooth brushing was rare. It was common by the 1930s, after which toothpaste sales leveled off even though the advertising, of course, continued. When fluoride toothpastes became available, advertising generated interest in better teeth and professional dental care. Later, a "plaque reduction war" (which first involved mouthwashes, and later toothpastes) brought a new awareness of gum disease and how to prevent it. The financial gains to the toothpaste industry were surely dwarfed by the benefits to consumers in the form of fewer cavities and fewer lost teeth.

Health claims induced changes in foods, in nonfoods such as 26 toothpaste, in publications ranging from university health letters to mainstream newspapers and magazines, and of course, consumer knowledge of diet and health.

These rippling effects from health claims in ads demonstrated the 27 most basic propositions in the economics of information. Useful information initially failed to reach people who needed it because information producers could not charge a price to cover the costs of creating and disseminating pure information. And this problem was alleviated by advertising, sometimes in a most vivid manner.

Other examples of spillover benefits from advertising are far 28 more common than most people realize. Even the much-maligned promotion of expensive new drugs can bring profound health benefits to patients and families, far exceeding what is actually charged for the products themselves.

The market processes that produce these benefits bear all the clas- 29 sic features of competitive advertising. We are not analyzing public service announcements here, but old-fashioned profit-seeking brand advertising. Sellers focused on the information that favored their own products. They advertised it in ways that provided a close link with their own brand. It was a purely competitive enterprise, and the benefits to consumers arose from the imperatives of the competitive process.

One might see all this as simply an extended example of the economics of information and greed. And indeed it is, if by greed one means the effort to earn a profit by providing what people are willing to pay for, even if what they want most is information rather than a tangible product. The point is that there is overwhelming evidence that unregulated economic forces dictate that much useful information will be provided by brand advertising, and only by brand advertising.

Of course, there is much more to the story. There is the question of how competition does the good I have described without doing even more harm elsewhere. After all, firms want to tell people only what is good about their brands, and people often want to know what is wrong with the brands. It turns out that competition takes care of this problem, too.

ADVERTISING AND CONTEXT

It is often said that most advertising does not contain very much information. In a way, this is true. Research on the contents of advertising typically finds just a few pieces of concrete information per ad. That's an average, of course. Some ads obviously contain a great deal of information. Still, a lot of ads are mainly images and pleasant talk, with little in the way of what most people would consider hard information. On the whole, information in advertising comes in tiny bits and pieces.

Cost is only one reason. To be sure, cramming more information into ads is expensive. But more to the point is the fact that advertising plays off the information available from outside sources. Hardly anything about advertising is more important than the interplay between what the ad contains and what surrounds it. Sometimes this interplay is a burden for the advertiser because it is beyond his control. But the interchange between advertising and environment is also an invaluable tool for sellers. Ads that work in collaboration with outside information can communicate far more than they ever could on their own.

The upshot is advertising's astonishing ability to communicate a great deal of information in a few words. Economy and vividness of expression almost always rely upon what is in the information environment. The famously concise "Think Small" and "Lemon" ads for the VW "Beetle" in the 1960s and 1970s were highly effective with buyers concerned about fuel economy, repair costs, and extravagant styling in American cars. This was a case where the less said, the better. The ads were more powerful when consumers were free to bring their own ideas about the issues to bear.

30

31

32

33

34

95

The same process is repeated over again for all sorts of products. 35
Ads for computer modems once explained what they could be used for.
Now a simple reference to the Internet is sufficient to conjure an elaborate mix of equipment and applications. These matters are better left
vague so each potential customer can bring to the ad his own idea of
what the Internet is really for.

Leaning on information from other sources is also a way to 36
enhance credibility, without which advertising must fail. Much of the
most important information in advertising—think of cholesterol and
heart disease, antilock brakes and automobile safety—acquires its force
from highly credible sources other than the advertiser. To build up this
kind of credibility through material actually contained in ads would be
cumbersome and inefficient. Far more effective, and far more economi-
cal, is the technique of making challenges, raising questions, and otherwise making it perfectly clear to the audience that the seller invites
comparisons and welcomes the tough questions. Hence the classic slogan, "If you can find a better whiskey, buy it."

Finally, there is the most important point of all. Informational sparse- 37
ness facilitates competition. It is easier to challenge a competitor through
pungent slogans—"Where's the beef?", "Where's the big saving?"—than
through a step-by-step recapitulation of what has gone on before. The bits-
and-pieces approach makes for quick, unerring attacks and equally quick
responses, all under the watchful eye of the consumer over whom the battle is being fought. This is an ideal recipe for competition.

It also brings the competitive market's fabled self-correcting 38
forces into play. Sellers are less likely to stretch the truth, whether it
involves prices or subtleties about safety and performance, when they
know they may arouse a merciless response from injured competitors.
That is one reason the FTC once worked to get comparative ads on
television, and has sought for decades to dismantle government or
voluntary bans on comparative ads.

"LESS-BAD" ADVERTISING

There is a troubling possibility, however. Is it not possible that in their 39
selective and carefully calculated use of outside information, advertisers have the power to focus consumer attention exclusively on the positive, i.e., on what is good about the brand or even the entire product
class? Won't automobile ads talk up style, comfort, and extra safety,
while food ads do taste and convenience, cigarette ads do flavor and
lifestyle, and airlines do comfort and frequency of departure, all the
while leaving consumers to search through other sources to find all the
things that are wrong with products?

In fact, this is not at all what happens. Here is why: Everything 40 for sale has something wrong with it, if only the fact that you have to pay for it. Some products, of course, are notable for their faults. The most obvious examples involve tobacco and health, but there are also food and heart disease, drugs and side effects, vacations and bad weather, automobiles and accidents, airlines and delay, among others.

Products and their problems bring into play one of the most 41 important ways in which the competitive market induces sellers to serve the interests of buyers. No matter what the product, there are usually a few brands that are "less bad" than the others. The natural impulse is to advertise that advantage—"less cholesterol," "less fat," "less dangerous," and so on. Such provocative claims tend to have an immediate impact. The targets often retaliate; maybe their brands are less bad in a different respect (less salt?). The ensuing struggle brings better information, more informed choices, and improved products.

Perhaps the most riveting episode of "less-bad" advertising ever 42 seen occurred, amazingly enough, in the industry that most people assume is the master of avoiding saying anything bad about its product.

Less-Bad Cigarette Ads

Cigarette advertising was once very different from what it is today. 43 Cigarettes first became popular around the time of World War I, and they came to dominate the tobacco market in the 1920s. Steady and often dramatic sales increases continued into the 1950s, always with vigorous support from advertising. Tobacco advertising was duly celebrated as an outstanding example of the power and creativity of advertising. Yet amazingly, much of the advertising focused on what was wrong with smoking, rather than what people liked about smoking.

The very first ad for the very first mass-marketed American ciga- 44 rette brand (Camel, the same brand recently under attack for its use of a cartoon character) said, "Camel Cigarettes will not sting the tongue and will not parch the throat." When Old Gold broke into the market in the mid-1920s, it did so with an ad campaign about coughs and throats and harsh cigarette smoke. It settled on the slogan, "Not a cough in a carload."

Competitors responded in kind. Soon, advertising left no doubt 45 about what was wrong with smoking. Lucky Strike ads said, "No Throat Irritation—No Cough . . . we . . . removed . . . harmful corrosive acids," and later on, "Do you inhale? What's there to be afraid of? . . . famous purifying process removes certain impurities." Camel's famous tag line, "more doctors smoke Camels than any other brand," carried a punch precisely because many authorities thought smoking was unhealthy (cigarettes were called "coffin nails" back then), and smokers were eager for reassurance in the form of smoking by doctors themselves. This particular ad, which was based on surveys of physicians, ran in one form or another from 1933 to 1955. It achieved prominence partly because physicians practically never endorsed non-therapeutic products.[1]

Things really got interesting in the early 1950s, when the first per- 46 suasive medical reports on smoking and lung cancer reached the public. These reports created a phenomenal stir among smokers and the public generally. People who do not understand how advertising works would probably assume that cigarette manufacturers used advertising to divert attention away from the cancer reports. In fact, they did the opposite.

Small brands could not resist the temptation to use advertising to 47 scare smokers into switching brands. They inaugurated several spectacular years of "fear advertising" that sought to gain competitive advantage by exploiting smokers' new fear of cancer. Lorillard, the beleaguered seller of Old Gold, introduced Kent, a new filter brand supported by ad claims like these: "Sensitive smokers get real health protection with new Kent," "Do you love a good smoke but not what the smoke does to you?" and "Takes out more nicotine and tars than any other leading cigarette— the difference in protection is priceless," illustrated by television ads showing the black tar trapped by Kent's filters.

Other manufacturers came out with their own filter brands and 48 raised the stakes with claims like, "Nose, throat, and accessory organs not adversely affected by smoking Chesterfields. First such report ever published about any cigarette," "Takes the fear out of smoking," and "Stop worrying . . . Philip Morris and only Philip Morris is entirely free of irritation used [sic] in all other leading cigarettes."

These ads threatened to demolish the industry. Cigarette sales 49 plummeted by 3% in 1953 and a remarkable 6% in 1954. Never again, not even in the face of the most impassioned anti-smoking publicity by the Surgeon General or the FDA, would cigarette consumption decline as rapidly as it did during these years of entirely market-driven anti-smoking ad claims by the cigarette industry itself.

Thus advertising traveled full circle. Devised to bolster brands, it 50 denigrated the product so much that overall market demand actually declined. Everyone understood what was happening, but the fear ads continued because they helped the brands that used them. The new filter brands (all from smaller manufacturers) gained a foothold even as their ads amplified the medical reports on the dangers of smoking. It

---

[1]The ad ran in many outlets, including The Journal of the American Medical Association, which regularly carried cigarette advertisements until the early 1950s. Incidentally, Camel was by no means the only brand that cited medical authorities in an effort to reassure smokers.

was only after the FTC stopped the fear ads in 1955 (on the grounds that the implied health claims had no proof) that sales resumed their customary annual increases.

Fear advertising has never quite left the tobacco market despite   51
the regulatory straight jacket that governs cigarette advertising. In 1957, when leading cancer experts advised smokers to ingest less tar, the industry responded by cutting tar and citing tar content figures compiled by independent sources. A stunning "tar derby" reduced the tar and nicotine content of cigarettes by 40% in four years, a far more rapid decline than would be achieved by years of government urging in later decades. This episode, too, was halted by the FTC. In February 1960 the FTC engineered a "voluntary" ban on tar and nicotine claims.

Further episodes continue to this day. In 1993, for example,   52
Liggett planned an advertising campaign to emphasize that its Chesterfield brand did not use the stems and other less desirable parts of the tobacco plant. This continuing saga, extending through eight decades, is perhaps the best documented case of how "less-bad" advertising completely offsets any desires by sellers to accentuate the positive while ignoring the negative. *Consumer Reports* magazine's 1955 assessment of the new fear of smoking still rings true:

99

> . . . companies themselves are largely to blame. Long before the current medical attacks, the companies were building up suspicion in the consumer by the discredited "health claims" in their ads . . . Such medicine-show claims may have given the smoker temporary confidence in one brand, but they also implied that cigarettes in general were distasteful, probably harmful, and certainly a "problem." When the scientists came along with their charges against cigarettes, the smoker was ready to accept them.

And that is how information works in competitive advertising.   53
Less-bad can be found wherever competitive advertising is   54
allowed. I already described the health-claims-for-foods saga, which featured fat and cholesterol and the dangers of cancer and heart disease. Price advertising is another example. Prices are the most stubbornly negative product feature of all, because they represent the simple fact that the buyer must give up something else. There is no riper target for comparative advertising. When sellers advertise lower prices, competitors reduce their prices and advertise that, and soon a price war is in the works. This process so strongly favors consumers over the industry that one of the first things competitors do when they form a trade group is to propose an agreement to restrict or ban price advertising (if not ban all advertising). When that fails, they try to get advertising regulators to stop price ads, an attempt that unfortunately often succeeds.

Someone is always trying to scare customers into switching 55
brands out of fear of the product itself. The usual effect is to impress
upon consumers what they do not like about the product. In 1991,
when Americans were worried about insurance companies going
broke, a few insurance firms advertised that they were more solvent
than their competitors. In May 1997, United Airlines began a new ad
campaign that started out by reminding fliers of all the inconveniences
that seem to crop up during air travel.

Health information is a fixture in "less-bad" advertising. Ads for 56
sleeping aids sometimes focus on the issue of whether they are habit-
forming. In March 1996, a medical journal reported that the pain
reliever acetaminophen, the active ingredient in Tylenol, can cause
liver damage in heavy drinkers. This fact immediately became the
focus of ads for Advil, a competing product. A public debate ensued,
conducted through advertising, talk shows, news reports, and pro-
nouncements from medical authorities. The result: consumers
learned a lot more than they had known before about the fact that all
drugs have side effects. The press noted that this dispute may have
helped consumers, but it hurt the pain reliever industry. Similar
examples abound.

100

We have, then, a general rule: sellers will use comparative adver- 57
tising when permitted to do so, even if it means spreading bad information about a product instead of favorable information. The mechanism
usually takes the form of less-bad claims. One can hardly imagine a
strategy more likely to give consumers the upper hand in the give and
take of the marketplace. Less-bad claims are a primary means by which
advertising serves markets and consumers rather than sellers. They
completely refute the naive idea that competitive advertising will
emphasize only the sellers' virtues while obscuring their problems.

Examining the Text

1. What points does Calfee make with his example of advertising for Kellogg's
All-Bran cereal? According to Calfee, what are the advantages and disadvantages of using ads to inform consumers about health issues?

2. According to Calfee, what are the "spillover benefits" of advertising?

3. What are some of the ways that free-market competition in advertising benefits consumers? Does Calfee see any reason for government or industry regulation of advertising?

4. *Thinking rhetorically:* How would you describe the tone of this article?
Considering the fact that Calfee is arguing an unusual position—that advertising is good for us—how does the tone of the article help him convey his arguments effectively? What other rhetorical strategies does Calfee use to make his
position persuasive?

For Group Discussion

This activity requires that each member of the group bring four or five ads to class—either from a magazine, newspaper, or brochure—in order to test Calfee's proposition that ads provide consumers with useful information. In your group, make a list of the useful information that each ad presents. That is, what helpful facts do you learn from the ad? Then discuss the other kinds of information or content presented in each ad. (You might reread Jib Fowles's "Advertising's Fifteen Basic Appeals" to get some ideas.) What conclusions can you draw from this comparison? Do your conclusions coincide with Calfee's claims? Are certain kinds of ads—or ads for certain products—more likely to contain helpful information?

Writing Suggestion

Calfee discusses the history of cigarette advertising, noting the predominance of "less-bad" claims and "fear advertising" in mid-twentieth-century cigarette ad campaigns. Find five or six recent cigarette advertisements in magazines or newspapers and analyze the information these ads present and the strategies they use to sell their product. Then write an essay in which you first summarize Calfee's discussion of the history of cigarette advertising; use quotations and paraphrases from the article to develop your summary. In the remainder of your essay, discuss what you see as the current state of cigarette advertising based on your analysis of recent ads.

Gender in Advertising

You're Soaking In It

JENNIFER L. POZNER

We begin this casebook on images of women and men in advertising with an article, originally published on the Web at Salon.com, *that presents the ideas of a recognized expert in the field, Jean Kilbourne. Kilbourne is the author of several books on advertising, including her most recent* Can't Buy My Love: How Advertising Changes the Way We Think and Feel. *She is also well known as the creator of award-winning documentaries such as* Killing Us Softly, Pack of Lies, *and* Slim Hopes. *She is a popular speaker on college campuses and in communities, where her message is that we should pay attention to the messages that advertising conveys, especially messages that are harmful to girls and women.*

In her publications and lectures, Kilbourne argues that we are inundated with ads telling us that products can meet our deepest needs, that we can be happier, more popular, more successful—more anything, it seems—simply by buying the right products. Kilbourne also draws attention to the damaging stereotypes of women and girls that are often found in advertisements, stereotypes that are all the more damaging because of the accumulated impact of the approximately three thousand ads that we see daily.

The article that follows begins by showing how Kilbourne's concerns are dealt with in the movie What Women Want, *starring Mel Gibson. Gibson plays the role of a chauvinistic advertising executive who experiences a significant change of heart when, through a bizarre electrocution experience, he gains the ability to hear the inner thoughts of the women around him. According to Pozner and Kilbourne, the movie perpetuates common misconceptions of the advertising business, as well as misrepresentations of men, women, and relationships.*

As you read, *note the effect of the interview format in most of this article. How does the question-and-answer structure of the article influence your understanding of Kilbourne's ideas? What's gained (and lost) by including Kilbourne's answers rather than just reporting on them?*

"Advertisers know what womanpower is," explains a self-promotional   1
pitch for the *Ladies' Home Journal*. The ad shows a stylish woman wired
to a mammoth computer that measures her whims with graphs, light
bulbs and ticker tape. The magazine insists that, like the machine, it has

its finger on the pulse of women's desires. Perk and breathlessness permeate its claim to be able to harness the many elements of "woman-power," including "sales power" ("She spots a bright idea in her favorite magazine, and suddenly the whole town's sold on it!"), "will power" ("Can you stick to a nine-day diet for more than four hours at a stretch?") and, of course, "purchasing power" ("Isn't it the power of her purse that's been putting fresh smiles on the faces of America's businessmen?").

That was 1958. Today advertisers are generally more sophisticated in their execution, but their primary message to and about women has remained fundamentally unchanged. To tap into our power, offer us a new shade of lipstick, a fresh-scented floor wax or, in the case of Mel Gibson's patronizing chick flick, *What Women Want*, L'eggs pantyhose, Wonderbras, or Nike Women's Sports gear.

The movie—No. 2 at the box office after a month in theaters—stars Gibson as Nick Marshall, a pompous advertising executive dubbed the "T&A King" for his successful reign over Swedish bikini-babe commercials. But Nick's campaigns leave female consumers cold and he loses an expected promotion to women's market whiz Darcy Maguire (Helen Hunt). Nick's boss explains that while he's more comfortable with Nick, men no longer dominate how ad dollars are being spent.

Once Nick acquires the ability to read women's minds—after an unfortunate incident with volumizing mousse, a hair dryer and a bathtub—a story unfolds that could only seem romantic to avid *Advertising Age* readers: Nick and his nemesis Darcy fall in love over Nike storyboards, brainstorming ways to convince consumers that "Nike wants to empower women" and "Nike is state-of-the-art, hardcore womanpower."

What Women Want is more than a commercial for Mars vs. Venus gender typing; it's a feature-length product placement, a jarring reminder that the entertainment media is up for grabs by the hawkers of hair spray and Hondas. Which is not to say that the news media is off limits. Take Disney's news giant, ABC. In November, after ABC accepted a hefty fee from Campbell's soup, journalist Barbara Walters and "The View" crew turned eight episodes of their talk show into paid infomercials for canned soup. Hosting a "soup-sipping contest" and singing the "M'm! M'm! Good!" jingle on-air, they made good on ABC's promise that the "hosts would try to weave a soup message into their regular on-air banter."

And in March, after Disney bought a stake in Pets.com, the company's snarky sock puppet mascot began appearing as a "guest" on "Good Morning America" and "Nightline." It was a sad day in news when Diane Sawyer addressed her questions to a sock on a stool with a guy's hand up its butt, but that's what passes for "synergy" in today's megamerged media climate.

How does advertising's increasing encroachment into every niche of mass media impact our culture in general, and women in particular?

103

Mothers Who Think asked pioneering advertising critic Jean Kilbourne, author of *Can't Buy My Love: How Advertising Changes the Way We Think and Feel.*

A favorite on the college lecture circuit, Kilbourne has produced 8 videos that are used as part of media literacy programs worldwide, in particular *Killing Us Softly,* first produced in 1979 and remade as *Killing Us Softly III* in 2000. She shares her thoughts here about advertising's effects on women, children, media and our cultural environment—and explains why salvation can't be found in a Nike sports bra.

In What Women Want, *Mel Gibson and Helen Hunt produce a Nike com-* 9 *mercial in which a woman runs in swooshed-up sportswear while a voice-over assures her that the road doesn't care if she's wearing makeup, and she doesn't have to feel uncomfortable if she makes more money than the road—basically equating freedom and liberation with a pair of $150 running shoes. Is this typical of advertising to women?*

Absolutely. The commercial in the movie is saying that women who are 10 unhappy with the quality of their relationships can ease their frustration by literally forming a more satisfying relationship with the road. There's no hint that her human relationships are going to improve, but the road will love her anyway.

Advertising is always about moving away from anything that 11 would help us find real change in our lives. In the funniest scene in the movie, when Mel Gibson finds out how much it hurts to wax his legs, he wonders, "Why would anyone do this more than once?" That's a very good question. But, of course, the film doesn't go there. The real solutions—to stop waxing or to challenge unnatural beauty standards or to demand that men grow up—are never offered. Instead, the message is that we must continue with these painful and humiliating rituals, but at least we can escape for a while by lacing on our expensive sneakers and going out for a run.

What Women Want *presents a pretty mercenary picture of advertising aimed at* 12 *women. You've studied the industry for decades. Does it seem accurate to you?*

It isn't far off. As in the film, advertisers were kind of slow to really 13 focus on women. Initially, they did it by co-opting feminism. Virginia Slims equated women's liberation and enslavement to tobacco with the trivializing slogan "You've come a long way, baby" in the '80s; a little while ago it ran a campaign with the slogan "Find your voice."

Then there were endless ads that turned the women's movement 14 into the quest for a woman's product. Was there ever such a thing as static cling before there were fabric softeners and sprays? More recently advertisers have discovered what they call "relationship marketing," creating ads that exploit a human need for connection and relationships, which in our culture is often seen as a woman's need.

Advertising and the larger culture often imply that women are failures if we 15
do not have perfect relationships. Of course, "perfect" relationships don't exist
in real life. Why are they so prominent in ads?

This is part of the advertising mentality. Think about *What Women* 16
Want—there's an ad at the heart of this film literally and figuratively.
Everybody lives in spectacular apartments, they're all thin and beautiful, and Mel Gibson makes this incredible instant transformation. He
starts out as a jerk, he's callous, he tells degrading jokes and patronizes
the women he works with, but because of his new mind-reading power
he gains immediate insight into women. He becomes a great lover in
the space of half an hour. At one point his daughter tells him he's never
had a real relationship in his life, but by the end of the film he has
authentic relationships with his daughter and his new love.

The truth is, most men gain insight into women not through 17
quick fixes but by having close relationships with them over time,
sometimes painfully. In the world of advertising, relationships are
instant and the best ones aren't necessarily with people: Zest is a soap,
Happy is a perfume, New Freedom is a maxipad, Wonder is a bread,
Good Sense is a tea bag, and Serenity is a diaper. Advertising actually
encourages us to have relationships with our products.

I'm looking at *TV Guide* right now and there's a Winston cigarette 18
ad on the back cover with a woman saying, "Until I find a real man, I'll
take a real smoke." There's another with four different pictures of one
man with four different women, and the copy reads, "Who says guys
are afraid of commitment? He's had the same backpack for years." In
another ad, featuring a young woman wearing a pretty sweater, the
copy says, "The ski instructor faded away after one session.
Fortunately the sweater didn't."

One automobile spot implied that a Civic coupe would never tell 19
you, "It's not you, it's me. I need more space. I'm not ready for a commitment." Maybe our chances for lasting relationships are greater with
our cars than with our partners, but surely the solution can't be to fall
in love with our cars, or to depend on them rather than on each other.

Basically, men can't be trusted but Häagen-Dazs never disappoints? Love is fleet- 20
ing but a diamond is forever? Sort of a recipe for lowered expectations, isn't it?

A central message of advertising is that relationships with human 21
beings can't be counted on, especially for women. The message is that

men will make commitments only reluctantly and can't be trusted to keep them. Straight women, and these are pretty much the women in ads, are told that it's normal not to expect very much or get very much from the men in their lives. This normalizes really abnormal behavior—with male violence at the extreme and male callousness in general—by reinforcing men's unwillingness to express their feelings. This harms men, of course, as well as women.

In What Women Want, *Mel Gibson is literally able to "get into the female* 22 *psyche," private thoughts and all, after he waxes his hairy legs and crams them into a pair of L'eggs pantyhose. Is it unusual for advertisers to imply that the essence of womanhood can be found in cosmetics and commercialism?*

Not at all. The central message of advertising has to be that we are 23 what we buy. And perhaps what's most insidious about this is that it takes very human, very real feelings and desires such as the need to love and be loved, the need for authentic connection, the need for meaningful work, for respect, and it yokes these feelings to products. It tells us that our ability to attain love depends upon our attractiveness.

By now most of us know that these images are unrealistic and unhealthy, that 24 *implants leak, anorexia and bulimia can kill and, in real life, model Heidi Klum has pores. So why do the images in ads still have such sway over us?*

Most people like to think advertising doesn't affect them. But if that 25 were really true, why would companies spend over $200 billion a year on advertising? Women don't buy into this because we're shallow or vain or stupid but because the stakes are high. Overweight women do tend to face biases—they're less likely to get jobs; they're poorer. Men do leave their wives for younger, more beautiful women as their wives age. There is manifest contempt and real-life consequences for women who don't measure up. These images work to keep us in line.

What do these images teach girls about what they can expect from themselves, 26 *from boys, from sex, from each other?*

Girls get terrible messages about sex from advertising and popular cul- 27 ture. An ad featuring a very young woman in tight jeans reads: "He says the first thing he noticed about you is your great personality. He lies." Girls are told that boys are out for sex at all times, and girls should always look as if they are ready to give it. (But God help them if they do.) The emphasis for girls and women is always on being desirable, not being agents of their own desire. Girls are supposed to somehow be innocent and seductive, virginal and experienced, all at the same time.

Girls are particularly targeted by the diet industry. The obsession with thinness is about cutting girls down to size, making sure they're not too powerful in any sense of the word. One fashion ad I use in my presentations shows an extremely thin, very young Asian woman next to the copy, "The more you subtract, the more you add."   28

Adolescent girls constantly get the message that they should diminish themselves, they should be less than what they are. Girls are told not to speak up too much, not to be too loud, not to have a hearty appetite for food or sex or anything else. Girls are literally shown being silenced in ads, often with their hands over their mouth or, as in one ad, with a turtleneck sweater pulled up over their mouth.   29

One ad sold lipstick with a drawing of a woman's lips sucking on a pacifier. A girl in a particularly violent entertainment ad has her lips sewn shut. Sometimes girls are told to keep quiet in other ways, by slogans like "Let your fingers do the talking" (an ad for nail polish), "Watch your mouth, young lady" (for lipstick), "Make a statement without saying a word" (for perfume), "Score high on non-verbal skills" (for a clothing store).   30

Let's talk about violence against women in ads. A controversy broke out during the Olympics when NBC ran a Nike commercial parodying slasher films, in which Olympic runner Suzy Favor Hamilton is chased by a villain with a chain saw. Hamilton outruns him, leaving the would-be murderer wheezing in the woods. The punch line? "Why sport? You'll live longer." The ad shocked many people, but isn't violence against women, real or implied, common in ads?   31

107

People were outraged that Nike considered this type of thing a joke. A recent Perry Ellis sequence showed a woman apparently dead in a shower with a man standing over her; that one drew protests, too. But ads often feature images of women being threatened, attacked, or killed. Sexual assault and battery are normalized, even eroticized.   32

In one ad a woman lies dead on a bed with her breasts exposed and her hair sprawled out around her, and the copy reads, "Great hair never dies." A perfume ad that ran in several teen magazines showed a very young woman with her eyes blackened, next to the text "Apply generously to your neck so he can smell the scent as you shake your head 'no.' " In other words, he'll understand that you don't really mean it when you say no, and he can respond like any other animal.   33

An ad for a bar in Georgetown with a close-up of a cocktail had the headline "If your date won't listen to reason, try a velvet hammer." That's really dangerous when you consider how many sexual assaults involve alcohol in some way. We believe we are not affected by these images, but most of us experience visceral shock when we pay conscious attention to them.   34

Are there subtler forms of abuse in ads? 35

There's a lot of emotional violence in ads. For example, in one 36
cologne ad a handsome man ignores two beautiful blonds. The copy
reads, "Do you want to be the one she tells her deep, dark secrets to?
Or do you want to be her deep, dark secret?" followed by a final
instruction: "Don't be such a good boy." What's the deep, dark secret
here? That he's sleeping with both of them? On one level the message is that the way to get beautiful women is to ignore them, perhaps mistreat them. The message to men is that emotional intimacy
is not a good thing. This does terrible things to men, and of course to
women, too.

There are also many, many ads in which women are pitted against 37
each other for male attention. For example, there's one ad with a topless woman on a bed and the copy, "What the bitch who's about to steal
your man wears." Other ads feature young women fighting or glaring
at each other. This means that when girls hit adolescence, at a time
when they most need support from each other, they're encouraged to
turn on each other in competition for men. It's tragic, because the truth
is that one of the most powerful antidotes to destructive cultural messages is close and supportive female friendships.

*Over the years, we've grown more accustomed to product placements in
movies, but* What Women Want *takes advertiser-driven content to a new
level. I tried to keep a running count, but there were so many I lost track:* 38
*Sears, L'eggs, Wonderbra, Macintosh, Martha Stewart, CNN, Meredith
Brooks and Alanis Morissette CD covers all get prominent plugs.*

The final commercial Gibson pitches to the Nike reps was similar in 39
*style, tone, and prime-time-friendly slogan to sports ads we've seen on TV
before. Would you be surprised if Nike's fake ad eventually traveled from the
big screen to the small screen? How did we get to a point where the whole
premise of a film rests on product placements?*

I wouldn't be surprised at all. In fact, the ad in the movie was made in 40
connection with Wieden + Kennedy, Nike's real-life ad agency. But
Nike doesn't really need to pay to broadcast the commercial on TV,
since this film was so successful at the box office—there couldn't be a
better launch for a commercial than this movie.

I think this is the wave of the future. As more and more people 41
use their VCR to skip the commercials when they watch television, the
commercials will begin to become part of the program so they can't be
edited out. So while you're watching "Friends," Jennifer Aniston will
say to Courteney Cox, "Your hair looks great," and Courteney will say,
"Yeah, I'm using this new gel!"

A number of media critics have dubbed the encroachment of advertising in   42
media, education and public spaces "ad creep." You've called it a "toxic cultural
environment." Can you explain that?

As the mother of a 13-year-old girl, I feel I'm raising my daughter in a   43
toxic cultural environment. I hate that advertisers cynically equate
rebellion with smoking, drinking, and impulsive and impersonal sex. I
want my daughter to be a rebel, to defy stereotypes of "femininity," but
I don't want her to put herself in danger. I feel I have to fight the culture
every step of the way in terms of messages she gets.

    Just as it is difficult to raise kids safely in a physically toxic envi-   44
ronment, where they're breathing polluted air or drinking toxic water,
it's also difficult or even impossible to raise children in a culturally
toxic environment, where they're surrounded by unhealthy images
about sex and relationships, and where their health is constantly sacrificed for the sake of profit.

    Even our schools are toxic—when McDonald's has a nutrition   45
curriculum, Exxon has an environmental curriculum, and kindergartners are given a program called "Learning to read through recognizing
corporate logos." Education is tainted when a student can get suspended for wearing a Pepsi T-shirt on a school-sponsored Coke day,
which happened in Georgia in 1998.

    The United States is one of the few nations in the world that think   46
that children are legitimate targets for advertisers. We allow the tobacco
and alcohol industries to use talking frogs and lizards to sell beer and
cartoon characters to sell cigarettes. The Budweiser commercials are in
fact the most popular commercials with elementary school kids, and Joe
Camel is now as recognizable to 6-year-olds as is Mickey Mouse.

What advice do you have for parents, for any of us, who want to counteract   47
this toxic cultural environment?

Parents can talk to their children, make these messages conscious. We   48
can educate ourselves and become media literate. But primarily we
need to realize that this is not something we can fight purely on an
individual basis.

    Corporations are forever telling us that if we don't like what's on   49
TV we should just turn it off, not let our kids watch tobacco ads or violent movies. We constantly hear that if parents would just talk to their
kids there would be no problem. But that really is like saying, "If your
children are breathing poisoned air, don't let them breathe."

    We need to join together to change the toxic cultural environment.   50
That includes things such as lobbying to teach noncorporate media literacy in our schools, fighting to abolish or restrict advertising aimed at

109

children, organizing to get ads out of our schools, banning the promotion of alcohol and tobacco, and other community solutions.

There are great media literacy projects in Los Angeles, New 51 Mexico, Massachusetts, and many places throughout the world. There's no quick fix, but I have extensive resources about media criticism groups, social change organizations, educational material, media literacy programs, and more available on my Web site. If they want, people could start there.

Examining the Text

1. Why do you think Pozner begins the interview with references to the movie *What Women Want* and to examples of product placement on TV networks? How do these examples set the stage for the interview with Kilbourne?

2. How does Kilbourne define "relationship marketing"? Which of the appeals discussed by Jib Fowles earlier in this chapter are used by "relationship marketing" ads?

3. Focusing on the issues of weight, dieting, and body image, in what ways does Kilbourne believe that advertising is responsible for causing harm to young girls? Why, according to Kilbourne, does advertising contribute to this problem?

4. What kinds of evidence does Kilbourne use to support claims she makes throughout this article? What evidence do you find particularly persuasive? Where in the article do you find yourself disagreeing with or doubting the validity of Kilbourne's claims?

5. The image on page 111, "Your Gaze Hits the Side of My Face," was created by the artist Barbara Kruger. Which of the themes discussed by Pozner and Kilbourne do you see reflected in this image?

6. *Thinking rhetorically:* Following up on the "as you read" question in the introduction to this article, what effect did the interview format of the article have on you as a reader? In general, what are some of the strengths and weaknesses of directly recording the answers of an interviewee rather than paraphrasing and commenting on them? In other words, what's gained and what's lost when we don't have the author—Jennifer Pozner—commenting on Kilbourne's answers?

For Group Discussion

Discuss what you think of the strategies that Kilbourne suggests for fighting the "toxic cultural environment" created by advertising. Which of these strategies do you think are the most likely to have an influence on the current state of advertising? Why would some strategies be more effective than others? Discuss any other strategies you can think of that allow ordinary people ("consumers") to have some impact on the content and techniques of advertising.

Writing Suggestion

As she answers questions in the interview, Kilbourne makes brief references to a number of advertisements that help to prove her points. For this assignment, look through magazines and newspapers for a single advertisement that you think either supports or contradicts one or more of Kilbourne's claims about "relationship marketing." Look for stereotypes, body images, violence, or other forms of advertising where abuses seem to occur. Begin your essay by providing a brief summary of Kilbourne's ideas. Then analyze the advertisement you've chosen. (You may want to review the "Reading Images" section in Chapter 1.) Be sure to connect your analysis of specific features of the ad to specific points that Kilbourne is making, either by providing quotations from Pozner's article or by summarizing Kilbourne's points in your own words.

"Your Gaze Hits Side of My Face," by Barbara Kruger. *(Courtesy of the Mary Boone Gallery, New York)*

Beefcake and Cheesecake: Insights for Advertisers

MARILYN Y. JONES, ANDREA J. S. STANALAND, AND BETSY D. GELB

Following up on Jean Kilbourne's discussion of advertising's cultural impact, this article presents the results of empirical research—that is, actual tests— on the ways that men and women respond to provocative ads. Like Kilbourne, Marilyn Y. Jones, Andrea J. S. Stanaland, and Betsy D. Gelb are interested in the effects of advertising on men and women in our society; however, the authors of this article look at the issue from the perspective of advertisers rather than consumers. In other words, Jones, Stanaland, and Gelb are less concerned with the social impact of provocative ads and more interested in whether the ads actually work: do these kinds of ads draw viewers in and ultimately sell products?

Another difference between this article and Kilbourne's research is that Jones et al. examine ads that have provocatively dressed male as well as female models: that is, "beefcake" as well as "cheesecake" ads. As the authors explain in their list of hypotheses, they expected to find differences both in viewers' attitudes toward the ads and in viewers' ability to recall specific information about the products being sold in the ads. In short, they expected that men and women would react differently to seeing beefcake and cheesecake ads.

This study was first published in the Journal of Advertising *in 1998. Like much academic writing, the article builds on previous research and attempts to resolve existing questions and test existing hypotheses. Indeed, as you can see in their list of references, Jones et al. draw on 45 previously published articles to provide the background and foundation for their own study.* **As you read** *this article, particularly the "Previous Research" section, be sure to underline and make marginal notes on the key findings of the existing research. With so many studies already done on advertising and gender, what issues still remain unresolved? What topics do academic researchers still see the need to pursue?*

Sex appeals in advertising now include eye-catching male models (Kuriansky 1995; Miller 1993) as well as cheesecake—sexy female models. Over the last 25 years, researchers investigating the effectiveness of sexy ads, most often cheesecake ads viewed by men, have reported mixed findings, in general concluding that such ads attract attention but do not improve either recall of or attitude toward the brand. The emergence of beefcake ads, ones with sexy male models, prompts the question of whether responses parallel those to cheesecake ads. Further, recent literature on differences between the sexes in responses to the same stimuli suggests that men and women may respond differently to any ad that makes a gender perspective salient.

Our study proceeded from two premises. The first was that we 2 need to know more about responses to cheesecake ads. Both men and women may have evolved in their views of what is appropriate since previous research was conducted; therefore, previous findings may no longer apply. The second premise was that we need to know more about beefcake ads, as no model of advertising effects predicts whether or under what circumstances men's and women's responses to beefcake ads parallel those to cheesecake ads.

We therefore studied how both male and female viewers of an ad 3 respond to advertising that is more versus less suggestive in its illustrations. We expected differences related to (1) the sex of the model and (2) whether the model is provocatively dressed. We expected those variables, interacting with sex of viewer, to affect attitudes toward the ad and the advertised brand, and also memorability of the ad and the brand.

The pattern of relationships expected was based on four overlap- 4 ping streams of research. The first important stream consists of studies of sexy models in advertising. The second pertains to the interpretation of, and reaction to, the pictorial components of an ad. The third stream is represented by the deconstruction literature, and has been applied to understanding how consumers read ads (Scott 1994a, b; Stern 1993). That perspective, which sees individual reaction to a communication as dependent on situation and context, has contributed to the position that communication is inherently gendered; that is, it contains cues that readers recognize as representing statements about gender (Stern 1993). The fourth research stream pertains to the general formulations of advertising response. Of specific interest was the dual mediation hypothesis (MacKenzie, Lutz, and Belch 1986) that reaction to an advertised brand is influenced by cognitive processing of advertised messages and the attitudes that such processing may in turn influence, but also that reaction is influenced directly by emotional response to the advertising.

PREVIOUS RESEARCH

Sexy Models in Advertising

The history of research in the field of sexy advertising has followed 5 advertising practice. Beginning more than 50 years ago, an advertiser might occasionally or routinely place a scantily clad female model in an ad offering a utilitarian product to men, assuming that attention to the ad would thereby increase. Once researchers began testing the efficacy of including such a model as an attention-getter, they simply followed advertising practice: they conducted their research using a sexy female model and an audience of men. They measured the effects on not only attention, but also other variables, such as brand name and copy point recall.

As sophistication increased, researchers added women to their pool of respondents and included measures of attitude toward the ad, realizing that for women the attitudes could well be negative (Morrison and Sherman 1972; Baker and Churchill 1977; Chestnut, LaChance, and Lubitz 1977; Peterson and Kerin 1977). Then psychological researchers prompted further complexity by showing the interrelationships of attitudes and cognitive variables. At roughly the same time, other researchers perceived that men as well as women might respond negatively to sexual images unrelated to the advertised product. More complex relationships were tested. As the next step, research with male models as well as female models appeared, with male and female respondents, primarily focusing on attitudes and finding differences depending on sex of respondent. 6

Our study adds to the stream of literature by measuring responses to beefcake and cheesecake ads by both men and women, and examining both attitudes and cognitive (memorability) variables. We measured attitude toward the ad and brand, as well as recall and recognition of brand, illustration, and copy. From the work of gender theorists such as Stern (1993), we expected to find differences between men's and women's responses to the same stimuli. 7

We proceeded from the idea that sexiness of a model pictured in an ad is linked to measures of responses to the ad and the brand, and that the relationships are moderated by the match between the sex of the viewer and the sex of the model. Measures of attitude response to advertising have demonstrated the utility of the dual-mediation hypothesis (MacKenzie, Lutz, and Belch 1986), which posits the following three sets of links: cognitions about the ad influence attitudes toward it and attitudes toward the brand; attitude toward the ad affects the cognitions people generate about the brand and also the attitude toward the brand; and brand cognitions influence attitude toward the brand. Other responses to advertising include memory measures, with memory depending on the amount of attention and thought given to an ad. 8

In general, the previous research supports the idea that sex of model and sex of viewer interact to influence response to advertising. However, the studies are not altogether consistent n their findings. One possible explanation is that sexiness has been operationalized in three 9

major ways: physical attractiveness, nudity, and rated sexiness/
suggestiveness. Hence, research results that appear to conflict may
actually reflect responses to significantly different stimuli.

Some studies have found that it is not the degree of sexiness   10
(whether that be nudity or rated suggestiveness) but the presence or
absence of a model that produces negative effects on recall and recognition (Alexander and Judd 1978; Judd and Alexander 1983). However,
that conclusion is called into question by O'Connor et al. (1986), who
found that brand recall did not diminish with the presence or absence
of a model. Recall does appear to decline as an ad contains more
nudity, but sexiness operationalized in a broader sense than nudity
may or may not reduce recall.

Increasing nudity and/or sexiness historically has been found to   11
influence attitude toward the ad. The most striking differences are
between men and women, with female respondents reacting more negatively than men to sexiness. However, these results are based largely
on studies employing only female models.

Visual Images in Advertising

A separate but related set of studies has considered the effects of visual   12   **115**
images. Mitchell (1986) and Mitchell and Olson (1981) show evidence
that the meanings derived from the pictures included with ads have a
direct effect on attitude toward the ad and an indirect effect on attitude
toward the brand. According to Mitchell (1986), the meanings conveyed by a picture in an ad may be affect laden and may influence
attitude toward the ad and, by extension, alter the direct link between
attitude toward the ad and attitude toward the brand as well as the
brand cognitions that contribute to attitude toward the brand. Scott
(1994a, b) notes that pictorial stimuli communicate meaning that they
do not explicitly "show," as consumers interpret visual content
through a dynamic system of symbols. One possibility, then, is that any
ad with a model prominently illustrated is making a gender-salient
statement based simply on the sex of the model. Another possibility is
that in the case of sexy ads, an advertiser is perceived as communicating a wish to associate a brand with a sexy man or a sexy woman.

Understandably, differences in responses have been found   13
between men and women. When Mick and Politi (1989) asked student
subjects to relate their thoughts and feelings about a suggestive ad with
a dominant visual content, the subjects reported a great variety of interpretations. Gender differences in interpretation were found and could
be traced back to differences in sensitivity to symbolic meanings within
the pictures. In contrast, Elliott et al. (1995) expected to find such differences but did not. They noted that many sexual images are ambiguous,

giving rise to interpretations that vary between sexes, although their study results did not support their expectations of interpretive differences. Plausibly, then, if interpretations yield beliefs that influence memory of the ad and attitudes toward it, those variables will be influenced by the sex of the respondent interacting with the degree of sexiness in the ad and the gender of the model.

Sex of the Model and Deconstruction Literature

Gender differences within the audience for advertising have frequently been associated with differences in response. Few studies, however, have examined differences generated by varying the sex of the model in the stimulus ads, because few have explicitly examined beefcake advertising.   14

Among researchers who have used sexy male models are Simpson, Horton, and Brown (1996), who found an opposite-sex effect: female viewers liked beefcake better than male viewers did. Their study involved neither a comparison with cheesecake nor extensive measurement of cognitive variables, and our research was intended to fill those gaps.   15

Some earlier studies (Belch et al. 1981; Sciglimpaglia, Belch, and Cain 1978) had used nude male models and nude female models and found that respondents reacted more negatively to models of their own sex than to those of the opposite sex. However, later studies using models that were attractive but not sexy produced different results. Patzer (1983) tested for differences between male and female viewers in liking for an ad with attractive (but not "sexy") models of each sex and found no difference by sex of viewer. Likewise, Caballero, Lumpkin, and Madden (1989) and Caballero and Solomon (1984) did not find an effect on purchase response for the viewer's sex in the presence of an attractive, but not sexy, model. The apparent lack of an opposite-sex effect for model attractiveness without sexiness suggests that the sexiness of the model may drive the effect.   16

More positive affective responses toward models of the opposite sex were found in studies by Belch et al. (1981), Sciglimpaglia, Belch, and Cain (1978), and Baker and Churchill (1977), particularly for a nude male model or a nude female model. Most prior work on gender differences supports an opposite-sex effect: sexy ads showing the opposite sex are viewed more favorably than are ads depicting a model of the viewer's own sex.   17

A broader conclusion, however, is that sexy ads evoke gender differences in measures of advertising effectiveness whether a study examines ads with same-sex illustrations, opposite-sex illustrations, or both. Explanations have alluded to a possible role of social and cultural factors in those differences. Scott (1994a, b) and Stern (1993) make the case for gender-specific interpretations of sexy advertising, and   18

Thompson and Hirschman (1995) note that widespread social constructions might give rise to the meanings people bring to sexy, and other gendered, stimuli. Stern and Holbrook (1994) explain that gender must be considered when attempting to understand a consumer's "meaning-making process," as gender will interact with cultural context to influence consumer responses to communication.

Elliott et al. (1995), using discourse analysis, analyzed the conversations of separate male and female focus groups about four sexy ads. Four male and four female focus groups were conducted, each moderated by someone of the same sex as its participants. The researchers concluded that both male and female participants responded positively to equality in sexual images or to perceived artistic sexuality, and responded negatively to sex-role stereotyping and the objectification of women. Interestingly, they found little comment on the objectification of men for the one ad that contained a sexy male image rather than a female image. One could hypothesize that male reactions to beefcake parallel female reactions to cheesecake. However, we might not expect that to be true in view of the political loading imposed on sexy ads with female models. Elliott and his coworkers observed that the focus group reactions appeared to take social and political themes into account. The same political/social themes were voiced by both male and female participants, and not generalized to the ads containing male models by either gender. Hence, though there seem to be gender-specific interpretations of advertising (cf. Scott 1994a, b) and cultural context seems to play a role (cf. Stern and Holbrook 1994), we cannot necessarily infer a parallel reaction effect. 19

117

Contemporary Models of Advertising Effectiveness

The literature also suggests the possibility that sexy ads are processed differently from ones with less distracting illustrations; that is, attention goes to the ad rather than the product. Differences in processing would explain findings such as those of Alexander and Judd (1978), whose male subjects had lower recall of brand names from ads showing a nude female model than from ads showing a landscape. Consistent with those results, other studies have found higher recall for (1) ads depicting a pasture versus a nude female model (Judd and Alexander 1983), (2) ads with lower erotic content than comparison ads (Weller, Roberts, and Neuhaus 1979), (3) ads deemed nonsexy as opposed to sexy ads (Severn, Belch, and Belch 1990), and (4) ads deemed nonsexual as opposed to sexual ads, though only male subjects were included in the study (Steadman 1969). 20

Only O'Conner et al. (1986) found lower recall for an ad with no model than for an ad judged to be high in sexuality. However, they did find higher recall for a low sexuality condition (an ad containing a nonsexy 21 model) than for a high sexuality condition. The discrepancy between the findings of O'Conner et al. and those of prior studies may be due to lack of control of stimuli; O'Conner et al. used actual ads judged as to sexuality, with no attempt to obtain uniform content, layout, or detail of copy.

Only Judd and Alexander (1983) and O'Conner et al. (1986) 22 designed their studies to examine the effect of interaction between sex of viewer and type of ad on memory; neither found such interaction. However, their operationalizations may have affected the results: Judd and Alexander looked at nudity without consideration of "sexiness," whereas O'Conner et al. did not use consistent stimuli. Also, none of the previously cited researchers used beefcake to prompt the cognitive responses of interest; reaction was to female models only.

By contrast, our expectation of memory differences is based on 23 theory about how ads are processed. Possibly viewers can be attracted by an eye-catching model and therefore associate favorable affect with the brand, but at the same time be annoyed by a sexist portrayal and feel unfavorable affect toward the ad. Alternatively, viewers can be puzzled by apparent incongruity between a sexy model and the product he or she is illustrating, experiencing unfavorable affect that is then associated with the brand. The theory suggesting the possibility of such scenarios comes from MacKenzie, Lutz, and Belch (1986), who tested four models of ad processing that included various paths between cognitive and affective processing of the ad itself and the cognitive and affective reactions to the brand. They demonstrated that not only do brand cognitions lead to brand attitudes, as posited in the most common models of advertising response, but that affective reactions to an ad influence brand attitudes both directly and indirectly, in the latter case by changing cognitions about the brand.

That is the dual mediation hypothesis, and a meta-analysis 24 (Brown and Stayman 1992) of the many studies that have examined the influence of attitude toward the ad on brand attitudes and cognitions found strong support for the paths hypothesized by the dual mediation model. The research is particularly pertinent because sexy advertising evokes feelings and thoughts about the ad itself that not only may reflect on attitudes toward the brand, but also may influence cognitive processing of it. Hence, men and women may differ in their response processes given a female or male model, provocatively clothed or not—the basic combinations tested in our study. Stern (1993) notes several information processing effects whereby gender may influence affective response to the ad, perceptions of an ad, and inference making. Meyers-Levy and Maheswaran (1991) bring additional complexity to the issue by suggesting that the different processing approaches employed by men and women afford another explanation for the expectation of different affective outcomes.

There is a precedent for attempting to blend such post-modern   25
viewpoints with a cognitive-based communications model. Sujan,
Bettman, and Baumgartner (1993) studied interplay between emotion-
evoking stimuli and consumer judgments of those stimuli. Their results
suggest that advertising cues often evoke autobiographical information;
the self-referencing is associated with an emotional loading, shifting
thought away from the product information in the ad. Further, autobiographical associations may carry over into evaluative judgments, such
as attitude toward the ad and even attitude toward the brand if a link is
established between the brand and the personal memories evoked.
Thus, gender differences might prompt different responses to sexy
advertising, including processing differences, because only ads using
models matching one's own gender prompt self-referencing (pointing
to a potential same-sex effect when cognition is measured).

On the basis of the literature, we tested a familiar idea in a more   26
comprehensive way than had been attempted previously. Using not
only cheesecake but also beefcake, and using not only affective but also
memory measures of advertising effectiveness, we tested the overall
idea that men and women respond differently to advertising, with the
sex of a model and degree of provocative dress of the model contributing to the differences.

We tested the following specific hypotheses.   27

119

H1:   The sex of a subject and the type of ad interact to influence
      men's and women's affective responses to ads.
      a. Women have less favorable attitudes than men toward
         cheesecake ads and brands advertised in cheesecake ads.
      b. Men have less favorable attitudes than women toward beef-
         cake ads and brands advertised in beefcake ads.
      c. Women have more favorable attitudes toward beefcake ads
         than toward cheesecake ads, but even more favorable atti-
         tudes toward ads with nonsexy male models.
      d. Men will have more favorable attitudes toward cheesecake
         ads than toward beefcake ads, but even more favorable atti-
         tudes toward ads with nonsexy female models.

H2:   The sex of a subject and the type of ad interact to influence
      men's and women's memory of advertising content.
      a. Women have lower recall and recognition scores than men for
         cheesecake ads.
      b. Men have lower recall and recognition scores than women for
         beefcake ads.
      c. Women have higher recall and recognition scores for beef-
         cake ads than for cheesecake ads, and higher recall and

recognition scores for nonsexy ads with a male model than for beefcake.

d. Men have higher recall and recognition scores for cheesecake ads than for beefcake ads, and higher recall and recognition scores for nonsexy ads with a female model than for cheesecake.

METHOD

Design and Stimuli

The hypotheses were tested in an experiment with five treatment levels, resulting in a five (type of ad) by two (gender of subject) between-subjects design. The dependent variables tested were recall and recognition of claims in the copy, of the illustration, and of the brand name, as well as attitude toward the ad and its elements ($\alpha = .89$) and attitude toward the brand ($\alpha = 90$).   28

The stimulus ads were created from two pretests. One pretest was used to find a gender-neutral product. Subjects rated 16 different products for their intrinsic masculinity and femininity and rated them for the sex of the usual buyer. Bicycles were selected from the test as being neither inherently feminine nor masculine and as being purchased by either male or female consumers.   29

In a separate pretest, student subjects rated 10 photos of male models and 10 photos of female models for sexiness of the model and attractiveness of the model. The photos used, selected from actual ads, included models wearing a variety of clothing (from conservative streetwear to swimwear) and in a variety of poses. For the sexy ad stimuli in the experiment, the male and female models (with comparable clothing and poses) considered attractive and having the highest sexiness ratings were used. For the nonsexy ad stimuli, male and female models with comparable clothing and poses rated attractive but nonsexy were selected. We were aware that bicycles seemed an unlikely match for a provocatively clothed model as the advertising illustration, but reasoned that previous research and frequent advertising practice have juxtaposed sexy illustrations with products for which their applicability is at least questionable. Further, bicycles were equally incongruous with the dress of the attractive but not sexy models, providing a control for the possible effect of perceived incongruity in the illustration across ads.   30

The ads, designed specifically for our study, promoted a fitness/cross-training bicycle. Each contained four claims (our flagship bike, powerful gearset, comfortable frame, and lightweight frame) as well as   31

the colors available, a headline, and the brand name. All ads were identical in terms of copy and layout, differing only in the picture included
with the bicycle. One of five pictures was used: a provocatively dressed
(sexy) male model, a sexy female model, a nonsexy male model, a nonsexy female model, and a landscape. As in prior studies (Steadman
1969; LaTour 1990; LaTour, Pitts, and Snook-Luther 1990), the landscape was included as a control.

Sample and Procedures

Approximately 300 undergraduate students at a major southwestern   32
university were enlisted as subjects in exchange for extra credit toward
their grade in a course. Students were chosen to be subjects because of
both availability and the compatibility of their age group and lifestyle
with the product category, bicycles.

The one ad given to each student was selected randomly: sexy   33
male model, sexy female model, nonsexy male model, nonsexy female
model, or landscape. The students were given 15 seconds to study the
ad and then told to put it in a manila envelope. They next filled out a
series of questionnaires in prescribed sequence, with several monitors
in the room to ensure that no one referred to the ad or to any preceding
form while filling out his or her answers.

The first section of the questionnaire measured attitudes by ask-   34
ing for degree of agreement or disagreement with statements about
perceptions of the brand and ad. It was followed by a blank layout of
the ad and a request that subjects write in information that they
remembered about the ad, a demonstration of recall. They also were
asked to write in the brand name and to describe in their own words
the picture in the advertisement. A final section of the questionnaire
tested for recognition of brand name and copy points with true/false
questions that included accurate and fictional statements.

Scores for attitude toward the ad and the brand were calculated   35
as the sum of responses to a set of five 7-point Likert scales measuring
strength of agreement or disagreement with statements such as "I
thought this was an interesting ad" (for attitude toward the ad) and "I
think the advertised bicycle is high quality" (for attitude toward the
brand). That approach to tapping attitudes (including terms such as
"likable," "quality," "interesting," and "good") is consistent with previous ad research on brand and ad evaluations (Edell and Staelin 1983;
Keller 1987). The adjectives selected were those used previously by
Baker and Churchill (1977) and by Bello, Pitts, and Etzel (1983).

Recall scores for each respondent were calculated by first coding   36
responses into 11 possible categories of ad content, such as "flagship
fitness bike," and then calculating the average number of correct items

mentioned per category. Recognition scores were the average number of correct responses to the eight true/false questions about ad claims, such as "the frame is a medium-weight frame."

Data were analyzed by ANOVA to determine the effect of the 37 independent variables on attitude toward the ad and the brand (affective responses) and on recall and recognition (cognitive responses) at the omnibus level. Planned simple and complex contrasts then were tested to pinpoint differences between specific sets or pairs of ads or sets of respondents (male vs. female). Initially, MANOVA had seemed appropriate, but we were unable to meet the assumption of homogeneity of variance–covariance matrices required for that technique.

RESULTS

A manipulation check verified that the sexy ads were, in fact, perceived 38 as sexy by subjects who saw them. Subjects who looked at an ad with a provocatively clothed model mentioned sexiness on their blank-page comments significantly more often than subjects who were shown a nonsexy ad (p < .0001). Figures 2.1 and 2.2 show the results in graphic form.

Results from ANOVA and a priori contrasts, show partial support 39 for both hypotheses. However, in general, the data show fewer significant results for cognitive responses and more for affective responses.

Consistent with H1, we found women to have less favorable 40 attitudes than men toward the cheesecake ad as well as the brand advertised in that ad. Also, male subjects had more favorable attitudes toward the cheesecake ad than to the beefcake ad. Those findings generally support the opposite-sex effect in the context of sexy stimuli. However, the differences seem to emerge primarily for the cheesecake ad. Male and female subjects showed no difference in their attitudes toward the beefcake ad or the brand advertised in it. Also, no difference appeared in the attitude scores of female subjects who saw a beefcake ad and those who saw an ad with a nonsexy male model.

Differences in attitude toward the ad and toward the brand 41 between women who saw a beefcake ad and women who saw a cheesecake ad are not statistically significant but are in the hypothesized direction. Similarly, differences in attitude toward the brand between men who viewed a cheesecake ad and men who viewed a beefcake ad are not statistically significant but are in the expected direction.

H2 has only limited support. Women had higher recognition 42 scores for the ad showing a nonsexy male model than for the beefcake ad; however, the contrast is not significant for the recall measure. Men

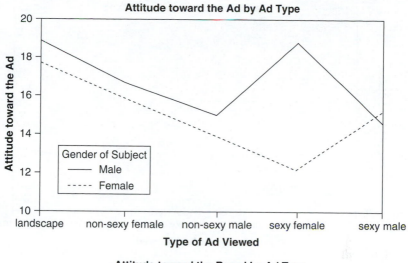

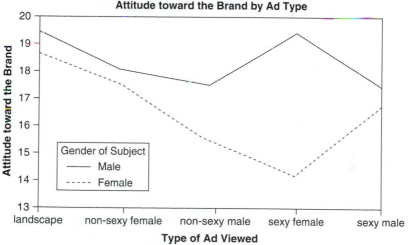

Figure 2.1 Results for Attitude Measures

had higher recall scores for the ad showing a nonsexy female model than for the cheesecake ad, but not higher recognition scores.

No other hypothesized memory differences were found. However, some findings opposite the ones expected can be seen in the tables. Women had *lower* recognition scores then men for the beefcake ad, and women viewing the cheesecake ad had *higher* recognition scores than women viewing the beefcake ad. Also, men had *lower* recall than women for the cheesecake ad.

123

43

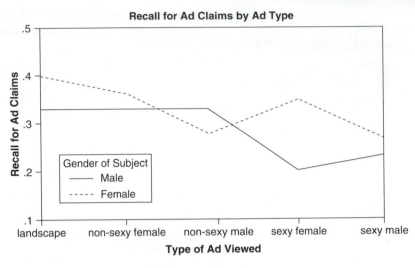

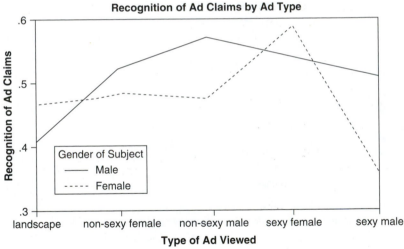

Figure 2.2 Results for Cognitive Measures

CONCLUSIONS AND IMPLICATIONS

The chief limitations of our study—the classroom setting and university student subjects—may limit the findings to a young adult advertising audience. However, students' attitudes toward advertising have been found to be consistent with those of the general population (Barnes 1982; Zanot 1984), and students are deemed appropriate subjects for basic research on causal mechanisms (Kardes 1996). Also, a young adult audience may be a likely target for bicycle ads and beefcake or cheesecake

44

ads. Nevertheless, given the limitations of the study, conclusions drawn from the results are only tentative.

Discussion of such conclusions begins with examination of the 45 questions that prompted the study: Do previous findings about reactions to cheesecake ads still hold, for men and for women, given changes in the social climate? Do those findings apply symmetrically to beefcake? Are responses to an ad with a sexy model in its illustration influenced by the interaction of the sex of a model with the sex of the viewer? If attitude toward the ad is influenced by such interaction, are cognitive measures likewise influenced? We discuss each of those issues in turn.

The findings support the previously noted negative influence of 46 cheesecake on women's attitudes toward the ad. However, men do not disparage beefcake. The results support the findings of Elliott et al. (1995) that a sexy male image evoked little comment. In our study, responses to beefcake differed from responses to an illustration of a fully clothed male model in only one hypothesized comparison. Scores on the recognition measure encompassing copy points, brand name, and illustration were higher for women who saw the clothed male model than for women who saw the beefcake ad.

The third issue guiding our study, the expectation that, for an ad 47 with a provocatively clothed model, the sex of that model and the sex of the viewer would interact to influence attitudes and cognitive responses, is supported but not as expected. Women who saw a cheesecake ad recognized ad content more and viewed the brand significantly more negatively than those who saw other illustrations. Cheesecake boosted men's attitude toward the ad, as expected, but caused no discernable reduction in measures of memory of the ad. However, beefcake evoked significantly lower recognition of ad contents among women than did cheesecake or other illustrations. Hence, contrary to our expectation, we cannot conclude that same-sex sexy ads provoke indignation and therefore interfere with memory of the ad copy and brand name. For women, indignation about a cheesecake ad instead appears to help memorability, but indignation is unlikely to be the effect the advertiser intended.

The interaction does appear, but not as consistently as expected. 48 Scores for men do not support the expectation that provocatively clothed models of one's own sex lead to disapproval that discourages cognitive processing. Possibly men simply are not interested in beefcake, and so processing is not influenced. The finding for women who viewed cheesecake was opposite the one hypothesized: cheesecake was more memorable than a nonsexy female model. Perhaps, disapproval of an illustration leads to a search in the ad copy for more to disapprove of.

In short, beefcake seems not to be as detrimental as cheesecake, 49 but, with an audience in the age category that might be most attuned to a sexy stimulus, we found that ads with sexy models offered few of the effects an advertiser would seek. Of course, a bicycle is not a product with sex-laden associations, and Simpson, Horton, and Brown (1996) found differences between products in responses to the degree of male nudity in an ad. It is interesting to juxtapose our findings with those of Campbell (1995), who studied consumer inferences of "manipulative intent" in ads with attention-getting tactics and found that such intent was most often inferred when the tactic did not fit the product category.

Clearly, the nonsexy ads seemed to do the most good with the least harm. Affective responses to such ads did not parallel women's negative responses to cheesecake, and cognitive responses did not parallel women's low level of recognition for beefcake. We found no evidence that attitude toward the brand is helped by a sexy model of either sex with audience members of either sex. 50

Our study has several theoretical implications. The nonsymmetrical patterns of results suggest the presence of (1) other meanings that are being brought to bear on the pictorial stimuli and (2) gender-specific interpretations of the stimuli. If a sexy picture has just an opposite-sex effect, we should always find a difference by gender of viewer—we do not. If a sexy model is always more fun to look at, men should prefer the sexy female model to the nonsexy one (they do), and women should prefer the sexy male model to the nonsexy one (they do not). Men and women, as Mick and Politi (1989) show, may perceive rather different qualities in such portrayals and may relate to the portrayals with different underlying needs and life experiences. Similar notions apply to the memory data—men and women may have studied the ads differently. For example, over all of the ads, recognition is higher than recall, but there are cases where recognition is no higher for a specific ad (women viewing a beefcake ad). That finding suggests increased elaboration on a selected subset of the information such that all that was examined (the particular subset) can be recalled. What we do not know is the nature of the thought process and why that subset was the focus of the attention. 51

From the perspective of advertising research, the obvious lesson is to exercise considerable care in audience selection when testing ads that might be characterized as sexy. Apparently, for sexy men as well as sexy women in ads there are some significant differences in responses. We expected and found male versus female differences in both attitudinal responses and ability to remember advertising claims. Those differences may not be critical for products targeted to one gender or the other, but caution must be used in testing advertising for a product for which one gender constitutes product users or decision influencers, and therefore is selected as the audience for the advertising research, but the other gender often performs the actual purchase. With beer, for 52 instance, brand preference among men is one goal, but women constitute the majority of supermarket beer purchasers (Dietrich 1992). If a male audience responds favorably to an ad test, a follow up among women may be necessary.

The limitation of our study to visual print ads provides issues to be investigated in future research. How might sexy models influence attitudes and memory differently in television commercials? Would we find similar effects when measuring reactions to sexy voices in radio spots? How resilient are resulting brand attitudes over time, especially in light of a variety of subsequent messages? Such questions might guide further efforts in the evolving research on sex appeals in advertising. 53

REFERENCES

Alexander, M. Wayne and Ben Judd, Jr. (1978), "Do Nudes in Ads Enhance Brand Recall?" *Journal of Advertising Research,* 18 (1), 47–50.

Baker, Michael J. and Gilbert A. Churchill, Jr. (1977), "The Impact of Physically Attractive Models on Advertising Evaluations," *Journal of Marketing Research,* 14 (November), 538–555.

Barnes, M. (1982), "Public Attitudes to Advertising," *International Journal of Advertising,* 1 (April–June), 119–128.

Belch, Michael A., Barbro E. Holgerson, George E. Belch, and Jerry Koppman (1981), "Psychophysiological and Cognitive Responses to Sex in Advertising," *Advances in Consumer Research,* Vol. 9, Andrew A. Mitchell, ed., St. Louis: Association for Consumer Research, 424–427.

Bello, Daniel C., Robert E. Pitts, and Michael J. Etzel (1983), "The Communication Effects of Controversial Sexual Content in Television Programs and Commercials," *Journal of Advertising,* 12 (3), 32–42.

Brown, Steven P. and Douglas M. Stayman (1992), "Antecedents and Consequences of Attitude toward the Ad: A Meta-Analysis," *Journal of Consumer Research,* 19 (June), 34–51.

Caballero, Marjorie J., James R. Lumpkin, and Charles S. Madden (1989), "Using Physical Attractiveness as an Advertising Tool: An Empirical Test of the Attraction Phenomenon," *Journal of Advertising Research,* 29 (4), 16–22.

———and Paul J. Solomon (1984), "Effects of Model Attractiveness on Sales Response," *Journal of Advertising,* 13 (1), 17–33.

Campbell, Margaret C. (1995), "When Attention-Getting Advertising Tactics Elicit Consumer Inferences of Manipulative Intent: The Importance of Balancing Benefits and Investments," *Journal of Consumer Psychology,* 4 (3), 225–254.

127

Chestnut, Robert W., Charles C. LaChance, and Amy Lubitz (1977), "The 'Decorative' Female Model: Sexual Stimuli and the Recognition of Advertisements," *Journal of Advertising*, 6 (4), 11–14.

Dietrich, Robert (1992), "Tracking the Invisible Men," *Progressive Grocer*, 71 (11), 69–82.

Edell, Julie A. and Richard Staelin (1983), "The Information Processing of Pictures in Print Advertisements," *Journal of Consumer Research*, 10 (June), 45–61.

Elliott, Richard, Abigail Jones, Andrew Benfield, and Matt Barlow (1995), "Overt Sexuality: A Discourse Analysis of Gender Responses," *Journal of Consumer Policy*, 18 (June), 187–217.

Judd, Ben B., Jr. and M. Wayne Alexander (1983), "On the Reduced Effectiveness of Some Sexually Suggestive Ads," *Journal of the Academy of Marketing Science*, 11 (2), 156–168.

Kardes, Frank R. (1996), "In Defense of Experimental Consumer Psychology," *Journal of Consumer Psychology*, 5 (3), 279–296.

Keller, Kevin Lane (1987), "Memory Factors in Advertising: The Effect of Advertising Retrieval Cues on Brand Evaluations," *Journal of Consumer Research*, 14 (3), 316–333.

Kuriansky, Judy (1995), "Sex Simmers, Still Sells," *Advertising Age*, 66 (special issue), 49.

LaTour, Michael S. (1990), "Female Nudity in Print Advertising: An Analysis of Gender Differences in Arousal and Ad Response," *Psychology & Marketing*, 7(1), 65–81.

———, Robert E. Pitts, and David C. Snook-Luther (1990), "Female Nudity, Arousal, and Ad Response: An Experimental Investigation," *Journal of Advertising*, 19 (4), 51–62

MacKenzie, Scott B., Richard J. Lutz, and George E. Belch (1986), "The Role of Attitude Toward the Ad as a Mediator of Advertising Effectiveness: A Test of Competing Explanations," *Journal of Marketing Research*, 23 (May), 130–143.

Meyers-Levy, Joan and Durairaj Maheswaran (1991), "Exploring Differences in Males' and Females' Processing Strategies," *Journal of Consumer Research*, 18 (June), 63–70.

Mick, David Glen and Laura G. Politi (1989), "Consumers' Interpretations of Advertising Imagery: A Visit to the Hell of Connotation," in Elizabeth C. Hirschman, ed., *Interpretive Consumer Research*, Provo, UT: Association for Consumer Research, 85–96.

Miller, Cyndee (1993), "They're Macho, and They're Back," *Marketing News*, 27 (24), 1.

Mitchell, Andrew A. (1986), "The Effect of Verbal and Visual Components of Advertisements on Brand Attitudes and Attitude Toward the Advertisement," *Journal of Consumer Research*, 13 (June), 12–24.

———— and Jerry C. Olson (1981), "Are Product Attribute Beliefs the Only Mediator of Advertising Effects on Brand Attitude?" *Journal of Marketing Research*, 18 (August), 318–332.

Morrison, Bruce John and Richard C. Sherman (1972), "Who Responds to Sex in Advertising?" *Journal of Advertising Research*, 12 (2), 15–19.

O'Connor, P.J., Aylin Baher, Bosco Gong, and Elyse Kane (1986), "Recall Levels of Sexuality in Advertising," *American Marketing Association Educators' Proceedings,* Terence A. Shimp, Subhash Sharma, George John, John A. Quelch, John H. Lindgren, Jr., William Dillon, Meryl Paula Gardner, and Robert F. Dyer, eds., Chicago: American Marketing Association, 2–5.

Patzer, Gordon L. (1979), "A Comparison of Advertisement Effects: Sexy Female Communicator vs. Non-Sexy Female Communicator," *Advances in Consumer Research*, Vol. 7, Jerry C. Olson, ed., San Francisco: Association for Consumer Research, 359–364.

————(1983), "Source Credibility as a Function of Communicator Physical Attractiveness," *Journal of Business Research,* 11 (2), 229–241.

Peterson, Robert A. and Roger A. Kerin (1977), "The Female Role in Advertisements: Some Experimental Evidence," *Journal of Marketing,* 41 (4), 59–63.

Reid, Leonard N. and Lawrence C. Soley (1983), "Decorative Models and the Readership of Magazine Ads," *Journal of Advertising Research,* 23 (2), 27–32.

Richmond, David and Timothy P. Hartman (1982), "Sex Appeal in Advertising," *Journal of Advertising Research*, 22 (5), 53–61.

Sciglimpaglia, Donald, Michael A. Belch, and Richard F. Cain (1978), "Demographic and Cognitive Factors Influencing Viewers' Evaluations of 'Sexy' Advertisements," *Advances in Consumer Research,* Vol. 6, William L. Wilkie, ed., Miami Beach: Association for Consumer Research, 62–65.

Scott, Linda M. (1994a), "Images in Advertising: The Need for a Theory of Visual Rhetoric," *Journal of Consumer Research*, 21 (September), 252–273.

————(1994b), "The Bridge from Text to Mind: Adapting Reader-Response Theory to Consumer Research," *Journal of Consumer Research,* 21 (December), 461–480.

Severn, Jessica, George E. Belch, and Michael A. Belch (1990), "The Effects of Sexual and Non-sexual Advertising Appeals and Information Level on Cognitive Processing and Communication Effectiveness," *Journal of Advertising,* 19 (1), 14–22.

Simpson, Penny M., Steve Horton, and Gene Brown (1996), "Male Nudity in Advertisements: A Modified Replication and Extension of Gender and Product Effects," *Journal of the Academy of Marketing Science*, 24 (3), 257–262.

129

Steadman, Major (1969), "How Sexy Illustrations Affect Brand Recall," *Journal of Advertising*, 9 (1), 15–19.

Stern, Barbara B. (1993), "Feminist Literary Criticism and the Deconstruction of Ads: A Postmodern View of Advertising and Consumer Responses," *Journal of Consumer Research*, 19 (March), 556–566.

————and Morris B. Holbrook (1994), "Gender and Genre in the Interpretation of Advertising Text," in *Gender Issues and Consumer Behavior*, Janeen Arnold Costa, ed., Thousand Oaks, CA: Sage Publications, 11–41.

Sujan, Mita, James R. Bettman, and Hans Baumgartner (1993), "Influencing Consumer Judgments Using Autobiographical Memories: A Self-Referencing Perspective," *Journal of Marketing Research*, 30 (November), 422–436.

Thompson, Craig J. and Elizabeth C. Hirschman (1995), "Understanding the Socialized Body: A Poststructuralist Analysis of Consumers' Self-Conceptions, Body Images, and Self-Care Practices," *Journal of Consumer Research*, 22 (September), 139–153.

Weller, Ralph B., C. Richard Roberts, and Cohn Neuhaus (1979), "A Longitudinal Study of the Effect of Erotic Content upon Advertising Brand Recall," *Current Issues and Research in Advertising*, James H. Leigh and Claude R. Martin, Jr., eds., Ann Arbor: The University of Michigan, 145–161.

Wise, Gordon L., Alan L. King, and J. Paul Merenski (1974), "Reactions to Sexy Ads Vary With Age," *Journal of Advertising Research*, 14 (4), 11–16.

Zanot, E. J. (1984), "Public Attitudes Towards Advertising: The American Experience," *International Journal of Advertising*, 3 (1), 3–15.

Examining the Text

1. In their summary of the history of research on sex advertising, Jones et al. discuss the "dual-mediation hypothesis" (paragraph 8). Restate this hypothesis in your own words. Does it seem like a logical and convincing hypothesis to you?

2. What key issues in existing scholarly work do the authors summarize in the "Previous Research" section? Based on their summaries of existing research, do you think they make an effective argument for the importance of their own research project?

3. The test conducted by the authors was intended to measure attitude, recall, and recognition. What meanings do each of these terms encompass? How is recall different from recognition?

4. What do the authors mean by "the opposite-sex effect" in advertising? Where do they see this effect in the results of their experiment?

5. *Thinking rhetorically:* Why do you think the authors use the words "cheesecake" and "beefcake" as shorthand terms for provocatively dressed female and male models? What effect does their use of these terms have on you as you read the article? Do you think other, more formal or academic terms would have been more effective?

For Group Discussion

The "Previous Research" section of the article provides an overview of four related strands of research having to do with beefcake and cheesecake advertising. In a small group, choose one of these research strands and, after rereading the section, summarize the key questions researchers have addressed, the methods they've used to find answers to these questions, and the results that they've come up with. As a group, prepare a brief (5-minute) presentation to give to the rest of the class that summarizes the key issues and ideas in the research strand you've examined.

Writing Suggestion

The structure and style of this article are quite consistent with writing in the social sciences. Results of empirical research, such as we find in this article, are most often organized in specific sections and present empirical data in tables and figures; they draw on previous research and use a highly academic style and vocabulary. Part of the underlying reason for this formula is that it establishes *ethos* or a sense of the authority and expertise of the authors.

131

In an essay, identify specific features of this article that you think help to establish the authority or *ethos* of the authors. In other words, what elements of the article make you inclined to believe that what the authors say is true? Select four or five features that you think lend credibility to the authors and devote a paragraph to each. In each paragraph, explain what the feature is, provide an example of it, and discuss how it establishes the *ethos* of the authors. You might conclude your essay by drawing comparisons to other styles and formats of writing—such as what we see in the other two articles in this section—in order to highlight the particular kinds of authority claimed in social science writing.

ADDITIONAL SUGGESTIONS FOR WRITING ABOUT ADVERTISING

1. Choose a magazine, television, or radio advertisement that you find particularly interesting, appealing, or puzzling, and write a narrative essay describing your response to the ad.

Begin by recording your initial impressions of the ad. What do you notice first, and why are you drawn to that element of the ad? What emotions or thoughts strike you as you first look at the ad? Then describe your step-by-step progress through the ad. Where does your eye go next? How do your thoughts or emotions change as you notice more of the ad? Finally, record your impressions after you've taken in all of the ad. How does this final impression differ from your first impression?

You might conclude your narrative by commenting on whether, based on your response, the ad achieves its objective of selling the product. In other words, do you think you responded as the designers of the ad intended?

2. Devise your own ad campaign for a product with which you're familiar, including several different ads, each appealing to a different audience.

After deciding on the product, briefly describe each audience group. Choose the form in which you want your advertisements to appear (magazine ads, TV commercials, audio presentations, billboards, or other forms and venues) and then decide on the persuasive methods that you want to use. Do you want to appeal to emotion or intellect or both? What motives will you try to reach? You might refer to Fowles's list of advertising's basic appeals.

Finally, design the ads and briefly explain the reasoning behind each design.

3. Choose recent issues of a women's magazine and a men's magazine, and compare and contrast the ads in each.

How many advertisements are there? What products are being advertised? What techniques are used in the ads and how do these techniques differ significantly between men's and women's magazines? What are the differences in the appeals the ads make? What are the differences in the images of men and women?

From your findings, draw conclusions about how advertisers envision and represent differences in gender. What (if any) stereotypes of men and women do the ads present?

4. Imagine that you are a member of a citizens' group working to improve the quality of advertising. What specific recommendations would you make and what standards would you want to see enforced? Illustrate your ideas with ads you can find that either meet or fall below these standards.

Internet Activities

1. On the Web, you'll find sites representing the products and services of almost all major U.S. corporations and of many smaller businesses as well. These corporate Web sites can be seen as extensive advertisements. Though they differ in style and strategy from television and magazine advertisements, they share the goal of informing consumers about a product or service and persuading consumers in their purchasing decisions.

At the *Common Culture* Web site, you'll find links to the sites of companies selling a variety of products. Choose one of those product categories and investigate the links. As you browse through the companies' Web sites, make a list of the kind of information that's offered there, the organization of the site, the graphics and other interactive elements that are used, the style and tone of the writing, and the mood created at the site. Then write an essay in which you describe the similarities and differences of two or more sites. What strategies do these sites use to promote the company's products and services? Which strategies do you find effective, and why? You might conclude your essay by commenting on the distinctive features of Web sites as advertisements. How are they different from magazine and television ads?

2. You've probably noticed that many Web sites contain advertisements—called "Web banners"—for other sites or for products and services offered by specific companies. These banners usually appear in the top portion of the Web page and invite viewers to click on an icon to get more information. Also on the Web are sponsor links and extra windows that open up to advertise products when one visits a Web site. At the *Common Culture* Web site, you'll find links to examples and additional information about Web advertising. Visit these links and take some time to browse the Web and familiarize yourself with the advertising strategies there. Then, write an essay in which you first describe the characteristics of advertising on the Web, and then compare and contrast Web advertising to television commercials and to print ads. What common features are shared by ads in these different media? How do the differences in media shape the content and style of advertisements?

Reading Images

The image entitled "Absolute End" on page CI-2 is taken from Adbusters (http://www.adbusters.org); it's one of their "spoof ads" that draws on familiar themes and motifs in advertising in order to undermine the messages that the ads themselves convey. Adbusters has spoofed such popular ad campaigns as Obsession perfume and the "Joe Camel" cigarette ads. The idea is to turn ads against themselves, to use the very style of the manufacturers' advertisements in exposing the harm that these ads and products can cause.

"Absolute End" is one of several spoofs of the Absolut vodka ads in which the shape of the vodka bottle is superimposed over some geographic location (for instance, New York's Central Park). Here, the familiar bottle shape (made familiar in part by the Absolut vodka ads themselves) is used as a chalk drawing on a pavement, calling to mind the chalk drawings that trace the shape of a murder victim's body.

Clearly, "Absolute End" is not an advertisement for Absolut vodka. However, it's not an ad directly against Absolut vodka, either. It seems, rather, to be an ad against alcohol advertising in general. The text in the image makes the message explicit:

> Nearly 50% of automobile fatalities are linked to alcohol. 10% of North Americans are alcoholics. A teenager sees 100,000 alcohol ads before reaching the legal drinking age.

In an essay, analyze the techniques used in this image to convey its message. For instance, consider how the perspective of the photograph influences your reaction to it: why is the viewer positioned above the scene that the photograph depicts? Consider also what's left out of the photograph: why is there no victim's body in this scene? Who is included in the scene, and why? Consider also the color scheme and other visual components of the image. Finally, be sure to discuss the text that's included: the "title" of the image and the three sentences that state its message.

Conclude your analysis by discussing whether or not you think a "spoof ad" like this one is an effective way to convey a message. What are the advantages and disadvantages of using a visual statement like this rather than a purely textual one (for instance, a newspaper article about alcohol, drunk driving, and advertising)?

3

Television

THE BOYS ALWAYS FOUND
SUNSET ON THE PRAIRIE A
PARTICULARLY MOVING
EXPERIENCE
Drawing by Glen Baxter; © 1991
The New Yorker Magazine, Inc.

© The New Yorker Collection 1991
Glen Baxter from cartoonbank.com.
All Rights Reserved.

We may laugh at these "boys" who stand in the middle of the barren
Southwest desert watching a sunset on TV as the real sun sets behind
them. Yet the joke is also on us because—like the cowboys—we might
often find ourselves more engaged, more entertained, and even more
emotionally touched by what we watch on television than by our own
experiences in real life.

Some critics even suggest that people regard what they see on television as more real than what goes on around them and thus virtually
narrow their world to what comes to them on "the tube." Paradoxically,
television's greatest benefit is its potential to broaden our experience, to
bring us to places we could never visit, to people we could never meet,
and to a range of ideas otherwise unavailable to many people.

135

This complex relationship between television, individual viewers, and society as a whole leads thoughtful people to examine closely the way television diverts our attention from what could be our own rich, nonmediated experiences; the way it entertains and informs us through otherwise inaccessible experiences; the way it shapes our perceptions of the world around us.

The readings in the first part of this chapter address some of the important questions raised in regard to this ubiquitous medium. How accurately does television represent reality? How strongly do its distortions of reality affect our ideas and behavior? Why do Americans spend so much time watching television? What essential needs and desires does television satisfy? To what extent does television intervene in our everyday lives, influencing families and communities, domestic space, and leisure time? Can watching TV actually make us smarter? Will new technological developments change how we watch television in the future?

The readings in the second part of the chapter address some of these questions by focusing on a particular type of television show: the comedy news or "infotainment" show. The three articles in this casebook are written in response to a shift in how Americans find out about what's going on in the world. Newspapers, radio, and nightly news shows on TV used to be the standard sources of information. With the advent of the Internet, people increasingly get their news from such Web sites as cnn.com and aol.com. More recently, people—and particularly young people—are turning to cable TV comedy shows such as *The Daily Show* and *The Colbert Report* to learn about current events, politics, the economy, and domestic and international news. To understand why these shows are so popular and what impact they're having on American culture, the authors draw comparisons to other, related artifacts: Russell Peterson's article compares *The Daily Show* and *The Colbert Report* to late-night mainstream comedy shows; Gerald Erion discusses their similarities and differences from conventional television news shows; and Jeffrey Jones discusses these shows in relation to mainstream journalism. We hope this casebook demonstrates that focusing on a particular type of TV show can yield diverse interpretations and complex insights.

As you read these articles, remember the television-entranced cowboys at the opening of the chapter. As you hone your own critical abilities, you will go beyond being a passive observer to become an active, critically engaged viewer.

The Cultural Influences of Television

Life According to TV

HARRY WATERS

*We begin this selection of readings with a report on a classic study of how
the world of television directly influences how people see the "real" world
around them. So says George Gerbner, a noted cultural critic and communications scholar. Gerbner and his staff spent over fifteen years studying the
televised programs America watches. Their results paint a damning picture
of the TV industry. In the following essay, Harry Waters summarizes
Gerbner's research about how the televised world matches up to "reality"
and to people's perception of reality. To that end, Gerbner breaks the televi-
sion-viewing audience into a number of different representative categories—
gender, age, race, and lifestyle, just to name a few—and he observes how
people in each category are portrayed in different television shows.*

*Frequently, Gerbner's results, as detailed by Waters, are surprising.
For example, contrary to most studies of the relationship between TV and
crime, which suggest that television causes people to become more violent,
Gerbner argues that the prevalence of crime on TV creates a "fear of victimization" in the viewer. This fear ultimately leads to a "mean-world syndrome" in which viewers come to see their social surroundings as hostile
and threatening. Waters balances Gerbner's conclusions with comments
from network officials who, not surprisingly, often take Gerbner to task.*

*As you read this selection, pay particular attention to the way
Waters maintains his objectivity by attributing most of the opinions and
conclusions to Gerbner and his assistants. Notice, too, how Waters' opinions
about Gerbner's research can be detected in phrasing such as "the gospel of
Gerbner," "tidy explanation," and "comforting."*

Since this is an article originally published in Newsweek, *a magazine that claims to report the news without bias, you might ask just how
objective so-called objective reporting really is.*

The late Paddy Chayefsky, who created Howard Beale, would have 1
loved George Gerbner. In "Network," Chayefsky marshaled a
scathing, fictional assault on the values and methods of the people
who control the world's most potent communications instrument. In
real life, Gerbner, perhaps the nation's foremost authority on the
social impact of television, is quietly using the disciplines of behavioral research to construct an equally devastating indictment of the
medium's images and messages. More than any spokesman for

a pressure group, Gerbner has become the man that television watches. From his cramped, book-lined office at the University of Pennsylvania springs a steady flow of studies that are raising executive blood pressures at the networks' sleek Manhattan command posts.

George Gerbner's work is uniquely important because it transports the scientific examination of television far beyond familiar children-and-violence arguments. Rather than simply studying the link between violence on the tube and crime in the streets, Gerbner is exploring wider and deeper terrain. He has turned his lens on TV's hidden victims—women, the elderly, blacks, blue-collar workers and other groups—to document the ways in which video-entertainment portrayals subliminally condition how we perceive ourselves and how we view those around us. Gerbner's subjects are not merely the impressionable young; they include all the rest of us. And it is his ominous conclusion that heavy watchers of the prime-time mirror are receiving a grossly distorted picture of the real world that they tend to accept more readily than reality itself.

The 63-year-old Gerbner, who is dean of Penn's Annenberg School of Communications, employs a methodology that meshes scholarly observation with mundane legwork. Over the past 15 years, he and a tireless trio of assistants (Larry Gross, Nancy Signorielli, and Michael Morgan) videotaped and exhaustively analyzed 1,600 prime-time programs involving more than 15,000 characters. They then drew up multiple-choice questionnaires that offered correct answers about the world at large along with answers that reflected what Gerbner perceived to be the misrepresentations and biases of the world according to TV. Finally, these questions were posed to large samples of citizens from all socioeconomic strata. In every survey, the Annenberg team discovered that heavy viewers of television (those watching more than four hours a day), who account for more than 30 percent of the population, almost invariably chose the TV-influenced answers, while light viewers (less than two hours a day), selected the answers corresponding more closely to actual life. Some of the dimensions of television's reality warp:

SEX

Male prime-time characters outnumber females by 3 to 1 and, with a few star-turn exceptions, women are portrayed as weak, passive satellites to powerful, effective men. TV's male population also plays a vast variety of roles, while females generally get typecast as either lovers or mothers. Less than 20 percent of TV's married women with children work outside the home—as compared with more than 50 percent in real life. The tube's distorted depictions of women, concludes Gerbner, reinforce stereotypical attitudes and increase sexism. In one Annenberg survey, heavy viewers were far more likely than light ones to agree with the proposition: "Women should take care of running their homes and leave running the country to men."

AGE

People over 65, too, are grossly underrepresented on television. 5 Correspondingly, heavy-viewing Annenberg respondents believe that the elderly are a vanishing breed, that they make up a smaller proportion of the population today than they did 20 years ago. In fact, they form the nation's most rapidly expanding age group. Heavy viewers also believe that old people are less healthy today than they were two decades ago, when quite the opposite is true. As with women, the portrayals of old people transmit negative impressions. In general, they are cast as silly, stubborn, sexually inactive, and eccentric. "They're often shown as feeble grandparents bearing cookies," says Gerbner. "You never see the power that real old people often have. The best and possibly only time to learn about growing old with decency and grace is in youth. And young people are the most susceptible to TV's messages."

RACE

The problem with the medium's treatment of blacks is more one of 6 image than of visibility. Though a tiny percentage of black characters come across as "unrealistically romanticized," reports Gerbner, the overwhelming majority of them are employed in subservient, supporting roles—such as the white hero's comic sidekick. "When a black child looks at prime time," he says, "most of the people he sees doing interesting and important things are white." That imbalance, he goes on, tends to teach young blacks to accept minority status as naturally inevitable and even deserved. To access the impact of such portrayals on the general audience, the Annenberg survey forms included questions like "Should white people have the right to keep blacks out of their neighborhoods?" and "Should there be laws against marriages between blacks and whites?" The more that viewers watched, the more they answered "yes" to each question.

WORK

Heavy viewers greatly overestimated the proportion of Americans 7 employed as physicians, lawyers, athletes, and entertainers, all of whom inhabit prime-time in hordes. A mere 6 to 10 percent of television characters hold blue-collar or service jobs vs. about 60 percent in the real work force. Gerbner sees two dangers in TV's skewed division of labor.

On the one hand, the tube so overrepresents and glamorizes the elite occupations that it sets up unrealistic expectations among those who must deal with them in actuality. At the same time, TV largely neglects portraying the occupations that most youngsters will have to enter. "You almost never see the farmer, the factory worker, or the small businessman," he notes. "Thus not only do lawyers and other professionals find they cannot measure up to the image TV projects of them, but children's occupational aspirations are channeled in unrealistic directions." The Gerbner team feels this emphasis on high-powered jobs poses problems for adolescent girls, who are also presented with views of women as homebodies. The two conflicting views, Gerbner says, add to the frustration over choices they have to make as adults.

HEALTH

Although video characters exist almost entirely on junk food and quaff 8 alcohol 15 times more often than water, they manage to remain slim, healthy and beautiful. Frequent TV watchers, the Annenberg investigators found, eat more, drink more, exercise less, and possess an almost mystical faith in the curative powers of medical science. Concludes Gerbner: "Television may well be the single most pervasive source of health information. And its over-idealized images of medical people, coupled with its complacency about unhealthy life-styles, leaves both patients and doctors vulnerable to disappointment, frustration and even litigation."

CRIME

On the small screen, crime rages about 10 times more often than in real 9 life. But while other researchers concentrate on the propensity of TV mayhem to incite aggression, the Annenberg team has studied the hidden side of its imprint: fear of victimization. On television, 55 percent of prime-time characters are involved in violent confrontations once a week; in reality, the figure is less than 1 percent. In all demographic groups in every class of neighborhood, heavy viewers overestimated the statistical chance of violence in their own lives and harbored an exaggerated mistrust of strangers—creating what Gerbner calls "mean-world syndrome." Forty-six percent of heavy viewers who live in cities rated their fear of crime "very serious" as opposed to 26 percent for light viewers. Such paranoia is especially acute among TV entertainment's most common victims: women, the elderly, nonwhites, foreigners and lower-class citizens.

Video violence, proposes Gerbner, is primarily responsible for 10 imparting lessons in social power: it demonstrates who can do what to whom and get away with it. "Television is saying that those at the bottom of the power scale cannot get away with the same things that a white, middle-class American male can," he says. "It potentially conditions people to think of themselves as victims."

At a quick glance, Gerbner's findings seem to contain a cause- 11
and-effect, chicken-or-the-egg question. Does television make heavy viewers view the world the way they do or do heavy viewers come from the poorer, less experienced segment of the populace that regards the world that way to begin with? In other words, does the tube create or simply confirm the unenlightened attitudes of its most loyal audiences? Gerbner, however, was savvy enough to construct a methodology largely immune to such criticism. His samples of heavy viewers cut across all ages, incomes, education levels and ethnic backgrounds—and every category displayed the same tube-induced misconceptions of the world outside.

Needless to say, the networks accept all this as enthusiastically 12
as they would a list of news-coverage complaints from the Ayatollah Khomeini. Even so, their responses tend to be tinged with a singular respect for Gerbner's personal and professional credentials. The man is no ivory-tower recluse. During World War II, the Budapest-born Gerbner parachuted into the mountains of Yugoslavia to join the partisans fighting the Germans. After the war, he hunted down and personally arrested scores of high Nazi officials. Nor is Gerbner some videophobic vigilante. A Ph.D. in communications, he readily acknowledges TV's beneficial effects, noting that it has abolished parochialism, reduced isolation and loneliness, and provided the poorest members of society with cheap, plug-in exposure to experiences they otherwise would not have. Funding for his research is supported by such prestigious bodies as the National Institute of Mental Health, the Surgeon General's office, and the American Medical Association, and he is called to testify before congressional committees nearly as often as David Stockman.

141

MASS ENTERTAINMENT

When challenging Gerbner, network officials focus less on his findings 13
and methods than on what they regard as his own misconceptions of their industry's function. "He's looking at television from the perspective of a social scientist rather than considering what is mass entertainment," says Alfred Schneider, vice president of standards and practices at ABC. "We strive to balance TV's social effects with what will capture an audience's interests. If you showed strong men being victimized as much as women or the elderly, what would comprise the dramatic conflict? If you did a show truly representative of society's total reality, and nobody watched because it wasn't interesting, what have you achieved?"

CBS senior vice president Gene Mater also believes that Gerbner   14
is implicitly asking for the theoretically impossible. "TV is unique in its
problems," says Mater. "Everyone wants a piece of the action.
Everyone feels that their racial or ethnic group is underrepresented or
should be portrayed as they would like the world to perceive them. No
popular entertainment form, including this one, can or should be an
accurate reflection of society."

On that point, at least, Gerbner is first to agree; he hardly expects   15
television entertainment to serve as a mirror image of absolute truth.
But what fascinates him about this communications medium is its
marked difference from all others. In other media, customers carefully
choose what they want to hear or read: a movie, a magazine, a best
seller. In television, notes Gerbner, viewers rarely tune in for a particular program. Instead, most just habitually turn on the set—and watch
by the clock rather than for a specific show. "Television viewing fulfills
the criteria of a ritual," he says. "It is the only medium that can bring to
people things they otherwise would not select." With such unique
power, believes Gerbner, comes unique responsibility: "No other
medium reaches into every home or has a comparable, cradle-to-grave
influence over what a society learns about itself."

MATCH

In Gerbner's view, virtually all of TV's distortions of reality can be attrib-   16
uted to its obsession with demographics. The viewers that prime-time
sponsors most want to reach are white, middle-class, female, and
between 18 and 49—in short, the audience that purchases most of the
consumer products advertised on the tube. Accordingly, notes Gerbner,
the demographic portrait of TV's fictional characters largely matches
that of its prime commercial targets and largely ignores everyone
else. "Television," he concludes, "reproduces a world for its own best
customers."

Among TV's more candid executives, that theory draws consider-   17
able support. Yet by pointing a finger at the power of demographics,
Gerbner appears to contradict one of his major findings. If female
viewers are so dear to the hearts of sponsors, why are female characters
cast in such unflattering light? "In a basically male-oriented power
structure," replies Gerbner, "you can't alienate the male viewer. But
you can get away with offending women because most women are
pretty well brainwashed to accept it." The Annenberg dean has an
equally tidy explanation for another curious fact. Since the corporate
world provides network television with all of its financial support, one
would expect businessmen on TV to be portrayed primarily as good
guys. Quite the contrary. As any fan of *Dallas, Dynasty* or *Falcon Crest*

well knows, the image of the company man is usually that of a menda-
cious, dirty-dealing rapscallion. Why would TV snap at the hand that
feeds it? "Credibility is the way to ratings," proposes Gerbner. "This
country has a populist tradition of bias against anything big, including
big business. So to retain credibility, TV entertainment shows businessmen in relatively derogatory ways."

In the medium's Hollywood-based creative community, the   18
gospel of Gerbner finds some passionate adherents. Rarely have TV's
best and brightest talents viewed their industry with so much frustration and anger. The most sweeping indictment emanates from David
Rintels, a two-time Emmy-winning writer and former president of the
Writers Guild of America, West. "Gerbner is absolutely correct and it is
the people who run the networks who are to blame," says Rintels. "The
networks get bombarded with thoughtful, reality-oriented scripts.
They simply won't do them. They slam the door on them. They believe
that the only way to get ratings is to feed viewers what conforms to
their biases or what has limited resemblance to reality. From 8 to 11
o'clock each night, television is one long lie."

Innovative thinkers such as Norman Lear, whose work has been   19
practically driven off the tube, don't fault the networks so much as the
climate in which they operate. Says Lear: "All of this country's institutions have become totally fixated on short-term bottom-line thinking.
Everyone grabs for what might succeed today and the hell with tomorrow. Television just catches more of the heat because it's more visible."
Perhaps the most perceptive assessment of Gerbner's conclusions is
offered by one who has worked both sides of the industry street.
Deanne Barkley, a former NBC vice president who now helps run an
independent production house, reports that the negative depictions of
women on TV have made it "nerve-racking" to function as a woman
within TV. "No one takes responsibility for the social impact of their
shows," says Barkley. "But then how do you decide where it all begins?
Do the networks give viewers what they want? Or are the networks
conditioning them to think that way?"

Gerbner himself has no simple answer to that conundrum.   20
Neither a McLuhanesque shaman nor a Naderesque crusader, he hesitates to suggest solutions until pressed. Then out pops a pair of
provocative notions. Commercial television will never democratize its
treatments of daily life, he believes, until it finds a way to broaden its
financial base. Coincidentally, Federal Communications Commission
chairman Mark Fowler seems to have arrived at much the same conclusion. In exchange for lifting such government restrictions on TV as
the fairness doctrine and the equal-time rule, Fowler would impose a
modest levy on station owners called a spectrum-use fee. Funds from
the fees would be set aside to finance programs aimed at specialized

143

tastes rather than the mass appetite. Gerbner enthusiastically endorses that proposal: "Let the ratings system dominate most of prime time but not every hour of every day. Let some programs carry advisories that warn: 'This is not for all of you. This is for nonwhites, or for religious people or for the aged and the handicapped. Turn it off unless you'd like to eavesdrop.' That would be a very refreshing thing."

ROLE

In addition, Gerbner would like to see viewers given an active role in 21
steering the overall direction of television instead of being obliged to passively accept whatever the networks offer. In Britain, he points out, political candidates debate the problems of TV as routinely as the issue of crime. In this country, proposes Gerbner, "every political campaign should put television on the public agenda. Candidates talk about schools, they talk about jobs, they talk about social welfare. They're going to have to start discussing this all-pervasive force."

There are no outright villains in this docudrama. Even Gerbner 22
recognizes that network potentates don't set out to proselytize a point of view; they are simply businessmen selling a mass-market product. At the same time, their 90 million nightly customers deserve to know the side effects of the ingredients. By the time the typical American child reaches the age of reason, calculates Gerbner, he or she will have absorbed more than 30,000 electronic "stories." These stories, he suggests, have replaced the socializing role of the preindustrial church: they create a "cultural mythology" that establishes the norms of approved behavior and belief. And all Gerbner's research indicates that this new mythological world, with its warped picture of a sizable portion of society, may soon become the one most of us think we live in.

Who else is telling us that? Howard Beale and his eloquent 23
alarms have faded into off network reruns. At the very least, it is comforting to know that a real-life Beale is very much with us . . . and really watching.

Examining the Text

1. Waters reports extensive studies by George Gerbner and his associates that show that heavy television viewers have a generally "warped" view of reality, influenced by television's own "reality warp" (paragraph 3). Which viewers do you think would be affected most negatively by these "warped" viewpoints, and why?

2. Gerbner's studies show that "55 percent of prime-time characters are involved in violent confrontations once a week; in reality, the figure is less than 1 percent" (9). While violent crime is known to rank as middle-class America's primary concern, most violent crime occurs in neighborhoods far removed from most middle-class people. How do you explain these discrepancies? Why is "violent confrontation" so common on television? How does the violence you see on television affect you?

3. Waters interviewed a number of people when he wrote this article for *Newsweek.* Collectively, they offer a variety of explanations for and solutions to the limited images television provides. Look closely at these suggested causes and solutions. Which seem most reasonable to you? In general, is Waters's coverage of the issue balanced? Why or why not?

4. *Thinking rhetorically:* Following up on the "as you read" question in the introduction to this article, what is your impression of the objectivity of this article? Where in the article do you see indications that the author is striving to be objective? Where do you see the author's opinions and biases coming through? In general, what is the relationship between objectivity and persuasiveness? That is, do you think it's easier or more difficult to be persuasive when you're also compelled to be objective?

For Group Discussion

This article was first published more than twenty-five years ago. With your group, look again at Gerbner's categories and discuss what significant recent examples suggest about the way current television programming represents reality. Do today's shows seem more accurate than those of ten years ago? As a class, discuss whether or not most viewers want more "reality" on television.

Writing Suggestion

The TV guide is a fine example of nonacademic but very common reading material in our culture. Millions of people read TV schedules every day and think nothing of it. This writing assignment asks you to reflect on *how* you read TV schedules and to interpret what meanings can be found in these common documents.

On page 146 is a reproduction of a page from the TV listings in our local (Santa Barbara, CA) newspaper, listing the televised offerings on Thursday, December 8, 2005. Begin writing about this document by describing it: What are its distinguishing features? How is the information organized? How does its appearance differ from the pages of this textbook? Next, take notes describing the strategies you use in reading this document: Where do you begin? Where does your eye go next? What factors influence your choices? Are there parts of the document that you ignore completely? Why? Finally, write down your thoughts about the content of this schedule: To what extent do the TV programs scheduled for this evening confirm or contradict Waters's claims in "Life According to TV"? As you bring these observations together in an essay, highlight what you see as the two or three most important features of TV schedules in general, based on your observations of this specific example.

TV WEEK

THURSDAY DECEMBER 8, 2005

KEY: 00 SANTA BARBARA   03 SANTA MARIA/SANTA YNEZ/LOMPOC

PRIMETIME

BROADCAST

Channel			6:00	6:30	7:00	7:30	8:00	8:30	9:00	9:30	10:00	10:30	11:00	11:30
USA	2	43	Law & Order: Criminal Intent: Ex Stasis. (cc) 961156		Law & Order: Special Victims Unit: Resilience. (cc) 825717		Law & Order: Criminal Intent: Shibboleth. (cc) 601137		Movie: "Dirty War" (2005) Tom Arnold. Terror attack around the Great. (cc) 604234				Movie: "Three Kings" (2005) Tom Arnold. 'R' hood. Music causes a program (cc) 654072	(11:35) Nightline 51427330
KBYT (ABC)	3	3	News 595		News 9175		Joey Joey's old friend. 8468	Will & Grace (N) 9205	The Apprentice: The Final Showdown. (N) 46669		(9:59) ER: All About Christmas Eve. (N) 55776717		News 7673040	Tonight Show
KSBY (NBC)	6	6	News 5595		News 9175									
TBS	7	45	Seinfeld (cc)	Seinfeld (cc)	Raymond	Raymond	Friends 510408	Friends 535243	Movie: ★★★ "Scorpion" (1986, Comedy) 'PG-13' (cc) 5498361				(11:16) "Stripes" 56345053	
KCAL	9	9	Be a Millionaire	9 on the Town 4021	Dr. Phil 37359		News (cc) 73779		News (cc) 86243		News (cc) 6746345	Sports Central 6887 0408	South Park (cc) 32934	South Park (N) 69601
KCET (PBS)	10	8	California's Gold 47311	Life and Times (N) 90141	The NewsHour With Jim Lehrer (N) (cc)		Tom Jones: The Legend The singer's hits. 794885		Bruce Springsteen and the E Street Band: Hammersmith Odeon, London 1975 1975 (concert, (N) (cc) 986601				Charlie Rose (N) 124137	
FOX 11-KKFX	11	11	Malcolm-Mid.	King of the Hill	The Simpsons	70s Show	The O.C. (N) (cc) 91175		Reunion: 1983. (N) (cc) 71311		News 8748625		News (cc) 5630240	Fear Factor 128137
KCOY (CBS)	12	26408	News (cc) 28408	King of the Hill	Entertainment Tonight 2304	The Insider (N) (cc) 6243	Survivor: Guatemala – The Maya Empire (N) (cc) 89717		CSI: Crime Scene Investigation: Still Life. (N) 79903		Without a Trace: When Darkness Falls. (N) (cc) 72040	Programa Pagado 410750	Programa Pagado 94799	Late Show-Letterman
KBEH	13		Atrevete 51396				Camino a la Fama 4041350		Amor en Custodia 14463175		La Chacala	Noticiero	Otra Mitad Sol	Hechos Noche
AZTECA	14		Los Machos 772224		Ventaneando 436865		El Cuerpo del Deseo 64021		Corazón Part.	Decisiones	Decisiones 87972		Noticias 30576	Titulares
KTAS (Tel)	15	1311	Noticias 1311	Nabi-Telemundo	La Tormenta 88601		Contra Viento y Marea 36175		La Esposa Virgen 15311		Aquí y Ahora 25798		Noticias C. C.	Noticiero Univ.
KPMR (Uni)	16	16	Noticias C. C.	Noticiero Univ	Piel de Otoño 25427		Everybody Hates Chris	Love, Inc. (N) (cc) 7345	Eva: Shelly And... 99243	Dura: Home Alone. 67779	Seinfeld: The Caddy. 55446	That '70s Show 31866	News 97048	Seinfeld (cc) 82137
KCOP (UPN)	44	13	The Bernie Mac Show	King of the Hill	The Bernie Mac Show	The '70s Show 5040	Everybody Hates Chris		The Apprentice: The Final Showdown. (N) 3359		(9:59) ER: All About Christmas Eve. (N) (cc) 18043427		News 1568408	Tonight Show
KNBC News	5		News (cc) 137	NBC Nightly News (cc) 717	Extra (N) (cc) 6330	Access Hollywood (N) 601	Joey Joey's old friend. 2750	Smallville: Lexmas. (N) 20663	Everwood (N) (cc) 40427		Will & Grace	Will & Grace	Sex and-City	Sex and-City
WB	5	7953	Yes, Dear 7953	Yes, Dear 8205	King	King	Smallville: Lexmas.	Wellness Hour	Paid Program	Community	News 57662	News 65300	Music Choice Concert 58885	
COX8	8		Education	In Focus	Community	Wellness Hour	Wellness Hour	Tuppayers and	Celebracion 20243		News 57662	Native 57862	Permaculture 58885	
COM 17-CMAC	17		Open Hearts Open Doors	SBPD Live	Ernie Solomon Show 540372		Santa Barbara City Council (cc) 920040					Undercover TV	Permaculture 58885	
City TV	18		The Rediscovery of York 34446		'70s Show	'70s Show	Cops 8251663		Cops 8270798		Cops 3510175	Cops 9705408	City Calendar 1138663	'70s Show
FX	19	77	King of the Hill	King of the Hill	'70s Show	Mary Anthony: A Life		Phillip Richardson 568934			Cops 4349359	Cops 4925779	'70s Show	'70s Show
COUNTY	20	20	(5) Board of Supervisors Hearing 9598892										Classic Arts Showcase	
CNN	22	50	Innovart-Educ	MimeWorks 9000966	Anderson Cooper 360 2069953				Larry King Live 69605		Creative	Creative	Science Writing Physics	
CNN Headln	23	51	Larry King Live 976068		Prime News Tonight 3157601		Showbiz Tonight 7604392		Prime News Tonight 7924156		Anderson Cooper 360 699092		Paula Zahn Now 2057137	
CNBC	24	48	Prime News Tonight 3157601	Phil of Future	That's-Raven		Apprentice: Martha Stewart		Mad Money 1532514		Nancy Grace 7627243		Headline News 1305088	
FOXNEWS	25	25	Mad Money 8302866	The Big Idea With Deutsch	On the Record-Van Susteren		The O'Reilly Factor 5065576		Special Report 5070240		The Big Idea With Deutsch		Paid Program	Paid Program
AMC	26	46	Hannity & Colmes 9728359		Movie: ★★ "The Mark Ligsoft" (1962) Katharine Hepburn. An old woman discovers a nephew. A Chicago cop. (cc) 524278						Your World With Neil Cavuto		Hannity & Colmes 8453137	
QVC	27	7	(5) Craftsman Workshop Holiday Special 8473048				Gifts for Her 1609966		Dennis Basso Boutique		Practical Presents 1642717		Great Tool Gifts 7454446	
TNT	28	28	NBA Basketball: Wizards at Pacers		NBA Basketball: Houston Rockets at Sacramento Kings. (Live) (cc) 186350						Inside the NBA (cc) 453088		Law & Order 918755	
NICK	29	70	All Grown Up	Danny Phant.	Oddparents	SpongeBob	Kim Possible: A Stitch in Time. (cc) 1264359		Full House	Fresh Prince	Roseanne (cc)	Roseanne (cc)	Roseanne (cc)	Cosby Show
DISNEY	30	69	Sister, Sister	Phil of Future	That's-Raven	That's-Raven				Phil of Future	Buzz-Maggie	Sister, Sister	That's-Raven	That's-Raven
Learning	31	59	Martha (N) 765224	Making Band	U.S. Marshals: Fugitive		U.S. Marshals: Fugitive		City Cops 452359		City Cops 455446	Punk'd 870514	U.S. Marshals: Fugitive	
Discovery	32	53	Cash Cab (N)	Cash Cab (N)	America's Next Top Model		I Shouldn't Be Alive 993791		Living With Tigers (cc) 939305		Into the Lion's Den 343412		MythBusters: Fugitive	
ANIMAL	33	71	The Planet's Funniest Animals	New Breed Vets (N) 42427			The Planet's Funniest Animals		The Planet's Funniest Animals		New Breed Vets 41798		The Most Extreme (cc) 40243	
ESPN	34	30	College Basketball: Georgetown at Illinois. (Live) (cc) 426408		SportsCenter (cc) 427137		NFL Live (N)	Outside-Lines	SportsCenter (cc) 440368		SportsCenter (N)	This Is Day	SportsCenter (cc) 395755	ESPN Holly.
ESPN 2	35	31	College Basketball: Massachusetts at Connecticut. 8124300		Quite Frankly With Smith		Rodeo: Wrangler National Finals – Seventh Round. From Las Vegas. 3487885				Lexus Gauntlet	Beat Down Sports Show	Lexus Gauntlet	NBA Action (N)
FOXSpts2	36		NHL Spotlight	HS Spotlight	Lexus Gauntlet	NHL Hockey: Mighty Ducks of Anaheim at Buffalo Sabres. 351982						So. Cal. Sports	So. Cal. Sports	Best-Sports
FOXSptHd	37	68	Fant. Football	Chris Myers	Break the Ice	NHL Hockey: Carolina Hurricanes at Los Angeles Kings. (Live) 133566					So. Cal. Sports	So. Cal. Sports	Beat Down Sports Show	
MTV	38	41	Making Band	Making Band	Making Band	Making Band	Making Band	Making Band	Making Band	Making Band	Making Band	Making Band	Real World Austin	Top 40 of 2005
VH1	39	41	America's Next Top Model		America's Next Top Model		America's Next Top Model		America's Next Top Model		America's Next Top Model		Breakback Mtn	Will & Grace (cc) 12542
LIFETIME	41	62	The Golden Girls	The Golden Girls 865137	Movie: ★★ "The Man Upstairs" (1992) Katharine Hepburn. An old woman hides a fugitive. 4845252		Movie: "One Special Night" (1999) Julie Andrews. Two strangers snowbound. 735 A frazzled parents two siblings at.				The Most Extreme (cc) 40243		It's Sew Easy 1590662	
HomeShop	42		Heidi Daus Fashion Jewelry 8297175				Harry & David		Estefan Music		Hal Lindsey	This Is Day		
Trinity	43	75	Bishop Jakes	This Is Day	Praise the Lord (cc) 658205		CSI: Crime Scene Investigation		Praise	Dr. Carl Baugh	Hal Lindsey	This Is Day	Praise the Lord (cc) 764476	
SPIKE	45	28	World's Wildest Police Videos		CSI: Crime Scene Investigation		CSI: Crime Scene Investigation		MXC 701137	MXC 79501	MXC 701137	TNA iMPACT! (N) (cc) 420750	World's Wildest Police Videos	

Television Addiction Is No Mere Metaphor

ROBERT KUBEY AND MIHALY CSIKSZENTMIHALYI

We all know that certain substances are addictive; indeed, we know that cigarettes, alcohol, and drugs are dangerous in large part because we can become addicted to them and end up using them to our own physical and psychological detriment. Certain activities, such as gambling, are also recognized as addictive. But can the activity of watching television be considered addictive? Are heavy television viewers "addicts" in the same way that alcoholics and long-term smokers are?

Robert Kubey and Mihaly Csikszentmihalyi address these questions in the following article, which was originally published in Scientific American. *Kubey and Csikszentmihalyi are both college professors: Kubey is the director of the Center for Media Studies at Rutgers University, and Csikszentmihalyi is the C. S. and D. J. Davidson Professor of Psychology at Claremont Graduate University. In this article, they combine their expertise in media studies and psychology in order to examine the phenomenon of "TV addiction."*

147

Although some social commentators see humor in the idea of couch potatoes "spudding out" in front of the television, Kubey and Csikszentmihalyi bring sociological and biological evidence to bear on their explanation of the addictive power television has over us. **Before you read,** *think about what the term* addiction *means to you. Do you know anyone who you think is "addicted" to television? What do you think are the causes and consequences of this addiction?*

Perhaps the most ironic aspect of the struggle for survival is how easily organisms can be harmed by that which they desire. The trout is caught by the fisherman's lure, the mouse by cheese. But at least those creatures have the excuse that bait and cheese look like sustenance. Humans seldom have that consolation. The temptations that can disrupt their lives are often pure indulgences. No one has to drink alcohol, for example. Realizing when a diversion has gotten out of control is one of the great challenges of life.

Excessive cravings do not necessarily involve physical substances. Gambling can become compulsive; sex can become obsessive. One activity, however, stands out for its prominence and ubiquity—the world's most popular leisure pastime, television. Most people admit to having a love–hate relationship with it. They complain about the "boob tube" and "couch potatoes," then they settle into their sofas and grab the remote control. Parents commonly fret about their children's viewing (if not their own). Even researchers who study TV for a living marvel at the medium's hold on them personally. Percy Tannenbaum of the University of California at Berkeley has written: "Among life's more embarrassing moments have been countless occasions when I am engaged in conversation in a room while a TV set is on, and I cannot for the life of me stop from periodically glancing over to the screen. This occurs not only during dull conversations but during reasonably interesting ones just as well."

Scientists have been studying the effects of television for decades, generally focusing on whether watching violence on TV correlates with being violent in real life (see "The Effects of Observing Violence," by Leonard Berkowitz; *Scientific American*, February 1964; and "Communication and Social Environment," by George Gerber, September 1972). Less attention has been paid to the basic allure of the small screen—the medium, as opposed to the message. 3

The term "TV addiction" is imprecise and laden with value judgments, but it captures the essence of a very real phenomenon. Psychologists and psychiatrists formally define substance dependence as a disorder characterized by criteria that include spending a great deal of time using the substance; using it more often than one intends; thinking about reducing use or making repeated unsuccessful efforts to reduce use; giving up important social, family, or occupational activities to use it; and reporting withdrawal symptoms when one stops using it. 4

All these criteria can apply to people who watch a lot of television. That does not mean that watching television, per se, is problematic. Television can teach and amuse; it can reach aesthetic heights; it can provide much needed distraction and escape. The difficulty arises when people strongly sense that they ought not to watch as much as they do and yet find themselves strangely unable to reduce their viewing. Some knowledge of how the medium exerts its pull may help heavy viewers gain better control over their lives. 5

A BODY AT REST TENDS TO STAY AT REST

The amount of time people spend watching television is astonishing. On average, individuals in the industrialized world devote three hours a day to the pursuit—fully half of their leisure time, and more than on any single activity save work and sleep. At this rate, someone who lives to seventy-five would spend nine years in front of the tube. To some commentators, this devotion means simply that people enjoy TV and make a conscious decision to watch it. But if that is the whole story, why do so many people experience misgivings about how much they 6 view? In Gallup polls in 1992 and 1999, two out of five adult respondents and seven out of ten teenagers said they spent too much time watching TV. Other surveys have consistently shown that roughly 10 percent of adults call themselves TV addicts.

To study people's reactions to TV, researchers have undertaken laboratory experiments in which they have monitored the brain waves (using an electroencephalograph, or EEG), skin resistance or heart rate of people watching television. To track behavior and emotion in the normal course of life, as opposed to the artificial conditions of the lab, we have used the Experience Sampling Method (ESM). Participants carried a beeper, and we signaled them six to eight times a day, at random, over the period of a week; whenever they heard the beep, they wrote down what they were doing and how they were feeling using a standardized scorecard. 7

As one might expect, people who were watching TV when we beeped them reported feeling relaxed and passive. The EEG studies similarly show less mental stimulation, as measured by alpha brainwave production, during viewing than during reading. 8

What is more surprising is that the sense of relaxation ends when the set is turned off, but the feelings of passivity and lowered alertness continue. Survey participants commonly reflect that television has somehow absorbed or sucked out their energy, leaving them depleted. They say they have more difficulty concentrating after viewing than before. In contrast, they rarely indicate such difficulty after reading. After playing sports or engaging in hobbies, people report improvements in mood. After watching TV, people's moods are about the same or worse than before. 9

Within moments of sitting or lying down and pushing the "power" button, viewers report feeling more relaxed. Because the relaxation occurs quickly, people are conditioned to associate viewing with rest and lack of tension. The association is positively reinforced because viewers remain relaxed throughout viewing, and it is negatively reinforced via the stress and dysphoric rumination that occurs once the screen goes blank again. 10

Habit-forming drugs work in similar ways. A tranquilizer that leaves the body rapidly is much more likely to cause dependence than one that leaves the body slowly, precisely because the user is more aware that the drug's effects are wearing off. Similarly, viewers' vague learned sense that they will feel less relaxed if they stop viewing may be a significant factor in not turning the set off. Viewing begets more viewing. 11

Thus, the irony of TV: people watch a great deal longer than they plan to, even though prolonged viewing is less rewarding. In our ESM studies the longer people sat in front of the set, the less satisfaction they said they derived from it. When signaled, heavy viewers (those who consistently watch more than four hours a day) tended to report on their ESM sheets that they enjoy TV less than light viewers did (less 12 than two hours a day). For some, a twinge of unease or guilt that they aren't doing something more productive may also accompany and depreciate the enjoyment of prolonged viewing. Researchers in Japan, the U.K. and the U.S. have found that this guilt occurs much more among middle-class viewers than among less affluent ones.

GRABBING YOUR ATTENTION

What is it about TV that has such a hold on us? In part, the attraction 13 seems to spring from our biological "orienting response." First described by Ivan Pavlov in 1927, the orienting response is our instinctive visual or auditory reaction to any sudden or novel stimulus. It is part of our evolutionary heritage, a built-in sensitivity to movement and potential predatory threats. Typical orienting reactions include dilation of the blood vessels to the brain, slowing of the heart, and constriction of blood vessels to major muscle groups. Alpha waves are blocked for a few seconds before returning to their baseline level, which is determined by the general level of mental arousal. The brain focuses its attention on gathering more information while the rest of the body quiets.

In 1986, Byron Reeves of Stanford University, Esther Thorson of 14 the University of Missouri and their colleagues began to study whether the simple formal features of television—cuts, edits, zooms, pans, sudden noises—activate the orienting response, thereby keeping attention on the screen. By watching how brain waves were affected by formal features, the researchers concluded that these stylistic tricks can indeed trigger involuntary responses and "derive their attentional value through the evolutionary significance of detecting movement. . . . It is the form, not the content, of television that is unique."

The orienting response may partly explain common viewer remarks 15 such as: "If a television is on, I just can't keep my eyes off it," "I don't want to watch as much as I do, but I can't help it," and "I feel hypnotized when I watch television." In the years since Reeves and Thorson published their pioneering work, researchers have delved deeper. Annie Lang's research team at Indiana University has shown that heart rate decreases for four to six seconds after an orienting stimulus. In ads, action sequences, and music videos, formal features frequently come at a rate of one per second, thus activating the orienting response continuously.

Lang and her colleagues have also investigated whether formal 16 features affect people's memory of what they have seen. In one of their studies, participants watched a program and then filled out a score sheet. Increasing the frequency of edits—defined here as a change from one camera angle to another in the same visual scene—improved memory recognition, presumably because it focused attention on the screen. Increasing the frequency of cuts—changes to a new visual scene—had a similar effect but only up to a point. If the number of cuts exceeded ten in two minutes, recognition dropped off sharply.

Producers of educational television for children have found that for- 17 mal features can help learning. But increasing the rate of cuts and edits eventually overloads the brain. Music videos and commercials that use rapid intercutting of unrelated scenes are designed to hold attention more than they are to convey information. People may remember the name of the product or band, but the details of the ad itself float in one ear and out the other. The orienting response is overworked. Viewers still attend to the screen, but they feel tired and worn out, with little compensating psychological reward. Our ESM findings show much the same thing.

Sometimes the memory of the product is very subtle. Many ads 18 today are deliberately oblique: they have an engaging story line, but it is hard to tell what they are trying to sell. Afterward you may not remember the product consciously. Yet advertisers believe that if they have gotten your attention, when you later go to the store you will feel better or more comfortable with a given product because you have a vague recollection of having heard of it.

The natural attraction to television's sound and light starts very 19 early in life. Dafna Lemish of Tel Aviv University has described babies at six to eight weeks attending to television. We have observed slightly older infants who, when lying on their backs on the floor, crane their necks around 180 degrees to catch what light through yonder window breaks. This inclination suggests how deeply rooted the orienting response is.

151

"TV IS PART OF THEM"

That said, we need to be careful about overreacting. Little evidence 20 suggests that adults or children should stop watching TV altogether. The problems come from heavy or prolonged viewing.

The Experience Sampling Method permitted us to look closely at 21 most every domain of everyday life: working, eating, reading, talking to friends, playing a sport, and so on. We wondered whether heavy viewers might experience life differently than light viewers do. Do they dislike being with people more? Are they more alienated from work? What we found nearly leaped off the page at us. Heavy viewers report feeling significantly more anxious and less happy than light viewers do in unstructured situations, such as doing nothing, daydreaming, or waiting in line. The difference widens when the viewer is alone.

Subsequently, Robert D. McIlwraith of the University of Manitoba 22 extensively studied those who called themselves TV addicts on surveys. On a measure called the Short Imaginal Processes Inventory (SIPI), he found that the self-described addicts are more easily bored and distracted and have poorer attentional control than the nonaddicts. The addicts said they used TV to distract themselves from unpleasant thoughts and to fill time. Other studies over the years have shown that heavy viewers are less likely to participate in community activities and sports and are more likely to be obese than moderate viewers or nonviewers.

The question that naturally arises is: In which direction does the 23 correlation go? Do people turn to TV because of boredom and loneliness, or does TV viewing make people more susceptible to boredom and loneliness? We and most other researchers argue that the former is generally the case, but it is not a simple case of either/or. Jerome L. and Dorothy Singer of Yale University, among others, have suggested that more viewing may contribute to a shorter attention span, diminished self-restraint, and less patience with the normal delays of daily life. More than twenty-five years ago, psychologist Tannis M. MacBeth Williams of the University of British Columbia studied a mountain community that had no television until cable finally arrived. Over time, both adults and children in the town became less creative in problem solving, less able to persevere at tasks, and less tolerant of unstructured time.

To some researchers, the most convincing parallel between TV and 24 addictive drugs is that people experience withdrawal symptoms when they cut back on viewing. Nearly forty years ago, Gary A. Steiner of the University of Chicago collected fascinating individual accounts of families whose set had broken—this back in the days when households generally had only one set: "The family walked around like a chicken without a head." "It was terrible. We did nothing—my husband and I talked." "Screamed constantly. Children bothered me, and my nerves were on edge. Tried to interest them in games, but impossible. TV is part of them."

In experiments, families have volunteered or been paid to stop 25 viewing, typically for a week or a month. Many could not complete the period of abstinence. Some fought, verbally and physically. Anecdotal reports from some families that have tried the annual "TV turn-off" week in the U.S. tell a similar story.

If a family has been spending the lion's share of its free time 26 watching television, reconfiguring itself around a new set of activities is no easy task. Of course, that does not mean it cannot be done or that all families implode when deprived of their set. In a review of these cold-turkey studies, Charles Winick of the City University of New York concluded: "The first three or four days for most persons were the worst, even in many homes where viewing was minimal and where there were other ongoing activities. In over half of all the households, during these first few days of loss, the regular routines were disrupted, family members had difficulties in dealing with the newly available time, anxiety and aggressions were expressed. . . . People living alone tended to be bored and irritated. . . . By the second week, a move toward adaptation to the situation was common." Unfortunately, researchers have yet to flesh out these anecdotes; no one has systematically gathered statistics on the prevalence of these withdrawal symptoms.

Even though TV does seem to meet the criteria for substance 27 dependence, not all researchers would go so far as to call TV addictive. McIlwraith said in 1998 that "displacement of other activities by television may be socially significant but still fall short of the clinical requirement of significant impairment." He argued that a new category of "TV addiction" may not be necessary if heavy viewing stems from conditions such as depression and social phobia. Nevertheless, whether or not we formally diagnose someone as TV-dependent, millions of people sense that they cannot readily control the amount of television they watch.

SLAVE TO THE COMPUTER SCREEN

Although much less research has been done on video games and com- 28 puter use, the same principles often apply. The games offer escape and distraction; players quickly learn that they feel better when playing; and so a kind of reinforcement loop develops. The obvious difference from television, however, is the interactivity. Many video and computer games minutely increase in difficulty along with the increasing ability of the player. One can search for months to find another tennis or chess player of comparable ability, but programmed games can immediately provide a near-perfect match of challenge to skill. They offer the psychic pleasure— what one of us (Csikszentmihalyi) has called "flow"—that accompanies increased mastery of most any human endeavor. On the other hand, prolonged activation of the orienting response can wear players out. Kids report feeling tired, dizzy and nauseated after long sessions.

In 1997, in the most extreme medium-effects case on record, 700 29 Japanese children were rushed to the hospital, many suffering from "optically stimulated epileptic seizures" caused by viewing bright flashing lights in a Pokemon video game broadcast on Japanese TV. Seizures and other untoward effects of video games are significant enough that software companies and platform manufacturers now routinely include warnings in their instruction booklets. Parents have reported to us that rapid movement on the screen has caused motion sickness in their young children after just fifteen minutes of play. Many youngsters, lacking self-control and experience (and often supervision), continue to play despite these symptoms.

Lang and Shyam Sundar of Pennsylvania State University have 30 been studying how people respond to Web sites. Sundar has shown people multiple versions of the same Web page, identical except for the number of links. Users reported that more links conferred a greater sense of control and engagement. At some point, however, the number of links

153

reached saturation, and adding more of them simply turned people off. As with video games, the ability of Web sites to hold the user's attention seems to depend less on formal features than on interactivity.

For growing numbers of people, the life they lead online may often seem more important, more immediate, and more intense than the life they lead face-to-face. Maintaining control over one's media habits is more of a challenge today than it has ever been. TV sets and computers are everywhere. But the small screen and the Internet need not interfere with the quality of the rest of one's life. In its easy provision of relaxation and escape, television can be beneficial in limited doses. Yet when the habit interferes with the ability to grow, to learn new things, to lead an active life, then it does constitute a kind of dependence and should be taken seriously. 31

Examining the Text

1. According to Kubey and Csikszentmihalyi, what factors distinguish TV addiction from simple TV viewing?

2. What biological evidence do Kubey and Csikszentmihalyi summon to support their claims of TV's addictive capabilities? What is the "orienting response," and how does it function in the context of TV viewing?

3. What do Kubey and Csikszentmihalyi mean when they ask, "In which direction does the correlation go?" How do they address the problem of correlation and causation in TV addiction?

4. According to Kubey and Csikszentmihalyi, in what ways are video games and computer use similar to and different from TV viewing? How do these similarities and differences affect the question of addiction that Kubey and Csikszentmihalyi discuss?

5. *Thinking rhetorically:* The title of Kubey and Csikszentmihalyi's article draws attention to the fact that many people use the term addiction as a metaphor. For instance, you might hear people saying that they're addicted" to watching "Survivor" or that they're "addicted" to Brown Sugar Cinnamon Frosted Pop-Tarts. What are some of the differences between using "addiction" as a metaphor and using it as a clinical term, as Kubey and Csikszentmihalyi do? Can you think of other terms that function as common metaphors in our culture, like "addiction" does?

For Group Discussion

In a group with several other students, choose an addiction about which you have some knowledge (for instance, gambling, smoking, or drinking alcohol). Make a list of all that you know about this addiction: who suffers from it, what problems it causes, why it occurs, how society has responded, what laws exist that address the addiction, what economic consequences it has, how it can be "cured," and so on. Then compare the list you've compiled to the facts about television addiction that Kubey and Csikszentmihalyi discuss in the reading.

Based on this comparison, do you think that excessive television viewing can genuinely be considered an "addiction"? Why or why not?

Writing Suggestion

For this assignment you'll need access to the Internet to research "TV Turn-Off Week." This annual event, described briefly by Kubey and Csikszentmihalyi, is organized by Adbusters. At *http://adbusters.org/campaigns/tvturnoff/* you can read more about this event, including personal accounts of people who participated and information about how the television media reported the event. You can also take a look at posters that people designed to publicize "TV Turn-Off Week," view a thirty-second TV "uncommercial" produced for the event, and read related articles. After reading through all this information, write an essay in which you argue either for or against the merits of "TV Turn-Off Week." Be sure to use quotations and/or statistics from the article by Kubey and Csikszentmihalyi in your argument. Feel free to include anecdotes or observations from your own experiences as a TV viewer to help bolster your position.

Watching TV Makes You Smarter

STEVEN JOHNSON

If your parents have ever complained that you watch too much TV, just tell them, "But Mom, Dad, watching TV is mentally stimulating and can actually make me smarter!" When they look at you in disbelief, refer them to the following article in which Steven Johnson makes precisely that argument: that watching TV—or at least, watching some of the shows currently on TV— gives you a good cognitive workout. The article, adapted from Johnson's bestseller, Everything Bad Is Good for You: How Today's Popular Culture Is Actually Making Us Smarter, *compares past and present TV shows and concludes that viewers today are required to exercise their mental faculties in order to make sense of complex, multilayered plots and characters.*

Although Johnson refers to many past and present shows in this article, his primary examples of intellectually challenging shows are 24, The West Wing, The Sopranos, *and* ER. *He argues that these shows combine the complicated plot threads of soap opera with the realistic characters and important social issues of nighttime drama. As a result, in any given episode of a show, viewers have to follow intersecting narrative threads that include many distinct characters, each with their own continuing story line. These shows often have fast-paced, specialized dialogue that's purposely difficult for viewers to follow. Watching the shows engages viewers in the pleasures of solving puzzles and unlocking mysteries, and so these shows provide a mentally stimulating hour of TV viewing—punctuated, of course, by commercial breaks.*

*It certainly goes against common perceptions of TV to suggest that watching shows is mentally stimulating; you're far more likely to find arguments like those presented in the earlier article by Harry Waters, that TV viewing can give you a skewed perception of reality. Because Johnson makes such an unusual argument, it's interesting to pay attention to the strategies he uses to try to convince readers that he's correct. **As you read,** notice the different kinds of evidence that Johnson uses to prove his point. What evidence do you find most convincing? What evidence do you find questionable?*

THE SLEEPER CURVE

Scientist A: Has he asked for anything special?
Scientist B: Yes, this morning for breakfast . . . he requested something called "wheat germ, organic honey and tiger's milk."
Scientist A: Oh, yes. Those were the charmed substances that some years ago were felt to contain life-preserving properties.
Scientist B: You mean there was no deep fat? No steak or cream pies or . . . hot fudge?
Scientist A: Those were thought to be unhealthy.

From Woody Allen's *Sleeper*

On Jan. 24, the Fox network showed an episode of its hit drama *24*, the real-time thriller known for its cliffhanger tension and often-gruesome violence. Over the preceding weeks, a number of public controversies had erupted around *24*, mostly focused on its portrait of Muslim terrorists and its penchant for torture scenes. The episode that was shown on the 24th only fanned the flames higher: in one scene, a terrorist enlists a hit man to kill his child for not fully supporting the jihadist cause; in another scene, the secretary of defense authorizes the torture of his son to uncover evidence of a terrorist plot.

But the explicit violence and the post-9/11 terrorist anxiety are not the only elements of *24* that would have been unthinkable on prime-time network television twenty years ago. Alongside the notable change in content lies an equally notable change in form. During its forty four minutes—a real-time hour, minus sixteen minutes for commercials—the episode connects the lives of twenty one distinct characters, each with a clearly defined "story arc," as the Hollywood jargon has it: a defined personality with motivations and obstacles and specific relationships with other characters. Nine primary narrative threads wind their way through those forty four minutes, each drawing extensively upon events and information revealed in earlier episodes. Draw a map of all those intersecting plots and personalities, and you get structure that—where formal complexity is concerned—more closely resembles *Middlemarch* than a hit TV drama of years past like *Bonanza*.

For decades, we've worked under the assumption that mass culture   3
follows a path declining steadily toward lowest-common-denominator standards, presumably because the "masses" want dumb, simple pleasures and big media companies try to give the masses what they want. But as that *24* episode suggests, the exact opposite is happening: the culture is getting more cognitively demanding, not less. To make sense of an episode of *24*, you have to integrate far more information than you would have a few decades ago watching a comparable show. Beneath the violence and the ethnic stereotypes, another trend appears: to keep up with entertainment like *24*, you have to pay attention, make inferences, track shifting social relationships. This is what I call the Sleeper Curve: the most debased forms of mass diversion—video games and violent television dramas and juvenile sitcoms—turn out to be nutritional after all.

I believe that the Sleeper Curve is the single most important new   4
force altering the mental development of young people today, and I believe it is largely a force for good: enhancing our cognitive faculties, not dumbing them down. And yet you almost never hear this story in popular accounts of today's media. Instead, you hear dire tales of addiction, violence, mindless escapism. It's assumed that shows that promote smoking or gratuitous violence are bad for us, while those that thunder against teen pregnancy or intolerance have a positive role in society. Judged by that morality-play standard, the story of popular culture over the past fifty years—if not 500—is a story of decline: the morals of the stories have grown darker and more ambiguous, and the antiheroes have multiplied.

The usual counterargument here is that what media have lost in   5
moral clarity, they have gained in realism. The real world doesn't come in nicely packaged public-service announcements, and we're better off with entertainment like *The Sopranos* that reflects our fallen state with all its ethical ambiguity. I happen to be sympathetic to that argument, but it's not the one I want to make here. I think there is another way to assess the social virtue of pop culture, one that looks at media as a kind of cognitive workout, not as a series of life lessons. There may indeed be more "negative messages" in the mediasphere today. But that's not the only way to evaluate whether our television shows or video games are having a positive impact. Just as important—if not more important—is the kind of thinking you have to do to make sense of a cultural experience. That is where the Sleeper Curve becomes visible.

TELEVISED INTELLIGENCE

Consider the cognitive demands that televised narratives place on   6
their viewers. With many shows that we associate with "quality"

entertainment—*The Mary Tyler Moore Show, Murphy Brown, Frasier*—the intelligence arrives fully formed in the words and actions of the characters on-screen. They say witty things to one another and avoid lapsing into tired sitcom clichés, and we smile along in our living rooms, enjoying the company of these smart people. But assuming we're bright enough to understand the sentences they're saying, there's no intellectual labor involved in enjoying the show as a viewer. You no more challenge your mind by watching these intelligent shows than you challenge your body watching *Monday Night Football*. The intellectual work is happening on-screen, not off.

But another kind of televised intelligence is on the rise. Think of 7 the cognitive benefits conventionally ascribed to reading: attention, patience, retention, the parsing of narrative threads. Over the last half-century, programming on TV has increased the demands it places on precisely these mental faculties. This growing complexity involves three primary elements: multiple threading, flashing arrows and social networks.

According to television lore, the age of multiple threads began 8 with the arrival in 1981 of *Hill Street Blues*, the Steven Bochco police drama invariably praised for its "gritty realism." Watch an episode of *Hill Street Blues* side by side with any major drama from the preceding decades—*Starsky and Hutch*, for instance, or *Dragnet*—and the structural transformation will jump out at you. The earlier shows follow one or two lead characters, adhere to a single dominant plot and reach a decisive conclusion at the end of the episode. Draw an outline of the narrative threads in almost every *Dragnet* episode, and it will be a single line: from the initial crime scene, through the investigation, to the eventual cracking of the case. A typical *Starsky and Hutch* episode offers only the slightest variation on this linear formula: the introduction of a comic subplot that usually appears only at the tail ends of the episode, creating a structure that looks like this graph. The vertical axis represents the number of individual threads, and the horizontal axis is time.

"STARSKY AND HUTCH" (ANY EPISODE)

A Hill Street Blues episode complicates the picture in a number 9 of profound ways. The narrative weaves together a collection of distinct strands—sometimes as many as ten, though at least half of the threads involve only a few quick scenes scattered through the episode. The number of primary characters—and not just bit parts—swells significantly. And the episode has fuzzy borders: picking up one or two threads from previous episodes at the outset and leaving one or two threads open at the end. Charted graphically, an average episode looks like this:

HILL STREET BLUES (EPISODE 85)

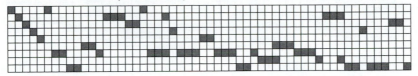

Critics generally cite *Hill Street Blues* as the beginning of "serious   10
drama" native in the television medium—differentiating the series from the single-episode dramatic programs from the '50s, which were Broadway plays performed in front of a camera. But the *Hill Street* innovations weren't all that original; they'd long played a defining role in popular television, just not during the evening hours. The structure of a *Hill Street* episode—and indeed of all the critically acclaimed dramas that followed, from "thirtysomething" to *Six Feet Under*—is the structure of a soap opera. *Hill Street Blues* might have sparked a new golden age of television drama during its seven-year run, but it did so by using a few crucial tricks that *Guiding Light* and *General Hospital* mastered long before.

Bochco's genius with *Hill Street* was to marry complex narrative   11
structure with complex subject matter. *Dallas* had already shown that the extended, interwoven threads of the soap-opera genre could survive the weeklong interruptions of a prime-time show, but the actual content of *Dallas* was fluff. (The most probing issue it addressed was the question, now folkloric, of who shot J.R.) *All in the Family* and *Rhoda* showed that you could tackle complex social issues, but they did their tackling in the comfort of the sitcom living room. *Hill Street* had richly drawn characters confronting difficult social issues and a narrative structure to match.

Since *Hill Street* appeared, the multi-threaded drama has   12
become the most widespread fictional genre on prime time: *St. Elsewhere, L.A. Law, thirtysomething, Twin Peaks, N.Y.P.D. Blue, E.R., The West Wing, Alias, Lost*. (The only prominent holdouts in drama are shows like *Law and Order* that have essentially updated the venerable *Dragnet* format and thus remained anchored to a single narrative line.) Since the early '80s, however, there has been a noticeable increase in narrative complexity in these dramas. The most ambitious show on TV to date, *The Sopranos*, routinely follows up to a dozen distinct threads over the course of an episode, with more than twenty

recurring characters. An episode from late in the first season looks like this:

THE SOPRANOS (EPISODE 8)

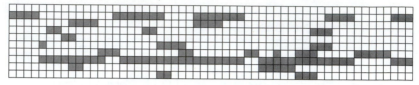

The total number of active threads equals the multiple plots 13
of "Hill Street," but here each thread is more substantial. The show doesn't offer a clear distinction between dominant and minor plots; each story line carries its weight in the mix. The episode also displays a chordal mode of storytelling entirely absent from "Hill Street": a single scene in *The Sopranos* will often connect to three different threads at the same time, layering one plot atop another. And every single thread in this "Sopranos" episode builds on events from previous episodes and continues on through the rest of the season and beyond.

Put those charts together, and you have a portrait of the Sleeper 14
Curve rising over the past thirty years of popular television. In a sense, this is as much a map of cognitive changes in the popular mind as it is a map of on-screen developments, as if the media titans decided to condition our brains to follow ever-larger numbers of simultaneous threads. Before "Hill Street," the conventional wisdom among television execs was that audiences wouldn't be comfortable following more than three plots in a single episode, and indeed, the "Hill Street" pilot, which was shown in January 1981, brought complaints from viewers that the show was too complicated. Fast-forward two decades, and shows like *The Sopranos* engage their audiences with narratives that make *Hill Street* look like *Three's Company*. Audiences happily embrace that complexity because they've been trained by two decades of multi-threaded dramas.

Multi-threading is the most celebrated structural feature of the 15
modern television drama, and it certainly deserves some of the honor that has been doled out to it. And yet multi-threading is only part of the story.

THE CASE FOR CONFUSION

Shortly after the arrival of the first-generation slasher movies— 16
Halloween, Friday the 13th—Paramount released a mock-slasher flick called *Student Bodies*, parodying the genre just as the "Scream" series would do fifteen years later. In one scene, the obligatory nubile teenage baby sitter hears a noise outside a suburban house; she opens the door to investigate, finds nothing and then goes back inside. As the door shuts behind her, the camera swoops in on the doorknob, and we see that she has left the door unlocked. The camera pulls back and then

swoops down again for emphasis. And then a flashing arrow appears on the screen, with text that helpfully explains: "Unlocked!"

That flashing arrow is parody, of course, but it's merely an exag- 17 gerated version of a device popular stories use all the time. When a sci-fi script inserts into some advanced lab a nonscientist who keeps asking the science geeks to explain what they're doing with that particle accelerator, that's a flashing arrow that gives the audience precisely the information it needs in order to make sense of the ensuing plot. ("Whatever you do, don't spill water on it, or you'll set off a massive explosion!") These hints serve as a kind of narrative hand-holding. Implicitly, they say to the audience, "We realize you have no idea what a particle accelerator is, but here's the deal: all you need to know is that it's a big fancy thing that explodes when wet." They focus the mind on relevant details: "Don't worry about whether the baby sitter is going to break up with her boyfriend. Worry about that guy lurking in the bushes." They reduce the amount of analytic work you need to do to make sense of a story. All you have to do is follow the arrows.

By this standard, popular television has never been harder to fol- 18 low. If narrative threads have experienced a population explosion over the past twenty years, flashing arrows have grown correspondingly scarce. Watching our pinnacle of early '80s TV drama, *Hill Street Blues*, we find there's an informational wholeness to each scene that differs markedly from what you see on shows like *The West Wing* or *The Sopranos* or *Alias* or *E.R.*

"Hill Street" has ambiguities about future events: will a convicted 19 killer be executed? Will Furillo marry Joyce Davenport? Will Renko find it in himself to bust a favorite singer for cocaine possession? But the present-tense of each scene explains itself to the viewer with little ambiguity. There's an open question or a mystery driving each of these stories—how will it all turn out?—but there's no mystery about the immediate activity on the screen. A contemporary drama like *The West Wing*, on the other hand, constantly embeds mysteries into the present-tense events: you see characters performing actions or discussing events about which crucial information has been deliberately withheld. Anyone who has watched more than a handful of *The West Wing* episodes closely will know the feeling: scene after scene refers to some clearly crucial but unexplained piece of information, and after the sixth reference, you'll find yourself wishing you could rewind the tape to figure out what they're talking about, assuming you've missed something. And then you realize that you're supposed to be confused. The open question posed by these sequences is not, "How will this turn out in the end?" The question is, "What's happening right now?"

The deliberate lack of hand-holding extends down to the 20 microlevel of dialogue as well. Popular entertainment that addresses technical issues—whether they are the intricacies of passing legislation, or of performing a heart bypass, or of operating a particle accelerator—conventionally switches between two modes of information in dialogue: texture and substance. Texture is all the arcane verbiage provided to convince the viewer that they're watching Actual Doctors at Work; substance is the material planted amid the background texture that the viewer needs make sense of the plot.

Conventionally, narratives demarcate the line between texture and substance by inserting cues that flag or translate the important data. There's an unintentionally comical moment in the 2004 blockbuster *The Day After Tomorrow* in which the beleaguered climatologist (played by Dennis Quaid) announces his theory about the imminent arrival of a new ice age to a gathering of government officials. In his speech, he warns that "we have hit a critical desalinization point!" At this moment, the writer-director Roland Emmerich—a master of brazen arrow-flashing—has an official follow with the obliging remark: "It would explain what's driving this extreme weather." They might as well have had a flashing "Unlocked!" arrow on the screen. 21

The dialogue on shows like *The West Wing* and *E.R.*, on the other hand, doesn't talk down to its audiences. It rushes by, the words accelerating in sync with the high-speed tracking shots that glide through the corridors and operating rooms. The characters talk faster in these shows, but the truly remarkable thing about the dialogue is not purely a matter of speed; it's the willingness to immerse the audience in information that most viewers won't understand. Here's a typical scene from *E.R.*: 22

[Weaver And Wright push a gurney containing a 16-year-old girl. Her parents, Janna and Frank Mikami, follow close behind. Carter and Lucy fall in.] 23

> *Weaver:* 16-year-old, unconscious, history of biliary atresia.
> *Carter:* Hepatic coma?
> *Weaver:* Looks like it.
> *Mr. Mikami:* She was doing fine until six months ago.
> *Carter:* What medication is she on?
> *Mrs. Mikami:* Ampicillin, tobramycin, vitamins a, d and k.
> *Lucy:* Skin's jaundiced.
> *Weaver:* Same with the sclera. Breath smells sweet.
> *Carter:* Fetor hepaticus?
> *Weaver:* Yep.
> *Lucy:* What's that?
> *Weaver:* Her liver's shut down. Let's dip a urine. [To Carter] Guys, it's getting a little crowded in here, why don't you deal with the parents? Start lactulose, 30 cc's per NG.
> *Carter:* We're giving medicine to clean her blood.

Weaver: Blood in the urine, two-plus.
Carter: The liver failure is causing her blood not to clot.
Mrs. Mikami: Oh, God. . . .
Carter: Is she on the transplant list?
Mr. Mikami: She's been Status 2a for six months, but they haven't been able to find her a match.
Carter: Why? What's her blood type?
Mr. Mikami: AB.
[This hits Carter like a lightning bolt. Lucy gets it, too. They share a look.]

There are flashing arrows here, of course—"The liver failure is causing her   24
blood not to clot"—but the ratio of medical jargon to layperson translation is remarkably high. From a purely narrative point of view, the decisive line arrives at the very end: "AB." The 16-year-old's blood type connects her to an earlier plot line, involving a cerebral-hemorrhage victim who— after being dramatically revived in one of the opening scenes—ends up brain-dead. Far earlier, before the liver-failure scene above, Carter briefly discusses harvesting the hemorrhage victim's organs for transplants, and another doctor makes a passing reference to his blood type being the rare AB (thus making him an unlikely donor). The twist here revolves around a statistically unlikely event happening at the E.R.—an otherwise perfect liver donor showing up just in time to donate his liver to a recipient with the same rare blood type. But the show reveals this twist with remarkable subtlety. To make sense of that last "AB" line—and the look of disbelief on Carter's and Lucy's faces—you have to recall a passing remark uttered earlier regarding a character who belongs to a completely different thread. Shows like *E.R.* may have more blood and guts than popular TV had a generation ago, but when it comes to storytelling, they possess a quality that can only be described as subtlety and discretion.

163

EVEN BAD TV IS BETTER

Skeptics might argue that I have stacked the deck here by focusing on   25
relatively highbrow titles like *The Sopranos* or *The West Wing*, when in fact the most significant change in the last five years of narrative enter- tainment involves reality TV. Does the contemporary pop cultural landscape look quite as promising if the representative show is *Joe Millionaire* instead of *The West Wing*?

I think it does, but to answer that question properly, you have to   26
avoid the tendency to sentimentalize the past. When people talk about the golden age of television in the early '70s—invoking shows like *The Mary Tyler Moore Show* and *All in the Family*—they forget to mention how awful most television programming was during much of that decade. If

you're going to look at pop-culture trends, you have to compare apples to apples, or in this case, lemons to lemons. The relevant comparison is not between *Joe Millionaire* and *M*A*S*H*; it's between *Joe Millionaire* and *The Newlywed Game*, or between *Survivor* and *The Love Boat*.

What you see when you make these head-to-head comparisons is that a rising tide of complexity has been lifting programming at the bottom of the quality spectrum and at the top. *The Sopranos* is several times more demanding of its audiences than "Hill Street" was, and *Joe Millionaire* has made comparable advances over *Battle of the Network Stars*. This is the ultimate test of the Sleeper Curve theory: Even the junk has improved.

If early television took its cues from the stage, today's reality programming is reliably structured like a video game: a series of competitive tests, growing more challenging over time. Many reality shows borrow a subtler device from gaming culture as well: the rules aren't fully established at the outset. You learn as you play. 27

On a show like *Survivor* or *The Apprentice*, the participants—and the audience—know the general objective of the series, but each episode involves new challenges that haven't been ordained in advance. The final round of the first season of *The Apprentice*, for instance, threw a monkey wrench into the strategy that governed the play up to that point, when Trump announced that the two remaining apprentices would have to assemble and manage a team of subordinates who had already been fired in earlier episodes of the show. All of a sudden, the overarching objective of the game—do anything to avoid being fired—presented a potential conflict to the remaining two contenders: the structure of the final round favored the survivor who had maintained the best relationships with his comrades. Suddenly, it wasn't enough just to have clawed your way to the top; you had to have made friends while clawing. The original *Joe Millionaire* went so far as to undermine the most fundamental convention of all—that the show's creators don't openly lie to the contestants about the prizes—by inducing a construction worker to pose as man of means while twenty women competed for his attention. 28

Reality programming borrowed another key ingredient from games: the intellectual labor of probing the system's rules for weak spots and opportunities. As each show discloses its conventions, and each participant reveals his or her personality traits and background, the intrigue in watching comes from figuring out how the participants should best navigate the environment that has been created for them. The pleasure in these shows comes not from watching other people being humiliated on national television; it comes from depositing other people in a complex, high-pressure environment where no established strategies exist and watching them find their bearings. That's why the 29 water-cooler conversation about these shows invariably tracks in on the strategy displayed on the previous night's episode: why did Kwame pick Omarosa in that final round? What devious strategy is Richard Hatch concocting now?

When we watch these shows, the part of our brain that monitors   30
the emotional lives of the people around us—the part that tracks subtle shifts in intonation and gesture and facial expression—scrutinizes the action on the screen, looking for clues. We trust certain characters implicitly and vote others off the island in a heartbeat. Traditional narrative shows also trigger emotional connections to the characters, but those connections don't have the same participatory effect, because traditional narratives aren't explicitly about strategy. The phrase "Monday-morning quarterbacking" describes the engaged feeling that spectators have in relation to games as opposed to stories. We absorb stories, but we second-guess games. Reality programming has brought that second-guessing to prime time, only the game in question revolves around social dexterity rather than the physical kind.

THE REWARDS OF SMART CULTURE   **165**

The quickest way to appreciate the Sleeper Curve's cognitive training   31
is to sit down and watch a few hours of hit programming from the late '70s on Nick at Nite or the SOAPnet channel or on DVD. The modern viewer who watches a show like "Dallas" today will be bored by the content—not just because the show is less salacious than today's soap operas (which it is by a small margin) but also because the show contains far less information in each scene, despite the fact that its soap-opera structure made it one of the most complicated narratives on television in its prime. With *Dallas*, the modern viewer doesn't have to think to make sense of what's going on, and not having to think is boring. Many recent hit shows—*24, Survivor, The Sopranos, Alias, Lost, The Simpsons, E.R.*—take the opposite approach, layering each scene with a thick network of affiliations. You have to focus to follow the plot, and in focusing you're exercising the parts of your brain that map social networks, that fill in missing information, that connect multiple narrative threads.

Of course, the entertainment industry isn't increasing the cogni-   32
tive complexity of its products for charitable reasons. The Sleeper Curve exists because there's money to be made by making culture smarter. The economics of television syndication and DVD sales mean that there's a tremendous financial pressure to make programs that can be watched multiple times, revealing new nuances and shadings on the

third viewing. Meanwhile, the Web has created a forum for annotation and commentary that allows more complicated shows to prosper, thanks to the fan sites where each episode of shows like *Lost* or *Alias* is dissected with an intensity usually reserved for Talmud scholars. Finally, interactive games have trained a new generation of media consumers to probe complex environments and to think on their feet, and that gamer audience has now come to expect the same challenges from their television shows. In the end, the Sleeper Curve tells us something about the human mind. It may be drawn toward the sensational where content is concerned—sex does sell, after all. But the mind also likes to be challenged; there's real pleasure to be found in solving puzzles, detecting patterns, or unpacking a complex narrative system.

In pointing out some of the ways that popular culture has 33 improved our minds, I am not arguing that parents should stop paying attention to the way their children amuse themselves. What I am arguing for is a change in the criteria we use to determine what really is cognitive junk food and what is genuinely nourishing. Instead of a show's violent or tawdry content, instead of wardrobe malfunctions or the F-word, the true test should be whether a given show engages or sedates the mind. Is it a single thread strung together with predictable punch lines every thirty seconds? Or does it map a complex social network? Is your on-screen character running around shooting everything in sight, or is she trying to solve problems and manage resources? If your kids want to watch reality TV, encourage them to watch *Survivor* over *Fear Factor*. If they want to watch a mystery show, encourage *24* over *Law and Order*. If they want to play a violent game, encourage Grand Theft Auto over Quake. Indeed, it might be just as helpful to have a rating system that used mental labor and not obscenity and violence as its classification scheme for the world of mass culture.

Kids and grown-ups each can learn from their increasingly 34 shared obsessions. Too often we imagine the blurring of kid and grown-up cultures as a series of violations: the nine-year-olds who have to have nipple broaches explained to them thanks to Janet Jackson; the middle-aged guy who can't wait to get home to his Xbox. But this demographic blur has a commendable side that we don't acknowledge enough. The kids are forced to think like grown-ups: analyzing complex social networks, managing resources, tracking subtle narrative intertwinings, recognizing long-term patterns. The grown-ups, in turn, get to learn from the kids: decoding each new technological wave, parsing the interfaces, and discovering the intellectual rewards of play. Parents should see this as an opportunity, not a crisis. Smart culture is no longer something you force your kids to ingest, like green vegetables. It's something you share.

Examining the Text

1. What does Johnson mean by the term the *Sleeper Curve?* How is this term related to the opening quotation from Woody Allen's movie, *Sleeper?*

2. In paragraph 5, Johnson makes a distinction between seeing the media "as a kind of cognitive workout, not as a series of life lessons." Explain this distinction in your own words. What TV shows might fall into the category of "cognitive workout"? What shows would be more likely to offer "life lessons"?

3. What does Johnson mean by "flashing arrows" in TV shows? What function do flashing arrows serve? How have they changed over the years?

4. According to Johnson, what kind of intellectual and social complexity does reality TV provide its viewers? Do you think Johnson's argument about reality TV is persuasive? Why or why not?

5. *Thinking rhetorically:* Following up on the "as you read" suggestion in the introduction to this article, think about the evidence that Johnson uses to support his claim that current TV shows are cognitively stimulating. Select one specific piece of evidence from the article that you find very convincing and one that you find unconvincing. Based on a comparison of these two pieces of evidence, what general conclusions can you draw about the characteristics of good and weak evidence?

For Group Discussion

In a small group, have one of the group members read aloud the last paragraph of the article, in which Johnson discusses how parents and children can benefit from "smart culture" on TV. Make a list of the benefits for kids and the benefits for parents. Then discuss whether you think each of the benefits can be realistically achieved by watching "smart TV." Draw on your own experiences and your own knowledge of TV programs in order to decide whether Johnson's argument is reasonable or whether he's overstating the positives of watching TV.

Writing Suggestion

Johnson provides some visual evidence to support his assertion that TV shows have become increasingly complex. The three graphs included in the article show the number of plot threads in single episodes of *Starsky and Hutch*, *Hill Street Blues*, and *The Sopranos*. A quick visual comparison of these graphs does indeed suggest that *The Sopranos* has more plot threads and more interweaving of these threads than the two earlier shows. Your assignment is to create a similar chart for a current TV show of your choice. Choose a show to watch, and as you're watching keep note of each time a new plot thread occurs or there's a reference to another thread. After the show is over, plot these elements on a simple chart in which the vertical axis represents each plot thread and the horizontal axis represents time. To make the task easier, label each plot thread on the vertical axis (something Johnson doesn't do). After you've finished the chart, write a paragraph in which you draw conclusions about the relative complexity of the show as compared to the three examples Johnson offers.

Gin, Television, and Social Surplus

CLAY SHIRKY

We conclude this selection of general readings about television with an article that points to both its past and its future. Clay Shirky draws an explicit contrast between Gilligan's Island *and* Wikipedia—*that is, between TV sit-coms and the participatory projects like* Wikipedia, *which are currently underway on the Internet. One of Shirky's key ideas is that television takes care of something that we have in surplus—time—by defusing it, whereas projects on the Internet draw on our free time more productively, engaging us in creative, collaborative activities.*

    This article has an interesting history: it is adapted from a talk that Shirky gave at a 2008 Web 2.0 conference and can be found online at a blog that Shirky developed to promote his latest book, Here Comes Everybody: The Power of Organizing Without Organizations. *The ideas here have been what we might describe as multiply mediated: oral presentation, online blog, print article. Shirky himself is equally multiple, so to speak. Here's how he describes his career on his homepage: "I have been a producer, programmer, professor, designer, author, consultant, sometimes working with people who wanted to create a purely intellectual or aesthetic experience online, sometimes working with people who wanted to use the internet to sell books or batteries or banking."* **Before you read the article,** *take a look at Shirky's homepage (http://www.shirky.com) and the blog he maintains (http://www.herecomeseverybody.org/) to read about some of his other projects, articles, and ideas.*

I was recently reminded of some reading I did in college, way back in 1 the last century, by a British historian arguing that the critical technology, for the early phase of the industrial revolution, was gin.

    The transformation from rural to urban life was so sudden, and so 2 wrenching, that the only thing society could do to manage was to drink itself into a stupor for a generation. The stories from that era are amazing—there were gin pushcarts working their way through the streets of London.

    And it wasn't until society woke up from that collective bender 3 that we actually started to get the institutional structures that we associate with the industrial revolution today. Things like public libraries and museums, increasingly broad education for children, elected leaders—a lot of things we like—didn't happen until having all of those people together stopped seeming like a crisis and started seeming like an asset.

It wasn't until people started thinking of this as a vast civic sur- 4
plus, one they could design for rather than just dissipate, that we
started to get what we think of now as an industrial society.

If I had to pick the critical technology for the twentieth century, 5
the bit of social lubricant without which the wheels would've come off
the whole enterprise, I'd say it was the sitcom. Starting with the Second
World War, a whole series of things happened—rising GDP per capita,
rising educational attainment, rising life expectancy and, critically, a
rising number of people who were working five-day work weeks. For
the first time, society forced onto an enormous number of its citizens
the requirement to manage something they had never had to manage
before—free time.

And what did we do with that free time? Well, mostly we spent it 6
watching TV.

We did that for decades. We watched *I Love Lucy*. We watched 7
Gilligan's Island. We watch *Malcolm in the Middle*. We watch *Desperate
Housewives*. *Desperate Housewives* essentially functioned as a kind of
cognitive heat sink, dissipating thinking that might otherwise have
built up and caused society to overheat.

And it's only now, as we're waking up from that collective ben- 8
der, that we're starting to see the cognitive surplus as an asset rather
than as a crisis. We're seeing things being designed to take advantage
of that surplus, to deploy it in ways more engaging than just having a
TV in everybody's basement.

This hit me in a conversation I had about two months ago. As Jen 9
said in the introduction, I've finished a book called *Here Comes
Everybody*, which has recently come out, and this recognition came out
of a conversation I had about the book. I was being interviewed by a
TV producer to see whether I should be on her show, and she asked
me, "What are you seeing out there that's interesting?"

I started telling her about the *Wikipedia* article on Pluto. You may 10
remember that Pluto got kicked out of the planet club a couple of years
ago, so all of a sudden there was all of this activity on *Wikipedia*. The
talk pages light up, people are editing the article like mad, and the
whole community is in an ruckus—"How should we characterize this
change in Pluto's status?" And a little bit at a time they move the
article—fighting offstage all the while—from, "Pluto is the ninth
planet," to "Pluto is an odd-shaped rock with an odd-shaped orbit at
the edge of the solar system."

So I tell her all this stuff, and I think, "Okay, we're going to have a 11
conversation about authority or social construction or whatever." That
wasn't her question. She heard this story, and she shook her head and
said, "Where do people find the time?" That was her question. And I
just kind of snapped. And I said, "No one who works in TV gets to ask

that question. You know where the time comes from. It comes from the cognitive surplus you've been masking for fifty years."

So how big is that surplus? So if you take *Wikipedia* as a kind of unit, all of *Wikipedia*, the whole project—every page, every edit, every talk page, every line of code, in every language that *Wikipedia* exists in—that represents something like the cumulation of 100 million hours of human thought. I worked this out with Martin Wattenberg at IBM; it's a back-of-the-envelope calculation, but it's the right order of magnitude, about 100 million hours of thought.   12

And television watching? Two hundred billion hours, in the U.S. alone, every year. Put another way, now that we have a unit, that's 2,000 *Wikipedia* projects a year spent watching television. Or put still another way, in the U.S., we spend 100 million hours every weekend, just watching the ads. This is a pretty big surplus. People asking, "Where do they find the time?" when they're looking at things like *Wikipedia* don't understand how tiny that entire project is, as a carve-out of this asset that's finally being dragged into what Tim calls an architecture of participation.   13

Now, the interesting thing about a surplus like that is that society doesn't know what to do with it at first—hence the gin, hence the sit-coms. Because if people knew what to do with a surplus with reference to the existing social institutions, then it wouldn't be a surplus, would it? It's precisely when no one has any idea how to deploy something that people have to start experimenting with it, in order for the surplus to get integrated, and the course of that integration can transform society.   14

The early phase for taking advantage of this cognitive surplus, the phase I think we're still in, is all special cases. The physics of participation is much more like the physics of weather than it is like the physics of gravity. We know all the forces that combine to make these kinds of things work: there's an interesting community over here, there's an interesting sharing model over there, those people are collaborating on open source software. But despite knowing the inputs, we can't predict the outputs yet because there's so much complexity.   15

The way you explore complex ecosystems is you just try lots and lots and lots of things, and you hope that everybody who fails fails informatively so that you can at least find a skull on a pikestaff near where you're going. That's the phase we're in now.   16

Just to pick one example, one I'm in love with, but it's tiny. A couple of weeks ago one of my students at ITP forwarded me a project started by a professor in Brazil, in Fortaleza, named Vasco Furtado. It's a Wiki Map for crime in Brazil. If there's an assault, if there's a burglary, if there's a mugging, a robbery, a rape, a murder, you can go and put a push-pin on a Google Map, and you can characterize the assault, and you start to see a map of where these crimes are occurring.   17

Now, this already exists as tacit information. Anybody who 18
knows a town has some sense of, "Don't go there. That street corner is
dangerous. Don't go in this neighborhood. Be careful there after dark."
But it's something society knows without society really knowing it,
which is to say there's no public source where you can take advantage
of it. And the cops, if they have that information, they're certainly not
sharing. In fact, one of the things Furtado says in starting the Wiki
crime map was, "This information may or may not exist some place in
society, but it's actually easier for me to try to rebuild it from scratch
than to try and get it from the authorities who might have it now."

Maybe this will succeed or maybe it will fail. The normal case of 19
social software is still failure; most of these experiments don't pan out.
But the ones that do are quite incredible, and I hope that this one succeeds, obviously. But even if it doesn't, it's illustrated the point already,
which is that someone working alone, with really cheap tools, has a
reasonable hope of carving out enough of the cognitive surplus,
enough of the desire to participate, enough of the collective goodwill of
the citizens, to create a resource you couldn't have imagined existing
even five years ago.

So that's the answer to the question, "Where do they find the time?" 20
Or, rather, that's the numerical answer. But beneath that question was
another thought, this one not a question but an observation. In this same
conversation with the TV producer, I was talking about *World of Warcraft*
guilds, and as I was talking, I could sort of see what she was thinking:
"Losers. Grown men sitting in their basement pretending to be elves."

At least they're doing something. 21

Did you ever see that episode of *Gilligan's Island* where they 22
almost get off the island and then Gilligan messes up and then they
don't? I saw that one. I saw that one a lot when I was growing up. And
every half-hour that I watched that was a half an hour I wasn't posting
at my blog or editing *Wikipedia* or contributing to a mailing list. Now, I
had an ironclad excuse for not doing those things, which is none of
those things existed then. I was forced into the channel of media the
way it was because it was the only option. Now it's not, and that's the
big surprise. However lousy it is to sit in your basement and pretend to
be an elf, I can tell you from personal experience it's worse to sit in your
basement and try to figure if Ginger or Mary Ann is cuter.

And I'm willing to raise that to a general principle. It's better to 23
do something than to do nothing. Even lolcats, even cute pictures of
kittens made even cuter with the addition of cute captions, hold out an
invitation to participation. When you see a lolcat, one of the things it
says to the viewer is, "If you have some sans-serif fonts on your computer, you can play this game, too." And that message—I can do that,
too—is a big change.

This is something that people in the media world don't under- 24
stand. Media in the twentieth century was run as a single race—consumption. How much can we produce? How much can you consume?
Can we produce more and you'll consume more? And the answer to
that question has generally been yes. But media is actually a triathlon,
it's three different events. People like to consume, but they also like to
produce, and they like to share.

And what's astonished people who were committed to the struc- 25
ture of the previous society, prior to trying to take this surplus and do
something interesting, is that they're discovering that when you offer
people the opportunity to produce and to share, they'll take you up on
that offer. It doesn't mean that we'll never sit around mindlessly watching *Scrubs* on the couch. It just means we'll do it less.

And this is the other thing about the size of the cognitive surplus 26
we're talking about. It's so large that even a small change could have
huge ramifications. Let's say that everything stays 99 percent the same,
that people watch 99 percent as much television as they used to, but 1
percent of that is carved out for producing and for sharing. The Internet-
connected population watches roughly a trillion hours of TV a year.
That's about five times the size of the annual U.S. consumption. One per
cent of that is 100 *Wikipedia* projects per year worth of participation.

I think that's going to be a big deal. Don't you? 27

Well, the TV producer did not think this was going to be a big 28
deal; she was not digging this line of thought. And her final question to
me was essentially, "Isn't this all just a fad?" You know, sort of the flagpole-sitting of the early twenty-first century? It's fun to go out and produce and share a little bit, but then people are going to eventually realize,"This isn't as good as doing what I was doing before," and settle
down. And I made a spirited argument that no, this wasn't the case,
that this was in fact a big one-time shift, more analogous to the industrial revolution than to flagpole-sitting.

I was arguing that this isn't the sort of thing society grows out of. 29
It's the sort of thing that society grows into. But I'm not sure she
believed me, in part because she didn't want to believe me, but also in
part because I didn't have the right story yet. And now I do.

I was having dinner with a group of friends about a month ago, 30
and one of them was talking about sitting with his four-year-old
daughter watching a DVD. And in the middle of the movie, apropos of
nothing, she jumps up off the couch and runs around behind the
screen. That seems like a cute moment. Maybe she's going back there to
see if Dora is really back there or whatever. But that wasn't what she
was doing. She started rooting around in the cables. And her dad said,
"What you doing?" And she stuck her head out from behind the screen
and said, "Looking for the mouse."

Here's something four-year-olds know: A screen that ships with- 31
out a mouse ships broken. Here's something four-year-olds know:
Media that's targeted at you but doesn't include you may not be worth
sitting still for. Those are things that make me believe that this is a one-
way change. Because four-year-olds, the people who are soaking most
deeply in the current environment, who won't have to go through the
trauma that I have to go through of trying to unlearn a childhood spent
watching *Gilligan's Island*, they just assume that media includes consuming, producing, and sharing.

It's also become my motto, when people ask me what we're 32
doing—and when I say "we," I mean the larger society trying to figure
out how to deploy this cognitive surplus, but I also mean we, especially, the people in this room, the people who are working hammer
and tongs at figuring out the next good idea. From now on, that's what
I'm going to tell them: We're looking for the mouse. We're going to look
at every place that a reader or a listener or a viewer or a user has been
locked out, has been served up passive or a fixed or a canned experience, and ask ourselves, "If we carve out a little bit of the cognitive surplus and deploy it here, could we make a good thing happen?" And
I'm betting the answer is yes.

173

Examining the Text

1. According to Shirky, what similar functions did gin and television sitcoms
serve when they were first introduced? Why do you think Shirky begins his
article with this analogy? Do you think that the analogy is effective despite the
significant differences between gin and television?

2. What does Shirky mean by a social or cognitive surplus? Do you agree that
time is currently a surplus?

3. In paragraph 15, Shirky writes, "The physics of participation is much more
like the physics of weather than it is like the physics of gravity." Take a look at
the sentences that follow and try to explain in your own words what Shirky
means. How does this statement contribute to his overall argument?

4. In paragraphs 12 and 13, Shirky presents a "back-of-the-envelope calculation" related to the number of hours people spend watching TV and the number of hours invested in a project like *Wikipedia*. Later in the article, he offers a
similar estimation. What effect do the numbers and statistics that Shirky provides have on your opinion of his argument? Does the fact that these numbers
are "guesstimates" rather than hard data have any impact on their relevance
for you?

5. What is the point that Shirky makes in his story of the four-year-old who
looks for the mouse for her television set? Why do you think Shirky leaves this
story until the end of his article? As a slogan, what does "we're looking for the
mouse" imply?

6. *Thinking rhetorically:* As we noted in the introduction, this article was initially a talk that Shirky presented at a conference. What signs of its beginnings as an oral presentation do you still see in the article? Do you think that these stylistic features help to advance or detract from Shirky's argument when it's presented in writing?

For Group Discussion

Toward the end of the article, Shirky returns several times to the idea that the Internet offers opportunities to participate and produce, whereas television offers only opportunities to consume. In a small group, list all the ways in which each of you has become more of a participant in broader social and cultural activities because of the Internet, whether it's creating a MySpace profile, posting videos on YouTube, or playing online games, for example. What benefits do you think you get from interacting on the Internet, and how are these different from the benefits you derive from watching TV? Based on your own experiences as participants and producers, do Shirky's predictions about the future seem persuasive to you?

Writing Suggestion

Shirky's basic premise about television—that it renders us passive consumers of media produced by others—may be undermined by new developments in the television industry that are aimed at engaging viewers and giving them more opportunities to interact with programs. In addition to shows that solicit our votes to affect or determine final outcomes (e.g., *Big Brother, American Idol*), many TV programs have Web sites where fans can contribute to discussions and find additional information about contestants and episodes (e.g., *Biggest Loser, Survivor*). ABC's *Lost* is well-known for the active participation of its fans in alternative forums, including Web sites, novels, podcasts, and other venues.

As a prewriting exercise for this assignment, make a list of the ways in which television programs use the Internet and other technologies to offer viewers more opportunities to interact and produce. Select what you see as the two or three most significant developments from this list and draft an essay in which you use these developments to argue against Shirky's claims about television. In your essay, discuss specific examples of interactive television programming—perhaps drawing on your own experience with these programs, as well.

Infotainment

Losing Our Religion

RUSSELL PETERSON

The first article in our case study on "infotainment TV" is adapted from the first chapter of Russell Peterson's 2008 Strange Bedfellows: How Late-Night Comedy Turns Democracy into a Joke. *As you can tell from the title and subtitle of the book, Peterson sees a clear mismatch between politics and comedy—or at least certain kinds of comedy. Jay Leno, David Letterman, and other mainstream late-night comedy hosts incur Peterson's criticism, whereas cable hosts Jon Stewart and Steven Colbert merit praise.*

Peterson draws a crucial distinction between cynicism and satire. As he puts it, "Unlike satire, which scolds and shames, [cynicism] merely shrugs" (paragraph 15). In other words, the satire of Stewart and Colbert are a kind of call to action, delivering a serious criticism of the political system, whereas the cynical and derisive political jokes of late-night comedy present a bleak and ultimately unproductive view of American democracy. Peterson knows something of the combination of politics and comedy: he's a former stand-up comedian and political cartoonist who currently teaches in the American Studies Department at the University of Iowa.

In drawing comparisons between late-night comedy and the comedy found on cable TV news shows, Peterson asks us to consider what we find funny. Toward the end of the article, he discusses two theorists—Sigmund Freud and Henri Bergson—who try to define the purpose of jokes and the function of laughter. **Before you read** *this article, think about the kinds of comedy and the individual comedians that you find funny. In particular, consider the late-night TV hosts and cable figures who Peterson discusses: Leno, Letterman, O'Brien, Stewart, and Colbert. Why do you appreciate the humor of some comedians but not of others?*

On the second Saturday after Easter, the city of Washington, D.C. wit- 1
nessed a miracle of sorts. The president of the United States appeared
before the assembled members of the White House Correspondents
Association accompanied by an uncanny doppelganger. This apparent
clone, who stood stage right of the commander in chief at a matching
podium, not only looked and sounded like George W. Bush, he seemed
to give voice to the president's subconscious thoughts: "Here I am at
another one of these dang press dinners: Could be home asleep, little
Barney curled up at my feet. Nooo. I gotta pretend I like being here.

Being here really ticks me off. The way they try to embarrass me by not editing what I say. Well, let's get things going so I can get to bed?"[1]

The president's double, actor Steve Bridges, did a heckuva job 2 reproducing his voice and gestures, and the crowd loved it. The members of the media elite erupted in laughter when George W. Bush's "inner voice" pronounced the first lady *"muy caliente."* It was the funniest and most elaborate presidential comedy routine since Bill Clinton's "Final Days" video, back in 2000.

But this wasn't the miracle, just a clever bit of stagecraft. The mir- 3 acle came after the Dueling Bushes routine, when Comedy Central's faux pundit Stephen Colbert stepped up to the lectern. What he said was not in itself so remarkable; the content of his routine was very much of a piece with the tongue-in-cheek right-wing pontificating seen four nights a week on *The Colbert Report*—a few of the jokes were even recycled from the show. What made his monologue startling—even awe-inspiring—was the fact that although the primary target of Colbert's ironic attack, the president of the United States, was sitting not six feet away from him, he pulled nary a punch. "The greatest thing about this man is, he's steady," proclaimed the comedian, with his impenetrable mock-sincerity. "You know where he stands. He believes the same thing Wednesday that he believed on Monday, no matter what happened Tuesday. Events can change; this man's beliefs never will." The president squirmed, his mottled face betraying the effort behind a strained smile. The audience, who had greeted the Bush/Bridges act with full-throated laughter, now sounded subdued, lapsing at times into uncomfortable silence. Colbert appeared undaunted. It was a brave and bracing performance, demonstrating what the comedian would call (in character) *muchos huevos grandes.*

That we live in a country where one can publicly criticize the head 4 of state is of course a kind of miracle in itself, one we perhaps too often take for granted. But to see *this* president—whose administration has specialized in intimidating critics and marginalizing dissent—mocked so mercilessly, to his face, in front of a cozy gathering of Washington insiders (who would suffer their own share of Colbert's satirical punishment that night), was like witnessing Moses calling down a plague of frogs on Pharaoh and his courtiers. That is, if Moses had been funny.

Yet the mainstream media, whose shindig this was, appeared to 5 leave all memory of Colbert's astonishing performance in the banquet hall, along with the parsley on their plates. Monday morning's *New York Times* ran a bubbly account of the president's "double" routine without so much as mentioning Colbert's name. Television news, both network and cable, followed suit, fawning over the video of the Bush "twins" as if it were the latest baby panda footage but avoiding any reference to the evening's controversial headliner.[2]

176

While the diners and the media corporations they represented 6
seemed to be experiencing selective amnesia, though, the Internet was
going Colbert-crazy. Liberal blogs sang his praises, while conservative
commentators condemned him for disrespecting the nation's chief
executive (something most of them had little problem countenancing
when that office was held by Bill Clinton). Someone launched a "Thank
You, Stephen Colbert" Web page, which in no time had registered the
gratitude of thousands of netizens who felt that President Bush had for
too long been treated far too gently by the mainstream press.[3]

When this cyber-rumbling began to grow too loud to ignore, a few 7
members of the diners' club decided they had better say something. But
they succeeded only in proving their critics right: the mainstream
media's belated response to Colbert was characterized by groupthink
and a preoccupation with style over substance. (Sure, his jokes pointed
out some unpleasant truths, but did he have to be so blunt about it?)
"The only thing worse than the mainstream media's ignoring Stephen
Colbert's astonishing sendup of the Bush administration and its media
courtiers," wrote *Salon's* Joan Walsh, "is what happened when they
started to pay attention to it." Indeed, from *Hardball's* human airhorn
Chris Matthews—who began his Siskel-and-Ebert bit with fellow irony-
challenged critic Mike Allen of *Time* magazine by asking, "Why was he
[Colbert] so bad?"—to Lloyd Grove of the *Daily News* to the *New York
Observer's* Christopher Lehman to alternative-media-emeritus Ana
Marie Cox (formerly of the Wonkette blog, now safely ensconced in the
media mainstream as a Time-Warner columnist, cable news bloviator,
and, incidentally, Mrs. Christopher Lehman), the pundit establishment
seemed to be on the same page. "The dreary consensus," noted Walsh,
was that "Colbert just wasn't funny."[4]

What is and isn't funny is of course a subjective judgment, but 8
there may have been more to this near-unanimity among the top tier of
television and print journalists—who happen to comprise most of the
guest list at events like the White House Correspondents Dinner—than
the fact that they all share remarkably similar tastes. "Why so defensive?" asked the *Washington Post's* media critic, Dan Froomkin. [5] Perhaps
it was because a mere comedian had not only embarrassed the press
corps's guest of honor but had also shown up his hosts by beating them
at what was supposed to be their own game: speaking truth to power.
The Fourth Estate is called that because it is meant to act as an extragov-
ernmental check on the judicial, legislative, and executive branches. But
the news media's compliant behavior in the wake of 9/11 and the run-up
to the invasion of Iraq, their failure to aggressively pursue a raft of
administration scandals, and even the cozy ritual of the Correspondents
Dinner itself belie that adversarial ideal. Colbert used the occasion to
backhandedly chide the press for their lazy complicity: "Here's how it

works: the president makes decisions. He's the decider. The press secretary announces those decisions, and you people of the press type those decisions down. Make, announce, type. Just put 'em through a spell check and go home. . . .Write that novel you got kicking around in your head. You know, the one about the intrepid Washington reporter with the courage to stand up to the administration. You know—fiction!"

It's hard to imagine a sharper critique of the press's failure to act as a watchdog, short of hitting Wolf Blitzer in the schnozz with a rolled-up newspaper. Colbert's real achievement, however, lies not in policing the standards of another profession but in asserting those of his own: for if "speaking truth to power" is part of the journalist's job, it is the satirist's primary mission—a higher calling, in fact, than merely being funny. 9

But if Colbert was just doing his job, why did it make the audience so uncomfortable? If this was just a case of satire fulfilling its function, why call it a miracle? Because, in spite of the fact that comedy *about* politics is now as common as crabgrass, political comedy—that is, genuine satire, which uses comedic means to advance a serious critique—is so rare we might be tempted to conclude it is extinct. Seeing it right there in front of God, the president, and the press corps was an astonishing moment, which stood out from the mundane rituals of politics and the press commonly seen on C-SPAN, *Meet the Press,* and the nightly news. It was like seeing an ivory-billed woodpecker alight on your satellite dish. 10

So "miracle" is indeed the word. Though some branded Colbert a heretic (the *Washington Post's* nominally liberal columnist Richard Cohen called him a "bully" for picking on the poor president), others saw him as a satirical evangelist, a Jonathan Edwards who took his text from the First Book of Jonathan Swift.[6] If the president and the press didn't laugh very much during the course of this sermon, it was because they recognized themselves as the sinners in the hands of an angry comedian. 11

Of course, it is possible that Colbert approached the dais with no mission in mind beyond making 'em laugh—though one suspects he and his writers are smart enough to know what they were getting into. Even if most of its practitioners would be loath to admit it, satire is a moral art. It calls on people and institutions to do their duty, as when Colbert scolded the press for their recent toothlessness: "Over the last five years you people were so good—over tax cuts, WMD intelligence, the effect of global warming," he said, wistfully. "We Americans didn't want to know, and you had the courtesy not to try to find out. Those were good times, as far as we knew." 12

This is the satirist as revivalist preacher, calling his congregation back to the True Faith. And in America—which, despite the efforts of the Christian Right, remains a secular nation—the name of that Faith is Democracy. Its holy book is the Constitution, its clergy the Supreme Court and our elected representatives, its congregants We the People, 13 its rituals voting and vigilance. Like other faiths—but unlike other governmental systems, which are held in place primarily through the threat of force—democracy depends on the devotion of its followers to sustain it. Some of the people, some of the time, must keep on believing that our electoral choices matter, that if we speak out our voices will be heard, that our representatives truly represent our interests. It's a tall order, but if we were to abandon all hope that democracy could endure—if democratic apathy reached the point of democratic atheism—our national faith would go the way of the cults of Baal, Zeus, Quetzalcoatl, and other unemployed divinities.

Thankfully, our civic religion has not yet reached its moment of   14
Nietzchean doom. But its tenets—equal justice for all; government of, by, and for the people—have been subjected to a subtle yet constant and corrosive barrage of blasphemous derision. It echoes from the office water cooler to the corner bar to the corridors of government itself. Most seductively, it rings out amidst the pealing laughter that emanates from millions of Americans' televisions each night.

THE LESSER OF TWO WEASELS: ANTI-POLITICAL COMEDY

While genuine satire arises from a sense of outrage, the topical jokes   15
heard in mainstream late-night monologues are rooted in mere cynicism. Unlike satire, which scolds and shames, this kind of comedy merely shrugs. Unlike Colbert, whose appearance at the Correspondents Dinner evoked a democratic revivalist, Jay Leno, David Letterman, and Conan O'Brien are evangelists of apathy.

The difference is easier to discern if we go back to a presidential   16
election year. So pick up that remote, hit rewind, and keep going, all the way back to 2004:

Political pundits are saying President George W. Bush has made gains
    in two key states: dazed and confused. (Letterman)
You see the pictures in the paper today of John Kerry windsurfing? . . .
Even his hobby depends on which way the wind blows. (Leno)
Earlier today, President Bush said Kerry will be a tough and hard-
    charging opponent. That explains why Bush's nickname for
    Kerry is "Math." (O'Brien)
Kerry was here in Los Angeles. He was courting the Spanish vote by
    speaking Spanish. And he showed people he could be boring in
    two languages. (Leno) [7]

A larger sampling would prove, as this selection suggests, that the   17
political jokes told by network late-night hosts aim, cumulatively, for a bipartisan symmetry. Although election season "joke counts" maintained

by the Center for Media and Public Affairs do not show a perfect one-to-one balance of jokes aimed at Democratic and Republican nominees, as the election got closer, a rough equity emerged, suggesting that George W. Bush was no more or less dumb than John Kerry was boring.[8] So it is in every presidential election year. Even in between, care is taken to target the abuse at "both sides," even if, during the Bush years, it has often meant resorting to time-worn Monica Lewinsky jokes. Maintaining this equilibrium is understood as one of the ground rules of the genre—a tenet so well established that an industry-specific cliché has arisen to describe those who embrace it: "equal-opportunity offenders."

The phrase, or the ideal it expresses, is typically brandished by late-night comics as a shield against charges of bias. But it is a paradigm embraced even more fervently by journalists who write about comedy. Bill Maher, Robin Williams, and Carlos Mencia—even an Israeli/Lebanese comedy team who bill their show as "The Arab-Israeli Comedy Hour"—have been celebrated in press accounts as equal-opportunity offenders. Being branded an EOO by the journalistic establishment is something like getting the Good Housekeeping Seal of Approval, though the honor is bestowed with some subjectivity. Sarah Silverman is praised by the *Milwaukee Journal Sentinel* for being one, and criticized by the *Houston Chronicle* for not being enough of one.[9]

To offend unequally, on the other hand, is offensive indeed. Page one of the August 22, 2004, *New York Times* Arts and Leisure section features a telling juxtaposition of two articles concerning topical comedy. At the top of the page, the *Times* frets that a few of those making jokes about President Bush have transgressed the boundaries of "just kidding" and crossed the line into genuine (gasp!) satire. Though Jon Stewart, for example, "has repeatedly insisted that he's nonpartisan," his jokes about the incumbent "have started to seem like a sustained argument with the president." A comedian using humor to express an opinion? *J'accuse!* Yet below the fold, the *Times* toasts *South Park* creators Matt Stone and Trey Parker's upcoming film, *Team America*, which promises to "take aim at sanctimonious right-wing nutjobs and smug Hollywood liberals alike." Parker takes the opportunity to assert his EOO bona fides: "People who go [to the film] will be really confused about whose side we're on. That's because we're really confused." Ah, that's what we like to see—fair and balanced comedy.[10]

Journalists' peculiar devotion to the equal-opportunity offender ideal results from a tendency to project their own profession's standards of objectivity onto comedians. Expecting Jay Leno to play by the same rules as Anderson Cooper is a bit like squeezing apples to get orange juice, but conventional wisdom seems to take this conflation of journalistic and comedic ethics for granted—the Pew poll, after all, asks its respondents to consider *The Tonight Show* and CNN side by

18

19

20

side. Comedians' own reasons for maintaining balance, however, have little to do with abstract notions of fairness; it's more a matter of pragmatism than idealism. As Jay Leno put it, once a comedian takes a political side, "you've lost half the crowd already." [11] These guys are in show *business*, after all, and it doesn't pay to alienate 50 percent of your potential viewers. Such bottom-line considerations, incidentally, help explain why *The Colbert Report* and *The Daily Show* can afford to be more politically "risky" than Leno's: a little over a million viewers—a narrowly interested but loyal core—amounts to a pretty respectable audience for a cable show like the *Report*, but for *The Tonight Show*, which averages six million viewers nightly, it would be a disaster. [12]

The bigger difference between the network and cable shows' humor has to do with what the jokes say, not how many of them are aimed at Democrats versus Republicans. On closer examination, the only political thing about the mainstream jokes quoted above is that they happen to be about politicians. They are personality jokes, not that different from the ones those same comedians tell about Paris Hilton or Ozzy Osbourne—just replace "dumb" and "boring" with "slutty" and "drug-addled." And unlike Colbert's jokes about Bush's inflexibility or his tendency to think with his "gut," the jokes told on the network shows rarely transcend the level of pure *ad hominem* mockery to consider how such personal traits might manifest themselves in terms of policy.   21

The bottom line of all the jokes about Bush's dumbness, Kerry's dullness, Al Gore's stiffness, Bob Dole's "hey-you-kids-get-outta-my-yard" crankiness, and so on is that all politicians are created equal—equally unworthy, that is—and that no matter who wins the election, the American people lose. Thus, despite their efforts to play it safe by offending equally (and superficially), the mainstream late-night comics actually present an extremely bleak and cynical view of American democracy.   22

What, then, is the secret of their appeal? Why do millions of us tune in, night after night, to be told—not overtly, but insinuatingly and consistently—that our cherished system of self-government is a joke? Perhaps because this confirms what we have always suspected: democracy is a nice idea but not, ultimately, a practical one. And if Americans doubt democracy, we hate politics. Politics is treated like an infection, or a tumor. It is to be avoided if possible, and when found lurking—in a sitcom writers' room, in an Oscar acceptance speech, in the funnies (*Doonesbury* has been exiled to the editorial pages of many of the papers that carry it)—it must be excised before it can infect the nation's body non-politic. Politics is *icky*.   23

Even our politicians disdain politics. A candidate can't go wrong by running against Washington, D.C., and all that it supposedly stands for. George W. "I'm from Texas" Bush successfully campaigned as an   24

181

anti-establishment "outsider"—and his dad was the president! Ronald Reagan got applause when he proclaimed that government was not the solution, but the problem—though he himself had just campaigned for, and achieved, the government's top job.[13]

Most Americans see nothing strange in this; for as much as we   25
like to wave the flag and pledge our allegiance to the republic for which it stands, as a people we regard our government, its institutions, and its representatives (save those who take care to inoculate themselves with anti-political rhetoric) with contempt. This feeling is reflected not only in our appallingly low voter turnout rates but also in our culture—particularly in our humor.

Which is why most of this country's "political" humor—from   26
Artemus Ward to Will Rogers, from Johnny Carson to Jay Leno, from Andy Borowitz to JibJab.com—has in fact been *anti*-political. "All politics is applesauce," Rogers once said, by which he did not mean that it was a tasty side dish with pork chops.[14] He meant that progress was the opposite of Congress, that the Democrats were worse than any other party except for the Republicans and vice versa, that six of one was half a dozen of the other. Will Rogers was an equal-opportunity offender.

Rogers's observation that "both parties have their good and bad   27
times . . . they are each good when they are out, and . . . bad when they are in" reappears almost seventy years later as Jay Leno's characterization of the 2000 election as a choice between "the lesser of two weasels." It appears again, in an "edgier" guise, when the *South Park* kids are given the opportunity to learn about democracy by nominating and voting for a new school mascot: "We're supposed to vote between a giant douche and a turd sandwich," Stan tells his parents, "I just don't see the point." His parents react with shocked sanctimony: "Stanley," scolds his mother, "do you know how many people died so you could have the right to vote?" Mom just doesn't get it.[15]

Whether the metaphor describes electoral choice as a contest   28
between a pair of rodents or between a feminine hygiene product and a piece of excrement, it's the same old joke. Anti-political humor is everywhere; clean or dirty, hip or square, as told by professionals over the airwaves and amateurs over the cubicle divider. In fact, what I think of as the quintessential anti-political joke is one I heard not from any television show but from my dad—and although this version dates from 1980, all that is necessary to make it work in any other presidential election year is to change the names:

> *Q:* If Jimmy Carter, Ronald Reagan, and John Anderson [that year's third-party threat] were all in a rowboat in the middle of the ocean, and the boat flipped over, who would be saved?
> *A:* The United States.

WHAT IS GOVERNMENT FOR? WHAT ARE JOKES FOR?

The implications of the rowboat riddle are fairly grim: no choice would   29
be better than the choice we have, and anyone who would presume to
be worthy of the people's vote deserves to drown like a rat. Yet this
nihilistic punch line is no more than a crystallization of the message
repeated night after night, joke after joke, by Jay, Dave, and Conan.
Late-night's anti-political jokes are implicitly anti-democratic. They
don't criticize policies for their substance, or leaders for their official
actions (as opposed to their personal quirks, which have little to do
with politics per se); taken as a whole, they declare the entire system—
from voting to legislating to governing—an irredeemable sham.

To understand the appeal of such anti-democratic heresy, it is help-   30
ful to start with a couple of fundamental questions. First, what is government for? The answer, according to the framers of the Constitution, is
to provide for the common defense, to promote the general welfare, and
so on. Or as Abraham Lincoln more succinctly put it, our government is
for the people—as well as by and of them. We, the people, choose our
government and therefore—indirectly, at least—are the government. The
U.S. is "us." Most of us learned this in elementary school.

183

When we grow up, however, this naïve faith in representative   31
democracy joins Santa Claus and the Easter Bunny on the scrap heap of
our childish beliefs. Even if we continue to believe, we tend to be a little
bit embarrassed about it. The majority of voters, in most election years,
would probably tell anyone who asked that they were holding their noses
as they entered the voting booth. We participate in the political process in
only the most minimal ways: we ignore local elections, few of us attend
caucuses or work as campaign volunteers, and between the first
Wednesday of November and the kickoff of the next season of attack ads,
we pay little attention to what our representatives do (unless there's a sex
scandal, of course). We treat democracy, our civic religion, only about as
seriously as what so-called C-and-E Christians (for Christmas and
Easter—the only occasions they bother to show up in church) treat theirs.
And of course the majority of those eligible to vote don't even bother.

Even lapsed voters may still profess faith in the democratic ideal,   32
but are likely to consider it lost to some more perfect past—before
Watergate, Irangate, or Monicagate; before PACs and lobbyists; back in
the days when politicians were statesmen, not these clowns you see
running for office nowadays. In just a century and a half, this version of
the anti-political argument goes, we've gone from Lincoln versus
Douglas to a douche versus a turd.

Of course, this is nostalgic nonsense; American leaders have been   33
failing to live up to their predecessors since Adams succeeded

Washington. The problem with the democratic ideal—with any ideal—is that reality will always fall short. Our candidates can never measure up to the Founding Fathers' patriarchal nobility, nor can our day-to-day experience of liberty, equality, and justice live up to the ringing words of the Declaration of Independence. Some years ago, Professor Louis Rubin dubbed the gap between the City on a Hill of our star-spangled dreams and the somewhat less utopian actualities of the nation we actually inhabit "the Great American Joke": "On the one hand there are the ideals of freedom, equality, self-government, the conviction that ordinary people can evince the wisdom to vote wisely, and demonstrate the capacity for understanding and cherishing the highest human values through embodying them in their political and social institutions. On the other hand there is the *Congressional Record*."[16] When you live in a country founded upon ideals—rather than the mere commonalities of tradition, language, and culture that formed the basis of older nations—you are doomed to perpetual disappointment.

But before further considering America's strained relation with its founding principles, let us turn to the second question: what are jokes for? This seemingly trivial query has in fact tested the cognitive powers of some pretty heavy-duty thinkers, from Aristotle to Immanuel Kant to Thomas Hobbes. Sigmund Freud provided one of the most useful contributions to this body of inquiry a century ago, in a book entitled *Jokes and Their Relation to the Unconscious.*[17] The purpose of joking, he theorized, is to help individuals cope with societal repression. At the core of all of Freud's work lies the assumption that even the most well-adjusted of us are carrying a heavy burden of hostility and sexual aggression. Bottling all that up can make us crazy, but if we allowed ourselves to express these impulses in an open and straightforward way, civilized society would be impossible—day-to-day life would resemble some unholy double feature of *Mad Max* and *Animal House*. So how do we get through the day? Freud identified a number of ways—many of which don't cost a hundred dollars an hour—including telling, and laughing at, jokes. Laughter is a safety valve for our anti-social drives. The rules of polite society (and the need to keep your job) prevent you from acting on your intensely felt desire to punch your boss in the teeth, but you can safely express that hostile impulse by imitating his stupid, jackass laugh for your coworkers during happy hour at the local bar.

Thus, laughter helps the individual cope with society. But might it also help society cope with the individual? According to Freud's contemporary, the philosopher Henri Bergson, the principal function of laughter is not so much to keep people sane as to keep them in line. "By laughter," he wrote, "society avenges itself for the liberties taken with it."[18] Whenever we laugh at someone whose comportment or behavior is somehow "wrong"—whether he or she is a nerd, a klutz, a pervert, a

34

35

ninny, or a fanatic—we reinforce what we consider to be "normal," non-laughable behavior. Laughter enforces conformity; it's the border collie that helps maintain the herd mentality.

How do these turn-of-the-twentieth-century Continental theories apply to contemporary American political comedy? First, and most obvious, laughing at political big shots is satisfying in the same way as laughing at your boss (because you can't punch the president, either). In fact, says Freud, if the target is big and important enough, the joke doesn't even have to be that good, "since we count any rebellion against authority as a merit" (a loophole *Saturday Night Live* has been exploiting for years).[19] Add to this basic truth the fact that America was born in rebellion and celebrates anti-authoritarianism in any form, from the Boston patriots' dumping tea in the harbor to Elvis's hip-swiveling impudence, and it's not hard to see how this point resonates with particular force in our culture.

Bergson's argument about laughter and social conformity speaks to one of the main sources of our democratic skepticism. If we take the idea that "all men are created equal" to be a fundamental American "norm" (and there is no principle we claim to hold dearer), then grasping at political power—seeking, that is, to escape the very equality that allows any one of us to run for office in the first place—is a violation of that norm. A fella (or even a gal) would have to think he's pretty hot stuff to sit in the House or Senate—to say nothing of the White House—and round these parts we don't cotton to folks what's too big for their britches. This is the central paradox of American representative democracy: the egalitarian idea that anyone can grow up to be president is inseparable from the notion that none of us deserves such an honor. This is why potential leaders of the free world go to such absurd lengths to look like someone you'd like to have a beer with: *I guess it's okay he wants to be president, as long as he doesn't think he's any better than us.*

Oddly enough, our devotion to the principles on which our government is founded—liberty (no one can tell me what I can and cannot do) and egalitarianism (none of us is any better than anyone else)—makes it impossible for us to believe in government itself. Government makes all kinds of demands on our liberty—we must pay our taxes, obey the laws, serve on juries, or even, at various points in our history, serve in the military. Moreover, it derives its authority to do all of this based on the unacceptably contradictory principle that our elected representatives, who supposedly serve at our pleasure, are also somehow the boss of us.

We carry this paradox, and the resentment that goes along with it, in the backs of our minds even as we cast our ballots, salute the flag, or send our children off to war. It is the shadow side of our patriotism; the doubt at the heart of our devotion; our secular, civic version of original sin. It's the small, insistent voice that grumbles, even as we recite the

36

37

185

38

39

Pledge of Allegiance or sing "The Star-Spangled Banner." *Yeah, right*. It is the voice of anti-political, anti-democratic heresy, echoing down the centuries, and from all across the political spectrum. It is the common complaint of left-wing anarchists like Abbie Hoffman (author of *Revolution for the Hell of It*), right-wing libertarians like anti-tax crusader Grover Norquist, civilly disobedient dropouts like Henry David Thoreau—even anti-state vigilantes like Timothy McVeigh.[20] In their own lighthearted way, late-night comics are torchbearers in this same anti-political parade. Unlike McVeigh, the damage they do is merely insidious, and largely invisible; but unlike Hoffman, Norquist, and Thoreau, they reach tens of millions of Americans each night.

DEFENDING THE FAITH: A PLACE FOR SATIRE?

In spite of its anti-democratic implications, anti-politics (and anti-political humor) is itself a bedrock American tradition: a contrarian habit as old as the republic itself. Atop this foundation of anti-political disdain, we have in recent decades been building a towering Fortress of Irony, reaching, by the turn of the twenty-first century, a point where it seems as if every communication is enclosed in air quotes. In contemporary America, sincerity is suspect, commitment is lame, and believing in stuff is for suckers. 40

Late-night comics did not invent the air-quote culture, anymore than they invented our anti-political sentiments, but they have played a leading role in proselytizing this cynical message. Election after election, night after night, joke after joke, they have reinforced the notion that political participation is pointless, parties and candidates are interchangeable, and democracy is futile. 41

This is not to suggest that comedy that takes politics as its subject matter is inherently destructive. Mocking our elected representatives and our institutions is an American birthright, and exercising that right is worthwhile, if only to maintain it. The problem is not the presence, or even the proliferation, of political comedy per se. The problem is that too little of it is actually "political" in any meaningful way. Genuine political satire, like good investigative journalism, can function as democracy's feedback loop. It can illuminate injustices, point out hypocrisy, and tell us when our government is not living up to its ideals, thereby raising the awareness that is the first step toward alleviating any of these problems. Real satire—such as Colbert's excoriation of the press and the president—sounds the alarm: something is wrong, people must be held to account, things must be made right. Anti-political humor—the far more common kind, practiced by Leno, Letterman, and O'Brien, among others—merely says, resignedly, "Eh, what are you gonna do?" 42

Yet the public, and especially the press, are so blinded by anti- 43
political disdain and unblinking devotion to the equal-opportunity
offender idea, that we have difficulty distinguishing genuine satire
from the ersatz kind, even when we see it. In a feature on *The Colbert
Report* (published several months before the Correspondents Dinner),
Newsweek stubbornly hangs on to the news media's beloved apolitical
paradigm: "[Though his] character is clearly a parody of God-fearing,
pro-business, Bush-loving Republicans . . . Colbert guards his personal
views closely, and if you watch the show carefully you'll see subtle digs
at everyone on the political-media map." With what seems like willful
naiveté, the magazine seizes on the host's rote disclaimer that his show
is strictly for laughs: "Despite the fact that politics is a primary inspiration and target, Colbert isn't interested in being political."[21]

Whether he's interested or not, though, Colbert's show *is* politi- 44
cal, in a way that the more traditional late-night programs—and, even
for all their enthusiastic offensiveness, the works of Stone and Parker—
are not. *The Colbert Report* is not an equal-opportunity offender. Neither
is *The Daily Show.* Nor, for that matter, is Bill Maher, who has definitely
met a man (or two) he didn't like. This is not to say that the *Report* is liberal propaganda, nor to deny that Colbert, Stewart, and Maher take
satirical shots at "both sides"—though perhaps it is worth considering
what would be so terrible about comedy that expresses a consistent
point of view. But the important difference between the smallish van-
guard of cable comics and the late-night mainstream is not so much a
matter of taking political sides as of taking politics seriously. It is the
difference between engaging with the subject and merely dismissing it.
Satire, at its best, is not just a drive-by dissing but exactly what the
Times accuses Jon Stewart of presenting: "a sustained argument."[22]
Consider the way Colbert deconstructs Bush's fetish for "resolve."
Watch how *The Daily Show* analyzes official rhetoric, as when Stewart
goes sound bite for sound bite with a videotaped politician, calling
attention to every outrage and evasion. Left or right, right or wrong,
fair or unfair, this is comedy that engages us in politics instead of offering us an easy out. It is a form of debate, not just entertainment; and as
such, it should be welcomed, not treated as "rude," or inappropriate.

Undoubtedly, many of the guests at the Correspondents Dinner— 45
including the president—would have had a more pleasant evening listening to the inoffensive humor of, say, Jay Leno. There's nothing wrong
with innocent laughter, of course. But insofar as our appetite for the
dismissive, plague-on-both-their-houses, progress versus Congress,
Tweedledum versus Tweedledee, pot-calling-the-kettle-black variety of
"political" humor reflects our fundamental doubts about the value of
political participation, and the viability of democracy, it is no laughing
matter.

187

NOTES

[1]The 2006 White House Correspondents Association Dinner was first broadcast on C-SPAN, April 29, 2006.

[2]Elisabeth Bumiller, "A New Set of Bush Twins Appear at Annual Correspondents' Dinner," *New York Times*, May 1, 2006, Lexis-Nexis, via Infohawk, http://web.lexisnexis.com.proxy.lib.uiowa.edu. On "followed suit," see Dan Froomkin, "The Colbert Blackout," *Washington Post*, May 2, 2006, http://www.washingtonpost.com/wpdyn/content/blog/2006/05/02/BL2006050200755.html (accessed March 14, 2007). See also Josh Kalven and Simon Maloy, "Media Touted Bush's Routine at Correspondents' Dinner, Ignored Colbert's Skewering," *Media Matters*, May 1, 2006; Julie Millican, "For Third Day in a Row, Good Morning America Touted Bush's White House Correspondents Dinner Skit While Ignoring Colbert's Routine," *Media Matters*, May 3, 2006, both available at http://mediamatters.org.

[3]Froomkin, "The Colbert Blackout"; "Thank You, Stephen Colbert" Web site, http://thankyoustephencolbert.org.

[4]Joan Walsh, "Making Colbert Go Away," *Salon*, May 3, 2006, http://www.salon.com/opinion/feature/2006/05/03/correspondents/index_np.html (accessed June 1, 2006), including Grove, Lehman, and Cox quotes; Mike Allen and Chris Matthews, *Hardball with Chris Matthews*, MSNBC, May 1, 2006.

[5]Dan Froomkin, "Why So Defensive?" *Washington Post*, May 4, 2006, http://www.washingtonpost.com/wp-dyn/content/blog/2006/05/04/BL2006050400967.html (accessed June 1, 2006).

[6]Richard Cohen, "So Not Funny," *Washington Post*, May 4, 2006, http://www.washingtonpost.com/wp-dyn/content/article/2006/05/03/AR2006050302202 html (accessed June 1, 2006).

[7]Letterman, retrieved from About.com Political Humor, "Late-Night Jokes about President Bush from 2004," comp. Daniel Kurtzman, http://politicalhumor.about.com/library/blbush2004jokes.htm (accessed June 1, 2006); Leno and O'Brien, retrieved from About.com Political Humor, "Late-Night Jokes about John Kerry," comp. Daniel Kurtzman, http://politicalhumor.about.com/library/bljohnkerryjokes. htm (accessed June 1, 2006).

[8]Center for Media and Public Affairs (CMPA), "Joke Archive, through August 24, 2004," http://www.cmpa.com/politicalHumor/archiveapri116th. htm (accessed March 14, 2007). President Bush held a commanding lead over Kerry for the year to date, but when Kerry became the presumptive and then official nominee, the numbers started to even out. Unfortunately, data for the months leading up to the election are unavailable, but in examining this and the other years' joke counts, the trend is clear.

[9]Alex Strachan, "Maher Targets Left and Right in Comedy Special," *Montreal Gazette*, Nov. 1, 2003; Doug Moore, "Williams' Act Has St. Louis Laughing at Itself," *St. Louis Post-Dispatch Everyday Magazine*, March 21, 2002; Gary Budzak, "Outspoken Honduras Native an Equal-Opportunity Offender," *Columbus Dispatch*, Jan. 6, 2005; Debra Pickett, "Middle East Duo Bets That Misery Loves Comedy," *Chicago Sun-Times*, June 6, 2003; Duane Dudek, "Blinded by the Bite; Silverman Skewers All with a Smile in 'Jesus,' " *Milwaukee Journal Sentinel*, Dec. 16, 2005; Bruce Westbrook, "Provocative Comedy:

No Magic in Silverman's 'Jesus,' " *Houston Chronicle*, Dec. 9, 2005, Lexis-Nexis, via Infohawk, http://web.lexis-nexis.com.proxy.lib. uiowa. edu.

[10]Jason Zengerle, "The State of the George W. Bush Joke," and Sharon Waxman, "The Boys from 'South Park' Go to War," *New York Times*, Aug. 22, 2004, national ed., Arts and Leisure, 1.

[11]Marshall Sella, "The Stiff Guy vs. the Dumb Guy," *New York Times Magazine*, Sept. 24, 2000, 74.

[12]*Tonight Show* viewership 6.4 million viewers, per Toni Fitzgerald, "Sunrise Surprise: The CBS Early Show," *Media Life*, March 1, 2007, http://www.medialifemagazine.com/artman/publish/article_10482.asp (accessed March 15, 2007); *Colbert Report* viewership approximately 1.2 million, *Daily Show's* 1.6 million, per Julie Bosman, "Serious Book to Peddle? Don't Laugh, Try a Comedy Show," *New York Times*, Feb. 25, 2007, Lexis-Nexis, via Infohawk, http://web.lexis-nexis. com.proxy.lib.uiowa.edu.

[13]In his first debate with Al Gore in 2000, Bush said, "I fully recognize I'm not of Washington. I'm from Texas." See Richard L. Berke, "Bush and Gore Stake Out Differences in First Debate," *New York Times*, Oct. 4, 2000. Reagan's "government is the problem" remark is from his First Inaugural speech, as printed under the headline "Let Us Begin an Era of National Renewal," *New York Times*, Jan. 21, 1981, Lexis-Nexis, via Infohawk, http://web.lexis-nexis.com.proxy.lib.uiowa.edu.

[14]Will Rogers, quoted in *Bartlett's Familiar Quotations*, 15th ed., ed. Emily Morrison Beck (Boston: Little, Brown, 1980), 765.

[15]Will Rogers, *The Best of Will Rogers*, ed. Bryan B. Sterling (New York: Crown Publishers, 1979), 55; Leno, *Tonight*, Nov. 6, 2000; *South Park*, episode 808, "Douche and Turd," first aired Oct. 27, 2004.

[16]Louis D. Rubin, "The Great American Joke," in *What's So Funny? Humor in American Culture*, ed. Nancy A. Walker (Wilmington, DE: Scholarly Resources, 1998), 109–110.

[17]Sigmund Freud, *Jokes and Their Relation to the Unconscious*, trans. James Strachey (New York: W. W. Norton, 1963).

[18]Henri Bergson, *Laughter: An Essay on the Meaning of the Comic*, trans. Cloudesley Brereton and Fred Rothwell (Los Angeles: Green Integer Books, 1999), 176.

[19]Freud, *Jokes*, 105.

[20]Abbie Hoffman (a.k.a. "Free"), *Revolution for the Hell of It* (New York: Dial Books, 1968). For a useful overview of the history of American anti-political sentiment, see Garry Wills, *A Necessary Evil: A History of American Distrust of Government* (New York: Simon & Schuster, 1999).

[21]Marc Peyser, "The Truthiness Teller," *Newsweek*, Feb. 13, 2006, Lexis-Nexis via Infohawk, http://web.lexis-nexis.com.proxy.lib.uiowa.edu.

[22]Zengerle, "The State of the George W. Bush Joke," 1.

Examining the Text

1. Peterson opens this article with an anecdote about Stephen Colbert's talk at the White House Correspondents Association dinner in 2006. Why does Peterson refer to the Colbert episode as a "miracle"? What significance does Peterson draw from the media's reactions to Colbert's jokes?

2. Peterson refers to the satirist as a kind of "revivalist preacher" (paragraph 13); what does he mean by this? What sort of revival does Peterson think Colbert and Stewart deliver? How is this understanding of satire related to the title of the article: "Losing Our Religion"?

3. According to Peterson, what are the key differences between the genuine satire of cable TV hosts like Colbert and the mere cynicism of mainstream late-night comedy? Why does Peterson consider it cynical to be an "equal-opportunity offender" like Leno, Letterman, and O'Brien are?

4. Peterson claims that "Late-night's anti-political jokes are implicitly anti-democratic." What examples does he provide to support this claim? Do you find the examples—and the claim itself—persuasive? Do you agree with Peterson's assessment of the anti-democratic sentiment that is "the shadow side of our patriotism" (paragraph 39)?

5. *Thinking rhetorically:* Peterson is clearly no fan of the George W. Bush administration; for instance, he states early in the article that this administration "has specialized in intimidating critics and marginalizing dissent" (paragraph 4). What effect does Peterson's clear political affiliation have on your response to the article? If you agree with Peterson's political stance, does it make you more likely to accept his analysis? If you disagree with his political stance, do you find yourself looking for reasons to disagree with his analysis as well?

For Group Discussion

According to Peterson, cable TV news shows like *The Daily Show* and *The Colbert Report* offer the possibility of "genuine political satire" (paragraph 42); it is "comedy that engages us in politics, instead of offering us an easy way out" (paragraph 44). In a small group, discuss the extent to which you agree with Peterson's argument. If you watch these shows, do you think that they've influenced your attitude toward politics? In your experience, do these shows present a substantively different view of politics than you see in late-night comedy or elsewhere on TV?

Writing Suggestion

Peterson makes a number of claims about the typical American attitude toward politics:

- "Politics is treated like an infection, or a tumor. It is to be avoided if possible . . ." (paragraph 23).
- "Even our politicians disdain politics. A candidate can't go wrong by running against Washington, D.C., and all that it supposedly stands for" (paragraph 24).
- "The majority of voters, in most election years, would probably tell anyone who asked that they were holding their noses as they entered the voting booth. We participate in the political process in only the most minimal ways" (paragraph 31).

To test these claims, interview several fellow students about their political attitudes, and write an essay in which you report on what you discovered from these interviews.

As a first step, draft a series of questions to ask; you might consider asking questions about actual political participation ("Have you ever volunteered for a campaign?"), about knowledge of politics ("Can you name the U.S. Representative for your home district?"), and about attitudes toward politics and politicians ("Do you think most politicians are honest?"). Remember that if you ask specific questions you're more likely to get interesting responses; for this reason, you should avoid simply asking "What's your attitude toward politics?"

After you've drafted your list of questions and selected your interviewees, conduct the interviews. If you interview people face-to-face or over the phone, be sure to take notes that you can use later as you write your essay; you might also choose to interview people via email, but keep in mind that their responses might not be as detailed as if they were speaking, and that you won't have the opportunity to ask follow-up questions.

After conducting the interviews, identify four or five key ideas that emerged and focus your essay on explaining those ideas. In other words, don't simply present the transcripts of the interviews, but rather use selected quotations from the interviews to support specific points you discovered.

Amusing Ourselves to Death with Television News: Jon Stewart, Neil Postman, and the Huxleyan Warning

GERALD J. ERION

While most people would agree that they watch television primarily to be entertained, the term "infotainment"—along with the range of news and educational shows on TV—implies that we can be simultaneously informed and entertained. In the article that follows, though, Gerald Erion argues that TV does a very poor job of informing us, particularly about important issues and events. Erion draws on the work of Neil Postman to argue that the medium of television simply can't represent serious public discourse: "Just as ventriloquism and mime don't play well on radio, 'thinking does not play well on television' (p. 90)." Erion here is quoting from Postman's book Amusing Ourselves to Death; *you can tell from the title of this book that Postman, and Erion, think we're making a critical mistake if we expect television to inform us about serious issues.*

However, Erion sees value in The Daily Show *precisely because it also critiques television. He argues that several features of the show offer a Postman-esque condemnation of television news, and he also draws on Stewart's controversial 2004 appearance on* Crossfire *to support his thesis that Stewart is quite critical of mainstream television.*

Erion teaches courses in philosophy and general education at Medaille College in Buffalo, New York. The article that follows first appeared in a collection of essays entitled The Daily Show and Philosophy, *in which authors applied various philosophical principles and approaches to study* The Daily Show. *As you read this article, pay attention to the connections that Erion draws between Neil Postman, Marshall McLuhan, Aldous Huxley, and finally Jon Stewart. How do the lines of influence operate?*

While *The Daily Show* is undoubtedly funny, it also provides an intriguing study of our contemporary media environment. Indeed, hidden within many of Jon Stewart's funniest jokes are implicit critiques of the way television tends to report its news and host its public discussions of important issues. For instance, Stewart's opening rundown of the news as television covers it doesn't merely ridicule the day's major players and events, but also makes fun of the way television gathers and presents the news. In this way, over-the-top graphics and music packages, attractive but superficial "Senior Correspondents," and all the other trappings of television newscasts become fodder for *The Daily Show's* writing staff. More than just a "fake news" program, *The Daily Show* offers a rare brand of humor that requires its audience to recognize a deeper, more philosophical criticism of contemporary television news. 1

From time to time, Stewart takes these implicit critiques of contemporary media and makes them explicit. Such was the case during his October 2004 appearance on CNN's since-cancelled *Crossfire*, when Stewart begged his hosts to "stop hurting America" with their substitution of entertaining pseudo-journalism for serious reporting and debate. Through this bold, format-breaking effort, Stewart highlighted the difference between thoughtful discussion and the theater of today's vapid television punditry. As we will see, Stewart's analysis of the present state of mass communication echoes that of the celebrated New York University media theorist Neil Postman, whose discerning insights ground some of Stewart's sharpest comic bits. 2

AMUSING OURSELVES TO DEATH

Neil Postman's *Amusing Ourselves to Death* is a book about the many forms of human communication and how those forms influence the 3 messages that we communicate to one another. Postman acknowledges a significant intellectual debt here to Marshall McLuhan, and sees his own thesis as something of a revised version of McLuhan's famous pronouncement that "the medium is the message."[1] However, Postman extends McLuhan's ideas in ways that are both distinctive and significant.

For example, consider Postman's discussion of smoke signals. 4 While the medium of smoke might be an effective way to communicate relatively simple messages over intermediate distances, many other types of messages can't be transmitted this way. Philosophical arguments, for instance, would be especially difficult to conduct with smoke signals because, as Postman puts it: "Puffs of smoke are insufficiently complex to express ideas on the nature of existence [or other philosophical concepts], and even if they were not, a Cherokee philosopher would run short of either wood or blankets long before he reached his second axiom. You cannot use smoke to do philosophy. Its form excludes the content."[2] So, the medium of smoke has a significant influence on the kind of content it can be used to communicate. At a minimum, smoke signaling restricts both the complexity and the duration of the messages it carries. Likewise, we shall see that *The Daily Show's* comedy often reflects the restrictions placed by our contemporary electronic media (including television) upon their content.

193

THE HUXLEYAN WARNING

Now, as Postman sees it, *all* media influence their content, and in a 5 multitude of different ways. He writes: "[Mine] is an argument that fixes its attention on the forms of human conversation, and postulates that how we are obliged to conduct such conversations will have the strongest possible influence on what ideas we can conveniently express" (p. 6). This goes not only for smoke signals, but also for speech and written language, and even for the electronic media that are so important in our contemporary lives.

Of particular interest here is the ubiquitous medium of television, 6 which Postman sees as a historic extension of such earlier media as the telegraph, photography, radio, and film.[3] How does television influence its content, according to Postman? His theory is complex, but in essence it maintains that television's inherent "bias" implies a tendency to render its content—even its most important news reports, political and religious discussions, and educational lessons—more *entertaining* than they would be otherwise, and consequently less serious, less rational, less relevant, and less coherent as well (pp. 67–80, 85–98).

The fact that television provides entertainment isn't, in and of itself, 7 a problem for Postman. He warns, however, that dire consequences can befall a culture in which the most important public discourse, conducted via television, becomes little more than irrational, irrelevant, and incoherent entertainment. Again, we shall see that this is a point often suggested by *The Daily Show's* biting satire. In a healthy democracy, the open discussion of important issues must be serious, rational, and coherent. But such discussion is often time-consuming and unpleasant, and thus incompatible with television's drive to entertain. So, it's hardly surprising to see television serving up important news analyses in sound bites surrounded by irrelevant graphics and video footage, or substituting half-minute ad spots for substantial political debates. On television, thoughtful conversations about serious issues are reserved for only the lowest-rated niche programs. Just as ventriloquism and mime don't play well on radio, "thinking does not play well on television" (p. 90).[4] Instead, television serves as a hospitable home for the sort of "gut"-based discourse celebrated by Stephen Colbert.[5]

When we grow comfortable with the substitution of televised entertainment for serious public discourse, we begin the process of (to use Postman's words) "amusing ourselves to death." As Postman explains, this form of cultural corrosion is like that described in Aldous Huxley's classic novel *Brave New World,* in which the citizenry is comfortably and willingly distracted by the pleasures of *soma,* Centrifugal Bumble-puppy, and the feelies (pp. vii–viii, 155–6). 8

POSTMAN AND TELEVISION NEWS

Postman and the writing staff of *The Daily Show* seem to agree that television's presentation of news tends to degrade its content in significant ways. Consider Postman's explanation of the ironic title of his chapter on television news, "Now . . . This:" "There is no murder so brutal, no earthquake so devastating, no political blunder so costly—for that matter no ball score so tantalizing or weather report so threatening—that it cannot be erased from our minds by a newscaster saying 'Now . . . this'" (p. 99). Thus, Postman maintains that the use of "Now . . . this" is a tacit admission of the incoherence of television news, and "a compact metaphor for the discontinuities in so much that passes for public discourse in present-day America" (p. 99). 9

Of course, Postman believes that television does more to the news than disrupt its coherence. Revisiting his general thesis about how television influences its content, Postman also claims that televised news is irrational, irrelevant, and trivial. As he explains, television presents us "not only with fragmented news but news without context, without consequences, without value, and therefore without essential seriousness; that is to say, news as pure entertainment" (p. 100). So, even weighty news subjects can become entertaining under the influence of television, 10 as the typical American newscast showcases a company of attractive reporters skipping from dramatic local stories to dramatic international stories, to celebrity gossip, to weather forecasts, to sports scores, to a closing story about babies or puppies or kittens. Commercials are scattered throughout. Music, graphics, and captivating video footage add touches of theater to the program. Quick transitions from one segment to the next ensure that audience members don't become bored—or troubled—for long.[6] Instead of useful and important information, then, viewers are treated to the impotent but entertaining trivia that Postman calls "disinformation," which isn't necessarily false but *misleading,* creating the *illusion of knowing* and undermining one's motivation to learn more (p. 107). Consequently, Postman writes, "Americans are the best entertained and quite likely the least well-informed people in the Western world" (p. 106).

THE DAILY SHOW AND TELEVISION NEWS

Now, as far as I know, the writing staff of *The Daily Show* doesn't publicly acknowledge Postman's influence. It's even possible that they've never heard of Postman. Nonetheless, it's clear that these general ideas about television news, whatever their sources, can help us to see the significance of some of the program's wittiest and most inspired jokes. *The Daily Show* is often described as a "fake news" program, but in fact, it's more than that. Much of its humor rests on Postman-like insights that highlight the peculiar ways in which the medium of television itself influences the news that it conveys. 11

For example, most episodes of *The Daily Show* begin with Stewart's rundown of the day's headlines as reported by the major television news programs. A comedy show that only does "fake news" might simply build jokes around the content of these headlines, or perhaps report fictional news stories in a humorous way. On *The Daily Show,* though, the way in which television seems destined to render its news as entertainment often serves as the basis for these opening segments. In recent years, Stewart and company have often joked about the major networks' coverage of natural disasters. In many of these cases, they simply replay absurd clips of television reporters standing outside during hurricanes, sitting in cars with giant thermometers during heat waves, or paddling canoes through inch-deep "flooded" city streets. Other segments mock the way hordes of television reporters cover celebrity weddings, arrests, and criminal trials. Segments like "International Pamphlet" and "The Less You Know" contain their own jokes but also poke fun at the shallowness of typical television news coverage. Exchanges between Stewart and his Senior Correspondents parody 12

their good-looking but sometimes ill-informed network counterparts.[7]
Even *The Daily Show's* clever graphics packages ("Mess O' Potamia,"
"Crises in Israfghyianonanaq," and so on) offer satirical imitations of the
logos, diagrams, and pictorial illustrations so essential to today's television newscasts. Moreover, Stewart himself has attacked the way television is compelled to report "breaking news" with what at times seems to
be inadequate or uncorroborated information, mere speculation, and no
editing whatsoever; shortly after the Washington, DC-area sniper shootings of 2002, he joked with CNN's Howard Kurtz: "By watching the 24-
hour news networks, I learned that the sniper was an olive-skinned,
white-black male—men—with ties to Son of Sam, Al Qaeda, and was a
military kid, playing video games, white, 17, maybe 40."[8] In these kinds
of segments, then, *The Daily Show* is clearly doing more than just "fake
news." It's also offering deep satire that relies on its audience's appreciation of the substance of Postman's thesis, that television has a significant
and sometimes adverse influence on the news content it reports.

At this point, one might be tempted to suggest that *The Daily Show* 13
simply reproduces the unfortunate transformation of reporting into
entertainment, as if *The Daily Show* were itself a source of news for its
audience members. For instance, Bill O'Reilly (host of the Fox News program *The O'Reilly Factor*) once famously dubbed viewers of *The Daily
Show* "stoned slackers" who "get their news from Jon Stewart."[9]
However, at least one prominent study by the Annenberg Public Policy
Center found that viewers of *The Daily Show* were *better* informed about
the positions and backgrounds of candidates in the 2004 U.S. Presidential
campaign than most others. Indeed, it's difficult to see how the deepest
Daily Show jokes could be appreciated by an audience unaware of the relevant social, political, and other newsworthy issues. As Annenberg analyst Dannagal Goldthwaite Young put it in a press release announcing the
Center's Election Survey results, *"The Daily Show* assumes a fairly high
level of political knowledge on the part of its audience."[10]

CONVERSATION AND *CROSSFIRE*

Postman's ideas about television also illuminate Stewart's infamous 14
October 15, 2004, appearance on CNN's *Crossfire*. First aired in 1982,
Crossfire was a long-running staple of CNN's lineup that featured curt
discussion by hosts and guests supposedly representing both left-wing
and right-wing positions on controversial political issues. Co-hosting for
Stewart's visit were the unsuspecting Paul Begala and Tucker Carlson,
neither of whom seemed prepared for what would become an extraordinary exchange. Instead of simply participating in a typical *Crossfire*-style
debate (described by more than one observer as a "shoutfest"), Stewart

quickly launched into a Postman-like criticism of the vapid and partisan punditry that passes for serious discussion on programs like *Crossfire*.

In fact, this theme is one that Stewart had explored before his *Crossfire* appearance. The recurring *Daily Show* segment, "Great Moments in Punditry as Read by Children," draws laughs simply by having children read from transcripts of shows like *Crossfire*. Moreover, during an interview with Bill Moyers, Stewart claimed that both *Crossfire* and its MSNBC counterpart *Hardball* were "equally dispiriting" in the way their formats degrade political discourse.[11] And in his interview with CNN's Howard Kurtz, Stewart foreshadowed his *Crossfire* appearance by chiding the news network for offering entertainers instead of "real journalists" and pleaded, "You're the news . . . People need you. Help us. Help us."[12]

On the *Crossfire* set, though, Stewart offered his most sustained attack against the shallow conversational style of television. Before either Begala or Carlson could catch his balance, Stewart was already begging them to "stop, stop, stop, stop hurting America" with their "partisan hackery," which he claimed serves only politicians and corporations and does nothing to help ordinary citizens make informed decisions.[13] "We need help from the media," Stewart said, "and they're hurting us." Carlson tried to counter Stewart's charges with the allegation that Stewart himself had been too lenient during the *Daily Show* appearance of 2004 Presidential candidate John Kerry. Stewart replied that there was a fundamental difference between journalism and comedy, snapping back, "I didn't realize that . . . the news organizations look to Comedy Central for their cues on integrity." And when Begala tried to defend the *Crossfire* format by claiming that it was a "debate show," Stewart pointed to Carlson's trademark bow tie as evidence that *Crossfire* is "doing theater, when you should be doing debate." Finally, Stewart charged, "You have a responsibility to the public discourse, and you fail miserably." Because of such remarks, Stewart's *Crossfire* appearance produced a rare opportunity for reflecting about the effects of television on public discourse. Indeed, the incident sparked much additional discussion in, for example, the *New York Times, Newsweek,* and countless electronic media outlets.

Once again, we can see that these are the sorts of criticisms developed by Postman in *Amusing Ourselves to Death.* His deepest discussion of such issues concerns ABC's controversial 1983 broadcast of the film *The Day After,* which depicts the bleak effects of a nuclear strike on the American Midwest. Given the film's grave subject matter, ABC decided to follow it with a roundtable discussion moderated by Ted Koppel and featuring such notable figures as Henry Kissinger, Elie Wiesel, Carl Sagan, and William F. Buckley.[14] With a serious theme and a guest list of unquestionable distinction, Koppel proceeded to march

15

16

197

17

his cast through a fragmented eighty minutes of "conversation" in which the participants rarely engaged one another on points of substance. Instead, they used their camera time to push whatever points they had decided to make beforehand, without regard to the contributions of their fellow participants. Postman writes:

> Each of the six men was given approximately five minutes to say something about the subject. There was, however, no agreement on exactly what the subject was, and no one felt obliged to respond to anything anyone else had said. In fact, it would have been difficult to do so, since the participants were called upon seriatim, as if they were finalists in a beauty contest. (p. 89)

To put it another way, this wasn't a genuine discussion, but a *pseudo-discussion* warped by television's drive to entertain. "There were no arguments or counterarguments, no scrutiny of assumptions, no explanations, no elaborations, no definitions" (p. 90), and yet each of these elements is essential to genuine and thoughtful dialogue. 18

So, how did ABC go wrong? According to Postman, the root problem remains that thoughtful conversation just isn't entertaining, and thus plays poorly on television. Televised discussions about even the most serious of subjects tend to be rendered in forms that are more amusing or dramatic than reflective. On this, both Postman and the writing staff of *The Daily Show* agree.[15] Moreover, CNN President Jonathan Klein cited Stewart's critique when he announced the cancellation of *Crossfire* in January 2005. In an interview with the *Washington Post,* Klein said, "I think [Stewart] made a good point about the noise level of these types of shows, which does nothing to illuminate the issues of the day." [16] 19

A HUXLEYAN MOMENT OF ZEN?

So, it appears that much of *The Daily Show's* sharpest comedy requires its audience to grasp a Postmanesque criticism of television news. In addition, Stewart himself seems to offer a more general critique of today's televised public discourse that is reminiscent of Postman's in several significant ways. This isn't to say, however, that Postman and Stewart are in perfect agreement. For one thing, Postman argues that the transformation of serious discussion into entertainment is all but inevitable when this discussion takes place on television. Stewart, on the other hand, seems to believe that television can do better. As we've seen, he has even appeared on CNN and used the news network's own programs to issue his call for reform. Postman and Stewart might also disagree about the suitability of television as a vehicle for sophisticated media criticism. Postman writes, for example, that any televised critique of television would likely be 20 "coopted" by the medium, and thus rendered in the typical fashion as mere entertainment (pp. 161–2).[1] In his eyes, television is simply incapable of carrying serious public discourse, including serious public discourse about mass communication itself. That Stewart has appeared on *Crossfire* and other such programs to address this issue suggests that he believes otherwise. No doubt this is a question worth further consideration, and through any medium capable of giving it a thoughtful hearing.

NOTES

[1]Marshall McLuhan, *Understanding Media: The Extensions of Man* (New York: McGraw-Hill, 1964); see especially pp. 7–21.

[2]Neil Postman, *Amusing Ourselves to Death: Public Discourse in the Age of Show Business* (New York: Penguin, 1985), p. 7. Subsequent citations will be made parenthetically in-text.

[3]Postman develops his sweeping history of American media in chapter 5 of *Amusing Ourselves to Death*, "The Peek-a-Boo World" (pp. 64–80).

[4]Postman acknowledges that, in other parts of the world (pp. 85–6) or in non-commercial contexts (pp. 105–6), television may serve different purposes. However, as he sees it, this does nothing to change the way that television most typically functions in contemporary American society.

[5]Colbert explained the importance of one's gut in the search for truth during his April 2006 White House Correspondents' Association Dinner performance: "Every night on my show, *The Colbert Report*, I speak straight from the gut, OK? I give people the truth, unfiltered by rational argument." On this point Colbert also compared himself to President George W. Bush, who sat at the head table just a few feet away from Colbert's podium:

> We're not so different, he and I. We both get it. Guys like us, we're not some brainiacs on the nerd patrol. We're not members of the Factinista. We go straight from the gut; right, sir? That's where the truth lies, right down here in the gut.
>
> Do you know you have more nerve endings in your gut than you have in your head? You can look it up. Now I know some of you are going to say, "I did look it up, and that's not true." That's because you looked it up in a book. Next time, look it up in your gut. I did, My gut tells me that's how our nervous system works.

[6]As Postman writes, "While brevity does not always suggest triviality, in this cast it surely does. It is simply not possible to convey a sense of seriousness about any event if its implications are exhausted in less than one minute's time" (p. 103).

[7]See also "Stephen Colbert's Guide to Dressing and Expressing Like a TV Journalist" in Jon Stewart, Ben Karlin, and David Javerbaum, *America (The Book): A Citizen's Guide to Democracy Inaction* (New York: Warner Books, 2004), pp. 142–3.

[8]*Reliable Sources*, CNN (November 2, 2002).

[9]*The O'Reilly Factor*, Fox News (September 17, 2004).

[10]"National Annenberg Election Survey" (press release), *Annenberg Public Policy Center* (September 21, 2004), p. 2.

[11]*Now,* PBS (July 11, 2003).

[12]*Reliable Sources,* CNN (November 2, 2002).

[13]*Crossfire,* CNN (October 15, 2004). All quotes below are from CNN's rush transcript of this episode.

[14]Postman actually cites Buckley's own legendary program *Firing Line* as a rare example of television as a "carrier of coherent language and thought in process" that "occasionally shows people in the act of thinking but who also happen to have television cameras pointed at them" (p. 91). *Firing Line* never received high ratings, though, and spent most of its 33 years on public television.

[15]Postman's son Andrew sums all of this up nicely in his "Introduction" to the 20th Anniversary Edition of *Amusing Ourselves to Death,* writing: "When Jon Stewart, host of Comedy Central's *The Daily Show,* went on CNN's *Crossfire* to make this very point—that serious news and show business ought to be distinguishable, for the sake of public discourse and the republic—the hosts seemed incapable of even understanding the words coming out of his mouth" (pp. xiii–xiv).

[16]Howard Kurtz, "Carlson & 'Crossfire:' Exit Stage Left & Right," *Washington Post* (January 6, 2005), C1.

[17]In the final chapter of *Amusing Ourselves to Death,* Postman describes a then-hypothetical but subversive anti-television television program that's eerily similar to *The Daily Show.* According to Postman, this program would serve an important educational purpose by demonstrating how television recreates and degrades news, political debate, religious thought, and so on. He writes: "I imagine such demonstrations would of necessity take the form of parodies, along the lines of 'Saturday Night Live' and 'Monty Python,' the idea being to induce a national horse laugh over television's control of the public discourse" (pp. 161–2). In the end, Postman rejects the idea of such a show as "nonsense," since he thinks that serious and intelligent televised discussion could never attract an audience large enough to make a difference.

Examining the Text

1. According to Erion, what are the key elements of Neil Postman's critique of television? Why does Postman think that television is ineffective at conveying serious content? Do you agree that "thinking does not play well on television" (paragraph 7)?

2. What examples does Erion provide to support his claim that the humor of *The Daily Show* "rests on Postman-like insights" (paragraph 11)? Do you find this evidence convincing?

3. Erion spends several paragraphs describing and commenting on Stewart's 2004 appearance on CNN's *Crossfire.* Why does Erion find this incident particularly revealing? How does the incident support Erion's claims that Stewart has the same view of television as Postman does?

4. *Thinking rhetorically:* Imagine for a moment that Erion is right and that *The Daily Show* does indeed deliver a Postman-infused, McLuhan-esque critique of television. Would that change the way that you watch *The Daily Show* (or the *Colbert Report*, or similar shows)? Do you think that Erion's purpose in writing this article is ultimately to add more legitimacy and philosophical sophistication to these kinds of shows? What other persuasive goals might Erion be trying to accomplish in this article?

For Group Discussion

Erion focuses his analysis on *The Daily Show* and on Jon Stewart's particular critique of television and news. In a small group, discuss the extent to which Erion's ideas apply to other comedy news shows such as *The Colbert Report* as well as to other "serious" television shows such as *Washington Week in Review.* Do these shows also deliver a Postman-like critique of television? What similarities and differences are there between these other shows and *The Daily Show?*

Writing Suggestion

Watch *The Daily Show* and *The Colbert Report* for a few nights (or look at their videos on the Web), and select one of the standard segments of one of these shows: for example, the Senior Correspondent report or "Great Moments in Punditry" on *The Daily Show,* "The Word" on *The Colbert Report,* or celebrity/ newsmaker interviews on both shows. Write down all of the details that you can about the segment: what are its key features, who participates, how long does it last, what specific topics does it take on?

After taking notes about a few instances of this segment, write an analysis in which you explore the messages conveyed by the segment. You should first summarize the key features of the segment, and then suggest how the segment works to deliver a satirical or critical view of television, politics, and/or journalism. In your analysis, draw on quotations and ideas from Erion's article as well as from the other two articles in this section of the television chapter.

"Fake" News versus "Real" News as Sources of Political Information: The Daily Show *and Postmodern Political Reality*

JEFFREY P. JONES

The article that follows was initially published in a 2007 collection entitled Politicotainment: Television's Take on the Real; *the book brings together essays that look at how politics is interpreted and represented in various forms of TV entertainment, including reality shows and drama series. A central premise of the book is that what we know about politics, politicians, and our entire political system is mediated through television; recalling Harry Waters' argument in the first article in this chapter,* Politicotainment *focuses on how television shapes and filters our view of reality.*

In this article, Jeffrey P. Jones writes about how The Daily Show *shapes our understanding of politics and political events. A professor at Old Dominion University, Jones has written widely about television, politics, and related topics. Here he draws a specific contrast between what we learn about politics through* The Daily Show *and what we learn through mainstream journalism. Toward the end of the article, Jones writes that "unhindered by the self-imposed constraints placed on reporters by the profession (as well as the co-dependent relationship that exists between government and the press),* The Daily Show *uses a fake news platform to offer discussions of news events that are informative and critical, factual and interpretive, thorough yet succinct" (paragraph 38).*

This statement concludes the close reading that occupies much of the article, in which Jones provides a detailed look at a specific episode of The Daily Show *in order to determine how accurate the show is. Surprisingly, he concludes that* The Daily Show *matches and even surpasses CNN's coverage of a particular campaign event. So although Jon Stewart or Stephen Colbert would be very unlikely to describe themselves as "journalists," they nevertheless perform some of the functions of mainstream journalists—and perhaps do a more effective job of it.*

Before you read *this article, make a list of journalists with whom you're familiar, whether from television, print, radio, or the Internet. How would you describe the work they do? What function does their work serve in our society? What particular skills and attributes do they need to perform effectively?*

A recurrent claim about young Americans is that they get more of their news about politics and current events from late-night television comedians than they do from the news media. This claim began with a statistic that appeared in a 2000 survey of the electorate conducted by the Pew Research Center for the People and the Press, which reported that 47 percent of people under thirty years old were "informed at least occasionally" about the presidential campaign by late-night talk shows.[1] Though there are numerous methodological and interpretive problems raised by this simple yet ultimately flawed statistic, journalists and other critics have nevertheless transformed it into a myth about young people and their news-consumption habits. Regardless of its accuracy, it seemingly explains why young people have increasingly turned away from traditional outlets of political communication, namely newspapers and television news (Mindich 2005). It also addresses journalistic concerns that audiences are attracted more to entertainment than serious public-affairs reporting, and what's worse, that they may not even be able to distinguish between the two. It also seemingly verifies fears of public ignorance of the political process (Delli Carpini and Keeter 1996), youth disengagement from politics (Buckingham 2000), a declining reading culture (Scheuer 1999), couch potato kids, the entertainmentization of politics (West and Orman 2003), and the cynicism that supposedly grips our society (Hart 1994; Chaloupka 1999).

This chapter begins, then, by examining and questioning this myth. But as with many myths that circulate in society, the critic's ability to refute the accuracy of the myth is not likely to diminish its popularity or widespread circulation. Instead, it may be more effective to show why the basic premise of the myth itself is incorrect. That is, in this instance, the idea that late-night comedic television does not (or cannot) impart important news or information about public affairs and thus, by definition, only traffics in the trivial, inane, or absurd. In this chapter, therefore, I turn the myth on its head by asking: What if the myth is true and young people *are* "getting their news" from popular late-night comedy programs such as *The Daily Show with Jon Stewart?* What is it they might learn about politics or current events from this show, and how does that compare with what they might learn about politics were they to watch more respected sources of news such as CNN instead? To begin answering this question, I compare a news item "reported" by *The Daily Show,* a fake news show that parodies a "legitimate" television news broadcast, with the same story as covered by CNN. I follow the Pew Center's lead by examining news reports of the 2004 presidential election, yet from broadcasts much later in the campaign when the viewing public is typically more raptly attuned. I analyze the type of information that is offered in the two reports and how the resulting meanings or "truths" compare.

I argue that even though *The Daily Show* is a fake news show, its faux journalistic style allows the show's writers and host to question, dispel, and critique the manipulative language and symbolizations coming from the presidential campaign while simultaneously opening up deeper truths about politics than those offered by the "objective" reporting of mainstream journalism. By actually showing the high levels of spin and rhetoric produced by the candidates and their campaigns, then offering humorous retorts that cut to the heart of the matter, *The Daily Show* offers its viewers particular (and perhaps more useful) "information" about the campaign that is often missing from "real" journalist reports on the news networks, and hence informs its viewers in ways that mainstream journalism rarely does. Given the extraordinary level of outright distortions, lies, and spin that dominated both the Republican and Democratic campaigns in this election, this chapter concludes that perhaps the postmodern notion that the "fake" is more

2

203

3

real than the "real" is not such an unsettling notion when it comes to citizens looking for truth in contemporary political communication on television. And, in turn, perhaps young citizens—if they do indeed get their information from political comedians on television—may not be as misinformed as the current myth suggests.

THE MYTH OF YOUNG PEOPLE AND KNOWLEDGE OF PUBLIC AFFAIRS

In February 2000, the Pew Research Center for the People and the Press 4 reported that 47 percent of people under the age of thirty were "informed at least occasionally" about the campaign or candidates by late-night talk shows (13 percent regularly and 34 percent sometimes). The poll was conducted from 4 to 11 January 2000, before any party primaries had taken place. In January 2004, the Pew Center repeated this survey (conducted 19 December 2003 through 4 January 2004), this time asking respondents if they "learned something" from comedy shows. Twenty-one percent of people under the age of thirty reported learning something from programs such as *Saturday Night Live* and *The Daily Show* (roughly the same number who learned something from the Internet). As the Pew study notes, "For Americans under thirty, these comedy shows are now mentioned almost as frequently as newspapers and evening network news programs as regular sources for election news." Furthermore, the report exclaims, "one out of every two young people (50%) say they at least sometimes learn about the campaign from comedy shows, nearly twice the rate among people age thirty–fourtynine (27%) and four times the rate among people fifty and older."[2]

Before taking these statistics at face value, however, we should 5 examine both the questions and the resulting statistics more closely. Certainly political insiders, heavy news readers/watchers, and political junkies are attuned to news so early in the campaign, for no other reason than to be able to handicap the upcoming horse race. As for the rest of the polity, however, the electoral contests in the small yet important states of Iowa and New Hampshire certainly receive much less of their attention because the party nominee is generally a forgone conclusion by the time most Americans have the opportunity to vote in their state primary election. Hence, for a poll to attempt to measure political knowledge and information about an election so early in the campaign is specious.

What is worse, though, is the wording of the question itself: 6 "informed at least occasionally." What does it mean to be "informed" about the campaign—knowledge of who is running for office, what their positions are on issues, who is ahead in the race, who has the biggest war chest, what gaffes have occurred to this point, the names of their wives, what type of underwear they prefer? At what level can most any type of nonfiction program—news reports, talk shows, documentaries, stand-up comedy, advertisements—provide *some* of this information? The question doesn't help us understand the underlying normative assumption of whether the respondent should know the differences between Al Gore's and Bill Bradley's positions on Social Security reform, or whether the respondent is simply expected to know their names and that they are running for office. Furthermore, the question asks "at least occasionally." Does that mean every day, once a week, or once a month, or does it suggest a regular and consistent pattern of consumption? Finally, what assumptions of intentionality are included here? Does the question seek to identify whether citizens brush up against news, or whether they intentionally turn to certain forms of programming for "information"? The survey results provide no answers to these questions. In short, the response to this question really only tells us two things—that comedians mine current affairs for humorous content, and that different programming types differ in their popularity among different demographic groups. It certainly does *not* measure whether the only or primary source of information about current affairs is obtained by watching late-night comedians on television.

Nevertheless, that hasn't prevented journalists from using the sta-   7   **205**
tistic to develop a full-blown myth about young people and their news consumption habits. For instance, CNN anchor Judy Woodruff began a question to *The Daily Show* host Jon Stewart by stating, "We hear more and more that your show and shows like your show are the places that young people *are getting their news*" (emphasis added)[3]. Ted Koppel, the anchor for ABC's late-night news show *Nightline* (a program that directly competes with these entertainment shows), similarly assailed Stewart by noting to his viewers, "A lot of television viewers, more, quite frankly, than I'm comfortable with, *get their news* from the comedy channel on a program called "'The Daily Show'" (emphasis added).[4] And perhaps most egregiously, *Newsday* reporter Verne Gay wrote, "A recent study from the Pew Center found that 8 percent of respondents *learned most everything they knew* about a candidate from shows like *The Daily Show* and *Saturday Night Live*" (emphasis added; Gay 2004).

As these quotes suggest, reporters have taken great liberty in revis-   8
ing and expanding what the statistic actually reveals. Yet the results of campaign knowledge test conducted on over 19,000 citizens in the summer and fall of 2004 by the University of Pennsylvania's National Annenberg Election Survey did little to temper the myth. The survey reported that "viewers of late-night comedy programs, especially *The Daily show* with Jon Stewart on Comedy Central, are more likely to know the issue positions and backgrounds of presidential candidates than people who do not watch late-night comedy," noting that *Daily Show* viewers

"have higher campaign knowledge than national news viewers and newspaper readers."[5] The survey concludes, "traditional journalists have been voicing increasing concern that if young people are receiving political information from late-night comedy shows like *The Daily Show,* they may not be adequately informed on the issues of the day. This data suggests that these fears may be unsubstantiated." The survey also points out, however, that "these findings do not show that *The Daily Show* is itself responsible for the higher knowledge among its viewers."

In summary, journalists and other critics of entertainment televi- 9 sion have propagated a myth based on dubious evidence that late-night comedy television programming is a central location for the delivery of news (and, by inference, misinformation, and ignorance about politics) for young people, a myth that competing quantitative evidence suggests is incorrect. What neither of these surveys reveals, however, is an assessment of the *content* of these shows—whether they offer viewers anything of value or are relatively meaningless, whether the information provided is accurate and truthful or biased and incorrect, or even how this material compares with other sources of information on public affairs. There is no qualitative assessment, only the assumption that what appears in these formats is not equivalent to that which could be obtained from traditional sources of political information. What follows, then, is an attempt to examine these questions directly, looking at how *The Daily Show* "reports" news and information, and its comparative value in light of reporting available on a more culturally acceptable and respected news source, CNN.

NEWS REPORTS BY *THE DAILY SHOW* AND CNN

Every weeknight (except Fridays), Comedy Central airs *The Daily Show,* 10 a mock news program and hybrid talk show that parodies television news for the first half of the program, then segues into a more typical talk-show interview between host Jon Stewart and a guest. The first half—the news segment—mimics the anchor-centered style of television news reporting, where Stewart narrates the day's top stories accompanied by video evidence. The news segment also uses the news convention of the anchor interviewing reporters "on location," in this instance, with Stewart talking to his faux "senior correspondents," who pretend to be reporting live via satellite (in front of a background image of, say, Baghdad or the White House). The primary interest of my investigation is this "news" segment of the show.

I examined one week of the program during the late stages of the 11 presidential campaign—4 to 7 October 2004—one week after the first presidential debate. I selected one program during this period as a representative text (Thursday, 7 October) for a close textual analysis. This limited selection allows for an in-depth analysis of the information and commentary provided, as well as a direct comparison with news reports from CNN. While the limited range of texts can be criticized as overly restricted, such a close reading of *The Daily Show* has not been conducted to date. Instead, existing studies have examined a broader range of texts from the program across numerous episodes and months of programming (see, for instance, Jones 2005a; and Baym 2005). Here, though, the intention is to make a direct comparison of two entire news reports on the same event. The selection of a single news report also limits the generalizability of my argument, yet the episode selected for scrutiny is not extraordinary. Rather, it is fairly representative, by my reading, of a typical *Daily Show* broadcast. Furthermore, the intentional circumscribing allows for the close reading of a text that cultural studies has proven to be of value. The episode selected illustrates the type of information provided in typical news reports by both *The Daily Show* and CNN, allowing us to compare not just the variety but also the quality of the reports and conclusions that can be drawn from them. The CNN reports come from three programs, all of which appeared on the same day as *The Daily Show* broadcast: *American Morning* (7 A.M.), *CNN Live Today* (10 A.M.), and *News from CNN* (12 P.M.).[6]

CNN began its 7 A.M. broadcast by reporting on Bush's campaign 12 appearances the previous day, as well as the release of the CIA's Iraq Survey Group report investigating the existence of weapons of mass destruction in Iraq. In reporting Bush's campaign stop in Pennsylvania, CNN White House Correspondent Elaine Quijano pointed out that the president made no mention of a new report by the Iraq Survey Group, which found no evidence of stockpiles of weapons of mass destruction in Iraq when the United States invaded in 2003. Still, Mr. Bush is standing by his decision, insisting that after September 11, the country had to assess every potential threat in a new light.

> (Video clip of President Bush speaking in Wilkes-Barre, Pennsylvania): Our nation awakened to an even greater danger, the prospect that terrorists who killed thousands with hijacked airplanes would kill many more with weapons of mass murder. We had to take a hard look at every place where terrorists might get those weapons. One regime stood out, the dictatorship of Saddam Hussein.

During the 10 A.M. report, CNN decided not to continue airing the 13 clip of Bush's speech, instead letting Quijano summarize the president's central point in the statement, as well as note the official White House "reading" of the report, attributed here to "administration officials."

But the president did not mention that new CIA report, which 14 found no weapons of mass destruction in Iraq when the United States invaded in 2003. Instead Mr. Bush repeated his argument that taking Saddam Hussein out of power has made the world safer. Administration officials say they believe the report shows Saddam Hussein was a threat that the United States needed to take seriously. They also say they believe it shows that he had the intent and capability to develop weapons of mass destruction.

By 12 P.M., CNN was simply reporting the release of the report as this: "Bush also defended the war in Iraq, just as the CIA prepares to report that Saddam Hussein did not have weapons of mass destruction or the means to produce them before U.S. troops invaded Iraq." 15

Jon Stewart also began his broadcast by announcing the release of the CIA report and noting its conclusions: 16

> Everything we've been waiting for happened today. The official CIA report, the Dulfer Report, has come out, the one they've been working on for the past two years. It will be the definitive answer on the weapons of mass destruction programs in Iraq, and as it turns out, not so much. Apparently, there were no weapons of mass destruction in Iraq, and their capabilities have been degraded, and they had pretty much stopped trying anything in '98. And both the president and vice president have come out today in response to the findings and said that they clearly justified the invasion of Iraq. Some people look at a glass as half full, while other people look at a glass and say that it's a dragon.

In this segment, Stewart provides roughly the same amount and type of information provided by CNN, but then goes out of his way to establish that despite clear and convincing evidence to the contrary, Bush and Cheney continue their act as either liars or highly delusional people; they see what they want to see. Here Stewart offers not just the facts, but also draws conclusions from those facts. Journalistic adherence to norms of objectivity generally prevents many reporters and anchors from looking across specific events to explicitly point out repeated patterns of deception or misjudgment by politicians and government officials (unless the reporting occurs in investigative or opinion-editorial pieces). *The Daily Show,* as a fake news program, is not limited by such professional constraints. Viewers are thus invited to focus on the most important aspect of this news event—that this is not just another investigation that proves the official reason for invading Iraq was misguided and wrong. Rather, the import is that the Bush Administration repeatedly refuses to admit its mistake. 17

CNN, on the other hand, simply repeats the administration's position, as is standard journalistic convention, Yet since numerous investigations have produced the same findings (which in the world of science and social science would amount to the establishment of "truth"), why should news media continue to repeat a position that has no basis in fact—just 18 because the government continues to assert the position? Is that "news-worthy," and if not, what news value is being fulfilled? Daniel Boorstin contends that assertions such as this amount to "pseudo-events," a story created by politicians and journalists that has no intrinsic value as a news event *per se,* but is only deemed as such by journalists in the era of "objec-tivity" (Boorstin 1960). Stewart refuses to play along and, again, ignores the administration's "reading" or justifications because they have no basis in reality (as determined by the numerous other officials, institu-tions, and nations that have concluded the same thing).

Stewart then turns his attention to a Bush campaign stop the day 19 before. "Let's begin tonight on the campaign trail," he says, while talk-ing over a video clip of President Bush in Wilkes-Barre, Pennsylvania. Bush is standing in front of a backdrop/banner with the words "A Safer America, A Stronger Economy" adorned over both of his shoul-ders. "Yesterday, President Bush's advisors alerted the networks he would be making a major policy speech in Wilkes-Barre, Pennsylvania. The subject . . . [*the graphic highlights the slogan "A Safer America"*]—no, not that. [*The graphic highlights "A Stronger Economy."*] Uh, wrong again. [*The graphic then shows a crossed-out slogan, superimposing the hand–scrawled mes-sage, "Recover from unbelievably poor debate performance."*]. That's it! That was the subject. Yes, in the week of his, let's call it 'weak' showing against Senator John Kerry on Thursday, the president and his handlers snook-ered the cable news networks into giving him one hour of free full-on campaign stop pabulum."

CNN also covered this campaign stop in all three of its morning 20 broadcasts. For both the 7 A.M. and 10 A.M. reports, Quijano simply referred to two campaign stops (one of which was in Pennsylvania), not-ing that Bush had "stepped up his attacks" and had come "out swinging hard against his opponent, "blasting" Kerry and delivering a "blistering assault on Kerry's record." The reporter seeks to summarize the tone and substance of the president's speeches, while characterizing him as on the offensive—exactly what the campaign hopes will be reported. Only the 12 P.M. broadcast noted the campaign's intentions in changing the focus of the speech. Wolf Blitzer introduced the subject by referring to Bush's "attempt to try to reestablish some political momentum," while the cor-respondent reporting the event pointed out the change in plans: "Well, Wolf, as you know, initially this was a speech that was supposed to focus on medical liability reform. But after President Bush's widely viewed disappointing performance in the first presidential debate, there was a difference in strategy, a change in strategy from the campaign. They changed this to sharp attacks against Senator Kerry and his record on the war on terror, as well as the economy."

CNN's reporting of this event is characterized by three tendencies 21 that political scientists argue are typical of news media's reporting in

209

elections: (1) elections are treated as a sports contest between two combatants (typically horse racing or, in this instance, boxing); (2) the press focuses on the campaign's strategies more than the issues themselves; and (3) the press often parrots the message that political campaigns want them to report, circulating the rhetoric and slogans without intensive scrutiny or criticism (see, for instance, Patterson 1993). Stewart also points out the campaign's strategy of deflecting attention from Bush's weak showing in the presidential debates by going on the offensive, but insists on calling attention to the manipulative aspects of the event itself—both the campaign's misleading the press about making a major policy statement (when the presence of the banner itself clearly shows the forethought and planning for this attack speech) and the oral and visual rhetoric that the campaign wants the news media to report and show its viewers. Stewart doesn't accept the contention that the speech is about national security or the economy and focuses instead on the artifice of the event. It is an artifice that the news media help create and facilitate by uncritically continuing to air the Bush speech live, even though the speech does not include the policy material they initially agreed merited free air time as a newsworthy *presidential* statement (as opposed to that of a candidate for office). As Stewart has noted about his show in an earlier interview, "What we try to do is point out the artifice of things, that there's a guy behind the curtain pulling levers" (Hedgpeth 2000). Here he does just that.

Stewart then shows several clips from the Bush speech that CNN 22 chose not to air in any of its three reports.

> *Stewart:* [Bush] began by throwing out the first pander.
> *Bush:* It's great to be in Wilkes-Barre, Pennsylvania. It's such an honor to be back here. It's great to be in a part of the world where people work hard, they love their families. . . .
> *Stewart:* [*said out of the side of his mouth*] Yeah, not like New York— family hating jackasses; lazy family haters.

CNN does not show this clip because, given the news values of 23 mainstream journalism, such statements by politicians are not newsworthy; they are typical of political speeches. For reporters assigned to follow the candidate's campaign, in fact, they have heard such statements countless times by this point in the campaign, said to different crowds in different places. For Stewart, however, the clip merits the viewers' attention because it shows that not only is the statement itself ridiculous, but that it is not beneath the president to pander to audiences. This is part of the overall point that Stewart attempts to make throughout the entire news segment—he continually asks the viewer to step outside the staged event to assess what information is available that might shed light on both presidential candidates' fundamental character as people and leaders.

Stewart continues covering the event by again showing another 24 clip that CNN chose not to air:

> *Stewart:* But then it was rival bashing time. Bush warmed up with a few insults aimed at the Democrats' number two man and his performance in Tuesday night's debate.
>
> *Bush:* America saw two very different visions of our country and two different hairdos. I didn't pick my vice president for his hairdo. I picked him for his judgment, his experience. . . .
>
> *Stewart:* [*showing a picture of a bald Dick Cheney*] which, sadly, is as good as his hairdo.

If pandering isn't enough, Stewart shows that it is not beneath 25 Bush to engage in *ad hominem* attacks. Again, CNN chose not to report this part of the president's speech, recognizing that attacks on one's opponents are simply part of electoral politics. Stewart, however, shows the clip not just to provide evidence of Bush's character and campaign style, but also to question the actual point that Bush is attempting to make so unproblematically—the quality of his administration's "judgment and experience" in the conduct of governmental affairs. Both CNN and *The Daily Show* have already provided evidence earlier in their broadcasts that the administration's "experience" of deciding to wage war, based on its "judgment" that there was trustworthy information to do so, was faulty. *The Daily Show,* however, is the only one to make the connection and point it out to viewers.

Like CNN, Stewart then focuses on the major policy statements 26 within Bush's speech.

> *Stewart:* Bush then moved onto his economic policy regarding Kerry.
>
> *Bush:* Now the Senator's proposing higher taxes on more than 900,000 small business owners. He says the tax increase is only for the rich. You've heard that kind of rhetoric before. The rich hire lawyers and accountants for a reason—to stick you with the tab.
>
> *Stewart:* Let me get this straight. Don't tax the rich because they'll get out of it? So your policy is, tax the hard working people because they're dumb-asses and they'll never figure it out? So vote for me, goodnight?

Only during its 12 P.M. broadcast did CNN report this aspect of 27 the president's speech, noting that Bush "also twisted Kerry's plan to

211

roll back the cut taxes for those making more than $200,000, describing it as a tax increase for more than 900,000 small businesses." The CNN report is critical at this juncture by pointing out the Bush campaign's distortion of Kerry's proposal (that is, rolling back Bush's tax cuts does not amount to a proposed tax increase). CNN's focus is on the rhetorical sleight of hand. But that is the extent of their report. Stewart, however, returns the focus to the president's rhetoric by carrying the point to its logical conclusion. He illuminates the contradictory nature of the populist statement by questioning what it is exactly that Bush is trying to articulate, while also reminding viewers of where Bush really stands on taxes and how his policies actually belie the rhetoric employed here. It merits noting that news programs rarely offer direct and damning evidence of contradictory statements or duplicitous comments. The convention they typically rely on is to quote someone else who will point this out (Tuchman 1978). CNN did not even air the actual clip, relying instead on its reporter to summarize Bush's statement. One might argue that CNN has done Bush a favor by *not* airing a statement that is logically somewhat ridiculous and, instead, doing the hard work of actually deciphering for the viewing audience what the president means, thereby making him look more presidential in the process.[7]

The only clip of the president's speech that CNN showed in all three of its broadcasts occurred in the 7 A.M report—his statement concerning the supposed threat posed by "the dictatorship of Saddam Hussein" (quoted above). *The Daily Show* also reported this part of the speech, but with much more scrutiny to what Bush actually said. Stewart here engages in a rhetorical back-and-forth with the video clip of Bush's statement, attempting to come up with the right answer for which nation it is *exactly* that threatens America with weapons of mass destruction: 28

> *Stewart:* Finally, the president brought the mood down a little, as only he can.
>
> *Bush:* After September 11, America had to assess every potential threat in a new light. We had to take a hard look at every place where terrorists might get those weapons and one regime stood out.
>
> *Stewart:* Well, that's true. It would be Saudi Arabia. Fifteen of the nineteen terrorists were actually from there.
>
> *Bush:* . . . the dictatorship of Saddam Hussein.
>
> *Stewart:* No, no. I don't think that's it. Um. Oh. It was Iran— proven Al-Qaeda ties, building up the nukes program. I think it was them.
>
> *Bush:* [*repeating the tape of Bush*] . . . the dictatorship of Saddam Hussein.

Stewart: No, no. I'm sure . . . [pause] . . . Pakistan. Top scientists sold nuclear secrets to . . .

Bush: [*repeating the tape of Bush*] . . . the dictatorship of Saddam Hussein.

Stewart: Could be Yemen. [*a graphic of a clock face with spinning hands is superimposed over a slightly faded image of Stewart, suggesting his thinking for quite some time of the possible countries, all the while Stewart thinks out loud*]. Oh . . . . Kazakhstan is actually a very dangerous . . . . Uzbekistan has always created problems in that region . . . . Turkey—very dangerous. Lebanon has some . . . . Qatar [*the graphic removes the clock face, and the camera focus on Stewart again becomes clear*] . . . Oh, oh, oh, North Korea. They have the bomb. Their leader is crazy. North Korea.

Bush: [*repeating the tape of Bush*] . . . the dictatorship of Saddam Hussein.

Stewart: [holding out his arms in front of him, like a robot, said in a slow monotone voice, with a staccato cadence]: The-dic-ta-tor-ship-of-Sad-dam-Hus-sein. Too-tired-to-fight-it. Must-learn. Re-pe-ti-tion.

Stewart scrutinizes the president's statement on its own terms—"in *every* place where terrorists might get those weapons": Saudi Arabia, Iran, Pakistan, North Korea, and so on. Then, through video repetition, Stewart highlights how the administration continues to repeat assertions over and over until the viewer is turned into an unthinking (or worn out) robot. In the speech itself, of course, Bush does not repeat the line. Yet Stewart recognizes that single speech events such as this do not constitute the reality that news media report and, in turn, help create. Instead, his use of manipulated video emphasizes the repeated pattern of administration efforts to establish something that is untrue, yet which citizens must work to resist because of its repeated assertion. As Stewart is quoted as saying, "We're out to stop that political trend of repeating things again and again until people are forced to believe them" (Armstrong 2003).

Stewart finishes the show's coverage of the Bush speech by returning one last time to a Bush pronouncement that was simply too good to pass up for its comedic value, yet also affirms the point about Bush's character that he has attempted to make throughout the telecast:

Stewart: But for all that, perhaps the most telling line of the speech came during Bush's seemingly innocuous segue into a story about his wife.

Bush: you're not going to believe this. It's a true story, or kind of true.

Stewart: [*said with sheepish grin*] George W. Bush—I can tell a lie.

30

Again, CNN doesn't air this clip because there is no news value   31
here—from their perspective, it is a meaningless aside unrelated to
either campaign strategy or policy stances. For Stewart, however, it not
only ties in nicely with the previous statement about Saddam Hussein
and 9/11, but it also neatly demonstrates *exactly* what is at stake in the
election of the president. Bush's proclivity to lie, in fact, was something
the news media generally ignored in the election campaign, yet was an
important criticism of Bush often addressed in numerous venues of
popular culture during the campaign—most famously in Michael
Moore's documentary film *Fahrenheit 9/11* (Jones 2005b).

Stewart concludes the news segment of the show by turning to an   32
event not widely covered by the news media—both John Kerry and Bush
soliciting votes by appearing on the afternoon therapy and relationship
talk show, *Dr. Phil.* Here he attempts to highlight the deeper truths at
work again, this time with the Democratic nominee:

> *Stewart:* But like Bush's speech, Kerry's *Dr. Phil* appearance had
> one moment that most clearly captured the essence of the can-
> didate.
>
> *Dr. Phil's Wife:* [*Video clip of the Dr. Phil Show, an interview with
> Senator Kerry conducted with the assistance of Dr. Phil's wife*]: Is
> one of your daughters more like you than the other?
>
> *Kerry:* Yes. No. That's . . . gosh . . . I'd like to . . . yes. But I guess
> . . . yes, the answer is yes.
>
> *Dr. Phil's Wife:* Which one do you think is more like you?
>
> *Kerry:* Well . . . um . . . I . . . that's why I hesitated, because I think
> in some ways my daughter Alexandra is more like me, but in
> other ways my daughter Vanessa is more like me.
>
> *Stewart:* [Burying his face into his hands, then moving his hands
> over his bowed head, gripping his hair, then the back of his
> neck. Stewart makes no comment, but simply looks at the cam-
> era with exasperation and dismay. The audience erupts in
> laughter.]

When presidential candidates first began appearing on such talk   33
shows with regularity in 1992, the news media covered these appearances as newsworthy events. They did so, in particular, because of the
unusual nature of the appearances, but also because the news media
disliked the "softball" questions offered up by these "illegitimate" non-
reporters (Debenport 1992). Because such appearances rarely feature
the candidates' saying much about their position on issues (focusing
more instead on personal matters), the news media now generally turn
a blind eye to these "campaign stops," treating them as *de rigueur* in the
hustle to reach disparate voter groups. *The Daily Show,* however, calls

attention to the spectacle performance not just for its groveling and humiliating aspects, but rather to highlight how such performances might actually tell us something important about the candidates. In this instance, Kerry confirmed everything the Bush campaign had said about him: that Kerry is unwilling to be pinned down on anything (despite how insignificant the matter), yet paradoxically will say anything to get elected if he believes that is what the audience wants to hear. That truth comes to light very clearly for viewers when the matter is something as trivial as reflecting upon the relationship with one's daughter. Viewers may not be able to discern whether Kerry is a flip-flopper on foreign-policy issues (say, for instance, his various votes on the Iraq war), but they can certainly recognize mealy-mouthed remarks when it comes to interpersonal relationships.

The Daily Show, therefore, has constructed a narrative, weaving   34
together campaign events to give the viewer insight into the candidates and who they might really be. This narrative is formulated from information derived from planned campaign events, yet woven together to tell a story that allows for evaluation of the candidates. Perhaps this is simply an entertainmentized version of a "news analysis" or "op-ed" journalism. But it is a particular brand of "reporting" that might illuminate for viewers the larger issues at stake beyond the isolated events   **215**
that typically dominate news reporting.

In summary, then, *The Daily Show* has provided viewers infor-   35
mation on several major political events that occurred the day before: the CIA report on weapons of mass destruction, Bush's campaign speech, and Kerry's appearance on a popular television program. The audience learns what the CIA report says, learns two of the main points in Bush's speech also reported by news outlets, and learns about Kerry's personal life. *The Daily Show* has not, therefore, short-changed viewers on information they would have seen by watching a "real" newscast.

Yet *The Daily Show's* audience also sees more material on these   36
events than that provided by CNN, learning things that CNN didn't report. First, *The Daily Show* highlights political rhetoric itself, showing the false statements, *ad hominem* attacks, pandering, and populist appeals of candidate Bush, not seeing such language as a "given" in politics, but instead as a disturbing quality that exemplifies the character of the politician. Second, and perhaps more important, the program offers viewers information they have heard before, yet are reminded of here as a means of making sense of the events covered in the daily news report: there were no weapons of mass destruction; the administration's actions exemplify its use of bad judgment because it went after the wrong regime; its economic policies are the opposite of what they say they are. Continually, Stewart will not let the viewer lose sight

of the greater truths at stake here. He is constantly keeping score, adding it all up, reminding the viewer of what this says about the candidates and the larger terms upon which they should be evaluated. In a single news report, the television news reporters rarely put things together in such a manner. And what the news media ignore may actually provide citizens with the type of meaningful information upon which they can base their electoral decisions. By Stewart's doing so in a typical news-reporting format, he demonstrates the failings of news media in informing viewers, drawing attention to how media serve as conduits for false information and image management, and how it would be easy for citizens to become the unthinking drones and robots that such unquestioned lies and manipulative imagery could lead them to become.

One might be tempted to criticize *The Daily Show* for selecting 37 damning video clips that are taken out of context and then used to ridicule or embarrass politicians, all for a laugh. As we have seen, however, the clips used by Stewart are no more out of context than the single clip shown by CNN. Both Stewart and CNN actually highlight the context of the speech—the poor debate performance, as well as the release of the CIA report—yet it is *The Daily Show* that provides even more depth to the speech by showing viewers more of it (six clips compared to one by CNN). Just because CNN and other news organizations make claims of neutrality and objectivity doesn't mean they aren't being selective in what they report and how they report it. Furthermore, Stewart reports the same events and highlights the same "newsworthy" items as CNN, including reaching many of their same conclusions. As journalism critics have pointed out, not only have the length of sound bites drastically decreased over the last twenty years, they are increasingly disappearing altogether from television news reports (despite a very large news hole with twenty-four-hour cable channels). Instead, reporters are simply summarizing what candidates and government officials say, then interpreting those comments in a conversation with the news anchor. Yet as we have also seen, those interpretations offer the viewer little in the way of substantive critical assessments because of the norms and conventions of the profession.

In short, *The Daily Show* has matched CNN's coverage of this par- 38 ticular campaign event, even surpassing it by providing viewers additional information about the candidates beyond policy positions and campaign strategies and maneuvers. Of course, CNN provides a wealth of information about national and world affairs that a comedy program like *The Daily Show* can never cover. Nor would I suggest that citizens could be fully informed by watching a comedy show that provides little more than ten minutes of "reporting." Nevertheless, if we are to assess the quality of information about the presidential campaign provided by a fake news show versus a real one (as the Pew study normatively asserts), then the analysis here suggests that *The Daily Show* can provide quality information that citizens can use in making informed choices about electoral politics.

FAKENESS, REALITY, AND THE POSTMODERN VIEWING PUBLIC

By most accounts, the institution of journalism is in a state of crisis in   39
America (Hachten 2005; Kovach and Rosenstiel 2001). As discussed above, the myth that young people get their news from late-night comedians is partly a desire to explain why young people, in particular, are turning away from broadcast news or print journalism as primary sources of news and information (Mindich 2005). With declining readership and viewership, the institution is economically challenged by dwindling advertising revenues as well as increased costs of production (Roberts et al, 2001; Seelye 2005a). Recent scandals related to professional norms and ethics (from story fabrication by Jason Blair at *The New York Times* and Stephen Glass at *The New Republic* to poor fact-checking on President Bush's Air National Guard records by Dan Rather at *CBS News*) have contributed to a decline in trust with news media consumers (Johnson 2003; Hachten 2005, 102–112). Concurrently, with new media technologies such as blogs and search-engine portals, citizens are questioning the top-down, gatekeeper role of news media and, instead, increasingly desire a more active role in the determination and construction of what constitutes news and who gets to make it (Gillmor 2004; Seelye 2005b). Furthermore, the press's timidity in questioning and thwarting overt propaganda efforts by the Bush Administration (as both *The New York Times* and *Washington Post* offered *mea culpas* for their lack of serious reporting on assertions and evidence by the Bush Administration in the run-up to the Iraq war) also weakens the news media's claim to serving as effective and trustworthy watchdogs to power (Younge 2004; Seeyle 2005c). Indeed, government propaganda combined with competition between news outlets that offer not just "competing views of the world, but different realities" (such as Fox News, *The New York Times,* and Al-Jazeera) leads to what Kristina Riegert calls the "struggle for credibility" with viewing audiences and voting publics (Riegert 2005).

Hence, what is also in crisis is the belief that news media provide a   40
realistic picture of the world. The public is well aware that both television and politics are spectacle performances and, indeed, that the press and government are two mutually reinforcing and constituting institutions.[8] News media are *part of* the political spectacle (Edelman 1988),

including journalists-cum-talk-show-pundits (who act more like lap-dogs to power than watchdogs of it), cheerleading embedded reporters, and patriotic news anchors who wear their hearts on their sleeves. An increasingly media-savvy public realizes that news programs such as CNN are no more "real" than *The Daily Show* is "fake." Yet mainstream news media continue to believe their claims to truth—and the authenticity of those claims—because of their *authority* to make them in the first place. It is an authority they have asserted (and the public has granted) through their title, special status, institutional-based legitimacy, access to power, and the means of production and distribution. But as Foucault also reminds us, "truth' is a type of discourse that societies accept and *make function as true*" (emphasis added; Foucault 1980, 132). And as postmodernists would have it, the "authentic" exists only in "the imaginings of those who yearn for it" (Webster 1995, 170). Were that to change, or should citizens come to believe that news is inauthentic, untrue, or just another form of constructed spectacle (that is, the credibility gap becomes a chasm), then they might yearn for other means of establishing truth and reality.

The institutional practice of journalism is a modernist means of 41
constructing knowledge of public life that for many years has been widely accepted. Increasingly, though, this means of taking account of the world is being questioned, if not discredited.[9] In a useful summary of postmodernist thinking, Frank Webster argues that,

> the modernist enthusiasm for genres and styles [of which news is one] is rejected and mocked for its pretensions [by postmodernists]. From this it is but a short step to the postmodern penchant for parody, for tongue-in-cheek reactions to established styles, for a pastiche mode which delights in irony and happily mixes and marches in a 'bricolage' manner. (Webster 1995, 169–170)

And in steps *The Daily Show*, with a tendency for just such postmod- 42
ern playfulness. But *The Daily Show* is "fake" only in that it refuses to make claims to authenticity (as demonstrated in the analysis above). But being fake does not mean that the information it imparts is untrue. Indeed, as with most social and political satire, its humor offers a means of reestablishing common-sense truths to counter the spectacle, ritual, pageantry, artifice, and verbosity that often cloak the powerful. The rationality of political satire is that it "reminds of common values," and "in its negative response to political excess, it serves to restore equilibrium to politics" (Schutz 1977, 327–28). Citizens know that public artifice exists, which is ultimately why the satire that points it out is funny—they just need someone skillful enough to articulate the critique. The type of fake-yet-real "reporting" performed by *The Daily Show* has led one

commentator to claim that *The Daily Show* is "reinventing political journalism" (Baym 2005). Perhaps more to the point, the postmodern audience that comprises its viewership and has made it popular are themselves reinventing what it is they want from political communication.

Though scholars often attack the press for its supposed cynicism 43 (for example, the way in which reporters point out the man behind the curtain), I contend that the press may not do this enough. Shelving journalistic conventions to get at important truths is less cynical than turning a blind eye to the manipulation by either contending that politics will always be this way or assuming that viewers *should* be informed enough or smart enough to connect all the dots themselves. A program like *The Daily Show* refuses to sit idly by while political lies and manipulative rhetoric go unchallenged (or, as Stewart says, "until it becomes true"). Unhindered by the self-imposed constraints placed on reporters by the profession (as well as the co-dependent relationship that exists between government and the press), *The Daily Show* uses a fake news platform to offer discussions of news events that are informative *and* critical, factual *and* interpretive, thorough *yet* succinct. Does that make it biased, unfair, or unbalanced? Not when the program sets its sights on the powerful. As Bryan Keefer, editor of Spinsanity.com, has argued, "the media need to understand that pointing out the truth isn't the same as taking sides."[10] This, of course, is what a fake news show is licensed to do, and why I contend that it provides such an important voice of political critique on the American political landscape (Jones 2005a).

In an opinion piece in the *Washington Post*, Keefer dares to speak 44 for his generation, justifying its changing relationship to traditional news media and its search for better alternatives. He contends that

> we live in an era when PR pros have figured out how to bend the news cycle to their whims, and much of what's broadcast on the networks bears a striking resemblance to the commercials airing between segments. Like other twenty-somethings, I've been raised in an era when advertising invades every aspect of pop culture, and to me the information provided by mainstream news outlets too often feels like one more product, produced by politicians and publicists. (Keefer 2004)

If the myth of young citizens turning to comedians for news and 45 information about politics ends up proving true, then as this analysis suggests, the fate of the republic doesn't seem in jeopardy if a comedy program like *The Daily Show* is a source for their knowledge of public affairs. As Keefer's comments suggest, at least when people watch a program that blatantly embraces its fakeness, they don't feel like they are being sold a bill of goods. Hence, the postmodern claim that the "fake" is more real than the "real" is perhaps not such an unsettling notion after all.

NOTES

[1]http://people-press.org/reports/display.ph3?Report ID=46.
[2]http://people-press.org/reports/display.php3?Report ID=200.
[3]"Jon Stewart," *Inside Politics,* CNN.com, 3 May 2002.
[4]Transcript of *Nightline,* ABC News, 28 July 2004 (accessed from Lexis-Nexis Academic Universe, 4 August 2004).
[5]http://www.naes04org.
[6]Transcripts of CNN, 7 October 2004 (accessed from Lexis-Nexis Academic Universe, 28 March 2005). I analyze three morning broadcasts of CNN to get some idea of the different ways that a news network reports a story, as well as how these brief reports are modified as the morning progresses.
[7]As one news analyst has noted, "Network newscasts hold to standard conventions, and in so doing, reduce Bush's sloppy, pause-saturated speech to a rightly constructed set of words that suggest clarity of thought and purpose." Such conventions, therefore, make the news media "susceptible to manipulation by the professional speech writers and media handlers who seed public information with pre-scripted soundbites and spin" (Baym 2005, 265).
[8]One only needs to look at popular narratives of either news media or the interactions of media and politics to see this recurrent theme. For examples, see films such as *Hero, Power, Broadcast News, A Face in the Crowd, Meet John Doe, The Candidate, Wag the Dog, Bulworth, Bob Roberts,* and *Dave.*

[9]Again, witness the movement toward blogging (and even the news media's embrace of it) as a manifestation of this questioning and reformulation. See, for instance, "The State (Columbia, S.C.) Launches Community Blog, Citizen Journalism Push," *Editor & Publisher,* 30 August 2005; and Saul Hansell, "The CBS Evening Blog," *New York Times,* 13 July 2005.
[10]One might be tempted to assert that this is exactly what competing "news" outlets like Fox News claim—that they are simply pointing our alternative truths. The crucial distinction between a program of political satire and a news organization like Fox that claims to be "fair and balanced," however, is their relationships to power. One is committed to critiquing power wherever it lies, while the other has proven its intentional commitment to supporting the powerful through highly orchestrated and sustained efforts by the media corporation's leadership (see Robert Greenwald's documentary *Outfoxed: Rupert Murdoch's War on Journalism*).

REFERENCES

Armstrong, S. 2003. "I Can Scratch the Itch." *The Guardian,* 17 March, p. 8.
Baym, G. 2005. "The Daily Show: Discursive Integration and the Reinvention of Political Journalism." *Political Communication* 22: 259–276.
Boorstin, D. 1960, *The Image: A Guide to Pseudo Events in America.* New York: Atheneum.
Buckingham, D. 2000. *The Making of Citizens: Young People, News and Politics.* London: Routledge.

Chaloupka, W. 1999. *Everybody Knows: Cynicism in America.* Minneapolis: University of Minnesota Press.

Debenport, E. 1992. "Candidates Try To Cut Media Filter." *St. Petersburg Times* (Florida), 11 June, p. 1A.

Delli Carpini, M.X., and Keeter, S. 1996. *What Americans Know About Politics and Why It Matters,* New Haven: Yale University Press.

Edelman, M. 1988. *Constructing the Political Spectacle.* Chicago: University of Chicago Press.

Foucault M. 1980. *Power/Knowledge: Selected Interviews and Other Writings, 1972–1977.* Brighton: Harvester Press.

Gay, V. 2004. "Not Necessarily the News: Meet the Players Who Will Influence Coverage of the 2004 Campaign." *Newsday,* 19 January, p. B6.

Gillmor, D. 2004. *We the People: Grassroots journalism, by the people, for the people.* Sebastopol, CA: O'Reilly.

Hachten, W.A. 2005. *The Troubles of Journalism.* 3rd ed. Mahwah, NJ: Lawrence Erlbaum Associates.

Hart, R.P. 1994. *Seducing America: How Television Charms the Modern Voter.* New York: Oxford University Press.

Hedgpeth, S. 2000. "Daily Show's Satiric Eye." *Plain Dealer* (Cleveland), 30 July, p. 61.

Johnson, P. 2003. "Trust of Media Keeps on Slipping." *USA Today,* 28 May.

Jones, J.P. 2005a. *Entertaining Politics: New Political Television and Civic Culture.* Lanham, MD: Rowman & Littlefield.

———— 2005b. "The Shadow Campaign in Popular Culture." In *The 2004 Presidential Campaign: A Communication Perspective* (pp. 195–216), edited by R Denton. Lanham, MD: Rowman & Littlefield.

Keefer, B. 2004. "You Call That News? I Don't." *Washington Post,* 12 September, p. B2.

Kovach, B., and Rosenstiel, T. 2001. *The Elements of Journalism: What Newspeople Should Know and the Public Should Expect.* New York: Crown.

Mindich, D.T.Z. 2005. *Tuned Out: Why Americans Under 40 Don't Follow the News.* New York: Oxford University Press.

Patterson, T.E. 1993. *Out of Order.* New York: Random House.

Rich, F. 2003. "Jon Stewart's Perfect Pitch." *New York Times,* 20 April, sec. 2, p. 1.

Riegert, K., with Johansson, A. 2005. "The Struggle for Credibility in the Iraq War." In *The Iraq War: European Perspectives on Politics, Strategy, and Operations.* London: Routledge.

Roberts, G.; Kunkle, T., and Layton, C. 2001. *Leaving Readers Behind: The Age of Corporate Newspapering.* Fayetteville: University of Arkansas Press.

Scheuer, J. 1999. *The Sound Bite Society: Television and the American Mind.* New York: Four Walls Eight Windows.

Schutz, C. 1977. *Political Humor: From Aristophanes to Sam Ervin.* New York: Fairleigh Dickinson University Press.

Seelye, K.Q. 2005a. "At Newspapers, Some Clipping." *New York Times,* 10 October, p. C1.

———. 2005b. "Why Newspapers Are Betting on Audience Participation." *New York Times,* 4 July.

———. 2005c. "Survey on News Media Finds Wide Displeasure," *New York Times,* 27 June.

Tuchman, C. 1978. *Making News: A Study in the Construction of Reality.* New York: Free Press.

Webster, F. 1995. *Theories of the Information Society.* London: Routledge.

West, D.M., and Orman, J. 2003. *Celebrity Politics.* Upper Saddle River, NJ: Prentice-Hall.

Younge, G. 2004. "Washington Post Apologizes for Underplaying WMD Scepticism," *The Guardian,* 13 August, p. 2.

Examining the Text

1. As Jones states, in 2000 the Pew Research Center reported that 47 percent of people under the age of thirty were "informed at least occasionally" about the campaign or candidates by late-night talk shows. Why does Jones refer to this statistic as a "myth"? What difference does it make, according to Jones, if this statistic is or isn't accurate?

2. In paragraph 12, Jones states that *The Daily Show* isn't limited by the same professional constraints that apply to mainstream journalism. What are those constraints? How does *The Daily Show*'s freedom from these constraints help it deliver more insightful, useful information, according to Jones?

3. Jones notes that *The Daily Show* episode that he observed included a number of video clips that did not appear on CNN and that traditional journalists would not deem "newsworthy" (e.g., Bush's opening remarks in his speech in Wilkes-Barre, Kerry's appearance on Dr. Phil). How does *The Daily Show* make these items relevant? Do you agree that these video clips provide important information about the candidates?

4. What evidence does Jones provide to prove that mainstream journalism is in a state of crisis? What does he mean by "authenticity" in this context?

5. *Thinking rhetorically:* Jones begins the article with a three-paragraph overview of his argument. What do you think of this as an opening strategy? Does it help or hurt your ability to understand the points that Jones makes later in the article? Rereading these opening paragraphs after having read the article, do you think that they provide an accurate summary?

For Group Discussion

Near the end of the article, Jones includes a quotation in which Bryan Keefer reflects on the way that his generation of "twenty-somethings" thinks about the news. Reread this quotation—and the entire last paragraph of the article—and consider the extent to which Keefer's perspective applies to your generation as well. Specifically, do your friends and fellow students see news as a "product, produced by politicians and publicists"? In a discussion with several fellow students, share your response to Keefer's quotation and your overall view of mainstream news.

Writing Suggestion

Replicate Jones's study on a more modest level by watching two different news shows on the same night, taking notes, and comparing their coverage of the events of the day.

Begin the assignment by selecting two news shows that you think will offer interesting similarities and contrasts; you might compare a comedy news show to a "serious" one, as Jones does, or you might choose shows that you think have different political biases.

Next, watch (and if you can, tape) the shows. As you're watching, make note of the order of the stories being discussed, how much time is spent on each story, and what information is conveyed in the story.

Review the summaries you wrote as you watched the shows in order to determine similarities and differences. Do some prewriting in response to the following questions: What conclusions can you draw from the order in which stories were presented and from the time allocated to each? Were there significant differences in the information that the two shows presented on the same stories? What kinds of stories were covered in one show but not in another?

After completing the prewriting activity, formulate a thesis that provides a general statement about the similarities and differences between the two news shows. In the body of your essay, support your thesis, as Jones does, with specific examples drawn from your observations of both shows.

ADDITIONAL SUGGESTIONS FOR WRITING ABOUT TELEVISION

1. This chapter concludes with three essays about the relatively new genre of comedy news shows. Choose another genre (such as reality shows, makeover shows, game shows, situation comedies, detective shows, cartoons, talk shows, soap operas, or live police dramas) and analyze the underlying presuppositions of this genre. What specific beliefs, actions, and relationships do these shows encourage? How and why do these shows appeal to the audience? If everything that you knew were based on your exposure to this genre of show, what kind of world would you expect to encounter, how would you expect people to behave toward each other, and what sort of values would you expect them to have? To support your analysis of the genre, use examples from specific shows, but keep in mind that your essay should address the genre or category of shows in general.

2. According to sociologists and psychologists, human beings are driven by certain basic needs and desires. Some of the articles in this chapter attempt to account for the powerful appeal of television in our culture, suggesting that we rely on television to fulfill needs that aren't met elsewhere. Consider some of the following basic needs and desires that television might satisfy for you or for the broader viewing public:

> to be amused
> to gain information about the world
> to have shared experiences
> to find models to imitate
> to see authority figures exalted or deflated
> to experience, in a controlled and guilt-free situation, extreme emotions
> to see order imposed on the world
> to reinforce our belief in justice
> to experience thrilling or frightening situations
> to believe in romantic love
> to believe in magic, the marvelous, and the miraculous
> to avoid the harsh realities of life
> to see others make mistakes

Referring to items on this list, or formulating your own list of needs and desires, compose an essay in which you argue that television succeeds or fails in meeting our basic needs and desires. Use specific television programs that you're familiar with as concrete evidence for your assertions.

3. As the articles on *The Daily Show* and *The Colbert Report* indicate, it's possible for people to interpret the messages of a television show in substantially different ways. Choose a show that you're familiar with and about which you think there can be multiple interpretations. You might think about older shows, such as *Star Trek* or *The Sopranos,* or more recent shows, such as *Family Guy* or *Lost*. You might want to watch a few episodes of the show (all of the ones mentioned above have past episodes available on video and DVD) just to remind yourself of the characters, setting, typical plot structure, and other details. Then write an essay in which your thesis states two (or more) possible interpretations of the show. In the body of the essay, explain what details of the show support each of these interpretations. You might conclude the essay by stating which interpretation you find most persuasive.

Internet Activities

1. Game shows have long been a popular television genre, and their popularity of late seems to be on the rise. One reason may be found in their similarity to reality TV shows, in that they allow for a degree of audience interactivity that scripted shows like dramas and comedies lack; after all, viewers can become participants on game shows and gain instant celebrity if they do well. Game shows also seem to appeal to our greed (or our desire to get rich quickly and without too much work) as well as to our competitive nature. In preparation for writing an essay on game shows, recall some of the ones that you've seen on TV, and check the *Common Culture* Web site for links to sites related to game shows. Then, write an essay in which you analyze the reasons why this television genre is appealing to viewers. As part of your essay, you might decide to compare and contrast game shows to reality television shows to determine the relative appeal of these two genres.

2. Although it's difficult to predict developments having to do with the Internet, a possibility discussed by experts is that television and the World Wide Web will, in some way, merge. Perhaps your TV screen will become your computer monitor, or you'll be able to order movies and view television shows through your computer and Internet connection. Already we see some early connections between the two media, for instance in the live Web casts that some TV shows are doing, or in exclusive Web casts (that is, programs or videos that are shown only on the Web and not on TV). In addition, most news and sports shows have companion Web sites that offer viewers additional information, pictures, interviews, etc. Consider some of these developments, discussed in further detail at the links provided at the *Common Culture* Web site. Then, write an essay in which you discuss the ways in which the Web competes with or complements television. Do the two media provide the same kind of information and entertainment, or do they offer fundamentally different viewing experiences?

Reading Images

The image at the bottom of page CI-2 is a still photograph of Nam June Paik's video installation artwork, entitled "TV Buddha Reincarnated." Paik is a well-known Korean–American artist whose works incorporate television, video, and other technologies in thought-provoking and aesthetically interesting ways. (If you're intrigued by "TV Buddha Reincarnated," you can find out more information about Paik and view some of his other work at the Artcyclopedia Web site [*http://www.artcyclopedia.com/artists/paik_nam_june.html*].)

The title of this piece—"TV Buddha Reincarnated"—refers to an earlier and simpler work by Paik, entitled "TV Buddha." In "TV Buddha," Paik positioned a statue of the Buddha looking at a television set; on top of the television set was a video camera, trained on the statue of the Buddha. In essence, the Buddha statue was "watching" himself (or itself) on television.

As you can see, "TV Buddha Reincarnated" incorporates more technologies than the earlier piece: there's a video camera, but also a telephone and a computer. The statue of the Buddha has been refashioned as well, with what appears to be an interior of wires, circuit boards, and batteries.

Begin an analytical essay about this image by first describing it as clearly and in as much detail as possible. Consider issues of perspective, color, positioning, shapes, sizes, and focal point. Next, identify what you see as the three or four most significant components of the work, whether it's the use of the Buddha statue as part of this piece (with the meditational and religious overtones that the statue conveys), the Buddha's high-tech (but seemingly antique) interior, the telephone, the video camera, the computer (replacing the television from the earlier "TV Buddha" piece), or some other component. In separate paragraphs, offer an interpretation of each of these components, attempting to explain what meaning they add to the work. Keep in mind that although what you see in this textbook is a photograph, "TV Buddha Reincarnated" was an installation piece (with the video camera turned on and recording). People viewing the work could walk around it and see it from different angles. You might want to comment on how this interactive viewing experience could change the meaning of different components of the work.

Finally, draw your analysis together in a statement that articulates what you see as the message of "TV Buddha Reincarnated." What story does this artwork tell? What point do you think Paik is trying to convey through this piece? In your conclusion, draw on any of the readings in the "Television" chapter that are relevant to your analysis.

4

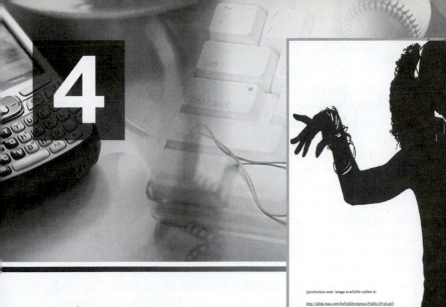

[production note: image available online at:
http://idisk.mac.com/kellykthompson/Public/iPod.gif]

Works with Mac or PC. Over a million

Popular
Music

A dancer, her arms outstretched, stands in stark silhouette against a vibrant fuchsia background. Electronic pulses from her graphically contrasting MP3 player reach her brain through earbuds as she gazes heavenward, eyes seemingly closed. The listener appears to be transported by the music, in a state of blissful trance.

By virtue of its sheer volume, rhythm, and encompassing presentation, music has the capacity to take us to completely different psychic spaces. It can lift us from our ordinary sense of reality and profoundly affect our moods, emotions, energy level, and even our level of sexual arousal. Furthermore, the lyrics, when combined with these powerful aural appeals, become all the more potent and suggestive, influencing our feelings of isolation or belonging, our relation to parents and friends, our attitudes toward authority figures, our notions about romance, and our views about gender and race.

The articles in this chapter discuss the ways in which people are "constructed" by what they hear—that is, how their beliefs, values, attitudes, and morals are shaped by the music they listen to. Some observers see this phenomenon as potentially dangerous since it encourages people—especially young people—to transgress the boundaries imposed by civilized society. However, other critics contend that popular music plays a very positive role in contemporary society since it allows people to voice feelings and ideas that would otherwise not be widely heard. This is especially the case with rap and hip-hop music, as several writers in the second section of this chapter observe. Originally created by and intended for young, African American inner-city audiences, hip-hop subsequently gained widespread acceptance, to the point that it became a major force in the recording industry, thus giving previously disenfranchised urban youth a more pervasive presence in the popular culture. However, some observers of pop-musical trends have begun to question the sustainability of hip-hop as a mainstream form, and this chapter also addresses the current debate over the question, "Is hip-hop dead" . . . or is it still a vital musical force to be reckoned with?

As you read these essays, perhaps hooked up to your iPod and blasting the latest Coldplay, Lil Wayne, Death Cab for Cutie, Rihanna, M.I.A., or Tupac posthumous release, you might consider the implications of music in your life: the reasons why you listen to certain kinds of music, the messages embodied in their lyrics and rhythm, and the pleasures and possible dangers inherent in letting popular music move you to a completely different frame of mind.

Is Hip-Hop Dead?

Rap and Race: It's Got a Nice Beat, But What About the Message?

RACHEL E. SULLIVAN

Over roughly three decades, hip-hop music has traveled from the Bronx, across the country, and around the world. Rap's roots are in New York's African American neighborhoods, but its audience is just as likely to be Caucasian suburbanites. In the following article, published in the Journal of Black Studies, *author Rachel Sullivan attempts to discern differences in attitude toward rap based on race. She wants to know, for example, whether Black adolescents are more committed to, and more knowledgeable about, hip-hop and its practitioners than White youths.*

As Sullivan develops her article, she closely scrutinizes earlier research on rap, which primarily explored rap's role as a form of resistance among Black listeners. In reviewing and analyzing previous research, Sullivan focuses on a key question: Does rap retain a role in racial identification even as its audience grows in size and racial diversity? The article details the result of a poll she conducted among young people—both Black and White—in a midwestern city.

As you read, notice how the author develops her background information and her hypotheses first before delving into the actual research she conducted. Why do you think it's important for her to acknowledge both the previous research and critique its shortcomings? How did her findings differ from her expectations, as stated at the beginning of the piece?

229

RACE AND RAP'S ROOTS

Rap music emerged in the mid-1970s in New York City. Since that period, it has grown from a New York phenomenon to a mainstay of popular music in the United States and around the world (McGregor, 1998). Most of the research on rap music explores its history and development as a social movement (Rose, 1991, 1994) and analyzes the content of lyrics (Henderson, 1996; Martinez, 1993, 1997; Pinn, 1999). Although these studies have contributed to our understanding of

1

hip-hop, they are more focused on music artists and less on rap fans.[1] Thus, this article marks a departure from much of the research because it focuses mostly on rap's listeners and their interpretations of rap, specifically racial differences in adolescents' opinions of rap.

In its early years, rap's fans were primarily Black and Latino; 2 however, the 1980s saw the popularity of rap music expand dramatically. Artists such as Run DMC, LL Cool J, Salt N' Pepa, and the Beastie Boys all gained popularity not only with urban African Americans and Latinos but also with White adolescents outside the inner city (Rose, 1994). By the late 1980s, rap was no longer viewed as a fad but as a distinctive musical form. In spite of the increasing numbers of White rap fans, many people still viewed rap consumers as African American.[2]

How these fans interpret and reinterpret rap music and how 3 important rap music is in their lives have not been thoroughly explored. Furthermore, studies on the potential differences that racial/ethnic groups may have are often limited in much of the literature. Given the racialized political themes in rap (Martinez, 1997), it is possible that rap's White fans may see rap in a different light. They may also try to avoid listening to rap that involves a more explicit critique of racism.

During the 1980s, genres of rap became more noticeable, and 4 many rappers turned to more overtly political themes.[3] They addressed gang violence, police brutality, and other politically charged issues, such as poverty and racism (Martinez, 1997). The more politically oriented rap became very popular in the late 1980s and early 1990s (Rose, 1991), a period that some refer to as the golden era of rap (Powell, 2000). The group Public Enemy was at the forefront of this movement with songs like "Fight the Power," "By the Time I Get to Arizona," and "911 is a Joke" (Drayton, Shocklee, & Sadler, 1990; Ridenhour, Shocklee, & Sadler, 1991; Shocklee, Sadler, & Ridenhour, 1989), all of which addressed the effects of White racism in the United States (Rose, 1991, 1994). Even "gangsta rappers" injected political views into their music; for example, Ice Cube's (1991) "How to Survive in South Central" criticizes the Los Angeles Police Department's treatment of African Americans.[4]

Although more overtly political rap lost popularity in the mid- 5 1990s, some critical discourse is still embedded in the lyrics of many recent rap songs. Nevertheless, rap's more critical voices have been marginalized in recent years. Some say that corporate control and marketing have deadened hip-hop's political edge (Powell, 2000). Rather than offering a critique of the postindustrial United States, which was more evident in early rap (Rose, 1994), rap's critical voice has faded into the background. Even though this may not be directly connected to rap's widening and "Whitening" audience, it is probably not coincidental.

From the start, the public viewed hip-hop culture and rap music 6
through a racist lens. Rappers and rap fans were often portrayed as men-
acing Black adolescents, and rap music was vilified as violent and misog-
ynistic (Feagin, Vera, & Batur, 2001; Rose, 1994). As Rose (1994) noted, rap
music has both overt and covert political dimensions: "Rap's poetic voice
is deeply political in content and spirit, but its hidden struggle—that of
access to public space and community resources and the interpretation of
Black expression—constitutes rap's hidden politics" (p. 145). She also
pointed out the "struggle between rappers' counter-dominant speech and
the exercise of institutional and discursive power against them." Rose
(1994) highlighted the role of institutional racism leveled against rappers,
who were given poor record contracts and forced into recording divisions
that had smaller budgets. Moreover, these same acts found it nearly
impossible to put together concert tours because insurance companies
refused to insure their concerts. These companies argued that rap acts
were a great risk because of their allegedly violent fans (Rose, 1994). Thus,
the struggle for rap artists and fans to gain respect has taken place in the
context of pervasive, institutionalized White racism.

Of particular interest are the criticisms leveled by White politi- 7
cians, almost all of whom viewed rap as producing potential victimizers. Vice President Dan Quayle attacked rapper Tupac Shakur for
promoting violence. President George H. W. Bush also voiced his antirap (anti-Black) sentiments when he criticized Ice-T and Body Count's
song "Cop Killer" (Rose, 1994). (Ironically, neither politician had heard
these albums; in fact, Dan Quayle did not even pronounce Tupac's
name correctly, and Bush failed to realize that Body Count was in fact a
heavy metal group.) President Bill Clinton also leveled similar charges
at rapper Sista Souljah, arguing that she advocated killing Whites
(Feagin et al., 2001). Other well-known political figures, such as Bob
Dole and Supreme Court nominee Robert Bork, have also added their
own critiques of rap music (Ogbar, 1999). All these criticisms of rappers
were made by politicians in a highly racialized (racist) context. Even
though many of their criticisms may have relayed legitimate concerns
about violence, their discussions also appealed to fears that these rappers would somehow incite violence among Black youth; moreover,
they appealed to Whites' fears of Black youth.

Rap music has long been the target of criticism from the popular 8
media, White politicians, and even some older African Americans.
Often, antirap sentiments are thinly veiled anti-Black comments.
Moreover, these antirap comments are often framed differently from
those attacking White musicians, as Binder's (1993) analysis of media
accounts indicates. Her study indicated that White heavy metal fans
were viewed as potential victims of the music, whereas predominantly
Black rap fans were viewed by media outlets as potential victimizers.

A small number of African American leaders have also criticized   9
rap on similar grounds. C. Deloris Tucker and Reverend Calvin Butts
have both argued that rap music promotes violence and misogyny and
have publicly criticized rap music on these grounds (Ogbar, 1999; Rose,
1994). White media outlets, possibly in search of African Americans to
make criticisms, have quickly picked up Black leaders' criticisms.

In the new millennium, critics from within the hip-hop commu-   10
nity have argued that many contemporary artists have abandoned
antiracism messages and focused instead on money and sexual
exploits (Powell, 2000). They go on to say that corporate control and the
desire to reach a "wider and Whiter" audience has led rap away from
overtly antiracist sentiments. Although hip-hop artists have always
been diverse and self-critical (Ogbar, 1999), criticism from within
hip-hop seems to have increased in recent years.

Although many leaders have argued about the effects of rap on   11
its fans, studies exploring effects of rap are few. This is partly because
the small body of research on hip-hop focuses more on artists, lyrical
content, and the history of hip-hop. Moreover, any social differences
(gender, age, race, social class, etc.) in fans that could be correlated with
influence are generally overlooked.

232

RACE AND RAP'S AUDIENCE

Debates regarding the effects of rap music are missing one very critical   12
voice—that of fans. While politicians and other community leaders argue
over "how corrupting" rap can be and researchers look at the themes and
history of the music, few people speak directly to rap fans asking them
what they feel about rap and how important it is in their lives.

In spite of the criticism, the popularity of rap continues to grow.   13
Billboard's top 100 albums of April 11, 1998, included thirteen rap
albums, whereas *Billboard*'s top 100 albums of January 20, 2001,
included twenty one rap acts.[5] Given the tremendous increase in rap's
popularity, it is evident that rap's White audience has grown dramatically. In the early 1990s, Public Enemy's Chuck D estimated that 60 percent of his audience was White (Rose, 1994). However, it is very difficult to make any precise estimates of the racial makeup of the rap
audience because no specific information has been collected.

Even though many people have made claims about rap music and   14
its effect on its listeners, research on music effects generally focuses on
young Whites and their attitudes about rock and roll, punk, or heavy
metal (Arnett, 1992, 1993, 1995; Fox, 1987; Gold, 1987; Rosenbaum &
Prinsky, 1991; Roe, 1995; Snow, 1987; Stack, Gundlach, & Reeves, 1994).
Jonathon Epstein's (1994) collection of essays, *Adolescents and Their Music:*

If It's Too Loud, You're Too Old, does include one essay on rap music, but this is surrounded by thirteen other essays all dealing with rock and heavy metal.

Many of the studies analyzing rap have been more qualitative 15 and theoretical, focusing on the role of rap music in popular culture (Fenster, 1995; Martinez, 1997) and its use as a form of resistance (Berry, 1994; Martinez, 1993; Pinn, 1996; Rose, 1991). However, these studies did not examine multiracial samples and did not ask specific questions focusing on the attitudes of rap's audience.

One study by Epstein, Pratto, and Skipper (1990) analyzed the 16 relationship between behavior problems and preference for rap and heavy metal music. This study indicates that preference for heavy metal and rap was highly correlated with race: 96 percent of those who preferred heavy metal were White, and 98 percent of those who preferred rap were Black. In addition, they found that preference for both forms of music was not associated with behavior problems.

Three studies have focused on young people's opinions of rap. 17 One study written by Berry (1994) concluded that rap helps low income African American youth develop empowering beliefs that help them connect with their culture and develop positive identities. However, the weakness of this study is that it does not give a detailed analysis of students' responses or the questions students were asked, so it is difficult to gain a thorough understanding of the students' attitudes. Moreover, the sample only included low income African Americans in an Upward Bound program.

The second study from *American Demographics* magazine reported 18 on a survey conducted by Teenage Research Unlimited (Spiegler, 1996). This study revealed that 58 percent of those younger than eighteen years and 59 percent of those eighteen to twenty years *liked* or *strongly liked* rap. This study also found that several fashions associated with hip-hop were considered "in" by twelve- to nineteen-year-olds. Seventy-eight percent of adolescents said that baggy clothes were in, 76 percent said pro sports apparel was in, and 69 percent said hooded sweatshirts were in. The author argued that rap has expanded the market for White designers such as Tommy Hilfiger and DKNY; moreover, style of dress has become a way for Whites to connect with Blacks without actually having any face-to-face contact. Although this indicates that there are racial differences, those differences were not the focus of the survey.

Finally, the most detailed study of rap's effect on adolescents was 19 conducted by Kuwahara (1992). This study found that 13.3 percent of Black college students listened to rap all the time, and 29.7 percent listened to rap often. Kuwahara also found that Black men had a stronger preference for rap than Black women. The analysis of White college students revealed that 51.6 percent of White men and 68.9 percent of White women

233

seldom or *never* listened to rap. When the two groups were compared, White students demonstrated less knowledge of rap acts regardless of their preference for rap music. However, Whites and Blacks did not differ much in their reasons for listening to rap. Both groups preferred the beat most and the message second. Drawing on qualitative responses from Black students, Kuwahara argued that rap music and the styles of dance associated with it serve as forms of resistance to the dominant culture. However, findings from this study may be dated. Rap's popularity has increased significantly since 1992, and the White audience for rap has increased (*The Source*, 1998).

Because of the rapid change in rap's popularity, it is necessary to   20
reevaluate youth's attitudes toward rap. More literature on rap is also needed because the current writings are few and many theoretical claims have not been substantiated through empirical work.

METHOD AND HYPOTHESES

To explore the relationship between racial identity and preference   21
for rap music, I conducted surveys in a small Midwestern city. I approached teenagers on a Saturday afternoon in a local mall and asked them to fill out a brief survey about the music they listened to. In creating this survey, I developed four major hypotheses related to racial differences in adolescents' reactions to and interpretations of rap music.

First, I predicted that Black adolescents would have stronger   22
preferences for rap music than White adolescents. Given the high percentage of African American rappers and rap's history of articulating concerns of Black youth, I expected that young African Americans would like rap music more than Whites. Moreover, at least two prior studies found this (Epstein et al., 1990; Kuwahara, 1992).

For the second hypothesis, I expected that Black respondents   23
would be more likely to agree with the statements, "Rap is a truthful reflection of society," "I find myself wearing clothes similar to rappers," and "I find myself using words or phrases similar to rappers." If Kuwahara's 1992 study is still accurate and Black students like rap music more than their White counterparts, then I expect that Black adolescents will incorporate rap music and rap acts into their everyday life to a greater extent than White adolescents.

Next, I hypothesized that Black adolescents would listen to a   24
wider variety of rap acts. In spite of rap's increasing popularity with Whites, I expected that Black adolescents will still be more knowledgeable about rap acts (Kuwahara, 1992).

Finally, I expected that Whites (who are rap fans) would be most   25
likely to say that rap has affected their opinions about racism. If rap

234

does act as an interracial socializer, then it may very well be that White fans learn about the effects of racism and discrimination through rap music. White adolescents may also be more affected because African American adolescents are more likely to have many more sources, such as parents, religious leaders, or peers, through whom they learn about racism. On the other hand, White adolescents are probably less likely to hear about racism through peers and family members; therefore, they may be most affected by rap. Although the study was generally guided by hypotheses, I also put an open-ended question at the end of the survey, asking rap fans why they listened to rap, which was designed to give the respondents an opportunity to express their feelings outside of the narrow categories that I previously provided.

FINDINGS

The response rate was very high: Only three adolescents refused to participate in the study. There were a total of 51 respondents—twenty-one Blacks, seventeen Whites, seven Latinos, and six who marked other categories. Nineteen of the respondents were girls and thirty two were boys, and the mean age of respondents was sixteen years old. The questionnaire included thirteen questions. Participants were asked their age, gender, and race as basic demographic questions. Then they were asked how much they liked rap on a scale ranging from ten (*It's my favorite music*) to one (*I don't like it at all*). Participants were also asked how many hours they listened to rap and which three rap artists they listen to most. The next four questions asked how rap had influenced them, and the final, open-ended question asked those who listened to rap why they listened. 26

Rap music appeared to be very popular within the sample. Overall, students rated rap 7.98 on the 10-point scale. The mean rating was 8.57 for Blacks, 7.18 for Whites, and 8.29 for Latinos.[6] However, the difference between racial groups was not statistically significant.[7] What was most surprising was that twenty two of the respondents gave rap a ten, saying that it was their favorite music. Within this group, racial differences were more evident: thirteen of these respondents were Black, three were Latino, four were White, and two marked multiple racial categories or no category.[8] This does provide some evidence that rap is more popular with African Americans; however, the difference did not appear to be significant in this sample. 27

Overall, respondents registered slight agreement with the statement, "Rap is a truthful reflection of society." Moreover, there were not strong racial differences. African Americans had a mean of 3.3, and Whites had a mean 3.1 (on a five-point scale where five represented *strongly agree*). So the hypothesis that Blacks would be more likely to agree with this statement was not confirmed. However, another finding 28

235

did come out of this particular question. Those who were rap fans were much more likely to agree that rap is a truthful reflection of society.[9]

The hypotheses that African Americans were more likely to agree 29 with the statements, "I find myself wearing clothes similar to rappers" and "I find myself using words or phrases similar to rappers" were supported. Black adolescents were much more likely to report wearing clothes similar to rappers, and they were somewhat more likely to say that they used words similar to rappers. Only one White respondent agreed that he wore clothes similar to rappers; however, eight Whites reported that they used words or phrases similar to rappers.

White fans were more likely to say that rap had affected their 30 opinion about racism than Black fans. However, what was even more interesting was that the overall agreement for Whites, regardless of whether they were fans, was higher than that of African Americans. Even though there were racial differences in agreement with this state-ment, overall the respondents moderately disagreed; they did not believe rap has had much of an effect on their opinions about racism.

The two open-ended questions in the survey provided the most 31 interesting answers. They were used to address the third hypothesis that Black adolescents would be more knowledgeable about rap. I asked the respondents to name their three favorite rap acts, and provided them with three blanks. African Americans did name a wider variety of rap acts; they named a total of twenty seven different acts, and only three answers were left blank. In contrast, White adolescents named only fifteen different acts, and left fourteen blanks. Racial differences in whom adolescents named as their favorite rap acts were small.[10]

Although I formulated no hypotheses about racial differences in 32 reasons for listening to rap music, some differences were evident. Whites, particularly young women, were much more likely to say that they lis-tened to rap because it had a "nice beat." Black adolescents gave more diverse responses, and the most common response was variations of "I like it." However, a significant number of African American adolescents gave responses that indicated that rap was an affirmation of their experi-ences. The following five responses were indicative of these responses:

Teach me things or tell me things about life. (Black male, 17)
Because it hits home, when I listen to it it's something I can relate to.
    (Black male, 18)
Because it tells the truth about how us Black people live being raised in
    the ghetto. (Black female, 15)
Because I like the way it sounds and some rapper just tell the truth and
    the way things really are. (Black female, 17)
Mostly because of the way they talk and state about people's real life.
    (Black female, 13)

Only one White respondent had a similar response: 33

Because some of the things the rappers rap about is the same type of shit that happens in everyday life to sombody [sic] from the hood. (White male, 18)

Even the response by this eighteen-year-old White male is written   34
in third person, indicating some distance between this young man and "sombody [sic] from the hood."

These statements indicate that there are some racial differences   35
in why African Americans and Whites listen to rap and how knowledgeable they are about rap. Unfortunately, the methodology limited the ability to probe on many of these questions, which could have provided more detailed answers and revealed more specific racial differences.

Overall, this survey indicates that the racial gap in adolescents'   36
desirability ratings for rap is closing. Nevertheless, racial differences in adolescents' perceptions of rap still exist. However, this survey is primarily exploratory. It does not include a random sample and does not allow us to further explore how Whites and Blacks are affected by and committed to rap.[11]

237

RAP'S RACIAL IMPLICATIONS

The most striking finding from this study is that the racial gap in pref-   37
erence for rap music is closing. Unlike the previous research (Epstein et al., 1990), this study shows that preference for rap was not significantly different for Blacks and Whites; however, this may be misleading. Black adolescents named more rap artists and were more likely to say that they wore clothes like rappers and used words or phrases similar to rappers. Moreover, African Americans were more likely to say that they listened to rap because it was truthful and taught them about life. Although White adolescents say they like rap, many of the White respondents in this survey had difficulty naming three rap artists, which indicated that they did not have a high level of commitment to the music. Rap may only be a fad and a phase, as indicated by this statement given when a respondent was asked why he listened to rap:

I used to but now I don't anymore. (White male, 16)

The responses to the open-ended questions on the survey sup-   38
port the idea that African Americans have higher commitment to rap. The wider variety of rap acts Black adolescents listed provides evidence that they have a broader knowledge of rap. Some of the White

respondents' answers to the question, "Why do you listen to rap?" indicated that Whites were listening to rap because it has a "good beat," so the message of the music was not as important as the sound. This leads me to believe that although Black and White adolescents are saying that they like rap, they may be getting two different messages from the same music. Many young African Americans appear to be looking at rap for its messages about life and its aesthetically pleasing sound, yet Whites seem to be listening almost exclusively because of the aesthetically pleasing sound. In many ways, these findings support Berry's (1994) and Martinez's (1997) arguments that rap is a form of resistance. Although young African American rap fans are not arguing that rap leads them into social protest, they seem to be indicating that it offers a counterdominant message that they use as an affirmation of their experiences.

Not only are rap music and hip-hop culture a potential form of 39 resistance, they may also have broad-reaching implications for identity development and maintenance. Although many may see music as a passing phase, it is often a source of information about one's group (or other groups), and it can also be a (re)affirmation of one's identity. This could be particularly true for young African Americans, who are less likely to have their experiences reflected in the dominant culture.

Therefore, future research needs to examine not just how much 40 adolescents report they like to rap but their knowledge and commitment to the music. Furthermore, the extent to which Black and White adolescents are getting different messages from the same rap songs must be clarified.

Because so many young Whites listen to rap, future research 41 should also focus on rap as an interracial socializer. Whites in this study (who were fans) indicated that rap had affected their opinions about racism. The survey did not measure how rap had affected their opinions of racism or how it has affected their opinions of African Americans more generally. However, rap as an interracial socializer may be detrimental for many reasons. First, many Whites who listen to rap may be motivated by curiosity. Rap may allow White adolescents to satisfy their curiosities without ever having face-to-face contact or interpersonal relationships with any African Americans, so rap can be a way for Whites to vicariously learn about African Americans. They may be able to satisfy curiosities about African Americans and even mimic what they may see as African American life without having an understanding or appreciation of African American experiences. Second, rap music does not reflect the diversity of African Americans. Rap often operates from the perspectives of young, urban, Black men. White adolescents may get a picture of African American life that is not inclusive of those who are older, from rural areas, or female (or other important social characteristics). The third reason this could be detrimental is because it may perpetuate prejudices, particularly the view that African Americans are materialistic and hedonistic, which could inadvertently promote stereotypes more than it dismantles them. Although rappers themselves are not fully accountable for how their music is interpreted, many fans may not be accessing alternative sources of information about African Americans. In addition, many rap songs are fictional and do not even represent the artists' true beliefs or those beliefs of African Americans in general. Rap, like any other cultural product, is also subjected to corporate control, which could potentially limit antiracist messages because those messages may not be as economically profitable.

I am not making the case that rap sends only negative messages to White adolescents. Many artists do have images that are less stereotypical (Ogbar, 1999); however, those voices are often less commercially successful. Rap would probably be best when combined with other forms of interracial socialization, particularly in a society that has been built on racism, sexism, and capitalism. Daily interactions or interactions that are not from media could be beneficial. 42

One of the more interesting findings in this study is the overall agreement with the statement that rap is a truthful reflection of society.[12] Future research has many questions to answer in this respect. If adolescents agree that rap is a truthful reflection of society, do they value rappers' opinions about political and social issues? Moreover, it is important to understand what aspects of rap adolescents think are truthful. Do young people believe what rappers say about topics such as gender, sexuality, racism, police brutality, wealth, and poverty? This may be very difficult to ascertain, given the ambivalence and the great diversity found within rap. This also has practical applications for political organizers who want to mobilize the hip-hop generation. 43

Rap music research has a very promising future. There is little work in this field, so virtually any aspect of rap music is open to research. Moreover, rap music and hip-hop culture are the products of the first generation to be raised in the postindustrial era (Rose, 1994). Research on racial formations and their effects on the post–baby-boomer generations need to be pursued further given the unique technological and social changes experienced by the hip-hop generation.[13] 44

Although this article focuses primarily on racial differences, future studies can focus on several other areas. Factors such as gender, class, age, and urbanicity affect the production and consumption of rap and preferences for rap. The area of racial differences also needs to be explored further. Many of the responses to this survey need elaboration. Precisely why and how there are racial differences in consumption of rap can be identified through in-depth interviews. In addition, 45

239

rap's effects on Latinos also need to be analyzed. Latino rappers, such as Mellow Man Ace, Kid Frost, Fat Joe, Cuban Link, and Cypress Hill (who have Black and Hispanic members), have made strong contributions to hip-hop, and much research, including this, does not explore Latino opinions. The role of rap as a form of interracial socialization should also be analyzed because such a large number of White adolescents are listening to rap, even those who are not fans cannot help being exposed to at least some rap. Adolescents' interpretations of rap songs must also be examined so researchers can better understand what they are listening to and why they think it is important or unimportant. Finally, more research must be done because rap is constantly changing.

Even though rap music is a relatively new phenomenon, it continues to expand. The current market for rap and hip-hop products is a lucrative business. What started out in the Bronx has spread nationwide. Although rap music is reaching a multiracial audience, this research indicates that Black and White adolescents are influenced by rap in different ways. These differences need to be further examined and interpreted. 46

240

NOTES

[1]It is important here to explain the difference between the term *rap* and *hip-hop*. In the movie *Rhyme and Reason* (Block, Spirer, & Sollinger, 1997), rapper KRS-One defines hip-hop as the cultural phenomenon that appeared in the mid- to late 1970s. Hip-hop culture is primarily organized around the experiences of urban, minority youth, and the primary expressions of hip-hop culture include rapping, break dancing, and graffiti art (Rose, 1994). Some also include DJing as the fourth pillar of hip-hop. So, rap music is a form of expression used by people within the hip-hop community or culture.

[2]It is interesting to note that the Puerto Rican members of the early hip-hop culture were ignored and forgotten by the popular media and many later rap fans.

[3]It is very difficult to make clear distinctions between the genres of rap. Some divide rap into East Coast and West Coast. East Coast rap generally comes from New York, and West Coast rap comes from Los Angeles and its surrounding cities. Dividing rap by coast has some merit because most rappers come from these cities, but it fails to address differences in rap beyond geographic subcultures. Moreover, the division also ignores the recent ascendance of rappers from the South. Others have used the terms *old school* and *new school*—old school rap would be anything before the late 1980s, and new school anything after that point. Rap has also been classified as gangsta rap, political rap, dance rap, fast rap (*The Source*, 1998), and gospel rap. We would also argue that materialistic rap and bravado rap should also be added to the list of rap genres.

[4]Ice Cube and other rappers have long been critical of the Los Angeles Police Department, which seems quite appropriate given the recent revelations about police brutality and misconduct in that department.

[5]Artists such as Snoop Doggy Dogg, Tupac, Notorious B.I.G., Eminem, and others have produced multiplatinum records.

[6]Because there were only seven Latinos in the study, it is difficult to make any accurate generalizations.

[7]All tests of statistical significance were conducted using chi-square. Results are significant if they have a p value of .05 or less.

[8]Only two of the Black respondents giving rap a ten were Black young women. In fact, only three of the twenty-two were females.

[9]Those who rated rap 6 or higher were considered to be fans.

[10]Black adolescents chose Master P as their favorite rap act followed by Tupac, Puff Daddy, Notorious B.I.G., and Ice Cube. The most popular rap artists, according to White adolescents, were Master P followed by Mase, Tupac, Puff Daddy, and Bone Thugs-n-Harmony.

[11]Commitment in this study is operationalized as: the ability to name rap artists, wearing clothes similar to rappers, using words or phrases similar to rappers, belief that rap is a truthful reflection of society, and listening to rap because it is truthful or teaches about life.

[12]This question was included in the survey because it is one main argument used to justify explicit and violent lyrics in rap.

[13]I intentionally avoid using the term *Generation X*; we find this term to be racially loaded. I argue that this term has been used almost exclusively to refer to young, middle-class, White men and their experiences. Personally, I prefer the *hip-hop generation*. Although many may think this is also racially loaded, hip-hop has always been a multiracial movement, which makes the term more inclusive.

REFERENCES

Arnett, J. (1992). The soundtrack of recklessness: Musical preferences and reckless behavior among adolescents. *Journal of Adolescent Research, 7,* 313–331.

Arnett, J. (1993). Three profiles of heavy metal fans: A taste for sensation and a subculture of alienation. *Qualitative Sociology, 16,* 423–443.

Arnett, J. (1995). Adolescents' uses of media for self socialization. *Journal of Youth and Adolescence, 24,* 519–533.

Berry, V. (1994). Redeeming the rap music experience. In J. Epstein (Ed.), *Adolescents and their music: If it's too loud you're too old.* New York: Garland.

Binder, A. (1993). Constructing racial rhetoric: Media depictions of harm in heavy metal and rap music. *American Sociological Review, 58,* 753–767.

Block, C. X., Spirer, P., & Sollinger, D. (1997). *Rhyme and reason* [Video recording]. Produced by City Block and Asian Pictures. West Hollywood, CA: Miramax Films.

Drayton, W., Shocklee, K., & Sadler, E. (1990). 911 is a joke. On *Fear of a Black Planet*. New York: Def Jam Records.

Epstein, J. S. (Ed.). (1994). *Adolescents and their music: If it's too loud you're too old*. New York: Garland.

Epstein, J. S., Pratto, D., & Skipper, J., Jr. (1990). Teenagers, behavioral problems, and preferences for heavy metal and rap music: A case study of a southern middle school. *Deviant Behavior, 11*, 381–394.

Feagin, J. R., Vera, H., & Batur, P. (2001). *White racism: The basics* (2nd ed.). New York: Routledge.

Fenster, M. (1995). Understanding and incorporating rap: The articulation of alternative popular musical practices within dominant cultural practices and institutions. *Howard Journal of Communications, 5*, 223–244.

Fox, K. J. (1987). Real punks and pretenders: The social organization of a counterculture. *Journal of Contemporary Ethnography, 16*, 344–370.

Gold, B. D. (1987). Self-image of punk rock and nonpunk rock juvenile delinquents. *Adolescence, 22*, 535–544.

Henderson, E. A. (1996). Black nationalism and rap music. *Journal of Black Studies, 26*, 308–339.

Ice Cube. (1991). How to survive in South Central. On *Boyz N the Hood* [Cassette]. Burbank, CA: Qwest Records.

Kuwahara, Y. (1992). Power to the people y'all: Rap music, resistance, and Black college students. *Humanity and Society, 16*, 54–73.

Martinez, T. (1993). Recognizing the enemy: Rap music in the wake of the Los Angeles riots. *Explorations in Ethnic Studies, 16*, 115–127.

Martinez, T. (1997). Popular culture: Rap as resistance. *Sociological Perspectives, 40*, 265–286.

McGregor, T. (1998). Worldwide worldwide. *The Source: The Magazine of Hip-Hop Culture & Politics, 100*, 109.

Ogbar, J. (1999). Slouching toward Bork: The culture wars and self-criticism in hip hop music. *Journal of Black Studies, 30*(2), 164–183.

Pinn, A. (1996). Gettin' grown': Note on gansta rap music and notions of manhood. *Journal of African American Men, 2*, 61–73.

Pinn, A. (1999). How ya livin'? Notes on rap music and social transformation. *Western Journal of Black Studies, 23*(1), 10–21.

Powell, K. (2000, October 9). My culture at the crossroads: A rap devotee watches corporate control and apolitical times encroach on the music he has loved all his life. *Newsweek*, p. 66.

Ridenhour, C., Shocklee, H., & Sadler, E. (1991). By the time I get to Arizona. On *Apocolypse 91 . . . The Enemy Strikes Back*. New York: Def Jam Records.

Roe, K. (1995). Adolescents' use of socially devalued media: Towards a theory of media delinquency. *Journal of Youth and Adolescence, 24,* 617–630.

Rose, T. (1991). "Fear of a Black planet": Rap music and Black cultural politics in the 1990s. *Journal of Negro Education, 60,* 276–290.

Rose, T. (1994). *Black noise: Rap music and Black culture in contemporary America.* Hanover, NH: Wesleyan University Press.

Rosenbaum, J. L., & Prinsky, L. (1991). The presumption of influence: Recent responses to popular music subcultures. *Crime & Delinquency, 37,* 528–535.

Shocklee, H., Sadler, E., & Ridenhour, C. (1989). *Fight the Power.* New York: Def Jam Records.

Snow, R. P. (1987). Youth, rock' n roll, and electronic media. *Youth and Society, 18,* 326–343. *The Source: The Magazine of Hip Hop Music, Culture & Politics.* (1998, January). Special 100th Issue.

Spiegler, M. (1996, November). Marketing street culture: Bringing hip-hop style to the mainstream. *American Demographics,* pp. 28–34.

Stack, S., Gundlach, J., & Reeves, J. (1994). The heavy metal subculture and suicide. *Suicide and Life Threatening Behavior, 24,* 15–23.

Examining the Text

1. The author states that debates regarding the effects of rap have tended to exclude the voice of fans. Other studies have been more "qualitative and theoretical." In trying to figure out the role of rap in society, why is it important to speak to fans of the music? Why is it important to examine rap on the basis of race? What insights can fans provide that might not be available by simply looking at music sales, concert attendance, fashion adoption, and so on?

2. Author Sullivan calls rap an "interracial socializer" (Paragraph 25). What do you understand by this term? What are the positive and negative consequences of using rap in this role? In your opinion, does music have the power to bring people of differing backgrounds together?

3. What specific racial differences did the author find in her study? How do these differ from the results she predicted in her hypotheses? Does anything about her study surprise you or challenge previously held beliefs or opinions?

4. If you had been asked the same questions as those surveyed for the article, what would your answers have been? Would your responses align with those surveyed, based on your cultural background?

5. *Thinking rhetorically:* Based on the tone and the format of this piece, who would you say its intended audience is? Provide textual evidence to support your contention that this article was written to enable hip-hop fans to understand better why they listen to the music. Do you think the author is trying to persuade readers to adopt a particular position; if so, what do you think that position is? Find samples in the text that illustrate the article's thematic core belief. By the end of the text, do you feel that the article provided satisfactory answers or raised more questions?

For Group Discussion

Historically, music has played an important role as a force for social change: in the civil rights, anti-Vietnam War, and labor movements, for example. Rap has also a social justice element to it. Discuss whether you think that role is diminished as rap becomes more mainstream or that the power of the lyrics will be lost when audiences cannot identify with its Black-oriented message.

Writing Suggestion

Imagine you are conducting research attempting to measure the influence of rap music on students at your school. Design fifteen to twenty questions that you think would be key to ask, and then administer your survey to as many students as is feasible. In an essay, explain the reasoning behind your choice of questions, making sure to explain your hypotheses and intended methodology, and then discuss the results of your study. Consider this question as a possible thematic center for your paper: Is your sample student population representative of the youthful American population at large, or is it significantly different?

The Miseducation of Hip-Hop

EVELYN JAMILAH

In this article, the author points to criticisms currently being leveled at rap music and hip-hop culture from within the community of African American educators. No one would deny that rap culture has unprecedented popularity among young people. Nevertheless, many of these observers believe that while the themes embodied in rap music may reflect real-life situations within America's inner cities, rap's influence may be ultimately counterproductive, causing Black students to perform worse in school—which, in turn, will perpetuate the negative economic and social conditions that rappers dramatize in their lyrics. Some observers go so far as to insist that young African American students turn away from this popular art form, while others suggest that some university courses focus their attention on rap to make some connections between this popular form and the work of Black historians, sociologists, urban psychologists, and so forth.

As you read this article, attempt to determine the author's own stance toward this topic. Does she play the role of dispassionate observer, merely recording journalistically the arguments swirling around this hotly debated topic, or can you detect a certain agenda, a rhetorical stance underlying her reportage? Note also your own reactions to points raised during this piece. The commentators presented in this article will probably cause you to have some emotional reaction; try to set your emotions aside momentarily, make note of specific points of agreement or disagreement as they arise.

When Jason Hinmon transferred to the University of Delaware two years ago from Morehouse College in Atlanta, the 22-year-old senior says he almost dropped out his first semester. 1

He says that for financial reasons, he came back here to his hometown. But in many ways, he had never felt so abandoned. 2

"I came to class and my professors didn't know how to deal with me," he says, between bites of his a-la-carte lunch. "I could barely get them to meet with me during their office hours." 3

Dark-hued, dreadlocked and, well, young, he says many of his mostly White professors figured they had him pegged. 4

"They took one look at me and thought that I was some hip-hop hoodlum who wasn't interested in being a good student," he says. 5

But if Hinmon represents the "good" students with grounds to resent the stereotype, there are faculty who profess there's no shortage of young people willing to live up—or down—to it. 6

"You see students walking on campus reciting rap lyrics when they should be reciting something they'll need to know on their next test. Some of these same students you won't see back on campus next semester," says Dr. Thomas Earl Midgette, 50, director of the Institute for the Study of Minority Issues at historically Black North Carolina Central University. 7

"These rap artists influence the way they dress," he continues. "They look like hoochie mamas, not like they're coming to class. Young men with pants fashioned below their navel. Now, I used to wear bell-bottoms, but I learned to dress a certain way if I was negotiating the higher education maze. I had to trim my afro." 8

The difference between today's students and their parents, faculty, and administrators is marked, no doubt. Technology's omnipresence—apparent in kids with little patience for anything less than instant meals, faster Internet information, and cellular ubiquity—is certainly at play when it comes to explaining the divide. 9

But what causes more consternation among many college and university officials is a music form, a culture, and a lifestyle they say is eating away at the morals, and ultimately the classroom experience, of today's college students. 10

Hip-hop—brash, vulgar, in-your-face hip-hop—is indisputably the dominant youth culture today. Its most controversial front men 11 floss mad ice (wear lots of diamonds and other expensive jewelry), book bad bitches (usually scantily clad, less than the take home kind of girl), and in general, party it up. Its most visible females brag about their sexual dexterity, physical attributes, and cunning tactics when it comes to getting their rent paid.

With college completion statistics at an embarrassing low and the 12 Black–White achievement gap getting wider by the semester, perhaps it's time to be concerned whether the culture's malevolent message is at play.

But can atrocious retention rates really be linked to reckless 13 music? Or do university officials underestimate their students? Is it that young folk today have no sense of history, responsibility, and plain good manners? Or are college faculty a bunch of old fogies simply more comfortable with Marvin Gaye's "Sexual Healing" than Little Kim's sexual prowess?

Is this no different than the divide we've always seen between 14 young people and their college and university elders? Or do the disparities between this wave of students and those charged with educating them portend something more disparaging?

THE GAP

At the heart of the rift between the two groups is a debate that has both 15 sides passionately disturbed.

Young people say they feel pigeonholed by an image many of 16 them don't support. They say the real rub is that their teachers—Black and White—believe the hype as much as the old lady who crosses the street when she sees them coming.

And they'd like their professors to consider this: They can listen 17 to the music, even party to it, but still have a response just as critical, if not more so, than their faculty and administrators.

Others point out that the pervasiveness of hip-hop's immoral 18 philosophies is at least partly rooted in the fact that the civil rights movement—the older generation's defining moment—surely did not live up to all its promises for Black America.

And further, they say it's important to note that not all hip-hop is 19 irresponsible. In fact, some argue that it's ultimately empowering, uplifting, and refreshing. After all, when was the last time a biology professor sat down with a Mos Def CD? How many can even pronounce his name?

Older faculty, administrators, and parents alike respond that the 20 music is downright filth. And anyone associated with it ought to have their mouths and their morals cleansed.

There's a real problem when a marijuana-smoking ex-con named 21
Snoop Doggy Dog can pack a campus auditorium quicker than Black
historian John Hope Franklin; when more students deify the late Tupac
Shakur and his abrasive lyrics than those who ever read the great
Martin Luther King Jr.'s "I Have a Dream" speech; when kids decked
out in sweats more pricey than their tuition complain that they can't
afford a semester's books; when the gains they fought so hard for are,
in some ways, slowly slipping away.

"I think what causes us the most grief is that hip-hop comes 22
across as heartless, valueless, nihilistic, and certainly anachronistic if
not atheistic," says Dr. Nat Irvin, president of Future Focus 2020, an
urban futures think tank at Wake Forest University in North Carolina.
"Anyone who would argue with that needs to take a look for themselves and see what images are prevalent on BET and MTV."

"But I don't think there's any question that the disconnect comes 23
from the fact that old folks don't have a clue. They don't understand
technology. The world has changed. And there's an enormous age gap
between most faculty on college campuses and the rest of America," he
says.

More than 60 percent of college and university faculty are over 24
the age of forty five. Meanwhile, nearly 53 percent of African
Americans are under thirty and some 40 percent are under twenty.

That means more than half of all Blacks were born after the civil 25
rights movement and the landmark *Brown vs. Board of Education* case.

"There's no big puzzle why these kids are coming with a different 26
ideology," Irvin, 49, says.

THIS IS WHAT BLACKNESS IS

It is universally acknowledged that rap began in New York City's 27
Bronx borough nearly thirty years ago, a mix of Jamaican reggae's
dancehall, America's funk music, the inner city's pent-up frustrations,
and Black folks' general propensity to love a good party.

Pioneering artists like the The Last Poets, The Sugar Hill Gang, 28
Kurtis Blow, and Run-DMC combined creative genius and street savvy
to put hip-hop on the map.

Its initial associations were with graffiti and party music, accord- 29
ing to Dr. Robin D. G. Kelley, professor of history and Africana studies
at New York University.

"Then in the late '80s, you begin to see more politicized manifes- 30
tations of that. BDP, Public Enemy . . . In essays that students wrote that
were not about rap music, but about the urban condition itself, they

would adopt the language. They would quote Public Enemy lyrics, they would quote Ghetto Boys," says Kelley, 38.

"This whole generation of Blacks in particular were trying to 31 carve out for themselves an alternative culture," he continues. "I saw a whole generation for the first time say, 'I don't want to go to corporate America. I don't want to be an attorney. I don't want to be a doctor. I don't want to get paid. I want to make a revolution.'"

"The wave that we're in now is all over the place," he explains. 32

But even hip-hop's fans stop short at endorsing some of the themes prevailing in today's music and mindset.

Kevin Powell, noted cultural critic and former hip-hop journalist, 33 says the biggest difference between the music today and the music at its onset is that "we don't own it."

"Corporate America completely commodified hip-hop," he says. 34 "We create the culture and corporate America takes it and sells it back to us and tells us, 'This is what Blackness is.'"

And while Powell, 34, says he is disappointed in some of the 35 artists, especially the older ones who "should know better," many students are their staunchest defenders.

Caryn Wheeler, 18, a freshman at Bowie State University, explains 36 simply that "every day isn't about love." Her favorite artists? Jay-Z, OutKast, Biggie Smalls, Tupac, and Little Kim, many of whom are linked to hip-hop's controversial side. "We can relate because we see what they are talking about every day," she says.

Mazi Mutafa, 23, is a senior at the University of Maryland College 37 Park and president of the Black Student Union there. He says he listens to jazz and hip-hop, positive artists and those who capture a party spirit. "There's a time to party and have fun, and Jay-Z speaks to that," he says. "But there needs to be a happy medium."

Interrupting, senior Christine Gonzalez, 28, says a lot of artists 38 like Jay-Z tend to be revered by younger students. "As you get older, you tend to tone down your style and find that happy medium," she says. "It's all a state of mind."

"People have to understand that Jay-Z is kind of like a 100-level 39 class—an intro to hip-hop. He brings a lot of people into its fan base," Mutafa chimes in. "But then you have groups like The Roots, which are more like a 400-level class. They keep you engaged in the music. But one is necessary for the other."

Erick Rivas, 17, a freshman also at the University of Maryland, 40 says he listens to Mos Def, Black Star, Mobb Deep, Wu-Tang Clan and sometimes other, more mainstream acts like Jay-Z. "Hip-hop has been a driving force in our lives. It is the soundtrack to our lives," he explains.

KEEPIN' IT REAL

But if hip-hop is the soundtrack to their lives, it may also mark the failure of it. 41

De Reef Jamison, a doctoral candidate who teaches African American history at Temple University in Philadelphia, surveyed 72 Black male college students last summer for his thesis. Then a graduate student at Florida, A&M State University, Jamison was interested in discovering if there are links between students' music tastes and their cultural identity, their grades, and other key indicators. 42

"While the lines weren't always so clear and distinct, I found that many of the students who had a low African self-consciousness, who overidentified with a European worldview and who were highly materialistic were often the students who listened to the most 'gangster' rap, or what I prefer to call reality rap," he explains. 43

As for grades, he says the gangster rap devotees' tended to be lower than those students who listened mostly to what he calls more conscious rap. Still, he's reluctant to draw any hard and fast lines between musical preference and student performance. 44

"I'd recommend that scholars take a much closer look at this," he says. 45

Floyd Beachum, a graduate student at Bowling Green State University in Ohio, surveyed secondary [school] students to try to ascertain if there was a correlation between their behavior and the music they listened to. 46

"The more hyper-aggressive students tended to listen to more hardcore, gangster rap," he says. "Those who could identify with the violence, the drive-by shootings, the stereotypes about women—many times that would play out in their lives." 47

But Beachum, who teamed up with fellow Bowling Green graduate student Carlos McCray to conduct his research, says he isn't ready to draw any sweeping conclusions either. 48

"Those findings weren't across the board," he says, adding that he believes school systems can play a role in reversing any possible negative trends. 49

"If hip-hop and rap influence behavior and you bring all that to school, then the schools should create a very different environment and maybe we'll see more individuals go against the grain," he says. 50

Even undergraduates say they must admit that they see hip-hop's squalid influence on some of their peers. 51

"It upsets me when some young people complain that they can't get a job, but when they go into that interview, they refuse to take off their do-rags, their big gold medallion, and their baggy pants," says 52

Kholiswa Laird, 18, a freshman at the University of Delaware. "But for some stupid reason, a lot of them feel like they're selling out if they wear proper clothes."

"That's just keepin it real," explains Davren Noble, 20, a junior at 53 the University of Delaware. "Why should I have to change myself to get a job? If somebody wants to hire me but they don't like my braids, then either of two things will happen: They'll just have to get over it or I just won't get the job."

It's this kind of attitude that many in higher education see as the 54 crux of the problem.

"We're not gonna serve them well in the university if we don't 55 shake their thinking about how dress is going to influence job opportunities," says Central's Midgette.

Noble, from Maplewood, N.J., is a rapper. And he says that while 56 he grew up in a posh suburb, he often raps about violence.

"I rap about positive stuff, too, but as a Black person in America, 57 it's hard to escape violence," he explains. "Mad Black people grew up in the ghetto, and the music and our actions reflect that."

For sure, art has been known to imitate life. Hip-hop icon Sean 58 "Puffy" Combs—who two years ago gave $750,000 to his alma mater, Howard University—is currently facing charges on his involvement in a Manhattan nightclub shooting last December. Grammy-winning rapper Jay-Z, also was connected with a night club dispute that ended with a record company executive being stabbed last year.

A BAD RAP?

A simple explanation for the boldness of much of rap's lyrics is that 59 "artists have always pushed the limits," Kelley says.

But what's more, there is a politically conscious, stirring, enrich- 60 ing side of hip-hop that many of its fans say is often overlooked.

"Urban radio stations play the same songs every day," says 61 Powell, a former reporter for *Vibe* magazine. "The media is ghettoizing hip-hop. They make it look passe."

Those often included in hip-hop's positive list are Lauryn Hill, 62 Common, Mos Def, Dead Prez, Erykah Badu, Talib Kweli, and other underground acts. Indeed, many of them have been active in encouraging young people to vote. Mos Def and other artists recently recorded a song in memory of Amadou Diallo, "Hip-Hop for Respect."

This is the side of hip-hop many young people say they'd like 63 their faculty to recognize. This is also the side that some people say faculty must recognize.

"There are scholars—I've seen them do this before—who will 64 make a disparaging remark about a whole genre of music, not knowing a doggone thing," NYU's Kelley says. "That's the same thing as saying, 'I've read one article on rational choice theory and it was so stupid, I dismissed the whole genre.' . . . People who are trained in their own fields would never do that with their own scholarship, and yet they are willing to make these really sweeping statements."

"And they don't know. They don't have a critical understanding 65 of the way the music industry operates or the way in which people engage music," he says. "But they are willing to draw a one-to-one correlation between the students' failure and music."

Some professors argue that another correlation should be 66 made: "My most serious students are the die-hard hip-hop fans," says Dr. Ingrid Banks, assistant professor of Black Studies at Virginia Tech. "They are able to understand politics because they understand hip-hop."

Banks says that more of her colleagues would be wise to better 67 understand the music and its culture. "You can't talk about Reagan's policies in the '80s without talking about hip-hop," says the 30-something scholar. "If you start where students are, they make these wonderful connections."

251

CURRICULAR CONNECTIONS

If the augmentation of hip-hop scholarship is any indication, academe 68 just may be coming around to at least tolerating this formidable medium.

Courses on hip-hop, books, essays, and other studied accounts of 69 the genre are being generated by a pioneering cadre of scholars. And while many people see that as notable, there's not yet widespread belief that academe has completely warmed to the idea of hip-hop as scholarship.

Banks, who has taught "Race, Politics and Rap Music in Late 70 Twentieth Century America" at the Blacksburg, VA, school, says she's experiencing less than a speedy response to getting her course included into the department's curriculum.

"I understand that it usually takes a while to get a course 71 approved, but there have been courses in bio-history that were signed off on rather quickly," she says.

But if academe fails to find ways to connect with hip-hop and its 72 culture, then it essentially will have failed an entire generation, many critics say.

"What's happening is that administrators and teachers are faced 73
with a real crisis. And that crisis they can easily attach to the music,"
Kelley says. "It's the way they dress, the way they talk. The real crisis
is their failure to educate; their failure to treat these students like
human beings; their failure to come up with a new message to engage
students."

"Part of the reason why there is such a generational gap is 74
because so few educators make an effort to understand the times in
which they live. You can't apply '60s and '70s methods to teaching in
the new millennium. You can't apply a jazz aesthetic to hip-hop
heads," says Powell, who lectures at seventy to eighty colleges and universities a year. "You have to meet the students where they are. That's
the nature of education. That's pedagogy."

And while Wake Forest's Irvin says he would agree with that sen- 75
timent, he also sees a role that students must play.

"What I see as being the major challenge that these kids will deal 76
with is the image of young, urban America," Irvin says. "Young people
need to ask themselves, 'Who will control their identity?'"

"If they leave it up to the media to define who they are, they'll 77
be devastated by these images," he says. "That's where hip-hop is
killing us."

Examining the Text

1. What judgment does Dr. Thomas Earl Midgette of North Carolina Central
University make about students he sees on campus? What judgment do you
make about Dr. Midgette—that is, do you agree with his belief that hip-hop
attitude and fashion might somehow contribute to academic and/or social
failure?

2. The article alludes to "technology's omnipresence." Describe this concept
and cite some concrete examples to support its validity. What effect does technology have on young people, according to this article, and how does Jamilah
associate technology with the generation gap that exists within school systems?

3. Where did rap music originate, according to the author? How did it come
about, and how did it evolve through subsequent decades? What form(s) does
rap take today?

4. *Thinking rhetorically:* Does the author have an underlying persuasive purpose in composing this piece? If so, what specific techniques does she use to
"win" the reader to her point of view. Cite evidence from the text to support
your conclusions.

For Group Discussion

Jamilah asks the question concerning hip-hop styles and attitude, "Is this no
different than the divide we've always seen between young people and their

college and university elders?" Based on your own experience as a member of the hip-hop generation (even if you're not a rabid fan of hip-hop), attempt to answer this question: Are the styles and behaviors of today the same as the bell-bottoms and Afros to which Dr. Midgette refers near the beginning of this article, or is there something more insidious in hip-hop culture and its effect on students?

Writing Suggestion

Write an essay in which you comment on Jamilah's statement, "There's a real problem when a marijuana-smoking ex-con named Snoop Doggy Dog can pack a campus auditorium quicker than Black historian John Hope Franklin; when more students deify the late Tupac Shakur and his abrasive lyrics than those who ever read the great Martin Luther King Jr.'s 'I Have a Dream' speech." As you formulate a thesis, decide first whether or not you agree with this statement by the author. Next, spend some time freewriting on the topic, letting your mind wander over a wide range of points of contention or agreement. Having accomplished this activity, begin to cut and paste those supporting points into an order that has a coherent logical development, and then fill in that framework with supporting paragraphs that contain concrete evidence and examples from your experience, reading, and music listening.

253

5 Things That Killed Hip-Hop

J-ZONE

A recent album by American hip-hop artist Nas appeared with the title, "Hip Hop Is Dead." In a late September radio interview, Nas commented, "Hip-hop is dead because we as artists no longer have the power." He went on to say, ". . . basically America is dead. There is no political voice. Music is dead. Our way of thinking is dead, our commerce is dead. Everything in this society has been done. That's where we are as a country." These comments, along with the album's title itself, sent a shock wave through the hip-hop community, with much argument on both sides flying through the blogosphere. Some argued that hip-hop as a musical subgenre is as vital and vibrant and authentic voice of the inner city as it ever was, while others pointed to declining sales and changing mainstream tastes to support Nas's claim of rap music's impending demise. The following article is one such opinion piece by a Queens, New York–based hip-hop artist named J-Zone, who is intimately familiar with all things hip-hop, having majored in music at the State University of New York, worked as head engineer, achieved prominence with several albums of his own music, and helped produce numerous releases for other artists.

*The article, "5 Things That Killed Hip-Hop" appeared as a posting on a popular rap-centered Web site, where the writing of a number of prominent hip-hop critics and artists frequently appears in blog form. The blog is a form of writing that arose in recent history and must increasingly be considered as a legitimate literary subgenre. An abridgment of the phrase "Web log," the blog represents a series of Internet posts containing entries on topics as varied as political opinion, depictions of events such as breaking news or cultural happenings, diary-like personal history, or other media-based communications such as video or art. While most blogs are mainly textual, the writing in them differs radically from the kinds of academic discourse you produce, and generally read, for your classes. **As you read** this article, therefore, pay attention to the ways in which J-Zone often purposely breaks grammatical rules and uses decidedly nonacademic language for rhetorical purpose; that is, engages the reader with a friendly, conversational, and easy-to-read tone, and to establish "street credibility" for himself, as he discusses the current state of hip-hop music in American culture.*

I realize that arguing about music is pointless cause we all got different opinions. A few people wanted my opinion on the "is hip hop dead?" matter and I just put my opinion on my sites. For some reason, it's gotten a lot of unexpected feedback, but what I'm saying isn't really new, nor is there is there a right or wrong answer to that question. If u agree with me that's cool, if you disagree that's cool too. It's music, not life and death. At the least, to read it is a way to kill some time. 1

Everybody's saying it. Nas titled his album that. People are debating and a few brothers asked me for my humble opinion. So as I watch the Celtics lose their 17th straight on Sportscenter, I'll do a music related blog for once. After all, it affects me right? 5 things I feel are the biggest culprits of rap's downfall. Well actually before I exercise my freedom of speech and somebody gets upset for nothing, let me clarify. 2

A. I am NOT saying that there isn't a batch of stellar records released yearly, or a group of dope producers delivering fly shit or a handful of rappers that still make you wanna listen. I also know music is subjective and it's all opinion. The great music of today may be on par with the great of yesterday, but in the grand scheme of things, the negatives far outweigh the positives. 3

B. There's 3 things you can never argue about ... Religion, Politics and Hip-Hop. Cause no matter your opinion, somebody will tyrannically oppose and get all fuckin emotional. It's just my humble opinion, relax. Who cares anyway? 4

C. For the record, the politics at major labels, press and radio are not listed here because they've been around since the beginning of 5 time. And we have ourselves to blame for not manning up to take control of those. Yo Flex, drop a bomb on that. OK, where was I?

CLANS, POSSES, CREWS & CLIQUES: WHO U WIT?

Safety in numbers. Movements, collaborations, big name guests, teams, crew beef, etc. The days of the solo roller are over. In the prime of rap, you were judged solely on your music. Rakim, Nas & Biggie (early on), LL, Kane . . . they all built their legend on music alone. Hell, Rakim had no guests on his first 4 albums. Sure there was Juice Crew, Native Tongues, Lench Mob crew, etc. But it wasn't mandatory. Then for some reason, in the mid-late 90's, it became totally necessary to have a movement. A crew with 1,000 different artists all on the same team. Touring together, crew t-shirts, beef with other crews, collaborations, etc. Not that that's a bad thing, but it's like people cannot identify with one artist; there has to be a movement or somebody else involved to validate them. Look at today's most successful artists. They all have a movement. Roc-A-Fella, Def Jux, Stonesthrow, Rhymesayers, G-Unit, Dipset, Wu-Tang, Hieroglyphics, Okayplayer, etc. Or if you're not part of a movement, you collaborate with other high profile artists. Doom, Danger Mouse, etc. It's all about cross-pollinating fan bases. You don't? You die. And for some reason, I see Da Youngstas album, *Da Aftermath*, as the beginning of this from a beat standpoint. That and Run DMC's *Down With The King* (both 1993) were the first albums I can remember to use a lot of different producers with totally different sounds. It worked back then, they were dope albums. But it wound up being a cancer. 6

Nowadays you need a Timbaland track, a Neptunes track, a Just Blaze track, a Dre track, a Kanye track for people to really care . . . and for the most part it sounds like a collection of songs, not an album. Why not let one of them just do the whole fuckin album? Can't please everybody, why make a futile attempt? Good albums are about a vibe. Wu-Tang was a movement, but it was cohesive and made sense because they all vibed together and RZA was the sonic glue. Sans *Illmatic, Ready to Die* and a few others, every single great rap album had a maximum of 3 producers and 3 guests. In this fascination with movements, name association and special guests, we've lost album cohesiveness and the focus on just music. It's no longer about how dope you are, it's who you rollin with and who's cosigning what you do. And usually 92% of the crew isn't up to par with the few star artists in the crew. Quantity rules, not quality. You can have a 5 mic album, but nobody cares unless there's a bunch of other people involved. 10 producers and 7 guests. And now so and so with a platinum album can put 7

255

his wack ass brother or cousin on and cheapen the game, cause they're part of the movement and its about who you with. Back in '88, Milk D said he had *"a great big bodyguard"* on *Top Billin*. But that was it. In 2007, there would be a Great Big Bodyguard solo album.

TOO MUCH MUSIC

Like the crew theory, this is about quantity. People want more, even 8 if it means a dip in quality. Some people can put out music quickly and do it well. Some people just want to bombard the market for the sake of doing it. Rakim did albums every 2 years. EPMD, Scarface and Ice Cube did it every year and that was considered fast. Nowadays, if you don't have 2 albums, 5 mix tapes and 10 guest appearances a year, you're slippin and people forget you. This attempt to keep up with the rush has cheapened the music. Now you have regular mixtapes marketed as albums, just a bunch of thrown together songs for the fuck of it. But to survive these days, you have to do that to stay in the public eye. There's far too many slim line case CD-R mix tapes out, and as important as mix tapes are to rap, the very vehicle that helped it grow is now playing a part in killing it. Now everybody has forgotten how to make cohesive projects, so we cover it up by labeling it as a mix tape. The value and pride that full length albums used to symbolize are no more. Mixtapes now triple the number official albums in artist's catalog and never has music seemed so cheap and fast food. Not to mention, when the majors went completely awry in the late 90's, the indie rap scene went out of control with too much product.

When I debuted in 1999, there were maybe 25–30 other indie 9 vinyl releases out that mattered. And mine was one of the only full-length albums. So it was only a matter of time before I got a listen, it didn't matter that I had no big names on my record and came outta nowhere. Try that now. To go to a store and see the foot high stack of one sheets for new records, mix CD's and DVD's dropping weekly makes you see you have a snowballs chance to survive in that world. Look at how many releases a week are on Hiphopsite, Sandbox, Fat Beats, UGHH, etc. The high profile artists get some attention, and everybody else gets ordered in ones and twos, if that. So today's new talent making his debut is in for an uphill battle. Great records go unnoticed. Rap is now a disposable art. Mr. Walt of Da Beatminerz once said, "You work 16 months on an album and get a 2 week window of opportunity. After that your record is as good as dead for most people." That sums it up.

TOO COOL TO HAVE FUN/NO BALANCE IN RAP

When rap stopped being fun, I knew we were in big trouble. Not too 10
many people are doin' music for fun anymore. Ask yourself, *"would I
still mess with music as a hobby if there wasn't any money in it?"* Too many
people would say no. We all wanna get paid. Shit, I got bills too, I love
money! But too many people just seem like they'd rather be doing
other shit. You read in interviews, *"I don't care about no rap, I'd rather be
hustling. I just do this cause I can."* Hey, whatever floats your boat, I can
relate, there's been artists like that since the beginning of time, but they
were never the majority until now. Having fun is nowhere near as
important as your life before you got signed. And there's plenty of battle MC's, political MC's and killer thugs but it seems there's not many
funny artists no more. Like on some Biz Mark, Humpty Hump, The
Afros shit. Not afraid to go to the extreme and have fun. God forbid
you use your imagination or rap about something not involving Hip
Hop, the hood, you bein' the shit, the end of the world or what color
your car interior is.

   I live in Queens, less than a mile from 50 Cent's old house. 11
Nobody really knows I make music over here. Some kid from over here
saw me in The Source a while back and said *"Yo I ain't know you was in
it like that, yo why you ain't tryin to pump your shit out here and let people
know, you should rep the hood? 50 did it."* Why should I? I'm not on the
block tryin to push weight, I'm out there walking to Walgreens for my
Grandmother, on my way to the park for a game of 21 or to watch a
game at the local high school. I'm a grown ass man with a college
degree and I like my neighborhood, but I choose to rap about my beat
up car, not dancing in clubs, women with bad hygiene and too many
kids or ball playin rappers with limited ball skills, cause I ain't a street
cat and I'd rather show the lighter side of life. And that was never a
problem back in the day.

   Okay those ain't completely new topics, but it's like rappin about 12
those things these days gets you marked as novelty rap. Biz rhymed
about a lot of this same shit back in the day, but it was still accepted as
legit Hip Hop. 2007? He could never do a song like *The Dragon*. Little
Shawn & Father MC rapped about the ladies with some R&B beats.
De La Soul were labeled as hippies. But all those dudes would beat yo
fuckin ass if you got out of line! They were soft by no means, they just
wanted to do the music they enjoyed, cause rap is supposed to be a
way to have fun and get away from the everyday stress, while not limiting yourself. The thing that made rap so dope in the "golden era" was
the balance of styles. You had clown princes like Biz, Humpty Hump,
Kwame and ODB later on. You had political brothers like X-Clan, PE,

Lakim Shabazz, Poor Righteous Teachers, Kam, etc. You had the explicit shit on Rap-A-Lot and the whole 2 Live movement in Miami. Hip-house like Twin Hype, new jack shit like Wrecks-N-Effect, the whole Native Tongues thing, the hard South Central LA shit, the Oakland funk . . . and they all co-existed, were all dope and they all had fun regardless of their style. King Sun made *On The Club Tip* and then did *Universal Flag*. Lakim Shabazz, Twin Hype and Wrecks-N-Effect had raw battle rap, Geto Boys and Ganksta Nip were hilarious, PE had the yin and yang of Chuck, and Flav and ODB was a ferocious battle MC.

Even the more serious political rap . . . everybody seemed to be   13
enjoying making music. Gangsta rappers had a fuckin sense of humor back then. Mob Style might have been the hardest group I've ever heard and they lived it. But them dudes also showed other sides and sounded like they enjoyed music, because it was an escape from everyday bullshit. Tim Dog, was hilarious and hard at the same time. Even if it was a joke to some, the shit was good listening. Suga Free is an ice cold pimp for real, but he has a sense of humor and approaches his music doin what he feels. Who says rappin about a girl with no teeth or going to the store with coupons ain't "real"? Everything is "real", people forget that. Everybody is so concerned with being feared and taken seriously, they can't come off those insecurities and do some guilty pleasure shit. Even the producers. If you can't show your other sides and bug out in your music, where can you do it? Stop being scared and break some fuckin rules. Put some 300 pound girls in your video for once! Laugh at yourself, dog, you ain't no killer 24/7. You ain't battling MC's and being a lyrical lyricist mixtape murder 24/7. Havin fun is almost hip-hop faux pas these days. Rap is dead without balance . . . period.

LAW & ORDER: MPC AND SAMPLING

"Boop Boop, it's the sound of the police!" Yup, the legal police. Hip-hop is   14
based in illegality, but not maliciously. Ironically, many people got into it to stay out of legal troubles, but technically this positive move is also seen as a life of crime by the powers that be. Mix tapes, remixes, sampling, parodies (somewhat) . . . the appeal of hip-hop was always rearranging the old to create the new. It's the lifeline of the music. One man's treasure is apparently another man's trash. In the wake of DJ Drama getting busted by the Feds for selling mix tapes that the labels and artists themselves approve and benefit from, it has never been more evident that the RIAA and their legal vendetta have just pulled

the IV. We all knew that the late 80's way of taking 8 bar James Brown loops and not clearing was bound to catch up to us. I can live with that. You have a platinum album and loop somebody's whole shit, break'em off some money and publishing, its only right. But then the lawyers and courts got tyrannical. Now 1/8 of a second sample can run you the risk of legal action. Ouch. I remember having a beat placed on a TV show and the music supervisor panicked after the fact because he swore the snare I used sounded like it was sampled. Wow. I understand melodies, but somebody can own a snare sound now?

This is pretty lousy, but to this point it only affected some of the 15 major label stuff and big corporate gigs. No more. MySpace is now shutting down pages that post remixes. WHAT!? I find that completely ass backwards. I know a few dudes that were warned, and others shut down without notice for posting remixes of major label songs with COMMERCIALLY AVAILABLE ACAPELLAS! WELL WHAT THE FUCK IS AN ACAPELLA AVAILABLE ON A RECORD FOR?! TO BE REMIXED! DING DING . . . MESSAGE! Now to take that remix and release it on a major label and make 50 grand is one thing. But to have fun with remixes and post them on a MySpace page, where ZERO DOLLARS can be made directly off of it, is completely harmless promotion for all parties involved. Not anymore.

Back in the day to be on a Kid Capri, Double R, S&S, Doo Wop, 16 Silver Surfer, etc. mixtape was the best thing to happen to an artist and their label. An unknown producer leaking a dope remix to a popular artists record was a way to get buzz and a way for the industry to find new talent. Taking pieces of old music and creating something new (like the Bomb Squad) wasn't looked upon with the seriousness of a gunpoint mugging. But in a day where album sales are down, no artists or labels are seeing any money, CD's have foolishly been raised in price, interpolating one line of *Jingle Bells* in your song can get you sued and you can't post a remix for promotional and listening purposes only . . . you can see the music and legal industries have officially declared war on rap as a knee jerk reaction to their own failures. And as idiotic and unjust as things have become, they have the loopholes of law on their side.

THE INTERNET

Talk about a double edged sword. Never has it been so easy to get your 17 music heard. If I make a dope beat, I can put it on my MySpace page and it's up in an hour (depending on the servers, it may be "processing" for about 3 years). No more spending money and wasting time for records and test presses. Now people in Arkansas that only have MTV and the Internet can hear my music. Limited distribution isn't as big a problem as before. Everybody is almost equal, and we all have MySpace pages. But look at the flipside: everybody is almost equal, and we all have MySpace pages. There is so much shit out and the internet lurks with a million people doing the same thing, it's virtually impossible to stand out. Back in the day, you had to work your way up in the business. Having a record was in most cases a privilege and a reward for your hard work. Catalog meant something. We're in an MP3 world now, and somebody in their bedroom is on an equal plane with somebody that's paid dues and worked hard. That's great for the kid with talent and no vehicle to get heard. That sucks for the no talent hacks on MySpace that post advertisements for their wack music on your comments page.

The Internet also killed rap's number one asset. Anticipation. 18 How many can remember buying a mixtape and hearing 3 dope joints from an upcoming album on a mixtape? You couldn't wait to cop the album. And you didn't hear the album 3 months in advance cause there was no way to spread it that fast. And in rare cases where the album leaked, you had to get a tape dub and even when you did, you still bought it. I remember hearing *Lots Of Lovin, Straighten It Out, TROY* and *Ghettos Of The Mind* from *Mecca & The Soul Brother* 2 months before it came out. But I couldn't find any other songs. That drove the anticipation up and got everybody talking. We were all eager to support. In 2007, the album would leak months in advance, you burn it and that's it. I'm not complaining cause that won't change things, but that was a large part of what appealed to me and many others about music, especially rap. No more. No artwork & physical CD to read the credits and shoutouts (remember those!?), no anticipation, it's old news by street date, the shit don't sell and here we are. Tower's closing, the legendary Beat Street is closed, Music Factory is a wrap . . . people don't realize that rap as we know it is done. Labels are fuckin suing common civilians for file sharing! A physical copy no longer matters unless you're a collector.

Back in the day, you would never see internet beef. It's just stupid 19 junior high shit. People leaving threats and talkin shit via MySpace, people getting hurt over e-beef at shows, kids on message boards flexin muscle and actin hard. Great! Now that we have a bunch of killers on wax, we got a bunch of em posting in forums. Cute. You can sit in a bedroom in Mexico and talk about knockin out somebody in Finland and it will never come back to you. Hip-hop bravado and the anonymity of the Web . . . it don't get more junior high. The Internet was the blessing and the curse of rap music. I may catch heat for this, but I think the best thing is to blow up the industry and start over.

There is still great music, and I will enjoy making this music til I pass on, even if only as a hobby. I will still be diggin for records, makin beats, playing instruments, and watching old movies for inspiration. But sometimes things need to fall apart to give birth to greater things. The fall of rap in its current state may give birth to something bigger and better. It's what I'm banking on, cause realistically, how much longer can it go down this road? I'm not saying go back in time. Classic rap artists may have been influenced by Cold Crush and Melle Mel, but they took that influence and added something different on to it to create something new, and until that principle can be followed again, I say fuck fixing an abandoned building. Hit it with a wrecking ball and rebuild!

Examining the Text

1. In his reason 5 section, the author cites "clans, posses, crews and cliques" as being at least partially responsible for hip-hop's decline. In what way have the increasing numbers of people involved in a song/album's production contributed to a lessening in musical quality, according to J-Zone? In your experience, is this phenomenon unique to hip-hop, or has it affected all forms of popular music, either positively or negatively, or both?

2. Hip-hop artist Lil Wayne was recently quoted in a *Rolling Stone* magazine article as saying he has recorded "somewhere in the thousands" of songs in recent years. The article concludes, "Wayne makes new songs the way you make lunch, and songs have a way of getting out" on Web sites and in stores. With the advent of inexpensive consumer-level music production, creating and distributing mixes in the form of digital playlists has increased dramatically in the last several years—not just for established artists such as Lil Wayne, but for lesser-known artists as well. How has the proliferation of "mixtapes"—compilations of songs recorded in a specific order, originally onto a compact audio cassette tape, but more recently in compact disk or MP3 format—negatively affected the overall quality of hip-hop, according to J-Zone? Does he suggest a solution to the problem of "too much music," or is the situation out of control and beyond repair, in his opinion . . . and in yours?

3. What does the author mean when he laments that there's "no balance in rap" anymore? What are some examples of a greater sense balance in hip-hop's "golden era," in the opinion of J-Zone? How does J-Zone's personal experience serve as an example of this phenomenon, and how might the situation be remedied, according to this article?

4. MPC devices (the acronym stands for MIDI Production Center or, more recently, Music Production Center) are electronic musical instruments produced by the Japanese company Akai and others, beginning around 1990. These devices allow contemporary music artists to sample short sequences of previously recorded music and insert those passages into their own tracks.

What is this author's opinion about sampling other people's work in hip-hop songs? How has the MPC phenomenon contributed to the impending "death" of hip-hop, in the view of author J-Zone?

5. *Thinking rhetorically:* Blogs are sometimes criticized as being highly charged expressions of opinion, frequently unsupported by evidence, disorganized, and lacking critical distance and balance. In what ways does "5 Things That Killed Hip-Hop" conform to this stereotype about blogs? In what ways does it disprove that criticism, both in its form and content?

For Group Discussion

The author presents a balanced commentary on the role the Internet has played on the current state of hip-hop, in his reason 1 section. What, in his view, are the positive effects of the cyberculture on hip-hop music and production, and in what ways has the Web negatively affected hip-hop? In small groups, expand this discussion beyond the boundaries of rap and hip-hop: how has the Internet affected popular music, the music industry, and your lives as consumers of, and listeners to, music? Make a two-column list of the various positive and negative Web-related factors, and, after reconvening the whole class, have each group report on its list of factors. In the full-class discussion, try to arrive at some consensus about the effect of the Web on popular music generally: on the whole, has it had a positive or negative effect?

Writing Suggestion

Go to one of the many popular blog sites on the Web and create a presence for yourself there. While it's important to remember that the style you use for your blog will differ dramatically from the language, style, and structure you use for your academic essays, one of the goals for any writing course is for you to get practice in a variety of styles, and blogging is increasingly becoming an accepted mode of discourse. For example, in the business community, numerous companies, agencies, and other institutions have begun creating a public relations presence by the use of blogs. Professional journalists, likewise, are becoming increasingly reliant on blogging, as are motion picture and music critics, for example. In this assignment, you will undertake to write a music-related blog for the rest of the current school term. Using this format, you will communicate your ideas on the current state of the music industry, to discuss your favorite kinds of popular music, to review recent albums, and to explore the various possibilities for accessing music, such as satellite and Web-based radio, file-sharing services (the legal ones, of course!), brick-and-mortar record emporiums, concerts, and so forth. Your instructor will promise not to grade your grammar, syntax, and organization; this will be a platform where those concerns are temporarily suspended, so that your imagination can range freely over whatever topic you find interesting.

Music and Contemporary Culture

The Money Note: Can the Record Business Be Saved?

JOHN SEABROOK

*The music business has always embraced the latest recording technology.
Over the decades, music has changed with the tide of technical innovation:
from sheet music to mechanical cylinders to 78 rpm records to 8-track and
cassette tapes and, most recently, to CDs and MP3s. In the following article
originally published in the* New Yorker *magazine, author John Seabrook
explains how the recorded music business moved from pressing long-playing
records to issuing music on compact discs, the latter representing a technology that held promise of more resilience than easily scratched vinyl records
and reduced production costs.*

*However, while the medium on which music is recorded has changed
over the years, the process of selecting and marketing talent altered little
since World War II. According to Seabrook, "a few guys still determine the
fate of many." By "the few," he means the artist and repertoire (A&R) men
celebrated as heroes by recording-industry insiders for recognizing and promoting the performers who go on to become stars. Yet, the success rate of the
A&R specialists is no greater than ten percent: for every one success, there
are nine failures, a rate that is less successful than a computer program
developed to determine pop music successes by scientists in Barcelona.
Although A&R men like the one profiled in Seabrook's article still retain a
high importance in the music industry, their ability to help propel future
stars to huge record sales has been dented by the ability of consumers to copy
CDs for sharing via the Internet. Seabrook says that young people in particular no longer think of purchasing music when it can be copied for free from
the Internet.*

*As you read, pay special attention to ways in which the author's
descriptive language conveys the visceral experiences involved in listening
to music, while at the same time informing the reader about popular music
history and economic trends.*

When he was a teen-ager, growing up in New York City in the 1970s,
Jason Flom wrote songs, sang, and played guitar for two rock bands,
which he named Relative Pleasure and Selective Service. But Flom's

dreams of rock stardom ended around the time he started working at Atlantic Records, in 1979, when he was nineteen, and began redirecting his energies into making other people stars. Now forty-two, he is one of the most successful record men of the past twenty years, scoring hits in genres as varied as heavy metal (Twisted Sister), Celtic pop (the Corrs), and rock (Matchbox 20, Sugar Ray). Altogether, his artists have sold more than a hundred million CDs.

In an era when many of the top-selling acts have "flava"—the   2 edgy sound of hip-hop artists and R&B singers and rap-metal groups, who emerge from niches and achieve broad recognition—Flom has continued to have success with pop music, that sweet, beguiling, never-too-challenging sound, which has been a record industry staple from Bing Crosby to Doris Day to Britney Spears. Flom's specialty is delivering "monsters"—records that sell millions of copies and become rainmakers for everyone else in the record business because they bring fans into the music stores. Successful record men are commonly said to have "ears," but prospecting for monsters requires eyes for star quality as well as a nose for the next trend. You have to be able to go to thousands of sweaty night clubs, and sit through a dozen office auditions each week, and somehow not become so jaded that you fail to recognize a superstar when you encounter one. Like the night in 1981 when Clive Davis, then the head of Arista Records, happened to go to a New York supper club and hear a nineteen-year-old gospel singer who was Dionne Warwick's cousin—Whitney Houston. Or the day when Bruce Lundvall, the head of Blue Note Records, had a routine office audition from a singer recommended by an employee in the accounting department—Norah Jones. Or the time in 1997 when Flom met Kid Rock, then an obscure m.c. who had made a couple of records that "stiffed" (sold poorly), in the basement of a Detroit disco at two-thirty in the morning. It is necessary to recognize that ineffable quality a great pop star communicates (Flom calls it "the thing"), but it isn't always necessary to love the way the music sounds. Chris Blackwell, who founded Island Records, told me that he didn't especially like listening to U2 when he first heard them play, in the early 1980s, but "I could see that they had something," and so he signed them to his label.

Why should the latent capacity for superstardom in pop, which is   3 perhaps the most egalitarian of art forms, be obvious to only a gifted few like Jason Flom—those great A&R (artist-and-repertoire) men whom the record industry celebrates as its heroes? (And they are invariably male.) After all, even the great record men are wrong much more often than they are right about the acts they sign (nine misses for each hit is said to be the industry standard). One wonders how much of the art of hitmaking is just dumb luck. Scientists in Barcelona say they have created a computer-based "Hit Song Science" that picks hits much more efficiently than a human can. There's even a Web site, hitsongscience.com, where aspiring pop stars can test themselves on a hit-o-meter.

American Idol, the popular *Star Search*-style Fox TV show, in which   4
the viewers pick their own stars by voting over the telephone, is considered a "reality show," but the democratic process is not the way stars are actually discovered. In the record business, a few guys still determine the fate of many.

One day last October, I was sitting with Flom in his office at   5
Atlantic, which is part of the Warner Music Group, at Sixth Avenue and Fifty-first Street, when he played me a song by a new artist he had recently signed to his label, Lava Records. (Flom began the label as a joint venture with Atlantic, and then sold his share to the company two years ago, for a reported fifty million dollars.) Lava has a roster of twenty-three artists, and Flom can afford to take "a big bet," as he puts it, on two or three new artists a year. The artist's name was Cherie, he explained, and she was a young French singer whose specialty was the sweeping pop ballad. She was a "belter," as they say in the business— one of those singers who doesn't hold back.

Flom often has a startled expression in his eyes, as if he were wait-   6
ing for something to go wrong—a look of disappointed optimism, the feeling that anyone who makes a career out of betting on talent must routinely suffer. But today he looked positively grim as he talked about the record business. Sales of recorded music in the United States have dropped by more than a hundred million units in the past two years, falling well below seven hundred million. The eighteen-year-old Canadian singer Avril Lavigne is the idol of ten-year-old girls across the country, but her debut album, "Let's Go," sold far fewer records in its first six months (four million) than did Alanis Morissette's debut album, "Jagged Little Pill" (seven million), which was released in 1995. Around the globe, the record business is 16 percent smaller than it was in 2000. Record labels blame the fans, for lacking the long-term loyalty to pop acts which record buyers used to have, and for engaging in wholesale "piracy" of music, either by copying CDs or by download-ing music illegally from the Internet. "There is no precedent for what's happening now in the music business," Flom said. "What would hap-pen if groceries suddenly became free, or hotels—do you think those businesses would survive?"

However, Flom brightened at the prospect of playing Cherie's   7
demo CD. "I guess you'd call her a diva," he said. "She's seventeen, and she's classically trained, but she sings these pop ballads—and she is phenomenal." He was excitedly hunting for the demo amid the stacks of disks that cover every surface in his office. "I honestly believe she is one of the most important artists I've ever signed." Seeing the

skeptical look on my face—a French pop star?—Flom quickly said, "She's also Jewish, and there aren't too many of them left in France, if you know what I mean, so it's a little different from being just French. And," he added, "she doesn't sound French when she sings."

Flom lacks the star quality that he divines in other people. He is neither tall nor physically imposing, and he seems more like a laid-back lawyer than like a record man (his father is Joseph Flom, a patriarch of the New York law firm Skadden, Arps, Slate, Meagher & Flom). He is a friend of Bill Clinton's and a generous supporter of the American Civil Liberties Union. He is not wild and crazy, although his office, like the offices of most record executives, is full of photographs of him posing with wild and crazy guys such as Kid Rock, who usually has his middle finger extended in the picture. During the 1980s, Flom tried living like a rock star, but when he was twenty-eight he checked into the Hazelden clinic, in Minnesota, for thirty days of rehab, and he hasn't had a drink or a line since. Now he lives with his wife and their two kids on the Upper West Side.

He had never heard Cherie sing before she and her manager, Jeff Haddad, turned up in his office the previous February, on Valentine's Day, for an audition. Haddad had given Flom his pitch, which, Haddad told me later, included this question: "There are maybe twenty people in the world who can deliver a song the way Faith Hill sings the Diane Warren song that is the theme in the movie *Pearl Harbor*, and out of those people how many can do it in four different languages?" Then Cherie performed two songs, one in French and the other in English; her only accompaniment was the noisy heating system in Flom's office. On the basis of that half-hour meeting, and Flom's gut feeling that the girl, whose real name is Cindy Almouzni, had that special quality which can move a massive amount of product, Flom signed her to a million-dollar, five-album contract, and was prepared to do everything that a major label like Warner can do to make an artist a big star— "Whatever it takes to put her over," Flom told me. He declined to say how much that would cost, but David Foster, another top hitmaker with Warner Music, told me, "It's basically a five-million-dollar bet. It might cost only five hundred thousand dollars to make the record, but it's so expensive to promote it. If you get on the *Today* show, you've got to get a band together, fly everyone in and put them up, and by the time you're done it has cost you fifty thousand dollars."

Last year, the *Wall Street Journal* ran a story about an unknown eighteen-year-old Irish singer named Carly Hennessy, whose debut CD, from Universal, was the subject of a $2.2–million marketing campaign yet wound up selling only 378 copies in its first three months. "If that happens to me," Flom said, "a lot of people are going to look at me funny." For the artist, the stakes were higher. "This is her shot. It's very rare for an artist to get a buildup like this and then, if things don't go well, come back from it and reinvent herself."

The song Flom played for me that day in his office, "My Way 11
Back Home," is a love ballad written for Cherie by the Canadian singer-songwriter Corey Hart, who has also composed songs for Celine Dion. The lyrics are solidly within the convention of self-help, which is one of the main tropes of the popular love ballad. The singer is finding her way through the darkness, and, in spite of winter storms, bitter cold, and loneliness, manages to reach high and touch the sky, and to find . . . My Way Back Home. It was a surprising choice from the man who gave the world Twisted Sister's "We're Not Gonna Take It," although perhaps this is Flom's genius—understanding how a conventional love ballad and a heavy-metal anthem stimulate the same adult-contemporary emotions. As Doug Morris, the head of Universal Music Group, who was Flom's mentor when Morris ran Atlantic, said to me, "The basic thing is you've got a singer, and you've got a song, and you put them together and it makes people feel good. And if they feel good enough they buy it! That's what it's all about! And it's a beautiful thing when you see it happen—the singer up there singing his song and all the fans are screaming for him. It makes me wanna cry when I see it."

And Cherie's voice was remarkably appealing. She had the vocal 12
power of Whitney Houston and the feel-good-around-the-edges shimmer of Shania Twain. But she wasn't a screamer; she could sustain the note at the end of a phrase without resorting to vibrato. She hit the high notes effortlessly, could soar from tragedy to triumph in a single breath, and seemed to inhabit the lyrics with complete sincerity. As the chorus rolled around for the second time, I sensed that the song was building toward an emotional climax that people in the record business sometimes refer to as "the money note"—that moment on the record which seems to have an almost involuntary effect on your insides. (According to researchers at Dartmouth who recently studied the brains of people listening to music, the brain responds physiologically to dramatic swoops in range and pitch.) The money note is the moment in Whitney Houston's version of the Dolly Parton song "I Will Always Love You" at the beginning of the third rendition of the chorus: pause, drum beat, and then "Iiiiiieeeeeeiiieeii will always love you." It is the moment in the Celine Dion song from *Titanic*, "My Heart Will Go On": the key change that begins the third verse, a note you can hear a hundred times and it still brings you up short in the supermarket and transports you from the price of milk to a world of grand romantic gesture—"You're here/There's nuthing I fear."

David Foster, the producer of "I Will Always Love You," who is 13
among the contemporary masters of the pop ballad (he has written and

produced songs for Natalie Cole and Toni Braxton, among others), says that he came up with the expression during a session with Barbra Streisand. "Barbra had hit this high note, and she wanted to know how it sounded because, although you'd think Barbra was real confident, she's not," he told me. "And I said, 'That sounds like money!'" He added, "And I don't mean money in the crass sense of that will make a lot of money, although that's certainly part of it. I mean expensive. It sounds expensive."

Cherie hit the money note with full force—"When I cry I'm   14
weak/I'm learning to fly." As her voice went up on "fly," an electric guitar came floating up with it, and the tone was so pure that a chill spread over my shoulders, prickling the skin. Flom pumped his fist when the moment hit, lifted his leg a little, and grimaced.

When the song ended, he asked me what I thought, and I admit-   15
ted that I had found the money note shattering. But would it produce the reaction Flom was looking for—the effect he had mimed for me earlier, by taking an imaginary wallet from his back pocket, fingering an imaginary bill, and slapping it down on an imaginary counter? What was to stop people from taking the money notes for free?

Flom pointed out that Cherie's music, like that of Norah Jones,   16
should appeal to older people, who are less likely to download music from the Internet. "But who knows?" he said. "It's difficult to compete with free. All I know is what I know—if the star is big enough, people will buy the album, because it's like a piece of the artist. But if the star doesn't have that kind of irresistible appeal then people just say, 'What the heck, I'll download the good songs.' So we just have to figure out how to make her a big star."

Five global music companies control more than 85 percent of the   17
record business. (The remaining 15 percent is divided among some ten thousand independent labels.) Universal Music Group, which is owned by Vivendi Universal, is the dominant player among the majors; then comes the Warner Music Group, a division of AOL Time Warner; Sony Music Entertainment; the Bertelsmann Music Group (BMG); and the EMI Group. From the early '70s to the mid-'90s, Warner was the leading company in the record industry, but by the end of 2002, with a 16 percent share of the domestic market, the company had fallen behind Universal, which had a 29 percent share.

The story of Warner Music is a parable for the music industry—a   18
tale of corporate dyssynergy. Over the course of the rock era, which began almost fifty years ago, virtually all the original record companies have been bought by larger media corporations. The industry has changed from an art-house business run by the founders of the labels—men with ears, like Ahmet Ertegun, a founder of Atlantic; Chris

Blackwell, of Island Records; and Jerry Moss, the co-founder, with Herb Alpert, of A&M Records—into a corporate enterprise run by managers, who in addition to making records have to worry about quarterly earnings and timely results.

Atlantic Records was co-founded in 1947 by the Turkish-born 19 Ertegun with money borrowed from the family dentist. He began by recording artists like Ray Charles and the New Orleans juke-joint bluesman Professor Longhair. In the 1950s, Ertegun, working with his partners—his brother Nesuhi and Jerry Wexler, a writer for Billboard— had a string of hit records with singers like Ruth Brown and Big Joe Turner, before the dominant power in the music business, CBS Records (now owned by Sony), discovered the commercial possibility of black R&B music. In the mid-1960s, Atlantic expanded into pop (Bobby Darin, Sonny and Cher) and, later, into rock (Buffalo Springfield). In 1968, Ertegun sold the label to Warner-Seven Arts, and the following year Steve Ross's Kinney National bought that company, creating Warner Communications. During the 1970s, the collection of Warner labels assembled by Ross and run by the legendary record man Mo Ostin (including Atlantic, Warner Bros., Reprise, Elektra, and Asylum), eclipsed those of CBS, and Warner became the leader of the record indus- try. Its acts included the Grateful Dead; Crosby, Stills, Nash & Young; the Eagles; Fleetwood Mac; and the Doobie Brothers. "Steve Ross's never got involved in anything we did," Ertegun, who continued to run Atlantic after its sale, told me. "He was just happy to see the results." But as Warner Communications grew—it merged with Time, in 1990, and AOL, in 2001—the music business faltered. Ross, who might have been able to run the labels effectively, died in 1992, and Gerald Levin took over.

269

The business rationale behind the record companies' role in these 20 huge conglomerations was that their corporate owners would use the cash generated by monster hits to pay for other parts of their opera- tions, and the companies would be able to survive the stiffs, thanks to their corporate backing. Corporate ownership also gave record men like Ertegun the financial resources to compete for expensive estab- lished acts like the Rolling Stones, whom he signed in the 1970s. However, it gradually became apparent that the corporate culture might not provide the best environment for nurturing new talent. Chris Blackwell, who sold Island to PolyGram in 1989 (he now has another independent label, Palm Pictures), told me, "I don't think the music business lends itself very well to being a Wall Street business. You're always working with individuals, with creative people, and the people you are trying to reach, by and large, don't view music as a commodity but as a relationship with a band. It takes time to expand that relationship, but most people who work for the corporations have three-year contracts, some five, and most of them are expected to produce. What an artist really needs is a champion, not a numbers guy who in another year is going to leave."

Moreover, the kind of controversy that often helps sell records is   21
not good for the corporate image. In the mid-nineties, Warner was well positioned to control the exploding rap market, through its half ownership of Interscope, a label that had been developed by the producer Jimmy Iovine and had recently signed Tupac Shakur. Interscope was allied with Death Row Records, the label run by Dr. Dre and Marion (Suge) Knight, which recorded seminal gangsta-rap acts like Snoop Doggy Dogg. But bad publicity from these acts was hurting Time Warner's other businesses and straining the political connections that the corporation needed in Washington. In 1995, Levin made the decision to sell the company's half share of Interscope, and it eventually became part of Universal. Iovine went on to amass a remarkable streak of hits, including records by Eminem and the rapper 50 Cent. Warner missed out on the rap boom almost entirely.

In the past three years, under the leadership of Roger Ames, a   22
suave, cigarette-smoking, fifty-two-year-old Trinidadian, who took over the Warner Music Group in 1999, the company has had major hits

with Linkin Park, Enya, and Faith Hill. Ames has also cut costs to improve profits. However, Warner is fourth among the majors in sales of new music and did not have a record on the list of Top Ten-selling albums in 2002:

1. "The Eminem Show"/Eminem, 7.6 million (Interscope).
2. "Nellyville"/Nelly, 4.9 million (Universal).
3. "Let's Go"/Avril Lavigne, 4.1 million (Arista, a BMG label).
4. "Home"/Dixie Chicks, 3.7 million (Sony).
5. "8 Mile"/Soundtrack, 3.5 million (Interscope).
6. "Missundaztood"/Pink, 3.1 million (Arista).
7. "Ashanti"/Ashanti, 3.09 million (Murder Inc., Universal).
8. "Drive"/Alan Jackson, 3.05 million (Arista Nashville).
9. "Up"/Shania Twain, 2.9 million (Universal).
10. "O Brother, Where Art Thou?"/Soundtrack, 2.7 million (Universal).

But is a winner-take-all strategy the best way to run a record   23
company—for any of the majors? Hitmaking is an imprecise method of doing business. Of thirty thousand CDs that the industry released last year in the United States, only 404 sold more than a hundred thousand copies, while twenty-five thousand releases sold fewer than a thousand copies apiece. No one seems to be able to predict which those 404 big sellers will be. The chairman of BMG, Rolf Schmidt-Holtz, told

Billboard in December, "We need reliable calculations of returns that are not based solely on hits because the way people get music doesn't go with hits anymore." He added, "We have to get rid of the lottery mentality."

I asked Flom whether he thought hits might become less impor- 24 tant to the record business. "That ain't gonna happen," he said. "If anything, hits can be more important than ever because you can make stars on a global scale now. If the star is big enough, people will want to buy the CD." When I repeated what Schmidt-Holtz had said, Flom looked momentarily stunned. Then he said, "Something must be getting lost in the translation there because the day we stop seeing hits is the day people stop buying records."

When Cindy Almouzni was eight, in 1992, the video of the 25 Whitney Houston song "I Will Always Love You" came out, accompanied by shots of the singer playing opposite Kevin Costner in the film *The Bodyguard*. Cindy was the youngest of three children in a religious household in Marseilles. Her parents are Sephardic Jews from North Africa. As a child, her father fled during the Algerian war and met his wife years later in France. When Cindy's mother was too busy to watch her, she would put her in front of music videos on TV. Cindy learned "I Will Always Love You," exactly the way Whitney sings it—the breathing, the key change in the third chorus—and she sang it over and over again. At first, she sang the song to herself, then to her family, and then in school. The summer that she was nine, she sang "I Will Always Love You" for several hundred people at a campground where the Almouznis went during August.

271

Her parents sent her to singing school, and after that she received 26 private lessons. She learned the songs of Jacques Brel and Edith Piaf, but she also continued to sing "I Will Always Love You." At fourteen, she won a local karaoke contest and went to Paris for a national competition. There, she met a record producer, who invited her to his studio to record a song he had written called "I Don't Want Nobody (Telling Me What to Do)." The vocals were remixed, and the song became a dance track, which wound up in the hands of Jeff Haddad, a languid, affable Californian. "I heard her sing, and she blew me away, and I thought, Let's do what we can to make this happen," Haddad told me. He flew to France to meet her parents, and they agreed to let him try to make their daughter a star.

Haddad is a manager, but, like many other people in the music 27 industry—producers, songwriters, engineers, lawyers—he functions as a filter between undiscovered talent and a major-label deal. He and Dave Moss, the owner of a small record label, put out a single of Cindy's dance song, and it became an international hit for Cherie Amore, as they decided to call her back in 2000 when there was a vogue for French house music. On the strength of that success, Haddad commissioned a British songwriter and producer named Paul Moessl to create a pop ballad for Cherie. Moessl wrote a song called "Older" ("My love is older than my years/It's wiser than your fears"). There was considerable interest in the demo, and Haddad scheduled a week of office auditions in L.A. and a week in New York with people like Tommy Mottola, who was then the head of Sony Music. It was cold in New York, and people were coughing and sneezing while Cindy sang. Jason Flom was the last record guy they saw. "Within thirty seconds of hearing her sing," he said, "I just knew." In Cherie, Flom encountered a singer whose artistic sensibility was derived from the kind of commercial music that record men like Flom produce—her flava was pop. He signed her within a week.

The traditional course in star-making is to begin with a local fan   28
base and gradually grow to global renown. Flom was proposing to market Cherie the other way around—she would appear on the scene as a "worldwide artist," with campaigns in France, Italy, England, and Spain, as well as in the United States. Although the music industry more or less invented the hit, it has struggled to make songs and artists into the kind of global properties that movies have become. (The recent film *X2* opened simultaneously in ninety-five countries.) Music is supposed to be the universal language, but pop depends on regional associations and on language, which is why the charts in France and Spain and Germany are so different from the pop charts in the United States.

Last summer, Flom presented his future star at the Warner Music   29
Group summit meeting held in Barcelona and attended by affiliates from more than a hundred and thirty countries. ("There were some affiliates from countries I didn't even know they had records in," Flom said.) Cherie was a hit, and Flom and Haddad decided that she should sing several of the tracks on her debut album in Spanish and French, as well as in English. They solicited songs from successful pop songwriters, like Kara Dioguardi and Paul Barry, and they hired producers who had scored hits in European and South American countries to work on possible singles for those countries.

Flom told me that in some ways Cherie's youth and obscurity   30
were advantages in making her into a worldwide sensation. Stars often balk at travelling to other countries to perform and don't want to keep up the relentless schedule of public appearances which is necessary to sustain a hit record. "The nice thing about Cherie is she's portable," Flom said. "She'll go places and do stuff if we think she should do it."

But, if Cherie truly is an extraordinary artist, why not build her   31
career more slowly? "In an era like this," Flom said, "when the audience has more distractions than ever, you have to reach critical mass to

put an artist over. And the outlets you need to do that, the Teen Peoples and whatever, are not going to take you seriously unless they know you are putting a major push behind it."

Of course, it was possible that Flom was wrong about Cherie's 32 talent. Perhaps she wasn't a great artist; maybe she was merely a great karaoke singer, and the audience would be able to tell the difference. On the other hand, maybe the current pop scene is a "karaoke world"—the phrase that the pop impresario Malcolm McLaren uses to describe contemporary pop culture—in which all the great artistic statements have already been made, and the newer artists are merely doing karaoke versions of their predecessors.

In November, I attended a marketing meeting in Flom's spacious 33 corner office to draw up an outline for launching Cherie's career, or, as they say in the business, "blowing her up." Seven Lava staff members were in attendance: Richard Bates, creative; Nikki Hirsch and Lee Trink, marketing; Aaron Simon, product management; Doug Cohen, video promotion; Janet Stampler, new media; and Lisbeth Cassaday, publicity. Before the meeting started, Aaron Simon told the others about the experience of having Cherie sing for him, in the office. "I was, like, 'Do you want me to close the door?'" he reported. "And she was, like, 'No, it's cool.' And she just did it right there. And it was, like—chills."

273

Flom began by saying that they hoped to take the first single, 34 probably a mid- to up-tempo dance number, to American radio in June 2003. When record guys hear fans complaining that pop music has become too commercial, they are often quick to blame radio. Radio doesn't play as much new music as it used to, they argue, and the music that is played has to fit into a certain format, which is based on research about what people like to listen to—or, at least, will tolerate. Many stations also carry between fifteen and twenty minutes of commercials an hour. ("If anyone said we were in the radio business, it wouldn't be someone from our company," Lowry Mays, the founder and C.E.O. of Clear Channel, which is the country's largest radio-station operator, with some hundred million listeners nationwide, told Fortune in March. "We're not in the business of providing well-researched music. We're simply in the business of selling our customers products.")

Cherie's music fits almost perfectly into the adult-contemporary 35 format, radio's largest; Flom thought that Cherie was tailor-made for New York's WLTW 106.7 Lite-FM, the city's most popular music radio station, which is owned by Clear Channel. Jim Ryan, a programming executive there, told me that when Flom played "My Way Back Home" for him, along with two other songs, during a car ride home from an industry event, he said, "Jason, I want to quit my job at Clear Channel and sign up on the Cherie bandwagon."

With luck, Flom went on, Cherie's first single would be a hit, and   36
would cross over from the light-FM stations to the Top Forty stations.
At that point, Lava would release the second single, a ballad. Flom was
also looking at other ways to promote Cherie. One was a Time Warner
DVD, a Batman movie called *Batman: Mystery of the Batwoman*; Cherie
was being animated in the film as a sexy singer whom Batman encounters in a late-night *boite*, and who sings a song called "Betcha Neva" (a
song that would be on Cherie's album). He added that there had been
tremendous interest in Cherie from "the soundtrack community," especially from makers of animated films, and reminded everyone that
Celine Dion's big break came with the theme song from the Disney
movie *Beauty and the Beast*. "I'm not saying she's another Celine, but
there's a road map there."

The group then discussed the possibility of getting Cherie a product-   37
endorsement deal with a company like Revlon. As the expense of blowing up an artist increases and the prospective payoff in record sales
becomes ever more in doubt the industry is shifting the cost of promoting
artists onto advertisers. Sting's 1999 album, "Brand New Day," an
Interscope release, sold sluggishly until the artist was featured in a Jaguar
commercial singing music from the album—and then sales took off.

274

The staff addressed the subject of "imaging" Cherie—what kind   38
of look the artist should affect. Cherie's personal style was a work in
progress. She was not a dressy kind of girl: she was partial to jeans.
Richard Bates, the art director, said that in examining the images of current pop stars, she had noticed that there was a middle ground
between Britney Spears and Shania Twain, which no one was trying to
fill. "The older singers are very polished and classy, and then it jumps
down to young and trashy—which we don't want her to be," he said.
The danger was that in trying to strike a balance between these
extremes you might wind up with nothing at all. In photos from
Cherie's first shoot, the artist, dressed in a sleeveless jersey and neat
jeans, well-scrubbed, her long hair pushed back from her face, looked
as if she were ready for a college interview.

Lee Trink talked about making Cherie a keyword on AOL Time   39
Warner's Internet service, and launching a "Who Is Cherie?" instant-
messaging campaign.

The staff was undecided on the use of what Lisbeth Cassaday   40
referred as "the 'd' word." Cassaday thought it was best not to call
Cherie a diva; Flom wasn't so sure. "I mean, she is a diva, right?" he
said. It was a conundrum. Operatic divas inhabit classic dramatic roles
like *Tosca* and *Madame Butterfly*, but pop divas, one way or another,
have to play themselves, which may be why pop divas wear out faster
than operatic divas. The constant blowing up they require eventually
causes them to explode.

Once the album went platinum—hit a million in sales—Flom   41
said, they would go to the media with the story of Cherie's life. Flom
reminded everyone that the artist was Jewish. He had heard that her
synagogue in Marseilles was burned recently, and, "while this should
obviously be treated as a very sensitive subject, we could go to Oprah
and pitch her as an artist who has suffered violence in her life as a
result of her religion."

Everyone nodded.   42

"You know. It's a story line."   43

In 1983, the president of PolyGram, Jan Timmer, introduced what   44
he hoped would become the new platform for the sale of recorded
music—the compact disk—at a recording-industry convention in
Miami. Technically, CDs were a big advance over vinyl and tape. On a
CD, music takes the form of digital strings of ones and zeros, which are
encoded on specially treated plastic disks. If the disk is properly cared
for, there is no "fidelity degradation"—none of those hisses and pops
that vinyl develops over time. The high-tech allure of the CD would
allow the industry to raise the cost of an album from $8.98 to $15.98
(even though CDs were soon cheaper to manufacture than vinyl
records), and the record companies would get a larger share of money
because the industry would persuade artists not to raise royalty rates,
arguing that the extra money was needed to market the new format to
customers.

Timmer's group was booed by record men in the audience that   45
day. This may have been because the co-inventors of the CD—Philips,
which was a corporate partner of PolyGram, and Sony—wanted a
patent royalty on the disks. The booing, however, also reflected the
music industry's long history of technophobia. A hundred years ago,
music publishers were trying to sue player-piano makers out of existence, fearing that no one would ever buy sheet music again. In the
1920s, the music industry sued radio broadcasters for copyright
infringement. Although history has repeatedly shown that new
technologies inevitably bring opportunities and create new markets,
the industry's attitude toward new technology remains hostile.
(Technophobia is also rampant in the film industry: in 1992, when
movie studios were suing Sony over the Betamax, claiming that it was
a threat to the film business, Jack Valenti, the president of the Motion
Picture Association of America, said, "The VCR is to the American film
producer and the American public as the Boston Strangler is to a
woman alone." Fortunately for the movie industry, it lost the Betamax
case: today, videos and DVDs account for more than fifty percent of a
studio's revenues.)

The CD, of course, turned out to be extremely popular with   46
record buyers. Many fans who already owned music on vinyl dutifully

275

replaced their records with CDs. By 1986, CD sales had climbed to a hundred million worldwide, and by the early '90s, hit albums on CD were selling in greater numbers than hit albums on vinyl had sold. In 1999, in what now looks like hubris, the industry's trade organization, the Recording Industry Association of America (R.I.A.A.), created a super-platinum prize with which to honor the new megahits—the Diamond Award, bestowed on records that sell more than ten million copies. (Flom has two Diamond Awards, for Matchbox 20's "Yourself or Someone Like You" and for Kid Rock's "Devil Without a Cause.") CDs also turned out to be a brilliant way of repackaging a label's "catalogue"—all the recordings that were no longer in production on vinyl. CDs spawned a generation of record executives whose skill was in putting together compilations of existing music, rather than in discovering new artists. Through the stock market crash of 1987 and the recession of the early '90s, the CD market grew steadily, until sales abruptly declined in 2001, by 6 percent, and then dropped 9 percent in 2002.

Lyor Cohen, the head of Island Def Jam, which is owned by Universal, thinks that the record industry would have been better off without the CD. "The CD kept the whole business on artificial life support," he told me. Without it, the old record industry would have died in the early '80s, and a new, more modern industry would have replaced it. But the CD preserved the status quo. "The record business became a commodity business, not a content-and-creation business," Cohen said. He rubbed his fingertips together. "What was lost was secchie—it means 'touch.' " 47

Unlike Jason Flom, who has always worked at a record label, Cohen got his start as an artist's representative; he co-managed the Beastie Boys and Public Enemy. Now forty-three, he is tall and speaks with a slight Israeli accent. On the morning I visited Cohen in his office, in Manhattan, he was dressed in jeans and an expensive-looking dress shirt and was puffing on a cigar. He propped his size-13 New Balance sneakers up on his desk as he spoke. 48

"The A&R guys at the record companies had gotten a little older and didn't feel like standing in the back of some filthy hole to listen to a new band," he said. "So, instead, they started repackaging stuff from when they were younger. We got the theme album—'Summer of Love,' 'Splendor in the Grass,' whatever—and by the end of the '80s most of the industry's profits were in catalogue." 49

Finally, CDs made piracy possible by making music much easier to copy. Had the platform never shifted from vinyl, the piracy problem wouldn't be nearly so bad. The zeal with which the labels flogged their catalogues on CD insured that a large amount of previously recorded music was rendered into digital form—almost none of it protected from 50 copying. "None of us wondered what the digitizing of sound waves would mean to our business," Stan Cornyn, a longtime Warner marketing man, wrote in *Exploding,* a recent history of Warner Music. "How fidelity degradation, which had held back some from making free tape copies, would no longer be a factor once sound waves got turned into digits. ... Digital sound, being so casually accepted into our world, was free to cause an epidemic. It would make data copying easy, clean, free, and something that felt about as immoral as killing an ant."

During the past decade, virtually every piece of popular music 51 ever recorded on CD has been "ripped," converted into a compressed digital file known as an MP3 (short for Moving Picture Experts Group Layer Three), and made available online, where anyone with a computer can get it. Once a song is converted into an MP3, it can be copied millions of times without any fidelity degradation. New music is ripped from CDs and uploaded as soon as the records come out (often before they come out, by studio technicians or by music journalists who receive advance copies). Music fans, who used to hear a song they liked on the radio, go to the record store, and buy the album, now hear a song they like on the radio, go to the Internet, and help themselves to it for free. Teenagers who were once the labels' best customers are now their worst enemies. "Younger fans, at whom pop music is aimed, tend to be comfortable with computers, which is why downloading hurts the best-selling hits more than other kinds of music," I was told by Hilary Rosen, the departing CEO of the RIAA. "As a result, records that might have sold eight million copies now sell five. Unfortunately, these blockbuster sales pay for the development of new artists—Kid Rock pays for all the others." In 2002, the industry shipped 33.5 million copies of the year's ten best-selling albums, barely half the number it shipped in 2000.

Whether or not the record business figures out how to make 52 money from MP3s, the format is here to stay. Just as CDs replaced vinyl, so will MP3s replace CDs. But, whereas CDs made the record business extraordinarily lucrative, MP3s are making it extraordinarily painful—a gigantic karmic correction that may lead to a bigger music business one day, although not before things get worse. Daniel Strickland, a twenty-three-year-old student at the University of Virginia, told me recently, "Maybe it's because I'm in college and I have an eighteen-year-old sister and a ten-year-old brother, but, let me tell you, nobody I know buys CDs anymore. My sister—she just gets on her computer, and she knows only two things, file sharing and instant messaging. She and friends go online, and one instant-messages the other, and says, 'Oh, there's this cool song I just found,' and they go and download it, play it, and instant-message back about it. My brother has never even seen a CD— except for the ones my sister burns."

Napster, the first widely used music-sharing software, appeared   53
in 1999. It was based on a program developed by a nineteen-year-old
college student named Shawn Fanning. Later that year, the R.I.A.A.
charged Napster with copyright infringement, and, after a hearing in
San Francisco, a California federal judge ruled against Napster and
eventually closed the service down. But that action did almost nothing
to diminish the availability of free music online; people simply began
to use other file-sharing programs, like KaZaA, Morpheus, Grokster,
and LimeWire. Unlike Napster, these programs, which operate on what
are known as P2P (peer-to-peer) computer networks, have no central
computer that keeps an index of all the files on the system. Instead, any
computer using one of these programs can search and share files with
any other computer using the same software. The number of people
downloading music files over P2P networks today is thought to be
many times greater than the number of people who used Napster at its
height; by some estimates, fifty million Americans have downloaded
music illegally.

The music industry has launched alternatives to the P2P   54
networks—legal, online music services like Emusic, Pressplay, and
Rhapsody. But so far these have failed to attract many fans, partly
because they require users to pay monthly subscription fees, rather
than selling individual songs and albums. Sony and Universal recently
sold Pressplay to Roxio, a software company, which is expected to give
its service a new, sexier-sounding name—Napster. Apple's iTunes
Music Store, which was launched in April, selling downloadable songs
for ninety-nine cents and albums for ten dollars, is the best-designed
and best-stocked of the legal services, and the company sold three million songs in the first month of operation. Although sales have fallen
sharply, other companies, including Microsoft, are reportedly planning
similar services. Meanwhile, the labels are quietly beginning to harvest
the marketing data on songs and artists that the illegal networks offer.
Warner Music Group worked with Big Champagne, a company that
mines data from the P2P networks, but Big Champagne's CEO, Eric
Garland, isn't allowed to talk about it. "We are still very much the mistress," he told me.

In 2001, the RIAA joined the film industry in bringing a copyright-   55
infringement suit against some of the larger P2P networks, including
Morpheus and Grokster. But suing peer-to-peer networks isn't as easy as
suing Napster; for one thing, there's no one to sue. (KaZaA is based on
software that was commissioned by two Scandinavian businessmen. The
programmers are Estonian. The right to license the program was acquired
by Sharman Networks, an Australian company that has no direct
employees and is incorporated in the Pacific island nation of Vanuatu.)
Also, P2P networks offer a wide range of legitimate applications for

research and businesses. In April, a federal judge in Los Angeles ruled that, because Morpheus and Grokster can be used for both legal and illegal purposes, the companies that distribute the software can't be sued for copyright infringement.

Last fall, several Microsoft programmers released a study of some of the social implications of P2P. They foresaw the networks converging into what the authors called "the Darknet"—a vast, illegal, anarchic economy of shared music, TV programs, movies, software, games, and pornography which would come to rival the legitimate entertainment industry. Unless the government does something about P2P, our entertainment industry could one day resemble China's, where piracy is endemic. With no means of support, many artists would be forced to stop working, and a cultural dark age would ensue. The movie industry, which is a bigger and more politically powerful force than the record business, has yet to see its profits eroded by illegal downloading, but it may be only a matter of waiting until DVD burners become the standard item in PCs that CD burners are now. Unlike the music industry, the film industry is incorporating copy protection into its digital recordings, but the Darknet is full of bright hackers determined to prove their mettle by breaking through the most robust encryption.

In the face of the recent legal setbacks in the RIAA's campaign against the P2P networks, the organization's war on piracy has shifted toward the people who steal music. In April, the RIAA named four university undergraduates in a multi-million dollar claim for copyright infringement, forcing them to pay between twelve thousand and seventeen thousand dollars each in fines. The day before the RIAA lost in the Grokster case, it won an important victory in a legal action against Verizon, when a federal judge in New York upheld a ruling that Verizon was required, under the 1998 Digital Millennium Copyright Act, to turn over to the RIAA the names of customers whom the record industry suspected of illegally sharing music files. (Verizon, which is in the business of selling broadband Internet connectivity, does not want to discourage potential customers, even if downloading music illegally is what they want broadband for.) Last week, the RIAA announced that it would begin preparing hundreds of lawsuits against individuals, charging the defendants up to a hundred and fifty thousand dollars per song. "It's easy to figure out whose computer is doing it," Hilary Rosen told me.

The record industry has also engaged in less conventional ways of harassing people who use P2P networks, including posting music files that are corrupt or empty, and has explored the legality of using software that temporarily "locks up" any computer that downloads it. Orrin Hatch, the chairman of the Senate Judiciary Committee, when asked a couple of weeks ago whether he favored passing legislation that would override federal anti-hacking laws, said that if other means of stopping illegal downloaders failed, "I'm all for destroying their machines. If you have a few hundred thousand of those, I think people would realize the seriousness of their actions."

Sir Howard Stringer, the chairman of the Sony Corporation of 59 America, calls downloaders "thieves." "That's a reasonably polite way of saying it," he observed recently. "A shoplifter is a thief. That actress wandering around Hollywood helping herself, she was a thief. She should have adopted the Internet defense—'I was downloading music in the morning, downloading movies in the afternoon, and then I thought I'd rustle a few dresses out of the local department store. And it's been a good day, and all of a sudden I'm arrested. How is that fair?'" Many people I met within the record industry seem to regard today's music fans with disapproval. Tom Whalley, the head of Warner Bros. Records, said, "I think the audience is less loyal today than it used to be. The artist has to prove him- or herself with every new album; it feels like you're starting over each time." Fans I spoke to had, for their part, almost nothing good to say about the record industry. "I think the record companies are greedy pigs," said Oliver Ignatius, a fourteen-year-old music fan who lives in Brooklyn and who knows as much about pop music as anyone I know. Ignatius is the type of fan a record guy would kill for: he downloads, but he also uses file-sharing services to discover new music and to research previously recorded material, and if he likes what he hears, he buys the CD. He keeps his CDs in scrapbook-size folders, like a collection of stamps or baseball cards. Oliver thinks that the price of a CD should be six dollars. The industry is currently drawing the line at ten dollars—the price of downloading an album from Apple's iTunes Music Store.

One could argue that the record industry has helped to create 60 these thieving, lazy, and disloyal fans. By marketing superficial, disposable pop stars, labels persuade fans to treat music as superficial and disposable. By placing so much emphasis on hit singles that fit into the radio formats, the record industry has created a fan who has no interest in albums. And the values of the people who share music illegally over P2P networks are, after all, rock-and-roll values: freedom, lack of respect for authority, and a desire for instant gratification—the same values that made so many people in the record business rich.

Still, one of the most galling things about the piracy problem, if 61 you happen to be in the record business, is that not only are the fans gleefully and remorselessly taking the hits you make; they are doing so because they think you deserve it—it's your payback for ripping off artists with years of "plantation accounting." "I hope it all goes down the crapper," Joni Mitchell said of the record industry in Rolling Stone last year. "I would never take another deal in the record business. . . .

I'll be damned if I'll line their pockets." The following month, in *W*, she called the record industry a "corrupt cesspool," saying that she was leaving the major-label system because "record companies are not looking for talent. They're looking for a look and a willingness to cooperate." (Mitchell's most recent album came out on Nonesuch, a Warner label.) As Malcolm McLaren observed to me, "The amazing thing about the death of the record industry is that no one cares. If the movie industry died, you'd probably have a few people saying, 'Oh, this is too bad—after all, they gave us Garbo and Marilyn Monroe.' But now the record industry is dying, and no one gives a damn."

In December, I went to Los Angeles to visit the recording studio   62
where work on Cherie's album was under way, and to meet the artist. Cherie had moved there in June, shortly after finishing school in France. The label had found her a house in Beverly Hills, and she was living there by herself, although Haddad was keeping a close watch over her. Her mother had come to help her settle in, but she had returned home to Marseilles.

Haddad briefed me on Cherie's schedule in L.A. "Her routine is   63
very intense, and it's all about her," he said. "She gets up early, and she works out at home, sometimes with her trainer, then she does her voice lessons, and she does her English lessons, and if she's recording, she spends afternoons and evenings at the studio, and if she isn't, she meets with agents and movie producers and a bunch of other people who are interested in her."

Westlake Studios is in Hollywood, in a one-story building with   64
blackout windows, at the corner of Santa Monica and Poinsettia. It's an expensive, state-of-the-art studio. These days, almost all the effects that were once only possible to create in a professional studio like this can now be achieved on a home computer with a software program. (A program called Pro Tools will even correct your voice when you sing off key.) Flom's reason for spending the money anyway, as I understood it, was: Anyone can make a record these days, but only a major label can make a really expensive record. This is what economists call "retreating upmarket," which is the classic response of an entrenched industry threatened with a disruptive technology.

Inside, Cherie, who had recently turned eighteen, was behind a   65
glass wall that separated the recording area from the control room. She was singing "pickups"—the bits of the song in which the vocal needed work. Most of the pickups were the "U" sounds, where Cherie sounded most French.

At the controls of an immense mixing board was Humberto Gatica,   66
a producer of hits by, among others, Celine Dion and Michael Jackson. Gatica had silver hair, a slight Spanish accent (he was born in Chile), and a voluble manner. Beside him, co-producing, was the songwriter

Paul Moessl, who had written Cherie's original demo, "Older," and was the co-writer of the song they were working on now, "Fool." The musicians had already recorded their parts—the label had bought the services of the best studio musicians, including the rock star Beck's father, David Campbell, who specializes in arrangements for strings. Moessl estimated that there were fifty thousand dollars' worth of strings on the record. Now Gatica was mixing everything together on the hundred-and-twenty-track system.

Moessl, who was in his early thirties and had lank blond hair, 67 said, "Did you pull down the crunchy loop?" referring to part of the complicated percussion mix.

"No," said Gatica, not taking his eyes off the flashing lights on the 68 console. "I just took a little pressure off the snare."

Moessl turned his attention to a volume on his lap, which was 69 entitled *The Book of Positive Quotations*. He was looking for ideas for lyrics for a new song he was writing with Cherie.

"If you are writing an artistic song, you write from inside your- 70 self," he said. "You say, oh, I don't know, 'My dog died today,' or something like that. But if it's a commercial song you look for uplifting things."

The recording of the album had not been going as smoothly as 71 Flom had hoped. For one thing, the songwriters were having trouble creating the right up-tempo number for Cherie—the song that would become the all-important first single. "Ballads are about love," Flom explained to me, "but, at least for the last twenty years, most dance songs are about sex. But Cherie doesn't sing about sex. She sings about love. So we need a dance song about love. 'Push Push in the Bush' is not the right song for Cherie."

Gatica, his back stiff from bending over the mixing board, seemed 72 to have become temporarily confused by all the sonic possibilities at his fingertips. He paused from his work, sat down with his head in his hands, and remained that way in silence for a minute or so. Cherie waited patiently for him to recover. Finally, he sat up and said, "I was riding in the car the other day, and an Annie Lennox song came on from ten years ago or so—and, man, it was brilliant. Brilliant production. But now the kids don't want that sound anymore." He threw his hands in the air. "They want simple! Like it's made in a garage! So you do an expensive production like this one, made in a facility like this that costs many thousands of dollars a day, and then you end up grunging it up so that it sounds like it was made in a garage."

Cherie finished her pickups and emerged from the recording 73 room. She wore a navy turtleneck, Levi's, black boots with pointed toes and stiletto heels, and silver bracelets on each wrist, which she twisted with her long, thin fingers. She wasn't as sultry as the animated Cherie in the Batman movie, but she was much more beautiful than she appeared in the label's first photo shoot, with dramatic cheekbones and striking dark eyes. When she smiled, her mouth went up in the middle but turned down at the corners, in a way that looked French. Her English was passable, and when she was stuck for a word, Haddad supplied it. She seemed like a nice, modest girl who was trying hard to please.

We went to a room at the back which was used as a place to hang out between sessions. There were candles burning, and plants, and low, comfortable furniture. Cherie said that she had never been interviewed before, but if she was nervous it added to her charm. I asked her about the feeling she is able to put into a song, adding that Flom had described it as "the thing." Cherie, her eyes bright, responded, "Yes! This is eet! It is the thing. That is exactly what it is—it's just this thing." She gestured toward her chest. "I don't know where it comes from, just comes from inside you—the thing." 74

As we were talking, I could hear Gatica shouting in Spanish as he worked on the word "learn," which sounded particularly Gallic, playing it over and over again, adding what were to me inaudible effects, and shouting some more. 75

"So now I will sing for you, it's O.K.?" Cherie asked. She stood up and launched into her lucky song—a Jacques Brel belter called "Quand on n'a que l'amour." The money note is the last note in the piece, and Cherie hit it perfectly, arms reaching to embrace her amour. Chills. 76

283

Flom arrived, wearing a suit, and hugged his star. They walked back into the control room, where Gatica was at work. The producer played the song. Flom listened with his head inclined downward, rocking with the beat back and forth, his fist cocked, ready to punch the air when he heard the money note. 77

But the note never came. When the song ended, Flom looked crestfallen. He said he missed some of the simplicity of the earlier demo. 78

"Right," Gatica said. "I am combing it now. The idea is to keep it fresh—transparent. Today, records are simpler. People will say this sounds like Whitney Houston. Well, it is a ballad. But we have to make it for a new generation." 79

They played the song again. "We have been very, very careful not to let the accent get in the way," Gatica said. 80

"Though you can still tell she's French," Flom said. 81

"You can tell?" the producer said, sounding alarmed. 82

"It's not that that's bad," Flom said. "She's French. Hey—it is a Romance language, after all." 83

Flom departed, and Gatica went back to work. Hours later, when I left, he was still at it. 84

On the subject of whether the record industry will survive, there 85
are optimists and pessimists. The optimists think record companies
will eventually figure out how to sell music over the Internet, and
when that happens, the market for music will be three times bigger
than it is now. The pessimists say that the industry has missed a crucial
opportunity to control the new distribution platform and that, unless
the government intervenes, the recording industry will disappear, and
the music business will return to what it was in the nineteenth century,
when publishing and performing were the main sources of revenue.
Chris Blackwell thinks the online music business will be a boon to
independent labels because manufacturing and distribution costs will
be much cheaper; Ahmet Ertegun says, "Yes, but independents still
have to get people to buy their records." And, with so much music out
there, artists will need more blowing up than ever.

Historically, popular music has been heavily influenced by its 86
format. In the nineteenth century, before Edison invented the
phonograph, the music business was a publishing enterprise in
which sheet music was the primary commodity. People performed
the music themselves, at home, usually on the piano. Songs were
made into hits by the popular performers who travelled around the
country putting on concerts and musicals. The length of the songs
varied. It was a singles business. When recorded music became
popular, early in the twentieth century, and the format changed to
the shellac 78-r.p.m. disk, popular songs became about three minutes long, which was as much time as a disk could hold. The invention of the LP—the 33-r.p.m. long-playing record—in the late 1940s
created the market for albums. For the record companies, albums
cost about the same as singles to produce, but they could be sold for
much more. In the CD era, the record industry all but killed off the
singles business.

MP3s might revive that business. For artists, this will mean that, 87
instead of making grand artistic statements with an album released
once every three or four years, they will focus their talent on individual
songs, which they will release every month or so. Moby, the popular
recording artist, told me he thought this would be a terrible development for artists, "because an album is so much more interesting artistically than a song." Fans will buy this music in part because it will
include goods and services like concert tickets and merchandise.
Traditionally, record labels have earned money only from the sale of
recorded music, but increasingly record companies may make deals
like the one EMI made last year with the British pop star Robbie
Williams, in which the label paid the artist some eighty million dollars
to become a full partner in all of Williams's earnings—from publishing,
touring, and merchandise, as well as from record sales.

As with CDs, MP3s will probably cause a boom in catalogue   88
sales. At the moment, because of traditional retailing constraints, only
a small fraction of a label's catalogue is for sale. In an online music
store, everything can be offered. Niche markets could become much
more important, and artists with small but loyal followings, who are
not economically viable in a winner-take-all market, might hold more
appeal. Danny Goldberg, a former president of Warner Bros. Records,
who is a founder of the independent Artemis Records, told me, "The
Internet will be good for Latin music, jazz, world, and anything that
sells five to ten thousand." The singer-songwriter Jimmy Buffett, who
decided to leave the major-label system and put out music on his own
label, Mailboat Records, told me that he thinks that more artists will
go into the music business for themselves. "At Mailboat, we have
three people, and we take care of our customers, and we handle the
shows, and everyone has a good time—it's just like the old record
business," he said.

Arguably, the most important function that record-industry pro-   89
fessionals perform—the task that people like Jason Flom, Jeff Haddad,
David Foster, Lyor Cohen, Humberto Gatica, and Paul Moessl are all
engaged in, one way or another—is filtering through the millions of
aspiring artists who think they can sing or play and finding the one or
two who really can. Record men of the future might not need to do
A&R; they might not even make records. They may prepare monthly
playlists of new songs or artists that will be beamed wirelessly to your
portable MP3 player. But their essential task—filtering—will remain
the same.

Everything depends on getting people to pay for recorded music   90
that they now get for free. When radio threatened the music business in
the 1920s and 1930s, the broadcasters agreed to pay a fee to the various
rights holders for the music they played, based on an actuarial accounting system. Rights holders' societies like Ascap administered those
payments. Some have argued that a similar system should be adapted
to the Internet, but many users would refuse to pay their share, and
would go on taking music for free. It may make more sense to address
the P2P problem with a government-imposed, statutory license, such
as many countries in Europe impose on TV owners. Anyone with an
Internet connection would be charged a few dollars a month, regardless of whether he downloaded music or not. That money would be
distributed to the rights holders, based on an online sampling system.
As Jim Griffin, a former executive at Geffen Records and a digital-
rights visionary, explained the concept to me, "You monetize anarchy.
Charge them five dollars a month to be thieves."

As the music business shifts online, the hitmakers may give way   91
to people who understand the financial restructuring that's needed.

285

In January, Sir Howard Stringer replaced Tommy Mottola, the head of Sony Music, with Andrew Lack, an executive from NBC with no previous experience in the record industry. The uber bosses of the record labels aren't even necessarily from the entertainment industry. Universal Vivendi is now run by Jean-René Fourtou, an expharmaceuticals executive; and the head of Bertelsmann is Gunter Thielen, who formerly ran the company's printing and industrial operations. In some ways, the record business of the future sounds more like a public utility than like a music company. It also doesn't sound like as much fun.

In April, Flom decided to postpone Cherie's record. Instead of coming out this summer, it will be released sometime during the first quarter of next year. "It's just taking them a lot longer in the studio than we had anticipated," he told me, and I had a vision of Gatica, the producer, driving himself to distraction with the crunchy loops. 92

I said that it seemed as though worldwide politics had given the lie to the idea of a "worldwide artist," especially if the artist is French. "They're not going to boycott the fucking album because she's French," Flom replied. Still, it was perhaps not the ideal time to break a worldwide artist named Cherie. 93

The last time I saw Flom, the numbers for the first quarter of 2003 had just come in, showing that the record industry's downward spiral was continuing. Sales were even lower than those of the first quarter of the disastrous previous year. The top-selling album in the country was a collection of songs sung by Kelly Clarkson, Fox's first "American Idol" winner, who has been discovered and blown up without much help from a record label—television made her a star. (Before too long, the United States' pop charts could begin to resemble Spain's, where seven of the spots on the Top Ten charts were recently occupied by reality-show contestants, causing real recording artists to complain that they aren't getting a fair shake.) And there was talk of a merger between BMG and Warner Music, which could mean that the man who called for the end of Flom's type of "lottery mentality," Rolf Schmidt-Holtz, could be Flom's boss. 94

Still, on this warm, springlike day, Flom seemed to be in a sunnier mood about the future than he had been when we first met, six months earlier. He had recently signed a new, all-girl country-rock group called Antigone Rising, whom he expected to be huge. And he was happily immersed in looking for the right song that would be the first single for Cherie, confident that sooner or later the perfect up-tempo love song would present itself. Jerry Wexler, one of Ertegun's partners at Atlantic, once said that artist-and-repertoire was just a fancy expression for putting a singer together with a song, and in this respect the record business does not seem to have changed at all. 95

Flom said he had even thought about trying to write a song for   96
Cherie himself. But this idea hadn't got very far.

"I can't imagine writing a song today," he said. "I don't know   97
where I'd start."

Can the record business survive?   98

Examining the Text

1. Beyond the implications of new technology and the recording industry's
response to it, what other issues does the author address in this article? On
reflection, do you believe that illegal downloading is the main issue confronting the recording industry? Why, or why not?

2. Author Seabrook quotes Jason Flom making the above statement: "If the
star is big enough, people will buy the album because it's like a piece of the
artist. But if the star doesn't have that kind of irresistible appeal, then people
just say, 'what the heck, I'll download the good songs.' So we just have to figure
out how to make her a big star." Looking back on recently successful bands and
singers, how much of their popularity do you think is owed to this kind of
"blowing up" by recording-industry executives like Flom? Using some of your
own favorite musicians as examples, examine whether you think Flom's statement is accurate: can record sales be driven by record companies' marketing
efforts?

3. Examine the quote from Clear Channel CEO Lowry Mays, who says: "We're
simply in the business of selling products." What does this imply about the role
of commercial radio and other media in the development and dissemination of
your favorite music? When you listen to a radio station that plays current
songs (as opposed to hits from the past), do you notice how many get frequent
plays? Do you ever consider that record companies might be influencing what
gets played on the radio; if so, do you object to such "manipulation"?

4. *Thinking rhetorically:* Based on the title, what sorts of information and
themes did you expect from the article? After reading it, did the article meet
your expectations? What specific persuasive techniques does the writer
employ with this article? By the end of the article, did these techniques alter
your views on whether or not the record business can be saved? If so, how; if
not, why not? Might the author have approached the subject using different
rhetorical strategies and still attained the same result for you?

287

For Group Discussion

By now, everyone knows that downloading copyrighted music from the
Internet is illegal, yet still it persists. Knowing that it is legally wrong has not
dissuaded the majority of Americans who still download music, seemingly
unconcerned about the ethical issues involved. In light of what you've read in
the article, discuss what would have to change in order for people to stop
downloading music. Are there steps that the recording industry should take?

Should universities and other providers of high-speed Internet connections be held responsible when users download music illegally? Alternatively, take a pro-downloading position and defend the rights of MP3-sharers to access music freely and without legal consequence.

Writing Suggestion

Imagine you are a record label executive faced with declining sales of CDs as a result of downloading from the Internet. Write a letter to the *New Yorker* magazine in which you defend recent efforts to sue networks like Napster as well as individual heavy users of file-swapping networks. Address how you're trying to win the battle in the court of public opinion as well as legally.

"Take Those Old Records Off the Shelf": Youth and Music Consumption in the Postmodern Age

DAVID HAYES

As a college student, you may be just old enough to remember the transition from recorded music on audiocassettes to the currently popular digitized formats such compact discs and iPods. However, the transition from cassette to CD to MP3 merely represents the most recent trend in recorded music manufacture and marketing. Before the cassette was eight-track and reel-to-reel tape, and along with that the long-playing album (LP), a black pizza-like contrivance etched with tiny grooves and played on a turntable with a needle stylus. Just when you thought the LP was mainly a relic of the past, relegated to garage sales, the dusty storerooms of curio shops, or the occasional cross-face scratch by an old-school turntablist DJ in a club . . . vinyl is back! This paper analyzes the reemergence of music recorded on vinyl LPs as a viable alternative format for music consumption in the digital age. Based on interviews conducted during field research on the emotional appeals of popular music, this article's author argues that youth consumers have begun to adopt the "retro" technology of LPs and turntables, in part as a means to resist industry-regulated and -dictated modes of music consumption, and for several other potential reasons, as the essay will explore.

As you read, pay attention to the critical lens through which the author views his research subject. This article occasionally but very pointedly makes reference to "postmodernism," a theoretical and/or philosophical term you may have heard but may not completely understand. In fact, it's easy not to understand what postmodernism means because the term has many significations and can be applied to a variety of disciplines, from architecture to art. However, in this article, Hayes appears to embrace a strand of postmodernism that observes contemporary individuals abandoning certain convention-driven assumptions, prejudices, and constraints to embrace the contradictions, humor, and profusion of pop and mass culture, both contemporary and historical. From this perspective, the usual "high" and "low" designations of cultural artifacts (Shakespeare = high; American Idol = low) are rendered pointless and unimportant, and everything becomes fair game for research analysis. One of the many features of this thread of postmodernism is the nostalgic re-embracing of all things "retro": artifacts and styles that might have been dismissed as "low" because they were passé, unworthy, or outmoded, such as "B-movies" from the '50s, '70s fashions such as bell-bottom hip-hugger pants, démodé hair styles (the moustache is back!), and antiquated technologies, such as vinyl recording . . . the latter being the subject for this article's examination.

Explanations for the music industry's current state of disarray often focus on the development and promotion of artists who seemingly lack the ability to produce albums in the sense that older generations of music fans knew them. Christina Aguilera, Nelly, Britney Spears, Justin Timberlake and many other contemporary musicians are commonly perceived as "singles" artists, adept at producing catchy songs but unable to make full-length recordings that sustain the interest of their audiences. Consequently, the argument goes, many youth consumers have turned their backs on the traditional economic practice of buying music, instead downloading favorite songs and compiling their own digital libraries on home computers, iPods, CD-Rs, and other mechanisms that enable reproduction, reordering, and (albeit legally dubious) redistribution.

1

   During recent field research on the effect of popular music on youth identity, I interviewed many teenage music fans who voiced this common discourse. Many of them complained that the contemporary music landscape was populated by untalented performers and profit-hungry executives interested only in producing material for "tween" and even younger audiences. They lamented the passing of (what they commonly perceived as) a golden age of recorded music: a time when artists released albums containing important statements, unfettered by the interference of record labels. According to their shared perspective, this epoch began with the arrival of the Beatles, Dylan and other musicians whose recording careers began in the early '60s and ended—resoundingly—with the suicide of

2

Nirvana's Kurt Cobain in 1994. Between these cultural bookends, albums by artists as diverse as Jimi Hendrix, Bruce Springsteen, and the Sex Pistols were cited as examples of recordings marked as authentic (versus the perceived inauthenticity of many contemporary releases). Perhaps not surprisingly, then, modern music was of little interest to more than one-third of the youth I interviewed—a subset of music fans fixated on music from previous eras to the degree that they privileged LPs and turntables over contemporary digitized formats and playback systems overwhelmingly endorsed by their peers.

According to their narratives, four distinct characteristics con- 3 tributed significantly to the development of their affective relation with vinyl: the appeal of LP jackets, custodianship of records, engagement in the listening experience (including participatory aspects of the turntable), and the quest for elusive vinyl recordings. Although these elements play an important role in these youth's consumption of vinyl and constitute a significant portion of my analysis, it is not the intent of this paper to debate the superiority or inferiority of LPs versus CDs. Instead, I attempt to engage the larger question of why these young people—many of whom were born well after the decline of vinyl—have turned to a listening practice that openly contradicts the benefits of digital recording. What is there in the crackles and pops of an LP that satisfies their desire for "authentic" music?

I argue that, through their retrogressive tastes and practices, these 4 youth effectively disrupt the music industry's efforts to define and regulate their consumer identities, thus restoring a degree of autonomy to an economic relation widely perceived to be over-determined by corporate objectives, youth-oriented marketing campaigns, legal action, and other forms of control advocated by the Recording Industry Association of America (RIAA). Furthermore, these acts of resistance help to mediate their status as problematic subjects, encouraged to consume new music frequently and profusely but classified as thieves when they resort to modes of distribution outside the control of Vivendi-Universal, Warner Music Group, EMI Group, Sony, and BMG (soon to merge into Sony BMG)—the five current controlling interests of the music industry. Caught between these two oppositional discourses, a growing number of youth music fans have become disillusioned with the industry's mechanisms of commerce and artists (such as Christina, Britney, and Justin) perceived to be inextricably linked to the economies of their labels. Consequently, they regard music from past eras as offering more sincere, authentic observations on the human condition—reflective of the artists' lived experiences and the artistic autonomy necessary to produce and distribute such works. In doing so, however, these young people ignore these recordings' indelible ties to the music industry's capitalistic framework.

POSTMODERNISM AND NOSTALGIA

While many of my pro-vinyl research participants knowingly privilege   5
vinyl to resist the industrial regulation of popular tastes and modes of
consumption, their shared practice also enables them to counteract two
of postmodernism's core tenets: our collective nostalgia for seemingly
simpler times and one of its attendant correlates, a perceived loss of
agency. Through their newfound interest in outdated technologies and
older recordings, these youth construct consumer identities that challenge the music industry's attempts to define and regulate behavior,
refusing the present and the commonplace in favor of the past and the
obscure. They are empowered by their declaration of (relative) autonomy from dominant contemporary modes of consumption to explore
new—or at least divergent—cultural arenas in which the consumer
structures his or her music preferences and not, as many of them perceive, the other way around. Thus freed to trawl through the virtually
endless back catalog of popular music, they select recordings based on
what they have read (in corporate periodicals like *Spin*, *Rolling Stone*,
and *Vibe*, independent periodicals like *MaximumRockNRoll* and *The
Source*, fanzines, online blogs, band Web sites, and other sources of
information), what catches their eyes (Franny, one of my research par-   **291**
ticipants, often bought LPs because of the jackets' alluring designs),
and what their budgets permit (bargains found in flea markets and
yard sales were commonly cited). While these criteria all contribute to
the development of increased personal agency among pro-vinyl music
fans, the constraint imposed by the last factor poses perhaps the most
significant challenge to the music industry's efforts at consumer regulation, for it directs these youth away from conventional retail outlets
(both large-scale corporations, such as HMV and Tower Records, and
local independent music stores) and toward alternative sources offering affordable, otherwise unavailable recordings.

However, before turning to the narrative of my research subjects   6
to examine how their fascination with vinyl contributes to the development of these and other aspects of personal agency, I wish briefly to
address the issue of nostalgia and its impact on representations of
music consumption in many contemporary popular culture texts.
Fredric Jameson's examination of postmodernism and the nostalgia
film provides a useful starting point as it addresses a similar seemingly
retrogressive cultural shift that is connected with practices of consumption. In "Postmodernism and Consumer Society," Jameson argues that
an increasing number of contemporary films engender nostalgic readings because they "reawaken a sense of the past" (8) through their uses
of tropes associated with older texts. For example, he posits that
George Lucas's *Star Wars* (1977) is a film that can be read in two (if not

more) ways. For older viewers, Lucas's characters recall the stalwart heroes, distressed heroines, and diabolical villains of '30s and '40s movie serials, although recognition of these references is unnecessary for younger audience members to appreciate the film as a self-contained experience. Lawrence Kasdan's *Body Heat* (1981) is also a nostalgia film, Jameson argues, because it straddles several temporalities. Although the story is contemporarily located, it is filled with allusions to Art Deco, film noir, and other stylistic elements that recall—at least for audiences cognizant of Kasdan's references—earlier works such as Billy Wilder's *Double Indemnity* (1944) and Tay Garnett's *The Postman Always Rings Twice* (1946). However, as Jameson points out, there is more to this reflexivity than simply remembering the past. He argues that "it seems ... exceedingly symptomatic to find the very style of nostalgia films invading and colonizing even those movies today which have contemporary settings, as though, for some reason, we were unable today to focus on our own present, as though we had become incapable of achieving aesthetic representations of our own current experience" (9).

I argue that music fans who have tossed aside Discmans and dusted off their parents' turntables are similarly affected by this post-modern malaise. As youth consumers, they are encouraged to adopt the latest trends in pop culture—from music to fashion to technology to diet—but are ultimately unable to integrate these experiences meaningfully into their lives before they are asked to embrace newer, supposedly superior products. For example, each Friday, filmgoers are presented with a new batch of releases that vie for their attention via elaborate marketing campaigns, yet many of these works, while offering immediately and easily accessible entertainment, are often perceived by audiences as empty or insignificant experiences after their consumption. Furthermore, as Will Straw observes, the advent of home entertainment technology has led to the perpetual presence of many otherwise forgettable films via the endless array of DVDs and VHS tapes available at any movie rental store ("Embedded Memories"). Their continual accumulation, he argues, acts as a drag on modern culture, making it difficult (if not impossible) for consumers to approach contemporary films without an intertextual reading often based upon a limited understanding of older films, genres, actors, directors, and other associated elements. To illustrate his argument, Straw cites Jay Roach's Austin Powers in *Goldmember* (2002), a film that demands at least passing knowledge of previously marginal genres such as blaxploitation, late-'60s British spy films (many of which, like *Our Man Flint* (1966) and *In Like Flint* (1967), were parodies of earlier Bond films) and other forms that have recently experienced renewed interest largely because of DVD re-releases. Thanks to studios' reissue

7

programs, the past is always present with us—albeit reframed according to contemporary sensibilities and appetites. Our nostalgic longing for older cultural texts has been fully leveraged by an entertainment industry that both recirculates its back catalog and produces new films, such as Quentin Tarantino's *Kill Bill: Vol. 1* (2003) and *Vol. 2* (2004), that invite, if not demand, recollection of their reference points. Are the makers of these films wrong to draw so extensively upon antecedents? Of course not, but one cannot deny their complicity in a recycling of tropes that has destabilized the arena of cultural production and reception, particularly for artists interested in exploring themes that illustrate who we are now and not then.

This brings me back to an examination of my research subjects' reconfigured habits of music consumption. Although these youth are relatively new enthusiasts for vinyl LPs (all were previous purchasers of CDs before their switch), they have adopted decoding practices that mimic those used by previous generations to purchase, experience, and respond to music. Like the audiences of nostalgia films, their consumption of cultural texts draws upon popular understandings of how these experiences were framed in (and by) the past. These representations are hard to escape, as they pop up in contemporary popular culture with alarming regularity. DJing practices aside (a phenomenon worthy of separate analysis), vinyl consumption has figured prominently in such recent films as *Almost Famous* (2000), the *Austin Powers* trilogy (1997, 1999, and 2002), *Ghost World* (2000), and *High Fidelity* (2000) as well as TV shows such as *American Dreams* (NBC), *The Simpsons* (Fox), and *That '70s Show* (Fox)—all, to varying degrees, works that trigger nostalgic readings. In these examples, listening to vinyl is primarily marked as a pleasurable experience, often as an opportunity for youth to assert their independence from parents (*Almost Famous, American Dreams, That '70s Show, The Simpsons* ["Whacking Day"]) and peers (*Ghost World, High Fidelity*) and/or as a prelude to sex (*Austin Powers, The Simpsons* ["The Way We Was"]). Many of these works romanticize the interaction between the listener and his or her music, emphasizing the care required in removing a record from its cardboard jacket, placing it on the turntable, and selecting a desired track. By contrast, when CD consumption is depicted in popular texts—a comparatively rare occurrence—the focus is almost always placed on sound rather than action, as if the disc magically cued itself.[1]

A series of scenes from Stephen Frears' *High Fidelity* provides a concise example of this discourse. When a customer of Championship Vinyl (note the store's name) asks for a copy of a particular Echo and the Bunnymen LP, clerk Barry (Jack Black) tells him, "The Killing Moon EP is almost impossible to find, especially on CD—yet another cruel trick played on all the dumb-asses who got rid of their turntables."

8

9

293

Soon afterward, clerk Dick (Todd Louiso) informs another customer (Sara Gilbert) that modern punk band Green Day is influenced by the Clash and Stiff Little Fingers—two groups that released the bulk of their work before the advent of CDs. To illustrate his point, Dick pulls an album by Stiff Little Fingers from the store racks and, as we watch him through the glass display case, bends down and carefully places the tone arm on the LP while watching for her reaction. This is followed by an exchange in which storeowner Rob Gordon (John Cusack), twirling a CD around his finger, tells Dick, "I will now sell five copies of The Three EPs by the Beta Band." Like Dick, Rob also bends down to cue the music but this time, the camera remains focused on the action above counter; we are not privy to the presumably familiar process of programming a CD player. Moments later, many of his customers are bobbing their heads to the music of the Beta Band. One customer asks, "Who is this?" as Rob and Dick smile knowingly at each other, smug in the assessment of their clientele's predictability.

In these scenes, Frears (re)constructs vinyl as an authoritative 10 mode of music consumption, positioning its enthusiasts (as personified by the staff of Championship Vinyl) as informed, hip music fans and those unaware of vinyl's superiority as either young enough to be excused for their ignorance (Dick's customer) or old enough to know better (Barry's customer). The latter category, according to Barry, is made up of "dumb-asses" gullible enough to switch over to CDs at the music industry's behest, and now are unable to track down recordings (such as Echo's The Killing Moon [1984] and Stiff Little Fingers) that are best experienced on vinyl. By contrast, today's dominant mode of music consumption is presented as mechanical and mundane; the Beta Band CD is played—we assume—by simply inserting it into a CD player. There is nothing rhapsodic about this action, for it requires neither an inordinate amount of attention, as Dick gave the Stiff Little Fingers LP, nor the cool assuredness demonstrated by Barry as he educated his customer on the music industry's hegemonic practices. Furthermore, through his framing of this scene, Frears implies that most contemporary music fans are easily duped into buying whatever is presented to them; with a push of the play button, Rob is able to convince his customers of the Beta Band's artistic merit, whereas Dick's introduction of Stiff Little Fingers is met with ignorance ("Is this the new Green Day?" asks one customer).

FORMAT AND THE MUSIC INDUSTRY

Although the position of authority granted to vinyl in *High Fidelity* 11 and the other works cited above appear to mark the re-emergence of a listening practice framed as the dominant mode of consumption for those informed enough to recognize its hipness, vinyl in fact never went away. Even after CDs surpassed LPs as the dominant medium in 1987, vinyl remained the format of choice for many die-hard collectors, independent musicians, and other fans drawn to its supposed sonic superiority, relative scarcity, and retrogressive technology. While many small (largely regional) labels continued to release music on 7" and 12" records throughout the '90s, locating their products was often a difficult task since mainstream retail outlets such as Tower Records and HMV shelved few if any LP releases after deleting previous stock. Faced with the industry's reconfiguration of music consumption, vinyl enthusiasts were limited to two main avenues of acquisition. First, a small number of independent retailers continued to stock vinyl releases—most often, limited pressings by small labels.[2] In many cases, these stores also contributed significantly to indigenous music scenes by promoting shows, supporting local artists, and selling tickets, t-shirts, fanzines, and other merchandise not handled by major retailers. Used record stores proved to be another dependable source for vinyl throughout the '90s, ironically a golden age for collectors during a period when many music fans replaced LPs with CDs.

Despite the continued availability of vinyl through these outlets, 12 the vast majority of the record-buying public supported the industry's claim that CDs provided improved fidelity while requiring less maintenance (as well as less precision when selecting a track). In 1983, two years after the CD's introduction, approximately 1.5 million units, or $17.2 million US in retail sales (Haring 47), were sold, compared to LP sales of 30 million units (White 3). Dannen, Goodman and Haring all offer unflattering pictures of industry executives colluding to systematically dismantle the record-buying public's consumptive habits by limiting the production of LPs, refusing retailers their option of returning unsold vinyl stock and artificially inflating the wholesale cost of CDs to guarantee increased profits. By 1989, these tactics finally brought about the format shift that the industry desired: CDs had all but eliminated LPs as a viable format, generating $2.69 billion US compared to vinyl sales of $232 million US (Haring 47).

At the turn of the millennium, though, vinyl sales began slowly to 13 recover as CD sales declined, a trend quantified by Nielsen SoundScan. According to year-end tallies published in Billboard, US CD unit sales dropped from 649,393,000 units in 2001 (Market Watch 2001) to 636,485,000 units in 2003 (Market Watch 2004)—an overall decline of 2 percent, while formats classified as "Other" (largely vinyl, but including a small number of DVD audio-albums [Jackson]) rose from 1,292,000 units sold in 2001 (Market Watch 2001) to 1,862,000 units sold in 2003 (Market Watch 2004): an increase of more than 30 percent.

Recognizing the growing interest in vinyl, HMV, Tower Records   14
and other large-scale music outlets have recently begun to stock the
White Stripes' Elephant (2003), Outkast's Speakerboxxx/The Love
Below (2003), and other limited-edition LPs. However, the prices
assigned these vinyl releases are often as much as 40 percent higher
than their CD equivalents—a serious impediment for prospective
buyers, considering that many CDs contain tracks that, largely due to
spatial limitations, are absent from their corresponding LP versions.
(It should also be noted that most major retailers' LP prices are significantly higher than those of most independently owned businesses.)
Perhaps not surprisingly, then, whenever most of the pro-vinyl youth
I interviewed chose to obtain a new release, they usually opted for the
CD version even though—as I stated earlier—this was a relatively
rare occurrence due to their general disdain for the contemporary
music scene.

THE CONSUMPTION OF VINYL BY YOUTH MUSIC FANS

Within this perilous cultural landscape, the pro-vinyl youth of my   15
research project attempted to regain a degree of agency seemingly nulli-
fied by contemporary modes of music consumption by turning to past
texts largely understood as authentic and meaningful. I first met many
of these youth during the summer of 2003 while conducting field-work
for a larger project on the affectivity of popular music: specifically, how
various subgenera of popular music inform youth understandings of
race, gender, and other social issues. To locate potential participants, I
visited three local music stores in the Canadian city of my field research
and placed advertisements requesting the involvement of teenagers
who would describe themselves as serious music fans (not that they
necessarily liked serious music, but that they were serious about the
importance of music in their lives), a category aptly describing the
twenty-three young people eventually selected for inclusion in my project. While the use of technology in music consumption was not initially
one of my primary research objectives, I became fascinated by eight of
my research participants' enthusiastic responses toward the consumption of music on vinyl. These eight also intermittently purchased new
and used CDs and downloaded music files from the Internet, but LPs
were their primary music format. Interestingly, there was no correlate
among the other fifteen I interviewed; none of them listened to LPs even
occasionally, relying instead exclusively upon a combination of purchased CDs and downloaded MP3s.

According to the responses of the eight pro-vinyl youngsters, 16 their decidedly retrogressive tastes and shared method of accessing and experiencing music reflected more than a mere dissatisfaction with contemporary youth culture. I argue that their practices, like the appetite for nostalgia films posited by Jameson, are responses to a postmodern malaise brought about by consumer capitalism. Faced with a constant barrage of new music produced for (and marketed at) their demography, these young people attempt to mark themselves as different by rejecting widespread practices of consumption maintained by the music industry's capitalistic framework. In its place, they attempt to construct alternative practices and attitudes that imply a deeper appreciation of music perceived as being distinct from the mechanisms of commerce regulating their peers' listening experiences. These re-inscriptions of consumer identity are ever present in the narratives of my research subjects, most of whom are highly aware of their complex— and often contradictory—understandings of music and the affectivity it engenders.

In accordance with the spectacle of imagery promoted by such 17 publications as *1000 Record Covers and Classic Rock Covers*, most of the pro-youth I interviewed cited the visual appeal of the LP jacket's 12"x12" cardboard canvas as an important reason for their attraction to vinyl. Franny (age eighteen), a fan of classic and alternative rock, stated, "I think a big deal is the cover art on old albums 'cause it's such a nice thing. I've got Abraxas by Santana. I don't even like the album. I just wanted the picture on the front. The record's kind of scratched, but who cares?" Similarly, Hank (age nineteen) argued that "there's something about having a piece of vinyl because it's a piece of art." Alec (age fourteen) stated his preference for the larger text and images printed on the LP jacket and inside sleeve, as opposed to the relatively diminished presentation of lyrics in a CD booklet. Furthermore, he described the aroma associated with LP cardboard jackets as "old fashioned" and "classy" (presumably referring to the moldiness of records kept in a damp environment), a distinction not evoked—at least for Alec—by plastic CD cases.

Although larger images and text on the LP jacket contributed to 18 the affectivity that vinyl engendered for these youth, most of their enthusiasm was reserved for the listening experience itself—in particular, their active involvement in negotiating the pops, skips, and crackles endemic to most second-hand records. However, rather than interpreting these sonic defects as impediments, most of these youth regarded them as integral to their consumption of music, valorizing these blemishes for the seeming authenticity with which they imbued the recordings. Of the eight pro-vinyl youth I interviewed, Alec was the most vocal in his appreciation of vinyl imperfections, stating: "It just makes me feel so complete listening to the LP. I love the crackling. It just makes me feel that this is what music was when it was made. This is the way it should be." Val (age sixteen) also suggested that less-than-pristine audio fidelity was connected to a sense of completeness in the listening experience:

> It sounds kind of corny, but when I'm listening to a record, I like the 19 atmosphere it gives my room. I can make my room in my image of what CBGBs might look like. I've got the posters up on the wall, and the lights are all low and everything, and I put a record on ... it's a nice vibe. You get that crackling sound, and it sounds cool.

Carl (age eighteen), a regular purchaser of used vinyl, opined: "If 20 I listen to the vinyl, I'll get more out of it than if I listen to a CD, because with a CD of an old band, it kind of seems more of a recreation than the music." Erica (age fourteen), a pop fan whose exposure to vinyl was limited to her parents' dusty collection, commented that LPs were "more authentic. It's kind of like the original." Although he preferred the convenience of a CD, John (age nineteen) acknowledged that "there's certainly a different sound on vinyl than CD—more of a rustic, old time sound."

Furthermore, several of the pro-youth and one member of my pro- 21 ject's wider subject pool took the audiophile's position that the digitization of analogue recordings cleaned up the music too well. They argued that the overall ambience of a recording session (such as the warmth of the studio, the physical presence of the artists, and other inaudible but nevertheless distinct aspects of a recording) was inaudible after each element of performance had been digitally separated and scoured during the encoding process. For example, Jonathan (age sixteen) claimed that an LP recording sounded better than its CD equivalent because of "a certain richness ... that you can just never get with a CD." Dan (age seventeen), a heavy metal fan who bought exclusively CDs, nevertheless agreed with Jonathan's assessment of the sonic differences between LP and CD recordings: "[Records] sound a lot different than CDs. They're not as clear. It just sounds better. It sounds like you're actually with (the musicians) when they're playing it." When asked why he was drawn to vinyl, Kyle (age fifteen) immediately cited "the quality of the music. It's crisp, and if you have it properly equalized with a good player and a good needle, it can sound a hundred times better than a CD."

As these comments suggest, many of my research participants felt 22 that format and authenticity were indelibly tied. Although the music preferences of these youth ran the gamut from Elvis to the Sex Pistols, there was a shared understanding that listening to their preferred artists on vinyl somehow constituted an experience more authentic than that offered by CDs. Because most of their favorite artists recorded the bulk of their work prior to the ascension of the CD and decline of the LP, these listeners understood vinyl recordings to be inextricably linked to the original studio session, as close as a music fan could get to the artist's actual performance. By contrast, they perceived CDs to be temporally disconnected from the music, approximations of a moment locked in time but ultimately unable to communicate its essence.

Issues of audio fidelity aside, these interpretations of format are   23
problematic for their disregard of the fact that vinyl recordings are also reproductions of sound and not, obviously, actual performances. As Simon Frith argues, whenever a temporally fixed performance (such as a Sidney Bechet solo) is remastered by a studio engineer and re-released by a record company for public consumption, what we get is not necessarily a version closer to the original performance but "a performance reconstructed according to today's sound values" (235). Since the advent of music digitization, as consumers we have been groomed by the music industry to expect clarity radically different from what audiences heard thirty years ago. When we play a CD, we expect each instrument to be distinct and crystal clear; it is then our job as listeners to assemble these parts, a process that I argue contributes significantly to our individual responses to a specific recording. I am not suggesting that these standards are wrong; they are simply reflective of the interplay between the industry's technological innovations and public expectations of sound. The more compelling question is: why have the eight pro-vinyl youth of my study rejected these popular understandings in favor of a listening experience that is predicated on sonic homogeneity and fragility, rather than heterogeneity and stability?

Based on their collective narratives, physical interaction and not   24
quality of sound appears to be the dominant factor in these youth's privileging of vinyl. Alec referred to his love of LPs as a "commitment" involving maintenance of the record through cleaning and careful handling, as well as changing his turntable's needle regularly. Jonathan also cited the care necessary to maintain an LP's condition, arguing that "a CD is flimsy and you can toss it around and it'll be fine [but] a record, you have to take care of." Similarly, Carl referred to the higher degree of responsibility involved in the handling of an LP: "I have a lot of respect for vinyl when I have it because I don't want to scratch it at all. I don't want to ruin it or ruin the case [sic] or anything, but with a CD, I can always make a new one or buy a new one."

Physical participation was also cited as an important part of the   25
listening experience. For many of these youth, the increased demands of carefully positioning the needle and flipping the record were seen as integral components to the enjoyment of music, practices not associated

with the relative ease of the CD player and its multi-disc, random select options. For Alec, the relative inconvenience of listening to vinyl was tantamount to dedication:

> Flipping the album—that's a pain when you're in bed and you're almost asleep and you're listening to the earphones and then it stops, and you've got to get out of bed to flip the album. I guess [flipping the album] is just one more part of the whole. With the CD, you can just click 'repeat' and stuff, but it's so much more the easier path you can take, rather than being committed to listening to the music that you love.

Franny also commented on her involvement in the act of playing   26
and listening to a vinyl LP, stating that "there's something nice about putting the record on and having to do the whole thing. There's something a lot more interactive about it than just throwing on a CD and skipping to the tracks." Even LP detractors recognized the increased level of participation required with an LP and turntable. Jeremiah (age eighteen), a fan of gangsta rap, acknowledged that LPs seemed "sturdy" but preferred CDs because "they're a lot easier to listen to. I have a six-disk changer, so I can just grab six of my favorite CDs and just switch them around. I got a remote. I don't have to go over or nothing" whereas with vinyl, he stated, a listener had to "open it up and flip it around. It takes too much time."

Jeremiah's comments aside, it is apparent that the increased level   27
of physical participation required with an LP is commonly regarded not as an inconvenience, but as an essential component of the listening experience. Although many of my subjects argued passionately that audio fidelity was the primary reason for their attraction to vinyl, I suggest that it is of secondary importance. These youth are not attempting to get as close as possible to the sound of the original studio performance. They aren't obsessed with hunting down first-generation master tapes to replicate the sensation of being next to Elvis in the Sun Studios in 1954 or with Bob Dylan during 1962's Columbia sessions; if that was the case, an argument could be made for privileging the digital re-mastering of older analogue recordings, most of which initially lacked a sense of sonic dimension due to the technological limitations of their day. Instead, these youth appear to favor the higher degree of participation endemic to the experience of listening to vinyl because it exists in opposition to the relative ease of programming CDs, selecting music files on home computers or portable digital music players, and other dominant modes of consumption. The act of cueing a turntable's tone arm involves a degree of dexterity not required in the activation of more contemporary technologies, engendering an acute awareness of participation among the pro-vinyl youth I interviewed. Similar to the

relation between a CD and the laser of its playback system, the resulting contact between stylus and groove is fixed, for once the needle enters the record's vinyl canal, it is locked in its path until the end of the side unless the listener intervenes. However, fragility also figures prominently in the consumption of vinyl; whereas advances in CD technology have virtually eliminated the potential for skipping (unless one is driving on a very bumpy road), a record enthusiast must tread carefully while the record is playing for fear of affecting the delicate contact between needle and LP. The temporal limitations of an LP's face also significantly distinguish the vinyl listening experience from more contemporary modes of consumption. Whereas no more than 25 minutes of music can be pressed onto each side of a record, a CD may hold more than 70 minutes of material, providing a sonic backdrop that can go on infinitely if a multidisk player is programmed appropriately. Comparatively, listening to one side of an LP is momentary, and I believe that youth drawn to its allure are conscious of the fragile, fleeting nature of their engagement.

While embracing a temporally limited, less mobile, more demand- 28 ing playback system may seem ludicrous in a culture where listening to music is often present to enrich other activities but is seldom the focus of attention, it has provided my research participants with opportunities to reinvigorate their consumption of music with a sense of personal agency. Within this alternative framework, they mark themselves as serious music fans actively involved in disrupting the music industry's attempts to regulate popular music trends and modes of consumption. Although their use of outdated technology might be viewed by their peers as quirky if not downright anachronistic, these youth are nevertheless empowered by their affective relation with vinyl, demonstrating throughout our interviews a degree of enthusiasm sadly lacking among even the most ardent CD purchasers. As they have demonstrated, the malaise of postmodernism is perhaps best counteracted by revisiting what we have previously discarded, for somewhere among our basements, attics, and garages possibilities might still exist for the reinscription of significance into a landscape of popular culture presently defined by the frequency and volume of consumption.

301

COLLECTING VINYL

In the concluding section of this paper, I wish to examine a final but 29 nevertheless significant aspect of the affective relation that vinyl engendered for three of my eight pro-vinyl research participants: the

hunt for recordings available exclusively on LP. Various music companies have loudly trumpeted their reissuing programs, regularly compiling unreleased tracks, b-sides, demos, and other rarities alongside
classic tracks on "limited edition" CDs or in lavishly illustrated, defini-
tively annotated box sets. Unless one's taste in music runs to the
extremely obscure, there is almost nothing that cannot be purchased on
CD today, either readily available in most communities or else an email
away. For vinyl aficionados, however, intense pleasure is derived from
the hunt for recordings that might be accessible if not for the limitation
of format. For example, although Hank downplayed his position
within the culture of record collecting, his comments revealed that
acquiring an extensive personal music library was indeed significant in
the construction of his identity as a committed music fan:

> A lot of people collect vinyl because they collect vinyl and they want to
> collect all of Frank Zappa's original first pressings and they spend their
> life looking for them, whereas I'd be happy with a pressing from 1989 of
> Joe's Garage that's not worth anything but still has the music on it. I also
> buy vinyl to sort of say, 'I have that on vinyl', where it's sort of harking
> back to the old days of having a collection.

302

Hank's words provide a fitting example of Will Straw's postula-   30
tion that record collectors use their libraries as a basis for social interaction with other enthusiasts, finding common points of reference based
on what is or isn't in a collection. Straw argues that the canonical bodies created and displayed by record collectors, overwhelmingly the
province of male music fans, are endemically tied to masculine notions
of social interaction and the use of domestic space as a signifier of
knowledge. As such, the male collector arranges his LPs in a manner
that emphasizes both the extent of his music library (size does matter
among connoisseurs) and the energy that he has invested in amassing
such a discriminating collection (rare or cherished items often receive a
prominent position either physically or canonically). Of course, the ful-
fillment of such an arrangement is realized only in the presence of
other similarly minded individuals as they flip through his acquisitions, confirming the collector's own good taste (and, implicitly, his
effort in developing it) and suggesting other material that might com-
plement the collection. By contrast, non-collectors are expected neither
to offer any more than the most cursory comment nor to state their own
preferences, since their minimal knowledge of the collecting culture
invalidates their opinions on music.

Like Hank, Jonathan and Kyle also valorized the effort required   31
in building a significant LP collection, rhapsodizing over the satisfaction of obtaining difficult-to-find vinyl pressings. As Jonathan

explained, "You have to put effort in tracking down the LP of certain albums, so the effort makes it seem like more of an experience. The extra effort solidifies how much you want to support that particular artist. Instead of the convenience of going down to one of the chain stores to pick up the CD, waiting for it makes it more exciting." He acknowledged that most of his favorite music was available on CDs, but argued that this "convenience" took away from the satisfaction of waiting for the right format to come along. Implicit in Jonathan's view was the audiophile's preference for the sound of music on vinyl, although this position was never formally articulated during our discussion of collections, which focused instead on the commitment required to stock his music library with specific LPs that were difficult—if not impossible at times—to attain.

As a fellow record collector, I can attest to the pleasure derived   32 from the limitations that Jonathan and his peers imposed upon themselves and, by extent, their collections. A record jacket might be in pristine shape while its accompanying LP might be damaged beyond playability, or else a mint-condition LP might be housed within a tattered, defaced jacket. A dealer might inflate the price to an unreasonable level, preventing even the most arduous fan from filling an aching gap in his collection. One might wait months or even years for the LP version of a certain recording to come along, but it is a later (and therefore less desirable) pressing. Perhaps the LP never materializes, although a CD version is readily available. These factors all contribute to the commitment of building a collection of vinyl recordings, as they constitute considerable restrictions that do not apply to the more relaxed practices of the CD buyer. It has been my experience that these demands are seldom appreciated by non-collectors who often are more interested in hearing anything within a certain genre of music than a specific recording or artist. If a casual music fan indicates any interest in the collector's acquisitions, he or she will usually suggest, "Put on some jazz," whereas a collector is prone to request a certain album by Miles Davis or, more likely, an artist generally regarded as obscure by those less knowledgeable.

The collector's pursuit of the elusive is another aspect of this   33 intense fascination with marginal music. For example, Kyle commented that finding certain LPs was even more satisfying because "they don't release things [on CD] that they released thirty years ago." Hank also referred to the unavailability of specific recordings, citing the example of Dan Hicks, a '70s country-rock artist whose albums have not yet been reissued on CD: "[The record companies] haven't released them, so it's kind of cool to have those and know that no one else is really listening to them unless they're a collector."

By tracking down vinyl versions of otherwise-unavailable record-   34 ings, collectors like Hank are disrupting the regulatory processes of the music industry on several levels. First, they are defying the industry's control of products according to marketability. I assume that the present lack of Dan Hicks CDs has little to do with evaluations of artistic merit; more likely, the absence of substantial contemporary demand for an artist achieving only minor status during his '70s heyday doesn't justify the production and promotion costs for Sony (the artist's former label). Thus, for Hank, unearthing Hicks's music was a project of excavation. He was able to recover music lost in time to all but the most committed fan and incorporate it in his collection alongside other favored artists. That most of his peers were unfamiliar with Hicks's work due to its obscurity was also important, for it cast Hank as a well-informed music collector who was able to function outside the industry's impositions. As Straw suggests, the "outsider" status cultivated by Hank highlights his considerable knowledge, but it is an identity not necessarily appreciated by many of his peers; in fact, Hank stated that other students viewed his taste in music as "another mark on the tally on stupid things [he's] done."

Why, then, does Hank attempt to mark himself as a knowledge- 35
able music fan when it causes more social problems than it solves? Why bother collecting the recordings of Dan Hicks and other forgotten artists when there is no one with whom to share them? I argue that, for the collector of marginalia, hunting for obscure recordings doubles as an act of resistance against the music industry's maintenance of a constructed popular music narrative. As Hank and Kyle both indicated, many historic recordings have yet to be released on CD, forcing consumers who have graduated from being casual listeners to being fans of specific genres and artists—especially those pre-dating the emergence of CDs in the '80s—to search for original vinyl pressings.

Although many small independent labels specialize in releas- 36
ing obscure material (Germany's Bear Family and NYC's Norton Records immediately come to mind), major labels tend to select items carefully from their consolidated back catalogues for re-issue treatment. The control of what music is and is not generally available to the public informs a popular music narrative that might be dubbed "the *Rolling Stone* history of rock and roll," due to the influence that that periodical wields in the construction of an industry-sanctioned canon of music. According to this widely accepted view, Elvis is credited with the birth of a youth-centric music that combined previous elements of R&B and country, paving the way for the Beatles, the Rolling Stones, and other rock acts of the '60s, punk bands of the mid-seventies, and grunge acts of the early '90s. Lost in this narrative, though, are the substantive works of artists associated with other forms and eras that disrupt the industry's linear history,

such as '40s R&B, '50s rockabilly, and '60s surf, garage (or "frat rock"), and soul music. Furthermore, the absence of these texts also presents the evolution of popular music largely as the product of musicians signed to contracts with major corporations, a view ignoring the involvement of countless artists achieving only regional success. Often recording only a song or two for small, independent labels, these musicians contributed significantly to the development of rock and roll and its numerous subgenera by expanding teen audiences, experimenting with musical forms and, perhaps most importantly, serving as models for other youth who would subsequently form their own bands. Most of those even fortunate enough to sign contracts with major labels were unable to parlay their relative successes into careers, but nevertheless their records still provide important insights into changing styles and popular tastes—not to mention the pleasure that they are still able to provide listeners. For Hank and Kyle, discovering these artists' recordings on vinyl (on either original pressings or reissues) is a liberating experience for it provides them with opportunities to consume music excluded from the industry's narrative history and, as a politicized act, assists in their willful disruption of the mechanisms of corporate capitalism.

Of course, all purchases—even those marked as disruptive—are still acts of consumption involving what Adorno described as the interplay between exchange value and use value. However, buying used vinyl—be it an old LP, 45 or 78—often occurs in an economic sphere in which the finer points of consumerism's regulatory characteristics are absent. The items sought by Hank and Kyle have been decommissioned, so to speak, since a record dealer with direct ties to major channels of production and distribution has already sold them at a previous point in time. Taxes have already been collected for the records, distributors have been paid for their products, artists have (presumably) been compensated, and so forth. However, these conditions of initial sale have little impact on the economic transaction that occurs when the record is sold for the second (or third . . .) time. For example, tax may or may not be collected by the used record dealer (for most regular customers, taxation is usually overlooked during a cash transaction), the sale may or may not be recorded, and so forth. Furthermore, the price of the record is highly arbitrary, reflecting the dealer's awareness or appreciation of the record as much as its collectable (or "book") value. Because prices for the same product can therefore fluctuate wildly from store to store, the consumer is thus able to shop around for a price that matches the exchange value that he or she feels is appropriate for a certain record.

Major retailers are also free to sell CDs at whatever price they choose, but relatively stable wholesale costs—set and maintained by

37 **305**

38

music corporations—are determining factors when executives weigh potential profit margins against the necessity of remaining competitive in a heavily populated market. Consequently, HMV, Tower Records, Wal-Mart, Target, and other businesses invariably offer the same product for approximately the same price, subsequently forcing smaller, often independently owned stores to follow suit. The consumer is left with few options if he or she desires a particular CD strongly enough: either pay the going rate or go without (or else download it, a practice with implications that far exceed the scope of this paper). By contrast, a music fan interested in used recordings is able to play a more active role in the process of acquisition by shopping around, haggling with dealers, and receiving discounts for frequent or large purchases. Furthermore, this consumer is also able to purchase music for a price that he or she might consider a bargain (i.e., less than what he or she was willing to pay), thus leveraging the use value attributed to a particular record against the exchange value that the merchant has assigned it.[3] For younger music fans like Kyle, these bargains provide an effective way to amass a collection of records cheaply and quickly. In fact, during our first interview Kyle arrived with a bag full of LPs culled from the dollar bin of a local used record store, excited by the notion that he could purchase intriguing music for such a low price. He refused the label of collector, though, stating that his growing vinyl library (approximately 100 records after a year of collecting) was meant solely for his listening enjoyment, not for archiving and maintaining indefinitely.

306

Despite differences in Hank and Kyle's approaches and intentions, 39 collecting vinyl has provided both young men with opportunities to experience works by artists marginalized or excluded by conventional narratives (for Hank, Dan Hicks and Frank Zappa; for Kyle, Iron Maiden and Propaghandi), thus contributing to a comprehension of popular music far more complex than the relatively conventional understandings of research participants whose consumption of music was limited to CD purchases and/or downloaded music files. Although their devotedness to arcane knowledge might be ridiculed in other fields—especially among youth—Will Straw observes that "record collecting . . . is almost never irredeemably nerdish" (10), concluding that the hipness commonly ascribed to this practice is substantiated by the development of personal music libraries and their inherent displays of knowledge and taste, as well as their resistance (or at least indifference) to dominant practices and aesthetic trends. For youth vinyl collectors like Hank, Kyle, and Jonathan, these associations figure prominently in the construction of social identities marked by independence, confidence, and an awareness of the historical foundations upon which contemporary youth culture is predicated.

CONCLUSION

For the eight pro-vinyl youth of my research project, locating and lis- 40
tening to LP recordings was largely a project of resistance. However,
while the equation that these music fans assumed to exist between
authenticity and format allowed them to circumvent dominant practices and tastes, it also contributed to their understanding of the past as
a site free from the tensions impacting the contemporary production
and consumption of cultural forms. Just as audiences for *Kill Bill*, the
Austin Powers trilogy, and other nostalgia films embrace the resurrected
tropes of blaxploitation, gore, film noir, and other film subgenera and
excuse the overt misogyny and racism of these texts as relics from our
politically incorrect past, none of the pro-vinyl youth I interviewed
stopped to consider any of the potential pitfalls inherent in the excavation of past music for present consumption. These youth were quick to
label many of today's artists as industry puppets, manufactured and
promoted by corporations intent on profit at the expense of artistic
integrity, whereas pre-CD works were almost uniformly understood to
be immune from the tensions of capitalism inherent in the signing,
writing, recording, producing, and distributing of an artist's music.
Consequently, the romanticism with which they regarded the past
effectively blurred their ability to critique the strengths and weaknesses of these older recordings—an evaluative process that they
eagerly used to define most modern music and its affective relation
with many of their peers. Furthermore, their predilection for retrogressive works and technologies often closed down opportunities to hear
new music produced either within or outside the industry's perime-
ters, and the absence of a viable, sustained youth market poses an even
bigger threat to the continued development of popular music than the
advent of online sharing of unlicensed music files.

    That said, despite these and other drawbacks inherent in their ret- 41
rogressive mode of consumption, involvement in the culture of vinyl—
from hunting down an obscure LP to cleaning it, playing it, listening to
it (and negotiating its pops and crackles), archiving it, and, perhaps
most importantly, talking about it with other similarly minded individuals—has enabled these young people to operate with a reinvigorated
sense of agency in an arena of cultural production and consumption
largely over-determined by corporate interests. Sadly, many of their
peers have yet to develop this degree of autonomy, quickly embracing
each new singing sensation simply because MTV has his or her video
in heavy rotation. Furthermore, this wider group's exposure to (and
subsequent understanding of) the sounds and practices of past generations are often limited to largely re-inscribed representations in *The
Wedding Singer* (1998), *Detroit Rock City* (1999), *Starsky and Hutch* (2004),

307

the *Austin Powers* trilogy, and other cinematic parodies in which erst-while cultural experiences are presented as stylistic faux pas for the amusement—rather than education—of youth audiences. In the face of these totalizing images, many youth vinyl enthusiasts are at least exploring the past on their own terms, setting their own agendas, and tracking down their own leads—from local store owners, peers, and (gasp) parents—rather than depending upon MTV, BET, VH1, or any other media outlet to structure their consumption of popular culture. Considering the chaotic state of contemporary music—music fans characterized as thieves by the RIAA, the meteoric rise and fall of celebrities via *American Idol* and *Making the Band*, the emergence of copyright-protected CDs—their backward glance is understandable, if not laudable.

NOTES

[1]One of the few examples of CD programming that comes to mind is that of George Michael's music video for "Freedom," in which a number of super-models program the musician's CD and listen to it while engaging in a number of sexually charged activities. While the music appears to produce an affective response for Cindy Crawford, Naomi Campbell, and others appearing in the video, the process of cueing the CD is presented as a detached, unemotional experience. An interesting contrast is provided by Oasis's video for "Wonderwall," which opens with a 45-rpm dropping from a turntable spindle to its revolving mat; although no human presence is discernible in this scene, the act is undeniably framed in romanticism and nostalgia.

[2]Most major cities are able to support at least one vinyl-centric music store. In Canada, Edmonton's Blackbyrd Myoozik, Montreal's Primitive Records, Toronto's Rotate This, and Vancouver's Zulu Records come to mind.

[3]From personal experience, I argue that the price a record collector feels is appropriate rises proportionately to the time that he or she has spent searching. What seemed outlandish five years ago might presently be regarded as acceptable if a particular record has proven impossible to locate. On that note, anyone reading this paper with a copy of Johnny Thunders' So Alone for sale should contact me post-haste.

WORKS CITED

1000 Record Covers. Ed. Michael Ochs. London: Taschen, 2002.

Classic Rock Covers. Ed. Michael Ochs. London: Taschen, 2001.

Dannen, Frederic. *Hit Men: Power Brokers and Fast Money inside the Music Business.* New York: Times Books, 1990.

Frith, Simon. *Performing Rites: On the Value of Popular Music.* Cambridge, MA: Harvard UP, 1998.

Goodman, Fred. *The Mansion on the Hill: Dylan, Young, Geffen, Springsteen, and the Head-on Collision of Rock and Commerce.* Toronto: Random House, 1997.

Haring, Bruce. *Off the Charts: Ruthless Days and Reckless Nights inside the Music Industry.* New York: Birch Lane Press, 1996.

High Fidelity. Dir. Stephen Frears. Perf. John Cusack, Jack Black, and Tom Louiso. Buena Vista, 2000.

Jackson, Cynthia (Nielsen SoundScan representative). "Re. Billboard's Album Format." E-mail to the author. 26 Mar. 2004.

Jameson, Fredric. "Postmodernism and Consumer Society." *The Cultural Turn: Selected Writings on the Postmodern, 1983–1998.* London: Verso, 1998.

Market Watch. *Billboard.* 29 Dec. 2001: 12.

——. *Billboard.* 10 Jan. 2004: 57.

Straw, Will. "Sizing up Record Collections: Gender and Connoisseurship in Rock Music Culture." *Sexing the Groove: Popular Music and Gender.* Ed. Sheila Whiteley. London: Routledge, 1997. 3–16.

——. "Embedded Memories." *Re/Evolution 3 Conference.* Concordia University, Montreal. 20 Mar. 2004.

White, Adam. Talent Almanac 1984. New York: *Billboard*, 1984.

Examining the Text

1. What four distinct characteristics, as defined by the author, have contributed to the development of young people's affective (i.e., emotional) relation with vinyl in the contemporary recorded music market? As a result of young vinyl consumers' "retrogressive tastes and practices," what effect might today's youth consumers have on the music industry, in Hayes' opinion?

2. The author provides a brief history of vinyl records in several of this article's body paragraphs, concluding that "vinyl in fact never went away." What is the somewhat circuitous history of vinyl in the late twentieth and early twenty-first century, according to Hayes?

3. In the course of his research study, the author distills and then lists several concrete reasons for which young "audiophiles" buy records on vinyl. Cite each of these specific reasons, and discuss them briefly.

4. *Thinking rhetorically:* The author of this article takes a social scientist's approach to his subject, conducting a research study to test his working hypotheses concerning youth consumption of vinyl recordings. Describe his research methods, and outline the conclusions at which he arrived in the course of his study. Does his research method seem sound, or can you perceive areas in which it needs to be refined and/or altered? Do his conclusions seem reasonable, based on the information presented?

For Group Discussion

In the concluding section of this essay, the author posits certain additional emotional rewards derived from the consumption of vinyl records, including a social dimension—i.e., sharing one's interests with friends having similar interests—and the pleasure derived from the various activities involved in the process of collection. In the whole-class setting, discuss whether or not you share these particular joys with the vinyl collectors described in this essay. Additionally, feel free to come up with an additional set of emotional pleasures derived from various aspects of popular music consumption.

Writing Suggestion

The author of this article refers to Jameson's study of contemporary "nostalgia film." He points to certain concrete examples, such as the original *Star Wars* (1977), which reminds older viewers of thirties and forties movie serials. He also refers to the Austin Powers movies, which demand "at least passing knowledge of previously marginal genres such as blaxploitation, late-60's British spy films ... and other forms that have recently experienced renewed interest largely because of DVD re-releases." Concludes Hayes, "Our nostalgic longing for older cultural texts has been fully leveraged by an entertainment industry that both recirculates its back catalog and produces new films, such as Quentin Tarantino's *Kill Bill* ... that invite if not demand recollection of their reference points." Similarly, he argues that music fans have "dusted off their parents' turntables" and turned to vinyl because, as youth consumers, they have been "encouraged to adopt the latest trends in pop culture—from music to fashion to technology to diet—but are ultimately unable to integrate these experiences meaningfully into their lives before they are asked to embrace newer, supposedly superior products." In an expository essay of five pages, explore the ways in which this phenomenon affects you: in what ways are you "seduced" by pop-cultural appeals to nostalgia—whether in music, film, or in other media—and/or in what ways do you resist the nostalgic "leveraging" described by Hayes in this article?

Sex and Drugs and Rock 'n' Roll: Urban Legends and Popular Music

IAN INGLIS

Urban legends are tales circulated widely in modern societies. While, in previous historical periods, such narratives were usually transmitted orally, nowadays many are discovered and disseminated by the mass media and are told as "true stories" that contain astounding, sensational, or bizarre details. Many urban legends achieve an enviable longevity: there are very few people in the Western world who have not heard of the vanishing hitch-hiker, the alligators lurking in the sewers, the funeral ashes mistakenly used as spices, or the babysitter terrorized by the madman upstairs. Popular music has proved to be an especially fertile ground for the propagation of such stories. Whether by word of mouth, through fanzines, or across the Internet, the often dramatic urban legends of popular music have been, and continue to be, generated to ever wider audiences. By examining some of the more familiar urban legends of popular music, the author of this essay aims to illustrate the roles that their persistent repetition perform, and to assess the social and cultural functions they fulfill.

As you read, note the deliberate formal structure and organization of this piece, characteristic of media studies scholarship. In his introductory section Inglis introduces the topic of urban legend generally, and then he "downshifts" to a focused and assertive thesis statement regarding urban legends in the popular music sphere. [Note about thesis statements: while you may sometimes want to avoid Inglis' blunt "I propose to"—or "I shall"—type of thesis declaration in your own academic essays, favoring instead an explicit assertion of your essay's main points, this is a perfectly legitimate and time-honored form of academic writing and has the advantage of letting the reader know exactly where the essay is heading.] Furthermore, the author breaks his supporting paragraphs into lists of qualities and characteristics, which lends specificity and credibility to his developing arguments and aids readers by providing discrete "packets" of information to digest as the arguments unfold.

311

Within contemporary communities where opportunities to engage in social interaction and technologies to assist such interaction have multiplied rapidly in recent years, rumor and gossip remain routine components of daily conversation. The development of the Internet has ensured that these exchanges are no longer limited to the interpersonal; stories are now transferred between sites rather than between acquaintances. In addition, the media's active promotion of the cult of celebrity allows for the public recognition of many more individuals about whom stories may be told and information exchanged.   1

The proliferation of sensational or dramatic or bizarre tales about those defined as "celebrities" falls into the general category of "urban legends." While it is true that the majority of traditional legends, or myths, have tended to be general in nature, difficult to source, and impossible to verify, there nonetheless exists a substantial collection of tales which are specific, detailed, and, at least in theory, open to verification. In order to illustrate these processes, I propose to explore one   2 particular arena in which such tales have flourished—the world of popular music. I shall examine the nature of the legends themselves, the motivations of those who relate them, and the social functions that their circulation serves.

THE URBAN LEGENDS OF POPULAR MUSIC

Urban legends have been defined as stories that "belong to the subclass   3 of folk narratives, legends believed, or at least believable" (Brunvald 3). Furthermore, these narratives are told and retold over years; they achieve an enviable longevity, despite the denials of the actors themselves or the accumulation of counter-evidence. Indeed, denials are often incorporated into the supporting evidence for many of these tales, via the argument that they are merely attempts to conceal an embarrassing truth; ironically, every additional denial only serves to extend the life of the story. Consider the following examples:

- *Led Zeppelin, the Shark and the Groupie.* While staying at the Edgewater Inn in Seattle in 1969 on their North American tour, Led Zeppelin and their road crew are visited in their hotel room by a red-haired, seventeen-year-old groupie named Jackie. She is tied to a bed and members of the group rape her with a live mud shark they caught while fishing from the balcony.
- *Paul Is Dead.* In the winter of 1966, at the pinnacle of the Beatles' success, Paul McCartney is killed in a car crash and replaced by an actor named William Campbell. The Beatles are able to continue their career (with the imposter) for several years, but provide numerous clues about the circumstances of Paul's death—on their album covers, in the lyrics of their songs, in films and photographs of the group.
- *The Rolling Stones, Marianne Faithfull and a Mars Bar.* In May 1967, the police raid Keith Richards's home in Sussex and arrest Richards, Mick Jagger, and art gallery owner Robert Fraser on drug charges. During the raid, the police discover a naked Marianne Faithfull lying across the sofa, while Jagger eats a Mars Bar that is protruding from her vagina.
- *Elvis Presley and the Rubber Hose.* In the early years of his career in the mid-1950s, Elvis Presley inserts a length of rubber hose down the front of his trousers before each stage performance in order to exaggerate the overtly sexual nature of his performance.
- *Bob Dylan's Unannounced Visit.* On a trip to London in the late 1980s, Bob Dylan contacts Dave Stewart of the Eurythmics, who

invites him to use his studio. However, Dylan goes to the wrong address, the house of a plumber whose name is also Dave. When the plumber returns from work, his wife greets him with the words, "Bob Dylan's here to see you . . . he's in the kitchen, having a cup of tea."

- *The Ohio Players and the Murder in the Studio.* When the Ohio Players are recording their 1976 hit single "Love Rollercoaster," someone is murdered in the studio during the recording sessions. The death scream is inadvertently captured on tape, and can be clearly heard during the track's percussion break.
- *The Dark Side of the Moon and The Wizard of Oz.* Pink Floyd's 1973 album *The Dark Side of the Moon* is composed, constructed, and recorded as a deliberate and calculated soundtrack to MGM's 1939 musical *The Wizard of Oz.* If played together, the music on the album and the action on the screen are perfectly synchronized.
- *The Beatles' Lost Album.* Shortly before the release of *Abbey Road* in September 1969, the master tapes of another planned album by the Beatles (*Hot as Sun*) are stolen from the home of producer George Martin and from the offices of EMI and Apple, and are held to ransom. The ransom is paid, but two of the tapes are destroyed and the third is accidentally erased while passing through the X-ray security equipment at Heathrow airport.
- *Elvis Presley's Faked Death.* Elvis Presley's apparent death at his Graceland home in August 1976 is a cleverly contrived deception. Disillusioned with the stresses and strains that accompany his position as the world's most famous entertainer, and unhappy with the circumstances of his personal life, Elvis fakes his own death and escapes into anonymity.
- *Stevie Nicks's Cocaine Habit.* By the mid-1980s, after years of cocaine addiction, Fleetwood Mac's Stevie Nicks has caused such severe damage to her septum that she is unable to inhale the drug nasally. The only way she can now satisfy her habit is via an enema and she engages a full-time employee to perform this duty for her.
- *Ozzy Osbourne and the Live Bat.* During Ozzy Osbourne's 1981 'Night Of The Living Dead' tour, a member of the audience in Des Moines, Iowa, throws a live bat on to the stage. Stunned, it lies motionless, and Osbourne, believing it to be a rubber toy, bites off its head. He's rushed to hospital and treated for rabies.
- *Motley Crue and the Replacement Nikki Sixx.* During the mid-1980s, Motley Crue's bassist, Nikki Sixx, is forced to quit the group for an extensive program of drug rehabilitation. The unknown Matthew Trippe is hired to secretly replace him and does so for

313

several years, even writing some of the group's most successful songs during this period. When Sixx returns, Trippe is sacked, with no reward, recognition, or acknowledgement.

• *Keith Richards and His Father's Ashes.*When Keith Richards's father, Bert, dies in 2002, his body is cremated. Later, Richards adds cocaine to the ashes, inhales the mixture, and announces "I snorted my father."

In form and content, these tales are distinguished by three recur- 4
ring characteristics that relate to their structural, ideological, and occupational dimensions.

First, unlike many of the more traditional urban legends, which 5
are largely unattributed, these are precise and detailed accounts. "The vanishing hitch-hiker," "the alligators roaming through the sewers," "the spider in the beehive hairstyle," "the funeral ashes mistakenly used as seasoning," and "the babysitter terrorized by the madman on the upper floor" are among the most recognizable and repeated urban legends, but lack any specific information about time, place, and person. In contrast, the myths of popular music come laden with details— dates, settings, addresses, names, ages, descriptions. And the details remain constant with each telling: the confectionery enjoyed by Jagger and Faithfull is always a Mars, never a Hershey or Kit-Kat bar; Paul McCartney's replacement is identified by name; Bob Dylan's visit is to a plumber, never to any other kind of tradesman; Led Zeppelin's groupie (always Jackie) visits them at the Edgewater Inn in Seattle, and never at any other location; it is only Stevie Nicks and never any other performer who suffers the indignities of a cocaine enema. In this sense, these stories have, over several decades, become more or less convincing replicas of historical truth, or "factoids."

Second, many of the tales exhibit a continuing fascination with 6
the perceived excesses of the rock and roll lifestyle. Musicians have long prided themselves on their bohemian tradition, their identification and exclusion of "squares," and their refusal to adopt conventional modes of behavior (Becker). In such circumstances, a stereotyped ideology of "sex and drugs and rock'n'roll" lends itself to stories of the fantastic, the outrageous, the unruly, and the shocking. The challenges issued to socially approved norms are illustrated by the declarations contained in many of its anthems: "Hope I die before I get old" (The Who), "Feel like letting my freak flag fly" (Crosby, Stills, Nash & Young), "Don't know what I want but I know how to get it, I wanna destroy" (The Sex Pistols), and "Rock'n'roll is here to stay, better to burn out than to fade away" (Neil Young) are just a few of the many examples in which a hedonistic and confrontational stance has been knowingly articulated by musicians themselves.

Third, the accounts are plausible. They may be unlikely, improbable, even incredible ... but their events are at least possible and the stories cannot therefore be dismissed out of hand. Within a fifty-year history "almost as unruly as the music itself, which is saying a lot" (R. Palmer 11), there have been more than enough recorded examples of financial ruin, sexual excess, violence, imprisonment, drug addiction, alcoholism, premature death, suicide, and mental illness to justify the frequent connections noted between the creative personality and emotional instability or psychological disturbance (Wills and Cooper 16–18). Given this history, the kind of stories discussed above tend to be greeted with less skepticism when told about popular musicians (individually and collectively) than would be the case if they were told about members of other professional groups. Put simply, they would not be believed elsewhere. Thus, the continuing generation and circulation of these tales both contributes to and benefits from a general perception that "undoubtedly rock'n'roll attracts some seriously unbalanced and deranged people, damaged and unstable" (Shapiro 213).   7

THE STORYTELLERS

315

It has been argued that: 8

> whatever the origins of urban legends, their dissemination is no mystery ... groups of age-mates, especially adolescents, are an important channel ... other paths of transmission are among office workers and club members, and among religious, recreational and regional groups. (Brunvald 4-3)

Informal, face-to-face exchanges of news and information, in casual conversations between peers, at home, in work or school, have been the major routes along which stories have been told and retold, and have also provided the basis for the "word of mouth" evaluations seen as so crucial to commercial success within all areas of the entertainment industry (Kent 40–77).   9

In a more stabilized form, but operating in much the same way, fanzines have become additional vehicles of transmission. Localized, defiantly independent, often highly idiosyncratic, they emerged, as part of a democratization of cultural resources through the 1970s and 1980s, as ideal mediums for the publication of novel, alternative, or "unofficial" readings. Occupying a cultural terrain that lies "somewhere between a personal letter and a magazine" (Duncombe 10), they provide opportunities for narratives to be introduced to, and tested by, a potentially sympathetic audience.   10

However, both of these have been overtaken (but not yet ren-   11
dered obsolete) since the 1990s through the Internet's capacity to allow
its users to go beyond mere interpersonal and subcultural exchanges to
instigate global, instantaneous transfers of ideas and information. The
character of communication and contact in "the network society"
(Castells) has, as a result, been fundamentally reconstituted, with
important consequences for the transmission of contemporary myths.

> In the past, rumoring has been discussed as a type of communication
> that was only possible with people who were already involved in the
> same social network or by way of direct physical contact. The Internet
> has changed the ways rumoring can happen, and has made possible
> rumoring between people who have never met or communicated before.
> (Fisher 159)

Nonetheless, whatever combination of storytelling styles is   12
employed—verbal, in print, online—the motivations of those who
engage in such discussions lie at the heart of any attempts to understand the stories' continued circulation. With this in mind, I wish to
propose a fourfold typology of storytellers.

316

1. *The Believer.* This is the person who genuinely believes—or, at   13
the very least, hopes—that the legend is true. Denials, often from the
protagonists themselves, are dismissed as evidence of a conspiracy theory to prevent the truth from being allowed to surface; the believer's
goal is to reveal that truth. There is a familiar literature—both fictional
(Lurie) and academic (Festinger, Riecken, and Schachter)—which
explores the consequences for believers who refuse to modify their
beliefs, even in the face of apparently incontrovertible evidence. In
exactly the same way that attempts to question accounts of alien
abduction and imminent UFO invasion, or the many reported sightings of Bigfoot and the Loch Ness Monster, only add to the vigor with
which those claims are defended, so too within popular music, suggestions that believers may be mistaken or misguided typically result in a
consolidation of the beliefs in question. The enduring belief that Elvis
Presley did not die, as demonstrated in the frequent and persistent
alleged sightings of the singer over thirty years, presents the most succinct example of this kind of response (Marcus; Denisoff and Plasketes;
Rodman). And, on the other hand, the enduring belief that Paul
McCartney did die continues to be upheld to this day by those believers who, for forty years, claim to have discovered clues, mistakes, and
incongruities to support their conclusion (Reeve; Patterson).

2. *The Cynic.* Conversely, the cynic knows or believes the story to be   14
false. In telling the story, he/she intends to illustrate the absurdity of the
myth, ridicule its logical inconsistencies, and emphasize the gullibility of

those who subscribe to it. Such attacks stem from a perception of believers as irrational and obsessive. They are seen as trying to:

> compensate for a perceived personal lack of autonomy, absence of community, incomplete identity, lack of power and lack of recognition . . . someone who is making up for some inherent lack. He or she seeks identity, connection and meaning via celebrities . . . [and] has fragile self-esteem, weak or non-existent social alliances, a dull and monotonous "real" existence. (Jenson 17-18)

Thus, the cynic's retelling of a myth frankly and deliberately 15 undermines a believer's retelling of the same myth. This cynicism illustrates a persistent, and largely negative, approach in the historical analysis of audiences' consumption of popular music that has expressed itself through the adoption of varying degrees of elitist commentary. Adorno's suggestion that pre-war listeners to popular music were "not merely turned away from more important music, but confirmed in their neurotic stupidity" (41) and Hoggart's description of the post-war audience for rock and roll in the United Kingdom as "a depressing group . . . most of them are rather less intelligent than average . . . they have no aim, no protection, no belief'" (248-49) may merely be two of the more familiar observations that are routinely reinforced by the storytelling motivations of the cynics.

3. *The Entertainer.* For the entertainer, the story is nothing more 16 than a diverting or unusual tale to be told to others; it is related in the same way that a joke is told. From the jongleurs and jesters of medieval Europe to the screen comedians of the contemporary age, a special status has been enjoyed by those persons with an ability to entertain and amuse others. This is as true in routine social interactions as it is in formalized encounters between performers and audiences: "laughter and smiling are actively used as resources in the course of social interaction . . . [they] are built into social life by participants in an intricate manner and are exchanged as part of a collaborative process" (Mulkay 107). Popular music, because of its familiarity and accessibility, thus provides an unusually broad, and continually expanding, range of topics around which such exchanges can happen and from which the entertainer can make his/her selection. In addition, the characteristic narrative form and the allegedly factual content of urban legends—as opposed to other comedic modes, including the one-liner, the "shaggy dog" story, the pun—is particularly attractive to the entertainer, since it reflects a basic property of comedy.

> Much comedy, no matter how funny, commonly uses a narrative form which is not essentially dissimilar from realist narrative in general . . . [it] has an outline, a narrative skeleton, which follows the norms of realism

317

in the minimal sense that the characters progress from point a to point b for a reason . . . [and] the spatial relationships between the two points are portrayed in a way roughly consistent with the laws of the known universe. (J. Palmer 113)

4. *The Expert.* For the expert, each retelling of a story increases the stock of "cultural capital" he/she possesses. In particular, the apparent access to knowledge or information or tastes not shared by others lends the expert a mark of distinction and, as Bourdieu has noted, "nothing more infallibly classifies than tastes in music" (18). The definition, offered by Jones, which sees urban legends as "tales circulated widely in modern society . . . generally transmitted orally . . . [and] told as 'true stories', often attributed to a friend of a friend" (439) is appropriate here, since it lends support to the way in which distinction is further increased if the expert can claim (as is often the case) a more personal association with the source, or the subject, of the story. Such moments of association are rare.

> The relationship between celebrities and fans is typically mediated through representation. Despite the increasing profusion of celebrities in society . . . encounters are comparatively rare. Stage, screen, audio transmission and print culture are the main institutional mechanisms that express the various idioms of celebrity culture. Each presupposes distance between the celebrity and the audience. (Rojek 46)

Because of their rarity, narratives in which the expert may appear to play a central role—by dint of intimacy, presence, or "insider" status—may work to increase the prestige he/she gains with each repetition of the tale, since, in effect, they reduce the distance between the subjects of a story and the tellers of a story, between celebrities and their audiences. This is true of all celebrity types, but particularly of celebrities in popular music.

> More than any other form of celebrity, the popular music celebrity . . . demonstrates the rapidity of dissipation of the power and influence of a public personality. The reason for part of this dissipation is the way in which the popular music industry has helped to construct itself as a symbol of change and transformation . . . the succession of apparent new images and sounds constitutes the representation of change that is often used by the culture at large as a representation of the vitality of the entire culture. (Marshall 183)

Thus, the continued distribution of urban legends within and around popular music derives from a variety of storytelling sources, each of which brings its own motivations (which may vary in intensity) and takes away its own rewards (which may vary in size and scale).

17

18

19

The classifications of believer, cynic, entertainer, and expert are not mutually exclusive and, moreover, may be adopted and adapted for specific occasions: the same person may believe that Stevie Nicks's well-documented cocaine addiction did lead to its bizarre consequences, dismiss the claim that a real murder was captured on a U.S. chart-topping single by the Ohio Players, enthusiastically relate Bob Dylan's visit to the unsuspecting plumber as a whimsical joke, and use the detected synchronicities between *The Dark Side of the Moon* and *The Wizard of Oz* as evidence of his/her musical expertise. Furthermore, there is, of course, no guarantee that the audience to whom these myths are told will understand them in the way they are explained by the storyteller: what may be presented as a joke may be perceived as a fact; what is told as an example of expert knowledge may be simply disbelieved.

THE SOCIAL FUNCTIONS OF POPULAR MUSIC'S URBAN LEGENDS

In the preceding section, I offered an analysis of the specific factors 20 influencing those storytellers actively involved in the generation of popular music's urban myths. Alongside their personal motivations, it is equally important to consider the functions that the legends serve within the popular music community, and also within society as a whole.

First, in a very simple way, such stories provide conversational 21 topics to assist in the establishment and maintenance of social relationships via interaction and communication. Earlier in this discussion, I referred to the ways in which rumor and gossip are routine components of daily interaction. By bracketing them together, I may have implied that the two are identical. This is not strictly true.

> Gossip is like gossip anywhere else in the world. Men and women say things about other men and women; accuracy is beside the point. Rumour-mongering is different. Rumours arise out of social situations containing affective alternatives: the accuracy or truth of the matter is important because ... [it] will affect future thought and action. (Burridge 130-31)

In this sense, the urban legends discussed above tend to be, in the 22 main, examples of gossip. Although individual storytellers may vociferously defend or attack the reliability of the accounts they present, ultimately any attempts to "prove" or "disprove" the allegations are irrelevant, since their "truth" or "untruth" is relatively unimportant. So too are the value judgments listeners may choose to impose on the stories they hear: the "revelations" about Elvis Presley's use of a rubber hose may be interpreted as a playful prank or offensive or lewd behavior; Stevie Nicks's anal intake of cocaine may invite sympathy or outrage. Fundamentally, both episodes exist as bizarre and sensational tales, readily incorporated into patterns of gossip that allow audiences to exchange intimate and idiosyncratic details of a celebrity's life. They satisfy some of the recurring needs which guide our use of the media and media-related activities—surveillance, personal identity formation, and the establishment of social relationships. Further, their longevity and the absence of a consistent "preferred reading" in response to the events they depict support the general assertion that "the purpose of gossip about celebrities is not to elevate or idealize them as exemplary individuals. The choice of figures about whom gossip will be exchanged is as likely to include those regarded with resentment or derision as those regarded as heroic" (Turner 107).

Second, these tales can be seen as modern variants of the deeper, often religious, myths about legendary places, people, and texts— Camelot, El Dorado, Atlantis; Jesus Christ, Confucius, Muhammad, Gautama Siddhartha; the Dead Sea Scrolls, the Holy Grail, the Gnostic Gospels. Whichever we choose to follow or explore, all contain a common characteristic: "It will be always the one, shape-shifting, yet marvellously constant story that we find, together with a challengingly persistent suggestion of more remaining to be experienced than will ever be known or told" (Campbell 3, emphasis added). If this inclination to seek guidance and enlightenment, to experience more, often from the discovery of hidden truths or lost documents, has been historically present in many spiritual communities, it is no less present across the terrain of contemporary popular culture. The remarkable success of Peter Jackson's 2001–2003 film trilogy of Tolkien's *The Lord of the Rings* and the global impact of *The Da Vinci Code* (Brown) indicate the presence of a significant audience for whom the intersections between myth and reality, legend and logic, the known and the unknown, are central cultural foundations.

Popular musicians have been quickly accommodated into these, and similar, discourses. The pilgrimage (there is no other word) made by hundreds of thousands of fans each year to Graceland reproduces many of the expectations and obligations that a Catholic will take to Lourdes, a Hindu to the Ganges, a Druid to Stonehenge, or a Muslim to Mecca. The transposition of the Beatles from pop stars to spiritual messiahs and the sanctification of Bob Dylan by those of his fans who regard him not merely as a singer-songwriter, but as a philosopher-king are, perhaps, the two most pressing examples of this tendency. And, clearly, some of the urban myths relate to these changes of status

23

24

very directly. The account of the Beatles' "missing" album, Hot as Sun, is less a tale of a few mislaid songs than it is of a legendary text whose truths and insights can never be recaptured. Dylan's arrival at the door of an unsuspecting plumber becomes a pseudo-Biblical parable in which we learn that any of us—however undeserving or unlikely—might one day meet our savior.

It may not be accidental that the rise of mass-mediated forms of entertainment (including popular music) has coincided with the decline of secular religion. Rojek's recognition of "inescapable parallels with religious worship, reinforced by the attribution by fans of magical or extraordinary powers" (53) is borne out by the repetition of urban legends in which popular music's people, texts, and places perform functions that are elevated far beyond the confines of mundane reality.

Third, there is a considerable number of urban legends whose primary social function is to allow for members of the public to engage in vicarious identification with the named protagonists and elements of their lifestyle. This should not be taken to mean that storytellers would wish to emulate the precise activities detailed in the stories, many of which are, after all, unpleasant, uncomfortable, and dangerous. Instead, the stories reflect an envy for the social and professional environment they describe—particularly for the freedom from constraints (material and behavioral) that wealth and fame allow popular musicians to enjoy. Performers thus become representatives of the communities constructed by their followers: "the musician becomes a blank slate on which the fans project their own desires, hopes, frustrations and unfulfilled pleasures" (Shapiro 216).

In this sense, it is not surprising that the largest single category of urban legends in popular music is about examples of sexual behavior; their popularity may be seen as evidence for the theory of catharsis, which argues that exposure to media depictions of sex or violence will act as a form of displacement therapy by providing a relatively harmless, fantasy outlet for potentially aggressive impulses that would otherwise remain unsatisfied (Feshbach).

So, while it is unlikely that many would wish to mimic Led Zeppelin's participation in a sexual assault that uses a mud shark, or would want to copy Marianne Faithfull and Mick Jagger in their consumption of a Mars bar, it may be more likely that these tales evoke a sense of envy for an unconventional and permissive lifestyle that is beyond scarcity and in which such behaviors are tolerated, even celebrated. And, within the world of urban legends, such behavior is not isolated; there are so many tales told of popular music and sexual excess that it has become one of the central components in the contemporary stereotype of the "rock star." In addition, and crucially, popular music's tacit encouragement of such behavior is not meaningless.

25

26

321

27

28

> By communicating certain meanings, or structures of meanings, it offers its audiences ways of seeing the world, of interpreting experiences; it offers them values that have a profound impact on the ways they respond to particular situations and challenges. (Grossberg 154)

In short, these stories allow for the construction of a homologous relationship between the real world of the storyteller (and listeners) and the perceived world that urban legends describe.   29

Fourth, some tales are employed individually to perform important political functions. Specifically, an urban legend may emerge to cope with an immediate and ideologically damaging situation. The clearest example of this is the recurring assertion that Elvis Presley faked his death, and is alive and well. Presley's life illustrated both the optimism of "the American dream" and the tragedy of "the American nightmare." Born in impoverished circumstances in Tupelo, Mississippi, the Memphis truck driver became the world's most celebrated entertainer and one of the iconic figures of the twentieth century. His career—on record, in movies, in cabaret—provided a ringing endorsement of the belief that, in the land of opportunity, nothing was impossible for those with talent, hard work, and a degree of good luck. When he died in 1977, drug-damaged, bloated, and obese, face down in a pool of vomit on the floor of his bathroom, his death seemed to be an equally emphatic demonstration of the poisonous and corrupting repercussions of his success as a popular musician.   30

To admit the circumstances of his death is therefore to undermine the legitimacy of a national ideology that promotes ambition, possession, and wealth—for what good are such attributes if they lead to a lonely and miserable end? But by choosing to deny his death and prolonging "the liberatory celebration of his life" (Gottdeiner 200), which is "confirmed" by the many reported sightings of him, that ideology is protected. In this case, although it clearly overlaps with the type of myth which functions as a religious/spiritual fable (in that Elvis, like Jesus, is "resurrected"), the urban legend is less about the extraordinary nature of Presley himself, and more about the maintenance of a political philosophy to which the singer himself, and many of his fans, fully subscribed.   31

Fifth, in their position as cultural texts, the materials of popular music (songs, performances, recordings) continually offer themselves for interpretation. "Meaning," however defined, is contingent, malleable, transitory, and reached only through subtle negotiation. The idea that any text, musical or otherwise, possesses a single, absolute "meaning" is difficult to sustain, since it rests on an assumption that it contains a deliberate message, which is decoded by the reader in the way it was encoded by the producer, and which is accepted   32 uncritically. Texts generate multiple meanings; "alternative readings" are equally valid. In the context of popular music, where, as indicated above, "word of mouth" reports, comparisons, and evaluations play a major role in the politics of consumption, this has helped to create a discourse in which not only alternative meanings, but alternative narratives, explanations, and histories are readily found. And the locations in which we come across many of these alternative accounts are in its urban legends.

Wolff has argued that "the reader, viewer or audience is actively   33 involved in the construction of the work of art . . . without the act of reception/consumption, the cultural product is incomplete" (95). Thus, the discovery that the scream during the percussion break in the Ohio Players' "Love Rollercoaster" is the sound of a murder completes the listeners' understanding of the track. The revelation that the Beatles' album covers from *Rubber Soul* to *Let It Be* contain visual and verbal clues that confirm Paul McCartney's death adds to our knowledge of the group's musical output in those years. And the disclosure that in *The Dark Side of the Moon* Pink Floyd fashioned a precise musical soundtrack to accompany The *Wizard of Oz* increases our estimation of the group's musical virtuosity.

323

> The reader is always right, and no one can take away the freedom to make whatever use of a text which suits him . . . the right to leaf back and forward, to skip whole passages, to read sentences against the grain, to misunderstand them, to reshape them, to embroider them with every possible association, to draw conclusions from the text of which the text knows nothing. (Enzensberger 11)

Popular music's capacity to sustain this type of urban legend pro-   34 vides the setting and the opportunity for an escape from the tyranny of imposed meaning, in which misunderstanding, reshaping, embroidery— "textual poaching" (Jenkins)—can take place.

CONCLUSION

In the detailed telling of the stories themselves, in the motivations of   35 the storytellers, and in the social functions they serve, the urban legends of popular music differ from other kinds of urban folklore. Those tales are essentially tales of warning: they are direct descendants of the traditional fairy tale, whose main function is to allow members of a community (particularly the young) to access the wisdom and experience of past generations in order to learn of the risks that exist in the wider world. The dangers faced by Little Red Riding Hood, Snow White, and Hansel and Gretel are exactly the same dangers awaiting today's unsuspecting youngsters; thus, the encounter with a vanishing hitch-hiker teaches us to be wary of strangers; the fate of the young babysitter reminds us to be vigilant at all times; the eating of the funeral ashes tells us to avoid impulsive actions.

By contrast, popular music's urban legends contain little in the 36 way of warning or guidance; they stand by themselves as independent narratives, told to amuse, to shock, to impress, rather than to educate. Indeed, they bear a remarkable similarity to the traditional tales, or "oral histories," related by storytellers in the communities of North Africa. Alongside the snake-charmers, acrobats, dancers, and other entertainers in Jemaa El Fna, the main square in Marrakech, the practice continues today:

> They're the most skilled of the entertainers ... their themes are love, death, conquest: the more melodramatic the better. Once a story's been declaimed, it's taken up by another teller and passed on to an ever-growing audience: a verbal chain letter, registering new shifts of emphasis each time it's retold. (Gladstone-Thompson 197)

In addition, they reflect the nature of popular music itself and its 37 social and professional practices, in which chaos and hedonism are routinely presented as equal partners:

> By any definition, being a professional musician can be a crazy way to make a living ... between bursts of hyperactivity can be periods of cataclysmic boredom. It takes a special effort to avoid this potentially hazardous rollercoaster. (Shapiro 213)
> No matter how one uses the music—the ultimate escape, soothe the pain, liberate the spirit, contemplate life, have fun, make passionate love—it remains an integral part of our lifescripts. (Friedlander 295)

Within an environment that (apparently) values risk, excess, sensu- 38 ality, and flamboyance and rejects a philosophy of deferred gratification in favor of the pursuit of immediate rewards, accounts of behaviors that display restraint and caution are therefore deemed inappropriate. In short, the urban legends of popular music effectively manipulate the (stereo)typical characteristics of performers and their associated lifestyle into convenient and familiar narrative forms that are generated and circulated by its followers and fans.

Whether they are accurate or inaccurate is irrelevant; whether 39 they are believed or disbelieved is unimportant. However disruptive, however contrived, however fanciful they may appear, their real signif-icance lies therefore not in their particular details, but in their general role as sources of images, ideas, and information which run counter to, undermine, and challenge "official" discourses. In creating their own narratives, interpretations, and explanations, those previously con-fined to roles as consumers of cultural texts are, individually and in collaboration with others, demonstrating their ability to also act as pro-ducers and distributors of cultural texts.

WORKS CITED

Adorno, Theodor W. *The Culture Industry*. London: Routledge, 1991.

Becker, Howard. *Outsiders*. New York: The Free Press, 1963.

Bourdieu, Pierre. *Distinction*. New York: Routledge, 1985.

Brown, Dan. *The Da Vinci Code*. New York: Bantam, 2003.

Brunvald, Jan Harold. *The Vanishing Hitchhiker: American Urban Legends and their Meanings*. New York: Norton, 1981.

Burridge, Kenelm. "Cargo." *Mythology*. Ed. Pierre Maranda. Harmondsworth: Penguin, 1972. 127–35.

Campbell, Joseph. *The Hero with a Thousand Faces*. Princeton, NJ: Princeton UP, 1949.

Castells, Manuel. *The Rise of the Network Society*. Oxford: Blackwell, 1996.

Denisoff, R. Serge and George Plasketes. *True Disbelievers: Elvis Contagion*. Somerset, NJ: Transaction, 1995.

Duncombe, Stephen. *Notes from Underground: Zines and the Politics of Alternative Culture*. London: Verso, 1997.

Enzensberger, Hans Magnus. *Mediocrity and Delusion: Collected Diversions*. London: Verso, 1992.

Feshbach, Seymour. "The Drive Reducing Function of Fantasy Behaviour." *Journal of Abnormal and Social Psychology* 50 (1955): 3-11.

Festinger, Leon, Henry W. Riecken, and Stanley Schachter. *When Prophecy Fails*. Minneapolis: U of Minnesota P, 1956.

Fisher, Dana R. "Rumoring Theory and the Internet: A Framework for Analyzing the Grass Roots." *Social Science Computer Review* 16. 2 (1998): 158–68.

Friedlander, Paul. *Rock and Roll: A Social History*. Boulder, CO: Westview, 1996.

Gladstone-Thompson, Anthony. "The City in the 1960s." *Marrakech: The Red City*. Ed. Barnaby Rogerson and Stephen Lavington. London: Sickle Moon Books, 2003.

Gottdeiner, Mark. "Dead Elvis as Other Jesus." *In Search of Elvis*. Ed. Vernon Chadwick. Boulder, CO: Westview, 1997. 189–200.

Grossberg, Lawrence. "Rock and Roll in Search of an Audience." *Popular Music and Communication.* Ed. James Lull. London: Sage, 1992. 152–75.

Hoggart, Richard. *The Uses of Literacy.* London: Chatto & Windus, 1957.

Jenkins, Henry. *Textual Poachers: Television Fans and Participatory Culture.* New York: Routledge, 1992.

Jenson, Joli. "Fandom as Pathology: The Consequences of Characterization." *The Adoring Audience: Fan Culture and Popular Media.* Ed. Lisa A. Lewis. London: Routledge, 1992. 9–29.

Jones, Alison. *Dictionary of World Folklore.* Edinburgh: Larousse, 1995.

Kent, Nicholas. *Naked Hollywood.* London: BBC Books, 1991.

Lurie, Mison. *Imaginary Friends.* London: Heinemann, 1967.

Marcus, Greil. *Dead Elvis: A Chronicle of Cultural Obsession.* New York: Doubleday, 1991.

Marshall, P. David. *Celebrity and Power: Fame in Contemporary Culture.* Minneapolis: U of Minnesota P, 1997.

Mulkay, Michael. *On Humour.* Cambridge: Polity, 1988.

Palmer, Jerry. *Taking Humour Seriously.* London: Routledge, 1994.

Palmer, Robert. *Rock & Roll: An Unruly History.* New York: Harmony, 1995.

Patterson, R. Gary. *The Walrus Was Paul.* Nashville, TN: Dowling Press, 1996.

Reeve, Andru J. *Turn Me On, Dead Man.* Ann Arbor. MI: Popular Culture Ink, 1994.

Rodman, Gilbert B. *Elvis after Elvis: The Posthumous Career of a Living Legend.* New York: Routledge, 1996.

Rojek, Chris. *Celebrity.* London: Reaktion Books, 2001.

Shapiro, Harry. *Waiting for the Man: The Story of Drugs and Popular Music.* London: Helter Skelter, 1999.

Tolkien J. R. R. *The Lord of the Rings.* London: Allen & Unwin, 1955.

Turner, Graeme. *Understanding Celebrity.* London: Sage, 2004.

Wills, Geoff and Cary L. Cooper. *Pressure Sensitive: Popular Musicians under Stress.* London: Sage, 1988.

Wolff, Janet. *The Social Production of Art.* London: Macmillan, 1981.

326

Examining the Text

1. How does the author define the term *urban legend* for the purposes of this article? What are some social factors contributing to the rise in urban legend lore in contemporary society, according to the author?

2. What are the three key "recurring characteristics" that, in their form and content, relate to the structural, ideological, and occupational dimensions of popular music-centered urban legends? What qualities do these pop-musical tales share with more "traditional" urban legends, and what traits distinguish rock and hip-hop urban legends with nonmusical ones?

3. In this article, the author proposes a "fourfold typology of storytellers"— that is, a breakdown of the characteristics of different groups responsible for creating and disseminating music-based urban legends. What are the personality qualities and motivations of each group of storytellers, and how does each go about contributing to the ever-growing body of urban legend?

4. Along with his analysis of pop-musical storytellers' personal dynamics, the author states that it is "important to consider the functions that the legends serve within the popular music community, and also within society as a whole." The author then lists and explains five functions that rock-centered legends might serve, either socially or psychologically, or both. Explain these functions and consider their validity based on your own experience and observation.

5. *Thinking rhetorically:* This article falls squarely within the genre of academic discourse called media studies. What is the author's intention of picking this topic in the first place, and what does he intend to prove by analyzing the subject in such exhaustive detail? By what methods does he achieve this result?

For Group Discussion

What are some of the "traditional" urban legends within the sphere of popular music, as presented by the author of this article? If you have heard any of these legends, feel free to amplify them in the small-group discussion setting, filling in any additional narrative material or "gory details" you may have heard. Next, add to this list any pop-musical urban legends *not* covered by Inglis in this piece, and relate that story with as much descriptive detail as you can. Finally, feel free to go beyond the sphere of popular music, relating any other urban legends that support—or perhaps even disprove—the author's assertions in this essay. After reassembling as a full class, have each group report its additional facts and stories and discuss the ways in which class members acquired this knowledge: did this material arrive in the ways predicted by Inglis in this piece, or are there additional ways of disseminating urban legends that the author may not have considered?

Writing Suggestion

Based on the lists generated in group discussion (see above) choose one of the dozens of pop-musical urban legends circulating on the Web and/or by word of mouth, and write a mini-research or "I-search" essay on it. The I-Search paper has a slightly different voice than the standard academic research paper, as modeled by the essay "Urban Legends and Popular Music." Where the writer of the standard research paper assumes a relatively detached and objective stance, as Ian Inglis did for this essay, the I-Search paper encourages you to assume a more visible role in the presentation. You might consider structuring your paper through several related sections: an introduction, in which you explain your reason for choosing the particular urban legend for analysis;

information you already know, or assumptions you have already made, about the legend in question; your search for additional information; and a summary of the new information you discovered. In the "search" section, you will pursue information about the urban legend mainly by searching the Web, but friends and acquaintances may serve as resources as well. As you write your essay, describe your search in the form of a narrative in which you highlight the key information you have found, and then conclude your essay by comparing your original knowledge and assumptions about the legend with the facts you finally revealed. If you were surprised and/or illuminated by any of your discoveries, you might describe that reaction in detail, in order to lend closure to your essay's conclusion.

In Perfect Harmony: Popular Music and Cola Advertising

BETHANY KLEIN

A recent article in USA Today *featured a list of "songs ruined by commercials": popular titles whose rights were purchased by companies advertising products from luxury cars to erectile dysfunction drugs in order to create in consumers' minds an instant identification with those products. In the* USA Today *story and in subsequent blogs, irate listeners report that their favorite songs—including Steve Miller Band's "Fly Like an Eagle," "Everlasting Love" by Natalie Cole, "Rock and Roll" by Led Zeppelin, "Lust for Life" by Iggy Pop, "Hush" by Deep Purple, "Our House" by Madness, and "Viva Las Vegas" (the latter for Viagra)—were permanently "destroyed" by their association with the products being hawked by the commercials, creating an unintentional 'backlash': resentment in the listening public toward the advertisers—and, by extension, the products being advertised. Resentment or not, there is no denying that popular music is now pervasive in the realm of marketing and that the pairing of already-popular songs with almost any kind of product helps lodge that brand in consumers' minds. This article by social scientist Bethany Klein examines how music provides a shortcut to branding. Through a systematic research process the author attempts to reveal the social and economic effects of corporations— especially corporate cola giants such as Coca-Cola and Pepsi—that insinuate themselves into popular music culture.*

As you read, note the ways in which advertisers attempt to make one brand of cola appear superior to the other. While most people would agree that there is virtually no qualitative difference between Coca-Cola and

Pepsi, marketers use a variety of techniques, many of them explored in this essay, to convince consumers otherwise. Further, the large cola companies use similar tactics to make their products appealing to the youth demographic. The author of this article, using interviews with advertising and music industry workers—along with an analysis of popular and trade press coverage of the relationships forged between popular musicians and the cola giants—demonstrates that Coke and Pepsi have positioned themselves as having a genuine connection to music culture, thus making the fizzy beverages appear "cool" to young listener–drinkers.

Popular music's relatively new relationship to advertising mirrors the   1
long-standing tension between fine art and advertising, "a century of uncertain courtship between artist and advertiser," in which artists are "eager to enter the agency, make a fast buck, and depart with independence intact" (Lears 133). Likewise, the negative reactions to the practice of song licensing in advertising parallel critiques about commercial art that arose in the early twentieth century, when "many observers perceived the forces of commerce to be adversely affecting the intents and practices of artists and to be encroaching inappropriately into realms of experience once deemed private" (Bogart 4). The modern use of music in commercials is a direct consequence of the early twentieth-century use of music in department stores: "Perhaps today's most prominent embodiment of their efforts, reflecting both the power and paradox of the alliance, is the use of music in television commercials" (Tyler 112–13). Though the presence of music in retail environments is a clear predecessor to the practice of licensing music for TV advertisements, the history of popular music is replete with relationships to commercial enterprise, all of which can be viewed as overtures to the current licensing mania. While commercial affiliations of popular musicians have become more widespread and conspicuous recently, the association has in fact existed since the dawn of rock and roll: in 1954, the King himself, Elvis Presley, loaned his voice to a radio jingle for Southern-Maid Donuts (Tayler).

Over the past decade, deregulation, digitization, and a general   2
increase in media commercialism have resulted in a radio industry that accommodates an ever-narrowing range of music and a music industry that, in the face of potential threats to record sales, is looking for alternative options to ensure financial viability. The turn to advertising is partly a reaction to dilemmas currently being confronted by the radio and music industries, yet the advertising industry comes with its own set of problems for recording artists and music culture.

Like early sponsors of cultural radio programs, who were "seen as patrons of the arts" (Bamouw 40), advertisers are praised for distributing music that might otherwise go unheard. However, the relationship is not equally beneficial, and the use of popular music in advertising threatens to empower commercial entities while devaluing cultural forms.

Through interviews with musicians, music supervisors, advertising creatives, and licensing managers, along with an analysis of popular and trade press coverage, this article explores the use of music in television commercials as a tool for branding. Coke's and Pepsi's relationships with popular music serve to highlight critical issues involving interactions between culture and commerce. 3

BANDS FOR BRANDS

Prior to the significant organizational, legal, and technological changes in both the radio and music industries that have produced an environment in which licensing to advertising is more common, music already represented an important weapon in the cola wars' arsenal. From Coke's classic 1971 commercial featuring hundreds of young people gathered on a hilltop to sing "I'd Like to Buy the World a Coke" to the more recent iTunes and Pepsi cross-promotion, music and cola, both products targeted primarily at a youth demographic, have endured a lengthy association. 4

Where relationships between popular musicians and advertisers have often been uneasy, reigniting high art debates about the consequences of commercial affiliation, Coke and Pepsi have positioned themselves as having a more genuine connection to music culture, as enthusiasts, champions, and partners. The two companies pursued this goal by creating advertising campaigns that were as much entertainment as sales pitch. In addition, the cola corporations have borrowed characteristics of rock music, such as authenticity and anti-authoritarianism, and applied them to their products, obscuring the archetype of preyed-upon artist and malevolent commercial interest often activated in the art versus commerce debate. The cola companies and popular music may appear to be in perfect harmony, but such relationships raise serious questions about the role of commerce in cultural production. By blurring the line between cultural and commercial interest, cola advertising contributes to an increasingly hyper-commercialistic media environment in the United States and abroad. 5

As the use of music and musicians in advertising has increased, a debate that was once reductive and obsessed with "selling out" has 6 become more nuanced and concerned with the details of a commercial campaign. The decision of artists to be involved with a commercial campaign can be viewed as a comment on the particularities of the campaign as well as on the artist. One element of the discussion surrounding popular music's use in advertising involves the type of product or service being advanced, where some products and companies provoke an extremely negative reaction for their use of music, while others are met with ambivalence or approval. Many of the musicians, music supervisors, licensing managers, and ad creatives I spoke with suggested that the use of licensed music was more suitable for some products and services than others. Certainly there are some products for which licensed music or musical spokespeople are logical components of conveying information. The specific selection of music or musician may still reflect marketing objectives, but, at a very basic level, it makes sense that a digital music-playing device like iPod would include licensed music in its television campaign. The natural fit between music and music-related products is one reason why a director of film and television for a collection of independent labels told me that she chose to pitch an especially picky band for an iPod campaign, despite the band's history of rejecting offers to license to advertising (Lanchart).

Further, even products more tangentially involved in our musical experiences have a sound reason to license music for use in advertising campaigns. For example, a product category that consistently licenses pre-existing music for its television commercials is automobiles, and for many consumers the car is where the majority of music listening occurs. But while automobiles may have a more natural connection to music than, say, vacuum cleaners, the reputation of the company and product also intervenes in the artist's decision-making process. That is, within the category of automobiles, various other distinctions are considered, some real and others a result of branding. Tricia Halloran, a music supervisor at HUM Music + Sound Design, explained that one of the bands she has worked with will license music to hybrid vehicles, but not to traditional gasoline-powered vehicles. In this example, there is a real difference, in terms of impact on the environment, between the products that this band will license to and those they would refuse. Some of the musicians I talked with described being more at ease licensing music to companies which they personally supported as consumers. Archie Moore of Velocity Girl rationalized that he was thinking about buying a VW bug when the group was approached to license "Sorry Again" to the company. Nick Krill of the Spinto Band, who licensed their song "Oh Mandy" to a Sears commercial, said, "I get my tools there just the same as everyone else," but then jokingly acknowledged the absurdity of an indie-rock group endorsing hardware:

"Although I would've probably got my tools at Tru-Value. Plug plug! I just got $100 to say that. "

In other cases, the difference between products that do or do not 8 fit with music licensing may be less easy to pin down. Brands that carry a cool cachet may appear to be less threatening in their use of popular music, and the "cool" of licensed music may seem a suitable match for the "cool" of the product. Continuing with the use of automobiles as example, it is notable that Volkswagen is regularly mentioned, in the press and in interviews I've conducted, as a company that, like Apple, has proven itself a good fit with music licensing. But whether Volkswagen as a company has values that are distinct in some real way from those of Pontiac or Cadillac is unclear; rather, Volkswagen's history of creative and innovative advertising has molded its positive reputation in the eyes of other creatives, in advertising and in music. Velocity Girl's Archie Moore admitted, "I feel kind of stupid for making the distinction, but we all agreed ... I think it was a company that we didn't have any problems with." The music selected for a campaign may then increase the product's or service's perceived hip character; that credible bands such as Stereolab and Luna had already licensed to Volkswagen also influenced Velocity Girl's decision. In such cases where the positive reputation of the company is not as clearly attached to the content of the product (Volkswagen was known as the Nazi car prior to its 1959 image overhaul courtesy of the Doyle Dane Bernbach agency's classic campaign), there was a time before cool, when the product was known only for its utility: a time before branding.

The colas fall squarely into this category, where the relationship 9 between product and music culture is one entirely based on construction. Let us not forget that Coke began its life as a patent medicine: hence, even the relationship between cola and "beverage" is a result of marketing, not kismet. The use of music culture to advertise a non-music-related product relies on the illusion of branding and the capability of advertising to construct a certain personality around a product. Yet, willing as subjects may be to accept the fruits of branding as natural and always already there, consumers are also capable of stepping back, recognizing the relationship for what it is. The process of branding may attempt to hide the capitalist logic that guides it, but commercial viewers are not simply or always passive dupes embracing any claim of personality that advertising throws their way, and advertisers have responded to consumer cynicism by raising the branding bar, encouraging our willingness to be duped, however temporarily, by marketing practices.

In describing advertising as a magic system, Williams identified a 10 cultural pattern in which the object itself is not enough to sell it; it must also be linked to some sort of personal meaning, the very essence of branding. Williams also described how advertising acknowledges and, indeed, applauds our skepticism, responding to critiques of advertising's false claims with a wink to the audience. Advertising strikes a careful balance between fooling the viewer and assuring the viewer that he or she is no fool. Branding strategies, which transform in reaction to viewer shrewdness, ensure that gut reactions persist despite a knowledge of intent; the result is an era of a cynical dominant ideology and cynical subjects, Sloterdijk's condition of "enlightened false consciousness, "here, as Zizek put it, "one knows the falsehood very well, one is well aware of a particular interest hidden behind an ideological universality, but still one does not renounce it" (29). There is a joy in allowing oneself to be taken for the branding ride that discourages renunciation and prevents a lucid and commonsensical response for even the quickest of viewers. Viewers may not necessarily or even often follow their viewing experience with a buying experience, but that does not stop them from experiencing the emotional manipulation aspired to by advertisers.

Indeed, ad creatives themselves, whose very job it is to construct 11 the personality around brands, and who, as a consequence, should have a greater awareness of the constructed nature of relationships between brands and personality traits, fall prey to the same illusions. A creative director I talked with related watching a commercial that used a song by indie group the Pernice Brothers, and hoping that the ad was for Target, which has successfully branded itself as the cool alternative to more square department stores, relying in part on popular music to achieve this end. Instead the commercial was produced for the decidedly less hip Sears, the realization of which bothered the creative director, though he ultimately caught himself buying in to branding techniques: "I guess if I got the Sears account, I might try to do the same thing, which is kind of funny . . . I guess I have gut reactions. . . . Target's a pure example of just how advertising can completely change your opinion of a company" (Carl). Like the Spinto Band, singer Joe Pernice reasoned that he already supported Sears as a consumer: "I like to build things, so I've bought a lot of Sears wrenches. I could honestly say I didn't have a problem with it."

Articulation—meaning both an expression and a joining 12 together—provides an entry point to understanding the process of branding, where the unity formed by articulation "is always, necessarily, a 'complex structure': a structure in which things are related, as much through their differences as their similarities" (Hall 44). I am interested in the use of articulation theory, as in McLeod's implementation of the term, as a way "to understand the transformations of cultural production" and to examine "how connections are made and why they are important" (14). The joining of music culture, through either a licensed track or the appearance of an artist, with a product or service in a commercial brings new connotations to both artist and company while naturalizing the relationship between the two. The value of articulating popular music to a product can be seen as especially important to advertisers competing with products similar, if not identical, in use-value, as is the case with cola.

Pepsi and Coke are examples of "parity products," where "marginally different products compete very closely, for the most part avoiding factual logical claims and relying on image management" (Huron 568); a close association with a style of popular music overrides the physical make-up of the product as the distinguishing mark. In presenting a product or service as engaged in a relationship with music culture, the distinction between popular music and commerce, and the lack of distinction between one brand and another, can both be hidden from view. One of the key foundations of the Cola wars is that the products are very similar and not basic necessities, so that image through advertising became essential to selling the products; advertising is not about what the product does but who the consumer is (Frank). In part because both companies needed to move outside the qualities of the products themselves to establish difference, Coke and Pepsi have perhaps the longest and most consistent relationship to popular music culture of any consumer product. As a result, an analysis of their histories with and strategies involving the use of popular music provides a revealing case study of how music is exploited for branding purposes. 13

334

COLA AND MUSIC DUETS

Coke transferred its advertising account to McCann Erickson in 1956, and popular music was immediately a part of the equation, with some of the earliest campaigns featuring performers like Connie Francis and the McGuire Sisters. These were hardly the trendiest performers available during these first days of rock and roll, but the early emphasis on popular music and musicians as sales pitch is notable. In 1963, Coke began its "Things Go Better with Coke" campaign and, while the original theme was performed by the Limeliters, the company soon invited dozens of popular musicians, including some at the time more controversial rock artists, to pen and perform a version of the "Things Go Better with Coke" theme song. Artists from the Troggs to Otis Redding, the Left Banke to Lulu, put their own mark on the song. Clocking in at ninety seconds apiece and sounding thematically and aesthetically very much like the artists' known work, with the exception of the recognizable chorus, these ads could easily be mistaken for chart hits. 14

The event that arguably sealed Coke's relationship to popular   15
music was the 1971 campaign featuring a group of wide-eyed multicultural young adults singing, "I'd like to teach the world to sing in perfect harmony/I'd like to buy the world a Coke and keep it company."
Two de-Coked versions, one by the Hilltop Singers and the other by the
New Seekers, went on to become chart hits. This was not the first time
in the history of advertising that a song that began life as a jingle was
reborn on the pop charts, but it may be the case that has been most
deeply lodged in our collective memory, not least by Coke itself, which
has returned to the campaign multiple times since.

Before "I'd Like to Teach the World to Sing" became a hit, Pepsi   16
also witnessed one of its ad themes cross over into the radio charts. The
theme to 1966's "Girlwatchers," Pepsi's Diet Coke campaign, became a
top 40 hit for the Bob Crewe Generation as "Music to Watch Girls By."
Compared to Coke, Pepsi was slow to use actual pop musicians,
though its campaigns did utilize youthful music. In the 1980s, Pepsi
made its affiliation to popular music more explicit, hiring some of the
most famous entertainers of the time, including Michael Jackson and
Madonna, to star in their commercials. These were two of the first spots
for which the premieres were treated not as advertising, but as must-
see programming. Over the next twenty years, artists ranging from Ray   **335**
Charles to Shakira joined the promotional crusade. Perhaps making up
for their late start in hiring actual artists, a 2002 Pepsi ad featured
Britney Spears traveling through Pepsi ads from the late 1950s to the
present, performing era-appropriate styles of music. Both companies
have made music such a focus of their advertising campaigns that pop
music history has to some extent been documented by the companies'
marketing histories.

The turn to music for marketing purposes in these two cases   17
served the purpose of reaching a desired market, since both popular
music and colas share a similar demographic. While both Coke and
Pepsi have long stressed youthfulness as a quality possessed by their
consuming demographic, in the past, the companies denied that their
advertising was specifically directed at youth. Of Pepsi's 1984 Michael
Jackson campaign, one journalist wrote, "the second of the two spots
clearly shows several preteen boys and girls holding caffeine-laden
Pepsi cans, an apparent break with a company policy that had kept
kids out of Pepsi television spots" (Brown C3), to which Pepsi's senior
vice president of creative services countered that the ad was meant to
attract their parents. By the 1990s, the colas were more honest about
their target demographic and tactics to reach them, a signal that concerns over and fears about marketing directly to children have
decreased dramatically in the U.S. In 1991, an article in *Advertising Age*
reported that Coke "said a music tie-in is a natural fit for Coca-Cola

since music appeals to the youth market, the primary target for soft drinks and for No. 1 brand Coca-Cola Classic in particular" (Fahey 1).

As Pepsi and Coke advertising has spread to other countries 18 around the world, both companies have continued to use music as a means of branding across all promotions. Corporate sponsorship of music acts in the UK started to grow in popularity about a decade after the approach became common in the United States, and Pepsi and Coke were early takers. In television advertising, too, the colas extended their approach to non-U.S. markets. Because these brands have relied so heavily on the globally recognized language of Western-style popular music, in many cases, the same ads that are shown in the United States are also broadcast internationally, with little or no adaptation. When spots have been created outside the U.S., music remains the focus and international broadcasting takes on new meaning; for instance, Pepsi's 1989 "Glasnost" spot, which featured Soviet scenes paired with a score by Soviet rock group Pogo, was not only shown in the Soviet Union, but during the Super Bowl in the United States, and later around the world ("Debut Set for Pepsi's"). Through the campaign, Soviet and non-Soviet viewers alike discover that, despite other cultural differences, there are at least two universals: rock music and cola, preferably consumed together. Not only is the articulation between popular music and cola activated, but it is also shown to be immune to national and cultural boundaries.

CASTING DOUBT ON THE PERFECT HARMONY

In a lament for contemporary music, Bob Dylan once noted, "You 19 know things go better with Coke because Aretha Franklin told you so ... The corporate world, when they figured out what [rock and roll] was and how to use it they snuffed the breath out of it and killed it" (Dylan). [It remains unclear whether his decision later to license "The Times They Are a-Changin'" to a Bank of Montreal ad and "Love Sick" to a Victoria's Secret ad was a sign of submission or indifference.] The use of music and musicians in advertising draws out tensions that have long been part of larger cultural discourses involving the division between art and commerce. Julien Temple, director of Neil Young's video for "This Note's for You," a mocking critique of commercial tie-ins, explained:

> The best pop music is the truth of someone singing powerfully about what they feel. If that's owned by a conglomerate of soft drink, it's like having an invisible Pepsi sign engraved on your forehead.

That's definitely part of the process of how pop music is being killed. It becomes useless because it's incorporated. Lots of record companies are chaining music down to where it's not very interesting and nobody can do anything different with it. This song is a piece of integrity, and the drink companies want to own it! (qtd in Reed 19)

The relationships between corporations and musicians have 20 ranged from sponsorships of tours and music programs, to the use of popular songs in ads, to, in some cases, the offer to pay artists for approved lyrical mentions of products, with each of these methods raising eyebrows to varying degrees in different markets. In 2003, the BBC's decision to allow Coca-Cola to sponsor its Radio 1 and Top of the Pops charts was met with disapproval. An article in the Guardian expressed the main questions: "Was it politically astute for the BBC to allow the mainstays of its youth programming to be associated with a product, as Chrysalis chief executive Phil Riley puts it, that 'rots kids' teeth'? Or for the BBC to be linked so closely with a multibillion-dollar corporate giant?" (Wells 8). This story would not have received any attention in the U.S., where not only is the top-rated American Idol sponsored by Coke, but the contestants prepare to perform in a Coke-themed lounge and appear in mini within-program commercials for Coke. Even in the absence of program sponsorship, however, the association between pop music, youth, and Coca-Cola already exists the world over, thanks to consistent articulation through advertising.

In the United States, the association is not simply commonplace 21 and accepted, but is often argued to be a sensible extension of standard capitalist practice. Common to the argument that relationships between companies and musicians are both positive and natural are claims that popular music is, after all, produced within a commercial system and bought and sold as a commodity. Press coverage often treats licensing to commercials as a sensible branching off of other types of commercial affiliation, such as tour sponsorship. Some of the musicians, music supervisors, and licensing managers I spoke with made comments that similarly suggested that it is hypocritical to be against licensing to advertising when tours are so often sponsored or when bands and band members are implicitly lending an endorsement to products they use. When I asked Jeff Price, co-founder and general manager of spin ART Records, whether he would discourage bands from licensing to a more controversial product, such as alcohol, he responded, "Do I have a problem if one of our bands is serving beer at a bar? No. So why would I have a problem with their music being used in those commercials?" But such a position conflates all commercial affiliation, when in fact there are many types and grades of commercial affiliation confronting musicians; as one journalist put it, "At every level there is a constant battle between the pride of the artist and the lure of Mammon" (Thorncroft 120). For each artist who is vocally anti-corporate, like Fugazi, or entirely incorporated, like Britney Spears, there are many more in between constantly negotiating their comfort zone within the commercial arena.

Buying a bottle of Coke and buying a compact disc may be simi- 22 lar experiences, but drinking cola and listening to music are not. When the experience with a product, as opposed to simply the purchase of a product, is taken into account, the division between art and commerce, though in many ways unstable and blurred, is also based on real perceptual and emotional differences. As it becomes more natural to hear, experience, and be exposed to music through advertising, potential negative consequences are invited: at worst, larger issues of cultural production, music distribution, and creative independence, and the impact that advertising as a vessel of popular music has on each of these areas, will evade inspection. Corporate sponsors already have "a strong influence over currents of thought in our society" (Barnouw 74); popular music is employed in television commercials as yet another instrument of control.

COLA'S STRATEGIC CAPTURE OF MUSIC CULTURE

23

Coke and Pepsi, with their advertising agencies, have utilized a number of strategies in attempting to avoid and alleviate tensions inherent in dealings between commercial and cultural entities. Both companies have partnered largely with artists for whom commercial affiliations are viewed by the public as less compromising, and both have drawn attention to the benefits of exposure through advertising, as well as the creativity of the advertising medium. Further, Coke and Pepsi have attempted to adopt qualities symbolic of rock and roll as a means of narrowing the gulf between the philosophies of corporations and of artists. Each of these strategies is examined more closely.

COMMERCIALISM-FRIENDLY MUSIC

In popular music, distinctions are continuously made between more 24 and less artistic genres, often around variables already involved in discourse of cultural difference, such as race, gender, and class. In the 1960s, the rock as art movement aligned rock music with other cultural products seemingly positioned in opposition to clear commercial ends. As Frith described it, "The belief in a continuing struggle between music and commerce is the core of rock ideology" (41). Ultimately, it is a certain variety of music—largely white, male, and middle-class rock music—that is most philosophically at odds with commercial affiliation and most open to charges of "selling out." "While it's not surprising that people as historically crass as [t]he Jacksons would sell their soul for a soft drink Michael wouldn't touch," wrote one journalist in 1987, "it's surprising that an artist of [David] Bowie's calibre would join the corporate ranks" (Gross S18). In fact, Bowie's involvement does stand out against the usual music selection of the colas, which tends towards more "commercial" artists or those for whom commercial affiliation has less of a stigma attached to it.

While the "Things Go Better with Coke" campaign included a number of rock bands, by the 1980s, Coke and Pepsi were using mostly pop and R&B songs and acts. For these artists, commercialism was not necessarily a bad word. As Madonna explained in 1989, "What I do is total commercialism, but it's also art. . . . I like the challenge of doing both, of somehow making art that is accessible and making commerce something artistic" (qtd in Holden 1). 25

In 1990, with rap growing in popularity, Pepsi was one of the first advertisers to seek out the endorsement of a rap artist, featuring Young MC in its "Cool Cans" spot (Foltz). While rap was not, at first, an easy sell to companies nervous about language and alienating part of their consumer base (Foltz), it was an obvious choice for the colas. Not only was much rap music already littered with commercial product shout-outs (essentially free endorsements), but, focused as the cola corporations were on reaching both the youth and minority markets, rap presented a way to reach both simultaneously. According to the New York Times, "Middle America's growing acceptance of a variety of cultures has also fueled the boom in urban-inspired ads and promotions aimed at youth ages twelve to twenty-four" (Day C2). 26

From the rap artist's perspective, an offer from Coke or Pepsi served as a kind of validation. As a New York brand consultant put it, "The fact that Coca-Cola is using urban music says more about where urban music has moved than where Coke has moved" (Howard 7B). In a country with a history of black artists not being treated the same as white artists, where black music trailed behind in radio, on MTV, and in sales for many years, despite being the obvious basis for much of the popular white music, marketers like the cola companies wasted little time taking advantage of black music's desire to be treated and exploited equally in the area of advertising. Yet whether these artists are truly treated equally by the corporations remains in question: In 2003, Pepsi withdrew its commercial featuring rapper Ludacris 27 because of complaints about obscene lyrics on his album. But Pepsi had featured artists before whose album material or behavior outside the commercial campaign would have been inappropriate for a television spot. As rap impresario Russell Simmons pointed out, by featuring the historically outrageous Ozzy Osbourne in an ad, Pepsi appeared hypocritical (Carr). Finally, when less commercial or more socially conscious rappers, like Common, have appeared in cola ads, they have been subject to the same, if subdued, critiques of selling out as have their rock counterparts.

Rap remains, alongside pop, the most common genre tapped by 28 the cola companies in terms of featuring actual musicians and preexisting music in their television spots. Rock-themed campaigns, like Coke's faux-documentary following the activities of an all girl rock band, tend to use composed music and fictional groups, partly because actual rock groups may be more hesitant to commit to a Coke campaign. The director of film and television for the Beggars Group reported receiving "Diet Coke and Coke pitches all the time; they're constantly looking for new artists," but the artists she represents have so far refused because they do not support the company (Lanchart). One of those groups, the Super Furry Animals, turned down an offer from Coke only to find the company respond by doubling the money to 1 million [pounds sterling] (Rhys); the band maintained their stance, but this example reveals a disconnect between corporations and musicians, where the former can hardly imagine that an offer would be rejected for any reason other than financial. Singer and guitarist Gruff Rhys explained, "Most of our peers think we are nuts," echoing the sentiments of other holdouts. "[I]t's been a lonely road resisting the chants of the rising solicitations," said the Doors' John Densmore (35), whose refusal to consent has prevented his willing former bandmates from reaping a fortune in licensing fees. Lately even Densmore has tempered his position, telling *Rolling Stone* that the Doors would consider licensing to an advertisement for "something technology-oriented, or some hybrid car or something" (qtd in Serpick 20).

As licensing to commercials has become more routine, there is a 29 greater rock presence in advertising, including cola campaigns: the Rolling Stones' "You Can't Always Get What You Want" and Queen's "I Want to Break Free" were used to promote Coke's C2 in 2004, Green Day covered Sonny Curtis's "I Fought the Law" for Pepsi's iTunes promotion that same year, and it was reported in November 2005, that Detroit garage-rocker Jack White of the White Stripes had inked a deal with Coke to compose music for an ad. White based his decision in some measure on his own status as a Coke drinker, echoing the above-mentioned sentiments of Velocity Girl's Moore, the Spinto Band's Krill, and Joe Pernice. But White also insisted that he would have found it strange to license a song for the campaign, a sign, along with the fan critique that has followed many of these deals, that commercial involvement for rock musicians is still a complex negotiation.

BENEFITS TO ARTISTS

The partnerships between the cola companies and musicians have been 30 framed by the corporations and sometimes in the press as beneficial to artists. For older artists, participating in commercial campaigns can spark a renewed interest in back catalogs; Ray Charles admitted being embarrassed by the Diet Pepsi ads he starred in (Bream), but the campaign did bring attention to the artist during a relative lull in his career. Often commercial campaigns coincide with artist events, such as album releases or tours, acting as a cross-promotional tool. The 1989 Pepsi ad featuring Madonna's "Like a Prayer" was broadcast before the album was even released. The premiere of the ad, broadcast simultaneously in forty countries, was described thus in the press release: "The groundbreaking deal is expected to change the way popular tunes from major artists are released in the future. Traditionally, new songs have been made public through heavy radio air-play. In an innovative twist, the Pepsi–Madonna deal uses television to provide unparalleled international exposure for her new single" (quoted in Siegel 77). It is interesting that this case was framed in terms of bypassing commercial radio since, at the time, U.S. commercial radio was nowhere near the disaster it is today for young artists, with ever-narrowing playlists, a plague of payola schemes, and practical if not technical oligopoly status.

341

    The benefit to artists today is often explained as a salve against 31 the hard times being experienced by artists, in terms of both commercial radio lock-outs and the perceived threat of the twin evils of dubious consequence, piracy, and downloading. As the guitarist from the Counting Crows explained of the band's turn in a Coke commercial, "It's just such a tough world. . . . The economy and pirating and downloading. It's not a great thing" (Laue 4go). Involvement in commercial campaigns has, for some artists, become not simply another way to gain exposure and make a living, but the only way.

    As a further enticement to artists, in at least some cases of cola 32 advertising, creative control is shared with the artist as a guarantee that the finished product will carry the artist's aesthetic and at times moral mark, occasionally in very bizarre ways. Michael Jackson, known for his belief in health food, agreed to do the Pepsi ad, but refused actually to consume the beverage or to appear to be consuming the beverage on camera (Gross S18). Jackson also "demanded that the TV spots display his face no more than four seconds and feature one spin, not two, in his commercial's dance routine" (Engardio 16). Sometimes musicians are able to step outside the role of performer and into another creative position. George Michael agreed to do a Diet Coke ad on such premises: "In luring Michael as pitchman, Coca-Cola gave him the freedom to create his own pitch," plus producer and co-director duties (Collins 3D). As reported in *Creativity*, it has become more common for a commercial campaign featuring musicians to position "its hitmakers literally at the core of the creative team" (Lyon 16). By handing some creative control over to the artists, the typical advertising model is ostensibly turned on its head: "instead of asking the musician to celebrate the brand, each commercial, in effect, celebrates the musician" (Lyon 16). Or, at least, that is what artists are led to believe.

ADVERTISING AS ENTERTAINMENT

The reason why creative control is a variable at all is because the cola corporations have consistently promoted their television advertising as entertainment, not just pitch. It is not uncommon for musicians involved in the campaigns to talk about the ads as though they were any other creative project. For instance, in the PR report for Kanye West's Pepsi ad, the artist thanked the corporation as he might a music producer: "From concept, to execution, to post-production and effects, to revisions—a lot of work went into this creative process. . . . I want to thank Pepsi for working overtime to see this through" ("Kanye West and Pepsi"). A writer for the *Boston Globe* considered the overlap between entertainment and advertising when he contended that viewers will be left wondering whether Madonna's Pepsi ad premiere will be "a) a great moment in music history; b) a great moment in broadcasting history; c) a great moment in advertising history; or d) the end of Western civilization as we know it" (Siegel 77). His befuddlement sounds outdated now that television advertising as entertainment is an accepted part of everyday life, as evidenced by, for instance, the treatment of Super Bowl commercials as popular texts (McAllister "Is Commercial Culture . . . "). 33

The premieres of cola ads have sometimes been handled by the media and public as genuine cultural events, with families gathering eagerly around their television sets and an enormous number of viewers watching simultaneously. In 2001, Britney Spears appeared in a Pepsi commercial that, like Michael Jackson's 1984 ad and Madonna's 1989 ad, was anticipated as if it were a feature film. Millions of viewers tuned in to see the pop princess sing the praises of the sugary beverage. The framing of commercials as events assists in distancing these spots from their marketing origins. Further emphasizing its entertainment 34 qualities, the Britney spot premiered on television during the Academy Awards, the highest cultural honor for filmic success in the U.S. And continuing the parallel between this spot and actual filmed entertainment, viewers could access, via Yahoo!, "behind-the-scenes footage of the commercial shoot, a 15-second 'teaser' preview, and Spears' diary documenting the making of the commercial" (Jeckell). Through the hiring of well-known directors—Michel Gondry has directed for Coke, Spike Lee for Pepsi—and an emphasis on storytelling over product placement, Coke and Pepsi have asserted themselves as more similar to film than to traditional advertising.

Promotion of music-focused cola ads as entertainment has been facilitated by the popularity of the music video format following MTV's 1981 inception. According to a 1985 story in the *New York Times*, "At every turn, the imagery and sound of the music video, the first new form television has yielded in decades, is having a pronounced effect. Only three years old, the notion of melding highly stylized, rapidly cut video montages with rock music is echoing throughout the popular culture" (Smith 29). Because "[m]usic videos are fundamentally commercial, designed to sell rock musicians, songs and albums," in fact taking their inspiration from the European new wave commercials of the 1970s (Smith 29), it makes sense that the aesthetic was so readily adopted for television ads. If MTV is the ultimate postmodern vehicle (see Kaplan), then by borrowing its aesthetic, advertising also adopts the postmodern position that collapses distinctions, including, self-servingly, the distinction between artistic and commercial intent. By the time Britney Spears was approached to appear in Pepsi ads, the association between cola advertising and entertainment was fully entrenched in (false) cultural consciousness, which explains how Britney Spears could declare, "I'm a big fan of Pepsi products and Pepsi commercials" ("Britney Spears and Pepsi-Cola") as casually as one of her fans might say, "I'm a big fan of Britney Spears," and country star Faith Hill could unselfconsciously report, "It is an honor to be involved with Pepsi, who over the years has successfully blended a superior product with quality music, talent, and creativity" ("Faith Hill To Star"). Spears and Hill described their involvement with Pepsi in the same terms artists use to discuss working with music producers and film directors, and in so doing helped to move the discussion of cola advertising from the consumer market to the art world.

THE ADOPTION OF "ROCK" QUALITIES

Frank described soda as "[a]nother product category that was quite thoroughly given over to hip advertising" and noted that "the best soda ads stressed the values of the counterculture rather than simple countercultural appearances" (163, emphasis in original). As well as offering benefits and a degree of creative control to artists, cola advertising has adopted characteristics borrowed directly from the rock and roll handbook: anti-authoritarianism, authenticity, and gravity, all in service of achieving the elusive but essential tag of "cool," are established through the choice of artist and overall aesthetic and message of the spots. As Dawn Hudson, senior vice president for strategy and marketing for Pepsi, explained, "We try to choose celebrities not because they are hot and big but because their personalities or what they are known for reinforces our brand" (Howard 7B). By adopting and then reinforcing "rock" qualities, the cola corporations are able to make their advertising more attractive to musicians and less offensive to fans.

An anti-authoritarian stance is often expressed through the selec-   37
tion of notorious artists. Although Pepsi has conveyed surprise at the controversies sparked by their campaigns, the company's marketing department must be aware of the potential for controversy when divisive artists are selected to pitch for them. When Madonna's video for "Like a Prayer" was released shortly after the Pepsi commercial that featured the song, conservative groups were up in arms over the images of cross-burning, stigmata, and, while not explicitly mentioned by the protestors, interracial love. Pepsi unsuccessfully requested that MTV withdraw the video and ultimately dropped the sponsorship of Madonna, removing the spot in the U.S. For a corporation to hire Madonna, who, as one journalist writes, is known for "stirring up just enough controversy to advance her career without tipping the balance of public opinion against her" (Holden 1) and not anticipate potential controversy, is either incredibly naive or, more likely, a savvy business move.

Less predictable than the Madonna debacle, but just as headline   38
making, was Michael Jackson's hospitalization after an on-set accident set his hair on fire. Again, by 1984, Jackson was already well-known as a bit of a crotch-grabbing freak; that this campaign might result in the establishment clucking disapprovingly was no mystery to Pepsi. In 1989, Mike Beindorff, Coca-Cola USA's vice president of advertising and associate director of marketing, described Pepsi's approach as "a high-risk, high-benefit strategy" (qtd in Davis 26), maintaining that Coke's method is less risky. Yet, even in the absence of massive scandals and controversies, Coke's approach and use of music have, since the 1960s, carried an anti-authoritarian message. A jingle by the Troggs or the Left Banke sends a different message than one by Connie Francis, who had endorsed the Cola only a few years earlier; surely these ads sounded to over-forties at the time much the same as the

noise being played on the radio. Likewise, the gathering of youth on the hilltop was a conspicuous representation of the counterculture movement, aligning Coke and Coke drinkers in opposition to the authority who would have you cut your hair and drink a glass of milk. Both companies continue the tradition today, hiring musicians who, on the surface, teeter on the brink of controversy, through explicit sexuality, graphic lyrical content, or attitude. Even Coke's fake girl band, featured in a recent campaign, adopts an anti-authoritarian stance through their outspoken, punky, devil-may-care attitudes.

For Coca-Cola, the most important and constant characteristic underscored by the ad campaigns is authenticity, epitomized by the slogan and "Hilltop" chorus "It's the real thing." Likewise, the concept of authenticity, even as it is revealed to be an ever-changing and indefinable construction, continues to be salient to the discourse surrounding rock and roll. As the self-described "real thing," Coke sidesteps questions of unholy mergers between art and commerce; it cannot be a threat to authenticity because Coke itself is the authentic cola. While other slogans have come and gone over the years, Coke has returned to the theme of "real" repeatedly, using the hilltop ad as a hallmark of that promise. In the 1980s, Coke used nostalgia for its own ad as a campaign theme, allowing us to catch up with the wide-eyed idealists who populated the original ad, now with children of their own (and, one imagines, jobs working for The Man). In 2005, Coke revived the song again for its "Chilltop" spot, which featured corny blues-rocker G. Love and friends performing what one reporter called a "horrendously lame cover" (Lazare 65) from a Philadelphia rooftop. A small group alone on a roof transforms the unity message of the original into a message of exclusivity, a subtle reminder of the malleability of brand and brand values. Though these later revivals of the ads could be generously labeled missteps, McCann Erickson's supposition that viewers had a nostalgic relationship to the original was probably correct: the spot, along with a disproportionately large number of other cola ads, regularly has a position on lists of best ads or most memorable ads. Other uses of the "real" by Coke include the late 1980s and early 1990s campaigns proclaiming that you "Can't beat the real thing" and a more recent Coke campaign comprised of mini-documentaries featuring young people seeking to "make it real" through the joint consumption of cola and authentic music experiences, a thematic continuation of Coke's 2003 campaign featuring "real people and celebrities in 'real' situations" (Howard 7B).

The lure of the "real" and "authentic" has not escaped Pepsi either. Particularly the company's early adoption of the rap sound to convey its message signaled a reliance on authenticity to sell the Pepsi brand. In order to convey the brand as authentic, it was important to

39

40

345

use music also perceived as authentic. Young MC dismissed imitations of rap music in commercials as "offensive," explaining, "If the point is to reach young people, an imitation isn't going to have the right effect. . . . Rap fans will know right away when the music isn't the real thing, and the advertising is going to turn them off" (qtd in Foltz D5). As noted earlier, one of the advantages of hiring nonwhite musicians is that, beyond appealing to consumers in minority markets, these artists often hold an appeal to mainstream, especially youth, consumers. The road to authenticity through minority marketing recalls Hebdige's claims about the role of the "other" in the formation of subcultures, where historically, subcultures have borrowed what are perceived as authentic aesthetic ideas, cultural products, and, by extension, outsider status from minority cultures. Authenticity has been adopted by colas across the spectrum as a means of distinguishing their brand, through music, from presumably fake competition.

The use of music by the cola corporations also lends gravity to the spots. Music is a strong emotional connector and, as Sarah Gavigan, founder of music house Ten Music, explained, "with every piece of music there is an emotion that went behind it and that's kind of what [advertisers are] borrowing, the emotion to go over the top of their visual." Through their reliance on music, Coke and Pepsi have taken the message that music can change the world, which may actually be true, and transformed it into the suggestion that cola can change the world. Surely the success of Coke's "Hilltop" ad resulted from its overt similarities to the Beatles Our World contribution of "All You Need Is Love"; both presented a throng of hippies singing to a global audience about making the world a better place. 41

Coke linked itself to peaceful protest again in 2004 in a spot that featured singer Sharlene Hector. As written in the *Observer*, "She softly, to the point of insipidly, sings the 1954 protest song 'I Wish I Knew How It Would Feel to Be Free' that the fabulous Nina Simone would make her own. A song that was once a powerful, delicate cry for equality and freedom has its guts ripped out and is presented as if it is Coke that can be the ticket to a higher spiritual place" (Morley 53). The forthcoming campaign featuring the composition of White Stripes' Jack White is reported to revolve around the theme of worldwide love, too. Certainly the messages themselves are well-intentioned, and no doubt some Coke employees support them, but cola is hardly the most obvious tool to achieve the objectives of peace and freedom. Similarly, Pepsi's dependence on notions of generational difference, as per their "Pepsi Generation" slogan and reliance on generation-defining artists like Madonna, implicates the beverage as somehow responsible for positive changes, as opposed to simply cashing in on them. 42

This combination of anti-authoritarianism, authenticity, and   43
social significance recalls both the original rock and roll ideological
position and, more generally, the modus operandi of the 1960s countercultural movement, arguably a loose basis for subsequent notions of
"cool" or "hip." The use of popular music and musicians in advertising
provides a branding shortcut to achieving these qualities.

CONCLUSIONS

Through their extensive histories with popular music, Coca-Cola and   44
Pepsi-Cola have succeeded in the ultimate goal of branding, effecting
an articulation between culture and commercial product. And
although such articulation is by its nature "a linkage which is not necessary, determined, absolute, or essential for all time" (Hall qtd in
Grossberg 53), with companies like Coke and Pepsi, it becomes difficult
to tease out which came first, the reputation of the colas or their association with popular music. In the end, the music–cola articulation acts
as a self-perpetuating machine, where otherwise finicky bands may be
willing to waive their no-commercials policy for Coke or Pepsi.
Through all of the strategies here discussed, Coke and Pepsi have effectively become part of music culture, as well as part of the larger culture
too; there are cola collectors, just as there are record collectors, and
Coca-Cola has garnered free lyrical mentions by artists including the
Beatles, the Kinks, and the Jam. If there is any doubt as to whether companies consider these references to be (usually) free and desirable
advertising, consider brand strategy agency Agenda Inc.'s "American
Brandstand" project, which tracks for its clients the presence of lyrical
mentions of brands in the Billboard Top 20 singles chart (Coca-Cola
was ranked twenty-second with sixteen mentions in 2005; in 2004,
Pepsi beat Coke eight mentions to one) ("American Brandstand"). But
what does it mean for the colas to be so deeply insinuated into music
culture? There are two concerns: what music is doing for the colas and
what the colas are doing to music. As this analysis of Coke and Pepsi
advertising has shown, popular music allows the cola corporations to
hide the physical content of their products, as well as the politics of
their business, behind a veil of fabricated cool. We may be well-advised
to listen to one reporter who suggested there should "be a law that the
grosser, greasier corporate companies such as Coca Cola, McDonald's,
and KFC are closely monitored by official, independent watchdogs
when it comes to the music they use in their commercials to disguise
the fact that they are indeed morally, technically, emotionally, and
nutritionally gross and greasy" (Morley 53). For their part, the Super

347

Furry Animals ultimately gave "Hello Sunshine," the song requested by Coca-Cola, to a video detailing human rights abuses produced by War on Want, a non-profit organization which campaigns against the causes of global poverty, and which has criticized the Coca-Cola company's impact on local communities.

As for what the colas are doing to music, while the totality of consequences is still becoming apparent, they are definitely playing a more prominent role in music culture and distribution. In response to the 1989 Madonna–Pepsi partnership, Leslie Savan commented on advertising as the new and future medium of music transmission, "But if that's the way to enter the pantheon, then what does that make Pepsi and Coke? They are the medium through which the word is passed. They are universal, speaking no languages and all languages. And each art/ad is like a prayer unto them" (90).

The universality to which Savan refers is evident in Coke and Pepsi's global campaigns: More than other American brands these products and their ad campaigns have spread worldwide, a process Pico Iyer has dubbed "Coca-Colonization." But the United States is not only exporting cola and music through these advertisements, it is also exporting ideas about the relationship between cultural and commercial interests, which is why this case study is also a cautionary tale. At a time when musicians and record companies are increasingly desperate to explore nontraditional revenue streams, it is important to examine even seemingly benign partnerships and to recognize that, whatever the potential benefits to artists in the short term, when musicians and corporations enter into an agreement, the resulting partnership is not a symmetrical one. Bear in mind how many of the musicians who have been involved in cola campaigns are barely a blip on the popular culture radar today, while the names Coke and Pepsi remain in lights.

Over the years the colas have developed what amounts to a real relationship with the music industry. Coca-Cola's 1991 "Pop Music" program saw the company joining with Sony Music to provide free mini-CDs to buyers of multipacks, and in 2004, through their partnership with the iTunes music store, Pepsi invited customers to download a free song with purchase of a soft drink. Such promotions call attention to the role of the cola corporations in the distribution of popular music. Josh Rabinowitz, director of music for Grey Worldwide, sees a future where record labels become obsolete and singles are released directly through product advertisements. While this type of system may offer solutions to some of the problems presented by major labels, it also offers its own set of concerns. One advertising copywriter I spoke with worried that as corporations like Starbucks become more successful in music distribution they might, like major labels, "think they know better than the artist" (Kovey). He imagined a Starbucks

45

46

47

executive commenting on the new Ron Sexsmith album, saying, "the xylophone is too jarring, so if he could remove those then we'd be more willing to put it in the store" (Kovey).

The impact of commercial interests on the cultural realm is already occurring, even without this sort of blatant wresting of control and power over the production of culture from the hands of artists. Writing of corporate sponsorship of the arts, McAllister asserted, "Art becomes less valued, less credible, and less engaging. Art begins to equal other commercial entities. Art equals the sitcom; art equals the 15-second spot" (The Commercialization 221). Likewise, the articulation between music culture and commerce holds a similarly detrimental capacity; as the association becomes more conventional, and viewers more apathetic to it, the self-standing value of music culture may become threatened. The discomfort and disapproval voiced by critics, music fans, and musicians about the increasingly comfortable relationships between artists and corporations is an indication of a genuine cultural dilemma. More so is the quieting of this discourse over time, as cessation of the debate suggests submission to corporate control. Rather than dismiss the art-versus-commerce divide as constructed and the "sell-out" debates as antiquated, it is important to acknowledge and investigate these tensions. When it seems a line has been crossed, it is not necessary to redraw the line, but to assess who is in control and to what end. It is through such scrutiny that relationships between cultural and commercial entities can be monitored, and the tide of hyper-commercialism stemmed.

48

ACKNOWLEDGEMENTS

An earlier version of this article was presented at the MeCCSA and AMPE joint annual conference in January 2006, Leeds, UK.

WORKS CITED

"American Brandstand." Agendainc.com 18 Apr. 2006 http://www.agendainc.com/brand.html.

Barnouw, Erik. *The Sponsor: Notes on a Modern Potentate.* New York: Oxford UP, 1978.

Bogart, Michele H. *Artists, Advertising, and the Borders of Art.* Chicago, IL: U of Chicago P, 1995.

Bream, Jon. "Ray Charles' Genius Leaves State Crowd Saying, 'Uh-huh.'" *Star Tribune* 5 June 1992: 4B.

"Britney Spears and Pepsi-Cola Ink Global Sponsorship and Advertising Pact." *PR Newswire* 6 Feb. 2001.

Brown, Merrill. "Just in Grammy Time: The Jackson Soda Sell." *The Washington Post* 28 Feb. 1984: C3.

Carl, Chris. Personal interview, 8 Oct. 2005.

Carr, David. "Hip-Hop Impresario Urges Pepsi Boycott." *The New York Times* 6 Feb. 2003: C5.

Collins, Monica. "George Michael Creates an Ad." *USA Today* 30 Jan. 1989: 3D.

Davis, Tim. "What Ever Happened to 'Be a Pepper'?" *Beverage World* Apr. 1989: 26.

Day, Sherri. "Pepsi Says Its Pop Music Stars Can Reach Minorities and the Mainstream at the Same Time." *The New York Times* 27 Aug. 2002: C2.

"Debut Set for Pepsi's 'Glasnost' Commercial." *Journal of Commerce* 20 Jan. 1989: 5A.

Densmore, John. "Riders on the Storm: Why the Doors Don't Open When Corporate Ads Come Calling." *The Nation* 8 July 2002: 33-36.

Dylan, Bob. Liner notes, *Biograph*. Columbia Records, 1985.

Engardio, Pete. "Cola Wars II: The Battle of the Books." *Business Week.* Books, 1 Dec. 1986: 16.

Fahey, Alison. "Coke's $100M Blast: Mini-CDs Star in Huge Summer Promotion." *Advertising Age* 11 March 1991: 1.

"Faith Hill to Star in New Pepsi Commercial: 'Joy of Cola' Spot to Debut on Academy Awards Telecast." *PR Newswire*, financial news, 13 March 2000.

Foltz, Kim. "Madison Ave. Turns an Ear to Rap Music." *The New York Times* 6 July 1990: D5.

Frank, Thomas. *The Conquest of Cool: Business Culture, Counterculture, and the Rise of Hip Consumerism.* Chicago, IL: U of Chicago P, 1997.

Frith, Simon. *Sound Effects: Youth, Leisure, and the Politics of Rock'n'Roll.* New York: Pantheon, 1981.

Gavigan, Sarah. Personal interview, 14 Nov. 2005.

Gross, Jonathan. "Pop Culture." *The Toronto Star* 11 Apr. 1987: S18.

Grossberg, Lawrence, ed. "On Postmodernism and Articulation: An Interview with Stuart Hall." *Journal of Communication Inquiry* 10.2, 1986: 45-60.

Hall, Stuart. "Race, Articulation, and Societies Structured in Dominance." *Race Critical Theories: Text and Context.* Ed. Philomena Essed and David Theo Goldberg. Malden, MA: Blackwell, 2002. 38–68.

Halloran, Tricia. Personal interview, 27 Oct. 2005.

Hebdige, Dick. *Subculture: The Meaning of Style.* London: Routledge, 1979.

Holden, Stephen. "Madonna Re-Creates Herself—Again." The New York Times. Section 2, 19 March 1989: 1.

Howard, Theresa. "Coke Turns to Urban Music Stars for Latest Ad Campaign." *USA Today* 13 Jan. 2003: 7B.

Huron, David. "Music in Advertising: An Analytic Paradigm." *The Musical Quarterly* 73, 1989: 557–74.

Jeckell, Barry A. "Spears' Pepsi Ad to Get Online Unveiling." *BPI Entertainment News Wire* 20 March 2001.

"Kanye West and Pepsi Take a Trip around the Globe: Grammy Award-Winning Artist Stars in New Commercial Directed by Spike Lee." *PR Newswire* 25 Aug. 2005.

Kaplan, E. Ann. *Rocking around the Clock: Music Television, Postmodernism and Consumer Culture.* London: Routledge, 1987.

Kovey, Fred. Personal interview, 18 Sept. 2005.

Krill, Nick. Personal interview, 18 Nov. 2005.

Lanchart, Jenn. Personal interview, 20 Oct. 2005.

Laue, Christine. "Still Flying High: The Counting Crows Find That Touring Is Helping Them Survive the Ups and Downs of the Music World." *Omaha World Herald* 3 Apr. 2003: 4go.

Lazare, Lewis. "Coke Ad Nothing Like Real Thing." *Chicago Sun-Times* 30 June 2005: 65.

Lears, Jackson. "Uneasy Courtship: Modern Art and Modern Advertising." *American Quarterly* 39, 1987: 133-54.

Lukacs, Georg. *History & Class Consciousness.* Trans. Rodney Livingstone. New York: Merlin Press, 1967 [1920].

Lyon, Rick. "The Partnership for a Drag-free America: Creatives and Music Superstars are Collaborating on the 'New Classics' as Never Before." *Creativity* 1 Dec. 1997: 16.

McAllister, Matthew P. "Is Commercial Culture Popular Culture? A Question for Popular Communication Scholars." *Popular Communication* 1, 2003: 41-49.

———. *The Commercialization of American Culture: New Advertising, Control, and Democracy.* Thousand Oaks, CA: Sage, 1996.

McLeod, Kembrew. *Owning Culture: Authorship, Ownership, & Intellectual Property Law.* New York: Peter Lang, 2001.

Moore, Archie. Personal interview, 17 Sept. 2005.

Morley, Paul. "Music on TV: Justin's Secrets and Fries: Paul Morley Imagines a World in Which Fast Food Giants Advertise Their Wares with an Appropriate Soundtrack of Chas'n'Dave, not Timberlake." *The Observer* 15 Aug. 2004: 53.

Pernice, Joe. Personal interview, 21 Apr. 2006.

Price, Jeff. Personal interview, 17 Oct. 2005.

Rabinowitz, Josh. Personal interview, 5 Dec. 2005.

Reed, Christopher. "The Media: Pop Too Near Beer After a Fight, MTV Has Agreed to Show a Music Video Mocking Some of Its Biggest Sponsors." *The Guardian* 29 Aug. 1988: 19.

Rhys, Gruff. Personal interview, 28 March 2006.

351

Savan, Leslie. "Commercials Go Rock." *Sound and Vision: The Music Video Reader.* Ed. Simon Frith, Andrew Goodwin and Lawrence Grossberg. London: Routledge, 1993. 85-90.

Serpick, Evan. "Doors Ride Again: Box Set, Movie, and Vegas Show in the Works for the Band's Fortieth Anniversary." *Rolling Stone* 4 May 2006: 20.

Siegel, Ed. "Madonna Sells Her Soul for a Song." *The Boston Globe* 2 March 1989: 77.

Smith, Sally Bedell. "There's No Avoiding Music Videos." *The New York Times.* Section 2, 10 March 1985: 29.

Tayler, Letta. "Rock Stars Move to Corporate Beat: Once Oil and Water, Musicians and Advertisers Have Now Joined Forces." *The Ottawa Citizen* 23 June 2003: D3.

Thorncroft, Antony. "Marketing and Advertising: UK Sponsorship at Last Goes Pop." *Financial Times* 18 Sept. 1986: I20.

Tyler, Linda L. "'Commerce and Poetry Hand in Hand': Music in American Stores, 1880-1930." *Journal of the American Musicological Society* 45, 1992: 75–120.

Wells, Matt. "Message in a Bottle of Pop: Last Week the BBC Ran into Trouble over the Sponsorship of Its Radio and Top of the Pops Chart Shows by Coca-Cola." *The Guardian.* Media Pages, 8 Dec. 2003: 8.

Williams, Raymond. "Advertising, the Magic System." *Problems in Materialism and Culture.* London: New Left Books, 1980. 170–95.

Zizek, Slavoj. *The Sublime Object of Ideology.* London: Verso, 1989.

Examining the Text

1. The author of this article contends that, although pop musicians have often been wary about "selling out" by allowing advertisers to use their songs, the corporate giants Coke and Pepsi "have positioned themselves as having a more genuine connection to music culture, as enthusiasts, champions, and partners." By what means have the two companies pursued this goal of enticing musicians to sell advertisers the rights to their songs?

2. Klein explains that Pepsi and Coke are examples of "parity products," meaning that there's virtually no actual qualitative difference between the colas, so the image projected through advertising has historically been essential to selling the products. What is the history of cola advertising, according to this article? How do these ad campaigns attempt to lure the coveted youth demographic?

3. Although one might expect musical artists to be labeled as "sellouts" for allowing their music to be used by advertisers, rock and hip-hop musicians have somehow avoided this label when linking their music to the two major cola brands. What accounts for this phenomenon, according to this article's author?

4. According to Klein, corporations lead recording artists to believe that licensing their music to advertisers and marketers will yield a number of benefits to them, both financially and professionally. What, specifically, are these "benefits," as enumerated by Klein?

5. *Thinking rhetorically:* Klein states that, in addition to offering some creative control to artists, cola advertising has adopted characteristics "borrowed directly from the rock and roll handbook" in order to make their bubbly soft drinks appealing to young people. What are the specific qualities evoked by rock/hip-hop-associated advertisements, and how does the evocation of these qualities lure young consumers? How does Klein organize her arguments in this section of the essay, in order to lend credibility her assertions?

For Group Discussion

The author of this article says that marketers and other commercial types generally applaud the practice of using popular songs to sell products, while cultural critics generally find fault with the practice: "Like early sponsors of cultural radio programs, who were 'seen as patrons of the arts' . . . advertisers are praised for distributing music that might otherwise go unheard. However, the relationship is not equally beneficial, and the use of popular music in advertising threatens to empower commercial entities while devaluing cultural forms." In small groups, list some specific ways in which advertising practices might be "devaluing" cultural artifacts, especially musical ones. In full-class discussion, have a representative of each group explain the list to the class. Then, in full-class discussion, attempt to arrive at some consensus regarding the effect of the commercial "co-opting" of popular songs and lyrics.

Writing Suggestion

The author of this article, while presenting a clear position vis-à-vis its subject, also takes great care to present both sides of the issue, allowing readers to form their opinions about the effects of advertising on artistic creation. On the one hand, artists should have the freedom to do whatever they want with their songs; as expressed by an individual in this article, "Do I have a problem if one of our bands is serving beer at a bar? No. So why would I have a problem with their music being used in those commercials?" On the other hand, this essay points out a clear and present danger in the prevalence of such practices: "Corporate sponsors already have 'a strong influence over currents of thought in our society' (Barnouw 74); popular music is employed in television commercials as yet another instrument of control." For the purposes of this assignment, explore the pros and cons of the pop music/advertising connection and then decide where your own sympathies lie. Then, in a persuasive essay, argue for that thesis. As author Klein does in this essay, you will want to present *both* sides of this controversy in an unbiased way, explaining in detail, and with supporting evidence, the merits of each point of view. You may even want to present the point of view that runs contrary to your own thesis position *first*, and then develop the material that supports your thesis, so that your essay moves in the direction of supporting your arguments while gently dismantling the points that run counter to your thesis. This is a particularly effective and subtle rhetorical strategy, since it draws in readers who may be "on the fence" about the subject, or even slightly opposed to your position, and then nudges them over to your position with clearly reasoned explanations and arguments.

ADDITIONAL SUGGESTIONS FOR WRITING ABOUT POPULAR MUSIC

1. Americans receive a great deal of information about important issues— for example, presidential elections, gender-role attitudes, the legalization of drugs—from popular music and the media that purvey it. Write an essay in which you examine the representation of one important social issue or problem through music. For instance, you might focus on how the United States' environmental policy, or inner-city poverty, or the health-care crisis, or the effects of religious fundamentalism, or the threat of international terror is represented in recent song lyrics, on AM and FM radio stations, and in videos on YouTube.

2. Write an essay in which you first construct a detailed description of a band or an individual performer whose music you know very well, and then analyze the themes embodied in that band's songs. Discuss the effects your band's or individual artist's music has on its listeners and some possible reasons for that band/artist's popularity or lack thereof with mainstream listeners.

3. Imagine that you've recently arrived in the United States from China or any other country that has a very restrictive Internet access policy. You surf the Web freely for the first time and find yourself watching several hours' worth of music clips on YouTube. Based on this initial viewing, write a description of the interests, attitudes, lifestyles, and customs of young Americans. Try to include information that you gather from everything you've seen during that hour—the videos, game shows, advertisements, promos for upcoming shows, and so on—and make sure that you render your descriptions in vivid detail, so that somebody from another country might visualize all the elements you describe.

4. Write an essay in which you discuss the relative advantages and disadvantages of several primary sources of popular music: television, radio, downloaded songs, record albums or compact discs, and videos—either on YouTube or on artists/bands' MySpace or other Web sites. Which of these media outlets do you think most effectively conveys the messages intended by contemporary recording artists, and why? Which source do you think trivializes the music, turning it into a popular product without redeeming social relevance? What are the advantages and disadvantages of each pop-music source?

Internet Activities

1. Visit the Web sites of some diverse musicians (possible options are available on the *Common Culture* Web site). Write an essay describing these sites. What features do these Web sites offer? What differences or similarities can you note in the presentations of the different musical genres? How would you account for these differences or similarities? For instance, is there anything offered on a Web site devoted to a rock group that isn't available on a jazz Web site? Are the Web site's features indicative of the genre in any way; that is, do the form, appearance, or layout of the site mirror the musical genre it presents?

2. With the advent of various forms of media on the Web, such as streaming radio broadcasts and YouTube videos, music has a new forum to reach an immediate, worldwide audience. Explore some sites that offer music from across the country and the world (options are available at the *Common Culture* Web site). Once you have sampled a diverse selection of music, write an essay categorizing and/or describing your findings. How is the availability of music on the Web changing how listeners access music and what they listen to? What type of music is available? Are any musical types represented more heavily than others? Are any music genres woefully lacking, in your opinion? How would you account for this representation (or lack thereof)?

Reading Images

Write an essay in which you compare and contrast the images of the two popular musicians, Tupac Shakur and Amy Winehouse, as illustrated on pages C1-3 and C1-4 in the color section of this book. In this type of essay, you want to spend some time describing each image, so that the reader has a sense of the key visual features of each. Next, you might explore the ways in which the superficial appearances of both illustrations are similar or different (depending on your "reading" of the pictures, following the directions toward the end of Chapter 1). Finally, you will want to show how the images' other elements (coloration, composition, text, and so forth, also as described in Chapter 1 of this book) work in similar or different ways to put forth the images' messages, which may be subtly implied or blatantly "in your face."

The problem with this kind of essay is one of organization. Since a comparison/contrast essay by its nature involves looking at both similarities and differences, make sure that you structure your paper so that you don't have to jump back and forth too much from issue to issue, point to point. While many writers, when writing comparison/contrast pieces, sometimes favor this approach, you might want to experiment with discussing *all* the elements of the Tupac image and *then* going on to the Winehouse, pointing out all its areas of likeness and dissimilarity. Ideally, your paper will flow smoothly and progress logically, while still covering all elements of likeness and dissimilarity.

Barbie and Ken
Branding
Photographer: Aaron
Goodman

"Conversion Barbie," by
Kimmy McCann

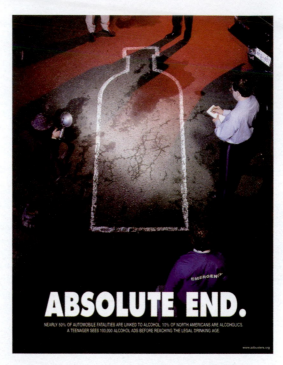

"Absolute End," by Adbusters Media Foundation

"TV Buddha Reincarnated," by Nam June Paik
Carl Solway Gallery, Cincinnati, Ohio. Photographers: Tom Allison
and Chris Gomien

Amy Winehouse
Corbis/Outline

Tupac Shakur
Getty Images/Time Life Pictures

Still photo from the film, *Johnny Mnemonic*
Picture Desk, Inc./The Kobal Collection

Brandi Chastain in her sports bra, by Reuters/Mike Blake;
Corbis/Reuters America LLC

"Knocked Up," 2007. Katherine Heigl and Seth
Rogen. Directed by Judd Apatow.
Suzanne Hanover/Universal; Picture Desk, Inc./Kobal
Collection

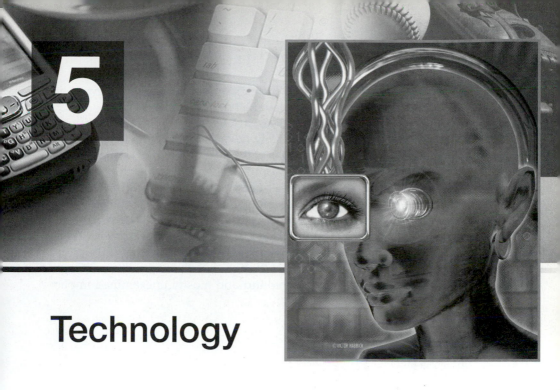

5

Technology

The image above seems to be clearly drawn from the realm of cyborgs and science fiction. After all, our eyeballs are not and could never be attached to a set of wires, or our eye sockets replaced with cybernetic implants. Or could they be? Although this computer-generated image is still a fiction, at least one real-life experiment comes pretty close to it. Steve Mann, a professor of electrical engineering at the University of Toronto, has designed a device called the EyeTap, a very high-tech set of computerized eyeglasses that cause the eye to function as if it were a digital camera. This eye/camera feeds images back into a computer, which can then process the images and can actually alter what the user sees (http://www.eyetap.org). Mann has also designed other kinds of wearable computers, devices that allow humans to change how they interact with their environments and to live in a computer-mediated reality.

The cyborg image—and even the EyeTap system—may both seem extreme, but how far are they really from other technologies that we use every day to enhance our lives and mediate our interactions with the world? Just thinking of our sense of sight, the technologies we commonly use range from simple eyeglasses and sunglasses to contact lenses and LASIK surgery. A wearable computer like the EyeTap is perhaps just the next logical step, one that harnesses the power of the computer to augment and alter the capabilities of the human eye. And why wouldn't a cybernetic implant be the next step after that?

But even if you never wear an EyeTap or have a computer implanted in your eye, you probably have a lot of experience with technologies that shape your everyday activities and augment your capabilities. For example, communications technologies like the Internet, instant messaging, and cell phones enable you to interact in an inexpensive and immediate way with people who are physically distant from you; video games let you experience unusual sorts of situations, challenges, and puzzles; and, of course, computers affect almost every aspect of our lives. Technologies like these are extremely influential because they're so common. Indeed, like the other subjects in *Common Culture*, technology exerts a profound and mostly unexamined impact on our lives.

Technology, Individuals, and Communities

Breaking Down Borders: How Technology Transforms the Private and Public Realms

ROBERT SAMUELS

One important premise of Common Culture *is that the culture all around us is worthy of investigation. Indeed, we believe that paying attention to the activities we are involved in every day is particularly important because these activities are highly likely to influence who we are, what we do, and what we value. Robert Samuels, a lecturer in the Writing Programs at UCLA, takes precisely this approach in the article that follows. Samuels reports on a mundane, everyday sort of event: a trip to his local Borders café. But in describing and analyzing what he sees at the café, he is able to draw conclusions about larger changes and challenges in our culture. Specifically, Samuels focuses his attention on the different technologies used by people at the Café, and he analyzes how the use of technologies blurs the borders between public and private and between work and play.*

*Samuels' article begins our chapter on technology, and the ideas he introduces here are taken up by the next two readings as well. So, **before you read**, make a list of the technologies you use on a regular basis, particularly those associated with media, communication, and culture: cell phone, computer, MP3 player, TV, VCR, DVD player, remote control, and other technologies like these. How do you think the technologies you regularly use have influenced the way you live your life? What would your everyday life be like without these technologies?*

It's a Tuesday morning and I'm walking through the Borders Café 1 just south of the UCLA campus in Westwood, CA. My plan is to find a table, drink my coffee, and read some of the novel that I just bought in the bookstore section. As I head for one of the few empty chairs, I pass by a man sitting at a table, the sports section of the *L.A. Times* spread out in front of him, a cup of coffee and a blueberry muffin to one side, his cell phone close at hand on the other side. He's wearing a t-shirt and shorts, but he might as well be in pajamas and slippers; it's as if he's in his own kitchen, reading his paper and having his breakfast, just following his morning routine.

I move past breakfast-man and notice a twenty-something 2 woman sitting in one of the five or six comfy upholstered chairs that Borders provides its customers. She's curled up cozily in the chair with one foot stretched out and resting on a matching upholstered footstool. Actually, the foot isn't resting; it's wagging back and forth in time, I assume, to the music that's coming through the headphones attached to her ears and her iPod. Keeping time to the music, she taps her yellow highlighter pen against the textbook that she's ostensibly reading. As I watch, she begins to hum out loud—it sounds like a wildly out-of-tune version of "Dancing Queen"—and then she abruptly looks up and stops humming, a bit startled, remembering that she's in Borders and not in her living room.

I sit at my own table with my coffee and novel, but I don't get past 3 the first page before I'm distracted by a woman at the table to my left who's talking on her cell phone. I see that she's also got her laptop computer open on the table and a magazine on her lap, but it's her phone conversation that's getting all of her attention—and, of course, the attention of everyone around her. We learn that she's terribly sorry but she has to cancel her job interview that Friday because of a doctor's appointment; our dismay is quickly alleviated when, in her next call, she tells a friend that, yes, the trip to Las Vegas that weekend is back on. The café, it seems, is her personal office.

Each of these people seems to have carved a little semi-private, 4 personalized space out of the larger public, commercial space of Borders Café. As people come and go, these spaces change, so that a time-lapse video of Borders Café would have to show it as not just one space but rather as an aggregate of small, shifting living rooms, kitchens, and offices (no bedrooms—yet!). And of course it's not just Borders; this kind of activity goes on at bookstores and coffee shops across the country. These new commercial public squares have become shared spaces that are neither private nor public. In fact, they compel us to redefine what private and public mean. The cell phone woman, for example, seems to have no problem sharing her Las Vegas plans with everyone sitting around her. But then I look around again and notice that I'm one of the few people who can actually hear her. Most of the other people here have headphones on and they're listening to their own iPods or MP3 players, perhaps precisely in order to avoid having to listen to conversations that should be private in the first place.

What I see at Borders convinces me that there are new rules for 5 how to act in public places and for how to socialize with and around one another. It's clear, as well, that none of these changes would have occurred without new technologies helping to break down borders. For instance, the telephone used to be firmly located in the private realm, physically attached to the kitchen wall or set on a desk in an office. Now, however, cell phones allow for a high level of mobility and access, and thus they help us transform any public place into a setting for a private conversation. The laptop, too, has not only transformed the desktop computer, but has also reinvented the desktop itself as any table or flat surface. Indeed, your very own lap becomes a desktop of sorts when you put your laptop computer on it.

With wireless technology, laptops and cell phones not only help   6
us cross back and forth between the public and the private, but they also function to undermine the distinction between work and play. For instance, people often jump quickly from doing work on their computers to emailing their friends and playing video games. Likewise, cell phones can combine work functions and play functions, incorporating games as well as digital cameras, video, and, of course, sound clips for ring tones. Some critics of new communication technologies argue that cell phones, laptops, iPods, and the other devices we take with us throughout our day encourage a high level of multitasking and prevent us from concentrating on any single activity. Thus, they argue, people not only become more superficial, but the constant switching between   **361**
work and leisure activities creates a fragmented sense of self and gives everyone a bad case of attention deficit disorder.

However, another way of looking at these new technologies is to   7
see how they allow people to re-center their sense of self by creating what can be called "personal culture." In other words, instead of seeing culture as a social and public activity, like going to a concert hall, devices like iPods and laptops allow people to take culture with them wherever they go. More importantly, instead of having to let the radio station tell them what to listen to or the newspaper limit their choice of news sources, people are able to personalize their own media and decide on their own what culture they want to consume.

Personal culture derives much of its power from the fact that   8
many of the new media devices are highly immersive: people on cell phones and laptops can become so involved in their own mediated worlds that they forget where they actually are and what they are supposed to be doing. Some states have laws now against driving while talking on a cell phone, but in addition to the physical danger there also may be a social cost. After all, we are social beings who live in public worlds, and therefore we cannot simply forget that other people exist. As I look around me at the people who have temporarily transformed Borders Café into a set of small personal spaces, I realize that although we're all together here there's very little chance that we'll interact with one another. Most of us are plugged in to technologies

that, while allowing us to personalize our environment, also effectively isolate us from our neighbors.

But is there really anything wrong with that? We adapt to our new 9 technologies and to the new spaces these technologies create; we adapt, in fact, by using more technologies. To tune out the cell phones, we put on our headphones. There seems to be no way of escaping from a technologically mediated environment, even in a place devoted to selling those old-fashioned, low-tech items called books. But, in Borders, at least, on this sunny Tuesday morning, we seem to be coping well enough even as the borders all around us are shifting and transforming.

Examining the Text

1. Why do you think Samuels begins his article with the detailed descriptions of three people he sees at Borders Café? What do you learn from these descriptions? How does this opening strategy help Samuels introduce his argument?
2. What does Samuels mean by "personal culture"? According to Samuels, how do technologies help us create "personal culture"?
3. Reread the last two paragraphs of the article. What do you think is Samuels' opinion of technology's influence on our culture?
4. *Thinking rhetorically:* Who do you think are the target readers of Samuels' article? And what do you see as its overall purpose? Point to specific features of the article that help you determine its audience and purpose.

For Group Discussion

Samuels discusses two different borders in this article: the border between public and private, and the border between work and play. In your group, choose one of these borders, and make a list of all the technologies that contribute to breaking down this border. You can begin with the technologies that Samuels himself describes; for instance, he discusses how the cell phone helps to break down the border between public and private as well as the border between work and play. Be sure to continue your list with examples of other technologies. Then list any technologies that you think help to maintain or increase the border. As a group, try to come to some general conclusions about the role of technology in the particular border area you're discussing.

Writing Suggestion

Samuels acts as an amateur anthropologist in this essay in the sense that he goes to a particular place, observes how people act there, and records and analyzes his observations in an article. Your assignment is to do something similar. Choose a place where people congregate: a coffee shop, a dorm lounge, an outdoor park or playground, a living room. Ideally the place you choose will be somewhere where you can sit and observe and take notes without being too distracted and without distracting others. Spend an hour or two at the place, watching to see what technologies people use and how the people interact with each other. Then write an essay modeled after Samuels' article. Begin the essay with a couple of detailed descriptions of specific people or activities you observed. In the body of the essay, discuss and analyze the ways that you saw technologies influence people's interactions. You might want to cite Samuels' article in your essay, perhaps in order to argue for or against the conclusions he draws.

The Judgment of Thamus

NEIL POSTMAN

If you've read Gerald Erion's article in Chapter 3, then you're already familiar with Neil Postman, the author of the following article. Erion's title—"Amusing Ourselves to Death with Television News"—is a direct reference to Postman's classic Amusing Ourselves to Death *(1985). In that book, Postman, who was a professor of "media ecology" at New York University, outlines the detrimental effects of television, on children as well as adults. Erion uses Postman's analysis to gain insight into the particular criticisms of television offered by Jon Stewart on* The Daily Show.

*The article that follows comes from one of Postman's later books—*Technopoly *(1992)—in which he extends his critique beyond the television screen to look more broadly at how technology influences our society. Although Postman was accused of being a technophobe, his argument here is more balanced: "Every technology is both a burden and a blessing; not either-or but this-and-that." Moreover, Postman believes that technological change is "ecological" in the sense that "One significant change generates total change." For Postman, the stakes are high when a new technology is introduced into a culture, and it is important that we think critically about technology if we are to live well with it.*

One reason we chose this article for Common Culture *is that we admire Postman's style of writing; we think that he crafted some particularly delightful phrases and sentences in this article.* As you read, *underline any segments of Postman's writing that you find especially pleasing to your stylistic sensibilities.*

You will find in Plato's *Phaedrus* a story about Thamus, the king of 1
a great city of Upper Egypt. For people such as ourselves, who are inclined (in Thoreau's phrase) to be tools of our tools, few legends are more instructive than his. The story, as Socrates tells it to his friend Phaedrus, unfolds in the following way: Thamus once entertained the god Theuth, who was the inventor of many things, including numbers,

calculation, geometry, astronomy, and writing. Theuth exhibited his inventions to King Thamus, claiming that they should be made widely known and available to Egyptians. Socrates continues:

> Thamus inquired into the use of each of them, and as Theuth went through them expressed approval or disapproval, according as he judged Theuth's claims to be well or ill founded. It would take too long to go through all that Thamus is reported to have said for and against each of Theuth's inventions. But when it came to writing, Theuth declared, "Here is an accomplishment, my lord the King, which will improve both the wisdom and the memory of the Egyptians. I have discovered a sure receipt for memory and wisdom." To this, Thamus replied, "Theuth, my paragon of inventors, the discoverer of an art is not the best judge of the good or harm which will accrue to those who practice it. So it is in this; you, who are the father of writing, have out of fondness for your off-spring attributed to it quite the opposite of its real function. Those who acquire it will cease to exercise their memory and become forgetful; they will rely on writing to bring things to their remembrance by external signs instead of by their own internal resources. What you have discovered is a receipt for recollection, not for memory. And as for wisdom, your pupils will have the reputation for it without the reality: they will receive a quantity of information without proper instruction, and in consequence be thought very knowledgeable when they are for the most part quite ignorant. And because they are filled with the conceit of wisdom instead of real wisdom they will be a burden to society."[1]

364

I begin my book with this legend because in Thamus' response 2 there are several sound principles from which we may begin to learn how to think with wise circumspection about a technological society. In fact, there is even one error in the judgment of Thamus, from which we may also learn something of importance. The error is not in his claim that writing will damage memory and create false wisdom. It is demonstrable that writing has had such an effect. Thamus' error is in his believing that writing will be a burden to society and *nothing but a burden*. For all his wisdom, he fails to imagine what writing's benefits might be, which, as we know, have been considerable. We may learn from this that it is a mistake to suppose that any technological innovation has a one-sided effect. Every technology is both a burden and a blessing; not either-or, but this-and-that.

Nothing could be more obvious, of course, especially to those 3 who have given more than two minutes of thought to the matter. Nonetheless, we are currently surrounded by throngs of zealous Theuths, one-eyed prophets who see only what new technologies can do and are incapable of imagining what they will *undo*. We might call such people Technophiles. They gaze on technology as a lover does on

his beloved, seeing it as without blemish and entertaining no appre-
hension for the future. They are therefore dangerous and are to be
approached cautiously. On the other hand, some one-eyed prophets,
such as I (or so I am accused), are inclined to speak only of burdens (in
the manner of Thamus) and are silent about the opportunities that new
technologies make possible. The Technophiles must speak for themselves, and do so all over the place. My defense is that a dissenting
voice is sometimes needed to moderate the din made by the enthusiastic multitudes. If one is to err, it is better to err on the side of Thamusian
skepticism. But it is an error nonetheless. And I might note that, with
the exception of his judgment on writing, Thamus does not repeat this
error. You might notice on rereading the legend that he gives arguments *for* and *against* each of Theuth's inventions. For it is inescapable
that every culture must negotiate with technology, whether it does so
intelligently or not. A bargain is struck in which technology giveth and
technology taketh away. The wise know this well, and are rarely
impressed by dramatic technological changes, and never overjoyed.
Here, for example, is Freud on the matter, from his doleful *Civilization
and Its Discontents*:

> One would like to ask: is there, then, no positive gain in pleasure, no
> unequivocal increase in my feeling of happiness, if I can, as often as I
> please, hear the voice of a child of mine who is living hundreds of miles
> away or if I can learn in the shortest possible time after a friend has
> reached his destination that he has come through the long and difficult
> voyage unharmed? Does it mean nothing that medicine has succeeded in
> enormously reducing infant mortality and the danger of infection for
> women in childbirth, and, indeed, in considerably lengthening the aver-
> age life of a civilized man?

Freud knew full well that technical and scientific advances are not to be   4
taken lightly, which is why he begins this passage by acknowledging
them. But he ends it by reminding us of what they have undone:

> If there had been no railway to conquer distances, my child would never
> have left his native town and I should need no telephone to hear his
> voice; if travelling across the ocean by ship had not been introduced, my
> friend would not have embarked on his sea-voyage and I should not
> need a cable to relieve my anxiety about him. What is the use of reducing
> infantile mortality when it is precisely that reduction which imposes the
> greatest restraint on us in the begetting of children, so that, taken all
> round, we nevertheless rear no more children than in the days before the
> reign of hygiene, while at the same time we have created difficult condi-
> tions for our sexual life in marriage. .... And, finally, what good to us is a

long life if it is difficult and barren of joys, and if it is so full of misery that we can only welcome death as a deliverer?[2]

In tabulating the cost of technological progress, Freud takes a   5
rather depressing line, that of a man who agrees with Thoreau's remark that our inventions are but improved means to an unimproved end. The Technophile would surely answer Freud by saying that life has always been barren of joys and full of misery but that the telephone, ocean liners, and especially the reign of hygiene have not only lengthened life but made it a more agreeable proposition. That is certainly an argument I would make (thus proving I am no one-eyed Technophobe), but it is not necessary at this point to pursue it. I have brought Freud into the conversation only to show that a wise man—even one of such a woeful countenance—must begin his critique of technology by acknowledging its successes. Had King Thamus been as wise as reputed, he would not have forgotten to include in his judgment a prophecy about the powers that writing would enlarge. There is a calculus of technological change that requires a measure of evenhandedness.

So much for Thamus' error of omission. There is another omission   6
worthy of note, but it is no error. Thamus simply takes for granted—and therefore does not feel it necessary to say—that writing is not a neutral technology whose good or harm depends on the uses made of it. He knows that the uses made of any technology are largely determined by the structure of the technology itself—that is, that its functions follow from its form. This is why Thamus is concerned not with *what* people will write; he is concerned *that* people will write. It is absurd to imagine, Thamus advising, in the manner of today's standard-brand Technophiles, that, if only writing would be used for the production of certain kinds of texts and not others (let us say, for dramatic literature but not for history or philosophy), its disruptions could be minimized. He would regard such counsel as extreme naïveté. He would allow, I imagine, that a technology may be barred entry to a culture. But we may learn from Thamus the following: once a technology is admitted, it plays out its hand; it does what it is designed to do. Our task is to understand what that design is—that is to say, when we admit a new technology to the culture, we must do so with our eyes wide open.

All of this we may infer from Thamus' silence. But we may learn   7
even more from what he does say than from what he doesn't. He points out, for example, that writing will change what is meant by the words "memory" and "wisdom." He fears that memory will be confused with what he disdainfully calls "recollection," and he worries that wisdom will become indistinguishable from mere knowledge. This judgment we must take to heart, for it is a certainty that radical technologies

create new definitions of old terms, and that this process takes place without our being fully conscious of it. Thus, it is insidious and dangerous, quite different from the process whereby new technologies introduce new terms to the language. In our own time, we have consciously added to our language thousands of new words and phrases having to do with new technologies—"VCR," "binary digit," "software," "front-wheel drive," "window of opportunity," "Walkman," etc. We are not taken by surprise at this. New things require new words. But new things also modify old words, words that have deep-rooted meanings. The telegraph and the penny press changed what we once meant by "information." Television changes what we once meant by the terms "political debate," "news," and "public opinion." The computer changes "information" once again. Writing changed what we once meant by "truth" and "law"; printing changed them again, and now television and the computer change them once more. Such changes occur quickly, surely, and, in a sense, silently. Lexicographers hold no plebiscites on the matter. No manuals are written to explain what is happening, and the schools are oblivious to it. The old words still look the same, are still used in the same kinds of sentences. But they do not have the same meanings; in some cases, they have opposite meanings. And this is what Thamus wishes to teach us—that technology imperiously commandeers our most important terminology. It redefines "freedom," "truth," "intelligence," "fact," "wisdom," "memory," "history"—all the words we live by. And it does not pause to tell us. And we do not pause to ask.

367

This fact about technological change requires some elaboration, 8 and I will return to the matter in a later chapter. Here, there are several more principles to be mined from the judgment of Thamus that require mentioning because they presage all I will write about. For instance, Thamus warns that the pupils of Theuth will develop an undeserved reputation for wisdom. He means to say that those who cultivate competence in the use of a new technology become an elite group that are granted undeserved authority and prestige by those who have no such competence. There are different ways of expressing the interesting implications of this fact. Harold Innis, the father of modern communication studies, repeatedly spoke of the "knowledge monopolies" created by important technologies. He meant precisely what Thamus had in mind: those who have control over the workings of a particular technology accumulate power and inevitably form a kind of conspiracy against those who have no access to the specialized knowledge made available by the technology. In his book, *The Bias of Communication*, Innis provides many historical examples of how a new technology "busted up" a traditional knowledge monopoly and created a new one presided over by a different group. Another way of saying this is that the benefits and deficits of a new technology are not distributed equally. There are, as it were, winners and losers. It is both puzzling and poignant that on many occasions the losers, out of ignorance, have actually cheered the winners, and some still do.

Let us take as an example the case of television. In the United States, where television has taken hold more deeply than anywhere else, many people find it a blessing, not least those who have achieved high-paying, gratifying careers in television as executives, technicians, newscasters, and entertainers. It should surprise no one that such people, forming as they do a new knowledge monopoly, should cheer themselves and defend and promote television technology. On the other hand and in the long run, television may bring a gradual end to the careers of schoolteachers since school was an invention of the printing press and must stand or fall on the issue of how much importance the printed word has. For four hundred years, schoolteachers have been part of the knowledge monopoly created by printing, and they are now witnessing the breakup of that monopoly. It appears as if they can do little to prevent that breakup, but surely there is something perverse about schoolteachers being enthusiastic about what is happening. Such enthusiasm always calls to my mind an image of some turn-of-the-century blacksmith who not only sings the praises of the automobile but also believes that his business will be enhanced by it. We know now that his business was not enhanced by it; it was rendered obsolete by it, as perhaps the clearheaded blacksmiths knew. What could they have done? Weep, if nothing else. 9

We have a similar situation in the development and spread of computer technology, for here too there are winners and losers. There can be no disputing that the computer has increased the power of large-scale organizations like the armed forces or airline companies or banks or tax-collecting agencies. And it is equally clear that the computer is now indispensable to high-level researchers in physics and other natural sciences. But to what extent has computer technology been an advantage to the masses of people? To steelworkers, vegetable-store owners, teachers, garage mechanics, musicians, bricklayers, dentists, and most of the rest into whose lives the computer now intrudes? Their private matters have been made more accessible to powerful institutions. They are more easily tracked and controlled; are subjected to more examinations; are increasingly mystified by the decisions made about them; are often reduced to mere numerical objects. They are inundated by junk mail. They are easy targets for advertising agencies and political organizations. The schools teach their children to operate computerized systems instead of teaching things that are more valuable to children. In a word, almost nothing that they need happens to the losers. Which is why they are losers. 10

It is to be expected that the winners will encourage the losers to   11
be enthusiastic about computer technology. That is the way of winners,
and so they sometimes tell the losers that with personal computers the
average person can balance a checkbook more neatly, keep better track
of recipes, and make more logical shopping lists. They also tell them
that their lives will be conducted more efficiently. But discreetly they
neglect to say from whose point of view the efficiency is warranted or
what might be its costs. Should the losers grow skeptical, the winners
dazzle them with the wondrous feats of computers, almost all of which
have only marginal relevance to the quality of the losers' lives but
which are nonetheless impressive. Eventually, the losers succumb, in
part because they believe, as Thamus prophesied, that the specialized
knowledge of the masters of a new technology is a form of wisdom.
The masters come to believe this as well, as Thamus also prophesied.
The result is that certain questions do not arise. For example, to whom
will the technology give greater power and freedom? And whose
power and freedom will be reduced by it?

I have perhaps made all of this sound like a well-planned con-   12
spiracy, as if the winners know all too well what is being won and what
lost. But this is not quite how it happens. For one thing, in cultures that
have a democratic ethos, relatively weak traditions, and a high recep-
tivity to new technologies, everyone is inclined to be enthusiastic about
technological change, believing that its benefits will eventually spread
evenly among the entire population. Especially in the United States,
where the lust for what is new has no bounds, do we find this childlike
conviction most widely held. Indeed, in America, social change of any
kind is rarely seen as resulting in winners and losers, a condition that
stems in part from Americans' much-documented optimism. As for
change brought on by technology, this native optimism is exploited by
entrepreneurs, who work hard to infuse the population with a unity of
improbable hope, for they know that it is economically unwise to
reveal the price to be paid for technological change. One might say,
then, that, if there is a conspiracy of any kind, it is that of a culture con-
spiring against itself.

In addition to this, and more important, it is not always clear, at   13
least in the early stages of a technology's intrusion into a culture, who
will gain most by it and who will lose most. This is because the changes
wrought by technology are subtle, if not downright mysterious, one
might even say wildly unpredictable. Among the most unpredictable
are those that might be labeled ideological. This is the sort of change
Thamus had in mind when he warned that writers will come to rely on
external signs instead of their own internal resources, and that they
will receive quantities of information without proper instruction. He
meant that new technologies change what we mean by "knowing" and

369

"truth"; they alter those deeply embedded habits of thought which give to a culture its sense of what the world is like—a sense of what is the natural order of things, of what is reasonable, of what is necessary, of what is inevitable, of what is real. Since such changes are expressed in changed meanings of old words, I will hold off until later discussing the massive ideological transformation now occurring in the United States. Here, I should like to give only one example of how technology creates new conceptions of what is real and, in the process, undermines older conceptions. I refer to the seemingly harmless practice of assigning marks or grades to the answers students give on examinations. This procedure seems so natural to most of us that we are hardly aware of its significance. We may even find it difficult to imagine that the number or letter is a tool or, if you will, a technology; still less that, when we use such a technology to judge someone's behavior, we have done something peculiar. In point of fact, the first instance of grading students' papers occurred at Cambridge University in 1792 at the suggestion of a tutor named William Farish.[3] No one knows much about William Farish; not more than a handful have ever heard of him. And yet his idea that a quantitative value should be assigned to human thoughts was a major step toward constructing a mathematical concept of reality. If a number can be given to the quality of a thought, then a number can be given to the qualities of mercy, love, hate, beauty, creativity, intelligence, even sanity itself. When Galileo said that the language of nature is written in mathematics, he did not mean to include human feeling or accomplishment or insight. But most of us are now inclined to make these inclusions. Our psychologists, sociologists, and educators find it quite impossible to do their work without numbers. They believe that without numbers they cannot acquire or express authentic knowledge.

I shall not argue here that this is a stupid or dangerous idea, only 14 that it is peculiar. What is even more peculiar is that so many of us do not find the idea peculiar. To say that someone should be doing better work because he has an IQ of 134, or that someone is a 7.2 on a sensitivity scale, or that this man's essay on the rise of capitalism is an A— and that man's is a C+ would have sounded like gibberish to Galileo or Shakespeare or Thomas Jefferson. If it makes sense to us, that is because our minds have been conditioned by the technology of numbers so that we see the world differently than they did. Our understanding of what is real is different. Which is another way of saying that embedded in every tool is an ideological bias, a predisposition to construct the world as one thing rather than another, to value one thing over another, to amplify one sense or skill or attitude more loudly than another.

This is what Marshall McLuhan meant by his famous aphorism 15 "The medium is the message." This is what Marx meant when he said,

"Technology discloses man's mode of dealing with nature" and creates the "conditions of intercourse" by which we relate to each other. It is what Wittgenstein meant when, in referring to our most fundamental technology, he said that language is not merely a vehicle of thought but also the driver. And it is what Thamus wished the inventor Theuth to see. This is, in short, an ancient and persistent piece of wisdom, perhaps most simply expressed in the old adage that, to a man with a hammer, everything looks like a nail. Without being too literal, we may extend the truism: To a man with a pencil, everything looks like a list. To a man with a camera, everything looks like an image. To a man with a computer, everything looks like data. And to a man with a grade sheet, everything looks like a number.

But such prejudices are not always apparent at the start of a technology's journey, which is why no one can safely conspire to be a winner in technological change. Who would have imagined, for example, whose interests and what world-view would be ultimately advanced by the invention of the mechanical clock? The clock had its origin in the Benedictine monasteries of the twelfth and thirteenth centuries. The impetus behind the invention was to provide a more or less precise regularity to the routines of the monasteries, which required, among other things, seven periods of devotion during the course of the day. The bells of the monastery were to be rung to signal the canonical hours; the mechanical clock was the technology that could provide precision to these rituals of devotion. And indeed it did. But what the monks did not foresee was that the clock is a means not merely of keeping track of the hours but also of synchronizing and controlling the actions of men. And thus, by the middle of the fourteenth century, the clock had moved outside the walls of the monastery, and brought a new and precise regularity to the life of the workman and the merchant. 16

"The mechanical clock," as Lewis Mumford wrote, "made possible the idea of regular production, regular working hours and a standardized product." In short, without the clock, capitalism would have been quite impossible.[4] The paradox, the surprise, and the wonder are that the clock was invented by men who wanted to devote themselves more rigorously to God; it ended as the technology of greatest use to men who wished to devote themselves to the accumulation of money. In the eternal struggle between God and Mammon, the clock quite unpredictably favored the latter.

Unforeseen consequences stand in the way of all those who think they see clearly the direction in which a new technology will take us. Not even those who invent a technology can be assumed to be reliable prophets, as Thamus warned. Gutenberg, for example, was by all accounts a devout Catholic who would have been horrified to hear that accursed heretic Luther describe printing as "God's highest act of 17

371

grace, whereby the business of the Gospel is driven forward." Luther understood, as Gutenberg did not, that the mass-produced book, by placing the Word of God on every kitchen table, makes each Christian his own theologian—one might even say his own priest, or, better, from Luther's point of view, his own pope. In the struggle between unity and diversity of religious belief, the press favored the latter, and we can assume that this possibility never occurred to Gutenberg.

Thamus understood well the limitations of inventors in grasping 18 the social and psychological—that is, ideological—bias of their own inventions. We can imagine him addressing Gutenberg in the following way: "Gutenberg, my paragon of inventors, the discoverer of an art is not the best judge of the good or harm which will accrue to those who practice it. So it is in this; you, who are the father of printing, have out of fondness for your off-spring come to believe it will advance the cause of the Holy Roman See, whereas in fact it will sow discord among believers; it will damage the authenticity of your beloved Church and destroy its monopoly."

We can imagine that Thamus would also have pointed out to Gutenberg, as he did to Theuth, that the new invention would create a vast population of readers who "will receive a quantity of information

without proper instruction... [who will be] filled with the conceit of wisdom instead of real wisdom"; that reading, in other words, will compete with older forms of learning. This is yet another principle of technological change we may infer from the judgment of Thamus: new technologies compete with old ones—for time, for attention, for money, for prestige, but mostly for dominance of their world-view. This competition is implicit once we acknowledge that a medium contains an ideological bias. And it is a fierce competition, as only ideological competitions can be. It is not merely a matter of tool against tool—the alphabet attacking ideographic writing, the printing press attacking the illuminated manuscript, the photograph attacking the art of painting, television attacking the printed word. When media make war against each other, it is a case of world-views in collision.

In the United States, we can see such collisions everywhere—in 19 politics, in religion, in commerce—but we see them made most clearly in the schools, where two great technologies confront each other in uncompromising aspect for the control of students' minds. On the one hand, there is the world of the printed word with its emphasis on logic, sequence, history, exposition, objectivity, detachment, and discipline. On the other, there is the world of television with its emphasis on imagery, narrative, presentness, simultaneity, intimacy, immediate gratification, and quick emotional response. Children come to school having been deeply conditioned by the biases of television. There, they encounter the world of the printed word. A sort of psychic battle takes place, and there are many casualties—children who can't learn to read or won't, children who cannot organize their thought into logical structure even in a simple paragraph, children who cannot attend to lectures or oral explanations for more than a few minutes at a time. They are failures, but not because they are stupid. They are failures because there is a media war going on, and they are on the wrong side—at least for the moment. Who knows what schools will be like twenty-five years from now? Or fifty? In time, the type of student who is currently a failure may be considered a success. The type who is now successful may be regarded as a handicapped learner—slow to respond, far too detached, lacking in emotion, inadequate in creating mental pictures of reality. Consider: what Thamus called the "conceit of wisdom"—the unreal knowledge acquired through the written word—eventually became the pre-eminent form of knowledge valued by the schools. There is no reason to suppose that such a form of knowledge must always remain so highly valued.

20   To take another example: In introducing the personal computer to the classroom, we shall be breaking a four-hundred-year-old truce between the gregariousness and openness fostered by orality and the introspection and isolation fostered by the printed word. Orality stresses group learning, cooperation, and a sense of social responsibility, which is the context within which Thamus believed proper instruction and real knowledge must be communicated. Print stresses individualized learning, competition, and personal autonomy. Over four centuries, teachers, while emphasizing print, have allowed orality its place in the classroom, and have therefore achieved a kind of pedagogical peace between these two forms of learning, so that what is valuable in each can be maximized. Now comes the computer, carrying anew the banner of private learning and individual problem-solving. Will the widespread use of computers in the classroom defeat once and for all the claims of communal speech? Will the computer raise egocentrism to the status of a virtue?

21   These are the kinds of questions that technological change brings to mind when one grasps, as Thamus did, that technological competition ignites total war, which means it is not possible to contain the effects of a new technology to a limited sphere of human activity. If this metaphor puts the matter too brutally, we may try a gentler, kinder one: Technological change is neither additive nor subtractive. It is ecological. I mean "ecological" in the same sense as the word is used by environmental scientists. One significant change generates total change. If you remove the caterpillars from a given habitat, you are not left with the same environment minus caterpillars: you have a new environment, and you have reconstituted the conditions of survival; the same is true if you add caterpillars to an environment that has had

none. This is how the ecology of media works as well. A new technology does not add or subtract something. It changes everything. In the year 1500, fifty years after the printing press was invented, we did not have old Europe plus the printing press. We had a different Europe. After television, the United States was not America plus television; television gave a new coloration to every political campaign, to every home, to every school, to every church, to every industry. And that is why the competition among media is so fierce. Surrounding every technology are institutions whose organization—not to mention their reason for being—reflects the world-view promoted by the technology. Therefore, when an old technology is assaulted by a new one, institutions are threatened. When institutions are threatened, a culture finds itself in crisis. This is serious business, which is why we learn nothing when educators ask, Will students learn mathematics better by computers than by textbooks? Or when businessmen ask, Through which medium can we sell more products? Or when preachers ask, Can we reach more people through television than through radio? Or when politicians ask, How effective are messages sent through different media? Such questions have an immediate, practical value to those who ask them, but they are diversionary. They direct our attention away from the serious social, intellectual, and institutional crises that new media foster.

374

Perhaps an analogy here will help to underline the point. In speaking of the meaning of a poem, T. S. Eliot remarked that the chief use of the overt content of poetry is "to satisfy one habit of the reader, to keep his mind diverted and quiet, while the poem does its work upon him: much as the imaginary burglar is always provided with a bit of nice meat for the house-dog." In other words, in asking their practical questions, educators, entrepreneurs, preachers, and politicians are like the house-dog munching peacefully on the meat while the house is looted. Perhaps some of them know this and do not especially care. After all, a nice piece of meat, offered graciously, does take care of the problem of where the next meal will come from. But for the rest of us, it cannot be acceptable to have the house invaded without protest or at least awareness. 22

What we need to consider about the computer has nothing to do with its efficiency as a teaching tool. We need to know in what ways it is altering our conception of learning, and how, in conjunction with television, it undermines the old idea of school. Who cares how many boxes of cereal can be sold via television? We need to know if television changes our conception of reality, the relationship of the rich to the poor, the idea of happiness itself. A preacher who confines himself to considering how a medium can increase his audience will miss the significant question: In what sense do new media alter what is meant by religion, 23 by church, even by God? And if the politician cannot think beyond the next election, then *we* must wonder about what new media do to the idea of political organization and to the conception of citizenship.

To help us do this, we have the judgment of Thamus, who, in the way of legends, teaches us what Harold Innis, in his way, tried to. New technologies alter the structure of our interests: the things we think *about*. They alter the character of our symbols: the things we think *with*. And they alter the nature of community: the arena in which thoughts develop. As Thamus spoke to Innis across the centuries, it is essential that we listen to their conversation, join in it, revitalize it. For something has happened in America that is strange and dangerous, and there is only a dull and even stupid awareness of what it is—in part because it has no name. I call it Technopoly. 24

NOTES

[1]Plato, p. 96.

[2]Freud, pp. 38–39.

[3]This fact is documented in Keith Hoskin's "The Examination, Disciplinary Power and Rational Schooling," in *History of Education*, vol. VIII, no. 2 (1979), pp. 135–46. Professor Hoskin provides the following story about Farish: Farish was a professor of engineering at Cambridge and designed and installed a movable partition wall in his Cambridge home. The wall moved on pulleys between downstairs and upstairs. One night, while working late downstairs and feeling cold, Farish pulled down the partition. This is not much of a story, and history fails to disclose what happened next. All of which shows how little is known of William Farish.

[4]For a detailed exposition of Mumford's position on the impact of the mechanical clock, see his *Technics and Civilization*.

375

Examining the Text

1. What are the two errors made by Thamus that Postman notes in the beginning of the article? Why do you think Postman begins by drawing attention to Thamus' errors?

2. What do you think of Postman's argument in paragraphs 10-11 that "the masses of people" are "losers" in the development and spread of computer technology? Are any of the repercussions he lists at the end of paragraph 10 demonstrably false? Given the fact that this article was written more than fifteen years ago, do you think Postman's observations are more or less true today?

3. In what ways is the practice of assigning grades in school a kind of "technology"? In what ways is grading "ideological"? What reasons does Postman give in paragraphs 13-15 for objecting to this practice, and what do you think of his argument?

4. Postman argues in paragraphs 19-20 that the television and the personal computer collide and conflict with traditional models of education by encouraging

children to develop different skills and approaches than they typically learn in the classroom. What do you think of his claims? If they're true, then how do you think television and computers should be effectively integrated into the classroom, if at all?

5. *Thinking rhetorically:* Why do you think Postman begins with the anecdote about King Thamus and extends this anecdote throughout the article? What is the effect of the repeated references to Thamus, Theuth, and Plato? Do these references help to bolster Postman's argument? Do his references to Freud, Thoreau, Gutenberg, and other famous thinkers and scholars serve a similar function?

For Group Discussion

Choose a technology that everyone in the group agrees is either mostly a blessing or mostly a burden; you might think of technologies related to travel (e.g., bicycle, airplane), household tasks (e.g., vacuum cleaner, microwave), health (e.g., eyeglasses, x-ray), communication (e.g., radio, Internet). After you've chosen the specific technology, make a list of all its "burdens and blessings." Does Postman's belief in the two-sided impact of technology hold true with the technology you're discussing? What can you learn about this technology by looking at both its positive and negative effects?

Writing Suggestion

Postman argues that "technology imperiously commandeers our most important terminology. It redefines 'freedom,' truth,' 'intelligence,' 'fact,' 'wisdom,' 'memory,' 'history'—all the words we live by. And it does not pause to tell us. And we do not pause to ask." For this writing assignment, choose one of these terms, or another similarly important and broad term, and explore the ways in which technology has changed its definition.

Here are several prewriting activities that can help you begin this assignment:

- Make a list of all the different types of technology that may impact the definition of the term; consider how technologies related to communication, entertainment, medicine, travel, education, politics, and family life, for example, cause us to differently define the term you've chosen.
- Write about how you imagine the term was defined in the nineteenth century (or earlier) before the advent of many of the technologies that strongly impact our lives today.
- Think of the way your own understanding of this term has evolved during your life. Have any of the technologies that you use frequently caused you to think differently about this term?

After completing these prewriting activities, compose an essay with a thesis that states both how the term you've chosen is currently defined and how technologies have influenced this definition. Support your argument with specific examples, drawn from your prewriting activities.

Applications

1. Gaming

The Labor of Fun: How Video Games Blur the Boundaries of Work and Play

NICK YEE

A 2007 Harris Interactive survey found that the average eight- to twelve-year-old played thirteen hours of video games per week, and the average thirteen- to eighteen-year-old played fourteen hours of video games per week. Moreover, the survey found that the experience of playing wasn't entirely enjoyable: 23 percent of youth said they that have felt "addicted to video games"; 44 percent of youth also reported that their friends are addicted to games.

In the article that follows, Nick Yee explores the reasons teenagers as well as young adults spend so much time playing video games. Yee is particularly interested in massively multiplayer online role-playing games (MMORPGs), and in the problems that arise when players spend too much time "playing." Yee's article harkens back to the argument made by Robert Samuels earlier in this chapter, but here Yee provides a specific and detailed analysis of one way in which borders between work and play are being broken down by video games, and he speculates on the effect of this dissolution of borders.

Nick Yee has a Ph.D. from Stanford and is currently a research scientist at the Palo Alto Research Center (PARC), with his work focusing on online games and immersive virtual reality. This article originally appeared in Games and Culture, *an international quarterly journal that publishes theoretical and empirical research about games and culture within interactive media.*

Before you read *this article, think about your own video game habits. Do a quick tally of the amount of time you've spent playing video games, including arcade games, computer and console games, and online role-playing games. Has the time you've devoted to games increased or decreased over the years? What gratifications or rewards do video games provide you? What motivates you to play them as often (or as infrequently) as you do?*

There's a cultural premise that work and play are an inherent 1 dichotomy. When we talk about video games, it's easy to frame them as sites of play and entertainment. The staggering amount of work that's being done in these games is often gone unnoticed, and it's this work that I would like to foreground. Video games play important roles in the increasingly blurred intersections of our social, economic, and political spheres, and articulating those blurred boundaries in the microcosm of video games reveals larger trends in our digitally mediated world. In this case, articulating the blurring of work and play in video games reveals how they may soon become indistinguishable from each other.

Every day, millions of players log onto a genre of video games 2 known as massively multiplayer online role-playing games (MMORPGs). These games allow players to interact with each other and explore a world in real-time 3-D graphics. Every player is represented by a customizable character, and communication between players typically occurs over typed chat. Game play in MMORPGs is both complex and somewhat open ended. It is unfortunate that the metaphors of swords and dragon slaying obscure and distract us from the true nature of the work that is being done. To that end, an example that employs corporate metaphors will be used that sidesteps these distractions while at the same time reveals the analogous work of dragon slaying.

Pharmaceutical manufacturing is one of many possible career 3 choices in the game *Star Wars Galaxies*. Some other career choices include bioengineering, architecture, fashion design, and cooking. Third-party career planning tools are available for the undecided.[1] Pharmaceutical manufacturers create their products by combining raw resources. These raw resources, such as chemicals or minerals, must be located using geological surveying tools and harvested using installations bought from other players skilled in industrial architecture. Resource gathering is a time-consuming process that involves traveling and constant maintenance. Typically, pharmaceutical manufacturers rely on dedicated resource brokers instead. The attributes of the final product (i.e., duration vs. potency) depend on the attributes of the resources used; however, resources vary in quality, accessibility, and availability. Thus, manufacturers must decide which products make the most advantage of the resources available to them and must also take into account the demands of the market.

Raw resources are converted into subcomponents and final 4 products using factories[2] (also provided by player architects). Mass production introduces a constant supply-chain management problem, and manufacturers must ensure a steady supply of needed resources in the correct proportions. With final products in hand, manufacturers now face the most difficult problem—each other. In *Star Wars Galaxies*, everything that is bought or sold has to be bought or sold by another player. The game economy is entirely player driven. Manufacturers must decide how broad or narrow their product line should be, how to price and brand their products, where and how much to spend on advertising, whether to start a price war with competitors or form a cartel with them. Manufacturing pharmaceuticals is not an easy task. It takes about three to six weeks of normal game play to acquire the abilities and schematics to be competitive in the market, and the business operation thereafter requires daily time commitment.

5   In other words, players in *Star Wars Galaxies* operate a pharmaceutical manufacturing business for fun. The work in dragon slaying is equally complex and is in fact more stressful due to time constraints, frequent crises, and management issues related to coordinating twenty to thirty players over typed chat in real time (Yee, 2005). In both cases, players invest a great deal of time in their virtual careers. The average MMORPG player spends twenty-two hours a week playing the game (Yee, in press). And these are not only teenagers playing. The average MMORPG gamer is in fact twenty-six years old. About half of these players have a full-time job. Every day, many of them go to work and perform an assortment of clerical tasks, logistical planning, and management in their offices; then they come home and do those very same things in MMORPGs. Many players in fact characterize their game play as a second job: "It became a chore to play. I became defacto leader of a guild, and it was too much. I wanted to get away from real life and politics and social etiquette followed me in!" (twenty-year-old male player) and "I stopped playing because I just didn't want to commit to the crazy raid times (six+ hours in the evening'?)" (twenty-seven-year-old female player).

6   As these players point out, the game can become an obligation. One player put it more explicitly: "Was more like work then fun. One day got burnt out trying to get exp for level 55 and quit" (twenty-two-year-old male player).

7   The central irony of MMORPGs is that they are advertised as worlds to escape to after coming home from work, but they too make us work and burn us out. For some players, their game play might be more stressful and demanding than their actual jobs. And the most tragic irony is that MMORPG players pay game companies on a monthly basis (between $10 and $15) to work and get burned out.

8   Of course, the success of MMORPGs requires a minimization of burnouts. For these games to succeed, the player has to perform the

work without becomin g aware of its true nature. But this in fact is the purpose of all video games—to train a player to work harder while still enjoying it. And most games, including MMORPGs, employ elaborate designs that derive from principles in behavioral conditioning (Skinner, 1938). The timing and layering of reward mechanisms in video games train players to derive pleasure from the work that is being done. Video games condition us to work harder, faster, and more efficiently. In the same way that TiVO trains us to become better TV watchers (Andrejevic, 2002), video games train us to become more industrious game workers. Some players do eventually grasp the underlying nature of this digital treadmill: "The problem is that it goes from enjoyable to just work so gradually that unless you step back for a while and evaluate you do not even realize you're working" (twenty-one-year-old male player).

But the success of MMORPGs and video games in general 9 demonstrates how seductive and concealed the treadmill can be. And although I have singled out behavioral conditioning, it is clear that other game mechanics (i.e., social prestige, competition, etc.) also play an important role in this process. The point remains however that video games are inherently work platforms that train us to become bet-ter workers. And the work being performed in video games is increas-ingly similar to actual work in business corporations.

Some may argue that game play can never constitute actual work 10 because no real economic value is being generated, but as others have shown, virtual goods have real value (Castronova, 2002; Dibbell, 2003). In fact, there are companies such as IGE whose business model revolves around accumulating and selling virtual currency.[3] Because of the amount of work involved to advance a character's abilities, there are also companies, like TopGameSeller,[4] that offer character leveling services—"Our primary work center is located in Shanghai, China. It's a 45,000 sq. ft. building that houses over 400 of our employees.... We assign two or three expert players to your character to do the leveling" (http://www.topgameseller.com/faq.htm). For these employees of IGE and TopGameSeller, playing and working have become the same thing.

It is ironic that computers were made to work for us, but video 11 games have come to demand that we work for them. What's clear is that video games are blurring the boundaries between work and play very rapidly. Beck and Wade (2004) suggested that the gamer genera-tion is acquiring skills and developing traits that will require busi-nesses to adapt to them, but I believe a much larger intersection is occurring. Video games are changing the nature of both work and play. It is not so much that businesses will need to adapt to gamers as much as that work and play are starting to become indistinguishable from each other. And the following quote from a thirty-year-old registered nurse who plays EverQuest with her husband leaves us with a haunting premonition of the consequences of this blurring:

> We spend hours—HOURS—every SINGLE day playing this damn game. My fingers wake me, aching, in the middle of the night. I have headaches from the countless hours I spend staring at the screen. I hate this game, but I can't stop playing. Quitting smoking was NEVER this hard.

Ultimately, the blurring of work and play begs the question—what does *fun* really mean?   12

NOTES

[1] For example, see http://swgcb.yogn.net/swg-cb.php.
[2] Factories in Star Wars Galaxies do not produce goods instantaneously. Instead, factory runs take anywhere from one to four hours.
[3] See http://www.ige.com.
[4] See http://www.topgameseller.com.

REFERENCES

Andrejevic. M. (2002). The work of being watched: Interactive media and the exploitation of self-disclosure. *Critical Studies in Media Communication, 19*, 230-248.

Beck, J., & Wade, M. (2004). *Got game: How the gamer generation is reshaping business forever.* Cambridge, MA: Harvard Business School Press.

Castronova, E. (2002). *Virtual words: A first-hand account of market and society on the cyberian frontier.* Retrieved May 15, 2005, from http://ssrn.com/abstract=294828

Dibbell, J. (2003). The unreal estate boom, *Wired,11* (I). Retrieved May 15, 2005. from http://www.wired.com/wired/archive/11.01/gaming.html

Skinner, B. F. (1938). *The behavior of organisms.* New York: Appleton-Century-Crofts.

Yee, N. (2005). *Dragon-slaying 101.* Retrieved May 15, 2005, from http://www.nickyee.com/daedalus/archives/000859.php

Yee, N. (in press). The demographics, motivations, and derived experiences of users of massively multiuser online graphical environments. *PRESENCE: Teleoperators and Virtual Environments.*

Examining the Text

1. What kinds of work activities take place in the extended example Yee provides in paragraphs 3 and 4, in which he describes the career choice of pharmaceutical manufacturing in the game Star Wars Galaxies? Why do you think players would choose this kind of virtual career if it involves so much "work"?

2. In paragraph 8, Yee states that the purpose of all video games is "to train a player to work harder while still enjoying it." Thinking of the video games that you know about and/or play, does this seem like a realistic description to you? According to Yee, how do principles from behavioral conditioning help video games achieve this purpose?

3. Why do you think Yee ends his article with a question? And with the particular question he asks—"what does *fun* really mean?"—what rhetorical goal do you think he's attempting to achieve? In other words, how would defining "fun" help advance an understanding of the ways that MMORPGs operate?

4. *Thinking rhetorically:* At several points in the article, Yee provides quotations from actual anonymous MMORPG players who have experienced game playing as work. What function do these quotations serve? Would the article have been as effective without them? What other kinds of evidence does Yee incorporate to advance his argument?

For Group Discussion

Yee points to several instances of irony in his article:

- "The central irony of MMORPGs is that they are advertised as worlds to escape to after coming home from work, but they too make us work and burn us out."
- "And the most tragic irony is that MMORPG players pay game companies on a monthly basis (between $10 and $15) to work and get burned out."
- "It is ironic that computers were made to work for us, but video games have come to demand that we work for them."

Although the dictionary definition of irony is "the use of words to convey a meaning that is the opposite of its literal meaning," it's more generally understood (*á la* Alanis Morissette) to indicate a certain kind of incongruity or discord between what actually happens and what one intends or expects to happen.

In a small group, discuss what you think of the ironies that Yee observes: escape that becomes tedious and tiresome, work that you have to pay for, and computers that you work for. Are these indeed ironic? Do they characterize your video game playing or that of people you know?

Writing Suggestion

Yee focuses his analysis on MMORPGs and the way they induce players to work and get players to be better workers. For this writing assignment, see if you can observe a similar breakdown of the work/play distinction in another arena.

You can choose a leisure activity that we typically think of as "play"—sports, music, TV—and indicate the ways in which this activity can sometimes be more like "work." Or you can start with an activity that we typically think of as "work" and explore how it can become more like "play." In either case, discuss how work and play are defined in this activity. You might consider drawing on interviews with actual participants, as Yee does, in order to explore the topic and provide evidence for assertions you make.

Good Video Games, the Human Mind, and Good Learning

JAMES PAUL GEE

Despite—or perhaps because of—the many hours that people spend playing video games, the media seems mostly to report on it as a negative phenomenon. The content of video games comes under fire for violence, profanity, sexual content, and other offenses; the connection between violent acts and violence in video games was subject to particular scrutiny after the Columbine High School shootings because the two killers frequently played games such as Doom *and* Wolfenstein 3D. *In addition to criticism of the content of video games, many social commentators express concern over the amount of time kids spend gaming; wouldn't that time be better spent, these critics ask, playing outdoors, socializing with friends, exercising creativity, and learning new things?*

The article that follows doesn't directly address these criticisms of video games, but it does provide an almost completely positive view that isn't often represented in mainstream media. What good can come of playing video games? James Paul Gee offers us a two-part answer to this question. First, the way video games work is analogous to the way the human mind works, and so studying video games can give us insight into our cognitive and intellectual processes. Second, video games offer principles for learning; because they engage young people in long, complex, and difficult tasks, educators can learn from video games how to teach effectively.

Gee is a scholar of education and linguistics whose most recent research has focused on video games. He has two recent books on the topic: What Video Games Have to Teach Us About Learning and Literacy *(2003) and* Why Video Games Are Good for Your Soul *(2007), from which the following reading is taken. One of a growing number of researchers who take video games seriously and see them as an important object of academic study, Gee is particularly concerned with how gamers develop learning and literacy by playing video games.*

*Throughout the article, Gee is unapologetically positive about video games and their potential to help us learn more about the human mind and about ourselves. Indeed, Gee is more critical of the traditional educational system than he is of video games. **As you read** this article, then, bear in mind the criticisms of video games that you're familiar with. Does Gee's article answer these criticisms?*

INTRODUCTION

This chapter has two main points to make and, in turn, it falls into two 1 main parts. My first point—a point some will find startling at first—is that good video games (by which I mean both computer games and games played on platforms like the Xbox, Cube, or PlayStation) represent a technology that illuminates how the human mind works. My second point follows, in part, from this first one. It is that good video games incorporate good learning principles and have a great deal to teach us about learning in and out of schools, whether or not a video game is part of this learning.

VIDEO GAMES AND THE MIND

Video games are a relatively new technology replete with important, 2 and not yet fully understood, implications (Gee 2003). Scholars have historically viewed the human mind through the lens of a technology they thought worked like the mind. Locke and Hume, for example, argued that the mind was like a blank slate on which experience wrote ideas, taking the technology of literacy as their guide. Much later, modern cognitive scientists argued that the mind worked like a digital computer, calculating generalizations and deductions via a logic-like rule system (Newell & Simon 1972). More recently, some cognitive scientists, inspired by distributed parallel-processing computers and complex adaptive networks, have argued that the mind works by storing records of actual experiences and constructing intricate patterns of connections among them (Clark 1989; Gee 1992). So we get different pictures of the mind: mind as a slate waiting to be written on, mind as software, mind as a network of connections.

Human societies get better through history at building technolo- 3 gies that more closely capture some of what the human mind can do and getting these technologies to do mental work publicly. Writing, digital computers, and networks each allow us to externalize some functions of the mind.

Though they are not commonly thought of in these terms, video 4 games are a new technology in this same line. They are a new tool with which to think about the mind and through which we can externalize some of its functions. Video games of the sort I am concerned with—games like *Half-Life 2*, *Rise of Nations*, *Full Spectrum Warrior*, *The Elder Scrolls III: Morrowind*, and *World of WarCraft*—are what I would call "action-and-goal-directed preparations for, and simulations of, embodied experience." A mouthful, indeed, but an important one.

To make clear what I mean by the claim that games act like the 5 human mind and are a good place to study and produce human thinking and learning, let me first briefly summarize some recent research in cognitive science, the science that studies how the mind works (Bransford, Brown, & Cocking 2000). Consider, for instance, the remarks below [in the quotes below, the word "comprehension" means "understanding words, actions, events, or things"):

> . . . comprehension is grounded in perceptual simulations that prepare agents for situated action (Barsalou, 1999a: p. 77)
> . . . to a particular person, the meaning of an object, event, or sentence is what that person can do with the object, event, or sentence (Glenberg, 1997: p. 3)

385

What these remarks mean is this: human understanding is not pri- 6 marily a matter of storing general concepts in the head or applying abstract rules to experience. Rather, humans think and understand best when they can imagine (simulate) an experience in such a way that the simulation prepares them for actions they need and want to take in order to accomplish their goals (Barsalou 1999b; Clark 1997; Glenberg & Robertson 1999).

Let's take weddings as an example, though we could just as well 7 have taken war, love, inertia, democracy, or anything. You don't understand the word or the idea of weddings by meditating on some general definition of weddings. Rather, you have had experiences of weddings in real life and through texts and media. On the basis of these experiences, you can simulate different wedding scenarios in your mind. You construct these simulations differently for different occasions, based on what actions you need to take to accomplish specific goals in specific situations. You can move around as a character in the mental simulation as yourself, imaging your role in the wedding, or you can "play" other characters at the wedding (e.g., the minister), imaging what it is like to be that person.

You build your simulations to understand and make sense of 8 things, but also to help you prepare for action in the world. You can act in the simulation and test out what consequences follow before you act in the real world. You can role-play another person in the model and try to see what motivates their actions or might follow from them before you respond in the real world. So I am arguing that the mind is a simulator, but one that builds simulations to purposely prepare for specific actions and to achieve specific goals (i.e., they are built around win states).

Video games turn out to be the perfect metaphor for what this 9 view of the mind amounts to, just as slates and computers were good metaphors for earlier views of the mind. To see this, let me now turn to a characterization of video games, and then I will put my remarks about the mind and games together.

Video games usually involve a visual and auditory world in which 10 the player manipulates a virtual character (or characters). They often come with editors or other sorts of software with which the player can make changes to the game world or even build a new game world. The player can make a new landscape, a new set of buildings, or new characters. The player can set up the world so that certain sorts of actions are allowed or disallowed. The player is building a new world, but is doing so by using and modifying the original visual images (really the code for them) that came with the game. One simple example of this is the way in

which players can build new skateboard parks in a game like *Tony Hawk Pro Skater*. The player must place ramps, trees, grass, poles, and other things in space in such a way that players can manipulate their virtual characters to skate the park in a fun and challenging way.

Even when players are not modifying games, they play them with 11 goals in mind, the achievement of which counts as their "win state" (and it's the existence of such win states that, in part, distinguishes games from simulations). These goals are set by the player, but, of course, in collaboration with the world the game designers have created (and, at least in more open-ended games, players don't just accept developer's goals, they make real choices of their own). Players must carefully consider the design of the world and consider how it will or will not facilitate specific actions they want to take to accomplish their goals.

One technical way that psychologists have talked about this sort of 12 situation is through the notion of "affordances" (Gibson 1979). An "affordance" is a feature of the world (real or virtual) that will allow for a certain action to be taken, but only if it is matched by an ability in an actor who has the wherewithal to carry out such an action. For example, in the massive multiplayer game *World of WarCraft*, stags can be killed and skinned (for making leather), but only by characters that have learned the Skinning skill. So a stag is an affordance for skinning for such a player, but not for one who has no such skill. The large spiders in the game are not an affordance for skinning for any players, since they cannot be skinned at all. Affordances are relationships between the world and actors.

Playing *World of WarCraft*, or any other video game, is all about such affordances. The player must learn to *see* the game world—designed by the developers, but set in motion in particular directions by the players, and, thus, co-designed by them—in terms of such affordances (Gee 2005). Broadly speaking, players must think in terms of "What are the features of this world that can enable the actions I am capable of carrying out and that I want to carry out in order to achieve my goals?"

So now, after our brief bit about the mind and about games, let's put the two together. The view of the mind I have sketched, in fact, argues, as far as I am concerned, that the mind works rather like a video game. For humans, effective thinking is more like running a simulation than it is about forming abstract generalizations cut off from experiential realities. Effective thinking is about perceiving the world such that the human actor sees how the world, at a specific time and place (as it is given, but also modifiable), can afford the opportunity for actions that will lead to a successful accomplishment of the actor's goals. Generalizations are formed, when they are, bottom up from experience and imagination of experience. Video games externalize the search for affordances, for a match between character (actor) and world, but this is just the heart and soul of effective human thinking and learning in any situation.

As a game player you learn to see the world of each different game you play in a quite different way. But in each case you see the world in terms of how it will afford the sorts of embodied actions you (and your virtual character, your surrogate body in the game) need to take to accomplish your goals (to win in the short and long run). For example, you see the world in *Full Spectrum Warrior* as routes (for your squad) between cover (e.g., corner to corner, house to house) because this prepares you for the actions you need to take, namely attacking without being vulnerable to attack yourself. You see the world of *Thief* in terms of light and dark, illumination and shadows, because this prepares you for the different actions you need to take in this world, namely hiding, disappearing into the shadows, sneaking, and otherwise moving unseen to your goal.

When we sense such a match, in a virtual world or the real world, between our way of seeing the world, at a particular time and place, and our action goals—and we have the skills to carry these actions out—then we feel great power and satisfaction. Things click; the world looks as if it were made for us. While commercial games often stress a match between worlds and characters like soldiers or thieves, there is no reason why other games could not let players experience such a match between the world and the way a particular type of scientist, for instance, sees and acts on the world (Gee 2004). Such games would involve facing the sorts of problems and challenges that type of scientist does and living and playing by the rules that type of scientist uses. Winning would mean just

13

14

15　　**387**

16

what it does to a scientist: feeling a sense of accomplishment through the production of knowledge to solve deep problems.

I have argued for the importance of video games as "action-and- 17 goal-directed preparations for, and simulations of, embodied experience." They are the new technological arena—just as were literacy and computers earlier—around which we can study the mind and externalize some of its most important features to improve human thinking and learning. But games have two other features that suit them to be good models for human thinking and learning externalized out in the world. These two additional features are: a) they distribute intelligence via the creation of smart tools, and b) they allow for the creation of "cross functional affiliation," a particularly important form of collaboration in the modern world.

Consider first how good games distribute intelligence (Brown, 18 Collins, & Duguid 1989). In *Full Spectrum Warrior*, the player uses the buttons on the controller to give orders to two squads of soldiers. The instruction manual that comes with the game makes it clear from the outset that players, in order to play the game successfully, must take on the values, identities, and ways of thinking of a professional soldier: "Everything about your squad," the manual explains, "is the result of careful planning and years of experience on the battlefield. Respect that experience, soldier, since it's what will keep your soldiers alive" (p. 2). In the game, that experience—the skills and knowledge of professional military expertise—is distributed between the virtual soldiers and the real-world player. The soldiers in the player's squads have been trained in movement formations; the role of the player is to select the best position for them on the field. The virtual characters (the soldiers) know part of the task (various movement formations), and the player must come to know another part (when and where to engage in such formations). This kind of distribution holds for every aspect of military knowledge in the game.

By distributing knowledge and skills this way—between the vir- 19 tual characters (smart tools) and the real-world player—the player is guided and supported by the knowledge built into the virtual soldiers. This offloads some of the cognitive burden from the learner, placing it in smart tools that can do more than the learner is currently capable of doing by him or herself. It allows the player to begin to act, with some degree of effectiveness, before being really competent—"performance before competence." The player thereby eventually comes to gain competence through trial, error, and feedback, not by wading through a lot of text before being able to engage in activity. Such distribution also allows players to internalize not only the knowledge and skills of a professional (a professional soldier in this case), but also the concomitant values ("doctrine" as the military says) that shape and explain how and why that knowledge is developed and applied in the world.

There is no reason why other professions—scientists, doctors, government officials, urban planners (Shaffer 2004)—could not be modeled and distributed in this fashion as a deep form of value-laden learning (and, in turn, learners could compare and contrast different value systems as they play different games).

Finally, let me turn to the creation of "cross-functional affiliation." 20 Consider a small group partying (hunting and questing) together in a massive multiplayer game like *World of WarCraft*. The group might well be composed of a Hunter, Warrior, Druid, and Priest. Each of these types of characters has quite different skills and plays the game in a different way. Each group member (player) must learn to be good at his or her special skills and also learn to integrate these skills as a team member within the group as a whole. Each team member must also share some common knowledge about the game and game play with all the other members of the group—including some understanding of the specialist skills of other player types—in order to achieve a successful integration. So each member of the group must have specialist knowledge (intensive knowledge) and general common knowledge (extensive knowledge), including knowledge of the other members' functions.

Players—who are interacting with each other in the game and via 21 a chat system—orient to each other not in terms of their real-world race, class, culture, or gender (these may very well be unknown or if communicated made up as fictions). They must orient to each other, first and foremost, through their identities as game players and players of *World of WarCraft* in particular. They can, in turn, use their real-world race, class, culture, and gender as strategic resources if and when they please, and the group can draw on the differential real-world resources of each player, but in ways that do not force anyone into preset racial, gender, cultural, or class categories.

This form of affiliation—what I will call cross-functional 22 affiliation—has been argued to be crucial for the workplace teams in modern "new capitalist" workplaces, as well as in modern forms of social activism (Beck 1999; Gee 2004; Gee, Hull, & Lankshear 1996). People specialize, but integrate and share, organized around a primary affiliation to their common goals and using their cultural and social differences as strategic resources, not as barriers.

GOOD VIDEO GAMES AND GOOD LEARNING

So video games, though a part of popular culture, are, like literacy and 23 computers, sites where we can study and exercise the human mind in ways that may give us deeper insights into human thinking and learning, as well as new ways to engage learners in deep and engaged learning. And, in fact, one of the biggest contributions the study of good video games can make is to illuminate ways in which learning works when it works best for human beings. In part, because they externalize the way in which the human mind thinks, good video games often organize learning in deep and effective ways.

Many good computer and video games, games like *Deus Ex, The* 24 *Elder Scrolls III: Morrowind,* or *Rise of Nations,* are long, complex, and difficult, especially for beginners. As we well know from school, young people are not always eager to do difficult things. When adults are faced with the challenge of getting them to do so, two choices are often available. We can force them, which is the main solution schools use. Or, a temptation when profit is at stake, though not unknown in school either, we can dumb down the product. Neither option is open to the game industry, at least for the moment. They can't force people to play, and most avid gamers don't want their games short or easy. Indeed, game reviews regularly damn easy or short games.

For people interested in learning, this raises an interesting ques- 25 tion. How do good game designers manage to get new players to learn their long, complex, and difficult games and not only learn them but pay to do so? It won't do simply to say games are "motivating." That just begs the question of "Why?" Why is a long, complex, and difficult video game motivating? I believe it is something about how games are designed to trigger learning that makes them so deeply motivating.

So the question is: How do good game designers manage to get 26 new players to learn long, complex, and difficult games? The answer, I believe, is this: the designers of many good games have hit on profoundly good methods of getting people to learn and to enjoy learning. They have had to, since games that were bad at getting themselves learned didn't get played and the companies that made them lost money. Furthermore, it turns out that these learning methods are similar in many respects to cutting-edge principles being discovered in research on human learning (for details, see Gee 2003, 2004, 2005 and the references therein).

Good game designers are practical theoreticians of learning, since 27 what makes games deep is that players are exercising their learning muscles, though often without knowing it and without having to pay overt attention to the matter. Under the right conditions, learning, like sex, is biologically motivating and pleasurable for humans (and other primates). It is a hook that game designers own to a greater degree— thanks to the interactivity of games—than do movies and books.

But the power of video games resides not just in their present 28 instantiations, but in the promises the technologies by which they are made hold out for the future. Game designers can make worlds where people can have meaningful new experiences, experiences that their places in life would never allow them to have or even experiences no human being has ever had before. These experiences have the potential to make people smarter and more thoughtful.

Good games already do this and they will do it more and more in the future. *Star Wars: Knights of the Old Republic* immerses the player in issues of identity and responsibility: What responsibility do I bear for what an earlier, now transformed, "me" did? *Deus Ex: Invisible War* asks the player to make choices about the role ability and equality will or won't play in society: If we were all truly equal in ability would that mean we would finally have a true meritocracy? Would we want it? In these games, such thoughtful questions are not abstractions; they are part and parcel of the fun and interaction of playing.   29

I care about these matters both as a cognitive scientist and as a gamer. I believe that we can make school and workplace learning better if we pay attention to good computer and video games. This does not necessarily mean using game technologies in school and at work, though that is something I advocate. It means applying the fruitful principles of learning that good game designers have hit on, whether or not we use a game as a carrier of these principles. My book *What Video Games Have to Teach Us About Learning and Literacy* (2003) lists many of these principles. Science educator Andy diSessa's book *Changing Minds: Computers, Learning, and Literacy* (2000) offers many related principles without ever mentioning video games.   30

391

There are many good principles of learning built into good computer and video games. These are all principles that could and should be applied to school learning tomorrow, though this is unlikely given the current trend for skill-and-drill, scripted instruction, and standardized multiple choice testing. The principles are particularly important for so-called "at risk" learners, students who have come to school under-prepared, who have fallen behind, or who have little support for school-based literacy and language skills outside of school.   31

The principles are neither conservative nor liberal, neither traditionalist nor progressive. They adopt some of each side, reject some of each, and stake out a different space. If implemented in schools they would necessitate significant changes in the structure and nature of formal schooling as we have long known it, changes that may eventually be inevitable anyway given modern technologies.   32

I list a baker's dozen below. We can view this list as a checklist: The stronger any game is on more of the features on the list, the better its score for learning. The list is organized into three sections: I. Empowered Learners; II. Problem Solving; III. Understanding. Under each item on the list I first give a principle relevant to learning, then a comment on games in regard to that principle, as well as some example games that are strong on that principle. I then discuss the educational implications of the principle. Those interested in more ample citations   33 to research that supports these principles and how they apply to learning things like science in school should consult the references cited in Gee (2003, 2004, 2005). I should point out, as well, that the first part of this chapter has already discussed some of learning principles that we don't need to discuss further below, since distributed knowledge and cross-functional affiliation are themselves powerful forms of social organization for learning and knowledge building. So is the way in which good video games teach players to look for and build affordances into their learning environments.

I. EMPOWERED LEARNERS

1. Co-design

PRINCIPLE: Good learning requires that learners feel like active agents   34
(producers) not just passive recipients (consumers).

GAMES: In a video game, players make things happen. They   35
don't just consume what the "author" (game designer) has placed before them. Video games are interactive. The player does something, and the game does something back that encourages the player to act again, in good games, players feel that their actions and decisions—and not just the designers' actions and decisions—are co-creating the world they are in and the experiences they are having. What the player does matters and each player, based on his other own decisions and actions, takes a different trajectory through the game world.

EXAMPLE: *The Elder Scrolls III: Morrowind* is an extreme exam-   36
ple of a game where each decision the player makes changes the game in ways that ensure that each player's game is, in the end, different from any other player's. But at some level this is true of most games. Players take different routes through *Castlevania: Symphony of the Night* and do different things in different ways in *Tony Hawk's Underground*.

EDUCATION: Co-design means ownership, buy in, engaged   37
participation. It is a key part of motivation. It also means learners must come to understand the design of the domain they are learning so that they can make good choices about how to affect that design. Do student decisions and actions make a difference in the classroom curriculum? Are students helping to design their own learning? If the answers are no, what gives students the feeling of being agents in their own learning? Forced and enforced group discussions are about as far as interactivity goes in most classrooms, if it goes that far. The whole curriculum should be shaped by the learners' actions and react back on the learners in meaningful ways.

392

2. Customize

PRINCIPLE: Different styles of learning work better for different peo- 38
ple. People cannot be agents of their own learning if they cannot make
decisions about how their learning will work, At the same time, they
should be able (and encouraged) to try new styles.

GAMES: Good games achieve this goal in one (or both) of two 39
ways. In some games, players are able to customize the game play to fit
their learning and playing styles. In others, the game is designed to
allow different styles of learning and playing to work.

EXAMPLE: *Rise of Nations* allows players to customize myriad 40
aspects of the game play to their own styles, interests, and desires. *Deus
Ex* and its sequel *Deus Ex: Invisible War* both allow quite different styles
of play and, thus, learning, too, to succeed.

EDUCATION: Classrooms adopting this principle would allow 41
students to discover their favored learning styles and to try new ones
without fear. In the act of customizing their own learning, students
would learn a good deal not only about how and why they learn, but
about learning and thinking themselves. Can students engage in such
customization in the classroom? Do they get to reflect on the nature of
their own learning and learning in general? Are there multiple ways to
solve problems? Are students encouraged to try out different learning
styles and different problem solutions without risking a bad grade?

393

3. Identity

PRINCIPLE: Deep learning requires an extended commitment and 42
such a commitment is powerfully recruited when people take on a new
identity they value and in which they become heavily invested—
whether this be a child "being a scientist doing science" in a classroom
or an adult taking on a new role at work.

GAMES: Good games offer players identities that trigger a deep 43
investment on the part of the player. They achieve this goal in one of
two ways. Some games offer a character so intriguing that players want
to inhabit the character and can readily project their own fantasies,
desires, and pleasures onto the character. Other games offer a relatively
empty character whose traits the player must determine, but in such a
way that the player can create a deep and consequential life history in
the game world for the character.

EXAMPLE: *Metal Gear Solid* offers a character (Solid Snake) that is 44
so well developed that he is, though largely formed by the game's
designers, a magnet for player projections. *Animal Crossing* and *Scrolls
III: Morrowind* offer, in different ways, blank-slate characters for which
the player can build a deeply involving life and history. On the other

hand, an otherwise good game like *Freedom Fighters* offers us characters that are both too anonymous and not changeable enough by the player to trigger deep investment.

EDUCATION: School is often built around the "content fetish," 45 the idea that an academic area like biology or social science is constituted by some definitive list of facts or body of information that can be tested in a standardized way. But academic areas are not first and foremost bodies of facts, they are, rather, first and foremost, the activities and ways of knowing through which such facts are generated, defended, and modified. Such activities and ways of knowing are carried out by people who adopt certain sorts of identities, that is, adopt certain ways with words, actions, and interactions, as well as certain values, attitudes, and beliefs.

Learners need to know what the "rules of the game" are and who 46 plays it. They need to know how to take on the identity of a certain sort of scientist, if they are doing science, and operate by a certain set of values, attitudes, and actions. Otherwise they have no deep understanding of a domain and surely never know why anyone would want to learn, and even spend a lifetime learning in that domain in the first place.

Ironically, when learners adopt and practice such an identity and 47 engage in the forms of talk and action connected to it, facts come free— they are learned as part and parcel of being a certain sort of person needing to do certain sorts of things for one's own purposes and goals (Shaffer 2004). Out of the context of identity and activity, facts are hard to learn and last in the learner's mind a very short time, indeed.

4. Manipulation and Distributed Knowledge

PRINCIPLE: As I suggested in the first part of this chapter, cognitive 48 research suggests that, for humans, perception and action are deeply inter-connected (Barsalou 1999a, b; Clark 1997; Glenberg 1997; Glenberg & Robertson 1999). Thus, fine-grained action at a distance—for example, when a person is manipulating a robot at a distance or watering a garden via a web cam on the Internet—causes humans to feel as if their bodies and minds have stretched into a new space (Clark 2003). More generally, humans feel expanded and empowered when they can manipulate powerful tools in intricate ways that extend their area of effectiveness.

GAMES: Computer and video games inherently involve action at 49 a (albeit virtual) distance. The more and better a player can manipulate a character, the more the player invests in the game world. Good games offer characters that the player can move intricately, effectively, and easily through the world. Beyond characters, good games offer the player intricate, effective, and easy manipulation of the world's objects, objects which become tools for carrying out the player's goals.

EXAMPLE: *Tomb Raider, Tom Clancy's Splinter Cell,* and *ICO* allow   50
such fine-grained and interesting manipulation of one's character that
they achieve a strong effect of pulling the player into their worlds. *Rise
of Nations* allows such effective control of buildings, landscapes, and
whole armies as tools that the player feels like "god." *Prince of Persia*
excels both in terms of character manipulation and in terms of everything in its environment serving as effective tools for player action.

One key feature of the virtual characters and objects that game play-   51
ers manipulate is that they are "smart tools." The character the player
controls—Lara Croft, for example—knows things the player doesn't, for
instance, how to climb ropes, leap chasms, and scale walls. The player
knows things the character doesn't, like when, where, and why to climb,
leap, or scale. The player and the character each have knowledge that
must be integrated together to play the game successfully. This is an
example of distributed knowledge, knowledge split between two things
(here a person and a virtual character) that must be integrated.

A game like *Full Spectrum Warrior* takes this principle much further.   52
In this game, the player controls two squads of four soldiers each. The soldiers know lots and lots of things about professional military practice; for
example, how to take various formations under fire and how to engage in
various types of group movements in going safely from cover to cover.
The player need not know these things. The player must learn other
aspects of professional military practice, namely what formations and
movements to order, when, where, and why. The real actor in this game is
the player and the soldiers blended together through their shared, distributed, and integrated knowledge.

EDUCATION: What allows a learner to feel that his or her body   53
and mind have extended into the world being studied or investigated,
into the world of biology or physics, for example? Part of the answer
here is "smart tools," that is, tools and technologies that allow the
learner to manipulate that world in a fine-grained way. Such tools have
their own in-built knowledge and skills that allow the learner much
more power over the world being investigated than he or she has
unaided by such tools.

Let me give one concrete example of what I am talking about.   54
Galileo discovered the laws of the pendulum because he knew and
applied geometry to the problem, not because he played around with
pendulums or saw a church chandelier swinging (as myth has it). Yet it
is common for liberal educators to ask children innocent of geometry
or any other such tool to play around with pendulums and discover for
themselves the laws by which they work. This is actually a harder
problem than the one Galileo confronted—geometry set possible solutions for him and led him to think about pendulums in certain ways
and not others. Of course, today there are a great many technical tools

available beyond geometry and algebra (though students usually don't even realize that geometry and algebra are smart tools, different from each other in the way they approach problems and the problems for which they are best suited).

Do students in the classroom share knowledge with smart tools? 55 Do they become powerful actors by learning to integrate their own knowledge with the knowledge built into their tools? The real-world player and the virtual soldiers in *Full Spectrum Warrior* come to share a body of skills and knowledge that is constitutive of a certain type of professional practice. Do students engage in authentic professional practices in the classroom through such sharing? Professional practice is crucial here, because, remember, real learning in science, for example, is constituted by *being a type of scientist doing a type of science* not reciting a fact you don't understand. It is thinking, acting, and valuing like a scientist of a certain sort. It is "playing by the rules" of a certain sort of science.

II. PROBLEM SOLVING

5. Well-Ordered Problems

PRINCIPLE: Given human creativity, if learners face problems early on 56 that are too free-form or too complex, they often form creative hypotheses about how to solve these problems, but hypotheses that don't work well for later problems (even for simpler ones, let alone harder ones). They have been sent down a "garden path." The problems learners face early on are crucial and should be well-designed to lead them to hypotheses that work well, not just on these problems, but as aspects of the solutions of later, harder problems, as well.

GAMES: Problems in good games are well-ordered. In particular, 57 early problems are designed to lead players to form good guesses about how to proceed when they face harder problems later on in the game. In this sense, earlier parts of a good game are always looking forward to later parts.

EXAMPLE: *Return to Castle Wolfenstein* and *Fatal Frame2: Crimson* 58 *Butterfly*. Although radically different games, each does a good job of offering players problems that send them down fruitful paths for what they will face later in the game. They each prepare the player to get better and better at the game and to face more difficult challenges later in the game.

EDUCATION: Work on connectionism and distributed parallel 59 processing in cognitive science has shown that the order in which learners confront problems in a problem space is important (Clark 1989; Elman 1991a, b). Confronting complex problems too early can lead to creative solutions, but approaches that won't work well for even simpler later problems. "Anything goes"—"just turn learners loose in rich environments"—"no need for teachers"—these are bad theories of learning; they are, in fact, the progressive counterpart of the traditionalists' skill-and-drill.

Learners are novices. Leaving them to float amidst rich experiences with no guidance only triggers human beings' great penchant for finding creative but spurious patterns and generalizations that send learners down garden paths (Gee 1992, 2001). The fruitful patterns or generalizations in any domain are the ones that are best recognized by those who already know how to look at the domain, know how the complex variables at play in the domain relate and inter-relate to each other. And this is precisely what the learner does not yet know. Problem spaces can be designed to enhance the trajectory through which the learner traverses it. This does not mean leading the learner by the hand in a linear way. It means designing the problem space well. 60

6. Pleasantly Frustrating

PRINCIPLE: Learning works best when new challenges are pleasantly frustrating in the sense of being felt by learners to be at the outer edge of, but within, their "regime of competence." That is, these challenges feel hard, but doable. Furthermore, learners feel—and get evidence—that their effort is paying off in the sense that they can see, even when they fail, how and if they are making progress. 61

GAMES: Good games adjust challenges and give feedback in such a way that different players feel the game is challenging but doable and that their effort is paying off. Players get feedback that indicates whether they are on the right road for success later on and at the end of the game. When players lose to a boss, perhaps multiple times, they get feedback about the sort of progress they are making so that at least they know if and how they are moving in the right direction towards success. 62

EXAMPLE: *Ratchet and Clank: Going Commando*, *Halo*, and *Zone of the Enders: The Second Runner* (which has different difficulty levels) manage to stay at a "doable," but challenging level for many different sorts of players. They also give good feedback about where the player's edge of competence is and how it is developing, as does *Sonic Adventure 2 Battle*. *Rise of Nations* allows the player to customize many aspects of the difficulty level and gain feedback of whether things are getting too easy or too hard for the player. 63

EDUCATION: School is often too easy for some kids and too hard for others even when they are the same classroom. Motivation for humans lies in challenges that feel challenging, but doable, and in gaining continual feedback that lets them know what progress they 64 are making. Learners should be able to adjust the difficulty level while being encouraged to stay at the outer edge of, but inside, their level of competence. They should gain insight into where this level is and how it is changing over time. Good games don't come in grade-levels that players must be "at." They realize that it doesn't matter when the player finishes or how he or she did in comparison to others—all that matters is that the player learns to play the game and comes to master it. Players who take longer and struggle longer at the beginning are sometimes the ones who, in the end, master the final boss most easily.

There are no "special" learners when it comes to video games. 65 Even an old guy like me can wander the plains of Morrowind long enough to pick up the ropes and master the game. The world doesn't go away, I can enter any time, it gives me constant feedback, but never a final judgment that I am a failure, and the final exam—the final boss—is willing to wait until I am good enough to beat him.

7. Cycles of Expertise

PRINCIPLE: Expertise is formed in any area by repeated cycles of 66 learners practicing skills until they are nearly automatic, then having those skills fail in ways that cause the learners to have to think again and learn anew (Bereiter & Scardamalia 1993). Then they practice this new skill set to an automatic level of mastery only to see it, too, eventually be challenged. In fact, this is the whole point of levels and bosses. Each level exposes the players to new challenges and allows them to get good at solving them. They are then confronted with a boss that makes them use these skills together with new ones they have to learn, and integrate with the old ones, to beat the boss. Then they move on to a new level and the process starts again.

GAMES: Good games create and support the cycle of expertise, 67 with cycles of extended practice, tests of mastery of that practice, then a new challenge, and then new extended practice. This is, in fact, part of what constitutes good pacing in a game.

EXAMPLE: *Ratchet and Clank: Going Commando, Final Fantasy X,* 68 *Halo, Viewtiful Joe,* and *Pikmin* do a good job of alternating fruitful practice and new challenges such that players sense their own growing sophistication, almost as an incremental curve, as the game progresses.

EDUCATION: The cycle of expertise has been argued to be the 69 very basis of expertise in any area. Experts routinize their skills and then challenge themselves with the new problems. These problems force them to open up their routinized skills to reflection, to learn new things, and then to integrate old and new. In turn, this new integrated package of skills, a higher level of mastery, will be routinized through much practice. Games let learners experience expertise; schools usually don't. The cycle of expertise allows learners to learn how to manage their own life-long learning and to become skilled at learning to learn. It also creates a rhythm and flow between practice and new learning and between mastery and challenge. It creates, as well, a feeling of accumulating knowledge and skills, rather than standing in the same place all the time or always starting over again at the beginning.

8. Information "On Demand" and "Just in Time"

PRINCIPLE: Human beings are quite poor at using verbal information 70 (i.e., words) when given lots of it out of context and before they can see how it applies in actual situations. They use verbal information best when it is given "just in time" (when they can put it to use) and "on demand" (when they feel they need it).

GAMES: Good games give verbal information—for example, the 71 sorts of information that is often in a manual—"just in time" and "on demand" in a game. Players don't need to read a manual to start, but can use the manual as a reference after they have played a while and the game has already made much of the verbal information in the manual concrete through the player's experiences in the game.

EXAMPLE: *System Shock 2* spreads its manual out over the first 72 **399** few levels in little green kiosks that give players—if they want it—brief pieces of information that will soon thereafter be visually instantiated or put to use by the player. *Enter the Matrix* introduces new information into its "on demand" glossary when and as it becomes relevant and useable and marks it clearly as new. The first few levels of *Goblin Commander: Unleash the Hoard* allows the player to enact the information that would be in the manual, step by step, and then the game seamlessly moves into more challenging game play.

EDUCATION: If there is one thing we know, it is that humans are 73 not good at learning through hearing or reading lots of words out of contexts of application that give these words situated or experiential meanings. Game manuals, just like science textbooks, make little sense if one tries to read them before having played the game. All one gets is lots of words that are confusing, have only quite general or vague meanings, and are quickly forgotten. After playing the game, the manual is lucid and clear because every word in it now has a meaning related to an action-image, can be situated in different contexts of use for dialogue or action. The player even learns how to readjust (situate, customize) the meanings of game-related words for new game contexts. Now, of course, the player doesn't need to read the manual cover to cover but, rather, can use it as reference work to facilitate his or her own goals and needs.

Lectures and textbooks are fine "on demand," used when learn- 74 ers are ready for them, not otherwise, Learners need to play the game a bit before they get lots of verbal information, and they need to be able to get such information "just in time" when and where they need it, and can see how it actually applies in action and practice. Since schools rarely do this, we are all familiar with the well-known phenomenon of students gaining As because they can pass multiple-choice tests, yet can't apply their knowledge in practice.

9. Fish tanks

PRINCIPLE: In the real world, a fish tank can be a little simplified eco- 75
system that clearly displays some critical variables and their interactions that are otherwise obscured in the highly complex ecosystem in the real world. Using the term metaphorically, fish tanks are good for learning: if we create simplified systems, stressing a few key variables and their interactions, learners who would otherwise be overwhelmed by a complex system (e.g., Newton's Laws of Motion operating in the real world) get to see some basic relationships at work and take the first steps towards their eventual mastery of the real system (e.g., they begin to know what to pay attention to).

GAMES: Fish tanks are stripped down versions of the game. Good 76
games offer players fish tanks, either as tutorials or as their first level or two. Otherwise it can be difficult for newcomers to understand the game as a whole system, since they often can't see the forest because of the trees.

EXAMPLE: *Rise of Nations'* tutorial scenarios (like "Alfred the 77
Great" or "The 100 Years War") are wonderful fish tanks, allowing the player to play scaled down versions of the game that render key elements and relationships salient.

EDUCATION: In traditional education, learners hear words and 78
drill on skills out of any context of use. In progressive education, they are left to their own devices immersed in a sea of complex experience, for example studying pond ecology. When confronted with complex systems, letting the learner see some of the basic variables and how they interact can be a good way into confronting more complex versions of the system later on. This follows from the same ideas that give rise to the well-ordered problems principle above. It allows learners to form good strong fruitful hypotheses at the outset and not go down garden paths by confronting too much complexity at the outset.

The real world is a complex place. Real scientists do not go out 79
unaided to study it. Galileo showed up with geometry, ecologists show up with theories, models, and smart tools. Models are all simplifications of reality and initial models are usually fish tanks, simple systems that display the workings of some major variables. With today's capacity to build simulations, there is no excuse for the lack of fish tanks in

schools (there aren't even many real fish tanks in classrooms studying ponds!).

10. Sandboxes

PRINCIPLE: Sandboxes in the real world are safe havens for children 80 that still look and feel like the real world. Using the term metaphorically, sandboxes are good for learning: if learners are put into a situation that feels like the real thing, but with risks and dangers greatly mitigated, they can learn well and still feel a sense of authenticity and accomplishment.

GAMES: Sandboxes are game play much like the real game, but 81 where things cannot go too wrong too quickly or, perhaps, even at all. Good games offer players, either as tutorials or as their first level or two, sandboxes. You can't expect newcomers to learn if they feel too much pressure, understand too little, and feel like failures.

EXAMPLE: *Rise of Nations'* "Quick Start" tutorial is an excellent 82 sandbox. You feel much more of the complexity of the whole game than you do in a fish tank, but risks and consequences are mitigated compared to the "real" game. The first level of *System Shock 2* is a great example of a sandbox—exciting play where, in this case, things can't go wrong at all. In many good games, the first level is a sandbox or close to it.

401

EDUCATION: Here we face one of the worst problems with school: 83 it's too risky and punishing. There is nothing worse than a game that lets you save only after you have gone through a whole long arduous level. You fail at the end and have to repeat everything, rather than being able to return to a save part-way through the level. You end up playing the beginning of the level perfectly over and over again until you master the final bits. The cost of taking risks, trying out new hypotheses, is too high. The player sticks to the tried and true well-trodden road, because failing will mean boring repetition of what he or she already well knows.

Good games don't do this. They create sandboxes in the begin- 84 ning that make the player feel competent when they are not ("performance before competence"), and thereafter they put a moratorium on any failures that will kill joy, risk taking, hypothesizing, and learning. Players do fail, of course; they die and try again, but in a way that makes failure part of the fun and central to the learning.

In school, learners, especially so-called "at risk" learners need 85 what Stan Goto (2003) has called "horizontal learning," that is, time to "play around," to explore the area they are about to learn, to see what is there and what the lay of the land is, before they are forced up the vertical learning ladder of ever new skills. They need always to see failure as informative and part of the game, not as a final judgment or a device to forestall creativity, risk taking, and hypothesizing.

11. Skills as Strategies

PRINCIPLE: There is a paradox involving skills: people don't like prac-   86
ticing skills out of context over and over again, since they find such
skill practice meaningless, but, without lots of skill practice, they cannot really get any good at what they are trying to learn. People learn
and practice skills best when they see a set of related skills as a strategy
to accomplish goals they want to accomplish.

GAMES: In good games, players learn and practice skill packages   87
as part and parcel of accomplishing things they need and want to
accomplish. They see the skills first and foremost as a strategy for
accomplishing a goal and only secondarily as a set of discrete skills.

EXAMPLE: Games like *Rise of Nations, Goblin Commander: Unleash*   88
the Hoard, and *Pikmin* all do a good job at getting players to learn skills
while paying attention to the strategies these skills are used to pull off.
Rise of Nations even has skill tests that package certain skills that go
together, show clearly how they enact a strategy, and allow the player
to practice them as a functional set. The training exercises (which are
games in themselves) that come with *Metal Gear Solid* and *Metal Gear
Solid: Sons of Liberty* are excellent examples (and are great fish tanks, as

well).

EDUCATION: We know very well that learning is a practice effect   89
for human beings—the conservatives are right about that, we humans
need practice and lots of it. But skills are best learned (often in sets) as
strategies for carrying out meaningful functions that one wants and
needs to carry out.

Sounding out letters, together with thinking of word families and   90
looking for sub-patterns in words, work best when they are seen as
functional devices to comprehend and use texts. It's not that one can't
get reading tests passed by drilling isolated skills out of context—one
certainly can. But what happens is that we then fuel the so-called
"fourth-grade slump," the long known phenomenon in which children
seem to do all right learning to read (decode) in the early grades (at
least in terms of passing tests), but then cannot handle the complex oral
and written language they confront later in the content areas of school,
e.g., science, math, social studies, etc. (Chall, Jacobs, & Baldwin 1990;
see the papers in the special issue of the *American Educator* 2003a
devoted to what they call the "fourth-grade plunge").

These children aren't learning to "play the game"—and the game   91
in school is ultimately using oral and written language to learn academic areas each of which uses language far more complicated than our
everyday vernacular forms of language. Learners need to know how
skills translate into strategies for playing the game.

III. UNDERSTANDING

12. System Thinking

PRINCIPLE: People learn skills, strategies, and ideas best when they 92
see how they fit into an overall larger system to which they give meaning. In fact, any experience is enhanced when we understand how it
fits into a larger meaningful whole. Players can not view games as "eye
candy," but must learn to see each game (actually each genre of game)
as a distinctive semiotic system affording and discouraging certain
sorts of actions and interactions.

GAMES: Good games help players see and understand how each of 93
the elements in the game fit into the overall system of the game and its
genre (type). Players get a feel for the "rules of the game"—that is, what
works and what doesn't, how things go or don't go in this type of world.

EXAMPLE: Games like *Rise of Nations, Age of Mythology, Pikmin,* 94
Call of Duty, and *Mafia* give players a good feel for the overall world
and game system they are in. They allow players to develop good intu-
itions about what works and about how what they are doing at the present moment fits into the trajectory of the game as a whole. Players
come to have a good feel for and understanding of the genre of the
game they are playing (and in *Pikmin's* case, this is a rather novel and
hybrid genre). *Metal Gear Solid* and *Metal Gear Solid: Sons of Liberty*
come with training exercises that strip away the pretty graphics to
make clear how the player is meant to read the environment to enhance
effective action and interaction in the game. If players stare at the
pretty fish in island paradise of *Far Cry,* they'll die in a minute. Players
have to think of the environment they are in as a complex system that
must be properly understood to plan effective action and anticipate
unintended consequences of one's actions.

403

EDUCATION: We live, in today's high-tech, global world, amidst 95
a myriad of complex systems, systems which interact with each other
(Kelly 1994). In such a world, unintended consequences spread far and
wide. In such a world, being unable to see the forest for the trees is
potentially disastrous. In school, when students fail to have a feeling
for the whole system which they are studying, when they fail to see it
as a set of complex interactions and relationships, each fact and isolated element they memorize for their tests is meaningless. Further,
there is no way they can use these facts and elements as leverage for
action—and we would hardly want them to, given that acting in complex systems with no understanding can lead to disasters. Citizens
with such limited understandings are going to be dangers to themselves and others in the future.

13. Meaning as action image

PRINCIPLE: Humans do not usually think through general definitions 96
and logical principles. Rather, they think through experiences they have
had and imaginative reconstructions of experience. You don't think and
reason about weddings on the basis of generalities, but in terms of the
weddings you have been to and heard about and imaginative reconstructions of them. It's your experiences that give weddings and the
word "wedding" meaning(s). Furthermore, for humans, words and
concepts have their deepest meanings when they are clearly tied to perception and action in the world.

GAMES: This is, of course, the heart and soul of computer and 97
video games (though it is amazing how many educational games
violate this principle). Even barely adequate games make the meanings of words and concepts clear through experiences the player has
and activities the player carries out, not through lectures, talking
heads, or generalities. Good games can achieve marvelous effects
here, making even philosophical points concretely realized in image
and action.

EXAMPLE: Games like *Star Wars: Knights of the Old Republic*, 98
Freedom Fighters, Mafia, Medal of Honor: Allied Assault, and *Operation
Flashpoint: Cold War Crisis* do a very good job of making ideas (e.g., con-
tinuity with one's past self), ideologies (e.g., freedom fighters vs. ter-
rorists), identities (e.g., being a soldier) or events (e.g., the Normandy
Invasion) concrete and deeply embedded in experience and activity.

EDUCATION: This principle is clearly related to the information 99
"just in time" and "on demand" principle above. For human beings the
comprehension of texts and the world is "grounded in perceptual simulations that prepare agents for situated action" (Barsalou 1999a: p. 77).
If you can't run any models in your head—and you can't if all you have
is verbal, dictionary-like information—you can't really understand
what you are reading, hearing, or seeing. That's how humans are built.
And, note, by the way, that this means there is a kinship between how
the human mind works and how video games work, since video games
are, indeed, perceptual simulations that the player must see as preparation for action, or else fail.

CONCLUSION

When we think of games, we think of fun. When we think of learning 100
we think of work. Games show us this is wrong. They trigger deep
learning that is itself part and parcel of the fun. It is what makes good
games deep.

For those interested in spreading games and game technology 101
into schools, workplaces, and other learning sites, it is striking to
meditate on how few of the learning principles I have sketched out
here can be found in so-called educational games. "Non-educational"
games for young people, such as *Pajama Sam, Animal Crossing, Mario
Sunshine,* and *Pikmin,* all use many of the principles fully and well.
Not so for many a product used in school or for business or workplace learning. It is often said that what stops games from spreading
to educational sites is their cost, where people usually have in mind
the wonderful "eye candy" that games have become. But I would
suggest that it is the cost to implement the above principles that is the
real barrier. And the cost here is not just monetary. It is the cost, as
well, of changing people's minds about learning—how and where it
is done. It is the cost of changing one of our most change-resistant
institutions: schools.

Let me end by making it clear that the above principles are not 102
either "conservative" or "liberal," "traditional" or "progressive."
The progressives are right in that situated embodied experience is
crucial. The traditionalists are right that learners cannot be left to
their own devices, they need smart tools and, most importantly, they
need good designers who guide and scaffold their learning (Kelly
2003). For games, these designers are brilliant game designers like
Warren Spector and Will Wright. For schools, these designers are
teachers.

405

REFERENCES

American Educator (2003a). Spring Issue. http://www.aft.org/
    pubs-reports/american_educator/spring2003/index.html.
Barsalou, L. W. (1999a). Language Comprehension: Archival memory
    or preparation for situated action. *Discourse Processes* 28: 61–80.
Barsalou, L. W. (1999b). Perceptual symbol systems. *Behavioral and
    Brain Sciences* 22: 577–660.
Beck, U. (1999). *World risk society.* Oxford: Blackwell.
Bereiter, C. & Scardamalia, M. (1993). *Surpassing ourselves: An inquiry
    into the nature and implications of expertise.* Chicago: Open Court.
Bransford, J., Brown, A. L., & Cocking, R. R. (2000). *How people learn:
    Brain, mind, experience, and school: Expanded Edition.* Washington, DC:
    National Academy Press.
Brown, J.S., Collins, A. & Duguid, D. (1989). Situated cognition and the
    culture of learning. *Educational Researcher* 18: 32–42.
Chall, J.S., Jacobs, V., & Baldwin, L. (1990). *The reading crisis: Why poor
    children fall behind.* Cambridge, MA: Harvard University Press.

Clark, A. (1989). *Microcognition: Philosophy, cognitive science, and parallel distributed processing*. Cambridge: Cambridge University Press.

Clark, A. (1997). *Associative engines: Connectionism, concepts, and representational change*. Cambridge: Cambridge University Press.

Clark, A. (2003). *Being there: Putting brain, body, and world together again*. Cambridge, MA: MIT Press.

Elman, J. (1991a). Distributed representations, simple recurrent networks and grammatical structure. *Machine Learning* 7: 195–225.

Elman, J. (1991b). *Incremental learning, or the importance of starting small*. Technical Report 9101, Center for Research in Language, University of California at San Diego.

Gee, J. P. (1992). *The social mind: Language, ideology, and social practice*. New York: Bergin & Garvey.

Gee, J. P. (2001). Progressivism, critique, and socially situated minds. In C. Dudley-Marling & C. Edelsky, Eds., *The fate of progressive language policies and practices*. Urbana, IL: NCTE, pp. 31–58.

Gee, J. P. (2003). *What video games have to teach us about learning and literacy*. New York: Palgrave/Macmillan.

Gee, J. P. (2004). *Situated language and learning: A critique of traditional schooling*. London: Routledge.

Gee, J. P. (2005). *Why video games are good for your soul: Pleasure and learning*. Melbourne: Common Ground.

Gee, J. P., Hull, G., & Lankshear, C. (1996).*The new work order: Behind the language of the new capitalism*. Boulder, CO: Westview.

Gibson, J. J. (1979). *The ecological approach to visual perception*. Boston: Houghton Mifflin.

Glenberg, A. M. (1997). What is memory for? *Behavioral and Brain Sciences* 20: 1–55.

Glenberg, A. M. & Robertson, D.A. (1999). Indexical understanding of instructions. *Discourse Processes* 28: 1–26.

Kelly, A. E., Ed. (2003). Theme issue: The role of design in educational research, *Educational Researcher* 32: 3–37.

Kelly, K. (1994). *Out of control: The new biology of machines, social systems, and the economic world*. Reading, MA: Addison-Wesley.

Newell, A. & Simon, H. A. (1972). *Human problem solving*. Englewood Cliffs, NJ: Prentice Hall.

Shaffer, D. W. (2004). Pedagogical praxis: The professions as models for post-industrial education. *Teachers College Record* 10: 1401–1421.

Examining the Text

1. According to Gee, how do video games illuminate our understanding of the human mind? In what sense are video games "a new tool with which to think about the mind"?

2. In your own words, what are affordances? How do they contribute to an understanding of how video games function? of how the human mind functions? Can you think of specific affordances in video games you've played or in other technologies you've used?

3. What does Gee mean by "distributed intelligence" and "cross-functional affiliation"? How do these concepts apply to video games? In what ways do they help enlighten us on how the human mind functions?

4. In applying video game principles of learning to educational contexts, Gee identifies three categories: empowered learners, problem solving, and understanding. Based on your reading of the principles, briefly summarize the key elements of each category. What does it mean, according to Gee, to create empowered learners, to teach problem solving, and to enhance understanding?

5. *Thinking rhetorically:* In the second half of the article, Gee lists thirteen principles, and he discusses each one in the same format: he defines the principle, he discusses how games enact the principle, he provides one or more specific examples of video games, and he applies the principle to traditional educational practice. Do you think that this highly structured approach helps Gee convey his points more effectively and clearly? What are the drawbacks of this approach? For instance, did you find the sections repetitive?

For Group Discussion

Gee focuses on what he calls "good" video games, though he never explicitly defines what he means by "good" or what a "bad" video game would be. In a small group, make a list of five or six video games that you all know about or have played. Then discuss what you think is "good" about each game. After this general discussion, compile a list of what your group thinks are the characteristics of a "good" video game, and share this list with the rest of the class.

Writing Suggestion

Choose any one of the thirteen principles that Gee discusses in the second half of the article and write an essay that expands on each section so as to create a more complete discussion of the principle.

In the Principle section, define the principle both in your own words and using quotations from Gee. If he refers to other researchers in this section, you might look up those books and articles and quote from them as well. In the Games section, again use your own words and quotations from Gee (and others) to explain how video games in general apply the principle you're discussing. In the Example section, provide two or three detailed examples and descriptions of specific games that enact the principle; you can work with some of the games identified by Gee, or you can use other games as examples. Finally, in the Education section, use your own words and quotations from Gee (and others) to explore how the principle is or isn't used in traditional educational settings; in this section, be sure to draw on your own many years of experience as a student to illustrate points you make.

2. Facebook, MySpace, and Social Networking

You Have Been Poked: Exploring the Uses and Gratifications of Facebook Among Emerging Adults

BRETT A. BUMGARNER

As we're writing this introduction in 2008, Facebook is the social networking service (SNS) of choice for students at the University of California at Santa Barbara, where we teach. Indeed, by all accounts, Facebook is extremely popular at most universities in the United States. With varying degrees of obsession, students create Facebook profiles, join groups, post photos, amass friends, and write on each other's walls. Exactly why students do what they do on Facebook is the subject of the article that follows.

After describing Facebook and briefly introducing several concepts that he wants to test—uses and gratifications theory, voyeurism, exhibitionism—Brett A. Bumgarner reports the results of his online survey of students at the University of North Carolina at Chapel Hill. Bumgarner can claim some degree of expertise on the topic since he was himself an undergraduate student at this university when he conducted the study; the report was written first as an Honors Thesis (Bumgarner received Highest Honors for his work). It was subsequently published in the journal First Monday *(http://www. uic.edu/htbin/cgiwrap/bin/ojs/index.php/fm/), a peer-reviewed journal on the Internet that publishes articles about the Internet.*

By the time you read this introduction, it may be that another online SNS has surpassed Facebook in popularity; or indeed, it may be that students will do without online social networking altogether—though that seems an unlikely option. **Before you read** *this article, then, do a little thought experiment on what life—and particularly student life—would be like without Facebook and other SNSs. What would be gained and what would be lost if you didn't have SNSs to use?*

INTRODUCTION

Since its inception in February 2004, Facebook (http://www.facebook. 1
com) has rapidly become not only one of the most popular Web sites for

social networking, but also one of the most popular sites overall. Facebook currently ranks as the sixth most trafficked site in the United States and the number one site for photo-sharing (Facebook, 2007). It has been featured in several national publications, including *Newsweek* (Schwartz, 2005) and *USA Today* (Kornblum and Marklein, 2006), and has injected the verb "facebook" into young America's lexicon (Francisco, 2005). According to Facebook spokesperson Chris Hughes (2005), Facebook is available at every university in the United States.

Despite the ubiquity of Facebook among the collegiate popula- 2 tion, little research has been done on Facebook itself as Facebook opened to the public only in early 2004. No studies have examined why students use Facebook or how it fulfills their needs. The purpose of this research project is to understand what motivates college students to use Facebook and how Facebook gratifies these motivations.

WHAT EXACTLY IS FACEBOOK?

According to its Web site, Facebook is "a social utility that enables 3 people to understand the world around them." Originally, people with a university email address could create profiles divulging information about themselves and search for people at their university or other universities. The exclusivity to those with university email addresses has since slackened, opening Facebook up to networks based around high schools, companies, and regions as well (Facebook, 2007).

409

Facebook is part of the current cultural phenomenon of social net- 4 working services (SNSs), Web sites that connect people. MySpace and Friendster are two other common SNSs, and scores more exist, such as MeetUp, Orkut, Tribe.net, and Ryze (Nagele, 2005).

By the time of Facebook's founding, social networking had already 5 become a blazingly hot new Internet trend. Mark Zuckerberg was able to capitalize on this trend when he launched Facebook on 4 February 2004 (Francisco, 2005). The site began at Zuckerberg's university, Harvard, and grew rapidly. Facebook had 4,300 users after only two weeks. In a month, Facebook had become such a hit that it started expanding to other universities. In a year, Facebook was available at universities in Europe (*Harvard Crimson*, 2005). Only twenty months after going public, Facebook had already expanded to every university in the United States and had an estimated value of $100 million (Francisco, 2005).

UNDERSTANDING THE FACEBOOK USER

To understand why people are motivated to use Facebook, it is impor- 6 tant first to understand the standard Facebook user. According to

comScore Media Matrix, people aged eighteen to twenty-four disproportionately use online communication methods (comScore, 2005). It is also
this eighteen to twenty-four demographic that constitutes 51 percent of
SNS users (Hltwise, 2005).

This places the typical Facebook user into the life stage sometimes 7
called emerging adulthood. Emerging adulthood is a transitory period
between adolescence and adulthood occurring from the age of eighteen
to the mid-twenties. At this age, people are experiencing freedom by
living on their own for the first time and not yet having a family of
their own or a career.

This life stage is significant. In 1950, the median ages of marriage 8
for men and women were twenty-two and twenty, respectively. In
2000, however, the median ages of marriage had risen by five years for
both genders. Since the rates of college attendance are now higher than
ever, families and decisions on career paths occur later in life than
usual (Arnett, 2004).

With the age of first marriage older than ever before, a gap is cre- 9
ated. This gap represents a time period when individuals are no longer
in their original families but are yet to be in their chosen, created families (Arnett, 2004).

To fill this gap, people are relying on their networks of friends for 10
support and to take on the role of a surrogate family. These networks
can form groups, donned "urban tribes" by journalist Ethan Watters,
and can be functional units that take on many of the roles that a traditional family would fill. Some of these groups care for each other when
sick, help each other move furniture, or loan each other money when
financial times are hard (Watters, 2003).

SNSs such as Facebook give emerging adults a way to maintain 11
and build their friendship networks. By connecting to people in the
same geographical area through SNSs, it's easier than ever for people
to connect to groups and join urban tribes (O'Murchu, et al., 2004).

USES AND GRATIFICATIONS THEORY

Uses and gratifications (UG) theory attempts to explain how people 12
use the media to gratify their wants and needs, what motivates their
behavior and what are the consequences of their uses of media. With
the advent of the Internet, this perspective seems even more relevant.
Audiences undoubtedly play an active role in the messages they
receive from the Internet because to find information, they must
actively seek it out (Bryant and Zillman, 2002).

Motivations and selection patterns have been studied across a 13
variety of media, such as quiz programs, radio serials, and newspapers
(Bryant and Zillman, 2002). McQuail (1972) studied users' motivations

for watching television and outlined four main needs that people use the media to satisfy. These were diversion, personal relationships, personal identity and surveillance needs. Diversion needs involve a need to escape or a need for emotional release. Personal relationship needs are motives to connect to others. Personal identity needs include use of the media to help people form, adjust, and understand their own identity. Finally, surveillance needs inspire use of the media for information and understanding of the audience's environment (McQuail, 1972).

FACEBOOK, VOYEURISM, AND EXHIBITIONISM

Facebook also provides a venue for voyeurism. People can peruse the profiles of various users, read about other users' interests, read their friends' comments on their walls or view their friends. People can even scroll through a user's photo albums and see all of the pictures that that user has uploaded of themselves and all of the pictures that other users have uploaded with that user in it. Profiles can link to other, sometimes more personal, Web sites about the user. Some profiles link to other photo albums or to online journals. 14

Facebook thus may cultivate what Calvert (2000) refers to as "mediated voyeurism." According to Calvert's definition, mediated voyeurism is: 15

> ... the consumption of revealing images of and information about others' apparently real and unguarded lives, often yet not always for purposes of entertainment but frequently at the expense of privacy and discourse, through the means of mass media and Internet. [1]

Voyeurism could be important in understanding the use of Facebook. Some motivations for engaging in mediated voyeurism that are applicable to Facebook are finding other people to relate to (Andrejevic, 2004), trying to gain knowledge about others, or boosting one's self-esteem by deriding others (Calvert, 2000). 16

Voyeurism wouldn't be possible without the existence of exhibitionism, or self-disclosure. Without people willing to put their profiles on Facebook, Facebook wouldn't exist. Different suggested motivations for this sort of exhibitionism include the need to clarify or express one's identity, the need to validate oneself within the social matrix, the need to disclose personal information as a means of developing a relationship and the need to exert social control (Calvert, 2000). 17

Facebook may operate as an outlet for exhibitionism. Through profiles, users can clarify their chosen identities. By establishing a large 18 network of friends, users can validate their social viability. In establishing a Facebook account, users leave open the opportunity for others to forge a relationship with them. And, in discriminating between whom to befriend or from whom to accept friendship requests, users exert social control.

METHODS

To understand what motivates emerging adults to use Facebook and   19
how Facebook fulfills these motivations, an online survey was conducted. The survey was designed to measure different possible motivations for using Facebook and the importance with which different uses of Facebook were ascribed.

SAMPLE

Participants were selected from the Facebook website at the University   20
of North Carolina at Chapel Hill. Ten profiles of undergraduates appeared on each page. The ten people whose profiles were listed on every other page were contacted by their listed school email address and asked to participate in the study. Profiles that were obviously not those of real students (*e.g.*, "Corn Cob Bob" or "Paris Hilton") were not used; the next valid profile was used in its place.

About one-fourth (N = 3,944 or 26.5 percent) of the undergradu-   21
ate population at UNC–CH on Facebook in summer 2005 were contacted. A total of 1,049 students responded to the questionnaire, resulting in a response rate of 26.6 percent.

MEASURES

The first part of the questionnaire measured how important partici-   22
pants considered their ability to perform thirty-eight specific actions on Facebook. Actions included "poking others," "writing on friends' walls" and "joining groups," among others. Participants were asked to rate how important they valued their ability to perform these actions on a five-point scale, with one being "very unimportant" and five being "very important."

The second part of the questionnaire measured the students'   23
motivations for using Facebook. Participants were asked to rate how much they agreed or disagreed with fifty statements on a five-point scale, with one being "strongly disagree" and five being "strongly agree." Potential motivations were designed to assess the dimensions

derived from previous discussions on emerging adults, uses and gratifications theory, voyeurism, and exhibitionism.

The questionnaire was pilot tested with a group of undergraduates, and revisions were made based on their feedback. 24

PROCEDURE

The selected participants were contacted by email. The email directed 25
the participants to a Web site where they could complete the questionnaire. After completing the questionnaire, the participants were given the option of providing contact information to be entered into a drawing for a dinner for two at a local restaurant, which 93 percent of respondents did. Reminder email messages were sent out to all participants who had not completed the questionnaire a week later, encouraging those who hadn't taken the questionnaire to do so. All questionnaires that were submitted within six days of initial contact were included in the analysis.

RESULTS

A principal components analysis was performed on the items measur- 26
ing how important respondents rated different uses for Facebook and respondents' motivations for using Facebook. The component analysis identified eight underlying components of uses and nine motivations. Items with component score coefficients higher than 0.6 were considered strongly correlated with the component and items with component score coefficients between 0.4 and 0.6 were considered moderately correlated with the component. Items with component scores below 0.4 were considered too weakly correlated with a component to be used for further analysis.

Because there was no obvious conceptual connection between the 27
five items loading on component eight in both sets of items, these components were not included in the analysis.

The items loading on each of the fifteen remaining components 28
were combined and weighted using their component score coefficients so that they complied with the same five-point scale with which they were initially measured. To do this, items were multiplied by their component score coefficients, added to the other items in that component grouping, and then divided by the sum of the component score coefficients. Thus, seven new items were created measuring the importance of different uses for Facebook (Table 1), and eight new items were created measuring different motivations for using Facebook (Table 2).

Table 1: Ranking of Facebook uses

Uses	Description	Mean	Standard deviation
Friend functions	Accepting, adding, browsing through, or reviewing friends; seeing how friends are connected; showing friends other individuals.	3.91	0.737
Personal information	Reading personal information, looking through photos, reading walls, etc.	3.78	0.701
Practical information	Course and contact information.	3.38	0.912
Regulatory functions	Features that offer users control over their accounts, i.e., updating info or photos, privacy settings or editorial control over walls.	3.32	0.901
Groups	Features related to Facebook groups.	2.55	0.804
Events	Finding or planning events.	2.34	1.039
Misc. features	Friend details; social timeline; "pulse"; poking; social Web visualization; being friends with high schoolers; etc.	2.08	0.712

Notes: N = 1,001. Items on a five-point scale: 1 – Very unimportant, 2 – Unimportant, 3 – Neither important nor unimportant, 4 – Important, 5 – Very important.

Table 2: Ranking of Facebook motivations

Motivation	Description	Mean	Standard deviation
Social utility	Using Facebook with friends; talking with others about Facebook.	3.91	0.691
Directory	Use as a directory and to keep track of people, such as for class information.	3.71	0.682
Voyeurism	Learning about others from a distance; comparing oneself to others.	3.13	0.731
Herd instincts	Usage because everyone else does; not wanting to be left out.	3.08	0.865
Collection and connection	Amassing friends; organizing friends; feeling connected to others.	3.04	0.759
Personal expression	Expressing oneself, such as to develop relationships; gaining feedback on oneself; having others understand oneself.	2.69	0.722
Initiating relationships	Meeting people, particularly for romantic or sexual reasons; finding parties or events.	1.98	0.652

Notes: N = 920. Items on a five-point scale: 1 – Strongly disagree, 2 – Disagree, 3 – Neutral, 4 – Agree, 5 – Strongly agree.

The first component was a conglomeration of various Facebook 29
features and was labeled "Miscellaneous Features." As is shown in
Table 1, these features were not valued highly by most Facebook users.

Component two, "Groups," was comprised of group-related items 30
except for "make fake profiles."

Component three, "friend functions," included friend-related fea- 31
tures, such as friend lists; adding, declining, or accepting friend
requests, and looking at the connections among friends.

"Look up people to show someone else who they are" is an inter- 32
esting item in that it loads on both components three and four. While
not exactly a feature of Facebook, it is using Facebook to find someone's profile and show a friend who they are. Because of this, the item
fits right in with the voyeuristic qualities of component four, personal
information. Many of these items involve using Facebook to gather
personal information about others, whether through their photos, the
personal information section of their profile or their wall.

Component five, "regulatory functions," is composed primarily 33
of features that offer users control over their accounts, such as the ability to update profiles or photos, privacy settings or editorial content
over one's wall. It is unclear why messaging others is also positively
related to these uses. However, this item loaded only moderately on
component five, whereas all of the other items loaded strongly.

Component six loads strongly on Facebook's course-related 34
features, but also on contact information. Thus, component six was
labeled "practical information."

Component seven, "events," loaded strongly with both finding 35
and planning events on Facebook.

Table 1 shows how Facebook users value each of the use compo- 36
nents. Friend functions ranks the highest. Personal information, practical
information and regulatory functions were all also valued by Facebook
users. Neither groups nor events seemed too important to Facebook
users, as both scored on the lower half of the scale. Miscellaneous
features served as a catchall for Facebook features deemed unimportant
by users.

Table 2 shows the different components for motivations for using 37
Facebook. The items for each component don't always smoothly fit
together under one clear motivation, so all of the items for each component were examined for overriding themes.

Component one, diversion, strongly mirrors McQuail's motiva- 38
tion of diversion. Diversion entails the use of Facebook as a means of
entertainment, escape or out of habit. Also, being motivated to use
Facebook out of curiosity loads moderately on this component.

Component two, personal expression, seems tied to the previously 39
discussed motivations for exhibitionism. One, it involves using Facebook

of a means of creating an identity and expressing it. Two, it involves the hope that others will understand and appreciate this identity. Three, it involves adjusting this identity based on how others react to it.

Component three, collection and connection, involves using 40 Facebook to collect friends, organize and conceptualize one's social network and feel more connected to others. As previously discussed, emerging adults have frequently changing social lives and may be in search of surrogate families or "urban tribes." Those motivated by collection and connection may be using Facebook to instill social stability into their lives and to feel connected to others.

The fourth component, directory, is the motivation of using 41 Facebook as an index or reference guide. People who are motivated to use Facebook for this use Facebook to find out how to contact someone, to allow others to contact them if they need to, or to find out who is in their classes so that they can contact them about schoolwork.

Component five, initiating relationships, primarily entails using 42 Facebook to initiate relationships, often romantic or sexual, or to find parties or other events.

The sixth component, voyeurism, is tied to the previously dis- 43 cussed motivations for voyeurism. These users use Facebook to keep track of people and because they're curious about what other people are up to. Voyeuristic users use Facebook to compare themselves to others. This motivation additionally entails using Facebook to learn about other people from a distance to achieve social efficacy.

Users motivated by the seventh component, social utility, use 44 Facebook as a social activity with friends and as a topic of conversation. These users build and strengthen relationships with Facebook. It is important to note that this is not the same as building or strengthening relationships *through* Facebook, however. This component also loads on putting a lot of effort into one's Facebook profile, but with a component coefficient of 0.404 and the cutoff point being 0.400, this loading is weak in comparison to the other two.

The ninth and final component, Herd Instinct, is simply the band- 45 wagon effect. These users use Facebook because everyone else does and they don't want to be left out.

Table 2 answers the question of why emerging adults are using 46 Facebook, with the most prevalent motivation being social utility. Directory and diversion are both also common motivations for using Facebook. The motivation of initiating relationships, on the other hand, is rather uncommon, as is the motivation of personal expression.

The motivation components were correlated with the original 47 thirty-eight use items (Table 3). Only items with a correlation of 0.4 or greater (p < 0.01) were included in the tables. In Table 3, we see which specific Facebook uses are correlated with the motivations.

Table 3: Correlations between Facebook motivations and specific Facebook uses

Specific uses	Motivations							
	Diversion	Personal expression	Collection and connection	Directory	Initiating relationships	Voyeurism	Social utility	Herd instinct
Update information	0.31	0.41	0.35	0.28	0.20	0.31	0.37	0.12
Get contact information	0.13	0.18	0.21	0.44	0.17	0.24	0.22	0.06
Read other's personal information	0.43	0.41	0.37	0.29	0.23	0.47	0.40	0.15
Writing on walls	0.41	0.35	0.42	0.22	0.21	0.29	0.37	0.12
Reading walls	0.48	0.39	0.42	0.19	0.26	0.42	0.39	0.18
Browse through photos of others	0.41	0.35	0.37	0.26	0.27	0.41	0.40	0.19
Look for photos of a specific person	0.37	0.35	0.35	0.31	0.31	0.43	0.38	0.20
Look at the groups of others	0.37	0.43	0.38	0.29	0.24	0.43	0.32	0.20
Review friend list	0.31	0.38	0.43	0.25	0.23	0.34	0.35	0.15
Browse through friends of others	0.38	0.39	0.43	0.25	0.27	0.44	0.39	0.28
Add friends	0.38	0.41	0.45	0.35	0.20	0.38	0.47	0.15
Look up people to show someone else who they are	0.39	0.28	0.31	0.34	0.15	0.40	0.53	0.16

Notes: N: 999–1,040. All items (Pearson product-moment correlation coefficients) are significant at $\rho < 0.01$. Correlations above .40 are highlighted. Only items with at least one correlation > 0.40 are included.

Neither herd instinct nor initiating relationships is notably cor- 48
related to any use. As could be expected, getting people's contact
information is notably correlated only with directory, updating one's
info is notably correlated only with personal expression, and reviewing one's own friend list is notably correlated only with collection
and connection.

Every item correlated above 0.40 with voyeurism involves 49
learning about other people through Facebook. It is even moderately
correlated with reading other people's walls but not with writing on
them.

Reading other people's walls is also the primary way in which 50
Facebook users gratify the motivation of diversion.

The highest correlation here is between social utility and looking 51
up people to show someone else who they are. Because social utility is
the most prevalent motivation for using Facebook, this relationship is
of special importance.

DISCUSSION

The most prevalent motivation for using Facebook is as a social activ- 52
ity. Typical Facebook users use and talk about Facebook with their
friends. They look at people's photos, read their profiles with their
friends and talk about them. They use Facebook to show their friends
who someone else is. Essentially, Facebook operates primarily as a
tool for the facilitation of gossip. It makes sense that Facebook would
be ideal for this kind of communication. With Facebook, those interested in gossip can bring up everything they need to talk about their
subjects, from photos to a list of their interests to the status of relationships.

Facebook users do have other motivations, too. Facebook works 53
handily as a directory of their friends' contact information, practically
eliminating the need for address books. And, if people need information about class and they can't think of any classmates offhand,
Facebook can offer them a list of their classmates and their contact
information. Thus, it shouldn't be surprising that the use of Facebook
as a directory is its second most prevalent use.

It's worth noting that these two motivations are likely to be applic- 54
able specifically to Facebook and not to SNSs in general. Because
Facebook is centered on colleges, people are more likely to already know
others in their Facebook directory or to be able to recognize them than on
SNSs that aren't geographically based, such as MySpace. Gossip is more
interesting when it involves people one knows, so other SNSs may not
work as well as a tool for gossip. Similarly, the contact information of

strangers on MySpace may be less useful than that of friends or class-mates on Facebook.

One motivation that may be more applicable to other SNSs is initiating relationships. Though seemingly uncommon on Facebook, this motivation may have more of a home on other SNSs where the purpose is to meet new people. 55

Diversion may be a motivation that is applicable to both Facebook and other SNSs. On Facebook, this motivation is gratified through such uses as browsing through people's photos or reading their profile. Of note is that walls play a seemingly large role in the gratification of this motivation, particularly with those using Facebook for entertainment. Reading and writing on other people's walls is the main way that people use Facebook for fun. 56

Both voyeurism and exhibitionism were revealed as motivations for using Facebook. However, using Facebook to create and express an identity is rather infrequent. Interestingly, there are a couple of items loading on this component that have to do with a motivation to be accepted by and connected to others, indicating that that those who engage in exhibitionistic behavior may be doing so as a means for acceptance, both on Facebook and in other venues. 57

Voyeuristic use of Facebook, on the other hand, is far more commonplace. The gratification of this motivation is exactly as would be expected: reading personal information, looking through photos, seeing who someone's friends are, reading walls, etc. 58

One might think that because of Facebook's ubiquity, it benefited greatly by the snowball effect—a couple of people got on Facebook, then a few more got on because it seemed like the thing to do, and then herd instinct led people to Facebook in droves. While that's not necessarily false, the data indicate that this is not a primary motivation for why people use Facebook. 59

Some people use Facebook to collect, organize and feel connected to friends. These users like to amass a large social network on Facebook and look over their collected friends. This isn't a particularly strong motivation for users, but it isn't a weak one either. 60

It is interesting to note that users tended to value personal information more than practical information, however, indicating that Facebook is valued less for utilitarian purposes and more for social purposes. 61

CONCLUSION

Facebook could potentially gratify a variety of motivations. People could use Facebook because they just transferred to a new school and want to find and meet new people, or to see who is in their art history 62

419

class so they can call them and find information about the next test. Some could use Facebook to discover a potential love interest's favorite music, to keep in touch with old friends from high school, to put off doing work, or just because everyone else is using Facebook.

Though all of these, to varying degrees, seem to be reasons why people use Facebook, the most prevalent way in which people use Facebook is as a social utility. Counter to what may be intuitive, the primary way in which Facebook contributes to socializing isn't by offering a medium through which people can meet and communicate with others. Instead, it's by acting as a virtual watering hole that dispenses information about peers. 63

NOTE

[1]Calvert, 2000, pp. 2–3.

REFERENCES

420

Mark Andrejevic, 2004. *Reality TV: The work of being watched*. Lanham, Md.: Rowman & Littlefield.

J.J. Arnett, 2004. *Emerging adulthood: The winding road from the late teens through the twenties*. New York: Oxford University Press.

Jennings Bryant and Dolf Zillmann (editors), 2002. *Media effects: Advances in theory and research*. Second ed. Mahwah, N.J.: Lawrence Erlbaum Associates.

Clay Calvert, 2000. *Voyeur nation: Media, privacy, and peering in modern culture*. Boulder, Colo.: Westview Press.

comScore Media Matrix, 2005. "The score: Reaching social animals," *iMedia Connection*, at http://www.imediaconnection.com/content/6515.asp, accessed 29 November 2005

Harvard Crimson, 2005. "How they got here," at http://www.thecrimson.com/article.aspx?ref=505941 accessed 4 December 2005.

Facebook, at http://www.facebook.com, accessed 19 April 2007.

Bambi Francisco, 2005. "The Facebook phenomenon," *Investor's Business Daily*, at http://www.investors.com/breakingnews.asp?journalid=32493493&brk=1, accessed 28 November 2005.

Hitwise, 2005. "Users rediscover the buzz of social networking." at http://www.hitwise.com/press-center/hitwiseHS2004/social_networking.html, accessed 28 November 2005.

Chris Hughes, 2005. E-mail to the author, accessed 16 October 2005.

Janet Kornblum and Mary Beth Marklein, 2006. "What you say online could haunt you," *USA Today* (9 March), pp. 1A+ and at http://

www.usatoday.com/tech/news/internetprivacy/2006-03-08-facebook-myspace_x.htm, accessed 15 November 2007.

Dennis McQuail (compiler), 1972. *Sociology of mass communications: Selected readings.* Harmondsworth: Penguin.

Chris Nagele, 2005. "Social networks research report," *Wildbit* at http://www.wildbit.com/wildbit-sn-report.pdf, accessed 12 November 2005.

Ina O'Murchu, John G. Breslin, and Stefan Decker, 2004. "Online social and business networking communities," *Digital Enterprise Research Institute* at http://64.81.85.64/4thgenportals/WebPortaldocs.nsf/DocTitles/Online_Social_and_Business_Networking_Communities_/$FILE/DERI-TR-20 accessed 14 November 2005.

John Schwartz, 2005. "High-tech hot spots," *Newsweek* (22 August), p. 64.

Ethan Watters, 2003. *Urban tribes: A generation redefines friendship, family, and commitment* New York: Bloomsbury.

Examining the Text

1. How does Bumgarner define "emerging adulthood" and why does he think SNSs such as Facebook are particularly relevant during this period in a person's life?

2. In his discussion of uses and gratifications theory in paragraph 13, Bumgarner briefly mentions several possible motivations that people have for using media: diversion, personal relationships, personal identity, and surveillance. To what extent do you think these motivations apply to Facebook as well as to other media that young adults use?

3. In his Discussion section at the end of the article, what distinctions does Bumgarner draw between Facebook and other SNSs? In what ways does Facebook's restriction to college campuses impact how young adults use this social networking service?

4. *Thinking rhetorically:* Bumgarner ends his article with a metaphor comparing Facebook to a watering hold around which people meet and converse. Reflecting on Bumgarner's findings in his survey, as well as on your own experiences with Facebook (or other SNSs), how well do you think this metaphor holds up? What problems do you see with describing Facebook as a "virtual watering hole"? More generally, do you think it's an effective strategy to end an article with a metaphor? Why or why not?

For Group Discussion

In his discussion of Tables 1 and 2, Bumgarner briefly describes seven components or categories that characterize the ways people use Facebook and seven components or categories that characterize the reasons people use Facebook. Choose one of these two sets of categories—that is, either uses or motivations—and list the seven components. In a small-group discussion, come to your own conclusions about how important these uses or motivations are in your use of Facebook (or other SNSs). Does your ranking of these components match the ranking that Bumgarner found in his survey? Can you think of any other important uses or motivations involved with Facebook?

Writing Suggestion

Bumgarner includes tables with data from his questionnaires. Take one of the tables and, after carefully studying it, write a four- or five-paragraph explanation of the significant information that the table conveys. You might organize your essay by identifying one key point for each paragraph of your essay; key points can include data from different answers, or comparisons of data across different columns. Make sure that you don't simply report numbers; rather, provide verbal descriptions that show what the numbers signify. You might also consider including quotations or paraphrases from Bumgarner's article to help you explain what the information in the table means.

Why Youth (Heart) Social Network Sites: The Role of Networked Publics in Teenage Social Life

DANAH BOYD

The following article pairs nicely with Bumgarner's empirical study of Facebook: Danah Boyd focuses here on another SNS (MySpace), targets a different group of users (fourteen- to eighteen-year olds), and uses a different method (ethnography) to approach the subject. Boyd also provides more background information and theoretical analysis of the role of SNSs in the lives of teenagers; that is, she delves more deeply into questions of gratification and motivation that Bumgarner addresses only briefly. Ultimately, though, both authors are interested in knowing more about why SNSs have become so popular so quickly, and what effect their use has on the current generation of teenagers and students.

Boyd is particularly interested in understanding the developmental and social forces that make teenagers inclined to turn to MySpace. She looks at the difficult processes teenagers have to face as they define their identities and learn social norms, and she considers as well the familial and cultural constraints on teenagers—the rules and regulations and restrictions that govern their lives. According to Boyd, MySpace and other SNSs help teenagers negotiate these difficulties and so serve an important and helpful function.

Boyd explains that as part of her research for this article, she talked to and hung out with many teenagers; she includes quotations from two of them as epigraphs to her article, and other quotations are interspersed throughout the article. In addition, though, Boyd did more traditional kinds of research, as you can see in her lengthy footnotes, and she quotes from scholars in various fields. **As you read** *this article, therefore, pay attention to the ways in which Boyd draws on different "experts" to illustrate or support various points that she makes.*

"If you're not on MySpace, you don't exist"– Skyler, 18, to her mom[1]

"I'm in the 7th grade. I'm 13. I'm not a cheerleader. I'm not the president of the student body. Or captain of the debate team. I'm not the prettiest girl in my class. I'm not the most popular girl in my class. I'm just a kid. I'm a little shy. And it's really hard in this school to impress people enough to be your friend if you're not any of those things. But I go on these really great vacations with my parents between Christmas and New Year's every year. And I take pictures of places we go. And I write about those places. And I post this on my Xanga. Because I think if kids in school read what I have to say and how I say it they'll want to be my friend." – Vivien, 13, to Parry Aftab during a "Teen Angels" meeting[2]

During 2005, online social network sites like MySpace and Facebook 1 became common destinations for young people in the United States. Throughout the country, young people were logging in, creating elaborate profiles, publicly articulating their relationships with other participants, and writing extensive comments back and forth. By early 2006, many considered participation on the key social network site, MySpace, essential to being seen as *cool* at school. While not all teens are members of social network sites, these sites developed significant cultural resonance amongst American teens in a short period of time. Although the luster has since faded and teens are not nearly as infatuated with these sites as they once were, they continue to be an important part of teen social life.

The rapid adoption of social network sites by teenagers in the 2 United States and in many other countries around the world raises some important questions. Why do teenagers flock to these sites? What are they expressing on them? How do these sites fit into their lives? What are they learning from their participation? Are these online activities like face-to-face friendships—or are they different, or complementary? The goal of this chapter is to address these questions, and explore their implications for youth identities. While particular systems may come and go, how youth engage through social network sites today provides long-lasting insights into identity formation, status negotiation, and peer-to-peer sociality.

To address the aforementioned questions, I begin by document- 3 ing key features of social network sites and the business decisions that lead to mass adoption, and then seek to situate social network sites in a broader discussion of what I call "networked publics." I then examine how teens are modeling identity through social network profiles so that they can write themselves and their community into being. Building on this, I investigate how this process of articulated expression supports critical peer-based sociality because, by allowing youth to hang out amongst their friends and classmates, social network sites are providing teens with a space to work out identity and status, make sense of cultural cues, and negotiate public life. I argue that social network sites are a type of networked public with four properties that are not typically present in face-to-face public life: persistence, searchability, exact copyability, and invisible audiences. These properties fundamentally alter social dynamics, complicating the ways in which people interact. I conclude by reflecting on the social developments that have prompted youth to seek out networked publics, and considering the changing role that publics have in young people's lives.

METHODOLOGY AND DEMOGRAPHICS

The arguments made in this chapter are based on ethnographic data 4 collected during my two-year study of United States-based youth engagement with MySpace. In employing the term *ethnography*, I am primarily referencing the practices of "participant observation" and "deep hanging out"[3] alongside qualitative interviews. I have moved between online and offline spaces, systematically observing, documenting, and talking to young people about their practices and attitudes.

While the subjects of my interviews and direct observations are 5 primarily urban youth (ranging in age, sex, race, sexuality, religion, ethnicity, and socio-economic class), I have also spent countless hours analyzing the profiles, blogs, and commentary of teenagers throughout the United States. Although I have interviewed older people, the vast majority of people that I have interviewed and observed are of high school age, living with a parent or guardian. There is no good term to reference this group. Not all are actually students (and that role signals identity material that is not accurate). Vague terms like "youth," "young people," and "children" imply a much broader age range. For these reasons, and in reference to the history of the term "teenager" in relation to compulsory high school education[4], I have consciously decided to label the relevant population "teenagers" even though the majority of individuals that I have spoken with are fourteen–eighteen. While strictly speaking, there are non-high school age individuals in this category, the vast majority of them are; I will focus primarily on that group.

Qualitatively, I have found that there are two types of non- 6 participants: disenfranchised teens and conscientious objectors. The former consists of those without Internet access, those whose parents succeed in banning them from participation, and online teens who primarily access the Internet through school and other public venues where social network sites are banned.[5] Conscientious objectors include politically minded teens who wish to protest against Murdoch's News Corp. (the corporate owner of MySpace), obedient teens who have respected or agree with their parents' moral or safety concerns, marginalized teens who feel that social network sites are for the cool kids, and other teens who feel as though they are too cool for these sites. The latter two explanations can be boiled down to one explanation that I heard frequently: *"because it's stupid."* While the various conscientious objectors may deny participating, I have found that many of them actually do have profiles to which they log in occasionally. I have also found numerous cases where the friends of non-participants create profiles for them.[6] Furthermore, amongst those conscientious objectors who are genuinely non-participants, I have yet to find one who does not have something to say about the sites, albeit typically something negative. In essence, MySpace is the civil society of teenage culture: whether one is for it or against it, everyone knows the site and has an opinion about it.

Interestingly, I have found that race and social class play little role 7 in terms of access beyond the aforementioned disenfranchised population. Poor urban black teens appear to be just as likely to join the site as white teens from wealthier backgrounds—although what they do on there has much to do with their level of Internet access. Those who only access their accounts in schools use it primarily as an asynchronous communication tool, while those with continuous nighttime access at home spend more time surfing the network, modifying their profile, collecting friends, and talking to strangers. When it comes to social network sites, there appears to be a far greater participatory divide than an access divide.

Gender appears to influence participation on social network sites. 8 Younger boys are more likely to participate than younger girls (46% vs. 44%) but older girls are far more likely to participate than older boys

(70% vs. 57%). Older boys are twice as likely to use the sites to flirt and slightly more likely to use the sites to meet new people than girls of their age. Older girls are far more likely to use these sites to communicate with friends they see in person than younger people or boys of their age.[7] While gender differences do exist and should not be ignored, most of what I discuss in this article concerns practices that are common to both boys and girls.

Fundamentally, this chapter is a case study based on ethnographic data. My primary goal is simply to unveil some of the common ways in which teenagers now experience social life online. 9

PROFILES, FRIENDS, AND COMMENTS

Social network sites are based around *Profiles*, a form of individual (or, less frequently, group) home page, which offers a description of each member. In addition to text, images, and video created by the member, the social network site profile also contains comments from other members and a public list of the people that one identifies as *Friends* within the network.[8] Because the popularized style of these sites emerged out of dating services, the profile often contains material typical of those sites: demographic details (age, sex, location, etc.), tastes (interests, favorite bands, etc.), a photograph, and an open-ended description of who the person would like to meet. The default profile is publicly accessible to anyone, but most social network sites have privacy features that allow participants to restrict who can see what. For example, MySpace allows participants to make their profiles Friends-only (and sets this as the default for those who indicate they are fourteen or fifteen years old) while Facebook gives profile-access only to people from the same school by default. 10

After creating a profile, participants are asked to invite their friends to the site by supplying their email addresses. Alternatively, they can look at others' profiles and add those people to their list of Friends.[9] Most social network sites require approval for two people to be linked as Friends. When someone indicates another as a Friend, the recipient receives a message asking for confirmation. If Friendship is confirmed, the two become Friends in the system and their relationship is included in the public display of connections on all profiles.[10] These displays typically involve photos and nicknames that link to their profile. By clicking on these links, visitors can traverse the network by surfing from Friend to Friend to Friend. 11

In addition to the content that members provide to create their own profiles, social network sites typically have a section dedicated to comments by Friends. (On Friendster, this section is called *Testimonials*; 12

426

on Facebook, it is called *The Wall*.) Because Friendster implemented this feature to encourage people to write testimonials about their friends for strangers to read, early adopters used this feature to write single messages *about* the person represented in the profile. Over time, reciprocity motivated people to write creative testimonials back and forth, creating a form of conversation;[11] this was particularly popular amongst people using Friendster for playful activities. For example, a profile representing table salt wrote long love odes about pepper on the profile representing pepper; pepper reciprocated and this went back and forth for weeks.

As teenagers began joining Friendster, they also used this section   13 to write *to* the profile owner, even though the testimonials were public. When MySpace implemented the same feature and called it *Comments* instead of *Testimonials*, writing to the person became status quo, particularly amongst younger participants. The following comments highlight the difference:

> "*Mark is a man among boys, a razor sharp mind towering over the general sludge.*" (*Testimonial on Friendster Profile of Mark, 27*)

> "*Are we still gonna go paintballing?*" (*Comment on MySpace Profile of Corey, 14*)

427

In essence, Corey's friend is writing a purportedly private mes-   14 sage to him in a public space for others to view. Corey will reply to the comment in-kind, writing the answer on his friend's profile. By doing this, teens are taking social interactions between friends into the public sphere for others to witness.

Although many sites include other common features,[12] the prac-   15 tices that take place through the use of the most prevalent three—profiles, friends and comments—differentiate social network sites from other types of computer-mediated communication. Furthermore, what makes these three practices significant for consideration is that they take place in public: Friends are publicly articulated, profiles are publicly viewed, and comments are publicly visible.

NETWORKED PUBLICS

Defining the term *public* is difficult at best.[13] *As an adjective*, it is com-   16 monly used in opposition to *private*. *When referring to locations*, public is used to signal places that are accessible to anyone (or at least anyone belonging to a privileged category like *adults*). *In reference to actions or texts*, public often implies that the audience is unknown and that strangers may bear witness.

As a noun, public refers to a collection of people who may not all   17
know each other but share "a common understanding of the world, a
shared identity, a claim to inclusiveness, a consensus regarding the collective interest."[14] In some senses, *public* is quite similar to *audience* as
both refer to a group bounded by a shared text, whether that is a world-
view or a performance.[15] These words often collide conceptually
because speaking to the public implies that the public is acting as an
audience.

When talking about *the* public, one must ask if there is only *one*   18
public. When United States President Bush addresses the public, he's
not conceptualizing the same public as Zimbabwe President Mugabe.
Likewise, it is not the same audience that hears both presidents. If,
instead, we talk about *a* public, it is possible to recognize that there are
different collections of people depending on the particular situation.[16]
Talking about *a* public also implies that there must be multiple *publics*
separated by social contexts. What then constitutes the boundaries of a
given public?

In this article, I move between these many different meanings of   19
public. Social network sites allow publics to gather. At the same time,
by serving as a space where speech takes place, they are also publics
themselves. The sites themselves also distinguish between public and
private, where public means that a profile is visible to anyone and private means that it is Friends-only.

The types of publics that gather on social network sites and the   20
types of publics that such sites support are deeply affected by the mediated nature of interaction. For these reasons it is important to distinguish
these sites as *publics*, not simply public, and *networked publics*, not simply
publics. While this latter term has been used to reference "a linked set of
social, cultural, and technological developments that have accompanied
the growing engagement with digitally networked media,"[17] I am primarily talking about the spaces and audiences that are bound together
through technological networks (i.e. the Internet, mobile networks, etc.).
Networked publics are one type of *mediated public*; the network mediates
the interactions between members of the public. Media of all stripes have
enabled the development of mediated publics.

The reason for differentiating networked publics from mediated   21
and unmediated publics has to do with fundamental architectural differences that affect social interaction. In unmediated environments,
the boundaries and audiences of a given public are structurally
defined. Access to visual and auditory information is limited by
physics; walls and other obstacles further restrain visibility. Thus
when I say that I embarrassed myself in public by tripping on the
curb, the public that I am referencing includes all of the strangers who
visually witnessed my stumble. The audience is restricted to those

present in a limited geographical radius at a given moment in time. The public that I conceptualize might also include all of those who might hear of my accident through word-of-mouth; although the likelihood of others sharing the event is dependent on my status in the public and the juiciness of the story. While I might think that the whole world must know, this is not likely to be true. More importantly, in an unmediated world, it is not possible for the whole world actually to witness this incident; in the worst-case scenario, they might all hear of my mishap through word of mouth.

Mediating technologies like television, radio, and newsprint 22 change everything. My fall could have been recorded and televised on the nightly news. This changes the scale of the public. Rather than considering all of the people who *did* witness me visually, I must also consider all of the people who *might* witness a reproduction of my fall. The potential audience is affected by the properties of the mediating technologies, namely *persistence, replicability*, and *invisible audiences*. Networked publics add an additional feature—*searchability*—while magnifying all of the other properties. While broadcast media take advantage of persistence, it is not as if anyone could go to the television and watch my fall whenever they wish; but if my fall is uploaded to YouTube or MySpace Video, this is possible.

429

These four properties thus fundamentally separate unmediated 23 publics from networked publics:

1. *Persistence:* Unlike the ephemeral quality of speech in unmediated publics, networked communications are recorded for posterity. This enables asynchronous communication but it also extends the period of existence of any speech act.
2. *Searchability:* Because expressions are recorded and identity is established through text, search and discovery tools help people find like minds. While people cannot currently acquire the geographical coordinates of any person in unmediated spaces, finding one's *digital body* online is just a matter of keystrokes.
3. *Replicability:* Hearsay can be deflected as misinterpretation, but networked public expressions can be copied from one place to another verbatim such that there is no way to distinguish the "original" from the "copy."[18]
4. *Invisible audiences:* While we can visually detect most people who can overhear our speech in unmediated spaces, it is virtually impossible to ascertain all those who might run across our expressions in networked publics. This is further complicated by the other three properties, since our expression may be heard at a different time and place from when and where we originally spoke.

In short, a mediated public (and especially a networked public)   24
could consist of all people across all space and all time. Of course, in
reality, it probably will not, even when a person desperately wishes to
have such attention. Still, the bounding forces of networked publics are
less constrained by geography and temporal collocation than unmediated publics. Because people are not accustomed to socializing when
they do not know the audience or the context, interactions in networked publics are often peculiar to newcomers who get frustrated
when what they intended is not what is interpreted.

These properties affect both the potential audience and the con-   25
text in which the expression is received. We will address this further in
the next section as we consider young people's engagement with social
network sites more specifically.

INITIATION: PROFILE CREATION

Teenagers typically learn about MySpace through their friends—they   26
join because a friend invites them to join. After creating an account,
they begin setting up their profile by filling in forms on the site. This
generates a generic profile with content like "favorite books" and
"about me." Before writing anything of depth, teens tend to look at others' profiles, starting with the friend who invited them. In viewing that
profile, they are offered links to their friends' MySpace Friends; and so
they can spend countless hours surfing the network, jumping from
Friend to Friend.

By looking at others' profiles, teens get a sense of what types of   27
presentations are socially appropriate; others' profiles provide critical
cues about what to present on their own profile. While profiles are
constructed through a series of generic forms, there is plenty of room
for them to manipulate the profiles to express themselves. At a basic
level, the choice of photos and the personalized answers to generic
questions allow individuals to signal meaningful cues about themselves. While the ability to identify oneself through such textual and
visual means is valuable, MySpace profiles also afford another level of
personalization.

Experimenting with the generic forms, a few early adopters dis-   28
covered that MySpace had failed to close a security hole. While most
other sites blocked HTML, CSS, and Javascript in their forms,
MySpace did not. Early adopters began exploiting this hole to personalize their pages by adding code to the form fields that changed the
background and added multimedia to their pages. There is no simple
way to make these modifications;[19] individuals must figure out what
CSS or HTML goes in what form. While the site itself does not offer

support, numerous other websites (most initially created by teenagers) emerged to provide code and instructions for modifying every aspect of a MySpace page. Individuals choose a desirable layout and then they are instructed to copy and paste the code into the appropriate forms. This code inevitably includes links back to the helper page.[20] A copy/paste culture emerged, as teens began trafficking in knowledge of how to *pimp out*[21] their profiles. Although most teens' profiles are altered, it is important to not assume technological literacy[22]—few teens hand-code their pages; most use a helper site or beg friends to do it for them.

Building an intricate profile is an initiation rite. In the early days of their infatuation, teens spent innumerable hours tracking down codes, trading tips, and setting up a slick profile. Through this process, they are socialized into MySpace—they learn both technological and social codes. While technological information gives them the wherewithal to craft a profile, the interpretation and evaluation of this performance is dictated by social protocols. MySpace profiles become yet another mechanism by which teens can signal information about their identities and tastes.

29

431

IDENTITY PERFORMANCE

In everyday interactions, the body serves as a critical site of identity performance. In conveying who we are to other people, we use our bodies to project information about ourselves.[23] This is done through movement, clothes, speech, and facial expressions. What we put forward is our best effort at what we want to say about who we are. Yet while we intend to convey one impression, our performance is not always interpreted as we might expect. Through learning to make sense of others' responses to our behavior, we can assess how well we have conveyed what we intended. We can then alter our performance accordingly. This process of performance, interpretation, and adjustment is what Erving Goffman calls *impression management*,[24] and is briefly discussed in the introduction to this volume. Impression management is a part of a larger process where people seek to *define a situation*[25] through their behavior. People seek to define social situations by using contextual cues from the environment around them. Social norms emerge out of situational definitions as people learn to read cues from the environment and the people present to understand what is appropriate behavior.

Learning how to manage impressions is a critical social skill that is honed through experience. Over time, we learn how to make meaning out of a situation, others' reactions, and what we are projecting of

30

31

ourselves. As children, we learn that actions on our part prompt reactions by adults; as we grow older, we learn to interpret these reactions and adjust our behavior. Diverse social environments help people develop these skills because they force individuals to re-evaluate the signals they take for granted.

The process of learning to read social cues and react accordingly   32
is core to being socialized into a society. While the process itself begins at home for young children, it is critical for young people to engage in broader social settings to develop these skills. Of course, how children are taught about situations and impression management varies greatly by culture,[26] but these processes are regularly seen as part of coming of age. While no one is ever a true master of impression management, the teenage years are ripe with experiences to develop these skills.

In mediated environments, bodies are not immediately visible and   33
the skills people need to interpret situations and manage impressions are different. As Jenny Sundén argues, people must learn to *write themselves into being*.[27] Doing so makes visible how much we take the body for granted. While text, images, audio, and video all provide valuable means for developing a virtual presence, the act of articulation differs from how we convey meaningful information through our bodies. This process also makes explicit the self-reflexivity that Giddens argues is necessary for identity formation, but the choices individuals make in crafting a digital body highlight the self-monitoring that Foucault so sinisterly notes.[28]

432

In some sense, people have more control online—they are able to   34
carefully choose what information to put forward, thereby eliminating visceral reactions that might have seeped out in everyday communication. At the same time, these digital bodies are fundamentally coarser, making it far easier to misinterpret what someone is expressing. Furthermore, as Amy Bruckman shows, key information about a person's body is often present online, even when that person is trying to act deceptively; for example, people are relatively good at detecting when someone is a man even when they profess to be a woman online.[29] Yet because mediated environments present reveal different signals, the mechanisms of deception differ.[30]

WRITING IDENTITY AND COMMUNITY INTO BEING

A MySpace profile can be seen as a form of *digital body* where individu-   35
als must write themselves into being. Through profiles, teens can express salient aspects of their identity for others to see and interpret. They construct these profiles for their friends and peers to view. (We

will complicate the issue of audience in the next section.) While what they present may or may not resemble their offline identity, their primary audience consists of peers that they know primarily offline—people from school, church, work, sports teams, etc. Because of this direct link between offline and online identities, teens are inclined to present the side of themselves that they believe will be well received by these peers.

The desire to be cool on MySpace is part of the more general desire to be validated by one's peers. Even though teens theoretically have the ability to behave differently online, the social hierarchies that regulate "coolness" offline are also present online. For example, it's cool to have Friends on MySpace but if you have too many Friends, you are seen as a *MySpace whore*. These markers of cool are rooted in the social culture of MySpace. One of the ways that coolness is articulated is through bulletin posts meant to attack those who have status online and offline. One such post is a satirical Top 10 list of *"How To Be Cool On Myspace,"* which includes material like *"Your MySpace name MUST contain symbols and incorrect spelling"* and *"All your blogs have to be about how bad your day was."* While this post is meant to dismiss these common practices, when these posts are spread around, they simultaneously reinforce these norms in the process of mocking them.

Part of what solidifies markers of cool has to do with the underlying Friend network. MySpace Friends are not just people that one knows, but public displays of connections.[31] While teens will typically add friends and acquaintances as Friends, they will also add people because it would be socially awkward to say no to them, because they make the individual look cool, or simply because it would be interesting to read their bulletin posts. Because Friends are displayed on an individual's profile, they provide meaningful information about that person; in other words, *"You are who you know."*[32] For better or worse, people judge others based on their associations: group identities form around and are reinforced by the collective tastes and attitudes of those who identify with the group. Online, this cue is quite helpful in enabling people to find their bearings.

The best indicator of an individual's close friends is their Top Friends; these are displayed directly on an individual's profile, while the rest of their Friends require an additional click. Individuals can choose which Friends will be displayed. While the Top Friends feature allows members to quickly get to and show off the profiles of their closest friends, the public nature of this display tends to complicate relationships. In short, the Top Friends feature is considered pure social drama:

> *"Myspace always seems to cause way too much drama and i am so dang sick of it. im sick of the pain and the hurt and tears and the jealousy and*

36

433

37

38

*the heartache and the truth and the lies.. it just SUCKS! . . . im just so
sick of the drama and i just cant take it anymore compared to all the love
its supposed to make us feel. I get off just feeling worse. i have people complain to me that they are not my number one on my top 8. come on now.
grow up. its freaking myspace."*—Olivia, 17

The reason that the Top Friends feature wreaks social havoc on   39
teens' lives is because there are social consequences in publicly
announcing one's friends, best friends, and *bestest* friends. Feelings are
hurt when individuals find that someone that they feel close with does
not reciprocate.

*"As a kid, you used your birthday party guest list as leverage on the play-
ground. 'If you let me play, I'll invite you to my birthday party.' Then, as
you grew up and got your own phone, it was all about someone being on
your speed dial. Well today it's the MySpace Top 8. It's the new dangling
carrot for gaining superficial acceptance. Taking someone off your Top 8 is
your new passive aggressive power play when someone pisses you off."*—
Nadine, 16

Yet, for all of the social discomfort, these Friends help provide   40
group structure, further indicating the meaningful identity markers of
the individual. In choosing Friends, teens write their community into
being; which is precisely why this feature is so loved and despised.

Identity can be seen as a social process that is fluid and contingent   41
on the situation.[33] On MySpace, an individual's perceived audience
frames the situation. While others might be present, the markers of cool
are clearly dictated by an individual's friends and peers. What teens
are doing here is conceptualizing an *imagined audience*.[34] While this
may seem peculiar, it is a practice that is commonplace for people like
writers and actors who regularly interact with the public through
mediating technologies. Without having cues about who will witness a
given expression, an imagined audience provides a necessary way of
envisioning who should be present. The size and diversity of this imagined community depends on the individual; some imagine acquiring
fans while others imagine a community that is far more intimate. . . .
Youth's views on audience are quite nuanced.[35] While some value the
possibility of a wide audience, actually attracting such audience can
introduce complications. At the same time, wanting a large audience
does not mean that a large audience will appear: online, everyone is
famous to fifteen people.[36]

Regardless of desires, it is impossible to see the actual audience   42
across all space and all time. At the same time, it is necessary to understand the scope of one's audience to properly present oneself. By imagining an audience, regardless of its accuracy, teens are able to navigate

the social situation required in crafting a profile. Because of the intricate connection between offline and online social worlds, the audience that teens envision online is connected to their social world offline, or to their hopes about the possible alternatives online. Yet, their audience online may not be who they think it is.

PRIVACY IN PUBLIC: CREATING *MY* SPACE

"My mom always uses the excuse about the internet being 'public' when she defends herself. It's not like I do anything to be ashamed of, but a girl needs her privacy. I do online journals so I can communicate with my friends. Not so my mother could catch up on the latest gossip of my life."—Bly Lauritano-Werner, 17[37]

For Lauritano-Werner, privacy is not about structural limitations 43 to access; it is about being able to limit access through social conventions. This approach makes sense if you recognize that networked publics make it nearly impossible to have structurally enforced borders. However, this is not to say that teens do not also try to create structural barriers.

435

Teens often fabricate key identifying information like name, age, 44 and location to protect themselves. While parents groups often encourage this deception to protect teens from strangers,[38] many teens actually engage in this practice to protect themselves from the watchful eye of parents.

Fabricating data does indeed make search more difficult, but the 45 networked nature of MySpace provides alternate paths to finding people. First, few teens actually lie about what school they attend, although some choose not to list a school at all. Second, and more problematically, teens are not going to refuse connections to offline friends even though that makes them more easily locatable. Parents simply need to find one of their child's friends; from there, it is easy to locate their own kid. While teens are trying to make parental access more difficult, their choice to obfuscate key identifying information also makes them invisible to their peers. This is not ideal because teens are going online in order to see and be seen by those who might be able to provide validation.

Another common structural tactic involves the privacy settings. 46 By choosing to make their profile *private*,[39] teens are able to select who can see their content. This prevents unwanted parents from lurking, but it also means that peers cannot engage with them without inviting them to be Friends. To handle this, teens are often promiscuous with who they are willing to add as Friends on the site. By connecting to anyone who seems interesting, they gain control over the structure. Yet, this presents different problems because massive Friending introduces a flood of content with no tools to manage it.

Another structural approach intended to confound parents is creating *mirror networks*. When Stacy's mom found her profile, she was outraged. She called the moms of two of Stacy's friends—Anne and Kimberly. All three parents demanded that their kids clean up their profiles and told them to tell their friends the same or else more parents would be called. Steamed by the prudish response of their parents, Stacy, Anne, and Kimberly reluctantly agreed to change their profiles. Then, they each made a second account with fake names and details. Here, they linked to each other's second profile and uploaded the offending material, inviting their friends to do the same. In doing so, they created a network that completely mirrored the network that their parents had seen. Their parents continued to check their G-rated profiles and the girls continued to lead undercover lives. 47

While deception and lockdown are two common structural solutions, teens often argue that MySpace should be recognized as *my* space, a space for teenagers to be teenagers. Adults typically view this attitude as preposterous because, as they see it, since the technology is public and teens are participating in a public way, they should have every right to view this content. This attitude often frustrates teenagers who argue that just because anyone *can* access the site doesn't mean that everyone *should*. 48

When teens argue for having *my* space in a networked public, they are trying to resolve the social problems that emerge because the constructions of public and private are different online and off. In unmediated spaces, structural boundaries are assessed to determine who is in the audience and who is not. The decision to goof off during lunch is often made with the assumption that only peers bear witness. In mediated spaces, there are no structures to limit the audience; search collapses all virtual walls. 49

Most people believe that *security through obscurity* will serve as a functional barrier online. For the most part, this is a reasonable assumption. Unless someone is of particular note or interest, why would anyone search for them? Unfortunately for teens, there are two groups who have a great deal of interest in them: those who hold power over them—parents, teachers, local government officials, etc.—and those who wish to prey on them—marketers and predators. Before News Corporation purchased MySpace, most adults had never heard of the site; afterwards, they flocked there to either to track teenagers that they knew or to market goods (or promises) to any teen who would listen. This shift ruptured both the imagined community and the actual audience they had to face on a regular basis. With a much 50 wider audience present, teens had to face a hard question: what's appropriate?

This problem is not unique to social network sites; it has been present in all forms of mediated publics. Consider Stokely Carmichael's experience with radio and television.[40] As an activist in the 1960s, Carmichael regularly addressed segregated Black and White audiences about the values and ideals of the burgeoning Black Power movement. 51

Depending on the color of his audience, he used very different rhetorical styles. As his popularity grew, he started attracting media attention and was invited to speak on TV and radio. This opportunity was also a curse because both Black and White listeners would hear his speech. As there was no way to reconcile the two different rhetorical styles he typically used, he had to choose. By maintaining his Black roots in front of white listeners, Carmichael permanently alienated White society from the messages of Black Power. Faced with two disjointed contexts simultaneously, there was no way that Carmichael could successfully convey his message to both audiences. 52

Teenagers face the same dilemma on MySpace. How can they be simultaneously cool to their peers and acceptable to their parents? For the most part, it is not possible. While most adults wish that kids would value what they value, this is rarely true. It is easy to lambaste teens for accepting the cultural norms of the "in" crowd, but social categories[41] and status negotiation[42] are core elements in teen life; this is part of how they learn to work through the cultural practices and legal rules that govern society. The behaviors that are typically rewarded with status in school are often resistant to adult values. On MySpace, teens are directly faced with peer pressure and the need to conform to what is seen to be cool. Worse, they are faced with it in the most public setting possible—one that is potentially visible to all peers and all adults. The stakes are greater on both sides, but the choice is still there: *cool or lame?* 53

437

Unfortunately, the magnified public exposure increases the stakes. Consider a call that I received from an admissions officer at a prestigious college. The admissions committee had planned to admit a young Black man from a very poor urban community until they found his MySpace. They were horrified to find that his profile was full of hip-hop imagery, urban ghetto slang, and hints of gang participation. This completely contradicted the essay they had received from him about the problems with gangs in his community, and they were at a loss. Did he lie in his application? Although confidentiality prevented me from examining his case directly, I offered the admissions officer an alternative explanation. Perhaps he needed to acquiesce to the norms of the gangs while living in his neighborhood, in order to survive and make it through high school to apply to college. 54

Situations like this highlight how context is constructed and 55
maintained through participation, not simply observation. When outsiders search for and locate participants, they are ill prepared to understand the context; instead, they project the context in which they relate
to the individual offline onto the individual in this new online space.
For teens, this has resulted in expulsions, suspensions, probations, and
being grounded.[43] In Pennsylvania, a student's parody of his principal
was not read as such when the principal found this profile on
MySpace; the student was removed from school and lawsuits are still
pending.[44] Of course, not every misreading results in the punishment
of youth. Consider the story of Allen and his daughter Sabrina. Because
Sabrina thinks her dad is cool, she invited him to join her on MySpace.
Upon logging in, Allen was startled to see that her profile included a
quiz entitled *"What kind of drug are you?"*, to which she had responded
"cocaine." Confused and horrified, Allen approached his daughter for
an explanation. She laughed and explained, *"it's just one of those quizzes
that tells you about your personality . . . but you can kinda get it to say what
you want."* She explained that she didn't want to be represented by
marijuana because the kids who smoked pot were lame. She also
thought that acid and mushrooms were stupid because she wasn't a
hippie. She figured that cocaine made sense because she heard people
did work on it and, *"besides Dad, your generation did a lot of coke and you
came out OK."* This was not the explanation that Allen expected.

Teens are not necessarily well-prepared to navigate complex 56
social worlds with invisible audiences, but neither are adults. While
Allen was able to talk with his daughter about other possible interpretations of her choice in presentation, he recognized that her profile was
not meant for such audiences. How could he teach her how to engage
in identity presentation while navigating multiple audiences? While
MySpace is public, it is unlike other publics that adults commonly face.
This presents a generational divide that is further complicated by
adults' mis-readings of youth participation in new media.[45]

BUT WHY *THERE*?

The power that adults hold over youth explains more than just compli- 57
cations in identity performance; it is the root of why teenagers are on
MySpace in the first place. In the United States, the lives of youth—
and particularly high school teenagers—are highly structured.
Compulsory high school requires many students to be in class from
morning to mid-afternoon; and many are also required to participate in
after-school activities, team sports, and work into the evening. It is difficult to measure whether today's high school teens have more or less

free time than previous generations, but the increased prevalence of single working parent and dual-working parent households implies that there are either more latchkey kids or more after-school programs watching these kids.[46] Given the overwhelming culture of fear and the cultural disdain for latchkey practices, it is likely that teens are spending more time in programs than on their own. Meanwhile, at home in the evenings, many are expected to do homework or spend time with the family. While the home has been considered a *private* sphere where individuals can regulate their own behavior, this is an adult-centric narrative. For many teens, home is a highly regulated space with rules and norms that are strictly controlled by adults.

Regardless of whether teens in the United States have the time   58
to engage in public life, there are huge structural and social barriers to them doing so. First, there is an issue of mobility. While public transit exists in some urban regions, most of the United States lacks adequate transportation options for those who are unable to drive; given the suburbanization of the United States, teens are more likely to live in a region without public transit than one with public transit. There is a minimum age for drivers in every state, although it varies from 16–18. A license is only one part of the problem; having access to a car is an entirely separate barrier to mobility. This means that, for many teens, even if they want to go somewhere they are often unable to do so.

American society has a very peculiar relationship to teenagers—   59
and children in general. They are simultaneously idealized and demonized; adults fear them but they also seek to protect them.[47] On one hand, there has been a rapid rise in curfew legislation to curb teen violence[48] and loitering laws are used to bar teens from hanging out on street corners, in parking lots, or other outdoor meeting places for fear of the trouble they might cause. On the other hand, parents are restricting their youth from hanging out in public spaces for fear of predators, drug dealers, and gangs. Likewise, while adults spend countless hours socializing over alcohol, minors are not only restricted from drinking but also from socializing in many venues where alcohol is served.

Moral entrepreneurs have learned that "invoking fears about   60
children provides a powerful means of commanding public attention and support."[49] This ongoing *culture of fear* typically overstates the actual dangers and obfuscates real risks in the process.[50] Yet, the end result of this is that youth have very little access to public spaces. The spaces they can hang out in are heavily controlled and/or under surveillance:

> "My [guardian] is really strict so if I get to go anywhere, it's a big miracle. So I talk to people on MySpace . . . I know she means well, I know she

doesn't want me to mess up. But sometimes you need to mess up to figure out that you're doing it wrong. You need mistakes to know where you're going. You need to figure things out for yourself."—Traviesa, 15

Many adults believe that these restrictions are necessary to pre-   61
vent problematic behaviors or to protect children from the risks of society. Whether or not that view is valid, restrictions on access to public
life make it difficult for young people to be socialized into society at
large. While social interaction can and does take place in private environments, the challenges of doing so in public life are part of what help
youth grow. Making mistakes and testing limits are fundamental parts
of this. Yet, there is a pervading attitude that teens must be protected
from their mistakes.

At the beginning of this chapter, I explained that I would use the   62
term teenagers to refer to youth of high school age living at home. In
doing so, I glossed over how problematic any definition of youth or
teenager is.[51] Yet, it is precisely the construction of teenager/youth in
opposition to adult that creates the power dynamic upon which most
of the challenges stated earlier hinge. The term teenager did not exist a
century ago. It was most likely coined in the 1920s or 1930s; and it first
appeared in print as a marketing term in 1941.[52] The notion of *young
adult* did exist and it primarily referenced young people who were
entering the workforce. By about fourteen, most young people began
laboring outside the home; they continued to live with their parents
and their income helped the family pay its costs. The workforce was a
critical site of socialization into adulthood for young people; very few
went to high school or college. This changed in the United States during the Great Depression. With too few jobs and too many adults needing employment, the labor movement joined social reformers who had
been urging the government to require high school attendance for
young people. While social reformers believed that young people were
not mature enough to be entering the workforce, the labor movement
was more interested in keeping young adults out of the workforce (and
off the streets). Together, they were able to convince Congress to pass
compulsory education and child labor laws.

While the appropriateness of this move can be debated, its effect   63
was clear: young people were neatly segregated from adults in all
aspects of their lives. Through funding structures, schools were
encouraged to consolidate into large institutions that could support at
least 100 students per year so that schools could support activities and
sports that kept youth from mixing with adult laborers in leisure as
well as work. The school reform that took place during this era created
the iconic American high school imagery that Hollywood popularized
around the world during the second half of the 20th century. Idealists

viewed high school as a place where youth could mature both intellectually and socially, but age segregation meant that young people were being socialized into a society that did not include adults. While peer socialization is obviously valuable and important, it is fundamentally different from being socialized into adult society by adults themselves; generations emerge and norms rapidly change per generation. By segregating people by age, a true dichotomy between adult and teen emerged.

The development of an age-segregated group also created a target demographic for marketers. Following World War II, organizations and corporations began explicitly targeting teens directly, appealing to the tastes and values generated in teen culture. Spaces like dance halls, roller rinks, bowling alleys, and activity centers began offering times for teens to socialize with other teens. (These spaces, once vibrant in the United States, are virtually extinct now.) Businesses welcomed middle and upper class teens with open arms because of their perceived consumer power. Products began to be designed explicitly for teens. This consumer process similarly reinforced separate youth and adult publics. 64

By late in the 20th century, shopping malls became the primary "public" space for youth socialization.[53] While shopping malls once welcomed teens, teens are primarily seen as a nuisance now. Shopkeepers are wary of teens because of shoplifting and they are often ejected for loitering. While the public spaces built around consumerism have become increasingly hostile to teenagers, they still rabidly market to them. In other words, teens are still a marketable demographic for products, even if there is little interest in providing services for them. 65

This dynamic, while overly simplified for brevity's Sake, does not properly convey the differences across different social groups within American society. It is primarily the story of white, middle class, suburban teens. Poor teens and people of color were never given access to these types of spaces in the first place. That said, commercialism has moved on to co-opt the spaces that these groups do traverse. The corporatization and glorification/demonization of hip-hop and "the 'hood" is one example of this.[54] As we move towards a more global market, multinational corporations are expanding on their desire to target niche groups of teens, simultaneously supporting the attitude that teens are both angels and demons. 66

Collectively, four critical forces[55]—*society, market, law, and architecture*—have constructed an age-segregated teen culture that is deeply consumerist but lacks meaningful agency. The contradictions run deep—we sell sex to teens but prohibit them from having it; we tell teens to grow up but restrict them from the vices and freedoms of 67

441

adult society.[56] Teenagers have navigated and challenged this hypocrisy over decades. Changes in society, market, and law have shifted the perception and treatment of youth. What emerged with the Internet was a radical shift in architecture; it decentralized publics.

While the jury is still out on whether or not the Internet is democratizing, online access provides a whole new social realm for youth. Earlier mediated communication devices—landline, pager, mobile—allowed friends to connect with friends even when located in adult-regulated physical spaces. What is unique about the Internet is that it allows teens to participate in unregulated publics while located in adult-regulated physical spaces such as homes and schools. Of course, this is precisely what makes it controversial. Parents are seeking to regulate teens' behavior in this new space; and this, in turn, is motivating teens to hide. 68

> *"A few of my friends won't even dare to tell their parents about their MySpace cause they know they'll be grounded forever. I know two kids who got banned from it but they secretly got back on."*—Ella, 15

Yet, putting aside the question of risk, what teens are doing with this networked public is akin to what they have done in every other type of public they have access to: they hang out, jockey for social status, work through how to present themselves, and take risks that will help them to assess the boundaries of the social world. They do so because they seek access to adult society. Their participation is deeply rooted in their desire to engage publicly, for many of the reasons we have discussed earlier. By prohibiting teens from engaging in networked publics, we create a *participation divide*,[57] both between adults and teens and between teens who have access and those who do not. 69

CONCLUSION

Publics play a crucial role in the development of individuals for, as Nancy Fraser explains, "they are arenas for the formation and enactment of social identities."[58] By interacting with unfamiliar others, teenagers are socialized into society. Without publics, there is no coherent society. Publics are where norms are set and reinforced, where common ground is formed. Learning society's rules requires trial and error, validation and admonishment; it is knowledge that teenagers learn through action, not theory. Society's norms and rules only provide the collectively imagined boundaries. Teenagers are also tasked with deciding how they want to fit into the structures that society provides. Their social identity is partially defined by themselves, 70 partially defined by others. Learning through *impression management* is key to developing a social identity. Teenagers must determine where they want to be situated within the social world they see and then attempt to garner the reactions to their performances that match their vision. This is a lifelong process, but one that must be supported at every step.

In today's society, there is a push towards privacy. It is assumed   71
that people are public individuals who deserve the right to privacy rather than the other way around. With an elevated and idealized view of privacy, we often forget the reasons that enslaved peoples desperately wished for access to public life. By allowing us to have a collective experience with people who are both like and unlike us, public life validates the reality that we are experiencing. We are doing our youth a disservice if we believe that we can protect them from the world by limiting their access to public life. They must enter that arena, make mistakes, and learn from them. Our role as adults is not to be their policemen, but to be their guide.

Of course, as Hannah Arendt wrote long before the Internet,   72
"everything that appears in public can be seen and heard by everybody and has the widest possible publicity."[59] What has changed with the emergence of new tools for mediating sociality is the scale and persistence of possible publicity. For most people in history, public life was not documented and distributed for the judgment of non-present others. Only aristocrats and celebrities faced that type of public because structural and social forces strongly limited the "widest possible publicity." Not everything could be documented and spreading information was challenging. Only the lives of the rich and famous were deemed important enough to share.

443

The Internet has irrevocably changed this. Teens today face a pub-   73
lic life with unimaginably wide possible publicity. The fundamental properties of networked publics—persistence, searchability, replicability, and invisible audiences—are unfamiliar to the adults that are guiding them through social life. It is not accidental that teens live in a culture infatuated with celebrity[60]—the "reality" presented by reality TV and the highly publicized dramas (such as that between socialites Paris Hilton and Nicole Richie) portray a magnified (and idealized) version of the networked publics that teens are experiencing, complete with surveillance and misinterpretation. The experiences that teens are facing in the publics that they encounter appear more similar to the celebrity idea of public life than to the ones their parents face.

It is not as though celebrities or teenagers wish for every conver-   74
sation to be publicly available to everyone across all time and space, but mediated publics take the simplest public expressions and make them hyperpublic. Few adults could imagine every conversation they

have sitting in the park or drinking tea in a café being available for such hyperpublic consumption, yet this is what technology enables. Unfortunately, there is an ethos that if it is possible to access a public expression, one should have the right to do so. Perhaps this is flawed thinking.

While we can talk about changes that are taking place, the long-term implications of being socialized into a culture rooted in networked publics are unknown. Perhaps today's youth will be far better equipped to handle gossip as adults. Perhaps not. What we do know is that today's teens live in a society whose public life is changing rapidly. Teens need access to these publics—both mediated and unmediated—to mature, but their access is regularly restricted. Yet, this technology and networked publics are not going away. As a society, we need to figure out how to educate teens to navigate social structures that are quite unfamiliar to us because they will be faced with these publics as adults, even if we try to limit their access now. Social network sites have complicated our lives because they have made this rapid shift in public life very visible. Perhaps instead of trying to stop them or regulate usage, we should learn from what teens are experiencing. They are learning to navigate networked publics; it is in our better interest to figure out how to help them.

75

NOTES

[1]Quote posted by her mother Kathy Sierra: http://headrush.typepad.com/creating_passionate_users/2006/03/ultrafast_relea. html

[2]Part of a conversation from December 2004 that motivated Parry Aftab (Executive Director of Wired Safety) to help teens use social network sites safely; story shared by one of her "Teen Angels" (http://www.teenangels.com)

[3]Geertz, Clifford. 1973. *The Interpretation of Cultures*. New York: Basic Books.

[4]Hine, Thomas. 1999. *The Rise and Fall of the American Teenager*. New York: Bard.

[5]In a private message, Mary Gray (Indiana University) shared that her research in Kentucky shows that rural teens have no access to MySpace because they access the Internet at schools and libraries, where MySpace is banned.

[6]There is nothing to confirm that the person being represented is the person behind the profile. Teens are most notorious for maliciously creating fraudulent profiles to bully the represented but it is equally common for teens to create profiles for their friends. Because one's friends are made visible on one's profile, teens complain that their profile is ruined if their best friend does not have a profile that can be listed as a Friend on the site.

[7]Lenhart, Amanda. 2007. "Social Networking Websites and Teens: An Overview." *PEW Internet and the American Life Project*, January 7.

[8]Defining a category through articulated boundaries is problematic (see: Lakoff, George. 1987. *Women, Fire, and Dangerous Things*. Chicago: University of Chicago Press). My effort to do so is to distinguish what is unique to this new style of site from previous types of social software. Although this definition brings some clarity, newer social software is beginning to implement these features into sites that are predominantly about video sharing (YouTube), photo sharing (Flickr), music tastes (Last.FM), etc. The social network sites that I discuss here are first and foremost about the friends network while these newer sites are primarily about media sharing or discovery.

[9]For legibility, when I am referring to the Friends feature on MySpace, I capitalize the term. When I am referring to people that individuals would normally talk about as their friends, I do not.

[10]For a more detailed analysis on the Friending process, see: boyd, danah, 2006. "Friends, Friendsters, and MySpace Top 8: Writing Community Into Being on Social Network Sites." *First Monday* 11(12).

[11]Boyd, Danah and Jeffrey Heer. 2006. "Profiles as Conversation: Networked Identity Performance on Friendster." In *Proceedings of the Hawaii International Conference on System Sciences (HICSS-39), Persistent Conversation Track*. Kauai, HI: IEEE Computer Society. January 4-7.

[12]Most social network sites support private messaging so that people can contact other members directly. Some sites support blogging and posting of videos. MySpace and Friendster have a bulletin feature where participants can post messages that all of their Friends can read. Other features that appear on social network sites include: instant messaging, teacher ratings, message boards, groups, and classified ads. Exactly how these features are implemented differs by site.

[13]For a primer on some of the key debates concerning 'public' and 'public sphere,' see Calhoun, Craig. 1992. *Habermas and the Public Sphere*. Cambridge, MA: MIT Press.

[14]Livingstone, Sonia. 2005. "Introduction" and "On the relation between audiences and publics." *Audiences and Publics: When Cultural Engagement Matters for the Public Sphere* (ed. Sonia Livingstone). Portland: intellect. 9.

[15]Livingstone, Sonia. 2005. "Introduction" and "On the relation between audiences and publics." *Audiences and Publics: When Cultural Engagement Matters for the Public Sphere* (ed. Sonia Livingstone). Portland: intellect. 9-41.

[16]Warner, Michael. 1992. "The Mass Public and the Mass Subject." *Habermas and the Public Sphere* (Craig Calhoun, ed.). Cambridge, MA: MIT Press. 377-401.

[17]Ito, Mizuko. (2007, in press) "Introduction," *Networked Publics*. Cambridge: MIT Press.

[18]Negroponte, Nicholas. 1996. *Being Digital*. New York: Vintage.

[19]While MySpace recognized this hole within hours, they did not close the loophole nor did they begin supporting the practice. They allowed it to exist as an underground copy/paste culture. They have banned specific code that puts the site and participants at risk. For example, they block javascript to make it harder for scammers to prey on members.

[20]While the original copy/paste sites were created by teenagers, it is not clear who runs the thousands of codes sites currently operating. Most make

445

money off of advertising so it is likely to be a business venture. Scammers looking to exploit participants' willingness to copy/paste anything probably run some as well.

[21]"Pimp out" is a slang term that basically means "make cool" (by teen standards). Pimped out profiles usually involve heavy modifications to the templates and numerous multimedia components. What looks pimped out to a teen is typically viewed as horrifyingly chaotic to adults. Technologists complain that the design resembles that of early homepages with blink tags and random colors. The best way that I've found to describe what these profiles look like is a highly decorated teenage bedroom wall or locker.

[22]Perkel, Daniel. 2006. "Copy and Paste Literacy: Literacy Practices in the Production of a MySpace Profile—An Overview." In *Proceedings of Informal Learning and Digital Media: Constructions, Contexts, Consequences*. Denmark. September 21-23.

[23]Davis, Fred. 1992. *Fashion, Culture and Identity*. Chicago: University of Chicago Press.

[24]Goffman, Erving. 1956. *The Presentation of Self in Everyday Life*. Edinburgh: University of Edinburgh.

[25]Goffman, Erving. 1963. *Behavior in Public Places*. New York: The Free Press.

[26]Briggs, Jean. 1999. *Inuit Morality Play: The Emotional Education of a Three-Year-Old*. New Haven: Yale University Press.

[27]Sundén, Jenny. 2003. *Material Virtualities*. New York: Peter Lang Publishing.

[28]See David Buckingham's introduction to this volume for a greater discussion of this.

[29]Berman, Joshua and Amy Bruckman. 2001. "The Turing Game: Exploring Identity in an Online Environment." *Convergence*, 7(3), 83-102.

[30]Donath, Judith. 1999. "Identity and deception in the virtual community." *Communities in Cyberspace* (Marc Smith & Peter Kollock, eds). London: Routledge.

[31]Donath, Judith and danah boyd. 2004. "Public Displays of Connection." *BT Technology Journal*, October 22(4), pp. 7 1-82.

[32]Like "guilt by association," this phrase is logically fallible, but people still judge others based on those around them. Shapiro, Irving David. 1996, "Fallacies of logic: argumentation cons." *ETC.: A Review of General Semantics*, Fall 33(3).

[33]Buckingham, David, 2007. "Introduction" to this volume, p ???

[34]Benedict Anderson coined the term "imagined community" to discuss nationality. In talking about "imagined audiences," I am drawing on his broader point about how communities can be socially constructed and imagined by those who see themselves as members. Anderson, Benedict. 1991. *Imagined Communities*. New York: Verso.

[35]To follow this thread, see Susannah Stern's chapter in this volume

[36]This riff on Andy Warhol's infamous comment has circulated the web; I am not sure where to properly locate its origin.

[37]Lauritano-Werner, Bly. 2006. "Reading My LiveJournal." *Youth Public Radio*. June 28. http://youthradio.org/society/npr060628_onlinejournal.shtml

[38]Farnham, Kevin and Dale Farnham. 2006. *MySpace Safety: 51 Tips for Teens and Parents*. Pomfret, CT: How-To Primers.

[39]Private profiles in MySpace are visible to Friends only. When strangers visit their page, they are shown the primary photo, name, location, age, and a saying. They must become Friends with that person to see the rest of the content.

[40]Meyrowitz, Joshua. 1985. *No Sense of Place*. New York: Oxford.

[41]Eckert, Penelope. 1989. *Jocks & Burnouts: Social Categories and Identity in the High School*. New York: Teacher College Press.

[42]Murray Milner, Jr., 2004. *Freaks, Geeks, and Cool Kids: American Teenagers, Schools, and the Culture of Consumption*. New York: Routledge.

[43]Koppelman, Alex. 2006. "MySpace or OurSpace?" *Salon*. June 8. http://www.salon.com/mwt/feature/2006/06/08/my_space/

[44]Poulson, Kevin. 2006. "Scenes from the MySpace Backlash." *Wired News*. February 27. http:/ /www. wired. com/ news/ politics/ 1,70254-0. html

[45]To follow this thread, see Susan Herring's chapter in this volume

[46]Johnson, Julia Overturf, Robert Kominski, Kristin Smith, and Paul Tillman. 2005. "Changes in the Lives of U.S. Children 1990-2000." Working Paper No 78, United States Census Bureau. November.

[47]Austin, Joe, and Michael Nevin Willard. 1998. "Introduction: Angels of History, Demons of Culture." *Generations of Youth: Youth Cultures and History in Twentieth-Century America* (ed. Joe Austin and Michael Nevin Willard). New York: New York University Press, 1-20.

[48]Ruefle, William and Kenneth Reynolds. 1995. "Curfew and delinquency in major American cities." *Crime and Delinquency* 41:347-363.

[49]Buckingham, David. 2000. *After the Death of Childhood*. Oxford: Polity, p. 11.

[50]Glassner, Barry. 2000. *The Culture of Fear: Why Americans Are Afraid of the Wrong Things*. Basic Book.

[51]See Buckingham's intro in this volume.

[52]The history in this paragraph is well-documented and cited in: Hine, Thomas, 1999. *The Rise and Fall of the American Teenager*. New York: Bard.

[53]Crawford, Margaret. 1992. "The World in a Shopping Mall." *Variations on a Theme Park: The New American City and the End of Public Space* (ed. Michael Sorkin). New York: Hill and Wang, p. 3-30.

[54]Forman, Murray. 2002. *The 'Hood Comes First: Race, Space, and Place in Rap and Hip-Hop*. Middletown, Connecticut: Wesleyan University Press.

[55]Lessig, Lawrence. 1999. *Code and Other Laws of Cyberspace*. New York: Basic Books.

[56]The contradictions and challenges of youth as a social construct are well articulated in Buckingham, David. 2000. *After the Death of Childhood*. Oxford: Polity.

[57]Jenkins, Henry. 2006. "Confronting the Challenges of Participatory Culture: Media Education for the 21st Century." White Paper for MacArthur Foundation.

[58]Fraser, Nancy. 1992. "Rethinking the Public Sphere: A Contribution to the Critique of Actually Existing Democracy." *Habermas and the Public Sphere* (Craig Calhoun, ed.). Cambridge, MA: MIT Press. 125.

[59]Arendt, Hannah. 1958. *The Human Condition*. Chicago: University of Chicago Press, 50.

[60]Halpern, Jake. 2007. *Fame Junkies: The Hidden Truths Behind America's Favorite Addiction*. Houghton Mifflin.

Examining the Text

1. At the end of the second paragraph, Boyd states that her purpose is to uncover lasting insights into "identity formation, status negotiation, and peer-to-peer sociality." In your own words, what do each of these terms mean? Why are they particularly important issues for teenagers to negotiate?

2. Boyd identifies Profiles, Friends, and Comments as the three essential features of social network sites. What reasons does she give for seeing these as the three most important features? Are there other elements of social networking sites that you think are also important to how they function for teenagers?

3. Why does Boyd think it's important to define the term *public*? What advantages does she see in articulating multiple "publics" (paragraph 26)? How does the mediated nature of *networked publics* cause us to experience them differently and to act differently in them?

4. How is the creation of profiles linked to "impression management"? According to Boyd, how does impression management happen differently in a mediated, networked environment than it does in the nonmediated physical world? Why would impression management in profiles be particularly appropriate for teenagers?

5. According to Boyd, how does MySpace (and other mediated networks) complicate the distinction between public and private? What problems do teenagers have to resolve as they "engage in identity presentation while navigating multiple audiences"?

6. *Thinking rhetorically*: Boyd seems to presuppose that her readers don't know very much about MySpace; for instance, she defines what Profiles are and how Friends lists work. If you don't see yourself as the intended target audience—for instance, if you have a great deal of knowledge and experience with MySpace—how does this influence the experience of reading Boyd's article? Were there sections of the article that you felt you could skim or skip altogether since you already knew what she was discussing? In general, how does choosing a target audience help Boyd determine what information to include in her article?

For Group Discussion

Boyd's article was published in 2007 and it presents the results of research done several years earlier. Given the speed with which the Internet and social networking, in particular, have developed and changed, to what extent do Boyd's observations still hold true? In a group with other students, identify two or three points Boyd makes that strike you as still relevant and true; that is, they still describe the current reality of teens and social networking. Identify two or three other points made by Boyd that strike you as dated and no longer valid; what technical or social changes have rendered these points incorrect? How would you modify the point so that it accurately describes the current social networking scene?

Writing Suggestion

Write an essay in which you compare and contrast the article by boyd with the previous article by Bumgarner. Be sure to consider not only the content but also the methods of each article. What is the approach of each author to the subject matter? What kinds of evidence does each author include in his or her analysis? How is each article organized, and how do the differences in organization affect the message of the article? You might conclude your comparison by stating from which article you think you learned more about online social networking.

ADDITIONAL SUGGESTIONS FOR WRITING ABOUT TECHNOLOGY

1. Samuels and Yee are both concerned with the ways that technologies redefine borders: between public spaces and private spaces, and between work and play. Write an essay in which you state your own opinion about technology's impact on one of these or on another border area—for instance, human/machine, child/adult, male/female. What are the key technologies that have helped to shape your understanding of these supposedly opposite terms? What technologies change the way you understand the distinction between these terms?

Drawing from the articles, you can use quotations that you agree with to support claims that you make, and you can also use quotations that you disagree with in order to provide you with material to argue against. Try to draw as well on your own experiences and observations with the technologies you're discussing.

2. Postman argues that technologies have important and fairly unpredictable impacts on society, and he provides several brief examples to support this claim. Write a research-based report in which you describe the history of a particular technology, emphasizing the impact that this technology has had on popular culture or on a specific subculture.

To choose a technology for your research topic, think in terms of categories; there are, for instance, technologies associated with music, movies, entertainment, health and medicine, science, communication, sports, cooking, cleaning, and so on. Once you've chosen a category that interests you, it should be easier to choose a specific technology. Do research both in the library and on the Web in order to find out when the technology was invented, how it evolved through the years, when its popularity grew and declined, and, most importantly, what impact it has had on the people who have used it. You might end your research report with speculations about the future of this technology: what new developments are in store for it, and in what new ways do you imagine will people use it in the future?

3. This is a tough assignment: go and play a video game. Actually, the tough part comes next: write an essay in which you analyze the video game you played. To prepare for this assignment, before you play the game you should review your notes from the two articles on video games in this chapter: Nick Yee's "The Labor of Fun" and James Paul Gee's "Good Video Games, the Human Mind, and Good Learning." In particular, with Yee's article, give some thought to the different motivations and effects of game playing that he discusses; with Gee's article, pay attention to the way he describes details of specific games and connects those details to larger interpretations of the games and their educational value.

Next, give some thought to the video game you choose to play. You might want to choose a game with which you're very familiar, so that you have a complete understanding of its characters, rules, scenarios, and strategies. On the other hand, you might want to choose a game that's entirely new to you so that you come to it from a fresh perspective.

After you've chosen a video game to play, go ahead and play—but as you're playing, pay attention to both the game and your reactions to it. This may require that you play the game more than once! Ultimately you want to walk away from the experience with something to say about the underlying premises of the game as well as about how playing the game affected you. After playing, be sure to jot down some notes about the most salient and interesting features of the game; you can use these notes as you develop your essay.

In writing your analysis of the video game you played, begin with a specific claim about the game, and use evidence from the game and from your experience of playing it to support the claim you make.

INTERNET ACTIVITIES

1. In this chapter, Bumgarner and Boyd offer analyses of two social networking systems currently online: Facebook and MySpace. A project by Jonathan Harris and Sep Kamvar, entitled "We Feel Fine" (http://www.wefeelfine. org/), explores the world of social networking somewhat differently, in an interactive visualization of data drawn from a range of social networking sites (e.g., MySpace, LiveJournal, Flickr). This assignment asks you to visit "We Feel Fine," explore it in detail, and write a response to it.

As you'll see when you visit the site, Harris and Kamvar focus on sentences having to do with feelings (i.e., sentences that contain the phrase "I feel" or "I am feeling"); they present multiple ways to view these sentences along with data about the people who have written the sentences. Be sure to explore the different ways of viewing the data as well as to read the descriptions of the project in the Missions, Movements, Methodology, and Findings sections. You might also take a look at another visualization project by Harris and Kamvar that explores the world of online dating: "I want you to want me" (http://iwantyoutowantme.org/).

Once you've thoroughly explored the site, write a response that addresses the following questions: What does "We Feel Fine" tell you about social networking in general? In what ways are the ideas presented in Harris and Kamvar's project related to the analyses offered in Bumgarner's and boyd's articles? In the Mission section, Harris and Kamvar describe "We Feel Fine" as "an exploration of human emotion on a global scale"; does this seem to you to be an accurate description? How do the different ways of viewing the data contribute to your understanding of social networking and self-representation on the Internet?

In the response that you write to these questions, consider including one or more screenshots from "We Feel Fine" to help you illustrate specific points.

2. While Facebook and MySpace offer opportunities for social networking, blogging sites provide more open-ended forums for writing about yourself, your interests, your witty observations and unique experiences. This assignment asks you to give blogging a try yourself. Visit Blogger (http://www.blogger.com) or one of the other free blogging sites on the Web and follow the directions there to get started with your own blog. If you have questions or run into problems setting up your blog, services like Blogger have excellent Help functions to guide you along.

Once you've got your blog set up, what should you write? Your teacher might have some specific suggestions for you, but we'd suggest that you start with the filter-style blog. That is, write an entry that has a link to a site on the Web that you find interesting or important or surprising or otherwise worthy of note. Along with the link, write a paragraph or two with your commentary on this link: why have you chosen it? Why should people visit the site you're linking to? After you've written one filter-style entry, try writing another one; perhaps you could write one filter-style entry each day for a week or two. You might conclude your blog-writing adventure by writing an entry analyzing your experience: what do you find worthwhile or problematic about writing in a blog? How is it different from writing for print? Do you think you might continue blogging in the future?

READING IMAGES

The color image on page CI-5 is a still photo from the 1995 film *Johnny Mnemonic*; the color image on page CI-6 comes from the 1999 film *The Matrix*. In both, we see depictions of "the human" and of "the technological." Your task in this analytical essay is to compare the ways that each image represents people, technology, and their relationship. If you've seen one or both of the movies, try to refrain from discussing them in your analysis; stick to the images and to the meanings they convey.

Look first at how "the human" is represented in each image: what are the similarities and differences in the human figures that the images include? Next, write about how "the technological" is represented: how do we know that these movies are about computer technology? How does each image represent technology? As you discuss each of these components, remember to consider color, dimension, contrast, perspective, focal point, and other issues discussed in the Reading Images section of Chapter 1.

Move next to a discussion of the relationship that each image creates between humans and technology. What words would characterize this relationship: harmonious? antagonistic? intimate? distant? Be sure to provide evidence from each image to support the assertions you make about it.

6

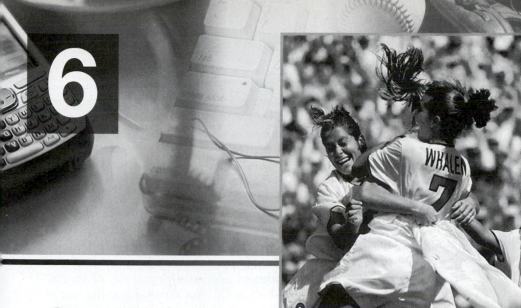

Sports and Games

The United States seems to be a nation obsessed with sports, an obsession nowhere more evident than in some fans' virtual addiction to sports statistics. Somewhere there's a statistics maven who knows the number of foot faults in the final 1956 Davis Cup match or the most triples by a left-handed batter during Tuesday afternoon World Series games. Fans crave statistics, no matter how minute, as a way of measuring the achievements of their favorite athletes and teams—and perhaps also as a way of holding the memory of never-to-be-repeated athletic performances.

It's not difficult to find further evidence of America's preoccupation with sports. Most daily newspapers allocate an entire section to sports reports and statistics; a number of national weekly and monthly publications concentrate exclusively on sports. Special sporting events such as the Super Bowl are consistently among the most highly rated TV broadcasts, and several cable networks are devoted solely to sports twenty-four hours a day. Americans play sports trivia games, call sports telephone hotlines, and participate in a multibillion dollar sports gaming industry; they display team logos on t-shirts, sweatshirts, baseball caps, and countless other articles of clothing. Many colleges and universities capitalize on the prominence of their sports programs to increase enrollments and donations.

Sports can affect fans in surprisingly intense ways. We all probably know people whose moods fluctuate with the fortunes of their favorite team, who might "bleed Dodger blue," as they say. Indeed, entire cities rejoice when their team brings home a championship, and our national mood lifts when an American underdog takes a medal at the Olympics or when the "Dream Team" squashes an opponent. Given this obsession, it's no wonder that professional athletes are among our most revered—and highly paid—citizens.

How can we explain the almost universal popularity of sports? The essays in the first part of this chapter offer views about the role of sports in American life in general, along with an insightful discussion of the ways in which American sports are affecting (or *in*fecting, in the opinion of some critics) cultures worldwide. The readings in this section examine various factors—physical ability, the influence of family and friends, climate and environment, even race and gender—that govern an individual's choice to participate in or follow a particular sport. The second group of essays, under the subheading "Games We Play," expands the focus of this chapter to examine the cultural effects of children's sports and certain board games, and examines the emergence of a particular card game—namely poker, of the no-limit hold 'em variety—as a peculiar type of national obsession.

Obviously, sports and games can influence the way we speak and the way we feel, our notions of teamwork and individuality, success and failure, and male and female roles. From sports and games we learn how to deal with pressure, adversity, and physical pain and we discover models of grace, skill, and style. As you read the essays in this chapter, think of the sports you play and watch, of the athletes or the card players you admire, of the role sports and games play (or have played) in your life.

Sports, Stars, and Society

Life on the Edge

WILLIAM DOWELL ET AL. (*TIME* MAGAZINE)

Fewer Americans are getting together for relaxed games of touch football or slow-pitch softball, and professional team sporting events are no longer attracting the large audiences of the past. Meanwhile, however, participation in high-risk extreme sports is on the rise. Increasing numbers of healthy, seemingly sane men and women are risking life and limb on a Sunday afternoon by jumping from a bridge or cliff or by climbing up a steep, sheer mountain face.

In this article, the authors examine the increasing popularity of extreme sports such as BASE jumping, paragliding, and so on, arguing that our current interest in dangerous sports stems from the fact that most Americans are living comfortable, safe lives. We seek out risk because it no longer seeks us—as in past eras when risks came routinely from war, famine, disease, and wild animals. In support of this argument, the authors point out the prevalence of other types of risk-taking behavior, which are common outside of sports, such as playing the stock market or engaging in unprotected sex.

As you read, think about the legitimacy of the authors' argument. Is there necessarily a connection between the popularity of extreme sports and risky behavior in other areas of social life? Is it fair to connect these behaviors to our generally comfortable lives? Can you think of other possible reasons for the rise in risky sporting behavior? Or are you persuaded by the connections these authors make?

"Five . . . four . . . three . . . two . . . one . . . see ya!" And Chance   1
McGuire, 25, is airborne off a 650-ft. concrete dam in Northern California. In one second he falls 16 ft., in two seconds 63 ft., and after three seconds and 137 ft. he is flying at 65 m.p.h. He prays that his parachute will open facing away from the dam, that his canopy won't collapse, that his toggles will be handy and that no ill wind will slam him back into the cold concrete. The chute snaps open, the sound ricocheting through the gorge like a gunshot, and McGuire is soaring, carving S-turns into the air, swooping over a winding creek. When he lands, he is a speck on a path along the creek. He hurriedly packs his chute and then, clearly audible above the rushing water, lets out a war whoop that rises past those mortals still perched on the dam, past the

commuters puttering by on the roadway, past even the hawks who circle the ravine. It is a cry of defiance, thanks and victory; he has survived another BASE jump.

McGuire is a practitioner of what he calls the king of all extreme 2
sports. BASE—an acronym for building, antenna, span (bridge), and earth (cliffs)—jumping has one of the sporting world's highest fatality rates: in its eighteen-year history, forty six participants have been killed. Yet the sport has never been more popular, with more than a thousand jumpers in the U.S. and more seeking to get into it every day. It is an activity without margin for error. If your chute malfunctions, don't bother reaching for a reserve—there isn't time. There are no second chances.

Still, the sport's stark metaphor—a human leaving safety behind 3
to leap into the void—may be a perfect fit with our times. As extreme a risk taker as McGuire seems, we may all have more in common with him than we know or care to admit. Heading into the millennium, America has embarked on a national orgy of thrill seeking and risk taking. The rise of adventure and extreme sports like BASE jumping, snowboarding, ice climbing, skateboarding and paragliding is merely the most vivid manifestation of this new national behavior. Investors once content to buy stocks and hold them quit their day jobs to become day traders, making volatile careers of risk taking. Even our social behavior has tilted toward the treacherous, with unprotected sex on the upswing and hard drugs like heroin the choice of the chic as well as the junkies. In ways many of us take for granted, we engage in risks our parents would have shunned and our grandparents would have dismissed as just plain stupid.

More than 30 percent of U.S. households own stocks of some form 4
or another, whether in investment accounts, mutual funds or retirement plans, up from 12 percent just ten years ago. While an ongoing bull market has lulled us into a sense of security about investing, the reality is we are taking greater risks with our money than any other generation in American history. Many of us even take this a step further, buying "speculative growth," i.e., highly risky Internet and technology stocks, breezily ignoring the potentially precipitous downside.

We change jobs, leaping into the employment void, imagining rich 5
opportunities everywhere. The quit rate, a measure of those who voluntarily left their most recent job, is at 14.5 percent, the highest in a decade. Even among those schooled in risk management, hotshot M.B.A.s who previously would have headed to Wall Street or Main Street, there is a predilection to spurn Goldman Sachs and Procter & Gamble in order to take a flyer on striking it rich quickly in dot.com land. "I didn't want someone in twenty years to ask me where I was when the Internet took off," says Greg Schoeny, a recent University of Denver M.B.A. who passed up opportunities with established technology firms like Lucent

to work at an Internet start-up called STS Communications. Schoeny is a double-dare sort who also likes to ski in the Rockies' dangerous, unpatrolled backcountry.

A full 30 percent of this year's Harvard Business School graduates   6
are joining venture-capital or high-tech firms, up from 12 percent just four years ago. "The extended period of prosperity has encouraged people to behave in ways they didn't behave in other times—the way people spend money, change jobs, the quit rate, day trading, and people really thinking they know more about the market than anyone else," says Peter Bernstein, an economic consultant and author of the best-selling *Against the Gods: The Remarkable Story of Risk*. "It takes a particular kind of environment for all these things to happen." That environment—unprecedented prosperity and almost a decade without a major ground war—may be what causes Americans to express some inveterate need to take risks.

There is a certain logic to it: at the end of a decade of American tri-   7
umphalism abroad and prosperity at home, we could be seeking to upsize our personalities, our sense of ourselves. Perhaps we as a people are acting out our success as a nation, in a manner unfelt since the postwar era.

Bungee Jumping at the X Games

The rising popularity of extreme sports bespeaks an eagerness   8
on the part of millions of Americans to participate in activities closer
to the metaphorical edge, where danger, skill and fear combine to
give weekend warriors and professional athletes alike a sense of
pushing out personal boundaries. According to American Sports
Data Inc., a consulting firm, participation in so-called extreme sports
is way up. Snowboarding has grown 113 percent in five years and
now boasts nearly 5.5 million participants. Mountain biking, skateboarding, scuba diving, you name the adventure sport—the growth
curves reveal a nation that loves to play with danger. Contrast that
with activities like baseball, touch football and aerobics, all of which
have been in steady decline throughout the '90s.

The pursuits that are becoming more popular have one thing in   9
common: the perception that they are somehow more challenging
than a game of touch football. "Every human being with two legs, two
arms is going to wonder how fast, how strong, how enduring he or
she is," says Eric Perlman, a mountaineer and filmmaker specializing
in extreme sports. "We are designed to experiment or die."

And to get hurt. More Americans than ever are injuring them-   10
selves while pushing their personal limits. In 1997, the U.S. Consumer
Products Safety Commission reported that 48,000 Americans were
admitted to hospital emergency rooms with skateboarding-related
injuries. That's 33 percent more than the previous year. Snowboarding
E.R. visits were up 31 percent; mountain climbing up 20 percent. By
every statistical measure available, Americans are participating in and
injuring themselves through adventure sports at an unprecedented rate.

458

Consider Mike Carr, an environmental engineer and paraglider   11
pilot from Denver who last year survived a bad landing that smashed
ten ribs and collapsed his lung. Paraglider pilots use feathery nylon
wings to take off from mountaintops and float on thermal wind
currents—a completely unpredictable ride. Carr also mountain bikes
and climbs rock faces. He walked away from a 1,500-ft. fall in Peru in
1988. After his recovery, he returned to paragliding. "This has taken
over many of our lives," he explains. "You float like a bird out there.
You can go as high as 18,000 ft. and go for 200 miles. That's magic."

America has always been defined by risk; it may be our predomi-   12
nant national characteristic. It's a country founded by risk takers fed up
with the English Crown and expanded by pioneers—a word that seems
utterly American. Our heritage throws up heroes—Lewis and Clark,
Thomas Edison, Frederick Douglass, Teddy Roosevelt, Henry Ford,
Amelia Earhart—who bucked the odds, taking perilous chances.

Previous generations didn't need to seek out risk; it showed up   13
uninvited and regularly: global wars, childbirth complications, diseases and pandemics from the flu to polio, dangerous products and

even the omnipresent cold war threat of mutually assured destruction. "I just don't think extreme sports would have been popular in a ground-war era," says Dan Cady, professor of popular culture at California State University at Fullerton. "Coming back from a war and getting onto a skateboard would not seem so extreme."

But for recent generations, many of those traditional risks have   14
been reduced by science, government or legions of personal-injury lawyers, leaving boomers and Generations X and Y to face less real risk. Life expectancy has increased. Violent crime is down. You are 57 percent less likely to die of heart disease than your parents; small-pox, measles and polio have virtually been eradicated.

Combat survivors speak of the terror and the excitement of playing   15
in a death match. Are we somehow incomplete as people if we do not taste that terror and excitement on the brink? "People are [taking risks] because everyday risk is minimized and people want to be challenged," says Joy Marr, 43, an adventure racer who was the only woman member of a five-person team that finished the 1998 Raid Gauloises, the grand-daddy of all adventure races. This is a sport that requires several days of nonstop slogging, climbing, rappelling, rafting and surviving through some of the roughest terrain in the world. Says fellow adventure racer

Tony Hawk

and former Army Ranger Jonathan Senk, 35: "Our society is so surgically sterile. It's almost like our socialization just desensitizes us. Every time I'm out doing this I'm searching my soul. It's the Lewis and Clark gene, to venture out, to find what your limitations are."

That idea of feeling bracingly alive through high-risk endeavor is   16
commonly echoed by athletes, day traders and other risk takers. Indeed, many Silicon Valley entrepreneurs are extreme-sports junkies. Mike McCue, 32, CEO and chairman of Tellme Networks, walked away from millions of dollars at his previous job to get his new company off the ground. It's his third start-up, and each time he has risked everything. In his spare time, McCue gets himself off the ground. He's also an avid rock climber. "I like to feel self-reliant and independent," he says. "And when I'm up there, I know if I make a knot wrong, I die."

Even at ground level, the Valley is a preserve of fearless entrepre-   17
neurs. Nirav Tolia passed up $10 million in Yahoo stock options to start epinions.com, a shopping-guide Web site. "I don't know if I would call it living dangerously," he says. "At Yahoo, I realized that money was not the driver for me. It's the sense of adventure."

Psychologist Frank Farley of Temple University believes that tak-   18
ing conscious risk involves overcoming our instincts. He points out that no other animal intentionally puts itself in peril. "The human race is particularly risk taking compared with other species," he says. He describes risk takers as the Type T personality, and the U.S. as a Type T nation, as opposed to what Farley considers more risk-averse nations like Japan. He breaks it down further, into Type T physical (extreme athletes) and Type T intellectual (Albert Einstein, Galileo). He warns there is also Type T negative, that is, those who are drawn to delinquency, crime, experimentation with drugs, unprotected sex, and a whole litany of destructive behaviors.

All these Type Ts are related, and perhaps even different aspects   19
of the same character trait. There is, says Farley, a direct link between Einstein and BASE jumper Chance McGuire. They are different manifestations of the thrill-seeking component of our characters: Einstein was thrilled by his mental life, and McGuire—well, Chance jumps off buildings.

McGuire, at the moment, is driving from Hollister to another   20
California town, Auburn, where he is planning another BASE jump from a bridge. Riding with him is Adam Fillipino, president of Consolidated Rigging, a company that manufactures parachutes and gear for BASE jumpers. McGuire talks about the leap ahead, about his feelings when he is at the exit point, and how at that moment, looking down at the ground, what goes through his mind is that this is not something a human being should be doing. But that's exactly what makes him take that leap: that sense of overcoming his inhibitions

and winning what he calls the gravity game. "Football is for pansies," says McGuire. "What do you need all those pads for? This sport [BASE jumping] is pushing all the limits. I have a friend who calls it suicide with a kick."

When a BASE jumper dies, other BASE jumpers say he has "gone 21 in," as in gone into the ground or gone into a wall. "I'm sick of people going in," says Fillipino. "In the past year, a friend went in on a sky-dive, another drowned as a result of a BASE jump, another friend went in on a jump, another died in a skydiving-plane crash. You can't escape death, but you don't want to flirt with it either." It may be the need to flirt with death, or at least take extreme chances, that has his business growing at a rate of 50 percent a year.

The jump today from the Auburn bridge, which Fillipino has 22 done dozens of times, is about as routine as BASE jumping can be. But Fillipino is a veteran with 450 BASE jumps to his credit. For McGuire, who has just 45, every jump is still a challenge. And at dawn, as he gets his gear ready, stuffing his chute and rig into a backpack so it won't be conspicuous as he climbs the trestles beneath the bridge (jumping from this bridge, as from many other public and private structures, is ille-gal), he has entered into a tranquil state, as if he were silently preparing himself for the upcoming risk.

461

When our Type T traits turn negative, though, there is a disturbing, 23 less serene element to America's being the risk nation. One chilling devel-opment is the trend of "barebacking," a practice in which gay men have unprotected sex with multiple partners. Jack, an avid proponent of bare-backing, argues that the risk of becoming HIV positive is outweighed by the rush of latex-free passion—especially in an era when, in his view, pro-tease inhibitors are on the verge of turning AIDS from a fatal disease into a chronic illness. "It's the bad boy in me getting off," he admits. "One thing that barebacking allows is a certain amount of control over the risk. In sex, we have the ability to face the risk and look it in the eye."

The Stop AIDS Foundation surveyed some 22,000 gay men in San 24 Francisco between 1994 and 1997, and during this period, the number of men who reported they always used condoms fell from 70 percent to 61 percent. "For some gay men, there is a sense of inevitability of becoming infected," says Michael Scarce, 29, a doctoral student in med-ical sociology who has been researching the barebacking phenomenon for the past two years. Scarce says that rather than living in fear and wondering when their next HIV test is going to return positive, some men create an infection ritual. "It really is a lifestyle choice," he says. "It comes down to quality of life vs. quantity of life."

This consequences-be-damned attitude may also be behind some 25 disquieting trends that surfaced in a report issued last week by the Substance Abuse and Mental Health Services Administration stating that the number of Americans entering treatment centers for heroin surged 29 percent between 1992 and 1997. "I'm seeking the widest possible range of human experience," says a recent Ivy League graduate about his heroin use.

The most notorious example of negative thrill seeking may have been when the Risk Taker in Chief, Bill Clinton, engaged in unprotected sex in the Oval Office. Experts point out that many people were forgiving of Clinton in part because they could identify with his impulsiveness. "Risky behavior has been elevated to new heights," argues Cal State's Cady. "There was never so much value put upon risk as there is now." 26

The question is, How much is enough? Without some expression of risk, we may never know our limits and therefore who we are as individuals. "If you don't assume a certain amount of risk," says paraglider pilot Wade Ellet, 51, "you're missing a certain amount of life." And it is by taking risks that we may flirt with greatness. "We create technologies, we make new discoveries, but in order to do that, we have to push beyond the set of rules that are governing us at that time," says psychologist Farley. 27

That's certainly what's driving McGuire and Fillipino as they position themselves on the Auburn bridge. It's dawn again, barely light, and they appear as shadows moving on the catwalk beneath the roadway. As they survey the drop zone, they compute a series of risk assessments. "It's a matter of weighing the variables," Fillipino says, pointing out that the wind, about fifteen m.p.h. out of the northwest, has picked up a little more than he would like. Still, it's a clear morning, and they've climbed all the way up here. McGuire is eager to jump. But Fillipino continues to scan the valley below them, the Sacramento River rushing through the gorge. 28

Then a white parks-department SUV pulls up on an access road that winds alongside the river. Park rangers are a notorious scourge of BASE jumpers, confiscating equipment and prosecuting for trespassing. Fillipino contemplates what would happen if the president of a BASE rig company were busted for an illegal jump. He foresees trouble with his bankers, he imagines the bad publicity his business would garner, and he says he's not going. There are some risks he is simply not willing to take. 29

Examining the Text

1. What do the authors mean when they state that the "stark metaphor" of BASE jumping "may be a perfect fit with our times" (3)?

2. In contrast to all the risk taking mentioned in this article, as a society we also engage in a lot of risk minimizing. Paradoxically, these efforts to ensure safety may be helping to spawn more thrill-seeking activities. Discuss examples of safety measures and risk minimizing in which we as a culture engage—both on the personal as well as on a political or public level.

3. Explain why the authors state that risk taking is perhaps America's "predominant national characteristic." Do you agree or disagree, and why? If this assertion is true, what are the positive and negative consequences of this characteristic for us as country?

For Group Discussion

While this article focuses on the risky characteristics of extreme sports—and uses this element of these sports to make connections to the larger cultural climate in America—another characteristic of extreme sports is noteworthy: nearly all of the sports discussed in this article are individual in nature. The rock climber, for example, tests her own individual abilities against the challenges posed by nature. Interestingly, the increasing popularity of these individual sports corresponds with the declining interest in playing and watching team sports. Use these ideas to theorize, as a group, about the possible significance of this shift from team to individual sports. Just as the *Time* article makes connections between sports and other cultural phenomena, ultimately using all of it to comment on human nature as it appears in America today, can you think of other cultural phenomena that might relate to this issue of individualism? Does this lead you to theorize some ideas about where we are or where we seem to be headed?

Writing Suggestion

It has been described here and elsewhere that an increasing number of Americans are choosing "the leisure pursuit of danger," spending their free time climbing slick rocks, steep mountains, and frozen waterfalls; paragliding; whitewater rafting; or even turning moderately dangerous sports such as downhill skiing into life-threatening endeavors such as extreme skiing. Conventional theories of personality suggest that these people might be acting on a "death wish," while others offer a more positive view of high-risk activities. For example, some researchers suggest that courting peril and undertaking potentially dangerous challenges are actually essential for the progress of societies and for the development of confidence, self-awareness, and a stronger sense of identity in an individual. In an essay, examine your own risk-taking behavior. Even if you're not a high-risk taker by any reliable psychological measure, you've undoubtedly taken a few risks in your life; for the purposes of this essay, risking might be defined as "engaging in any activity with an uncertain outcome," such as asking someone for a date or taking on a new and difficult challenge. To begin this writing assignment, recall a time when you took a risk and describe that event in concrete detail, as though you were writing a short story. Next, make a smooth transition into a section in which you reflect on and assess both the positive and negative effects of this experience. From this examination you should arrive at some conclusions regarding the ways in which this event revealed your own degree of risk-taking behavior, and/or helped to shape you as an individual. Finally, go back and construct an opening paragraph, using that conclusion as the basis for your essay's thesis statement, and voila! . . . you have an autobiographical narrative essay.

Champion of the World

MAYA ANGELOU

Maya Angelou is a well-known poet, novelist, and performer. Born in 1928 and raised in the segregated South, Angelou persevered through countless hardships to become one of the country's most revered authors and cultural leaders. Angelou read her poem, "On the Pulse of Morning," at the 1993 inauguration of President Bill Clinton.

The selection that follows is from Angelou's first volume of autobiography, I Know Why the Caged Bird Sings *(1969). She relates an important recollection from childhood about the night in the 1930s when world heavyweight champion Joe Louis, nicknamed the "Brown Bomber," defended his boxing title against a White contender. Much of Angelou's narrative is made up of the words and feelings of the local Black community gathered in her Uncle Willie's store to listen to the broadcast of that highly publicized match. Angelou shows how her neighbors' hopes and fears and their image of themselves as a people were intimately connected to the fortunes of Louis, one of a very few Black heroes of the day. Her narrative reveals that a "simple" sporting event can be of intense significance for a group of people who see it as a symbol of personal victory or defeat.*

Before you read, *recall any experience you've had or heard about in which a sporting event took on an emotional power and significance far greater than the event itself would seem to warrant. Whether this event is one that you participated in, watched, or read about, think about how and why sports can have such an intense influence on people's lives.*

The last inch of space was filled, yet people continued to wedge themselves along the walls of the Store. Uncle Willie had turned the radio up to its last notch so that youngsters on the porch wouldn't miss a word. Women sat on kitchen chairs, dining-room chairs, stools, and upturned wooden boxes. Small children and babies perched on every lap available and men leaned on the shelves or on each other. 1

The apprehensive mood was shot through with shafts of gaiety, as a black sky is streaked with lightning. 2

"I ain't worried 'bout this fight. Joe's gonna whip that cracker like it's open season." 3

"He gone whip him till that white boy call him Momma." 4

At last the talking finished and the string-along songs about razor 5
blades were over and the fight began.

"A quick jab to the head." In the Store the crowd grunted. "A left 6
to the head and a right and another left." One of the listeners cackled
like a hen and was quieted.

"They're in a clinch, Louis is trying to fight his way out." 7

Some bitter comedian on the porch said, "That white man don't 8
mind hugging that niggah now, I betcha."

"The referee is moving in to break them up, but Louis finally 9
pushed the contender away and it's an uppercut to the chin. The contender is hanging on, now he's backing away. Louis catches him with a
short left to the jaw."

A tide of murmuring assent poured out the door and into the 10
yard.

"Another left and another left. Louis is saving that mighty right . . ." 11
The mutter in the Store had grown into a baby roar and it was pierced
by the clang of a bell and the announcer's "That's the bell for round
three, ladies and gentlemen."

As I pushed my way into the Store I wondered if the announcer 12
gave any thought to the fact that he was addressing as "ladies and gentlemen" all the Negroes around the world who sat sweating and praying, glued to their "Master's voice."

There were only a few calls for RC Colas, Dr. Peppers, and Hires 13
root beer. The real festivities would begin after the fight. Then even the
old Christian ladies who taught their children and tried themselves to
practice turning the other cheek would buy soft drinks, and if the
Brown Bomber's victory was a particularly bloody one they would
order peanut patties and Baby Ruths, also.

Bailey and I laid coins on top of the cash register. Uncle Willie 14
didn't allow us to ring up sales during a fight. It was too noisy and
might shake up the atmosphere. When the gong rang for the next
round we pushed through the near-sacred quiet to the herd of children
outside.

"He's got Louis against the ropes and now it's a left to the body and 15
a right to the ribs. Another right to the body, it looks like it was low . . .
Yes, ladies and gentlemen, the referee is signaling but the contender
keeps raining the blows on Louis. It's another to the body, and it looks
like Louis is going down."

My race groaned. It was our people falling. It was another lynch- 16
ing, yet another Black man hanging on a tree. One more woman
ambushed and raped. A Black boy whipped and maimed. It was
hounds on the trail of a man running through slimy swamps. It was a
white woman slapping her maid for being forgetful.

465

Joe Louis, Champion of the World

The men in the Store stood away from the walls and at attention. 17
Women greedily clutched the babes on their laps while on the porch the
shufflings and smiles, flirtings and pinching of a few minutes before
were gone. This might be the end of the world. If Joe lost, we were back
in slavery and beyond help. It would all be true, the accusations that we
were lower types of human beings. Only a little higher than apes. True
that we were stupid and ugly and lazy and dirty and, unlucky and
worst of all, that God Himself hated us and ordained us to be hewers of
wood and drawers of water, forever and ever, world without end.

We didn't breathe. We didn't hope. We waited. 18

"He's off the ropes, ladies and gentlemen. He's moving towards 19
the center of the ring." There was no time to be relieved. The worst
might still happen.

"And now it looks like Joe is mad. He's caught Carnera with a left 20
hook to the head and a right to the head. It's a left jab to the body and
another left to the head. There's a left cross and a right to the head. The
contender's right eye is bleeding and he can't seem to keep his block
up. Louis is penetrating every block. The referee is moving in, but
Louis sends a left to the body and it's an uppercut to the chin and the
contender is dropping. He's on the canvas, ladies and gentlemen."

Babies slid to the floor as women stood up and men leaned 21
toward the radio.

"Here's the referee. He's counting. One, two, three, four, five, six, 22
seven . . . Is the contender trying to get up again?"

All the men in the store shouted, "NO." 23

"—eight, nine, ten." There were a few sounds from the audience, 24
but they seemed to be holding themselves in against tremendous pressure.

"The fight is all over, ladies and gentlemen. Let's get the micro- 25
phone over to the referee . . . Here he is. He's got the Brown Bomber's
hand, he's holding it up . . . Here he is . . ."

Then the voice, husky and familiar, came to wash over us—"The 26
winnah, and still heavy-weight champeen of the world . . . Joe Louis."

Champion of the world. A Black boy. Some Black mother's son. 27

He was the strongest man in the world. People drank Coca-Colas 28
like ambrosia and ate candy bars like Christmas. Some of the men went
behind the Store and poured white lightning in their soft-drink bottles,
and a few of the bigger boys followed them. Those who were not
chased away came back blowing their breath in front of themselves like
proud smokers.

It would take an hour or more before people would leave the 29
Store and head home. Those who lived too far had made arrangements
to stay in town. It wouldn't do for a Black man and his family to be
caught on a lonely country road on a night when Joe Louis had proved
that we were the strongest people in the world.

467

Examining the Text

1. Unlike the other selections in this chapter, which offer fairly objective analyses of sport, Angelou relates a personal recollection. What conclusions about the influence of sports on culture, and specifically on African American culture in the 1930s, can you draw from her story? Has that influence changed significantly over the last sixty years?

2. In paragraphs 16 and 17, Angelou describes her own thoughts about the prospect of Louis losing the match. After rereading these paragraphs, what do you think they contribute to the overall meaning and drama of the story? How are they connected to the final paragraph?

3. What is the effect of the concluding paragraph in the story? How would Angelou's message be different if she had not ended it this way?

For Group Discussion

Angelou's recollection demonstrates in vivid detail how a sporting event can take on much larger significance, how people can invest a great deal of emotion in the performance of an athlete or team. In small groups, discuss the specific ways in which the emotions described in this reading might parallel—and/or differ from—reactions to the recent election of Barack Obama within the political sphere.

Writing Suggestion

In her narrative, Angelou describes how Joe Louis was an inspiration and sign of hope for African Americans in the 1930s. Choose another athlete who you think has similarly been an inspiration to his or her fans or has served as a role model. In an essay, discuss the qualities that make that person a particularly good model. At the same time, if you think that athlete has negative qualities, you may cite these as well in analyzing how he or she has influenced fans.

The Unbeautiful Game

ADAM GOPNIK

A student journalist for a Tennessee college newspaper recently posted an article with the provocative title, "What's Wrong with the NFL?" In it, the writer pointed to the transgressions of a number of players—from Michael Vick's dog-fighting scandal to "Tank" Johnson's firearms convictions—and went on to conjecture about the reasons many pro footballers have become so degraded. The college reporter concluded that salaries were to blame: some players have contracts of over one hundred and fifty million dollars, which in their minds gives them license to behave in increasingly outrageous ways; other players misbehave out of a deep resentment because they are working just as hard as—or harder than—the multi-millionaire players but are earning the league minimum salary. The following article, this one from the New Yorker *magazine, draws similar conclusions about the relationship between money and the degradation of pro football, but Adam Gopnik's article takes the college newspaper posting several steps further. In this piece Gopnik examines the ways in which football has become "unbeautiful" . . . but he does it from the point of view of spectators and fans. Using a game between the New York Jets and the Houston Texans as a backdrop, the author observes that the attitude of those who watch pro football has soured in recent years. To support this contention, Gopnik analyzes his own experience and also reviews a number of books that have been written about pro football in the past several decades, including John Feinstein's* Next Man Up: A Year Behind the Lines In Today's NFL, *and* Moving the Chains: Tom Brady and the Pursuit of Everything *by Charles P. Pierce, along with several others.*

As you read, notice the way the author interweaves his present experience watching the Jets game, his reflections on his experience as a fan, and his reportage on the books he brings in as evidence. Because this is an example of magazine journalism and not a piece of academic research, the author can synthesize a number of secondary sources without having to employ citation conventions such as the MLA and APA styles. Furthermore, he can bring in his personal experience to a degree that one rarely sees in academic research papers. Nevertheless, the author brings to bear on his subject a wealth of analysis, critical thinking, and organizational skill in developing his thematic points about the ways in which football has changed—and ultimately the ways that watching football still provides meaning for its millions of fans.

Joe Namath is late. Promised for a twelve-thirty press "availability" in the lounge of the press box at Giants Stadium, in East Rutherford, New Jersey—that vital place where the fulcrum of the First Amendment, free food, is celebrated by reporters for hours on end every Sunday morning when the Giants or the Jets are in town—Namath finally wanders into the noiseless, sealed-glass press box around one-fifteen, when the Jets' game against the Houston Texans is already under way. The crowd in the press box has to decide whether to stick with the dullish game or go out and meet the greatest superstar (O.K., the only superstar) this hexed team has ever produced. A small line of reporters hisses out of the press box toward the lounge, like helium leaking from a balloon. 1

The tiny, intent circle gathers around Namath, who, at sixty-three, has aged into a cartoon version of his younger self. His schnoz, always notable, has become more so; he now looks weirdly like Joe Pepitone, that other, lesser New York swinger of the sixties. His salt-and-pepper hair is swept back, his face, after years in Florida, is leathery, and he wears oversized chestnut-tinted sunglasses, right out of a disco movie. His slouch has become a full question mark of a slump, but his genial, barracuda smile is intact, as are the elaborate schoolboy manners that lead him to refer to the men who mentored him by both their names and their nicknames. "I think that, after my family, Coach Paul 'Bear' Bryant was the biggest influence on me," he says, or, "I think the credit for creating that image"—of the quarterback as playboy—"has to go to Sonny Werblin. I mean, David A. 'Sonny' Werblin." 2

469

Joe talks for a bit about his new autobiography, one of two he has published. ("I certainly had help with it, but I wrote most of it myself this time.") But the reporters are looking elsewhere. 3

"What do you think of Eli?" one asks. 4

"Well, I think Eli has everything going for him except maybe his facial expressions and the way he carries himself," Namath jokes. (Eli Manning, the Giants' talented, inconsistent quarterback, has an unfortunate wide-eyed, golly-gee look for all occasions, like Opie, on the old Andy Griffith show, if he were to see Floyd the barber in a Halloween mask.) 5

"You don't think he has a leadership look?" the reporter says, leaning in eagerly. 6

"Now, I didn't say that." Namath laughs, seeing the approaching 7
headline clearly and ducking it. "I think he's got all the talent—I just
said maybe people misinterpret the way he looks."

I've been a Jets fan for forty years, and it's hard for me to believe 8
this full hand of good fortune. Namath, beyond reason or even the
bonds of fandom, got me through some bitter bits of my mixed-up adolescence. I loved him, we all loved him, not just for his famous upset
win in Super Bowl III but for his slouch and his white shoes and his
quick release—that upper body torquing around to shoot the ball out
to George Sauer, Jr., never needing to have the back foot planted—and
for the mildly Homeric drama of his career. Crippled early in his football life by bad knees of a kind the surgeons just don't make anymore,
he would disappear for half a season, reappear to throw for four hundred yards and four or five touchdowns, and then disappear again into
a welter of missed games and interceptions. As with Bobby Orr, his
great on-ice contemporary, his fragility was part of his resonance.

Someone asks Namath if he believes that Chad Pennington is in a 9
slump. Pennington, the Jets' current and gallant incumbent, is recover-
ing from two shoulder surgeries and has had a couple of off games.
Namath is suddenly intent. "No, he's a good quarterback," he says seriously. "I've only watched him this year as a fan, on television. I haven't
had a chance to break down the passing game to see if Chad's going to
the right spots or going to the wrong receiver." You sense that the distinction the old quarterback is making—between watching as a fan and
actually watching—is, for him, larger than he can quite explain. It isn't
just that he hasn't watched as attentively as he might have; watching
"as a fan, on television," means that he hasn't really watched at all.

Pennington, it turns out, after everyone has traipsed back to the 10
warm silence of the press box, is breaking out of his slump, courtesy of
the slow-footed Houston secondary. Pennington throws—well, not
strikes, exactly, but something like special-delivery messages, rising up
on his toes to send them spinning nicely, dartlike, into his receivers'
arms. The Jets pull out to a twenty-point lead.

Yet, astonishing as that is, what is really astonishing is to be 11
reminded again of how different this game looks depending on where
you see it from, on where you're standing (or sitting) while you watch
it. When you watch a pro football game from the Crimean War general's viewpoint of the press box, you can see what's going to happen.
On television, the quarterback peers out into the distance within the
narrowed frame of the midfield camera and for a moment everything
seems possible; the viewer can't know if there's a wideopen man fifty
yards deep or if there is nothing ahead of Pennington but despair—
four men crowding two receivers, who aren't even bothering to wave
their arms. The drama of the game on TV lies in finding out.

On the field, the quarterback backpedals, rolls right and takes a 12
look, and what is available—or not—is, within half a second, pitifully
evident. If you're watching live, Namath's point comes home; on television you see free will instead of a series of forced choices, mostly bad.
The quarterback, the gallant general, peering out, in command,
becomes, in reality, a stitch in the pattern already woven, his fate nearly
sealed before he gets to fiddle with it. (Which is why coaches always refer
to heroic quarterbacks as though they were mere middle-management
executives, making "good" and "bad" decisions in the pocket.)

The real excitement of the game on the field lies in the sudden 13
moments of frenzied improvisation, most often by the linebackers and
especially by the safeties, who on television mainly appear at the end
of the play to make a hit or swipe vainly at a pass. The Jets' safety Kerry
Rhodes, for instance, whose excellence is much cited but mostly invisible to one at home in front of the set, becomes the most entertaining
player to watch—racing the width of the field to cover an open
receiver, running like a man chasing his hat as it blows down the street
on a windy day, not running in tandem but running to get there, before
it's gone. Now, on a routine pass, Pennington is brought down hard,
and writhes on the ground in agony. The entire stadium goes silent. But
then he is bouncing up again, ready to go, and pumping his fists to
excite the crowd.

471

After the game, which the Jets hold on to win, 26–11, there is relief 14
in the locker room; Pennington is fine. The players, naked and semi-
naked, hold forth on the game, a ritual that we normalize (gotta beat
those deadlines) but in which any half-awake anthropologist would
spot something significant: the reporters being put in their place by the
players' sheer physicality, and the players being put in their place by
the reporters' being able to enforce their availability. Pete Kendall, the
Jets' left guard, is talking about Pennington's near-miss. "Let's say, he
was intently verbalizing," he says, sumo wrestler's body jiggling and
eyes ever so slightly alert. "Did I see it? No, I had no idea what was
happening. That's good for an offensive lineman. If you can watch
what's happening to your quarterback, you're not doing your job." He
smiles, tightly and pointedly, and goes back to putting on his pants.

All sports change depending on your point of view, but perhaps 15
none change so much as pro football. There is the familiar Sunday-
afternoon television—quarterback-centered, replete with instant
replays, each play a brief drama of courage and determination, a family entertainment, the original reality television. There is the actual
game, seen on the field, where the offensive and defensive lines meet in
a pit that is a kind of black hole of heaving, battling bodies—who
knows exactly what's going on in there. Rumors of fingers broken and
eyes gouged come back, and it is hard not to believe them. (In his new

book about football, *The Blind Side*, Michael Lewis explains that one of the most famous images in football memory—Lawrence Taylor's wild gesturing for help after breaking Joe Theismann's leg in two places— came about less from L.T.'s unexpected empathy for a stricken colleague than from his fear of getting caught in the pileup himself.) And there is the game as it has been presented, magnificently, by Ed Sabol and his family at N.F.L. Films, all caped Darth Vader-ish heroes, steam rising from mouths in the Green Bay winter; dramatic orchestral music and slow-motion long passes arcing lazily over and over in the midafternoon sky before they come racing to earth in someone's outstretched, praying hands. (A moment that in the stadium would just whiz by, unmusically.)

This makes pro football the original silly putty of the big media, 16 reshaped each year to entice an ever-larger audience—and at the same time sporadically mysterious, alluring, a weird mixture of violence, showman's calculation, and some kind of intense, medieval-tournament-like heraldry (those capes! those helmets! those cheerleaders!) and gallantry. Even when you try to be hard-headed about the game, some bit of color springs out. Alan Yost, a meat-and-potatoes financial journalist who writes most often for the *Wall Street Journal*, points out, in his new book about the finances of the sport, *"Tailgating, Sacks and Salary Caps,"* and with magical correctness, that the success of "Monday Night Football" derived in part from its lighting: all those shadowless fields and gleaming helmets. But when you try to be romantic about pro football its reality comes back: the snapping sound of Theismann's fibula, the nearly parodic corporatism that infects the game. The N.F.L. actually employs a special squad of sidelines watchers—"clothes Nazis," the players call them—to be sure that no coach ever strays from wearing officially sanctioned merchandise, right down to the skin, at game time. (Coaches can no longer wear a suit on the sidelines.)

Anything this self-consciously dressed up is asking to be dressed 17 down. And there was a time when pro football, seen from inside the locker room, offered the material for a kind of affable, blue-collar comedy, as an alternative to the nostalgic pieties of baseball and the urban realism that seems to halo basketball. It played the same role that its daddy sport, rugby, still plays throughout the world: the funny, dirty one. George Plimpton's 1966 *Paper Lion* and its even better sequel, *Mad Ducks and Bears*, like Dan Jenkins's roughly contemporary novel "Semi-Tough," are not just funny. They are about being funny, about the N.F.L. as a place where one is able to be funny. It's the laughter and the conversation, Plimpton explains to a baffled friend at one point about his love for the company of pro football players.

There's no laughter now. John Feinstein's new book on Brian 18 Billick and the Baltimore Ravens, *Next Man Up: A Year Behind the Lines in*

Today's NFL, employs the same premise as the best of all books about pro football, Roy Blount, Jr.,'s *About Three Bricks Shy of a Load*, an account of the 1973 season of the young Pittsburgh Steelers, the year after the Immaculate Reception game but before they won a Super Bowl. Feinstein takes the Ravens and their 2004 season as his subject, and the cast of characters is remarkably similar. There's an oppressed proletariat of special-teams players, a hard-pressed and overpaid first-round-draft-pick quarterback (Terry Bradshaw in Blount, Kyle Boller in Feinstein), a bunch of struggling linemen, and a tight-lipped, humorless, defensive-minded coach (Chuck Noll for the Steelers).

Blount's account of a year within an N.F.L. team thirty years ago 19 was essentially festive and high-spirited; Feinstein's is unrelievedly gloomy, tense, and depressing. "Next Man Up" refers to the cavalier cry of the coaches when yet another player goes down with a severe injury, and his tales are all of players belittled, bruised, and generally beleaguered, hoping to hang on long enough—five years is the run-up time to free agency these days—for a major payday. (And the paydays are major; twenty-five- and forty-million-dollar contracts come and go in his pages.) In part, of course, this difference in tone reflects a differ-ence in taste. Blount saw what he wanted to see and didn't see what he didn't want to see; there are no prizes on Parnassus for fair play. By his own account, he missed the fact that "Jefferson Street" Joe Gilliam, the Steelers' third-string quarterback, was not a free spirit but a heroin addict, and that the Steelers, at least by retrospective legend, were pio-neers in steroid abuse. Feinstein, on the other hand, sees what a dili-gent, intelligent, yet mainly humorless reporter is likely to see: a tangle of ambitions, injuries, and extremely short career expectancies, inter-rupted by sudden onsets of very big money. The closest thing to a hero in Feinstein's book is the offensive coordinator, Matt Cavanaugh, who, we know from almost the first page, is going to be fired at the end of the season for failing to do enough for the Ravens' offense, not that there is much he could have done. Cavanaugh is a sympathetic and unostentatious man, and, knowing his fate as we do, we wince with Feinstein every time this decent guy comes onstage to get kicked around one more time by the radio talk-show hosts and the owner and the other coaches.

It doesn't sound like fun, you figure out in the end, because it 20 isn't fun. Where it seemed natural for Blount to identify with the play-ers, and be warily sympathetic to the coach, Feinstein identifies with the owner and the coaches and is warily sympathetic to the players. He empathizes with them sufficiently to defend, at length, the linebacker Ray Lewis from the charge of murder, during a melee in Atlanta after the 2000 Superbowl, when in fact he was no more than a reluctant wit-ness, but it's obvious that the culture of the players is alien to him, as it

473

would be to most outsiders. The atmosphere is closed, guarded, and immensely knowing about the media; the artless charm with which Bradshaw or Dwight White confided in Blount would just not be possible now. With the best will in the world, there is very little you can squeeze out of the players that has not been pasteurized first by the agents and the league and the players' entourage, and by the players' understanding, essentially true, that the reporter is on nobody's side but his own. "Hang-around time," the old journalists' and sportswriters' favorite, is rarely part of the game now.

It is the owners, curiously, who are more eager to have their struggles and dramas narrated. Feinstein has the obnoxious Redskins' owner, Dan Snyder, drop into the narrative from time to time like Snidely Whiplash, to sneer and roll his mustache, while the Ravens' owner, Steve Bisciotti, who let Feinstein into the locker room, is very nearly made the hero of the book. Though Bisciotti does seem like a more level headed man than most N.F.L. owners, at one moment Feinstein relates a ritual and needless bit of humiliation that Bisciotti inflicted on Billick, shortly after he became the sole owner of the team. "You have some bad habits," he says to him. "For example, you always address me as 'young man' when you see me, and my wife as 'young lady.' . . . I'm about to become the owner of this team—your boss—and you greet me the same way you greet some kid coming up to you for an autograph. That's disrespectful." The insolence of wealth will creep out, as Dr. Johnson said. 21

The sour tone of so much of Feinstein's book isn't peculiar to Feinstein. Charles P. Pierce, a Boston sportswriter, who has the tools to pull a Blount, and the desire to do it, too, has written his own yearlong, hang-around account, this one about the Patriots and their star quarterback, Tom Brady—*Moving the Chains: Tom Brady and the Pursuit of Everything*—but his book, though better written, isn't much more fun than Feinstein's, mostly because Pierce has to write around his hero rather than through him. Brady is no Alex Karras. "I always figured that being a little dull was part of being a pro," Johnny Unitas is quoted as saying (in a new biography, "Johnny U.," by the former Time sportswriter Tom Callahan). "Win or lose, I never walked off a professional football field without first thinking of something boring to say." Brady resembles Unitas in this as in so much else. At one point, Pierce actually has to admit, "What Brady said reads more banal than it sounded at the time." The Patriots' coach, Bill Belichick, meanwhile, is so buttoned-up and close-mouthed that he makes both Chuck Noll and Brian Billick sound like Shecky Greene. (Belichick on Brady: "He does a lot of things well. He makes a lot of good plays. He makes a lot of good throws.") 22

Even books not precisely about the N.F.L. but about the path to getting there have something strained and unhappy in them. In *The Blind Side*, Michael Lewis, an expert storyteller, can stop telling stories 23 long enough to make a case for a complicated point in a convincing way, and one of the points he is making here is about the narrowed focus that football demands. His protagonist, a poor black kid named Michael Oher, is discovered to have "ideal" left-tackle potential, and he's taken in by an evangelical family who help nurture him—the story is basically "Gigi" without Louis Jourdan or the songs: "Thank Heaven for Very Big Boys." But where, for this football-loving reader, Lewis's baseball book was enlivening and cheering, his football book—about the making of a behemoth who may or may not get to the N.F.L.—is oddly sad. (The story of Gigi, who probably wouldn't have made starting courtesan, either, is a pretty sad one, too.)

Partly what drains the joy from the inner game of pro football these days is the same as what drains the joy from much of American life: there's a lot of money to be made by a few people, and a lot less for everybody else. The money in pro football comes in two flavors: more than you can imagine and less than you might think. The base pay for players is much higher, of course, than it is in the real world—the minimum for a rookie is almost three hundred thousand dollars—but the disproportion is real, too, and though the players maybe ought to be grateful for having as much as they do, like the rest of us they can't help being resentful for not having as much as they might. For every Chris McAlister, a shut-down cornerback making eight million a year, there is a Mike Solwold, a long snapper who after three seasons in the N.F.L. has already been cut or waived six times by four teams, and who has the bad luck in the Ravens camp to recover from an injury before he gets cut. (If he had still been injured, the Ravens would have had to pay him compensation.) 24

Feinstein reminds the reader that this here-today, gone-tomorrow rule is part of life in the N.F.L.; there is no, or very little, "guaranteed" money in pro football—the players work, and can be fired, "at will"—and, while a few upper-crust performers get to keep their signing bonus, most players are a snapped knee ligament away from street clothes. (Pierce reports that seventy-eight percent of N.F.L. players are unemployed, bankrupt, or divorced within two years of leaving the game, and those are the guys who make it.) Billick says grimly, about cutting players, "Whenever I have to make these cuts, I always think about what Clint Eastwood said in *Unforgiven*: 'When you kill a man, you not only are ending his life, you're taking away everything he ever had or is going to have.'" "The unhappiness that you feel among the players in all these books is hardly the misery of the oppressed, but it is something more familiar these days, the rancor of the near-miss. Why them and not us? is a radical question. Why the guy at the next locker and not me? a bitter one. 25

One way of dealing with the difference between the players and their experience—and, occasionally, their income—and everyone else's is to advance into a world of abstract manipulation where the players 26

475

are best appreciated as lines of numbers or as groupings of pixels. The kids do it through Electronic Arts Sports and its video games, where they make up their own teams and even their own players, and have as much allegiance to the dancing dots as we did to Joe Namath and Matt Snell. The grownups achieve the same effect, deep participation at a precarious distance, by becoming obsessed with the statistical analysis of sports. It is no accident, probably, that, as baseball salaries get bigger, a good deal of baseball writing has become more decorously removed from actual baseball into the numbers world (although Bill James, who started it all, has moved at last into management).

Pro football, however, has traditionally resisted statistical analysis. 27 Again and again, someone, like the fine sportswriter Allen Barra, has tried to match Bill James and write a football abstract, and, again and again, the enterprise has failed. One might think that the betting interest in pro football—which Yost estimates at more than a billion dollars per season—would lead to an ever more avid appetite for numbers, but the kind of analysis that Barra et al. are able to do is, although powerfully suggestive, weakly predictive. Football analysis is trickier than the baseball kind because football really is a team sport: every baseball act is colored by the context in which it takes place—the stadium and the situation—but football acts are the context in which they take place. A running back whose team wins every time he runs for a hundred yards is almost certainly busy running out the clock in the second half; he runs for a hundred yards because his team has already won. Unlike in baseball, all eleven guys on the field are involved in every play, and who deserves the credit or blame is harder to know than it looks.

Now, though, intricate analysis seems to have come to pro foot- 28 ball, through the good offices of the Internet and its capacity for the micro-niche, and the Web site Footballoutsiders has thrown off a book, the annual *Pro Football Prospectus*, which is apparently catching on. Football analysis has triumphed by combining the kind of detached statistical crunching that James pioneered with close amateur break-downs of Namath's "films." The two things taken together—the actual visual pattern of each play and the numerical representation of it—enable one to escape the contexts and "grade" the individual acts of the ballplayers to get a sense of who is doing what how well on every play.

The point of statistical analysis has never been to crunch numbers 29 but to challenge the conventional wisdom about how teams win and lose, and the football analysts are doing that now. Their conviction (much simplified) is that in the N.F.L. you pass to win and run to sustain a victory—though the average running play nets four yards, the median nets only three—and that most of the more conservative, hardnosed football strategies, like the one-run, bunt-and-sacrifice strategies in baseball, look canny and play dumb. There is even a strong, heretical movement under way against automatically punting on fourth down. (The irony of sophisticated analysis is that, while it tends to run counter to what the shouting heads on television pontificate about, it tends, ultimately, to go along with what the ignorant fans in the stands are screaming for: swing for the fences, go for it on fourth, etc.)

People within the game, though, still talk about brute physical 30 effort, and how much it matters. The two-yard runs, after all, are being played not in a video game but in a real world where the energy and will to get beaten up is a capital sum reduced by expenditure; those two-yard runs expend it. So the closeup view, emphasizing physical domination, isn't necessarily false, though it may be badly argued. The insiders may miss the pattern and still get the point. (Bill James himself has said—half as a joke, but only half—that he thought what brought the Red Sox back in 2004 was "veteran leadership." In the pure world of analysis, veteran leadership was long thought to be an explanatory principle on a par with water sprites and the rotation of the zodiac.) As our efforts to explain and predict are baffled, we retreat into pure pleasure. Then the question becomes: Enjoy what, how? Fortunately, a new book helps lead us back to becoming the armchair aesthetes we were all along. *In Praise of Athletic Beauty*, by Hans Ulrich Gumbrecht, who is a professor of comp lit at Stanford, is the book, and football the central **477** game. Much of the book sounds like the kind of guide to the aesthetic of sports that would be written by someone named Hans Ulrich Gumbrecht; long passages improve by being read in a light German accent. "Looking at empty stadiums," he remarks of his love of Stanford Stadium, "I suspect that stadiums 'stage' or 'make present' what Martin Heidegger once identified as the most elementary philosophical question: why there is something at all, opposed to nothing? On many levels and in multiple settings, stadiums materialize, and make us part of, this ultimate ontological contrast."

Nonetheless, Gumbrecht really is a fan, and he is trying to make 31 sense of a fan's experience. Instead of focusing on the easy cases— everybody can admire divers and gymnasts and the lacier kind of ice skaters—he takes for his subject the aesthetic of ballgames, which, he points out, began to become central to Western life as spectator sports only a century ago. His central thesis, to round it out a little crudely, is that we watch sports not out of identification with the players but out of a kind of happy absorption in someone else's ability: "The euphoria of focused intensity seems to go hand in hand with a peculiar quietness. I am at peace with the impression that I cannot control and manipulate the world around me. So intensely quiet do I become and so quietly confident, at least during the seconds when my favorite football team is talking through its next play in the huddle, that I feel I can let go and let come (or not) the things that I desire to come."

In other words, when we watch Joe Namath or Chad Pennington 32
or even Eli complete a pass what we feel isn't pathetic and vicarious
but generous and authentic: we give up a bit of ourselves in order to
admire another. We're broadened, not narrowed, by our fandom. Our
connection with our heroes is through an act of imagination, and the
act of imagination, not the connection, is what is worth savoring and
saving. (Stephen Dubner, before he struck gold with *Freakonomics*,
wrote a book about going in search of the Steelers' star runner Franco
Harris that made exactly this point; so did Frederick Exley's *A Fan's
Notes*, for that matter, where the narrator's obsession with Frank
Gifford helped him discover himself.)

These sentiments are what our grandfathers would have called 33
noble and manly, and certainly have something to do with what
makes us fans, whether the kind who tailgate in the cold or the kind
who compile stats in the overheated apartment. But is it possible to
divorce, or elevate, our aesthetic and imaginative interest so entirely
from our tribal and rooting interest? We can't be aesthetes without
also being fans. Even in the press box, many of us aren't really football fans; at least some of the time we're Jets fans or Giants fans or
Sea-hawks fans, and the connection between the team's fate and the
fan's fate isn't quite so beautifully disinterested as the formula suggests. My ideal game is not one in which the Jets and the Patriots are
engaged in a sterling contest where Pennington and Brady trade
coups and the final score is determined in overtime by an inspired
play. It's one in which the Jets pull ahead, 35-0, in the first quarter and
then coast to victory on a muddy field, as Brady slips and falls. This
may be many things, some of them forgivable, but generous and
broadening it isn't.

What makes the bald rooting interest forgivable, maybe, is the 34
near-certainty that the ideal game is never, or almost never, going to
happen. The essential experience of watching sports is experiencing
loss; anyone who has consoled a twelve-year-old after a Jets loss, or
been a twelve-year-old in need of consolation, knows this. Since loss
and disappointment are the only fixed points in life, maybe the best we
can say is that pro football, like anything else we like to watch, gives us
a chance to organize those emotions into a pattern, a season, while
occasionally giving us the hope of something more. The Jets don't
always lose—just nearly always. When they do better, we feel better.
That's the margin, or sideline, on which we live.

Examining the Text

1. This article begins with a long description of an encounter with professional
football legend Joe Namath, and this encounter leads to the author's expressing
a significant thematic point regarding the difference between watching football

live versus on television. In what ways do the two viewing experiences differ, in Gopnik's opinion?

2. The author of this article calls pro football "the original silly putty of the big media." How does this image of a children's toy—a flesh-colored silicone plastic blob that can be molded into a variety of shapes and lift newsprint off a sheet of paper—relate to the venerable American game of football, in Gopnik's view?

3. One of the subthemes of this article is that the image of football has changed over time. In a previous era, notes the author, football carried a connotation of being a somewhat quirky alternative to other sports. How does the author describe football's former identity in this article, and how has that identity changed, in his opinion?

4. Toward the end of this article, Gopnik provides some reasons why statistical analysis of professional football games is a less than satisfying pursuit—unlike baseball, which provides a wealth of enjoyable material for "stats geeks." However, the author ends this article on an upbeat note, positing a point of view that explains the real "beauty" in watching a variety of sporting activities, including football. On whose writing does he base this exaltation of sports fandom, and what are the specific propositions of this viewpoint?

5. *Thinking rhetorically*: This article's author contends that football in contemporary America is, on balance, "less fun"—and correspondingly more "unbeautiful"—than it was in previous eras. Examining the techniques with which he develops this persuasive position, what sorts of evidence does Gopnik provide to support this key thematic point? How does this mass of evidence add up to a convincing explanation for the decline in professional football's fun quotient?

For Group Discussion

Gopnik concludes this article by proposing that an essential experience of sports fandom is "experiencing loss." In this he seems to echo the Buddhist notion that every human life includes a certain experience of sickness, loss, and ultimately death—his point being that being a sports fan gives one practice in coping with these issues. Says Gopnik, "Since loss and disappointment are the only fixed points in life, maybe the best we can say is that pro football, like anything else we like to watch, gives us a chance to organize those emotions into a pattern, a season, while occasionally giving us the hope of something more." Discuss your own experience as a sports fan: what affective (i.e., emotional, psychological, and even spiritual) functions has being aligned with a certain team provided for you?

Writing Suggestion

In your grammar through high school experience, you undoubtedly had the wonderful opportunity to write one, if not literally hundreds, of book reports: short documents in which you proved to your teacher that you actually read a certain text, by summarizing the contents of the book and perhaps doing some rudimentary analysis as well. This article by Adam Gopnik might be seen as a kind of glorified—or at least extended—book report, in that he folds into his discussion a description of several books, all of them dealing with sports fandom generally, and professional football specifically. However, he goes *way* beyond your typical middle school book report, because he summarizes and analyzes these texts in service of a larger purpose: namely, to understand historical changes in professional football, and to arrive at some conclusions about emotional rewards and challenges of watching sports. This assignment asks you to undertake a similar task: in a piece of writing that transcends the traditional book report, choose and develop a sport-related topic and find several texts to help you explore and develop that hypothesis. Since you probably won't have time to read a wheelbarrow full of books, feel free to find shorter texts on the Web and through electronic journals on library databases. In some ways, your writing will resemble an academic research essay in that it will synthesize secondary sources; however, unlike an academic research paper, though, this synthesis will appear more informal and journalistic, and might incorporate more elements of personal experience, as Gopnik does. Also, you are excused from using MLA or APA documentation formats for the purposes of this assignment, although you will still, of course, need to identify and attribute your sources rigorously, as Gopnik does.

Discipline and Push-Up: Female Bodies, Femininity, and Sexuality in Popular Representations of Sports Bras

JAIME SCHULTZ

On a warm summer day it's common to see women runners, cyclists, or those simply out strolling or socializing wearing sports bras. The garment has become nearly as ubiquitous and socially acceptable as shorts and is worn equally for athletic and sedentary activities. But it hasn't always been that way, as Jaime Schultz explains in this comprehensive article tracing the evolution and public perception of the sports bra. Schultz describes the 1999 World Cup final in which a player removes her shirt, and then the author launches into an analysis of media—and by implication, public—reaction to this act. Schultz uses the public reaction as a way of examining broader societal attitudes toward women in sports, including issues of sexism, power, breast infatuation, eroticism, and the objectification of the female body.

Through this broader lens, Schultz attempts to determine whether the public display of Brandi Chastain's sports bra was simply a continuation of a tradition of (men) soccer players removing (and sometimes swapping) jerseys at the end of an important game or an erotic act . . . or was it a symbol of the progression of women's sports? Interpreting Chastain's act is, like understanding art, open to numerous theories, which Schultz seeks to explore in this article, recently published in the Sociology of Sports *journal.*

As you read, notice how Schultz uses soccer player Chastain as an anchor for the article, continuing to review the broader issues with a reference to the World Cup final. Although this is an academic work, the author seeks to inform and take the reader on an exploration of those wider, societal issues through a single event—Chastain's jersey removal—that was (and continues to be) relatively well-known. Most people can identify with a major sporting event televised to a mass audience, in this case one with forty million viewers. This makes the shirt-removal event an ideal, easily identifiable central point around which to examine the various thematic points that Schultz raises.

It is true that a clue to a woman's view of her femininity might be found in her choice of underwear?

(Benson & Esten, 1996, p. 26)

On July 10, 1999, over 90,000 people gathered in the Pasadena,   1
California, Rose Bowl to watch the U.S. women's soccer team play China in the final game of the World Cup. It was the largest crowd that ever gathered to watch a women's sporting event. An estimated 40 million television viewers tuned in as well, making it the most watched soccer game, men's or women's, in U.S. history (Longman, 1999, p. D1). The peak 18.8 Nielsen rating of the Women's World Cup final more than doubled the previous high for a televised soccer match in the U.S., the 1994 men's World Cup match between the United States and Brazil, which registered a 9.3 rating (Kimball, 1999).

What spectators observed, either from their bleacher seats or on   2
their television sets, was 120 minutes of spectacular, tense, and ultimately scoreless play between the two teams. As a result, a penalty kick shoot out determined the 1999 World Cup champion. Five players from each team took their turns shooting against the opposing goalkeeper. With the score tied at 4–4, Brandi Chastain was the tenth and final player to take her penalty kick. A goal by Chastain would mean victory for the U.S. Chastain placed the ball on the designated penalty spot, twelve yards away from the goal line. Not daring to look at Chinese goalkeeper Gao Hong, Chastain approached the ball and struck it with her left foot. Hong dove in futility. Chastain's shot hammered against

the side paneling of the net, just inside the right goal post, and secured the win for the U.S. women's soccer team.[1]

Spectators and viewers next witnessed an image that would pervade the media and cultural memories for months, even years to come. As one writer put it, "the ball had barely settled into the net when [Chastain] whipped off her jersey and stood there clad—from the waist up, anyway—only in her black sports bra" (Kimball, 1999). As Chastain celebrated with teammates in her black Nike Inner Actives sports bra, she was immediately and simultaneously lauded, ogled, scrutinized, and criticized for her actions. Debates over whether the bra exposure was acceptable or unacceptable, spontaneous or calculated, celebratory or opportunistic were played out in the media and at proverbial water coolers at the national and the international levels.

Just over two weeks after the World Cup final, Githens (1999) wrote that the image of Chastain in her sports bra was, "so startling . . . that it graced the front pages of numerous newspapers the next day, the cover of *Newsweek* and *Sports Illustrated* and, as of last week, racked up more than seventy Web site mentions on the Internet." Chastain was named one of *People* magazine's twenty most intriguing people of 1999 and one of *Street & Smith's* 100 most powerful sports figures (Penner, 2000, p. D1). In the interview round of the 1999 Junior Miss America pageant, contestants were asked whether Chastain's bra display had set a negative example for young girls. So much attention to Chastain's actions after her final goal raises the question: why all the fuss about a sports bra? That seemingly simple question serves as the foundation on which I construct this article.

The sports bra seems to be a relatively uncomplicated though, nonetheless, important garment. The invention of the commercial sports bra in 1977 was a significant advancement for physically active women. Design innovations led to the creation of a garment that allowed women greater support and comfort in their various types of movement. Despite its humble origins as an enabling technology, the sports bra has since been invested with new and varied cultural meanings and currencies. These meanings reflect shifts in ideals of femininity, the increasing acceptance of athletic female bodies, and the subsequent sexualization of those bodies. In addition, the bodily display of sports apparel in nonathletic settings has allowed the sports bra to become an item of fashion, as well as function.

In this article, I examine popular mediated representations of sports bras, specifically advertisements and what I call "iconic sports-bra moments." These moments pertain to Brandi Chastain's celebration of the U.S. women's soccer team's victory in the 1999 World Cup, as well as to reactions her celebration inspired. My analysis of these representations relies on the methodology that McDonald and Birrell (1999) refer to as "reading sport critically," a critical cultural studies approach that "focuses analytical attention on specific sporting incidents and personalities and uses them to reveal a nexus of power that helps produce their meaning" (pp. 283–284). In their anthology *Reading Sport*, Birrell and McDonald (2000) argue that incidents such as the Tonya Harding–Nancy Kerrigan figure skating spectacle (Braughman, 1995), the sexual harassment of Lisa Olson (Disch & Kane, 2000), and the Billie Jean King–Bobby Riggs "Battle of the Sexes" (Spencer, 2000) can be read as texts, offering unique points of access for interrogating the ideological production of power.

In particular, Birrell and McDonald (2000) recommend that schol- 7 ars attend to the mediated accounts produced around specific incidents because the "easiest way to get to ideology is through the media" (p. 11). In addition, the narratives that circulate around sporting personalities provide material for reading sport critically. Indeed, as Vande Berg (1998) argues, the mass media is primarily responsible for the construction of modern sporting celebrities. Andrews and Jackson's (2001) *Sports Star* attests to the role of the media complex in manufacturing and promoting the celebrity status of sports figures in an increasingly global cultural economy. The essays in *Sport Stars* constitute critical studies of sporting personalities, such as Wayne Gretzky (Jackson, 2001) and Cathy Freeman (Bruce & Hallinan, 2001), interrogated largely through attention to mediated representations of these individuals (see also Whannel, 2002). My intent in the first part of this article is to critically read the narrated reports of Brandi Chastain, her World Cup celebration, and the associated iconic sports-bra moments, paying particular attention to patriarchal power relations embedded in these cultural texts.

483

These power relations are also located in advertising discourse. In 8 the second part of this article, I draw from advertisements for sports bras that I found in women's health and fitness magazines, particularly *Women's Sport and Fitness*. Several scholars have argued that such magazines often promote oppressive, patriarchal notions of femininity using the rhetoric of well-being and empowerment (Duncan, 1994; Duquin, 1989; Eskes, Duncan, & Miller, 1998; Hargreaves, 1994; Leath & Lumpkin, 1992; Markula, 1995, 2001). White and Gillett (1994) similarly argue that bodybuilding magazines marketed to men (re)construct dominant masculine ideologies. Based on their critical decoding of advertisements in *Flex* magazine, White and Gillett (1994) propose that the "visual and narrative texts represent the male muscular body as a 'naturalized' embodiment of power, authority, and natural superiority" (p. 33). That this masculine ideal is "taken for granted as desirable affirms the insecurity of the reader who does not measure up to the envied image on the page" and pursuit of this standard is frequently inimical to men's health (p. 26). Likewise, the visual and narrative content of sports-bra advertisements convince female readers that the consumption of their products will assist in obtaining the particular ideal of femininity—one that is active, slender, and toned, and often difficult or impossible to achieve.

The representations I examine construct the sports bra as much more than a piece of athletic apparel for women. Although I do not call the utility of the garment into question, I suggest that the way it is considered, discussed, and framed in popular media results in the construction of the sports bra as an eroticized item. By extension, the breasts the bras cover, and the female bodies of which those breasts are a part, are similarly held up for scrutiny. The bra is constructed as an object of sexual desire, a means of disciplining the breast (both for the purposes of exercise and an objectifying gaze[2]) and disciplining the body. I further argue that these popular representations homogenize and normalize ideals of femininity that are considered achievable through technologies of disciplined body management. 9

After briefly discussing the evolution of the sports bra, I organize this article under the guise of a rhetorical disrobing. I begin with the act of removing one's shirt so that the sports bra is publicly exposed. The next layer I examine is the sports bra itself, specifically as it is constructed and understood as both functional and fashionable. Then, I analyze the implications that popular representations of sports bras have on women's breasts. Finally, I discuss the ways that these representations work to discipline women's bodies—bodies that are at once externally bound and internally managed by the sports bra. I refer to this organizational structure as a guise, for it implies that one might peel back the layers of discursive dress and reveal some naked truth about what the sports bra really means. I do not suggest that the sports bra has a singular or unitary meaning that can be uncovered through careful analysis; various contextualizations of the garment inspire a multiplicity of meanings (Birrell & McDonald, 2000, p. 11). Meaning is also dependent on the individuals who interpret the texts, and I do not presume to know how historical subjects will decode the moments or advertisements (Duncan, 1990; Fiske, 1989; Hail, 1980). Instead, I argue that there is one meaningful strand I find in popular representations of the sports bra that suggests the garment can be considered an eroticized object. More important, when the sports bra is infused with sexual connotations, those connotations are in turn associated with the bodies of women who wear the garment. 10

484

A HISTORICAL FOUNDATION

The history of women's undergarments has inspired a considerable amount of research (see, for example, Benson & Esten, 1996; Carter, 1992; Ewing, 1972; Ewing, 1978; Ferrell-Beck & Gau, 2002; Reyburn, 11

1971; Saint-Laurent, 1966). More often than not, however, the role that undergarments have played in the lives of active women has gone unexamined. In particular, it seems that what to do with one's breasts is a dilemma that has plagued the physically active female throughout time. For example, the Amazons, a legendary tribe of women in ancient Greece, were believed to have cut off their right breasts to facilitate archery (Yalom, 1997, p. 23). In less extreme cases, women worked merely to stabilize their breasts during activity. Women in ancient Rome supported their breasts by wearing bands around their chests or binding their breasts with a length of cloth or leather (Phillips & Phillips, 1993, p. 137). A vase from the fifth century BCE depicts Atalanta, a female athlete from Greek mythology, wearing an outfit akin to the modem bikini. Likewise, Lee (1984) argues that a fourth-century mosaic found in Sicily depicts ten bikini-clad women partici-pating in athletic competition. Part of the bikini costume is a "fairly wide band which is worn high under the arms, and appeared designed to strap down the breasts for vigorous activity" (Lee, 1984, p. 62).

Women also used corsets as a means of stabilizing their breasts, 12 though the primary purpose of the garment was to constrict waistlines. In Minoan Crete, women wore laced corsets that supported their breasts but left them bare (Benson & Esten, 1996, p. 49). Corsets reached the pinnacle of their popularity in the Victorian Era, when they served to discipline the entirety of women's torsos, including the hips, abdomen, and breasts. Even with the restricting technology of corsetry, some women did manage to participate in sports; the traditional use of rigid stays in corsets, however, made movement difficult and even dangerous. Delaney (1998) writes that women competing in the 1887 Wimbledon tennis tournament had to retire to the dressing rooms between matches to "unhitch their bloody corsets. As they endeavored to twist, turn and lunge on the courts, the women were repeatedly stabbed by the metal and whale bone stays of the cumbersome gar-ments." Though as early as 1837, Madam George had introduced a "Callisthenic Corset" that was "totally devoid of bone," to avoid such injuries during exercise (in Carter, 1992, p. 36).

The advent of elastic was a boon for the athletic, yet still-corseted 13 woman. In 1911, a significantly named "sports corset" was one of the first such undergarments to incorporate the flexible material (Phillips & Phillips, 1993, p. 138). Ewing (1972) argues that the 1914 tango craze inspired a "dancing corset." Constructed with elastic insets, the danc-ing corset facilitated movement, not just for the tango but also for other energetic dances, including the Charleston, Turkey Trot, and Bunny Hop (Carter, 1992, p. 90). Additional items were designed for other spe-cific physical activities, such as an elastic skating girdle, which was introduced by the Treo Company in 1915.

Farrell-Beck and Gau (2002) note that, although the first patent   14
for a brassiere was filed in 1863, it was not until the 1920s that
brassieres began to replace corsets as the favored undergarment of
women in the U.S. With the introduction of the brassiere, support for
breasts came from above (via shoulder straps) rather than from below,
as corsets previously provided. Like corsets, brassieres were adapted to
suit active women's lifestyles. For example, bras were incorporated
into swimwear. Farrell-Beck and Gau (2002) found that brassieres for
athletic women were patented as early as 1906 for acrobatic dancing
and other theatrical use, yet the style did not seem to catch on (p. 31). It
was not until the late 1970s that a bra specially designed for athletic
women would achieve popular acceptance and commercial success.
The advancements of women in sport, coupled with the fitness boom
of the 1970s, undoubtedly contributed to the need for equipment
specifically designed for female athletes.

In 1977, runners Hinda Miller and Lisa Lindahl created a proto-   15
type for the modern sports bra. Inspiration for the garment came when
the two women considered the utility of jockstraps for male athletes.
"We said," recalled Miller, "what we really need to do is what men
have been doing: pull everything close to the body" (Sharp, 1994,

p. 25). Originally dubbed the "Jockbra," Miller and Lindahl created the
sports bra by sewing two jockstraps together. The front panels of the
bra were made from the two oval jockstrap pouches and compressed
the breasts to the ribcage. The women used the waistband of the jockstrap to construct the bra's wide elastic band that encircled the torso.
The over-the-shoulder straps were reconfigured from the leg straps
and crossed in the back to further stabilize the breasts and keep the
straps from slipping down (Barr, 1997). The original appellation of the
garment was changed to JogBra when storeowners in South Carolina
found Jockbra offensive (Purdie, 1988, p. 63).[3] In the first year of production, 25,000 sports bras were sold (Nyad & Hogan, 1998, p. 49). In
1998, the sports bra industry rang up $412 million in retail sales (Peck,
1999), and statistics for sports bra sales in 2002 showed that the garment comprised 6.1 percent of the $4.5 billion bra market (Dolbow,
2002, p. 9). Based on these figures, it seems safe to claim that the sports
bra has become a popular garment.

It is difficult to dispute the benefits of the sports bra in the lives of   16
physically active women; it constitutes something of a technological
revolution. The sports bra has taken on symbolic importance as well,
becoming emblematic of the progress of women's sports. Hinda Miller,
one of the inventors of the sports bra, said that the garment has been
"as important to the growth of women's sports as the passage of Title IX"
(Peck, 1999), and others agree, calling it the "cloth symbol of Title IX"
(Gerhart, 1999, p. C01).

Despite the undeniably positive utility and symbolic significance   17
of this piece of apparel, popular representations of sports bras give rise
to competing meanings. One frequent mediated construction of the
sports bra is that it can be construed as a sexualized article that contributes to the objectification of female bodies.

Brandi Chastain's celebration of the U.S. women's 1999 World   18
Cup victory provides a salient example of the ways in which the popular media sexualizes sports bras and athletic female bodies. When
Brandi Chastain immediately ripped off her jersey after scoring the
game-winning goal, she provided the world with both a topic for public debate and the most enduring image of the 1999 World Cup. Who
can forget the image of Brandi Chastain, her muscular body clenched
and her emotion undeniably euphoric, clad from the waist up in only
her black Nike Inner Actives sports bra?

TEMPEST IN A B-CUP

*"Where were you when Brandi Chastain ripped off her shirt?". . . For a
certain generation of teenage girls, the Brandi question will someday resonate with the same timbre as does the Kennedy question for the Boomer
parents.*

(McKee, 2000, p. W4)

It appears that Brandi Chastain's celebration will persist in our cultural   19
memory for some time to come, though our interpretations of the incident vary. For some, the moment was empowering—the spectacle of a
strong woman excelling at her sport—and representative of how far
women's sports have come. For others, the moment seemed to signify
public acceptance of a new version of femininity. The repeated publication of Chastain in her sports bra legitimized an athletic, strong, active,
and autonomous female form. Still others read the gesture with a more
skeptical eye, suggesting that the moment was calculated to increase
either the marketability of the Nike bra or of Chastain herself. Thus,
Brandi Chastain was concomitantly framed as a triumphant athlete, a
poster girl for the success of Title IX, a paragon of changing feminine
ideals, and a calculating opportunist. Despite competing readings of
Chastain's celebration, discourse consistently turned to what it meant
for Chastain to take off her shirt, and how the public did or should
understand the display of a woman in her bra.

Though it is impossible to objectively read the moment, Chastain's   20
gesture seemed instantaneous after the goal; it appeared spontaneous
rather than designed. Chastain had already begun to take off her jersey
in the minuscule amount of time it took for the announcer to declare

"goal!" In less than two full seconds after her shot sailed past the Chinese goalkeeper, Chastain had yanked her jersey over her head and fallen to her knees with fists raised in triumph. Chastain has claimed the moment was nothing more than "temporary insanity" (see for example, Ackerman, 1999, p. 42; Brown, 1999; Davies, 1999, p. 10; Saporito & Willwerth, 1999, p. 58), and after analyzing the moment, I suggest that her gesture bears little resemblance to a seductive act.

Popular discourse, however, frequently constructed an eroticized 21 account of the incident. A significant number of writers used the term "striptease" in stories relating Chastain's gesture (see, for example, Bartolomeo, 2000; Harvey, 1999; Hickey 1999; Hummer, 2000; Jones, 2000; Kent, 2000; Kimball, 1999; Kimball, 2000; Middleton, 2000; Smoron, 1999). Similarly, the maneuver has been referred to as a "peel-down" (Peck, 1999), a "strip-down" (Brodeur, 1999), a "provocative gesture" (Ackerman, 1999, p. 42), a "half Monty" (Penner, 1999, p. D1), and designated as "the most brazen bra display this side of Madonna" (Tresniowski, 1999, p. 56). Such terms suggest that Chastain acted with the deliberate intention of titillating onlookers. Supporting this contention, some authors were also quick to include mention that several weeks before the 1999 World Cup, Chastain had appeared in *Gear*, a men's magazine. In her *Gear* pictorial, Chastain posed naked, save her cleats and strategically placed soccer balls. Chastain's decision to appear as she did in *Gear* was juxtaposed with her World Cup celebration and used to undermine both her athletic accomplishment and the sincerity of her revelry.

488

That male athletes seem to have set the precedent for this type of 22 divestiture further complicates the "Brandi bra moment" (Gerhart, 1999, p. C01; Riley, 2000). Andre Agassi and Pete Sampras have flung their sweat-drenched shirts into the stands after tennis matches. Dennis Rodman did the same after several professional basketball games. It is in soccer, however, that the action most frequently occurs. The practice is so widespread in men's soccer that Federation Internationale de Football Association (FIFA), soccer's international governing body, deemed it illegal to take off one's shirt in celebration (Payne, 1999). "Men do it all the time," said Roger Rogers, editor of *Women's Soccer World Magazine*. "It wasn't as though [Chastain] didn't have a bra on. It certainly would be discriminating to suggest a woman can't do it if a man does" (Welts & Oldenburg, 1999, p. 1A).

The resultant discrimination, however, is not based on whether 23 female athletes should have the same public disrobing rights as male athletes, but, rather, what is made of those athletes once their tops come off. Male athletes who doff their shirts do not come under the same media scrutiny that Brandi Chastain inspired.[4] There seems to be a dimension of sexuality connected with a woman who removes her jersey that is not found with male athletes who do the same. Addressing tennis player Goran Ivanisevic's ritual of "yanking off" his shirt en route to winning the 2001 Wimbledon tournament, Givhan (2001) wrote that he was reminded of Chastain's "impromptu striptease." Givhan continued,

> Her personal unveiling was one of those cultural touchstones, a moment when talk of female athleticism, body image and the objectification of women all converged. With Ivanisevic, the only talk is pretty much "Nice biceps." One wishes that Chastain had been greeted with simply "Nice six-pack."
>
> (Givhan, 2001, p. C02)

Other public responses to the mediated aftermath of Chastain's 24 celebration attended to this double standard. For example, Mead (1999) astutely noted that, "Girl Takes Top Off . . . is freighted with an entirely different symbolic weight" than "Sports Figure Takes Top Off" (p. 25). Ann Hollander (1978), an art and dress historian, proposes that, for women, the removal of the shirt or blouse has always signified an erotic invitation. So whether or not Chastain's gesture was calculated becomes somewhat irrelevant. Despite the many ways her celebration is read, the act of removing her shirt is largely understood as a public disrobing equivalent to a striptease. It seems the public views Chastain's gesture as an erotic invitation that begs repeating.

489

Shortly after the 1999 Women's World Cup, a commercial appeared 25 on ESPN. The commercial showed Chastain playing football with three men, including professional basketball player Kevin Garnett. When Chastain scored, all three men turned to her and waited. Finally Garnett broke the silence, asking Chastain, "What's with the shirt?" The men expected that Chastain would celebrate the football goal as she did the soccer goal in the World Cup—by taking off her shirt. It was not Chastain's sporting abilities that the men seemed to admire, but her body. Such anticipation suggests that sport offers another venue in which men can look forward to a woman undressing. These expectations are not limited to carefully orchestrated television commercials. Chastain wrote of a similar incident in which "this guy yells down from a railing three floors up in a hotel: 'Hey Brandi, what's up with the shirt?'" (Chastain, 1999, p. 76). Likewise, in a parking lot before a San Francisco 49er's game, a man asked Chastain, "Are you going to take off your shirt?" Chastain obliged by lifting up her sweatshirt to reveal a 49er's jersey (Harvey, 1999, p. D2).

An incident in the 2001 U.S. Major League Soccer (MLS) All-Star 26 game attested to the persistent association of Chastain, the removal of one's top, and the sports bra. In this game, two male players performed what they called "tributes" to Brandi Chastain (Mahoney, 2001, p. D10). First, Jim Rooney and then, later, Landon Donovan took off their jerseys when they scored in the MLS All-Star game. As previously mentioned, this celebratory reaction is somewhat common among male soccer players. This time, however, both men took off their jerseys to reveal black Nike sports bras. When Rooney stripped, teammate Mamadou Diallo caressed his sports bra. When Donovan revealed the bra, he was shown "prancing" about the field (Wagman, 2001).

Like other popular mediated representations of sports bras, a com- 27 plicated network of power relations lie below the surface of the seemingly uncomplicated actions of Donovan and Rooney. Chastain's celebratory actions in the 1999 World Cup emulated those of male soccer players. Because she is a woman, however, her actions came under scrutiny not usually associated with men taking off their jerseys. The effect of Chastain's emulation is sexualized. When men mimicked Chastain's actions, however, in a complex case of male soccer players imitating a female soccer player imitating the ritual behavior of male soccer players, the effect was comical. Jack Edwards, one of ABC's commentators for the game, remarked of Rooney, "Not the most beautiful sight we've ever seen, but certainly one of the more humorous" (Jones, 2001, p. D9). To dismiss Rooney and Donovan's actions as simply humorous, however, is to ignore more important implications. Though Rooney commented that it was "just a good laugh for us" (Gardner, 2001), the men's actions also involve misogyny. By mocking a significant moment in women's sports, the male athletes detracted from the moment's importance, reducing it to an incident of frivolity. In addition, the use of humor is one way of diffusing potential threats. Consider the following elements: soccer (a traditionally male sport), the Rose Bowl (a traditionally male venue), and taking off one's jersey upon scoring (a traditionally male style of celebration). Now substitute women in all these male-centered traditions and there is apt to be a sense of threat. Perhaps a humorous tribute to Chastain is one way that male athletes feel they can reassert their dominance when that power is contested.

Though Chastain was recalled in this incident, the media did not 28 reinvoke the same type of rhetoric in reporting it. Donovan and Rooney were described as "taking off" (Eisenberg, 2001), "whipping off" (Leonard, 2001), "ripping off" (Mahoney, 2001, p. D10), and "removing" (Gardner, 2001) their jerseys to reveal black Hike sports bras. The actions of the male players are not described as "stripteases" or "peeldowns." The language, significantly, is not overtly sexualized as in the case of Chastain, though the men's antics certainly pointed to a sexual dimension of removing one's shirt. Furthermore, the acts of Donovan and Rooney removing their shirts are not enough to invoke memories of Chastain. It is only when the bodies are coded with the sports bras that particular meanings are generated, making the gestures comical and, consequently, able to detract from the seriousness of women's sport. Masculine markers, such as referring to Rooney as "balding" (Jones, 2001, p. D9), pronounce the incongruity between the men and the bras. The conventional masculinity of Donovan and Rooney is important. Ian Bishop, also a member of the MLS All-Star game, said he never considered wearing a sports bra like his teammates. Bishop said, "Me with long hair, people would have thought other things" (Eisenberg, 2001). The combined feminine codings of long hair and a sports bra on a man might negate the humor of the gesture and call his gender and sexuality into question.

WHAT LIES BENEATH

In the case of Donovan and Rooney, the media give the sports bras primacy after the removal of their jerseys. In the case of Brandi Chastain, however, it is somewhat more difficult to discern whether her 1999 World Cup celebration is better understood as the act of a woman taking off her shirt or about the exposure of her bra. The act of displaying the bra and the bra itself are two separate, yet closely conjoined, aspects of Chastain's celebration. After the World Cup, photos of Chastain in her sports bra appeared in magazines throughout the world. The image of the sports-bra-clad Chastain made the covers of *Time, Newsweek,* and *Sports Illustrated*—all in the same week. When Chastain's picture graced the cover of *Sports Illustrated,* the magazine's managing editor, William Colson, deemed it, "the greatest picture of a sports bra in the history of publishing" (Hyman, 1999). To Colson, it was neither a picture of a great athlete nor a memorable moment in sports history. Instead, his reading of the cover photograph concentrated on the bra. Chastain and her team's accomplishment became secondary to the undergarment, so much so that the public still attends to her, not as an athlete, not as the woman who scored the winning goal in the 1999 World Cup, but simply as "that girl in the sports bra" (see for example, Crothers, 2000, p. 64). The reduction of Chastain to "that girl in the sports bra" was reinforced at the 2000 Olympics in Sydney, Australia. As the U.S. women's soccer team played Norway in the Sydney Football Stadium, several spectators held up signs that read, "Show us your sports bra" (More Brandi, Please, 2000).

Like Brandi Chastain, many women do not seem to mind whether 30 their sports bras are visible to the general public, perhaps because, in recent history, the sports bra has marked a categorical elision of function and fashion. As function, the sports bra falls under the heading of "sports equipment." Like shoes or bicycles specifically designed for

29

491

women, the sports bra has allowed women to more fully enjoy physically active lives. As fashion, however, the sports bra takes on different meanings. The sports bra might be seen as simply another item of lingerie, as in several mediated cases of Brandi Chastain. Nevertheless, Chastain has also increased the public acceptance of the bra as a piece of outerwear. Mike May, of the Sporting Goods Manufacturers Association, said that Chastain "made it OK for women to wear sports bras without anything else on top" (Hiestand, 1999, p. 3C). As a piece of lingerie, the sports bra can be seen as a fashionable dressing down of the female body. Conversely, when worn without a covering top, the sports bra can also be construed as fashionable dressing up of the female body as well.

The act of dressing, of wearing clothes and adopting one fashion or another, is both a cultural practice and a semiotic system. As cultural practice, it has become increasingly popular and acceptable for a woman to wear a sports bra as she would any other shirt. Payne (1999) wrote that although "such bras are designed for sports, they have become big business fashion items on and off the field with more and more women using them uncovered as casual wear." Similar articles attest to the use of sports bras as stand-alone wear. For example, a 2000 article in *Women's Sport and Fitness* asked, "When is a sports bra really an athletic top?" The answer: "Whenever the hell *you* want it to be" (Bartolomeo 2000, p. 42).[5] 31

In the semiotic system of fashion, the sports bra has become a way for female athletes and nonathletes alike to present a particular type of image. Susan Willis (1990) writes that women who wear workout clothes outside of an athletic setting "unabashedly define themselves as workout women. In making a public body statement, a woman affirms herself as someone who has seized control over the making and shaping of her body" (p. 7). Therefore, a woman might appear publicly in her sports bra to assert her identity as a workout woman. Wearing workout apparel outside of a physically active context allows women to convey the ways that they have disciplined and managed their bodies, and by extension, their lives. 32

SHAPING UP (AND OUT)

The sexualization of sports bras, and women who wear them, did not begin and end with these iconic sports-bra moments. Sports-bra advertisements offer another site for investigating how particular meanings of the garment are generated. One such meaning emphasizes the ways in which bras inevitably draw attention to women's breasts. As a result, advertisements for sports bras often play on the importance of presenting female breasts in ways that are considered attractive, particularly to an objectifying gaze. 33

Bras are essentially for and about breasts in some way or another. 34
The first bra a girl owns is a "training bra"—whether it is the girl or her
breasts that are being trained is open to interpretation. Throughout her
lifespan, a woman's breasts might be supported, separated, squeezed
together, shoved forward, rounded out, flattened down, or pushed up by
the bra she chooses to wear. Bras can create the illusion of breasts where
very little or none exist. Bras can also give the impression of an absence of
breasts if that effect is desired. Bras construct bodily silhouettes to suit
ephemeral fashions—from the minimized bustline of the 1920s to the pro-
jectile profile of the 1950s. Iris Marion Young (1990) writes that bras objec-
tify and normalize breasts, molding them to suit an ideal (p. 195). The
sports bra is not exempt from the normalizing and disciplining nature of
other bras. On the surface, it might seem that the sports bra is unconcerned with creating a socially desirable shape for women's breasts, as the
general principle of the garment is to compress the breasts for protection
and comfort during physical activity. Based on my analysis of sports-bra
advertisements, however, I propose that the sports bra is implicated in the
creation and maintenance of dominant cultural ideals of women's breasts.

There are several ways in which advertising discourse constructs 35
women's breasts as objects for scrutiny. It is interesting that this objectification often comes packaged in the rhetoric of empowerment. Myra
Macdonald (1995) writes that in the 1980s and 1990s advertisers "happily
made use of concepts that had acquired new status thanks to the feminist
and other civil liberties movements." In addition to empowerment,
Macdonald also noted that values such as "'freedom,' 'independence,'
and 'pleasure' . . . were reduced to matters of lifestyle and consumption"
(p. 92). Advertisements for sports bras are no exception. For instance,
early sports-bra advertising advocated empowerment through physical
activity. Bras with names such as "You Can Do It Running Bra" and
"Bound to Win" suggest as much. Themes of empowerment were
stressed in the first sports-bra ad (Jogbra, 1979), which articulated a
woman-centered approach to the garment by asserting, "no man-made
sporting bra can touch it." For the purpose of this article, however, I am
interested in examining the ways in which women are encouraged to use
their breasts as symbols of agency, control over their sexuality, and as
indicative of overall body management. This encouragement is conveyed as another way in which women might be empowered by a sports
bra. Writing specifically about Nike, Cole and Hribar (1995) argue that in
the postfeminist imagery, "a popular knowledge of empowerment" is
embedded in the intersection of bodily maintenance and the consumption of athletic-lifestyle products (p. 362).

Bodily maintenance, particularly conveyed as concern for the 36
appearance of women's breasts, tends to pervade sports-bra advertisements. For example, several present-day ads discuss the importance of

493

combating the "uniboob." The term *uniboob* refers to the simultaneous flattening and seeming lack of division between the two separate breasts. An ad for Lucy.com (2000), titled "The Uniboob Epiphany," provided a vignette of a woman in a gym who learns that the company has a sports bra to liberate her from the insidious uniboob. The ad concluded with a heroic Lucy declaring, "I will not rest until all the boobs in the world stand as strong and as proud as the women who bear them."[6] Liberation is thus connected not only to the right bra but also to the best possible presentation of women's breasts, making both active lifestyles and women's bodies objects of consumption.

Likewise, an ad for the Champion Jogbra (2000) invoked memories of Brandi Chastain by depicting a female soccer player in a black bra. The text of the ad stated, "Our latest innovation has a unique cup design that eliminates 'uniboob.' " The woman in the ad attests to this claim, as her gravity-defying breasts remain round, firm, and separate from one another as she performs a "bicycle-kick" maneuver that places her in the air, back parallel to the ground and chest pointed skyward. In the context of physical proficiency and autonomy, this advertisement, and others like it, constructs the ability to put forth a bifurcated bosom as an empowering act for women. 37

494

Not only should women worry about the uniboob, according to advertisements, but they should also be concerned with the prominence of their breasts. As stated earlier, the initial intent of the sports bra was to support the breasts by compressing them to the chest. The first sports-bra ad attested to the importance of compression, stating, "Jogbra's unique design holds breasts close to the body" (Jogbra, 1976). Similarly, a 1985 Jogbra ad avowed that the "minimized profile is critical" for participation in sports. The technique of compression, however, seems no longer valued (at least in advertisements), because, with compression, breasts lose their shape and appear smaller. Twenty years after its first advertisement appeared, Jogbra (1996) advocated a different selling point by stating, "Only abs should be flat. . . . Now, a sports bra that respects and defines your natural shape." It seems curious that a natural shape does not simply exist, but that it must be defined. This ad kills two birds with one bra, as it presents readers with idealized messages about both breasts and stomachs. Thus, the ideal breast shape is normalized, and, by extension, so is the ideal body type. The athletic but obviously breasted female body is naturalized, disguising the discipline necessary to achieve that body. 38

Concern for the shape of one's breasts is also expressed through medicoscientific discourse. An advertisement from Nike (1999) displayed a female figure with her breasts exposed.[7] Superimposed across her body was the question, "After years of exercise, what kind of shape will your breasts be in?" The ad continued, "breasts are held up by non-elastic Cooper's ligaments. And once they stretch, they don't snap back." As 39 such, breasts require Nike's Inner Actives bra to combat this risk. Not only will the Nike bra keep the Cooper's ligaments from stretching, but it will also work without "smashing you down." Other advertisements for sports bras make similar claims. Jogbra (1986) asserted that their "sports bra is scientifically designed to comfortably redistribute breast mass. . . . lessening the gravity pull that tears delicate breast tissue." A sports-bra advertisement from Lily of France (1979) declared that, "running is good for every part of you but two." Therefore, women understand that what might be beneficial for most of their bodies can be a detriment to those parts that signify sexual difference. The advertisements appeal to women's internalization of self-discipline and control while warning that sexual desirability is threatened without their products.

This concern for the shape of one's breasts also indicates that 40
beauty is conferred by a particular age. Young (1990) writes that, "breasts are the symbol of feminine sexuality, so the 'best' breasts are like the phallus: high, hard, and pointy" (p. 190). Flattened breasts signify prepubescence—a stage of development in which girls are not yet fit to be objects of sexual desire. On the other hand, stretched or sagging breasts suggest old age. Like the young girl, the older woman is also not culturally considered an object of sexual desire. The sports bra, like other bras, is concerned with promoting a sexuality that most

495

appeals to the masculine gaze. As an object of consumption, the sports bra plays on and reinforces hegemonic notions of femininity. Sports-bra advertising and the repeated publication of Brandi Chastain in her sports bra represent the dominant icons of consumer culture, including youth, physical attractiveness, and health (Hargreaves, 1987, p. 150). These icons are about more than women's breasts—they construct a bodily ideal for women, as well. Popular representations of sports bras homogenize and normalize a particular feminine standard, requiring women to discipline not just their breasts but also their bodies.

BREASTED BODIES

There is a considerable amount of discipline required to achieve the 41
femininity normalized by popular representations of sports bras. The women in these representations are slender, toned, and fit. Indeed, writers of both scholarly and popular texts have suggested that this type of body marks a new version of ideal femininity. M. Ann Hall (1996) writes, "Popular discourse today, at least in North America, invokes a normative ideal of female beauty that is slim, strong, sinuous, athletic and healthy" (p. 60; see also, Bordo, 1993; Maguire & Mansfield, 1998; Markula, 1995; Spitzack, 1990). Race is omitted from discussions of the culturally constructed ideal of feminine beauty Hall articulates, but it

seems clear that the ideal is also White. I found no popular representations of sports bras that were associated with women of color. It also seems safe to assume that the body is coded as middle to upper class. The Nike Inner Actives bra Chastain wore in the World Cup retails for $40–$50. The average sports bra costs around $30. In addition, the investment of time and money required to discipline one's body to work towards this feminine standard is substantial. Therefore, the beauty ideal is not only gendered, but also raced and classed as well.

This normative ideal of female beauty has been directly connected to discussions of Brandi Chastain. Sullivan's (1999) *Time* magazine article, "Goodbye to Heroin Chic. Now It's Sexy to Be Strong," proposed, "perhaps the botters' [soccer players] out-front sexuality will prompt all their come-lately fans—girls and boys both—to reconsider what constitutes healthy, full-bodied femininity" (p. 63). Likewise, the "new aesthetic" Chastain exemplifies "appears to be replacing the traditional dewy paradigm," according to one article in the *Wall Street Journal* ("Comment, 2000, p. A24). Brubach (1996) also speculated on the increasing acceptance of strong female bodies in the 1990s. Brubach, however, suggested that this ideal might be as damaging as other models of femininity, asking, "will the tyranny of the body built for sports be any less punishing—or any healthier—than the tyranny of the body built for fashion?" (p. 48). Like Chernin's (1981) "tyranny of slenderness," involving eating disorders and cultural preoccupations with body size, the discipline required for "the body built for sports" can be damaging to a woman's physical and psychological well being (Park, 1994). The disciplinary practices required for athletic femininity can be tyrannical and the homogenized images of women in their sports bras contribute to powerful forms of docility and normalization. 42

In *Discipline and Punish*, Michael Foucault (1977) theorizes that disciplinary power used by institutions, such as prisons, hospitals, and schools, produces "docile bodies" that are compliant with societal regimes of power. Using the metaphor of Jeremy Benthama's Panopticon, Foucault argues that, in modern society, discipline has been transformed from external force or coercion to internal self-surveillance. Sandra Lee Bartky (1988) argues that Foucault's formulation is "blind" to the ways in which disciplinary practice "turns a female body into a feminine one" (p. 78). Bartky purposes that power emanating from sources such as friends, media, and beauty experts should be considered in the production of docile female bodies. 43

Scholars have attended to the disciplinary regimes of diet, exercise, and sport to interrogate the production of docile bodies (see, for example, Andrews, 1993; Bordo, 1993; Cole, 1994; Johns & Johns, 2000; Spitzack, 1990; Theberge, 1991). Duncan (1994) argues that textual mechanisms in *Shape* magazine result in women's obsessive self-monitoring, furthering 44 the ends of patriarchy and detracting from the empowering possibilities of an active and healthy lifestyle. Eskes, Duncan, and Miller (1998) found that ideologies of empowerment espoused in the rhetoric of women's fitness magazines are "framed in such a way that true health is bypassed for the sake of beauty" (p. 340). Maguire and Mansfield (1998) contend that aerobic exercise "perpetuates the objectification of female bodies, organizing the reshaping of their bodies so that they are (hetero) sexually appealing" (p. 134). Others have argued that the sexualization and objectification of the seemingly transgressive physiques of female bodybuilders recuperate those bodies under the masculine gaze (Balsamo, 1994; MacNeill, 1988). As such, potentially liberating physical activity instead reinforces patriarchal views of femininity and maintains the gendered subordination of women.

The unidirectional consideration of the production of docility, 45 however, often ignores women's agency (Deveaux, 1994; Hall, 1996). Rather, as Markula (1995) argues in her study of aerobicizers, women do not completely internalize the panoptic power arrangement, but instead actively "question the body ideal and are particularly skeptical about the media presentation of exercising women" (p. 449; see also Collins, 2002; Hall, 1993; Lenskyj, 1994; Lloyd, 1996). Whereas individuals negotiate the meanings of cultural texts, the empowering potential of sport and exercise is jeopardized when those physical activities are cast as a means of achieving dominant and oppressive feminine ideals.

497

The popular representations of sports bras are implicated in the 46 (re)production of these ideals of femininity. For figures such as Brandi Chastain and the women in sports-bra advertisements, female strength, power, and autonomy are often subverted into sexualized attractiveness. Like others, Solomon (2000) posited that athletic female bodies have come to constitute what we culturally consider to be an attractive form of femininity. As Solomon argued, however, "The increasing acceptance of powerful women's bodies has been matched by a frantic attempt at containment. Yes, buff is beautiful—but only as long as its function is to be gawked at by guys." Unrestrained female power disrupts culturally gendered hierarchies. By reformulating that power as (hetero) sexually attractive, these popular mediated representations of sports bras help to restrain it, reining that power in under an objectifying gaze.

All this is not to say that the production of particular feminine 47 ideals is only enacted through and by mediated images of sports bras. Though these popular images do ideological work by normalizing and sexualizing a specific type of femininity, it is not a simple case of cause and effect. Bordo (1993) argues that bodies become disciplined through "the practices and bodily habits of everyday life" and not only through images that represent ideal femininity (p. 16). Likewise, Bartky (1988) writes that the "disciplinary power that inscribes femininity on the female body is everywhere and it is nowhere; the disciplinarian is every-one and yet no one in particular" (p. 74). The discipline required to strive for an athletic, feminine ideal should not be seen emanating only from an external, coercive force, such as popular mediated representations. Yet the images of women in their sports bras offer one of the many ways of examining how we continually consider, interpret, construct, perpetuate, and revise our ways of thinking about femininity and female bodies.

CONCLUSION

I began this article curious about why there was so much fuss over a 48 sports bra. There is no singular or elementary answer to this question. Perhaps one of the issues that complicate this analysis is that, as Brandi Chastain celebrated the World Cup victory in 1999, what she revealed was much more than a sports bra. To some, Chastain revealed the body of a female athlete in all its unabashed, muscular glory. To others, Chastain's divesture was akin to a striptease, revealing a female body proffered for masculine consumption. A number of onlookers felt Chastain's gesture was not revealing at all, but rather the way soccer players have tradition-ally celebrated goals. Other spectators felt that Chastain revealed her bra—not a piece of sports equipment, but a piece of lingerie that has tradi-tionally been a source of titillation. Certain individuals read the moment as a symbol of the progress of women's sports, whereas there were those who felt saddened that a significant moment in that progress was cheap-ened by a bawdy display. A portion of those witnessing Chastain's cele-bration understood it as an example of the commodification of sports and athletic bodies. Others interpreted the action as a woman calculating to capitalize on the moment in one of the few venues open to women athletes—that is, marketing her (hetero) sexuality. In short, what was revealed at the moment Brandi Chastain removed her soccer jersey was what Michael Messner (1994) terms the "contested ideological ter-rain" that has come to characterize the female athlete and her body.

It is a mistake to think that the iconic sports-bra moments and 49 advertisements mentioned in this article are just about the sports bras. In some representations, such as those of Brandi Chastain, we must consider the process by which the sports bra is made visible. A significant portion of the population seemed to lack the frame of reference for understanding a woman removing her shirt in public, or else their frames of reference led them to equate the removal with a provocative gesture. Once the sports bra can be seen publicly, either by disrobing or by wearing it without a covering shirt, the garment is often sexualized. Brassieres of all sorts are sexualized, but the sports bra presents an interesting case because it is simultaneously lingerie, sports equipment, and a fashion statement. In addition, sports bras have traditionally compressed women's breasts for comfort and protection in physical activity. Sports-bra advertisements, however, show women that they can buy garments that will shape their breasts into ways considered sexually attractive. Finally, popular representations of sports bras offer a gateway into larger issues about women's bodies. Mediated images of sports bras homogenize and normalize a particular feminine ideal. Although this ideal is about strength and fitness, it is packaged in ways that reproduce the traditional gender order. The disciplinary practices that produce these strong and fit bodies are recaptured through sexualized discourse. As such, athletic versions of femininity are not seen as threats, but as particular bodies rendered acceptable to the objectifying gaze.

NOTES

[1]For a complete story of the 1999 Women's World Cup, see Longman's (2000) *The Girls of Summer: The U.S. Women's Soccer Team and How It Changed the World*. For an analysis of media discourses surrounding the 1999 World Cup, see Christopherson, Janning, and McConnell (2002).

[2]In this article, I will use the term *objectifying gaze* to refer to the practices of surveillance that construe women as objects of sexual desire. My conceptualization of this term is particularly informed by the work of Laura Mulvey (1975, 1981).

[3]JogBra was sold to Playtex apparel in 1990. JogBra is now a division of Champion Products (Barr, 1997).

[4]It should be noted that Linda Medalen, a female player on the Norwegian national team, also removed her jersey after scoring a goal in an earlier round of the 1999 World Cup, though the act received little media attention.

[5]Public acceptance of a woman in a sports bra without a covering top is not unanimous. For example, in Tampa, Florida, high school officials deemed it "inappropriate" for female runners to wear sports bras without a shirt (Rozel, 2002). An official at a track meet in Wisconsin disqualified a relay team from Stevens Point Area Senior High School because one runner wore a sports bra (Runner Disqualified for Illegal Bra, 2002).

[6]For more on lucy.com's advertising see Baar (2000), p. 6.

[7]This advertisement turned out to be rather controversial. As a result, the advertisement that revealed the model's breasts only appeared in magazines that went to subscription holders. Magazines sold in stores or at newsstands, as well as those in magazines geared toward a younger audience, such as *Seventeen* and *YM*, were altered so that the model's hair hung down over her breasts.

REFERENCES

Ackerman, E. (1999, July 26). She kicks. She scores. She sells. *U.S. News & World Reports*, p. 42.

Andrews, D.-L. (1993). Desperately seeking Michel: Foucault's genealogy, the body, and critical sport sociology, *Sociology of Sport Journal,* **10**, 148–167.

Andrews, D.L., & Jackson, S.J. (Eds.). (2001). *Sport stars: The cultural politics of sporting celebrity,* London: Routledge.

Barr, A. (2000, June 19). Lucy on the web with sports bras. *Adweek,* p. 6.

Balsamo, A. (1994). Feminist bodybuilding. In S. Birrell & C.L. Cole (Eds.), *Women, sport, and culture* (pp. 341–352). Champaign, IL: Human Kinetics.

Barr, M. (1997, November 11). Women runners full of praise for sports bra. *The Plain Dealer,* p. 4E. Retrieved October 5, 2001, from the LexisNexis database.

Bartky, S.L. (1988). Foucault, femininity, and the modernization of patriarchal power. In I. Diamond & L. Quinby (Eds.), *Feminism and Foucault: Reflections on resistance* (pp. 61–86). Boston: Northeastern University Press.

Bartolomeo, J. (2000, January/February). Sports style: Underwear busts out. *Women's Sport & Fitness,* p. 42.

Bell, G. (2001, July 29). A little All-Star and a lot of spectacle. *The New York Times,* p. 8–10.

Benson, E., & Esten, J. (1996). *Un-mentionables: A brief history of underwear,* New York: Simon & Schuster.

Birrell, S., & McDonald, M.G. (Eds.). (2000). *Reading sport: Critical essays on power and representation.* Boston: Northeastern University Press.

Bordo, S. (1993). *Unbearable weight: Feminism, western culture, and the body.* Berkeley: University of California Press.

Braughman, C. (1995). *Women on ice: Feminist essays on the Tonya Harding/Nancy Kerrigan spectacle.* New York: Routledge.

Brodeur, N. (1999, August 26). World cup bra incident uplifts girls. *The Seattle Times,* p. B1. Retrieved October 5, 2001, from the LexisNexis database.

Brown, S.-S. (1999, July 18). Nike bra gets good exposure. *Denver Rocky Mountain news,* p. 2S. Retrieved October 5, 2001, from the LexisNexis database.

Brownmiller, S. (1984). *Femininity.* New York: Linden Press/Simon & Schuster.

Brubach, H. (1996, June 23). The athletic esthetic. *New York Times Magazine,* pp. 48; 50–51.

Bruce, T. & Hallinan, C. (2001). Cathy Freeman: The quest for Australian identity. In D.L. Andrews & S.J. Jackson (Eds.), *Sport stars: The cultural politics of sporting celebrity* (pp. 257–270). London: Routledge.

Carter, A. (1992). *Underwear: The fashion history.* New York: Drama.

Champion Jogbra (2000, September). Get in shape. *Women's Sport & Fitness,* p. 62.

Chastain, B. (1999, October 25). A whole new ball game. *Newsweek*, p. 76.

Cherain, K. (1981). *The obsession: Reflections on the tyranny of slenderness.* New York: Harper and Row.

Christopherson, N., Janning, M., & McConnell, E.-D. (2002). Two kicks forward, one kick back: A content analysis of media discourses on the 1999 Women's World Cup soccer championship. *Sociology of Sport Journal*, 19, 170–188.

Cole, C.L. (1994). Resisting the canon: Feminist cultural studies, sport, and technologies of the body. In S. Birrell & C.L. Cole (Eds.), *Women, sport, and culture* (pp. 5–29), Champaign, IL: Human Kinetics.

Cole, C.L., & Hribar, A. (1995). Celebrity feminism: Nike style, post-Fordism, transcendence, and consumer power. *Sociology of Sport Journal*, 12, 347–369.

Collins, L.H. (2002). Working out the contradictions: Feminism and aerobics. *Journal of Sport & Social Issues*, 26, 85–109.

Comment: The fair sex. (2000, May 11). *Wall Street Journal*, p. A24.

Crothers, T. (2000, July 3). Spectacular takeoff. *Sports Illustrated*, pp. 64–67.

Davies, T. (1999, July 26). Brandi's brazen celebration. *Maclean's*, p. 10.

Delaney, A. (1998, March 31). How we got rid of the bloody corsets and other tales of women's sports. *On the Issues: The Progressive Women's Quarterly*. Retrieved September 1, 2002 from http://www.il.proquest.com/products/pt-product-genderwatch.shtml

Deveaux, M. (1994). Feminism and empowerment: A critical reading of Foucault. *Feminist Studies*, 20, 223–247.

Disch, L., & Kane, M.-J. (2000). When a looker is really a bitch: Lisa Olson, sport, and the heterosexual matrix. In S. Birrell & M.-G. McDonald (Eds.), *Reading sport: Critical essays on power and representation* (pp. 108–143). Boston: Northeastern University Press.

Dolbow, S. (2002, January 14). Champion sports bra: Not for jocks. *Brandweek*, p. 9.

Duncan, M.C. (1990). Sports photographs and sexual difference: Images of women and men in the 1984 and 1988 Olympic games. *Sociology of Sport Journal*, 7, 22–43.

Duncan, M.C. (1994). The politics of women's body images and practices: Foucault, the panopticon, and *Shape* magazine. *Journal of Sport & Social Issues*, 18, 48–65.

Duquin, M.E. (1989). Fashion and fitness: Images in women's magazine ads. *Arena Review*, 13, 97–109.

Eisenberg, J. (2001, August 1). Rooney: Cross my heart, wearing a bra "not that bad." *The Palm Beach Post*, p. 8C. Retrieved October 5, 2001, from the LexisNexis database.

Eskes, T.-B., Duncan, M.C., & Miller, E.M. (1998). The discourse of empowerment: Foucault, Marcuse, and women's fitness texts. *Journal of Sport & Social Issues*, 22, 317–344.

Ewing, E. (1972). *Underwear: A history*. New York: Theatre Arts Books.

Ewing, E. (1978). *Dress and undress: A history of women's underwear*. New York: Drama Book Specialists.

Farrell-Beck, J., & Gau, C. (2002). *Uplift: The bra in America*. Philadelphia: University of Pennsylvania Press.

Fiske, J. (1989). *Television culture*. New York: Methuen.

Foucault, M. (1977). *Discipline and punish: The birth of the prison*. New York: Pantheon Books.

Gardner, C.-F. (2001, July 29). A stripped down showing by stars. *Milwaukee Journal Sentinel*, p. 11C. Retrieved October 5, 2001, from the LexisNexis database.

Gerhart, A. (1999, July 14). Cashing in on world cups. *Washington Post*, p. C01.

Githens, L. (1999, July 27). A show of support. *The Buffalo (New York) News*. Retrieved September 1, 2000, from the LexisNexis database.

Givhan, R. (2001, July 13). Winner takes (off) all. *The Washington Post*. p. C02.

Hall, M.A. (1993). Feminism, theory and the body: a response to Cole. *Journal of Sport & Social Issues, 17*, 98–105.

Hall, M.A. (1996). *Feminism and sporting bodies*. Champaign, IL: Human Kinetics.

Hall, S. (1980). Encoding/decoding. In S. Hall (Ed.), *Culture, Medical, Language* (pp. 128–138). London: Hutchinson.

Hargreaves, J. (1987). The body, sport and power relations. In J. Horne, D. Jary, & A. Tomlinson (Eds.), *Sport, leisure and social relations* (pp. 139–159). London: Routledge & Kegan Paul.

Hargreaves, J. (1994). *Sporting females: Critical issues in the history and sociology of women's sports*. London: Routledge.

Harvey, R. (1999, December 2). With so much exposure, Brandi can bare her soul. *Los Angeles Times*, p. D2.

Hickey, P. (1999, July 18). Juneau, Habs might be a nice fit. *The Gazette (Montreal, Quebec)*. Retrieved October 5, 2001, from the LexisNexis database.

Hiestand, M. (1999, October 28). Moment spurs a movement. *USA Today*, p. 3C.

Hollander, A.L. (1978). *Seeing through clothes*. New York: The Viking Press.

Hummer, S. (2000, September 29). Soccer's fairy-tale story has silver end. *The Atlanta Journal and Constitution*, p. 8E.

Hyman, M. (1999, July 26). The 'babe factor' in women's soccer. *Business Week*, p. 118. Retrieved October 5, 2001, from the ABI/INFORM Global database.

Jackson, S.J. (2001). Gretzky nation: Canada, crisis and Americanization. In D.-L. Andrews & S.J. Jackson (Eds.), *Sport stars: The cultural politics of sporting celebrity* (pp. 164–186). London: Routledge.

Jogbra. (1979, March). No man-made bra can touch it. *WomenSports*, p. 21.

Jogbra. (1985, April). Jogbra: The most important profile in sports history. *Women's Sport & Fitness*, p. 70.

Jogbra. (1986, March). *Women's Sport & Fitness*, p. 9.

Jogbra (1996, May/June). *Women's Sport and Fitness*, p. 49.

Johns, D.P., & Johns, J.-S. (2000). Surveillance, subjectivism, and technologies of power. An analysis of the discursive practice of high-performance sport. *International Review for the Sociology of Sport*, 35, 219–234.

Jones, G.L. (2000, February 1). Women's team agrees to 'historic' deal. *The Sporting News*. Retrieved June 13, 2002, from http://tsn.sportingnews.com/voices/grahamel.jones/20000201-p.html

Jones, G.L. (2001, July 29). Rooney gives full support. *Los Angeles Times*, p. D9.

Kent, M. (2000, August 13). Women's sexual revolution runs into knee-jerk response from male reactionaries. *Scotland on Sunday*, p. T13. Retrieved October 5, 2001, from the LexisNexis database.

Kimball, G. (1999, July 15). Getting tuned into women's soccer. *The Irish Times*. Retrieved October 5, 2001, from the LexisNexis database.

Kimball, G. (2000, July 4). Soccer; a case of overexposure; Chastain still defines Cup win. *The Boston Herald*, p. O60. Retrieved October 5, 2001, from the LexisNexis database.

Leath, V.M., & Lumpkin, A. (1992). An analysis of sportswomen on the covers and in feature articles of *Women's Sports & Fitness Magazine*, 1975–1989. *Journal of Sport & Social Issues*, 16, 121–126.

Lee, H.M. (1984). Athletics and the bikini girls from Piazza Armerina. *Stadion*, 10, 45–77.

Lenskyj, H. (1994). Sexuality and femininity in sport contexts: Issues and alternatives. *Journal of Sport & Social Issues*, 18, 356–376.

Leonard, T. (2001, July 31). Having too much fun at All-Star showcase. *The Record (Bergen County, New Jersey)*, p. S8. Retrieved October 5, 2001, from the LexisNexis database.

Lily of France. (1979, August). Running good for every part of you but two. *Women's Sports*, p. 8.

Lloyd, M. (1996). Feminism, aerobics and the politics of the body. *Body & Society*, 2, 79–98.

Longman, J. (1999, July 12). Women's world cup: Day in the sun for the girls of summer after a riveting championship run. *New York Times*, p. D1.

Longman, J. (2000). *The girls of summer: The U.S. Women's Soccer Team and how it changed the world*. HarperCollins Publishers.

lucy.com. (2000, September). The uniboob epiphany. *Women's Sport & Fitness*, p. 52.

503

Macdonald, M. (1995). *Representing women: Myths of femininity in the popular media*. London: Edward Arnold.

MacNeill, M. (1988). Active women, media representations, ideology. In J. Harvey & G. Cantelon (Eds.), *Not just a game: Essays in Canadian sports sociology* (pp. 195–212). Alona, MB: University of Ottawa Press.

Maguire, J. & Mansfield, L. (1998). "No-body's perfect": Women, aerobics, and the body beautiful. *Sociology of Sport of Journal*, 15, 109–137.

Mahoney, R. (2001, July 29). Donovan reveals skins, skills; Chastain imitators cap All-Star game. *The Washington Post*, p. D10.

Markula, P. (1995). Firm but shapely, fit but sexy, strong but thin: The postmodern aerobicizing female bodies. *Sociology of Sport Journal*, 12, 424–453.

Markula, P. (2001). Beyond the perfect body: Women's Body Image Distortion in fitness magazine discourse. *Journal of Sport & Social Issues*, 25, 158–179.

McDonald, M.G., & Birrell, S. (1999). Reading sport critically: A methodology for interrogating power. *Sociology of Sport Journal*, 16, 283–300.

McKee, S. (2000, July 7). On sports: Joie de soccer. *Wall Street Journal*, p. W4.

Middleton, C. (2000, September 29). Golden goal sinks golden girls. *The Daily Telegraph*, p. 41. Retrieved October 5, 2001, from the LexisNexis database.

Mead, R. (1999, July 26). The talk of the town. *The New Yorker*, p. 25.

Messner, M.A. (1994). Sports and male domination: The female athlete as contested ideological terrain. In S. Birrell, & C.L. Cole (Eds.), *Women, sport and culture* (pp. 65–80). Champaign, IL: Human Kinetics.

More Brandi, please. (2000, September 30). *The San Diego Union-Tribune*, p. 2. Retrieved October 12, 2003, from the LexisNexis database.

Mulvey, L. (1975). Visual pleasure and narrative cinema. *Screen*, 16(3), 6–18.

Mulvey, L. (1981). Afterthoughts on 'Visual pleasure and narrative cinema' inspired by 'Duel in the Sun' (King Vidor, 1946). *Framework*, 15, 12–15.

Neporent, L. (1994, February). Fit for a woman. *Women's Sport & Fitness*, pp. 76–83.

Nike (1999, September/October). After years of exercise, what kind of shape will your breasts be in? *Women's Sports & Fitness*, pp. 96–97.

Nyad, D., & Hogan, C.-L. (1998). Women: Empowered by the evolution of sports technology. In A. Bush (Ed.), *Designs for sports: The cult of performance* (pp. 46–67). New York: Princeton Architectural Press.

Park, R.J. (1994). A decade of the body: Researching and writing about the history of health, fitness, exercise and sport, 1983–1993. *Journal of Sport History*, 21, 59–82.

Payne, S. (1999, July 19). Shirts off to sports bras soccer star's topless turn puts undergarment in spotlight. *The Toronto Sun*. Retrieved October 5, 2001, from the LexisNexis database.

Peck, S. (1999). The bra: Brandi's public peeldown turned the spotlight on the humble sports bra. Retrieved September 20, 2001, from *car/1999/feat_bra1.html"* http://www.justforwomen.com/features/year/1999/feat_bra1.html

Penner, M. (1999, July 11). Bare facts make these two heroes. *Los Angeles Times*, p. D1.

Penner, M. (2000, September 12). Moment's over; now U.S. soccer hero Chastain can get back to game. *Los Angeles Times*, p. D1.

Phillips, J., & Phillips, P. (1993). History from below: Women's underwear and the rise of women's sport. *Journal of Popular Culture, 27,* 129–148.

Purdie, L. (1988, January/February). Function first. *Women's Sport & Fitness*, p. 63.

Reyburn, W. (1971). *Bust-up*. Englewood Cliffs, NJ: Prentice-Hall, Inc.

Riley, L. (2000, September 21). Bra's support not universal. *The Hartford (Connecticut) Courant*, p. A1. Retrieved October 5, 2001, from the LexisNexis database.

Rozel, L.A. (2002, June 3). Athletes are strapped by sports bra flap. *The Tampa Tribune*. Retrieved August 9, 2002, from the LexisNexis database.

Runner disqualified for illegal bra. (2002, May 31). Retrieved June 3, 2002, from http://news.findlaw.com/legalnews/sports/index.html

Saint-Laurent, C. (1966). *A history of ladies underwear*. London: Michael Joseph.

Saporito, B., & Willwerth, J. (1999, July 17). Flat-out fantastic. *Time*, pp. 58–64.

Sharp, D. (1994, September). The women who took the jounce out of jogging. *Health*, p. 25.

Smoron, P. (1999, July 25). A nice Hamm. *Chicago Sun Times*, p. 6. Retrieved October 5, 2001, from the LexisNexis database.

Solomon, A. (2000, April 19–25). Our bodies, ourselves. Retrieved September 12, 2002, from http://www.villagevoice.com/issues/0016/solomon2.php

Spencer, N.-E. (2000). Reading between the lines: A discursive analysis of the Billie Jean King vs. Bobby Riggs "Battle of the Sexes." *Sociology of Sport Journal, 17,* 386–402.

Spitzack, C. (1990). *Confessing excess: Women and the politics of body reduction*. Albany, NY: State University of New York Press.

Sullivan, R. (1999, July 19). Goodbye heroin chic. Now it's sexy to be strong. *Time*, p. 62.

Theberge, N. (1991). Reflections on the body in the sociology of sport. *Quest, 43,* 148–167.

Tresniowski, A. (1999, July 26). Soccer's happiest feat. *People Magazine*, pp. 54–60.

Vande Berg, L.R. (1998). The sports hero meets mediated celebrityhood. In L.-A. Wenner (Ed.), *MediaSport* (pp. 134–153). London: Routledge.

Wagman, R. (2001, August 9). All-Star sports bra frivolity damages MLS public image. *SoccerTimes*. Retrieved October 5, 2001, from http://www.soccertimes.com/wagman/2001/aug09.htm

Wells, M., & Oldenburg, A. (1999, July 13). Sports bra's flash could cash in. *USA Today*, p. 1A.

Whannel, G. (2002). *Media sport stars: Masculinities and moralities.* London: Routledge.

White, P.G., & Gillett, J. (1994). Reading the muscular body: A critical decoding of advertisements in *Flex* magazine. *Sociology of Sport Journal*, 11, 18–39.

Willis, S. (1990). Working out. *Cultural Studies*, 4, 1–18.

Yalom, M. (1997). *A history of the breast.* New York: Random House.

Young, I.-M. (1990). *Throwing like a girl and other essays in feminist philosophy and social theory.* Indianapolis: Indiana University Press.

Examining the Text

1. In what ways does Schultz link the practical aspects of the sports bra with its role as an erotic garment? Do you agree with the author's position that it both enables women to participate in sports yet carries with it a certain eroticism? Why, according to Schultz, does the popular media regard the sports bra as an "object of sexual desire, a means of disciplining the breast . . . and disciplining the body?"

2. How does the historical background on the mechanics of brassieres and sports—specifically the various methods women have used to compete athletically, unhindered by their breasts—tie in with current societal perceptions of women's undergarments? What does the response to Chastain publicly exposing her sports bra indicate to you about how the media regard the behavior of women players versus men players?

3. Why do you think the media used words like "striptease," "peel-down," "strip-down," and similar terms to describe Chastain's actions in taking off her jersey but referred to the Donovan and Rooney jersey-removals as "ripping off," "whipping off," and "removing"? What does the difference in the descriptions used tell you about gender, power, and sexual contexts of language? And why do you think that Ian Bishop, a teammate of Rooney and Donovan's, chose not to participate in mocking Chastain? What does his response imply about sexual stereotypes?

For Group Discussion

1. As a group, discuss how sexual stereotypes are found in sports. You might begin by listing a range of possible stereotypes, and then go on to discuss the ways in which these stereotypes affect (a) the sport; (b) women's participation in sports in general. What suggestions does the group have to overcome sexual stereotypes of the type identified by Schultz in the article?

2. Reread the section that begins with the heading, "Tempest in a B-Cup," and discuss whether you believe that, on reflection, Chastain's action in removing her jersey helped or hindered public perceptions about women's sports. Be mindful, that in some cultures, it would be frowned upon (or even illegal) for women to participate in sports. Contrast that to the apparent sexual objectification of women athletes in the United States.

Writing Suggestion

Title IX of the U.S. Civil Rights Act requires schools to provide equal access for girls and boys in school sports and is credited with an upsurge in girls and women participating in a range of athletic activities. Develop a thesis and write an essay discussing the question of whether you think that equality in sports has been achieved. Conversely, you might defend a position asserting that such equality can never be achieved in our society. As you develop your argument, consider all of the ways in which you either agree or disagree with the notion of equality. To provide evidence for your arguments in the body paragraphs of your paper, you might conduct research using the following: the sports section of your daily newspaper, sports coverage on television, sports franchises, gender of coaches, athlete incomes by gender, and other sources to inform your essay.

Games We Play

Jack of Smarts: Why the Internet Generation Loves to Play Poker

JUSTIN PETERS

Poker has leapt from dimly lit back rooms inhabited by avuncular cigar-chewers to the bright lights of TV broadcast and tech-savvy Generation X-ers weaned on Game Boys and surfing the Internet, according to author Justin Peters. He lays out a poker-related generation gap in this article first published by the Washington Post. *In it, age and perceptions about poker are key elements as the author documents how his own changing attitude to the card game parallels a broader shift that has taken place as a result of Internet poker and the televising of poker tournaments. Peters speculates that poker was declining in interest to the younger generation . . . until the Internet changed that, perhaps forever.*

Peters argues that fear of being perceived as a "novice" kept his generation out of traditional venues of poker games in the past, but that with the advent of anonymous online poker, younger players could participate without any potential embarrassment. The author also attributes the rising popularity of poker to the renewed interest by TV producers who, he says, have figured out a formula for showing poker on television. These combined factors have led to new players entering the professional circuit—and winning big! The author concludes that the qualities essential in a good poker player are aligned with traits that a generation exposed to hours of video games and computer-use already possess. Peters believes that members of his generation are playing poker to such a degree that it has transcended mere novelty into popular entertainment and even parody.

As you read, think about how your own perceptions and images of poker players have been formed. For instance, do you recall aged relatives playing poker at holiday times, or yourself playing as a child for candy or play money? Conversely, did televised poker spark your awareness of the game for the first time? How do your memories/perceptions relate to the stereotypes described by Peters? How successful is the author in making his experience relate to your own as a reader?

Before this year, my only experience with poker was at basketball camp 1
when I was twelve. We played during rest periods with Skittles for

chips and about seven different wild cards per hand. Although fun, the game paled by comparison to other leisure pursuits, such as sleeping, and I never gave it much thought after that. Yet during the past year, I have unexpectedly changed my tune. I've joined a weekly card game. I waste hours surfing online poker sites. I try to drop poker phrases like "bad beat" and "the nuts" into casual conversation. When I won $140 at the table in February, I spent weeks regaling everybody I knew with chapter and verse of my victory. Most reacted with raised eyebrows and condescension, but similarly afflicted friends of mine understood, greeting the story with measured awe, as if I were Amarillo Slim.

These days poker—specifically Texas hold 'em, the best version of 2 the venerable game—is enjoying an unexpected renaissance among Americans in general, and twenty-somethings in particular. It is newly ubiquitous on television: The World Series of Poker, a single event which took place last May, is replayed on ESPN with obsessive frequency ten months after it ended. The World Poker Tour, another set of tournaments located in casinos around the country, got picked up by the Travel Channel last year. In the fall, Bravo introduced its heavily promoted "Celebrity Poker Showdown" program, betting on viewers being riveted by a fifth-street showdown between Timothy Busfield and Coolio. But perhaps anecdotal evidence speaks louder: Three years ago, when I was a sophomore at Cornell University, there wasn't a game to be had. By the time I graduated, I could choose from several different games every night of the week.

Every generation gambles, but how they gamble says something 3 about the spirit of the age. Why are yuppies-in-the-making suddenly interested in poker, a game most of us grew up associating with either paneled basements and cheap cigars or Rococo Old West saloons filled with bolo-tied card sharps? The answer may be that the popular image of the game has undergone a subtle recasting—one with a great attraction to ironic youngsters like me who find in the game the same slightly glamorous, slightly seedy, go-getter spirit that characterized the Internet boom. It makes sense that today's college-educated young adults, especially young men, choose poker. Strategy oriented, individualistic, and embedded in a nice masculine mythology, poker is the perfect game for the revenge-of-the-nerds generation looking to square their intelligence with their inner maleness.

BOOMTOWNS TO POKER BLOGS

Poker first appeared in the United States in the 1820s, brought to New 4 Orleans by French immigrants who called the game poque. It traveled up the Mississippi River and spread throughout the country, soon becoming an underground national pastime, baseball for the unathletic. As the century turned, poker maintained its popularity, but lost its phenomenon status. Though television shows like *Maverick* in 1957 and the 1971 mini-series *The Gambler* later mythologized the poker players of the good old days—the dandified 1840s gambler, kind to women and merciless to cheaters—no one looked for glory or drama in modern poker anymore. To callow youth like me, the game looked like just another thing that Babbitty men did, like the Rotary club, or golf. People's dads played poker.

And then we started playing poker, too. Like everything else with   5 my generation, technological innovation helped enable our new hobby. By the late '90s and early 2000s, dozens of online casinos had sprung up, allowing the Internet to tap its full potential as a twenty-four-hour gaining paradise. Free from the annoying sanctions of the U.S. Penal Code, these offshore virtual Monte Carlos offered interested parties the opportunity to wager 'round the clock. Especially popular were online poker rooms, where you could play—for money, real or fake—against all comers. For many would-be players, the fear of looking like confused novices in front of a room full of old hands used to keep them from the tables. Now, the online poker rooms provide a convenient place to learn and refine the game at home with no one watching. More recent arrivals are the poker blogs shilling for their favorite sites, swooning over their favorite pros, and telling their stories about the hands that got away.

Televised poker is also a lot better than it used to be. For too long,   6 TV executives were unsure how to treat their poker coverage, cramming it into late-night time slots on cable sports networks. This was odd, as poker belongs in the same dubious semi-sport category as eating contests or spelling bees. Not only did it require no physical prowess, but due to prolonged exposure to tobacco, free drinks, and fluorescent lights, many of the game's finest players appear to be chronic palpitators and arrythmiacs. Little wonder that it never got good ratings on ESPN or the *Wide World of Sports*. But with the Travel Channel, formerly the repository of such stinkers as *Busch Gardens Revealed* and *Incredible Vacation Videos*, poker met its perfect match. The station has been the prime propagator and beneficiary of the poker craze with its *World Poker Tour* viewing block, which sends viewers casino-hopping around the world to a new poker tournament each week, open to all comers for a modest entrance fee. In its breathless approximation of legitimate sports coverage, the production is hilariously WWFesque in a way that appeals perfectly to ironic twenty-somethings: lots of gaudy money shots, a blonde "sideline reporter" who conducts exit interviews with ousted players, and "expert" announcers coming off as campy parodies of real sportscasters, with their nicknaming and jargonese. Well-placed cameras reveal each player's hole cards, allowing viewers at home to revel in omniscience even as they attempt to follow the thought processes of the bettors and sharpen their own skills at home.

Indeed, some of the best self-taught players, variants of 1990s computer nerds, are finding success in the pro poker circuit. The reigning World Series champion is a chubby, eagle-eyed twenty-eight-year-old Tennessee accountant with the Dickensian name of Chris Moneymaker. Moneymaker had learned the game just three years earlier and perfected his tricks by playing Internet poker obsessively. The 2003 World Series was his first professional event, and he beat hundreds of long-time professionals, walking away with $2.5 million, and the near-worshipful admiration of millions of delusional amateurs like myself. 7

BASEBALL FOR THE UNATHLETIC

The myth and aura of the game have perhaps never before been in such perfect accord with the aspirations of a generation. In the post-tech-boom years, the archetype of male success and cool mixes laddish cockiness and financial acumen. To my friends, blackjack seems like a game for those who trust their fate to chance or byzantine card-counting schemes. Slots are for the old, the overweight, and certain right-wing morality mavens. But poker, you see—for us poker has cache. Most forms of gambling depend on chance, but poker requires skill, and it's easy to believe that the player with the strongest will is going to win, leaving weaker minds to will in his wake. 8

511

Many of us were introduced to the modern face of poker by the 1997 movie *Rounders*, starring Matt Damon as a debt-ridden poker prodigy, which developed something of a cult status on many college campuses. *Rounders* popularized the act of reading someone's "tell"—the unique facial or bodily tics that unintentionally reveal his hand. At some games, table banter is nonexistent; the players just look at each other, trying in vain to "read" the table's reactions. It's this mental aspect of the game that attracts so many young players. "Before *Rounders*, I just thought of poker as something they played in saloons in Westerns, and boring five-card draw," says Arthur Wellington, a poker-obsessed student at Lehigh University in Pennsylvania. "[The movie] made me realize there was a lot more to the game than just betting on cards turned over." 9

My friends and I play every week, sometimes many times a week. A revolving cast of (young, male) characters show up at the games. We are all terrible. Everybody adopts a different persona. I am nearly silent during the game, hoping to project an image of cool rival examination and categorization of everyone else's reactions—a masterful command of the art of the "read." The reality is rather different. Usually I'm just thinking about how hungry I am, or I'm distracted by the TV. But the reality doesn't matter. 10

One guy, Jesse, is known for buying in, busting out, and repeating   11
the cycle multiple times in the course of one night's action, without giving the matter a second thought. He cheerfully admits that he is down
several hundred dollars since he began playing, and he never seems
too out of sorts about it, but sometimes I picture him alone, at home,
having crises of conscience, staring mournfully at his empty wallet and
shaking his head wordlessly.

A few of us have higher ambitions for our game, partly stirred by   12
an increased diet of televised poker. Although my friend Jake Collins
had only rarely played before this summer, he is now set on becoming a
professional player. I spent several weeks with him this summer in and
out of various West Coast motels, where the only consistent televised
entertainment we could find was poker tournaments. Thus stoked,
Collins is taking a scientific approach to his play, keeping detailed
charts and notebooks on his play patterns; despite real progress, he
knows he's got a long way to go before he can shoot with the big guns.
He speaks with hushed admiration of professional players' Svengali-
like ability to get inside other players' heads: "Those guys are so good."

FIVE-CARD NERDS

Another cult film on college campuses, the recent remake of Ocean's   13
Eleven, pokes fun at the desire of young people like me and my friends
to be cool poker players. The opening scene has Brad Pitt's character, a
been-around poker hand, coaching a series of Hollywood pretty boys
in the finer aspects of the game. Part of the joke is that the actors playing the pretty boys are themselves Hollywood pretty boys (a pre-
Punk'd Ashton Kutcher, Joshua Jackson) who don't know much about
the game—upon being dealt a hand, Topher Grace gleefully blurts
"Fellas! Fellas! Check this! All . . . reds!" Pitt just shakes his head.

You know something is a trend when it's not only being advanced   14
by popular culture, but satirized by it. Neophytes like me imagine that
the best players possess the qualities we saw or wanted to see in our
father figures: mental toughness, boldness, steadfastness. Plus, the game
requires no muscle tone, physical stamina, or quick reflexes–making it a
perfect match for a generation that grew up blasting away videogame
monsters with the twitch of a thumb and now workdays parked in front
of a computer screen. We may not have pecks, but we have the "read."

Examining the Text

1. What's the author's contention about poker appealing to his particular generation? Do you personally identify with his description of his generation?
How would you characterize the tone and style of this piece? Do you believe

that an older writer who had interviewed poker players of the author's generation could have written with the same tone and style?

2. Reexamine the article to see how the author links the following themes: technology, the generation gap, and issues of manliness. Do you agree with Peters' specific assertions regarding those themes? Could there be other reasons, unexplored in the article, for the apparent rising popularity of poker?

3. Do you think it reasonable for Peters to call the current popularity of poker a "craze," which might suggest a less than lasting appeal? Do you agree or disagree with him? What kind of emotional response does this article give you? Does it resonate with you and/or hold your interest? Why, or why not?

4. Do you believe that the author is right in saying that it's the "mental aspect" of poker that draws in so many younger players? If not, what additional factors might be responsible for poker's new appeal?

For Group Discussion

Survey your class (anonymously, if possible) to discover how many people have played online poker, gone to a casino to play poker, or play regularly for money at friends' homes. As a group discuss the article's central themes ("mental aspect," "fear of embarrassment," "technology") and assess whether those are the reasons that poker is drawing in new players. Review the survey results and then revisit the discussion to see if actual poker players in the class were more or less inclined to agree with the author. Discuss additional reasons for the current poker "craze" that group members may have raised during the discussion.

Writing Suggestion

If you're a poker player of the type described in the article, write an essay in which you lay out how you got attracted to playing poker (either online or in card rooms) and what the continued attraction is to playing. Gambling can be addictive; in your essay be sure to explain how you have approached that issue. If you're not a poker player, conduct research to put the rising number of poker players into a broader perspective of other gambling types. How does it compare to horse-betting, roulette, lotteries, and so on? You'll want to also examine the rapid growth of Indian-owned casinos across the nation. In either essay, be sure to examine the question of whether you think the current popularity of poker is harmless, potentially harmful, or neither.

The Search for Marvin Gardens

JOHN MCPHEE

Shortly before author John McPhee published the following piece, there appeared in Newsweek *magazine a story about Atlantic City, an urban area in New Jersey renowned for its boardwalk, gaming industry presence, expansive beachfront—and the physical model for the popular board game Monopoly. The* Newsweek *article was written to commemorate the one-hundredth anniversary of the Atlantic City boardwalk's construction, but it did not carry a celebratory tone; to the contrary, it depicted the New Jersey city as a model of neglect, urban blight, and social decay. The McPhee article, "The Search for Marvin Gardens," in some ways echoes the tone of the* Newsweek *piece, but it is written in a very different style. The former story is an example of investigative journalism, with a very clear thesis and concrete supporting evidence; the McPhee story is an example of what is known in academic circles as creative nonfiction: a writing sub-genre that uses the devices of literature (storytelling, figurative description, metaphor, and implied meaning) to craft memoirs, stories, and essays that are based in actual fact.*

"The Search for Marvin Gardens" is an example of the "segmented essay" creative nonfictional form. Unlike the traditional academic essay with which you are undoubtedly familiar—focused and assertive thesis statement, body paragraphs structured to develop that thesis with evidence, and examples organized in a coherent, linear way—the segmented essay purposely presents information in a disjointed way. Reading segmented essays requires more active engagement by the reader, since the thesis—the point of the writing—is never overtly stated but is rather suggested by the material in the segments and by the organization of the segments. In this way, the segmented essay resembles literature as much as exposition since it works by ambiguity, allowing for a multiplicity of possible "correct" interpretations. **As you read** *this essay, notice the ways in which the author moves back and forth between two related subtopics—the board game Monopoly, played at the tournament level by the author, and the city of Atlantic city, on which the board game was originally based—to suggest thematic meanings that are never overtly stated.*

Go. I roll the dice—a six and a two. Through the air I move my token, the flatiron, to Vermont Avenue, where dog packs range.   1

The dogs are moving (some are limping) through ruins, rubble, fire damage, open garbage. Doorways are gone. Lath is visible in the crumbling walls of the buildings. The street sparkles with shattered glass. I have never seen, anywhere, so many broken windows. A sign— "Slow, Children at Play"—has been bent backward by an automobile. At the lighthouse, the dogs turn up Pacific and disappear. George Meade, Army engineer, built the lighthouse—brick upon brick, six hundred thousand bricks, to reach up high enough to throw a beam twenty miles over the sea. Meade, seven years later, saved the Union at Gettysburg.   2

I buy Vermont Avenue for $100. My opponent is a tall, shadowy figure, across from me, but I know him well, and I know his game like   3 a favorite tune. If he can, he will always go for the quick kill. And when it is foolish to go for the quick kill, he will be foolish. On the whole, though, he is a master assessor of percentages. It is a mistake to under-estimate him. His eleven carries his top hat to St. Charles Place, which he buys for $140.

The sidewalks of St. Charles Place have been cracked to shards by 4 through-growing weeds. There are no buildings. Mansions, hotels once stood here. A few street lamps now drop cones of light on broken glass and vacant space behind a chain-link fence that some great machine has in places bent to the ground. Five plane trees—in full summer leaf, flecking the light—are all that live on St. Charles Place.

Block upon block, gradually, we are cancelling each other out—in 5 the blues, the lavenders, the oranges, the greens. My opponent follows a plan of his own devising. I use the Hornblower & Weeks opening and the Zuricher defense. The first game draws tight, will soon finish. In 1971, a group of people in Racine, Wisconsin, played for 768 hours. A game begun a month later in Danville, California, lasted 820 hours. These are official records, and they stun us. We have been playing for eight minutes. It amazes us that Monopoly is thought of as a long game. It is possible to play to a complete, absolute, and final conclusion in less than fifteen minutes, all within the rules as written. My oppo-nent and I have done so thousands of times. No wonder we are sitting across from each other now in this best-of-seven series for the interna-tional singles championship of the world.

On Illinois Avenue, three men lean out from second-story win- 6 dows. A girl is coming down the street. She wears dungarees and a bright-red shirt, has ample breasts and a Hadendoan Afro, a black halo, two feet in diameter. Ice rattles in the glasses in the hands of the men.

"Hey, sister!"
"Come on up!"
She looks up, looks from one to another to the other, looks them flat in the eye.
"What for?" she says, and she walks on.

I buy Illinois for $240. It solidifies my chances, for I already 7 own Kentucky and Indiana. My opponent pales. If he had landed first on Illinois, the game would have been over then and there, for he has houses built on Boardwalk and Park Place, we share the rail-roads equally, and we have cancelled each other everywhere else. We never trade.

In 1852, R. B. Osborne, an immigrant Englishman, civil engineer, 8 surveyed the route of a railroad line that would run from Camden to Absecon Island, in New Jersey, traversing the state from the Delaware

515

River to the barrier beaches of the sea. He then sketched in the plan of a "bathing village" that would surround the eastern terminus of the line. His pen flew glibly, framing and naming spacious avenues parallel to the shore—Mediterranean, Baltic, Oriental, Ventnor—and narrower transsecting avenues: North Carolina, Pennsylvania, Vermont, Connecticut, States, Virginia, Tennessee, New York, Kentucky, Indiana, Illinois. The place as a whole had no name, so when he had completed the plan Osborne wrote in large letters over the ocean, "Atlantic City." No one ever challenged the name, or the names of Osborne's streets. Monopoly was invented in the early 1930s by Charles B. Darrow, but Darrow was only transliterating what Osborne had created. The railroads, crucial to any player, were the making of Atlantic City. After the rails were down, houses and hotels burgeoned from Mediterranean and Baltic to New York and Kentucky, Properties—building lots—sold for as little as six dollars apiece and as much as a thousand dollars. The original investors in the railroads and the real estate called themselves the Camden & Atlantic Land Company. Reverently, I repeat their names: Dwight Bell, William Coffin, John DaCosta, Daniel Deal, William Fleming, Andrew Hay, Joseph Porter, Jonathan Pitney, Samuel Richards—founders, fathers, forerunners, archetypical masters of the quick kill.

9   My opponent and I are now in a deep situation of classical Monopoly. The torsion is almost perfect—Boardwalk and Park Place versus the brilliant reds. His cash position is weak, though, and if I escape him now he may fade. I land on Luxury Tax, contiguous to but in sanctuary from his power. I have four houses on Indiana. He lands there. He concedes.

10   Indiana Avenue was the address of the Brighton Hotel, gone now. The Brighton was exclusive—a word that no longer has retail value in the city. If you arrived by automobile and tried to register at the Brighton, you were sent away. Brighton-class people came in private railroad cars. Brighton-class people had other private railroad cars for their horses—dawn rides on the firm sand at water's edge, skirts flying. Colonel Anthony J. Drexel Biddle—the sort of name that would constrict throats in Philadelphia—lived, much of the year, in the Brighton.

11   Colonel Sanders' fried chicken is on Kentucky Avenue. So is Clifton's Club Harlem, with the Sepia Revue and the Sepia Follies, featuring the Honey Bees, the Fashions, and the Lords.

12   My opponent and I, many years ago, played 2,428 games of Monopoly in a single season. He was then a recent graduate of the Harvard Law School, and he was working for a downtown firm, looking up law. Two people we knew—one from Chase Manhattan, the other from Morgan, Stanley—tried to get into the game, but after a few rounds, we found that they were not in the conversation and we sent

them home. Monopoly should always be *mano a mano* anyway. My opponent won 1,199 games, and so did I. Thirty were ties. He was called into the Army, and we stopped just there. Now, in Game 2 of the series, I go immediately to jail, and again to jail while my opponent seines property. He is dumbfoundingly lucky. He wins in twelve minutes.

Visiting hours are daily, eleven to two; Sunday, eleven to one; evenings, six to nine. "NO MINORS, NO FOOD, Immediate Family Only Allowed in Jail." All this above a blue steel door in a blue cement wall in the windowless interior of the basement of the city hall. The desk sergeant sits opposite the door to the jail. In a cigar box in front of him are pills in every color, a banquet of fruit salad an inch and a half deep—leapers, co-pilots, footballs, truck drivers, peanuts, blue angels, yellow jackets, redbirds, rainbows. Near the desk are two soldiers, waiting to go through the blue door. They are about eighteen years old. One of them is trying hard to light a cigarette. His wrists are in steel cuffs. A military policeman waits, too. He is a year or so older than the soldiers, taller, studious in appearance, gentle, fat. On a bench against a wall sits a good-looking girl in slacks. The blue door rattles, swings heavily open. A turnkey stands in the doorway. "Don't you guys kill yourselves back there now," says the sergeant to the soldiers. 13

"One kid, he overdosed himself about ten and a half hours ago," says the M.P. 14

The M.P., the soldiers, the turnkey, and the girl on the bench are white. The sergeant is Black. "If you take off the handcuffs, take off the belts," says the sergeant to the M.P. "I don't want them hanging themselves back there." The door shuts and its tumblers move. When it opens again, five minutes later, a young white man in sandals and dungarees and a blue polo shirt emerges. His hair is in a ponytail. He has no beard. He grins at the good-looking girl. She rises, joins him. The sergeant hands him a manila envelope. From it he removes his belt and a small notebook. He borrows a pencil, makes an entry in the notebook. He is out of jail, free. What did he do? He offended Atlantic City in some way. He spent a night in the jail. In the 1930s, men visiting Atlantic City went to jail, directly to jail, did not pass Go, for appearing in topless bathing suits on the beach. A city statute requiring all men to wear full-length bathing suits was not seriously challenged until 1937, and the first year in which a man could legally go bare-chested on the beach was 1940. 15

Game 3. After seventeen minutes, I am ready to begin construction on overpriced and sluggish Pacific, North Carolina, and Pennsylvania. Nothing else being open, opponent concedes. 16

The physical profile of streets perpendicular to the shore is something like a playground slide. It begins in the high skyline of Boardwalk hotels, plummets into warrens of "side-avenue" motels, 17

517

crosses Pacific, slopes through church missions, convalescent homes, burlesque houses, rooming houses, and liquor stores, crosses Atlantic, and runs level through the bombed-out ghetto as far— Baltic, Mediterranean—as the eye can see. North Carolina Avenue, for example, is flanked at its beach end by the Chalfonte and the Haddon Hall (908 rooms, air-conditioned), where, according to one biographer, John Philip Sousa (1854–1932) first played when he was twenty-two, insisting, even then, that everyone call him by his entire name. Behind these big hotels, motels—Barbizon, Catalina—crouch. Between Pacific and Atlantic is an occasional house from 1910—wooden porch, wooden mullions, old yellow paint—and two churches, a package store, a strip show, a dealer in fruits and vegetables. Then, beyond Atlantic Avenue, North Carolina moves on into the vast ghetto, the bulk of the city, and it looks like Metz in 1919, Cologne in 1944. Nothing has actually exploded. It is not bomb damage. It is deep and complex decay. Roofs are off. Bricks are scattered in the street. People sit on porches, six deep, at nine on a Monday morning. When they go off to wait in unemployment lines, they wait sometimes two hours. Between Mediterranean and Baltic runs a chain-link fence, enclosing rubble. A patrol car sits idling by the curb. In the back seat is a German shepherd. A sign on the fence says, "Beware of Bad Dogs."

Mediterranean and Baltic are the principal avenues of the ghetto. 18 Dogs are everywhere. A pack of seven passes me. Block after block, there are three-story brick row houses. Whole segments of them are abandoned, a thousand broken windows. Some parts are intact, occupied. A mattress lies in the street, soaking in a pool of water. Wet stuffing is coming out of the mattress. A postman is having a rye and a beer in the Plantation Bar at nine-fifteen in the morning. I ask him idly if he knows where Marvin Gardens is. He does not. "HOOKED AND NEED HELP? CONTACT N.A.R.C.O." "REVIVAL NOW GOING ON, CONDUCTED BY REVEREND H. HENDERSON OF TEXAS." These are signboards on Mediterranean and Baltic. The second one is upside down and leans against a boarded-up window of the Faith Temple Church of God in Christ. There is an old peeling poster on a warehouse wall showing a figure in an electric chair. "The Black Panther Manifesto" is the title of the poster, and its message is, or was, that "the fascists have already decided in advance to murder Chairman Bobby Seale in the electric chair." I pass an old woman who carries a bucket. She wears blue sneakers, worn through. Her feet spill out. She wears red socks, rolled at the knees. A white handkerchief, spread over her head, is knotted at the corners. Does she know where Marvin Gardens is? "I sure don't know," she says, setting down the bucket. "I sure don't know. I've heard of it somewhere, but I just can't say where." I walk on, through a block of shattered glass. The glass crunches underfoot like coarse sand. I remember when I first came here—a long train ride from Trenton, long ago, games of poker in the train—to play basketball against Atlantic City. We were half black, they were all black. We scored forty points, they scored eighty, or something like it. What I remember most is that they had glass backboards—glittering, pendent, expensive glass backboards, a rarity then in high schools, even in colleges, the only ones we played on all year.

I turn on Pennsylvania, and start back toward the sea. The windows of the Hotel Astoria, on Pennsylvania near Baltic, are boarded up. A sheet of unpainted plywood is the door, and in it is a triangular peephole that now frames an eye. The plywood door opens. A man answers my question. Rooms there are six, seven, and ten dollars a week. I thank him for the information and move on, emerging from the ghetto at the Catholic Daughters of America Women's Guest House, between Atlantic and Pacific. Between Pacific and the Boardwalk are the blinking vacancy signs of the Aristocrat and Colton Manor motels. Pennsylvania terminates at the Sheraton-Seaside—thirty-two dollars a day, ocean corner. I take a walk on the Boardwalk and into the Holiday Inn (twenty-three stories). A guest is registering. "You reserved for Wednesday, and this is Monday," the clerk tells him. "But that's all right. We have *plenty* of rooms." The clerk is very young, female, and has soft brown hair that hangs below her waist. Her superior kicks her. 19

He is a middle-aged man with red spiderwebs in his face. He is jacketed and tied. He takes her aside. "Don't say 'plenty,'" he says. "Say 'You are fortunate, sir. We have rooms available.'" 20

The face of the young woman turns sour. "We have all the rooms you need," she says to the customer, and, to her superior, "How's that?" 21

Game 4. My opponent's luck has become abrasive. He has Boardwalk and Park Place, and has sealed the board. 22

Darrow was a plumber. He was, specifically, a radiator repairman who lived in Germantown, Pennsylvania. His first Monopoly board was a sheet of linoleum. On it he placed houses and hotels that he had carved from blocks of wood. The game he thus invented was brilliantly conceived, for it was an uncannily exact reflection of the business milieu at large. In its depth, range, and subtlety, in its luck-skill ratio, in its sense of infrastructure and socio-economic parameters, in its philosophical characteristics, it reached to the profundity of the financial community. It was as scientific as the stock market. It suggested the manner and means through which an underdeveloped world had been developed. It was chess at Wall Street level. "Advance token to the nearest Railroad and pay owner twice the rental to which he is otherwise entitled. If Railroad is unowned, you may buy it from the Bank. Get out of Jail, free. Advance token to nearest Utility. If unowned, you may buy it from Bank. If owned, throw dice and pay owner a total ten 23

519

times the amount thrown. You are assessed for street repairs: $40 per house, $115 per hotel. Pay poor tax of $15. Go to Jail. Go directly to Jail. Do not pass Go. Do not collect $200."

The turnkey opens the blue door. The turnkey is known to the 24 inmates as Sidney K. Above his desk are ten closed-circuit-TV screens—assorted viewpoints of the jail. There are three cellblocks—men, women, juvenile boys. Six days is the average stay. Showers twice a week. The steel doors and the equipment that operates them were made in San Antonio. The prisoners sleep on bunks of butcher block. There are no mattresses. There are three prisoners to a cell. In winter, it is cold in here. Prisoners burn newspapers to keep warm. Cell corners are black with smudge. The jail is three years old. The men's block echoes with chatter. The man in the cell nearest Sidney K. is pacing. His shirt is covered with broad stains of blood. The block for juvenile boys is, by contrast, utterly silent—empty corridor, empty cells. There is only one prisoner. He is small and black and appears to be thirteen. He says he is sixteen and that he has been alone in here for three days.

"Why are you here? What did you do?"
"I hit a jitney driver."

520

The series stands at three all. We have split the fifth and sixth 25 games. We are scrambling for property. Around the board we fairly fly. We move so fast because we do our own banking and search our own deeds. My opponent grows tense.

Ventnor Avenue, a street of delicatessens and doctors' offices, is 26 leafy with plane trees and hydrangeas, the city flower. Water Works is on the mainland. The water comes over in submarine pipes. Electric Company gets power from across the state, on the Delaware River, in Deepwater. States Avenue, now a wasteland like St. Charles, once had gardens running down the middle of the street, a horse-drawn trolley, private homes. States Avenue was as exclusive as the Brighton. Only an apartment house, a small motel, and the All Wars Memorial Building—monadnocks spaced widely apart—stand along States Avenue now. Pawnshops, convalescent homes, and the Paradise Soul Saving Station are on Virginia Avenue. The soul-saving station is pink, orange, and yellow. In the windows flanking the door of the Virginia Money Loan Office are Nikons, Polaroids, Yashicas, Sony TVs, Underwood typewriters, Singer sewing machines, and pictures of Christ. On the far side of town, beside a single track and locked up most of the time, is the new railroad station, a small hut made of glazed firebrick, all that is left of the lines that built the city. An authentic phrenologist works on New York Avenue close to Frank's Extra Dry Bar and a church where the sermon today is "Death in the Pot." The church is of pink brick, has blue and amber windows and two red doors. St. James Place, narrow and twisting, is lined with boarding houses that have wooden porches on each of three stories, suggesting a New Orleans made of salt-bleached pine. In a vacant lot on Tennessee is a white Ford station wagon stripped to the chassis. The windows are smashed. A plastic Clorox bottle sits on the driver's seat. The wind has pressed newspaper against the chain-link fence around the lot. Atlantic Avenue, the city's principal thoroughfare, could be seventeen American Main Streets placed end to end—discount vitamins and Vienna Corset shops, movie theatres, shoe stores, and funeral homes. The Boardwalk is made of yellow pine and Douglas fir, soaked in pentachlorophenol. Downbeach, it reaches far beyond the city. Signs everywhere—on windows, lampposts, trash baskets—proclaim "Bienvenue Canadiens!" The salt air is full of Canadian French. In the Claridge Hotel, on Park Place, I ask a clerk if she knows where Marvin Gardens is. She says, "Is it a floral shop?" I ask a cabdriver, parked outside. He says, "Never heard of it." Park Place is one block long, Pacific to Boardwalk. On the roof of the Claridge is the Solarium, the highest point in town—panoramic view of the ocean, the bay, the salt-water ghetto. I look down at the rooftops of the side-avenue motels and into swimming pools. There are hundreds of people around the rooftop pools, sunbathing, reading—many more people than are on the beach. Walls, windows, and a block of sky are all that is visible from these pools—no sand, no sea. The pools are craters, and with the people around them they are countersunk into the motels.

The seventh, and final, game is ten minutes old and I have hotels 27 on Oriental, Vermont, and Connecticut. I have Tennessee and St. James. I have North Carolina and Pacific. I have Boardwalk, Atlantic, Ventnor, Illinois, Indiana. My fingers are forming a "V." I have mortgaged most of these properties in order to pay for others, and I have mortgaged the others to pay for the hotels. I have seven dollars. I will pay off the mortgages and build my reserves with income from the three hotels. My cash position may be low, but I feel like a rocket in an underground silo. Meanwhile, if I could just go to jail for a time I could pause there, wait there, until my opponent, in his inescapable rounds, pays the rates of my hotels. Jail, at times, is the strategic place to be. I roll boxcars from the Reading and move the flatiron to Community Chest. "Go to Jail. Go directly to Jail."

The prisoners, of course, have no pens and no pencils. They take 28 paper napkins, roll them tight as crayons, char the ends with matches, and write on the walls. The things they write are not entirely idiomatic; for example, "In God We Trust." All is in carbon. Time is required in the writing. "Only humanity could know of such pain." "God So Loved the World." "There is no greater pain than life itself." In the women's block now, there are six blacks, giggling, and a white asleep in red shoes. She is drunk. The others are pushers, prostitutes, an auto thief, a burglar caught with pistol in purse. A sixteen-year-old accused of murder was in here last week, These words are written on the wall of a now empty cell: "Laying here I see two bunks about six inches thick, not counting the one I'm laying on, which is hard as brick. No cushion for my back. No pillow for my head. Just a couple scratchy blankets which is best to use it's said. I wake up in the morning so shivery and cold, waiting and waiting till I am told the food is coming. It's on its way. It's not worth waiting for, but I eat it anyway. I know one thing when they set me free I'm gonna be good if it kills me."

How many years must a game be played to produce an 29 Anthony J. Drexel Biddle and chestnut geldings on the beach? About half a century was the original answer, from the first railroad to Biddle at his peak. Biddle, at his peak, hit an Atlantic City streetcar conductor with his fist, laid him out with one punch. This increased Biddle's legend. He did not go to jail. While John Philip Sousa led his band along the Boardwalk playing "The Stars and Stripes Forever" and Jack Dempsey ran up and down in training for his fight with Gene Tunney, the city crossed the high curve of its parabola. Al Capone held conventions here—upstairs with his sleeves rolled, apportioning among his lieutenant governors the states of the Eastern seaboard. The natural history of an American resort proceeds from Indians to French Canadians via Biddles and Capones. French Canadians, whatever they may be at home, are Visigoths here. Bienvenue Visigoths!

My opponent plods along incredibly well. He has got his fourth 30 railroad, and patiently, unbelievably, he has picked up my potential winners until he has blocked me everywhere but Marvin Gardens. He has avoided, in the fifty-dollar zoning, my increasingly petty hotels. His cash flow swells. His railroads are costing me two hundred dollars a minute. He is building hotels on States, Virginia, and St. Charles. He has temporarily reversed the current. With the yellow monopolies and my blue monopolies, I could probably defeat his lavenders and his railroads. I have Atlantic and Ventnor. I need Marvin Gardens. My only hope is Marvin Gardens.

There is a plaque at Boardwalk and Park Place, and on it in relief 31 is the leonine profile of a man who looks like an officer in a metropolitan bank—"Charles B. Darrow, 1889–1967, inventor of the game of Monopoly." "Darrow," I address him, aloud. "Where is Marvin Gardens?" There is, of course, no answer. Bronze, impassive, Darrow looks south down the Boardwalk. "Mr. Darrow, please, where is Marvin Gardens?" Nothing. Not a sign. He just looks south down the Boardwalk.

My opponent accepts the trophy with his natural ease, and I 32 make, from notes, remarks that are even less graceful than his.

Marvin Gardens is the one color-block Monopoly property that is   33
not in Atlantic City. It is a suburb within a suburb, secluded. It is a
planned compound of seventy-two handsome houses set on curvilin-
ear private streets under yews and cedars, poplars and willows. The
compound was built around 1920, in Margate, New Jersey, and consists
of solid buildings of stucco, brick, and wood, with slate roofs, tile roofs,
multimullioned porches, Giraldic towers, and Spanish grilles. Marvin
Gardens, the ultimate outwash of Monopoly, is a citadel and sanctuary
of the middle class. "We're heavily patrolled by police here. We don't
take no chances. Me? I'm living here nine years. I paid seventeen thousand dollars and I've been offered thirty. Number one, I don't want to
move. Number two, I don't need the money. I have four bedrooms, two
and a half baths, front den, back den. No basement. The Atlantic is
down there. Six feet down and you float, A lot of people have a hard
time finding this place. People that lived in Atlantic City all their life
don't know how to find it. They don't know where the hell they're
going. They just know it's south, down the Boardwalk."

Examining the Text

1. In the segment devoted to the history of Atlantic City and the invention of
the game of Monopoly, McPhee refers to a number of business "tycoons" and
land speculators: "Dwight Bell, William Coffin, John DeCosta, Daniel Deal,
William Fleming, Andrew Hay, Joseph Porter, Jonathan Pitney, Samuel
Richards—founders, fathers, forerunners, archetypal masters of the quick kill."
Why does he provide such an exhaustive list people whose names we've never
heard before, and what does he mean when he calls them "masters of the quick
kill"? Is he really "reverential" about them, or does he have some other meaning in mind?

2. This essay is constructed through a series of disjointed scenes that are nevertheless related because they all deal with Atlantic City—either in the
Monopoly game or in the real world, on the East Coast of the United States.
One such scene occurs in a New Jersey jail and ends by discussing certain laws.
What specific activities and/or conversations take place in the jail during this
segment, and what implied point might the author be making in his discussion
of bathing suit statutes at the end of the segment?

3. The long segment beginning with "the physical profile of the streets" is
largely descriptive. What is being portrayed in this portion of McPhee's article,
and how does this depiction contrast with the abstract, geometric orderliness
of the Monopoly board?

4. According to the author, the game of Monopoly was "brilliantly conceived."
What was the particular genius of the game's inventor, in the opinion of
McPhee, and what is the seemingly timeless and universal appeal of this game?

5. *Thinking rhetorically*: How does the narrator characterize himself: what do you
learn about his personality, his profession, his personal history, his likes, dislikes,

obsessions, and so forth? What specific methods does the author use to deliver information about himself and/or to manipulate your feelings toward him?

For Group Discussion

This piece seems on the surface to be describing several completely different objects and locations, and to move back and forth between those items in a choppy, nonlinear way, like a movie quick-cutting between unrelated scenes. In the group discussion setting, address each segment of the essay individually, attempting to identify what, specifically, the author is talking about in each segment of this piece, and how each of these pieces contributes to your overall sense of the essay's meaning.

Writing Suggestion

John McPhee's article "The Search for Marvin Gardens" suggests in its unusual arrangement that there are many possible ways to set up an effective essay. Although there is great merit in the "standard" layout of expository essays—introduction and thesis statement, body paragraphs containing supportive evidence and argument organized in a logical sequence, and a conclusion that ideally adds something new—alternative essay forms are increasingly becoming a part of academic writers' palettes. McPhee's creative nonfictional discussion of Atlantic City—both in the Monopoly game and in the real world—works by relating two seemingly disconnected topics, cutting back and forth between them as an experimental filmmaker might intercut scenes. Ultimately, some clear meanings emerge from this dynamic tension between scenes, although the essay never makes a focused and assertive thesis statement in the way a conventional academic essay should. For this assignment, you are hereby issued creative license to construct your own segmented essay on a topic of your own choice. Perhaps, using the McPhee piece as a model, you might consider exploring your hometown, using disjointed scenes ultimately to build for the reader a sense of the place and its inhabitants. Enjoy the process—but keep in mind that, although the segmented essay may be a valid and lively expository form, some of your professors may reasonably want *only* conventional academic discourse. Make sure you know your audience—i.e., your teacher—before submitting such alternative forms!

The Meaning of Life

JILL LEPORE

This article by historian Jill Lepore is part historical profile, focusing on the life and recreational inventions of game maker Milton Bradley, and part social commentary, examining one of Bradley's games: the Game of Life, in all its variants through time. A synopsis of the history portion of the piece goes something like this: in the same year Abraham Lincoln was elected president, twenty-three-year-old Milton Bradley invented his first board game, called The Checkered Game of Life, in which a player starts on a square labeled Infancy and usually ends at Happy Old Age . . . usually, but not always: even when the player is headed for Happiness, she can end up at Ruin. This early version of the game made Milton Bradley a brand name, and to celebrate its centennial, in 1960 the company released the Game of Life, which many people alive today have played: the one with the little plastic toy cars with holes in them where the "family member" pegs go. Now, in the new millennium, there is a new game in the planning stages, this one called The Game of Life: Twists & Turns. With each new version of the game, Lepore shows how the rules, structure, and text of the game reflects—and perhaps even helps to construct, in some small way—the prevalent values of the era in which it appears.

As you read, notice the way that historians construct their arguments. A social scientist might devise a questionnaire or survey to conduct a statistical analysis on prevailing attitudes within a culture, but historian Lepore catalogues historical facts relevant to the development of this game through various eras, and from this evidence draws conclusions about the ways in which social values evolve through time.

In 1860, the year Abraham Lincoln was elected President, a lanky, long-nosed, twenty-three-year-old Yankee named Milton Bradley invented his first board game, on a red-and-ivory checkerboard of sixty-four squares. He called it The Checkered Game of Life. Play starts at the board's lower-left corner on an ivory square labeled Infancy—illustrated by a tiny, black-inked lithograph of a wicker cradle—and ends, usually but not always, at Happy Old Age at the upper right, though landing on Suicide with a noose around your neck is more common than you might think, and means, inconveniently, that you're dead. "The game represents, as indicated by the name, the checkered journey of life," Bradley explained, in his Rules of the Game. There are good patches, and bad, in roughly equal number. On the one hand: Honesty, Bravery, Success. On the other: Poverty, Idleness, Disgrace. The wise player will strive "to gain on his journey that which shall make him the most prosperous, and to shun that which will retard him in his progress." But even when you're heading for Happiness you can end up at Ruin: passed out, drunk and drooling, on the floor of a seedy-looking tavern where Death darkens the door disguised as a debt collector straight out of "Bleak House"—the bulky black overcoat, the strangely sinister stovepipe hat. 1

The Checkered Game of Life made Milton Bradley a brand name. His company, founded in 1860, survived his death in 1911, the 2

Depression, two World Wars, and even my mother, who worked there in the 1940s. In 1960, to celebrate its centennial, the Milton Bradley Company released a commemorative Game of Life. It bears almost no resemblance to its nineteenth-century namesake. In Life, players fill teensy plastic station wagons with even teensier pastel-pink and blue plastic Mommies and Daddies, spin the Wheel of Fate, and ride the highway of Life, earning money, buying furniture, and having pink and blue plastic babies. Along the way, there are good patches: "Adopt a Girl and Boy! Collect Presents!" And bad: "Jury Duty! Lose Turn." Whoever earns the most money wins. As the game's ad slogan has it, "That's Life!"

If, like me, you played the 1960 version of Life while wearing bell- 3 bottoms and listening to a 45 of Elton John's "Rocket Man," you have a pretty good idea of what happened to Milton Bradley's nineteenth-century game about vice, virtue, and the pursuit of happiness: it was reinvented as a lesson in Cold War consumerist conformity, a kind of two-dimensional Levittown, complete with paychecks and retirement homes and dental bills. Inside the game box are piles and piles of paper (Life is . . . paperwork!): fake automobile insurance, phony stock certificates, pretend promissory notes, and play money, seven and a half million dollars of it, including a heap of mint-green fifty-thousand-dollar bills, each featuring a portrait of Milton Bradley near the end of his days—bearded, aged, antique.

In the board-game industry, the 1960 Game of Life, which has 4 sold thirty-five million copies, is like that portrait of Old Man Bradley: a giant with gray whiskers, enjoying a very Happy Old Age. Only a handful of games have had as long a shelf life. (Who still plays Park and Shop, another game sold by the Milton Bradley Company in 1960, whose object was "to outsmart the other players by parking your car in a strategic place, completing your shopping quickly and being the first to return home"?) Beginning in 1992, Hasbro, the Rhode Island-based toy company that had acquired Milton Bradley eight years earlier, revised Life, slightly, to market it to the baby-boomer parents who had grown up with it: the station wagons became minivans, and, a few miles down life's highway, you could have a midlife crisis. Over the years, Hasbro has sold custom editions as movie and television tie-ins; if you have time on your hands, and a boundless tolerance for the cloying edginess of Nickelodeon, you can play the Game of Life in Bikini Bottom SpongeBob SquarePants Edition. Or not.

Last year, Hasbro asked, "What would the Monopoly game be 5 like if it were invented today?" and released Monopoly Here & Now, with new game pieces that include a cell phone, a box of French fries, and a laptop. This year, Hasbro is asking the same question of Life. Its answer, the Game of Life: Twists & Turns, will hit stores this summer.

But maybe a better question than "What would Life look like if it were invented in 2007?" is "How did Milton Bradley come to invent a game of life in the first place?" How, in other words, did Life begin?

"I, Milton Bradley, . . . have invented a new Social Game," 6 Bradley declared on his patent application. But the genealogy of the Checkered Game of Life stretches back centuries. Bradley's invention is descended from a family of ancient Asian games—members of a genus that R. C. Bell, in his amazing compendium *Board and Table Games from Many Civilizations* (1960), labelled "square board race games"—whose common ancestor is probably a thousand years old. In India, Jnana Chaupar (the "game of knowledge") is played much like the Checkered Game of Life: land on a virtue and you get to climb a ladder toward the god Vishnu and karmic liberation; land on a vice—or karmic impediment—and you're swallowed by a snake. (Beginning in 1892, Jnana Chaupar was sold in Britain as Snakes and Ladders; in the United States, it survives today as Chutes and Ladders.)

How young Milton Bradley, on the eve of the Civil War, came to 7 adapt an ancient Asian game to a red-and-ivory checkerboard featuring an American vision of the good life is nearly impossible to piece together from the scant documents about his life that survive. (Bradley kept a meticulous diary and, throughout his life, preserved his correspondence, which formed the basis of James J. Shea and Charles Mercer's 1960 biography of Bradley, *It's All in the Game*, and which, at the time, were housed at the company headquarters, in Springfield and East Longmeadow, Massachusetts. Sometime between then and when I visited those archives, in 2006, the papers were lost or destroyed.) But he didn't have to look half a world away to imagine that life would make a good board game. There were plenty of examples closer to home.

That life's a game that can be played well, or badly, is a very old idea 8 and, at least in the last few centuries in the history of Western civilization, a commonplace one. The people in Thomas More's *Utopia* (1516) play a game of life, "not unlike our chess," consisting of "a battle between the virtues and the vices." How to win, and whether you're playing against yourself or against God or Satan, are matters of considerable philosophical speculation. "Man's life's a game at tables," read a seventeenth-century epitaph, "and he may / Mend his bad fortune, by his wiser play." The young Milton Bradley, too, believed that "the journey of life is governed by a combination of chance and judgment." His game works the same way: there's what you spin, and there's where you choose to go. The Checkered Game of Life is a game of destiny checked by strategy.

But Bradley came from a family ruled, for generations, by nothing 9 so much as an angry God. The Bradleys had been in New England since 1635, when Daniel Bradley, an apothecary's son, settled in Salem,

Massachusetts. Their sufferings were Biblical. Daniel was killed by Indians in 1689, six years before Abenakis captured his fifteen-year-old son, Isaac. In 1697, another son, his wife, two of their children, and three more Bradley children died in an attack on Haverhill in which Hannah Bradley, the wife of still another of Daniel's sons, was taken captive. She escaped, only to be captured again in 1704 and carried to Canada; on the journey, she gave birth to an infant who was killed when her captors poured hot embers into its mouth. Her husband, Joseph Bradley, trudged after her through waist-high snows, with his dog, to pay her ransom and bring her home. The next time an Indian came to her door, Hannah shot him. (She lived to be ninety, but her old age was probably more haunted than happy.) In 1739, two of the next generation of Bradleys, Samuel and Jonathan, were cut off in their youth in an ambush in New Hampshire. By the time Jonathan's direct descendant Milton was born, nearly a century later, and given the name of the Puritan author of *Paradise Lost*, the family's fortunes had not gained much against adversity.

Still, the story of Bradley's ancestors was a story not of failure but of fate: God had chosen to visit them with affliction, and there was nothing they could do but praise Him. They would have had little patience for the eighteenth-century coffeehouse debate over which game life is most like. By the end of the century, the debate had become a cliche. "Sure, life's a game of cricket," a Bostonian joked in 1785. "Yet death has hit my wicket." 10

Milton Bradley's ancestors might have agreed with the English poet Nathaniel Cotton, who, in 1794, complained that the metaphor itself was heretical: 11

> That life's a game, divines confess; This says at cards, and that at chess; But if our views be center'd here, Tis all a losing game, I fear.

Profane or no, it was only a matter of time before the quip that life's a game inspired someone in England to make it a game. A board game called the New Game of Human Life was first sold in London in 1790. In an age still very much under the influence of John Bunyan's *Pilgrim's Progress* and Samuel Johnson's 1751 essay "Voyage of Life," it's hardly an accident that the New Game of Human Life was engraved and inked by a London printer who specialized in making maps: its Life is a journey along a twisty path from Infancy to Immortality, with eighty-four stops on the road, one for each year, in which the players' (or pilgrims') progress is speeded up by virtue and slowed down by vice. Land on the Duellist, at the square marked 22 (the twenty-second year of your life), and you'll be sent back to age 3 (for acting like a child); land on the Married Man, at 34, and you get to advance to the Good Father, at 56. Whoever dies first wins. 12

Like most "new" games, the New Game of Human Life was an 13
old game tarted up. It adapted its board and rules from a game called
the Royal Game of Goose, which was invented in Florence in the six-
teenth century, and was itself descended from a class of board games
that R. C. Bell calls "spiral race games." (The oldest spiral race game
may be the Hyena Game, played by Arabs in Sudan, in a groove traced
in the sand with a stick and involving a race between pebbles representing the players' mothers, who leave their village and head to a well
at the spiral's center, where they must wash their clothes and return
home before a hyena catches them.) By the 1720s, English printers had
adapted the spiral race game to the idea that life is a voyage in which
travellers are buffeted between vice and virtue. It was this central
Christian allegory that (as its instructions asserted) gave the New
Game of Human Life its "UTILITY and MORAL TENDENCY." Parents
were advised to play with their children and "request their attention to
a few moral and judicious observations explanatory of each Character
as they proceed & contrast the happiness of a Virtuous & well spent
life with the fatal consequences arriving from Vicious & Immoral
pursuits."

The New Game of Human Life showed up in the United States at 14
least as early as 1798 and apparently had a long life here. Had Milton
Bradley's long-suffering forebears condoned games (which, as
Puritans, they did not), they might have liked the New Game of
Human Life. At least they would have recognized its logic: life is a voyage that begins at birth and ends at death, God is at the helm, fate is
cruel, and your reward lies beyond the grave.

529

All of which combine to make it, by our board-game standards, 15
unbearably dull. There's no strategy, just dutiful to-ing and fro-ing, in
abject obedience to the Rules of the Game and the spin of the teetotum, a
numbered, six-sided top used in place of dice, which many nineteenth-
century Americans shunned as immoral. Even worse, there's a disquieting absence of adversaries; you're racing against the other players,
but you're not competing against them, the way you are in, say,
Monopoly, when you can charge them exorbitant rents. And, as for parents offering up "a few moral and judicious observations" at each
square, I have tried this—giving my best impression of an eighteenth-
century parent—and all I can say is: no dice. When my six-year-old
landed on the Docile Boy, at square 9, I asked him, "Do you know what
'docile' means?"

"No." 16

"It means you should do what I say, you little blister." 17

"Yeah, right. Um, your roll." 18

The next games of life played in the United States, the Mansion of 19
Bliss and the Mansion of Happiness, were both produced in England,

beginning around 1800. They look a lot like the New Game of Human Life—spiral race games adapted to the pilgrimage of life—and they're just as awful to play. Both represent immortality, life's final destination, as a heavenly mansion, which was then a popular Christian conceit. "O Lord! Deliver us from sin," one American evangelical prayed in 1814, "and when we shall have finished our earthly course, admit us to the mansion of bliss and happiness."

In the U.S., the Mansion of Bliss never really took off, despite the fact that the phrase "the mansion of bliss" was also used as an admiring term for a woman's breasts. But the Mansion of Happiness had a more successful American career. It was sold in the United States at least as early as 1806. An American edition appeared in 1843, based on revisions to the English game made by Anne Wales Abbott, the editor of a Boston-based juvenile serial called *The Child's Friend and Family Magazine*, and it went on to become one of the century's most popular and enduring games. [20]

The Mansion of Happiness is abundantly pious. The rules begin: [21]

> At this amusement each will find, A moral fit t'improve the mind;, It gives to those their proper due,, Who various paths of vice pursue,, And shows (while vice destruction brings), That GOOD from every virtue springs., Be virtuous then and forward press,, To gain the seat of HAPPINESS.

Whether it's amusing is more difficult to say. The Mansion of Happiness is one of those games which are hard to finish, mostly because the wages of sin are so harsh—"Whoever becomes a SABBATH BREAKER must be taken to the WHIPPING POST and whipt" (a retreat of six squares)—that you're forever going backward and losing turns. However popular the Mansion of Happiness was with the parents who purchased it, many of the game boards that survive in archives are in such suspiciously good condition that at least one historian has wondered whether children—who must, invariably, have been given the game as a gift—could ever bear to play it. After all, its rules read like a sermon: "Whoever possesses AUDACITY, CRUELTY, IMMODESTY, and INGRATITUDE, must return to his former situation till his turn comes to spin again, and not even think of Happiness, much less partake of it." [22]

Before he invented the Checkered Game of Life, Milton Bradley had scarcely begun to think of happiness. The only son of an insolvent, itinerant craftsman, he was born in Vienna, Maine, in 1836. When he was about ten, his hapless father, Lewis, invested what little money he had in a process for turning potatoes into starch, just months before the American potato crop was devastated by the same blight that drove hundreds of thousands of Ireland's poor farmers to immigrate to the United States. This, in turn, lowered the wages at factories like the textile mills in [23]

Lowell, Massachusetts, where Lewis Bradley was forced to move his family in 1847 to take a job that paid eighty-five cents a day.

While his father worked in the mills, Bradley attended Lowell's 24
grammar school and high school. After graduation, he was admitted to the Lawrence Scientific School in Cambridge, but he had to drop out when his father left Lowell for Hartford in search of a better job. By 1856, Bradley had made his way to Springfield, Massachusetts, where he found work as a mechanical draftsman. Four years later, he started a lithography business and brought out an immensely popular election-year lithograph of a clean-shaven Abraham Lincoln. Just when it seemed that the young striver had finally crawled his way to Success, he nearly sank into Ruin: Lincoln grew a beard, making Bradley's inventory worthless.

After he manufactured enough boxes of the Checkered Game of 25
Life to make a sales trip, Bradley travelled to New York, walked into a stationery store, and, his biographers recount, said to the manager, "How do you do, sir. I am Milton Bradley of the Milton Bradley Company of Springfield. I have come to New York with some samples of a new and most amazing game, sir. A highly moral game, may I say, that encourages children to lead exemplary lives and entertains both old and young with the spirit of friendly competition. May I demonstrate how it is played?"

531

The Checkered Game of Life is deceptively simple. Twirl the tee- 26
totum and move your counter around the board, collecting points by landing on any of the eight point-value squares. Whoever earns a hundred points first wins. Some squares help you along, little lithographed hands pointing the way, as when Perseverance leads you to Success, worth five points. Spinning a 2 from the red square between Ruin and Fat Office forces you to land on Suicide and die, but almost any spin from nearly every other square involves a decision, a choice among as many as eight possible moves. Unlike the New Game of Human Life or the Mansion of Happiness, the Checkered Game of Life requires you to make decisions, lots and lots of them. It's best to have a plan.

Most players try to go to School, which allows you to jump to 27
College (worth five points), heading, slowly, toward the top of the board and Happy Old Age, worth a whopping fifty points. But your chances of going to School are not good: from your starting position, at Infancy, you have to spin either a 3 or a 6. You might end up at Poverty instead. But don't despair. "It will be seen that poverty lies near the cradle," Bradley wrote in the Rules of the Game, explaining why he had placed Poverty just two squares from Infancy. But because "in starting life it is not necessarily a fact that poverty will be a disadvantage, so in the game it causes the player no loss." Even if you skip School altogether, you may be rewarded by landing on Honesty, and sent from there directly to Happiness (worth five points).

It's possible to win the Checkered Game of Life without ever 28 reaching Happy Old Age—after all, lots of people die young—but it's not easy. And, as Bradley warned, "Happy Old Age is surrounded by many difficulties": land on Idleness, and you'll be sent to Disgrace at the very bottom of the board, which means that you have to climb back up all over again. Here's another word of advice: Don't enter Politics if you can possibly avoid it. You'll go to Congress and earn five points, but you'll be carried away from Happy Old Age and you'll woefully increase your chances of landing on Crime and ending up in Prison, where you lose a turn, "For any person who is sent to prison is interrupted in his pursuit of happiness."

In his application to the U.S. Patent Office, Bradley insisted that 29 his game was "intended to forcibly impress upon the minds of youth the great moral principles of virtue and vice." But the Checkered Game of Life is at least as dark as its predecessors and more ruthless. (It has another distinction, too: it was enjoyed as much by adults as by children). In the Mansion of Happiness, landing on TRUTH—which you can't avoid if a spin of the teetotum sends you there—advances you six squares; in the Checkered Game of Life, Truth exists, and you can choose to seek it out, but it has no value. Bradley's game rewards Industry and Perseverance with Wealth and Success. It has no use for Patience or Charity, which aren't even on the board. (For a time, the game promoted betting on the stock market, with a square called Speculation.) The Checkered Game of Life isn't a race to heaven; it's a series of calculations about the best route to collect the most points, fastest. Accumulate, or fail.

Milton Bradley sold at least forty thousand copies of his game in 30 its first year, and decided to sell Games for Soldiers, a portable set of games (including the Checkered Game of Life, backgammon, checkers, dominoes, and chess). It found a place in the knapsack of many a Union soldier.

"You could never in a million years sell it today," Mel Taft, a for- 31 mer vice-president of research and development at the Milton Bradley Company, said about Bradley's Checkered Game, when I spoke to him by phone a few months ago. In 1959, when Taft and his colleagues were preparing for the company's centennial, they never seriously considered reviving Bradley's original game. It was so obviously and so dreadfully dated—it even had a square for Intemperance. They decided, instead, to hire a California firm famous for starting the hula-hoop craze to develop a new game of life. I asked both Taft and Reuben Klamer, who was an inventor of the 1960 game, if either of them had ever played the Mansion of Happiness. They hadn't heard of it. But the board game that the Milton Bradley Company released in 1960 as the Game of Life actually looks a good deal like the Mansion of Happiness, just with lots of pieces of plastic attached to it. It's a serpentine race game, a path representing the voyage of life, from high-school graduation to retirement. (In Life, you never die; you just quit working.) There are plenty of differences. In Life, some squares offer rewards ("Contest Winner! Collect $5000!"), and others mete out penalties ("Buy Furniture. Pay $2000"), but none are morally freighted; the game lacks any sense of life as a battle between vice and virtue. The object of the two games is different, too: at Life's Day of Reckoning, you count your cash, not your good deeds. And Life's most important squares are its red-letter "PAY DAY!"s.

What you earn on those paydays depends, in large part, on a cru- 32 cial choice you make on your very first move: will you go to college, or take a job? If you start work, you can collect paychecks right away; if you go to college, you have to pay tuition, but you earn more when you eventually do start getting paychecks. After that, there are occasional financial decisions to be made—do you want to buy life insurance? would you like to invest in the stock market?—but these, and the piles of papers and plastic babies, serve mainly as a distraction from the play's basic passivity. Like the Mansion of Happiness, Life is a journey along a (mostly) fixed path, where only one thing matters. And, like all earlier spiral race games of life, the Game of Life is essentially about fate—not whether you're fated to enter Heaven but whether you're fated to retire to Millionaire Acres. If the Checkered Game of Life brings together choice and chance, the Game of Life has only one real fork in the road: work or study.

533

Life vaulted over the rest of Milton Bradley's inventory to 33 become the company's flagship game, but it drew criticism, especially as years passed. The game is so relentlessly amoral and cash-conscious that a 1990s redesign team, eager to make it less so, pretty much gave up. When I visited Hasbro in February, a game designer told me that whenever people tried to make the game less about "having the most money it got really complicated." They did add Life Tiles, which allow players to accomplish things and do good deeds, except that the only way to be rewarded for your virtue is in the game's only currency: cash. Save an Endangered Species: collect $200,000. Solution to Pollution: $250,000. Open Health-Food Chain: $100,000. Recently, some of the old Life Tiles and the board's rewards have been replaced. You used to be able to get $100,000 for winning a Nobel Prize; now you can earn the same money for going on a reality TV show. But it's hard to tinker with success. "With this product there is so much nostalgia, there's only so much we can change," the Hasbro designer Dan Sanfilippo said.

Exactly because the 1960 Game of Life is so hard to change, 34 Hasbro is about to launch its new, new, new game of human life. The

Game of Life: Twists & Turns is not a checkerboard of choices; it's not a fixed and fated path. There is, instead, a plethora of paths. The Twists & Turns game board is divided into four squares—Learn It, Live It, Love It, and Earn It—through each of which a colored path snakes its way. Players decide how they want to spend their time—going to school, having kids, hanging out, travelling, whatever. You begin using a tiny plastic skateboard as a game piece; if you like, and if you earn enough, you can convert it to a sports car. You can play for five minutes or five hours; you can play till *American Idol* comes on. There are multiple places to begin, each called Start, but there's no place on the board called "Happy Old Age" or "Immortality" or "Millionaire Acres" or even, simply, "Finish." This is actually the game's selling point: it has no goal. Life is . . . aimless. (The game's box shouts, "A THOUSAND WAYS TO LIVE YOUR LIFE! YOU CHOOSE.") When you do decide to stop, whoever ends up with the most Life Points wins, but, heck, winning isn't everything. And, after all, you get as many points for scuba diving in the Great Barrier Reef, or for donating a kidney to a loved one, as for getting a Ph.D.

Money is a big part of the Game of Life: Twists & Turns. But there's no cash. Instead, each player gets a Life-Visa-brand "credit card" to insert in the game's electronic Life Pod, which keeps track of Life Points—earn more, spend more! "We are not marketing to kids," a Visa spokesman, Michael Rolnick, has said, responding to complaints about the Visa-Hasbro deal. "We are helping to educate kids. It's never too early." Hmm. Let's just say that Twists & Turns has a rather forgiving attitude toward the highly leveraged player. "If you're bankrupt in Monopoly, you're watching," a Hasbro Games vice-president, George Burtch, says. "In this game, you can be hugely in debt, but you're still playing!" In the Mansion of Happiness, there's a square for that kind of thing. It's called the Road to Folly. 35

After Milton Bradley's early success with the Checkered Game of Life, he pursued other interests. In the late 1860s, he had another big hit with croquet, whose rules he patented and whose equipment manufacture he perfected just as a fever for the game swept the nation, not coincidentally, on the heels of the claim that croquet was . . . just like life. "Croquet is the game of life, you see," says a character in a Harriet Beecher Stowe novel published in 1871, after which another agrees, "One may read all sorts of life-histories in the game. Some go on with a steady aim and true stroke, and make wickets, and hit balls, yet are croqueted back ingloriously or hopelessly wired and lose the game, while others blunder advantageously and are croqueted along by skillful partners into all the best places." 36

After croquet, though, Milton Bradley dropped the ball. In an era when success made the man—when to fail was to be a failure—Bradley, 37 to some degree, spurned his own achievement. He reached Fat Office, and he left it behind. Far more than most Yankee businessmen of his generation, he came to reject the notion that where you go in life is simply a matter of where you steer yourself. There were such things, in Bradley's mind, as lousy starts, rotten luck, and bad cards. "The journey of life is governed by a combination of chance and judgment," he wrote in 1866. As he grew into his middle years, he apparently came to believe that some people had been given better chances than others. Beginning in the late 1860s, Bradley devoted himself to the nascent kindergarten movement, a social and political reform as much as an educational one, which insisted that very young children could learn through art and play, a kind of learning that would set them up not only for future academic success but for happiness, too. The push to offer education to four-, five-, and six-year-olds was essentially a nineteenth-century equivalent to Head Start, in which reformers worked to establish free kindergartens for the children of the poor. Enthralled by the movement's philosophy, Bradley turned his energies toward manufacturing crayons, colored paper, color wheels, flash cards, and watercolors. He invented the one-armed paper cutter. In 1869, he entered the publishing business with *The Paradise of Childhood*, a lavishly illustrated manual for kindergarten teachers, adapted from the philosophy of the movement's German founder, Friedrich Froebel. Starting in 1893, Bradley published the monthly *Kindergarten News*.

535

As he aged, Bradley earned a reputation for taking naps in his office; he ordered the presses in his factory stopped for an hour and a half around lunch every day, so as not to disturb him. In 1910, the year before he died, his colleagues presented him with a book of tribute essays titled *Milton Bradley, A Successful Man*. But, writing in 1902, Bradley reflected that, of all he had done, he was especially proud of his (often unprofitable) educational inventions: "In using the word success, I do not wish to confine its meaning to that cheap interpretation which sees only the glitter of gold or the glamour of illusive fame. In my case, I cannot overestimate the feeling of satisfaction which has been with me all these years at the thought that I . . . have done something, if only something prosaic in character, to place the kindergarten on its present solid foundation." It was a lesson that a child could have drawn from playing the Checkered Game of Life: Beware of Ambition! It sounds good, but if you land there, you are promptly sent to Fame, a square that not only has no value in itself but also puts you perilously close to Jail, Prison, and Suicide. [38]

When Bradley was a young man, he had written in his Rules, "In starting life, it is not necessarily a fact that poverty will be a disadvantage, so in the game it causes the player no loss." But near the end of his life he seems to have come to believe that he had been wrong. He may [39] even have regretted that he had placed Poverty so close to Infancy, and made the chances of getting to School no better than one in three. The kindergarten movement was about beating those odds, or bettering them. It promised a kind of redemption. Maybe Milton Bradley saw in making crayons for kindergartners not only their second chance but his, too.

Examining the Text

1. Historian Jill Lepore begins this article by describing the first version of the Game of Life, called The Checkered Game of Life. Summarize the author's description of the game and then explain how, in Lepore's view, the strategies and goals of The Checkered Game of Life reflect concerns of Americans at that period of our history.

2. By way of contrast to the first question, describe the 1960's version of The Game of Life and explain what Lepore means when she says this new version of the game "was reinvented as a lesson in Cold War consumerist conformity, a kind of two-dimensional Levittown . . . " [Hint: Levittown is a town in New York State that was built shortly after the end of World War II and represents the prototype mass-produced suburban housing tract in America].

3. By this article's account, in 1959 the Milton Bradley Company at first did not seriously consider reviving The Game of Life, because it "was so obviously and so dreadfully dated—it even had a square for Intemperance." However, they did end up hiring the "California firm famous for starting the hula-hoop craze" to update the Game of Life. How did this development firm make the game more appealing to mid-twentieth-century players, and how did this game reflect cultural changes that had taken place?

4. *Thinking rhetorically*: Toward the middle of this article the author discusses the pre-twentieth-century versions of The Game of Life and simultaneously provides a lengthy and detailed history of Milton Bradley, who supposedly invented the game. List some key points in that historical progression before the 1960's version was released. What underlying themes about Bradley, the game and, ultimately, pre-twentieth-century American culture emerge through this historical account? What rhetorical methods does the author employ to make these thematic conclusions convincing?

For Group Discussion

This article's author says the Hasbro toy company currently has plans to issue a Life-like game for the new millennium. As in previous eras, the designers plan to invest the game with qualities that will make it appealing to today's young people, and perhaps their parents as well. What are the currently planned revisions to The Game of Life, as enumerated by Lepore? In group discussion, come up with some other revisions to The Game of Life that might even *more* effectively reveal aspects of contemporary American culture, and explain why you propose these new rules and/or structures for this venerable game.

Writing Suggestion

Pick a board game you know well, either from your childhood or from your contemporary recreational life. It can be something as nostalgic as the childishly simple Candyland, something martial, such as the popular Parker Brothers game of global domination, Risk, or something more cerebral, such as chess. With your chosen game as your essay's centerpiece, produce a writing that is similar in tone and structure to Jill Lepore's "The Meaning of Life." You may have to do a bit of research online to discover and present historical facts, as Lepore did in this piece, and be sure to attribute any of this secondary material to your original source. Like Lepore, however, you do not necessarily have to use an academic citation format such as MLA or APA to cite your sources— that is, unless your teacher instructs you to do so! From the historical facts you gather, come to some conclusions about the ways in which your game might reflect and/or construct cultural attitudes. What, for instance, might the game of Risk be saying about Americans' willingness—some might even say eagerness— to go to war in other parts of the world?

Fixing Kids' Sports

PETER CARY, RANDY DOTINGA, AND AVERY COMAROW

The following article was originally published in the journal Science & Society. *In it, the authors explore the changing face of children's team sports in the United States. The authors document the increasing seriousness applied to youth sports such as baseball, soccer, basketball, and softball, and contrast this with a corresponding decline in family activities like dinners together and vacations.*

In addition to the emergence of "select" and "elite" programs designed to tap the most talented youngsters in a particular sport, the authors also note that children are specializing in just one sport, playing more frequently and spending large amounts of time (as well as money) traveling to distant tournaments and competitions. As a result, the article states, children are becoming injured, disillusioned, and, ultimately, abandoning sports they formerly enjoyed. Experts, including a pediatrician, a parks administrator, a sports director, and others, lend support to the authors' position on what's happening to kids' sports. They also use former professional player Cal Ripken, Jr., who has expertise both as a player and a sports parent, in support of the article's central theme.

As you read, notice the writers' technique of using statistics to establish the legitimacy of claims they make in the article. Also, note how the quotes used at the beginning of the article signal clearly to the reader the direction the article will take. Quotes used throughout the story underscore the particular slant of the article, which urges readers to agree with the premise that youth sports in the U.S. need a new approach. Consider your own response to these techniques: did you appreciate the wealth of hard evidence, or did you feel as though you were being positioned or manipulated by the authors to agree with their position?

Fred Engh has seen it all. A wiry former college wrestler and father of 1
seven, Engh has been a baseball dad, a coach, an athletic director, and, for nearly thirty years, an evangelist out to fix youth sports. Mention any ugliness at a kids' sporting event, and Engh, the founder of the National Alliance for Youth Sports, can counter with tales even worse. There's the father telling the kid, "You little bastard, you could never get anything right." Or the beefy guy, captured on video, telling his young baseball player, "I'm gonna get you tonight because you let me down, buddy." Or the one that started Engh on his crusade, the kid pitching in a local recreation league, who, after every pitch, grabbed his elbow and winced. When the umpire stopped the game, the boy's father and coach came out to the mound. "What's wrong?" he asked the boy. "It's my arm; it hurts," said the child, crying. "Son," said the coach, "this is a man's game. Now stay in there and pitch."

Cal Ripken Jr., the former Baltimore Orioles star shortstop and a 2
father of two, has his own catalog of youth sports at their worst. He has seen coaches use what he calls the "loopholes" just to get wins. They will, in the younger leagues, tell players not to swing the bat because of the likelihood that the pitcher will throw more balls than strikes. Soon the bases are loaded. "So," Ripken continues, "you exploit the baserunning, and you create an environment that is frustrating to the defensive team, especially the pitcher. He starts crying. He's thinking, 'How terrible that all these kids are crossing the plate on passed balls and wild pitches and they are stealing on me. It's not fair; it's not fair.' And they break the kids down emotionally, and that's how you win."

On a plane not long ago, Ripken read Engh's *Why Johnny Hates* 3
Sports and found himself highlighting passage after passage. "I was struck by how the things he wrote about were things I cared about," Ripken recalls. He arranged to meet with Engh, and last week they got together again to talk. The topic: How to give kids' sports back to the kids.

That Ripken, a perennial all-star, would find common ground 4
with Engh, a sixty-eight-year-old grandfather of thirteen, isn't quite as surprising as it may sound. Just about anyone who has spent time around youth sports these days has had a bad experience or has heard of plenty more. A survey of 3,300 parents published in the

January/February issue of *SportingKid* magazine last year found that 84 percent had witnessed "violent parental behavior" toward children, coaches, or officials at kids' sports events; 80 percent said they had been victims of such behavior. A survey in South Florida in 1999 of 500 adults found 82 percent saying parents were too aggressive in youth sports, and 56 percent said they had personally witnessed overly aggressive behavior. An informal survey of youngsters by the Minnesota Amateur Sports Commission found 45 percent saying they had been called names, yelled at, or insulted while playing. Twenty-two percent said they had been pressured to play while injured, and an additional 18 percent said they had been hit, kicked, or slapped while participating. Not surprisingly, the dropout rate of all children from organized sports is said to be 70 percent.

Suffer the family. In the past decade, some disturbing new trends 5 have emerged. Children are starting in sports younger, specializing in one sport earlier, and may play the same sport year-round. The consequences of such activity are not yet fully understood, but sports physicians say stress injuries among kids are way up, and coaches say some of the most talented athletes drop out by their teens. And for many parents, the demands of toting kids to practice, travel games, and tournaments are taking a big toll on what used to be called family life. In the past twenty years, says Alvin Rosenfeld, a New York psychiatrist who specializes in adolescents, structured sports time has doubled while family dinners have been cut by a third and family vacations have decreased 28 percent. "There's been a huge growth in youth sports," says Paul Roellig, a Virginia coach and parent. "The question nobody's asking is, is this a good thing?"

Perhaps it all began way back in 1929, when the owner of a 6 Philadelphia factory set out to stop neighborhood youths from breaking his windows. He got a friend to organize a youth football league to keep the kids busy. Five years later, they named their club after the legendary Temple University football coach, Glenn Scobie "Pop" Warner. About the same time, in Williamsport, PA, a sandpaper plant worker named Carl Stotz decided to organize a league for the little kids left out of sandlot play. It came to be called "Little League." The first pitch was thrown on June 6, 1939.

From those humble beginnings, kids' sports exploded. Pop Warner 7 Football came to enroll more than 225,000 children in thirty six states. Little League has 2.5 million kids playing in fifty states. Babe Ruth League baseball, whose younger divisions now bear Cal Ripken's name, has 945,000 players and, like Little League, a World Series of its own.

The real boom in youth sports, however, was driven by soccer. 8 Here was a sport—unlike batting a pitched ball or shooting a basketball through a high hoop—that any tot could play. In 1964, the

American Youth Soccer Organization was formed in Torrance, Calif. Its founding principles included the ideas that every kid had to play at least half of every game and that teams had to be balanced in talent to ensure fairness. Soccer leagues grew like kudzu. In 2003, the Sporting Goods Manufacturers Association reported that 6.1 million kids from ages six to seventeen played soccer more than twenty five days a year. All told, more than 26 million, or two thirds of America's youth, play a team sport in America.

The boom in youth sports coincided with the suburbanization of 9 America, but it was stoked by the maturing of the baby boom generation and its unprecedented focus on its children. Parenting became "the most competitive sport in America," says Rosenfeld, the psychiatrist. "Soccer mom," meanwhile, came to conjure up more than just the image of a mother shuttling her kids to and from practice. "It's the culture," says Andrew Holzinger, athletic programs coordinator for Palm Beach County, FL. "Maybe all I wanted to do was have my daughter kick the soccer ball around because she's driving me crazy. But Soccer Mom gets out to the field, and she has a new personality. She gets to bond with the other parents about the lousy call, or 'Why is this an 11 o'clock game; I told them to schedule it earlier.' Soccer Mom, she gets to have her own sport."

Child abuse. As parents got more involved, some got *too* 10 involved, and things turned ugly. By the mid-'70s, Engh had seen enough. His daughter played on a softball team whose coach was caught urging his girls to shoplift for him, Engh says. And then, coaching his own son's baseball team, he ran into the father who told his boy with the sore elbow to stay in there and pitch. This was nothing more, Engh says, than "legalized child abuse."

He decided to do something about it. By 1980, he began working 11 out of a tiny second-floor office in West Palm Beach, creating a training manual for coaches. The idea: to make team sports less pressurized, safer, and more child friendly. Engh still remembers the day when the bank called and told his wife, Michaele, they were $440 overdrawn. With seven kids to feed, Engh thought it was the end. Then he opened his mail, and in it was his first order for the new manual, a check for $732. He never looked back.

Today, Engh's National Alliance for Youth Sports has certified 2.1 12 million volunteer coaches. But that, he says, isn't enough; everyone in youth sports—administrators, coaches, officials, parents—should be trained and sensitized. Indeed, one evening in February 2000, the Jupiter-Tequesta Athletic Association in Florida packed more than 1,500 parents into a stadium to watch a video on how to be a good sports parent, pick up a handbook, and sign a sportsmanship pledge—or their children could not play. Engh's National Alliance has even created a program to teach basic skills to kids as young as 3, so they can enjoy sports from the start. Near Buffalo, NY, the town of Hamburg adopted all of the alliance programs. "The coaches used to show up like, 'We're going to war here,'" says Tim Jerome, president of the junior football league. "It was pretty bad." Verbal abuse, shoving matches, parents misbehaving; it's all "changed dramatically," he says.

"The one thing people need to understand," Engh emphasizes, "is that they don't need to put up with this anymore." Mike Murray agrees. "Here in Northern Virginia," says Murray, a high school coach, teacher, and a director of youth baseball training programs, "you've seen a real cultural shift. All the things you'd want, people policing themselves. I think in large part people have bought into this." Murray is a trainer for another organization, the Positive Coaching Alliance. The alliance shares many of the same goals as Engh's organization— and even some of the same tips—but their approaches are different. Engh's organization wants all volunteers trained and certified; the Positive Coaching Alliance is focused more on the zen of coaching.   13

The PCA is the brainchild of a soft-spoken former college basket-ball player named Jim Thompson. While studying at Stanford University Business School in the mid-1980s, he found himself coaching his son's baseball and basketball teams. Seeing too many "negative interactions" between coaches and players, he recalled his earlier experiences working at the Behavioral Learning Center in St. Paul, MN. There he had learned the power that positive reinforcement had on severely disturbed children. He wrote a book called *Positive Coaching*, which stressed some basic principles: Athletes perform best when they feel good about themselves. The way to keep them confident is with positive comments. Athletes so motivated will be confident, try hardest, take chances, and play "over their heads." And when that happens, the team wins.   14

Thompson's manuscript made its way to Phil Jackson, then the head coach of the Chicago Bulls. Jackson, recalling his own trying years in youth sports, was struck: "It fused a lot of my thinking," he said. He decided to test Thompson's theory at the pro level. At the time, Jackson was riding one of his players, Horace Grant, pretty hard, and their relationship had fallen apart. Jackson tried the positive approach, and things turned around. Jackson, now with the Los Angeles Lakers, became the PCA's national spokesman.   15

Its influence has been sizable. The PCA's sixty five trainers have run workshops for 100 youth sports organizations, training an estimated 60,000 coaches and parents. "I can tell you the first year we ran PCA programs the number of coaches being ejected from games was cut drastically," says Tim Casey, former vice president of Chicagoland Pop Warner football conference. The Dallas Parochial League, with 3,500 fifth to eighth graders enrolled in eleven sports, began offering PCA workshops   16

541

to all coaches. In basketball, "our most volatile sport," says athletic director B. J. Antes, technical fouls dropped from over hundred to twenty six
in three years. This year, PCA workshops will no longer be optional,
Antes says. "It's too darned important not to make it mandatory."
Coaches say they like the PCA's "dual goal" approach: striving to win,
but using sports to teach life lessons. PCA workshops stress "honoring
the game," mastering sports skills, and shrugging off mistakes. "The
way I see the world of youth sports," Thompson says, "is that the win-at-
all-costs mentality is the root of all evil."

Studies confirm this. A survey last summer at the National PTA   17
Convention in Charlotte, NC, found 44 percent of parents saying that
their child had dropped out of a sport because it made him or her
unhappy. These parents were not wimps. In fact, 92 percent of the
respondents said sports were either important or very important to the
overall development of their children. But 56 percent said that youth
sports were too competitive, nearly half said that organized youth sports
need to be completely revamped, and half said if they could change one
thing, they would want their coach to be less focused on winning. Many
surveys support this conclusion: Most kids would prefer to play a lot on
a team that loses than sit on the bench of a team that wins.

542

For all the progress that the Fred Enghs and Jim Thompsons have   18
made, however, they have yet to address a development of the '80s and
'90s that has swept up many families. Known as travel teams, they are
formed of the best players in a league or a community, may be coached
by a volunteer parent or a well-paid coach, and travel to other towns—
and sometimes even other states—to play teams of their own caliber.
Also known as elite, select, or club teams, they're found in virtually
every town in the nation.

At their best, travel teams provide young players with professional-   19
level coaching, better competition, and even family bonding. "The clubs
get very tight. They like each other; they travel with each other; they go
on trips. It becomes much more of a long-term social thing as well as a
competitive thing," says Craig Ciandella, California director of United
States Specialty Sports Association baseball, which has 1,300 teams.
Many young athletes believe their clubs give them the accelerated development they need to make the high school varsity or go beyond. "It's no
longer a myth: If your kid wants to make a high school team, he has to
play club ball," says Jim Tuyay, a tournament director with the California
Beach Volleyball Association. "They're getting the training and the attention that the normal rec leagues are not providing."

Pressure. Travel teams can be nothing if not intense. They may   20
practice twice a week and play twice more. They can travel one, two,
three hours each way for games, chewing up entire Saturdays or weekends. "It becomes a way of life. It winds up being what you do on

weekends. You don't go away; you don't go on vacation; you do baseball. I wouldn't have had it any other way," says Ciandella. And most
kids playing on elite teams are encouraged to play the same sport again
in one, two, or three more seasons—even if they are playing other
sports. Some are told—and believe—that if they don't play, say, soccer
year-round, they will fall behind their peers.

One effect is even more pressure in the early years. Children now   21
play travel hockey at the age of seven, and baseball tournaments are organized featuring pitchers as young as eight. "Where we live, travel soccer
starts at the U-9 [eight-year-old] level," says Virginia father Roellig. If you
resist, he says, "you will be told, 'Your kids will quickly fall behind and
not make the team when they are ten.' If you want your kid to play in
high school, you have to start [travel] at ten, and if you want to travel at
ten, you have to play travel at eight." Roellig says his community recently
started a U-5 soccer program. Called the "Little Kickers," children can
play at age three and a half. In 2003, it enrolled fifty kids, he says; now it
has more than 150. "It's an arms race," complained one soccer mom in
Washington, D.C.

Some wonder whether things have not gotten out of hand. Roellig,   22
who coaches soccer, has three children, ages ten, fifteen, and sixteen—all
involved in sports. His fifteen-year-old daughter, a high school freshman, plays year-round soccer and two other sports to boot. In the spring,
she plays high school and travel soccer. In the summer she attends
camps, does a basketball league, and has August soccer practice. In the
fall, she has travel soccer and field hockey. And in the winter, she plays
indoor travel soccer and basketball. Most nights she gets home at 7:00 or
7:30 from practice, has to eat and do her homework. She may make it to
bed by 10 p.m., but she has to get up at 5:40 for school. "What gives is the
homework and the sleep," Roellig says, adding that his daughter often
looks exhausted. "If I had to do it again as a parent, I'd definitely scale
back sports," he says. "I think I'm doing more harm than good."

He's not alone. Holzinger, the parks administrator in Palm Beach   23
County, oversees 120 athletic fields and issues permits for their use by
sixty-five different youth organizations. Only 2 to 5 percent of children
under the age of thirteen, he believes, qualify as "elite" athletes. But in
his region, the proportion of kids being placed on "elite" teams has
grown to 25 to 30 percent of the athletic pool in the area. It's not that
more kids have become better athletes; more parents are simply insisting that their kids be enrolled on select teams. "As we see these children
as elite players, we stop thinking of them as children," Holzinger says.
"You're not a child; you're my defensive line that nobody ever gets
through. So if someone gets through, you let me down." The 25 percent
of kids who shouldn't be on the select teams, in other words, frustrate
the team and the coach. Parents get down on the coach because the team

isn't winning, and coaches sometimes take it out on the kids. Or some kids simply ride the bench. "You, the kid," Holzinger explains, "are now becoming frustrated with a sport, and it's a sport you loved. Past tense."

Much of the problem, Holzinger and others say, stems from 24 coaches. "You'd be surprised," Holzinger says, "by how many parents are really impressed when a coach tells them, 'I'll have your child in a scholarship; stick with this program.'" What parents don't understand, and what the coaches don't tell them, are the real numbers. Dan Doyle, a former collegiate basketball player and head coach, is the executive director of the Institute for International Sport at the University of Rhode Island. For his forthcoming book, *The Encyclopedia of Sports Parenting* (to be published in September 2005), Doyle's research team surveyed young basketball players. Using data from nationally affiliated basketball leagues, they estimated that the total number of fourth-grade boys playing organized basketball was about 475,000. At the same time, the team found, only 87,000 teens were playing basketball as seniors in high school. Of the 87,000, they say, 1,560 will win Division I college scholarships, 1,350 will get Division II scholarships, and 1,400 more will play at Division III schools. And of those 4,310, about 30 will make it to the National Basketball Association. An additional 130 will play pro ball in Europe.

In soccer, the odds are even longer because so many colleges 25 recruit foreign players. "It's not a worthy objective at the fourth- or fifth- or sixth-grade level," Doyle says, "which is what some of these coaches are telling them. You know, 'If you don't play for me you're not going to get to college.'" And tennis? Doyle found that there are approximately three million males between ten and eighteen worldwide aspiring to be top tennis players. How many make money on the pro circuit? 175. "The professional aspiration," he says, "it's just crazy."

Equally crazy, experts say, is the idea that child stars can be cre- 26 ated by starting early. "It doesn't matter when you start a sport. If you start at three, it doesn't necessarily help," says Paul Stricker, a pediatric sports medicine specialist in San Diego. "Kids develop sports skills in a very sequential manner, just like they do sitting up and walking and talking. Parents and coaches just don't understand that sequence. They feel that after they're potty trained, if they practice something enough they'll get it." Parents, some coaches say, are often fooled by "early maturers," kids who are big and well-coordinated at a young age. But often it's the late bloomers, who had to work longer and harder at sports, who turn into the stars.

Breakdown. Pushing kids to play sports too early and too often 27 can result in pain and worse. Since he began his specialty practice in 1991, Stricker says, "I've had at least a 30 to 40 percent increase in overuse injuries like stress fractures and tendinitis. Those are things we just didn't see much in kids previously." Stress fractures, which occur when kids overtax their bones, are common. "These only come from forces that are repetitive," Stricker explains. "The bone breaks down faster than it can build up." Tendinitis is also common, especially in pitchers and swimmers, because young muscles aren't strong enough yet to keep up with adult training regimens. In young pitchers, Stricker says, "the growth plate gets pulled apart like an Oreo cookie."

28 The American Academy of Pediatrics has taken note. "Those who participate in a variety of sports and specialize only after reaching the age of puberty," the academy said in a statement four years ago, "tend to be more consistent performers, have fewer injuries, and adhere to sports play longer than those who specialize early."

29 What overeager parents should really worry about, some experts say, is burnout. Jim Perry is director of athletics at La Quinta High School in Westminster, Calif., a public school where club sports are hugely popular. He says he recently read an article about a national powerlifting championship for kids as young as nine. "What nine-year-old gets up in the morning and says, 'I want to be powerlifting'?" he asks. "That came about because of a coach or a parent." Perry says many kids, so pushed, tire of sports by the time they reach high school. "It's not a matter of [club sports] sucking talent away [from high school]. They're driving high-end kids away from athletics in general," he says. "They're sick and tired of playing 135 travel baseball games a year by the time they're twelve years old. They're sick of playing 100 soccer games a year before they ever set foot in high school. They don't need it anymore."

30 Besides, it's not yet proven that year-round play, travel teams, and specialization make better athletes. "Most of today's top professional athletes didn't even think to specialize in just one sport until they were in high school, around the age of fifteen," says Rick Wolff, chairman of the Center for Sports Parenting at the University of Rhode Island. Cal Ripken, for one, attributes his success on the diamond partly to playing three sports into high school. Soccer taught him footwork and balance, he says. Basketball gave him explosiveness and quick movements. "I think athleticism is developed," he says, "by everything you do." For that reason, he tells his ten-year-old son, Ryan, "put down your glove" when spring baseball is over.

31 All the emphasis on winning, perversely, can make for inferior skills. The Virginia Youth Soccer Association, with 138,000 registered players, recently posted a long note on its website from Technical Director Gordon Miller assailing "overly competitive travel soccer." In their zeal to win games, Miller warned, some Virginia travel teams emphasize the wrong things. Big kids are recruited and taught to kick the ball long down the field instead of being taught to make tight, short passes and ball-handling skills. "You don't encourage flair, creativity, and passion for

the game," he says, emphasizing that it is in practice, not games, that young athletes develop their skills. Studies show, Miller says, that in a typical game a player on average has the ball in his or her control for only two to three minutes. "The question is, 'Is playing all of these matches the best way to develop players?'" he asks. "And the answer is, 'No.'"

If we could only start over—that's one of Fred Engh's dreams. 32 Engh has been traveling and speaking abroad, hoping to learn from others and to find countries where it's not too late to fix things. In the course of his travels, he came across the tiny Caribbean nation of Dominica, a place where organized youth sports do not yet exist. The Dominicans agreed to let Engh and his Alliance for Youth Sports start a complete roster of kids' sports there, from scratch. Engh told Ripken of the venture. Ripken says he was intrigued by the idea of starting a youth sports program with the slate entirely clean. "I never thought there was a place on this planet that hadn't played baseball as an organized sport," he says. "Maybe I could help participate in something like that—rebuilding the joy of baseball."

DROPPING OUT

546

Although the number of kids ages six to seventeen rose by more than seven million between 1990 and 2002, the most popular team sports lost significant numbers of players.

(Millions of players)
Basketball

1990	20
1998	22
2002	18

Soccer

1990	12
1998	14
2002	13

Softball

1990	12
1998	9
2002	6

Baseball

1990	10
1998	8
2002	7

Source: American Sports Data Inc., Sporting Goods Manufacturers Association

Examining the Text

1. In what ways do the authors appear to support the contention of Fred Engh that youth sports need fixing? Do you think this article is about the mission of Engh to reform kids' sports, or does it represent a broader criticism of youth sports? What role does Engh play in the article; could it have been written without any mention of him?

2. Look carefully at the statistics the authors quote. What information do they convey? Do you think those statistics provide a complete picture? What other perspectives might benefit by the inclusion of some statistics or other hard data?

3. The technical director of the Virginia Youth Soccer Association is quoted as saying that "overly competitive travel soccer" doesn't encourage "flair, creativity, and passion for the game." In your opinion, is it reasonable to draw conclusions about travel soccer based on the comments of one particular technical director? How might the inclusion of several other sports program directors' opinions have altered the tone and/or argumentative position and credibility of this article?

4. Parents seem to come in for much criticism in this article, yet the authors appear to have not spoken to anyone representing parents. Do you think this was a deliberate omission on their part? If so, why? If not, do you think hearing from parents would have altered your perception of the article? Based on the way the authors wrote the story and the emphasis given in the article, do you believe they have succeeded in addressing the source of the problem? Does the article offer a viable solution to the problems it highlights?

547

For Group Discussion

How many people in your group played sports regularly as kids? How many do so now? If, as the authors of this article predict, a significant number of your group members have stopped playing organized sports, discuss whether the reasons cited by the author match the reasons put forward by members of your group. In the opinion of your group members, are there other reasons why youngsters stop playing baseball, soccer, and other team sports?

Writing Suggestion

As an exercise in critical thinking and writing, develop an essay that counters the arguments put forth in this article. You might begin by making a list of all the statistics the authors use in their story about kids' sports, noting what categories they fall into. You might proceed to conduct some research via the library and the Internet, trying to find statistics that contradict the statistics used in the article. For example, one survey by the Minnesota Amateur Sports Commission reportedly found that 45 percent of participants had been called names, yelled at, or insulted while playing for a youth team. The explicit goal of this assignment will be to conduct research and write a persuasive essay in which you defend the role of competitive team sports. Explain why you think there are benefits for children from specializing at a young age, practicing frequently, and taking part in tournaments. Use the statistics you find to support your arguments.

ADDITIONAL SUGGESTIONS FOR WRITING ABOUT SPORTS

1. Using Maya Angelou's "Champion of the World" as a model, write a narrative in which you tell of a past experience with sports, either as a spectator or as a participant, that had a significant effect on your life. Perhaps this experience revealed something about yourself that you didn't realize, helped you to better understand someone else, taught you an important lesson, or corrected a misconception that you had. Or perhaps you're not certain what effect the experience had, and can use this assignment to speculate on its significance.

2. Attend a local sporting event, and bring a notebook and, if possible, a tape recorder or video camera. Observe and take notes about how the people around you behave, what they do and say, what they wear, how they relate to one another, what interests or bores them, when they seem satisfied or disappointed. Note also how their behavior is different from what it would likely be in other contexts. Try to be an impartial observer, simply recording what you see in as much detail as possible. From your notes, write an extended description of one or several typical spectators, and then draw some conclusions about why people enjoy watching sports. You may also want to discuss the psychological benefits and/or harm that being a spectator might cause.

3. Choose a sport or a game with which you're very familiar, either because you play it or watch it regularly. Reflect on your experience playing or watching this sport/game, and write down some of your recollections. Think about what you've learned from this activity, and how it has affected other areas of your life. Next, write an essay in which you show how this particular sport has influenced your beliefs, attitudes, and values. Be as specific as possible and try to show precisely how and why the sport/game has influenced you.

4. Many of the writers in this chapter discuss the impact of professional sports on individuals and on society as a whole. Referring to essays in this chapter, construct your own argument about the influence of professional sports. As a prewriting exercise, make lists of the beneficial and the detrimental influences of professional sports on our society. Try to come up with specific examples to illustrate each of the items on your lists. Working from those lists, develop a persuasive argument about the influence of sports on our society.

Internet Activities

1. Professional athletes are often role models in our society. As a prewriting exercise for this assignment, list some of the reasons why this is so, especially for young people. Also list the ways in which athletes might be good role models, as well as some of the reasons other professionals (for example, teachers or government leaders) might actually be better role models.

Next, visit the links to information about professional athletes, provided at the *Common Culture* Web site, to official and unofficial homepages of individual athletes. After browsing through these links, choose an athlete who you think is either a good or a bad role model. Do further research on this athlete, looking up interviews and articles about him or her in the library. From this information, write a brief biography of the athlete, focusing on the kind of role model he or she is.

2. Professional sports teams are in the business of making money, and the World Wide Web is increasingly becoming a venue for advertising and marketing. It's no surprise, then, that all of the major professional sports teams now have their own Web sites. Go to the *Common Culture* Web site for links that you can follow to visit the homepages of professional teams in baseball, football, men's basketball, women's basketball, and hockey. Choose a Web site for one team and read the site carefully and completely. Make a list of the information that the site offers, including statistics, pictures, news and "inside information," schedules, and so on. Then analyze the ways in which the information offered at the site is intended to promote or "sell" the team. Is the site addressed to current fans of the team, or is it intended to cultivate new fans? How effectively do you believe the Web site is in advertising and marketing the team it represents?

Reading Images

Brandi Chastain, shown in the photo on p. CI-7, is famous for her game-winning shot during the women's World Cup soccer tournament a few years back. But perhaps she is more famous for what happened after the game—in a moment of unbridled joy, she removed her jersey and bounded joyfully on the field in a sports bra, helping to make such apparel some of the most recognizable items of clothing in the country at that moment in pop-cultural history. She received so much notoriety for this single act that Brandi Chastain was moved to create her own Web site in response to the furor. The site, which she calls, "It's Not About the Bra," can be found at http://www.itsnotaboutthebra.com/

In an essay, "read" the images in this text and on Chastain's Web site to uncover and discuss the sociocultural messages they contain. Look carefully at all elements of the graphics. Discuss possible meanings implicit in the colors and the central images of Chastain. However, don't be content merely to focus on the central images: study the background "negative space" as well, to ascertain how the entire composition combines to create meaning. Note also the juxtaposition of image and text, along with messages contained in the text itself.

If you wish, you may take this discussion a step further by addressing a central issue raised by the pictures: namely, the commodification of sport. Some purists believe that sports are tainted by commercialism. They might therefore point to commercial use of the images that depict Chastain in her Nike sports bra and charge that by capitalizing on this pure moment of sport-centered bliss, the spirit of competition is reduced to a crass attempt to sell. Consider this issue, examining your own feelings about the pros and cons of commercialism in sport, and then develop a thesis that takes a persuasive stance with regard to this issue.

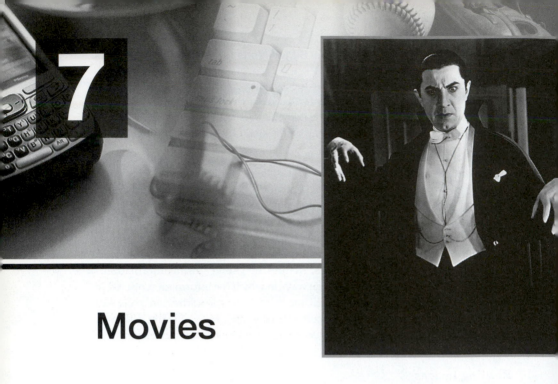

Movies

It's Friday night. You park in an exhaust-filled subterranean garage or a vast asphalt lot surrounding a mall. You make your way into the neon-lit megaplex, where you and a companion or two pay half a day's salary for tickets, an industrial-size bucket of popcorn, and a couple of ten-gallon sodas. You wind your way through a maze of corridors to the theater of your choice, where a psychedelic montage filling the screen is soon replaced by the first of an interminable series of quick-cutting previews as you bathe in rolling quadraphonic surround sound. You sink into your space-age stadium plastic seat and kick back, surrendering to the waves of sound and images. . . .

Such is moviegoing in the new millennium. Gone are the nickel matinee and the discount double feature, newsreels, cartoons, and comic short subjects, and the drive-in, where many a pair of teenagers learned human anatomy in the back seat of a Chevy.

The external trappings of the moviegoing experience may have changed, but the reasons people go are still pretty much the same: to get out of the house and escape the routine of their daily lives; to be part of a communal group sharing an experience; to find a romantic setting where conversation is at a minimum; to indulge, for one night, in an orgy of junk food; and, above all, to be entertained and, perhaps, touched emotionally. So strong is the draw of motion pictures that Americans fork over billions of dollars a year on domestic movies alone, despite the increasing availability of home entertainment through DVD rental services such as Netflix.

As there are many reasons for going to the movies, so there are many ways of explaining their popularity and studying their influence within the fabric of contemporary culture. From a sociological perspective, movies can reflect, define, or even redefine social norms, and—in the work of politically focused filmmakers such as Michael Moore—depict urgent social problems within the relative safety of the big screen. From a psychological perspective, viewers identify with the character and project their own feelings into the action, giving them a deep emotional connection to a protagonist along with feelings of tension and, ultimately release. From a literary perspective, movies can be interpreted in terms of genres—horror movies, or crime dramas, or menaced-female stories—or in terms of plot, characterization, imagery, and so forth. From an economic perspective, movies may be seen primarily as a consumable product, defined solely by the marketplace. To the cultural critic, this economic influence might seem to be negative, reducing a potentially powerful artistic form to the lowest common denominator. The capitalist observer might see such forces as positive, however, because they encourage the worldwide spread of American cultural values. Finally, from a semiological perspective, movies are ripe with symbolic imagery, from the multiple associations possible in a character's name to the way images are juxtaposed in the editing.

This chapter introduces film criticism arising from several of these views. The first readings focus on the social impacts and implications of film. The second part of this chapter looks closely at two moviemakers who have had a tremendous impact, not only on the film scene, but on modern culture as well. The first, Judd Apatow, gained critical acclaim through his short-lived television series *Freaks and Geeks,* and went on to produce some of the most popular comedies of our time, including *The 40-Year-Old Virgin, Knocked Up,* and *Superbad,* all of which reflect to a high degree the preoccupations of Americans in this unique period in history. The second cutting-edge filmmaker, Quentin Tarantino, gave us *Pulp Fiction,* arguably the most influential film of the postmodern era, along with other important releases such as the *Kill Bill* series and the low-pop-culture-inspired *Death Proof,* part of the Rodriguez/Tarantino *Grindhouse* collaboration. While the films of these two individuals couldn't be more different in style and content, they are nevertheless related, since each tells us much about ideas, fears, concerns, and impulses deeply implanted in American culture as we move into the new millennium.

Film and American Culture

The Way We Are

SYDNEY POLLACK

If anyone knows American moviemaking, it's Sydney Pollack. A director of more than sixteen films—including The Way We Were, Tootsie, Out of Africa, *and, most recently,* The Interpreter, *starring Nicole Kidman and Sean Penn—a producer of numerous films, including the recent* Michael Clayton, *and an occasional actor (including, for you trivia buffs, an appearance on the television megahit* The Sopranos*), Pollack has had an unparalleled opportunity to observe the changing tastes of the American viewing public and the movie industry's response to those changes. In the following article, a transcript of an address Pollack delivered at a conference about the influence of the popular media on American values, Pollack suggests that changes in the moral fabric of our society are responsible for the kinds of movies we see today, not vice versa.*

When he looks at contemporary America, Pollack finds a conspicuous lack of the "kind of scrupulous ethical concern for the sanctity of life" that prevailed in past decades and was reflected in motion pictures of the time, when there were less frequent and less graphic scenes of violence, when characters were esteemed for their humility and personal integrity, and when explicit sexuality was found only in "stag" films, not in mainstream theaters. Many people today, Pollack notes, are nostalgic for the "old values" and believe that movies should encourage the return of these values rather than reflecting current values. Pollack disagrees, however, pointing out that, although screenwriters and directors may want their movies to reflect some moral content, the economics of the industry require first and foremost that movies be entertaining, and therefore, they must appeal to a buying audience whose values may be very different from those of the reformers.

As you read, consider whether you agree with Pollack's notions of artistic integrity, especially his assertions that a filmmaker's prime goal should be to entertain an audience and that movies simply reflect the surrounding society. Is it possible that, in responding to their audience's changing tastes, filmmakers also "construct" public attitudes toward violence, sexuality, and so forth by pushing their explicitness further and further?

Six weeks ago, I thought I was going to be happy to be a part of this conference, which shows you how naive I am. The agenda—for me at least—is a minefield. Normally, I spend my time worrying about specific problems and not reflecting, as many of you on these panels do. So I've really thought about this, and I've talked to anyone who would listen. My colleagues are sick and tired of it, my wife has left for the country and even my agents—and these are people I pay— don't return my phone calls. By turns, I have felt myself stupid, unethical, a philistine, unpatriotic, a panderer, a cultural polluter, and stupid. And I've completely failed to solve your problems, except in one small way. You have delayed by at least six weeks the possibility of my contributing further to the problems you see.

I know your concerns have to do with American values and 2 whether those values are being upheld or assaulted by American enter- tainment—by what I and others like me do. But which values exactly?

In the thirties, forties, and fifties, six men in the Valley, immi- 3 grants really, ran the movie industry. Our society was vastly different. The language of the movies was a language of shared values. If you put forward a virtuousness on the part of your hero, everybody responded to it.

When Sergeant York, played by Gary Cooper, refused to endorse 4 a breakfast cereal, knowing he'd been asked because he'd won the Medal of Honor, he said: "I ain't proud of what I've done. You don't make money off of killing people. That there is wrong." We expected him to behave that way.

553

But society's values have changed. That kind of scrupulous, ethi- 5 cal concern for the sanctity of human life doesn't exist in the same way, and that fact is reflected in the movies. There's a nostalgia now for some of the old values, but so many people embrace other expressions of values that it's hard to say these other expressions aren't reality.

Their idea of love, for example, is a different idea of love. It's a 6 much less chaste, much less idealized love than was depicted in the earlier films. We are seeing some sort of return to the ideal of marriage. There was a decade or two when marriage really lost its popularity, and while young people are swinging toward it again, I don't believe one could say that values have not changed significantly since the thir- ties, forties, and fifties.

Morality, the definitions of virtue, justice, and injustice, the sanc- 7 tity of the individual, have been fairly fluid for American audiences in terms of what they choose to embrace or not embrace.

Take a picture like *Dances With Wolves*. You could not have made it 8 in the thirties or forties. It calls into question every value that existed in traditional Westerns. It may not reflect what everybody thinks now, but it expresses a lot of guilty reevaluation of what happened in the West, the very things shown in the old Westerns that celebrated the frontier.

If we got the movies to assert or talk about better values, would 9 that fix our society? Well, let me quote Sam Goldwyn. When he was told by his staff how poorly his studio's new—and very expensive—film was doing, Sam thought a minute, shrugged, and said, "Listen, if they don't want to come, you can't stop them."

Now that's as close to a first principle of Hollywood as I can come. It informs everything that we're here to discuss and it controls every solution that we may propose. 10

OUT OF HOLLYWOOD

Before they can be anything else, American movies are a product. This is not good or bad, this is what we've got. A very few may become art, but all of them, whatever their ambitions, are first financed as commodities. They're the work of craftsmen and artists, but they're soon offered for sale. 11

Whether we say that we're "creating a film" or merely "making a movie," the enterprise itself is sufficiently expensive and risky that it cannot be, and it will not be, undertaken without the hope of reward. We have no Medicis here. It takes two distinct entities, the financiers and the makers, to produce movies, and there is a tension between them. Their goals are sometimes similar, but they do different things. Financiers are not in the business of philanthropy. They've got to answer to stockholders. 12

554

Of course, the controlling influence in filmmaking hasn't changed in 50 years: it still belongs to the consumer. That's the dilemma and, in my view, what we're finally talking about. What do you do about culture in a society that celebrates the common man but doesn't always like his taste? 13

If you operate in a democracy and you're market-supported and driven, the spectrum of what you will get is going to be very wide indeed. It will range from trash to gems. There are 53,000 books published in this country every year. How many of them are really good? Tired as I may be of fast-food-recipe, conscienceless, simple-minded books, films, TV, and music, the question remains, who is to be society's moral policeman? 14

Over the course of their first 30 or 40 years, the movies were a cottage industry, and the morality that was reflected in them was the morality of the early film pioneers. Now, film studios are tiny divisions of multinational corporations, and they feel the pressure for profits that happens in any other repeatable-product business. They look for a formula. Say you get the recipe for a soft drink and perfect it; once customers like it, you just repeat it and it will sell. More fortunes have been lost than made in the movie business pursuing such a formula, but 15 unfortunately today, more junk than anything else is being made pursuing it. And film companies are folding like crazy.

Since we are in the democracy business, we can't tell people what they should or shouldn't hear, or support, or see, so they make their choices. The market tries to cater to those choices, and we have what we have. 16

MAKING FILMS

Are American films bad? A lot of them surely are, and so are a lot of everybody else's, the way a lot of anything produced is bad—breakfast cereals, music, most chairs, architecture, mail-order shirts. There probably hasn't been a really beautiful rake since the Shakers stopped making farm implements. But that is no excuse. 17

I realize that I am a prime suspect here, but I'm not sure that you really understand how odd and unpredictable a business the making of films actually is. It just doesn't conform to the logic or rules of any other business. It's always been an uneasy merger of two antithetical things: some form of art and sheer commerce. 18

If the people who make films get the money that is invested in them back to the people who finance them, then they'll get to make more. We know that the business of films is to reach as many people as possible. That works two ways; it's not just a market discipline. You have to remember that most of us who are doing this got into it for the romance, the glory, the applause, the chance to tell stories, even to learn, but rarely for the money. The more people you reach, the greater your sense of success. Given the choice, I'd rather make the whole world cry than seventeen intellectuals in a classroom. 19

But, paradoxically, if you are the actual maker of the film—not the financier—you can't make films and worry about whether they'll reach a large audience or make money, first, because nobody really knows a formula for what will make money. If they did, I promise you we would have heard about it, and studios would not be going broke. Second, and much more practically, if you spent your time while you were making the film consciously thinking about what was commercial, then the real mechanism of choice—the mechanism that is your own unconscious, your own taste and imagination, your fantasy— would be replaced by constant reference to this formula that we know doesn't work. 20

So the only practical approach a filmmaker can take is to make a film that he or she would want to see. This sounds arrogant, but you try to make a movie for yourself, and you hope that as many people as 21 possible will like it too. If that happens, it's because you've done something in the telling of the story that makes people care. One of the things that makes a film distinct from other American business products is this emotional involvement of the maker. A producer of auto parts can become pretty emotional about a sales slump, but it isn't the same thing. His product hasn't come from his history; it isn't somehow in the image of his life; and it lacks mystery. It is entirely measurable and concrete, which is certainly appropriate in the manufacture of auto parts. I wouldn't want to buy a carburetor from a neurotic, mixed-up auto manufacturer.

Fortunately for those of us in film, no such standards apply. Quite 22 the contrary, in fact. No matter what his conscious intentions are, the best part of what the filmmaker does—the part, when it works, that makes you want to see the film—doesn't come from a rational, consciously controllable process. It comes from somewhere inside the filmmaker's unconscious. It comes from making unlikely connections seem inevitable, from a kind of free association that jumps to odd or surprising places, conclusions that cause delights, something that creates goose pimples or awe.

This conference has suggested a question: While you're actually 23 making the movie, do you think about whether or not it will be doing the world any good? I can't answer it for filmmakers in general. For myself, candidly, no, I don't.

I try to discover and tell the truth and not be dull about it. In that 24 sense, the question has no significance for me. I assume that trying to discover the truth is in itself a good and virtuous aim. By truth I don't mean some grand, pretentious axiom to live by; I just mean the truth of a character from moment to moment. I try to discover and describe things like the motives that are hidden in day-to-day life. And the truth is rarely dull. If I can find it, I will have fulfilled my primary obligation as a filmmaker, which is not to bore the pants off you.

Most of us in this business have enormous sympathy for 25 Scheherazade—we're terrified we're going to be murdered if we're boring. So our first obligation is to not bore people; it isn't to teach.

Most of the time, high-mindedness just leads to pretentious or 26 well-meaning, often very bad, films. Most of the Russian films made under communism were of high quality in terms of craft, but they were soporific because their intent to do good as it was perceived by the state or an all-knowing party committee was too transparent.

I'm sure that you think the person in whose hands the process 27 actually rests, the filmmaker, could exert an enormous amount of control over the film's final worthiness. The question usually goes like this: Should filmmakers pander to the public, or should they try to elevate public taste to something that many at this conference would find more acceptable? Is the job of an American filmmaker to give the public what it wants or what the filmmaker thinks the public should have? This doesn't leave much doubt as to what you think is the right answer.

But framing your question this way not only betrays a misunderstanding of how the filmmaking process works but also is just plain wishful thinking about how to improve society. I share your nostalgia for some of those lost traditional values, but attempting to reinstall them by arbitrarily putting them into movies when they don't exist in everyday life will not get people to go to the movies or put those values back into life. I wish it were that simple.   28

ENGAGING AN AUDIENCE

This conference is concerned with something called popular culture   29
and its effect on society, but I am concerned with one film at a time and its effect. You are debating whether movies corrupt our souls or elevate them, and I'm debating whether a film will touch a soul. As a filmmaker, I never set out to create popular culture, and I don't know a single other filmmaker who does.

557

Maybe it's tempting to think of Hollywood as some collective   30
behemoth grinding out the same stories and pushing the same values, but it's not that simple. Hollywood, whatever that means, is Oliver Stone castigating war in *Born on the Fourth of July* and John Milius celebrating it in *The Wind and the Lion*. It's Walt Disney and Martin Scorsese. It's Steven Spielberg and Milos Foreman. It's *Amadeus* and *Terminator* and hundreds of choices in between.

I don't want to defend Hollywood, because I don't represent   31
Hollywood—I can't, any more than one particular writer can represent literature or one painter art. For the most part, the impulse toward all art, entertainment, culture, pop culture, comes from the same place within the makers of it. The level of talent and the soul, if you'll forgive the word again, is what finally limits it.

At the risk of telling you more than you need to know about my   32
own work, I make the movies I make because there is in each film some argument that fascinates me, an issue I want to work through. I call this a spine or an armature because it functions for me like an armature in sculpture—something I can cover up and it will support the whole structure. I can test the scenes against it. For me, the film, when properly dramatized, adds up to this idea, this argument.

But there are lots of other ways to go about making a film, and   33
lots of other filmmakers who do it differently. Some filmmakers begin knowing exactly what they want to say and then craft a vehicle that

contains that statement. Some are interested in pure escape. Here's the catch. The effectiveness and the success of all our films is determined by exactly the same standards—unfortunately, not by the particular validity of their message but by their ability to engage the concentration and emotions of the audience.

Citizen Kane is an attack on acquisition, but that's not why people 34
go to see it. I don't have any idea if the audience that saw *Tootsie* thought at any conscious level that it could be about a guy who became a better man for having been a woman; or that *The Way We Were*, a film I made twenty years ago, may have been about the tension between passion, often of the moment, and wisdom, often part of a longer view; or that *Out Of Africa* might be about the inability to possess another individual and even the inability of one country to possess another. That's intellectual and stuffy. I just hope the audiences were entertained.

I may choose the movies I make because there's an issue I want to 35
explore, but the how—the framing of that issue, the process of finding the best way to explore it—is a much more mysterious, elusive, and messy process. I can't tell you that I understand it; if I did, I would have a pep talk with myself and go out and make a terrific movie every time.

I would not make a film that ethically, or morally, or politically 36
trashed what I believe is fair. But by the same token, I feel an obligation—and this is more complicated and personal—to do films about arguments.

Orson Welles in
Citizen Kane

I try hard to give each side a strong argument—not because I'm a fair guy but because I believe it's more interesting. Both things are going on.

I do the same thing on every movie I make. I find an argument, a couple of characters I would like to have dinner with, and try to find the most fascinating way to explore it. I work as hard as I can to tell the story in the way I'd like to have it told to me.   37

What is really good is also entertaining and interesting because it's closer to a newer way to look at the truth. You can't do that consciously. You can't start out by saying, "I am now going to make a great film."   38

The virtue in making a film, if there is any, is in making it well. If there's any morality that's going to come out, it will develop as you begin to construct, at every moment you have a choice to make. You can do it the honest way or you can bend it, and the collection of those moments of choice is what makes the work good or not good and is what reveals morality or the lack of it.   39

I've made sixteen films. I've had some enormous successes and I've had some colossal failures, but I can't tell you what the difference is in terms of what I did.   40

AN AMERICAN AESTHETIC?

559

In some circles, American films suffer by comparison with European films precisely because a lot of our movies seem to be the product of little deliberation and much instinct. It's been said of European movies that essence precedes existence, which is just a fancy way of saying that European movies exist in order to say something. Certainly one never doubts with a European film that it's saying something, and often it just comes right out and says it.   41

American films work by indirection; they work by action and movement, either internal or external, but almost always movement. Our films are more narratively driven than others, which has a lot to do with the American character and the way we look at our lives. We see ourselves and our lives as being part of a story.   42

Most of our movies have been pro the underdog, concerned with injustice, relatively anti-authority. There's usually a system—or a bureaucracy—to triumph over.   43

More often than not, American movies have been affirmative and hopeful about destiny. They're usually about individuals who control their own lives and their fate. In Europe, the system was so class-bound and steeped in tradition that there was no democratization of that process.   44

There's no prior education required to assimilate American movies or American culture. American culture is general, as opposed   45 to the specificity of Japanese or Indian culture. America has the most easily digestible culture.

Our movies seem artless. The best of them keep us interested 46 without seeming to engage our minds. The very thing that makes movies so popular here and abroad is one of the primary things that drives their critics to apoplexy, but seeming artlessness isn't necessarily mindlessness. There's a deliberate kind of artlessness in American movies that has come from a discipline or aesthetic long ago imposed by the marketplace. Our movies began as immigrants' dreams that would appeal to the dreams of other immigrants, and this aesthetic has led American films to transcend languages and cultures and communicate to every country in the world.

THE FILMMAKER'S RESPONSIBILITY

It has been suggested to some extent in this conference that I ought to 47 study my own and American filmmakers' responsibilities to the public and to the world. I realize I have responsibilities as a filmmaker, but I don't believe that they are as a moralist, a preacher, or a purveyor of values. I know it's tempting to use filmmaking as such, but utility is a poor standard to use in art. It's a standard that has been and is still used by every totalitarian state in the world.

My responsibility is to try to make good films, but "good" is a 48 subjective word. To me at any rate, "good" doesn't necessarily mean "good for us" in the narrow sense that they must elevate our spirits and send us out of the theater singing, or even that they must promote only those values that some think are worth promoting.

Good movies challenge us, they provoke us, they make us angry 49 sometimes. They present points of view we don't agree with. They force us to clarify our positions in opposition to them, and they do this best when they provide us with an experience and not a polemic.

Somebody gave the okay to pay for *One Flew Over the Cuckoo's* 50 *Nest, Driving Miss Daisy, Stand By Me, Moonstruck, Terms of Endearment*, and *Amadeus*, and despite conventional wisdom that said those films could not be successful, those decisions paid off handsomely because there are no rules. Studio executives and other financiers do exceed themselves. They take chances. They have to, and we have to hope that they'll do it more often.

What we see in movie theaters today is not a simple reflection of 51 today's economics or politics in this country but is a sense of the people who make the movies, and they vary as individuals vary. So what we really want is for this very privileged process to be in the best hands possible, but I know of no force that can regulate this except the moral climate and appetites of our society.

What we're exporting now is largely a youth culture. It's full of 52 adolescent values; it's full of adolescent rage, love, rebelliousness, and a desire to shock. If you're unhappy with their taste—and this is a free market—then an appetite has to be created for something better. How do we do that? Well, we're back to square one: the supplier or the consumer, the chicken or the egg? Let's not even ask the question; the answer is both.

Of course filmmakers ought to be encouraged toward excellence, 53 and audiences ought to be encouraged to demand it. How? That's for thinkers and social scientists to figure out. I have no idea. But if I had to play this scene out as an imaginary dialogue, I might say that you must educate the consumer first, and the best places to start are at school and at home. And then you would say that that is my job, that popular entertainment must participate in this education. And I would say, ideally, perhaps, but I do not think that will happen within a system that operates so fundamentally from an economic point of view. On an individual basis, yes, one filmmaker at a time; as an industry, no. An appetite or market will have to exist first.

That's not as bad as it sounds, because in the best of all possible 54 worlds, we do try to satisfy both needs: entertain people and be reasonably intelligent about it. It can be done, and it is done more often than you might think. It's just very difficult.

561

It's like the two Oxford dons who were sitting at the Boarshead. 55 They were playwrights, grousing because neither one of them could get produced, neither one could get performed. One turned to the other and said, "Oh, the hell with it. Let's just do what Shakespeare did—give them entertainment."

Examining the Text

1. What is Pollack's point in paragraph 8? How does *Dances With Wolves* call "into question every value that existed in traditional Westerns," and how does it reflect a change in society's values? Is *Dances With Wolves* a good example of the kind of movie that critics would say contributes to the decline in American values? Why do you think Pollack mentions it so early in his speech?

2. Pollack says there "probably hasn't been a really beautiful rake since the Shakers stopped making farm implements" (paragraph 17). What does his point say in terms of questioning whether American films are "bad"? Do you find his analogy persuasive?

3. When Pollack asserts that he'd "rather make the whole world cry than seventeen intellectuals in a classroom" (19), what is he implying about his—and other filmmakers'—motivations? Do you think most creative people feel this way?

4. Pollack describes his interest in making "films about arguments" and giving "each side a strong argument" (36). What does he mean? Do you think movies that balance two sides of an "argument" are "more interesting" than those with clear-cut "good guys" and "bad guys"?

For Group Discussion

Pollack himself does not make the kinds of graphically violent movies that critics claim have a negative influence on American society. Nonetheless, he argues that "scrupulous, ethical concern for the sanctity of human life doesn't exist in the same way [it did in the past], and that fact is reflected in the movies." As a group, list examples from current events and recent films that demonstrate this lack of concern for human life. As a class, consider whether, based on these examples, you agree with Pollack that movies only reflect the values of society and do not contribute to their creation.

Writing Suggestion

Rent and watch one or more of Pollack's films (titles other than those mentioned in the headnote include *They Shoot Horses, Don't They?*, *Three Days of the Condor*, and *The Electric Horseman*). In an essay analyze Pollack's work as a reflection of contemporary American life. What themes or messages do you discover beyond his aim to tell a good story? Does he succeed in his stated goal of presenting an "argument"?

The Politics of Moviemaking

SAUL AUSTERLITZ

Politics and power have always been fodder for the camera. From the barely veiled depiction of newspaper titan Randolph W. Hearst in Citizen Kane *to the exploration of Richard Nixon's dark scheming in* All the President's Men, *Hollywood has unabashedly looked to real life as the basis of scripted entertainment. More recently, the following* MovieMaker *article contends, political documentaries have enjoyed a renaissance. So, too, have feature films with allegorical themes related to contemporary American political life. In the article, author Saul Austerlitz explores films both direct and documentary, such as Michael Moore's* Fahrenheit 911, *and fictional, such as* Mystic River, *for references to partisan politics.*

While filmmakers like Moore are virulently anti-administration and anti-corporation, even mainstream Hollywood movies in recent years have embraced scripts which, while less overt in their tone and intended message, are still anti-establishment. The article deals mainly with films that appear to question the current administration, and especially its foreign policies. Only one film, The Passion of the Christ, counteracts the so-called New Left's near-monopoly of politically themed movies, according to the author.

Finally, the article raises the question of whether the public's apparent interest in films with a political bent represents a new direction for cinema audiences, a groundswell of opposition to current governmental policies, an angry outcry by liberal film directors and producers—or all of the above. As **you read**, *look for comments the author makes in relation to both the public's perception and filmmakers' responses to the terrorist attacks of September 11, 2001, and uncover any biases the author may have toward these impressions and events.*

Public enemy's Chuck D once famously remarked that hip-hop was   1
like street CNN, informing its listeners of what was *truly* happening in their neighborhoods, their country and around the globe. In the post-September 11th era, when the actions of politicians and the lives of faraway strangers have come to be urgent matters even for those dis-affected by, or bored with, politics, the need for an uncensored voice is greater than ever.

It is often said that art is at its most successful when politics is at   2
its most reactionary; that times of political unrest and conservative government often impel artists to do their best work. Hip-hop's role as a funnel for current affairs has largely fallen by the wayside. But in the past three years, a tidal wave of films, from studios and indies world-wide, have filled the gap.

Encompassing everything from Michael Moore's *Fahrenheit 9/11*   3
and Errol Morris' *Fog of War* to Gus Van Sant's *Elephant* and Quentin Tarantino's *Kill Bill*, there has been a recent shift toward engaging with partisan political content among moviemakers, and a willingness among moviegoers to support these films. Part of this is the rebirth of documentaries, which are unashamed to take a political slant. The other segment of this reawakening is the political content that has found its way into mainstream Hollywood moviemaking. Examples range from the overt anti-Bushism of *The Manchurian Candidate* to subtler musings on the instinct toward revenge in Clint Eastwood's *Mystic River*.

Since the astonishing "this-could-only-happen-in-a-movie" twists   4
and turns of the 2000 election, and even more so since the terrorist attacks of September 11th, the U.S. has been a country divided. With the 2004 election upon us, it is increasingly clear that the American elec-torate is segmented into two equal and increasingly opposite parts. Democrats, still enormously bitter about the election that got away (and about a president who ranks among the most radically conservative in

recent memory) have chosen the box office as a shadow ballot, a place for disgruntled liberals to vote with their wallets. *Fahrenheit 9/11* capitalized brilliantly on this, with Moore and the Weinstein brothers marketing the film in such a way that weekend box office numbers served as a stand-in election. Cultural commentators made much of the close relationship between *Fahrenheit* and Mel Gibson's *The Passion of the Christ*, both box office smashes, one for the left and one for the right. But what truly united the two films was the sense of responsibility they engendered in their base audience. Liberals didn't just *want* to see *Fahrenheit 9/11*, they *had* to see it in order to spite President Bush and prove that liberals, far from a dying breed, had the clout to turn a fairly radical antiadministration rant into a blockbuster. With the enormous success of these politically-oriented films, the stunning possibility arises: Will movies play a decisive role in determining the outcome of this year's presidential election? By the time you read this, the answer may be clear.

MOVIES: THE NEW CNN

Film's role as "The New CNN" is best illustrated by the startling surge 5 in interest in documentary films. Cinema's hold on audiences for the last century is often described as a search for escape, a desire to return to the comfort of the womb in the darkness of the movie theater. But it's clear that, today, growing numbers of politically astute filmgoers are choosing to go to the movies to be faced with a clearer version of reality than what they get from their local news. One of the major reasons film is the new CNN is because the old CNN and its competitors, Fox News, MSNBC and the network news programs, have proved so derelict in their duty. In their effort to deliver the news as speedily as possible, television news has presented a highly distorted vision of contemporary reality, one that favors mindless patriotism and quasi-overt support of the Bush administration in lieu of hard-hitting journalism. Those looking for a more carefully drawn portrait of the world have been required to turn to other sources, namely their local arthouse theaters. "I think there's much more technology now to do films, to use entertainment as a *platform for advocacy*," says Robin Bronk, editor of the political essay collection *If You Had Five Minutes with the President*. "There is an infinite number of outlets for filmmakers now to make their voices heard."

Among documentarians, two primary tacks have been taken in 6 wrestling with the issues of the moment: some, like Moore, tackle them straight on; others, like Morris, choose allegory and metaphor. Morris' 2003 doc, *The Fog of War*, is a movie-length interview with former

Secretary of Defense Robert McNamara. McNamara served in Lyndon Johnson's cabinet and was widely seen (and reviled) as the architect of Johnson's strategy for pursuing the war in Vietnam. Morris structures the film around thirteen essential tenets regarding the appropriate pursuit of war, gleaned from McNamara's musings.

Coming in the immediate aftermath of the American invasion of Iraq, *The Fog of War* was seen by many as an explicit rebuke of the Bush administration for their blatant disregard of world opinion, their willingness to bend the truth about the aims and effects of the war, and for the Vietnam-like quagmire that Iraq threatened to become. Seeing McNamara, once a titan of world affairs, admired and despised in equal measure, now searching for forgiveness, one could not help but imagine a future Morris film starring Donald Rumsfeld. 7

INCONSISTENCY AND PASSION: *FAHRENHEIT 9/11* AND *CONTROL ROOM*

Moore's *Fahrenheit* brooked no such trafficking in metaphorical ponderings. Starting at the beginning, namely election night 2000, it's a polemic, passionate and messy screed against Bush and his merry gang of adventurers. It's the anti-CNN, a collection of clips that are shocking primarily because the American public had not previously seen them. Moore is less a great moviemaker than a terrific researcher, digging out diamonds from the rough of the 24-hour news universe. To see Bush in that Florida classroom on the morning of September 11, so terrifyingly unsure of how to comport himself, or footage of American soldiers wounded in Iraq, is to realize the enormous abyss between perception and reality in contemporary politics. 8

565

Fahrenheit 9/11 is an inconsistent film, with certain segments, like that about the Saudi menace, poorly argued and reeking of reckless conspiracy-mongering. Moore, ever the isolationist defender of the working class, blames the Saudis for American troubles in language that is eerily reminiscent of the "Buy American" anti-identification with the working class, however, also allows him to see the class-based nature of the American volunteer army. When a recruit from Moore's hometown says that parts of Iraq reminded him of Flint, it speaks volumes about the experiences of the American working poor. The film finds an icon of contemporary political disillusionment in Lila Lipscomb, a conservative Michigan homemaker radicalized by the death of her son in Iraq. Her unalloyed anger at an administration that went to war under false pretenses and sacrificed her son to no purpose made Lipscomb a paragon of liberal fury. At the Democratic National 9

Convention, videos were shown between speeches of lifelong Republicans describing their motivations for leaving the GOP—a sign of the Democrats borrowing Moore's strategies of convincing swing voters that the party of moderation is their own.

Another surprising hit earlier this year, *Control Room*, directed by 10 Jehane Noujaim, tackled the Iraq war and the concomitant media coverage and grossed close to $2 million. Rather than embed with an American military unit, missing the forest for the trees, *Control Room* details the work done by Arabic-language news channel Al Jazeera. Situated in Doha, Qatar, media center of the American Central Command, Al Jazeera reporters did their utmost to deliver a fuller portrayal of the horrors of the facts considerably to deliver a heroic version of Al Jazeera (overlooking their highly skewed reporting on the Israeli-Palestinian conflict and their tasteful look away from the atrocities perpetrated by Hussein's regime). Whether this Al Jazeera is fact or fiction is debatable, but what is remarkable is the overwhelming desire on the part of the viewing public for an unsullied news source, real or otherwise. *Control Room* was a hit because of the thirst for unfiltered truth about Iraq, whatever the truth quotient of the film itself. Noujaim's film was wish fulfillment for an American populace tired of the evasions and distortions of truth, from Ari Fleischer to the New York *Times*.

NOT FAIR AND BALANCED: *OUTFOXED* AND *UNCOVERED*

Producer-Director Robert Greenwald's *Outfoxed* put the lie to the Fox 11 News Channel's claims of "fair and balanced" coverage. Detailing the channel's numerous ties to leading conservatives, and the policy memos outlining the means by which news coverage is skewed to place Republicans in the best possible light, *Outfoxed* was a damning indictment of Fox News in particular, and the cable news media in general. The prolific Greenwald has also released two other films of notable interest in recent months: a newly updated version of the 2000 election doc *Unprecedented* (directed by Joan Selker and Richard Ray Perez) and the Iraq war study *Uncovered*. *Unprecedented* is a frankly partisan accounting of Bush v. Gore detailing Republican machinations to limit the Florida recount and preserve Bush's minuscule statewide lead. *Unprecedented* also presents the surprising thesis that the Gore campaign would have benefited from calling for a statewide recount; their desire to limit the recount to Democrat-heavy counties may have cost them the election.

Another crucial subject left primarily untouched by the main- 12
stream media, and told properly by documentary filmmakers, is that of
the Arab-Americans detained by the government after September 11.
Alison Maclean and Tobias Perse's *Persons of Interest* requires only the
barest necessities to tell its story. In a stark, unfurnished room reminiscent of a prison cell, or maybe a torture chamber, a series of witnesses
appear to testify before the camera. In addition to their verbal testi-
monies, which speak of visits in the night, lengthy spans in jail, and
families without loved ones, the camera records the testimony of their
bodies. We get their anguish and confusion about what has happened
to them and what continues to happen to them. Maclean and Perse
reveal the flip side of national security's post 9/11 crackdown—its brutal impact on those innocent individuals noted as "persons of interest."
"We wanted to puncture the mendacity around the Justice Department
and the war on terror," says Perse. "They wern't even investigating
most of the people they were arresting."

MURDER AND REVENGE: *KILL BILL* AND *MYSTIC RIVER*

On the fictional side, the events of September 11, Afghanistan, and Iraq 13
were reflected through the prism of films about political maneuvering,
violence, revenge, and death. Revenge was a constant, from *Kill Bill*'s
Bride to *Mystic River*'s Jimmy to *Man on Fire*'s bitter Secret Service
agent Creasy. *Kill Bill* and *Mystic River* were both baroque fantasies of
revenge on one's sworn enemies, the murderers of one's children—
potent metaphors for the American psyche after the deaths of close to
3,000 people on September 11, 2001. Clint Eastwood's *Mystic River* presented a more complex, nuanced version of the thirst for revenge, with
Sean Penn's Jimmy deciding, with much hesitation, to kill the man he
believes murdered his daughter, only to discover that he has killed an
innocent man. *Mystic River* reflected the anxiety that the wars in
Afghanistan, and Iraq, were glorified revenge-seeking missions, where
the U.S. struck out blindly at the unseen, misunderstood enemy in the
hopes of soothing a tormented breast. Eastwood does not stint on the
anguish of loss, though; the scene of Jimmy being dragged away by a
phalanx of police officers, flailing wildly while screaming, "Is that my
daughter in there?," is among the rawest, deepest depictions of grief
ever on-screen.

The desire to fight a just war against sworn enemies, and to van- 14
quish them once and for all, was a factor in the enormous appeal of
Jackson's *Lord of the Rings* trilogy. The source material, J.R.R. Tolkien's

novel, was a refighting of World War II in elfish garb, but the film could not help but look to Afghanistan and Iraq for metaphorical resonance. The wars of Middle Earth were tinged with a naïve, boy's-magazine quality, but the trilogy's aura of evocative doom, and the gloom of a world locked in a desperate struggle for the future, resonated deeply.

EXPLORATIONS OF VIOLENCE: *ELEPHANT*

Gus Van Sant's *Elephant*, another exploration of the impulse of violence, fictionalized the events of the Columbine shootings, depicting a day in the life of what appears to be a fairly regular American high school. The Columbine connection, while obvious, overshadows the film's deeper concern, which is the eruption of violence from within the framework of mundane daily life. The protagonists echoed Dylan Klebold and Eric Harris for many, but with a little tweaking, they could just as easily have been Mohamed Atta and Zacarias Moussaoui— seemingly normal young men who secretly sought revenge on a world that rendered them deeply angry. Cultural critics have often remarked that dreadful events like the Holocaust or the bombing of Hiroshima and Nagasaki cannot be depicted artistically in a head-on fashion; their horrors are too deep to be adequately represented.

The events of September 11 are impossible to be shown in such a fashion as well, for the above reasons as well as the fact that we have all already seen them depicted as such. To have seen the second tower of the World Trade Center collapse live on television, and to know that one has just witnessed the death of thousands of people is a sensation too overpowering to ever be recreated no matter how acute the film wizardry. Knowing this, *Elephant* does not attempt to do so, but Van Sant powerfully summons the ordinariness of workaday American life in order to utterly shatter it beyond repair.

The image of a world permanently altered is a subtext of Martin Scorsese's historical epic *Gangs of New York*. The bitter gang warfare between the Nativists, led by Daniel Day-Lewis's flag-covered Bill the Butcher, and the Dead Rabbits, led by Leonardo DiCaprio's Amsterdam Vallon. Amsterdam, another revenge-seeker (Bill had killed his father some years prior) leads his gang into a final showdown with the Nativists, and the battle is raging at full blast when, unexpectedly, history erupts. The draft riot of 1863, pitting Confederate-tilting New Yorkers against the fatcats seeking to draft them for Union cannon fodder, and against the African Americans they irrationally blame for the outbreak of war, breakout, and the petty gang warfare is place permanently on hold. *Gangs of New York* powerfully summons the sense of personal concerns subsumed by the tidal wave of history. In the film's unforgettable closing image, Amsterdam, standing in a small cemetery across the water from Manhattan, remarks that "For the rest of time, it would be like no one even knew we were here." Over his dialogue, Scorsese places a fast-forward history of New York, as reflected in its skyline—the buildings growing progressively higher until the World Trade Center emerges as its peak, then the towers disappearing, while the cemetery is simultaneously covered in weeds and growth until it, too, vanishes. This image is simultaneously enormously consoling and powerful, and deeply saddening; it is a comfort to know that even the most jagged wounds are eventually healed by the passage of time and the amnesiac qualities of history, but it is also distressing beyond words to conceive of a time when the struggles and losses that defined all our lives will be forgotten beyond recall.

ISOLATIONIST ANXIETY: *THE VILLAGE*

Contemporary politics are also about fear—fear of terrorism, fear of what 18 the next day will bring, fear-mongering by savvy politicians. M. Night Shyamalan has always been a moviemaker whose primary concerns are fear and death, so it comes as little surprise that *The Village* is a remarkably contemporary evocation of the climate of isolationist anxiety. His film concerns a small enclave of individuals living in an isolated hamlet surrounded by foreboding woods. The villagers are deathly afraid of the creatures that lurk just outside the boundaries of their community, and have incorporated rules to govern their interaction with them. They fervently believe that if only they can separate themselves fully from the rest of the world, no harm can befall them—a comfortingly false belief similar to that of many Americans, liberal and conservative, after September 11.

Michael Koresky, an editor at *Film Comment*, points out "What 19 *Fahrenheit 9/11* proved was that the direct address with politics in film is the only through-road to the American consciousness. Shyamalan's *The Village* is arguably a more complex, more highly allegorical investigation of isolationism and social complacency in the contemporary U.S., and its outright rejection proved that cloaking politics in metaphor sadly no longer suffices in our CNN and Fox News 'reality' TV-burdened, barely literate climate."

CONTEMPORARY POLITICS: *THE MANCHURIAN CANDIDATE*

Demme's remake of the 1964 classic *The Manchurian Candidate* takes on 20 the contemporary political climate through the prism of politics itself.

As in the original, a powerful, domineering mother pushes her weakling son forward as a vice-presidential candidate for her own nefarious purposes. Where the original concerned the Soviet menace and presented the spectacle of a McCarthyesque, anti-Communist hatemonger revealed to be a Communist shill himself, the 2004 version features a shadowy multinational corporation, Manchurian Global.

Like a through-the-looking-glass version of Halliburton, Man- 21
churian looks to secretly commandeer the wheel of American political discourse, and attempts to do so via a secretly controlled vice-presidential candidate. Once elected, he will be, as one wag points out in the film, "The first bought and paid for vice president of the United States." Using the televisions in practically every scene as a contemporary Greek chorus, *The Manchurian Candidate* presents the specter of a world one step beyond ours, with terrorist attacks a weekly affair, and a government dedicated to fighting shadowy wars across the globe. Liev Schreiber's politician patsy contains echoes of George W. Bush (third-generation political scion, lightweight tool of his political masters) and Dick Cheney (that bought-and-paid-for comment deliberately touches on fears of Cheney's ongoing relationship with the defense gaint Halliburton). Demme's film is resolutely fictional, but freed from the requirement of truth-telling. *The Manchurian Candidate* reaches for deeper truths about the Bush administration's penchant for fear-mongering as a means of maintaining the reins of political discourse.

THE MOVIE THEATER AS CULTURAL MIRROR

In the past four years, politics have moved significantly closer to home. 22
The ability of many Americans to thoroughly tune out politics as irrelevant to their daily existence has evaporated, and this new reality has seeped into the world of cinema as well. A movie, being a collective endeavor, is often an expression of shared hopes and worries and of ideas bubbling underneath the surface of contemporary life. Films have long served as a barometer of American life, reflecting the complex, tangled web of fears and desires angling for superiority. The 2000 election, the events of September 11 and their aftermath, the invasions of Afghanistan and Iraq, and the actions of the current administration have all found their way onto American movie screens in coded, allusive form, as well as through factual documentation. Increasingly, Americans are looking to moviemakers for answers and for direction, in a manner reminiscent of the impact of counterculture films like *Easy Rider* and *Hearts and Minds* on the Vietnam generation. "I do think there's something about the way people are engaging with these films," says Perse. "They want to interact with these films."

The movie theater has become the mirror in which Americans can truly see themselves. What they see, unsurprisingly, is far from simple. Much of the passionate advocacy found in recent films has been in anticipation of the upcoming presidential election, generally considered by most observers to be the most important (and bitterly fought) since 1968. The outcome of that election will place these films into clearer focus, and establish them as an expression of the groundswell of populist opposition to the Bush administration, and to the war in Iraq, or as an ultimately futile and unrepresentative explosion of liberal bitterness. Only time—and the ballot box—will tell.

Examining the Text

1. What is the author saying about the role film is playing in the American public's desire for news? Do you agree with the author's contention about this new "public information" role of movies? In your opinion, can a given movie, which has a relatively long gestation period, truly provide a meaningful way of analyzing current events compared to radio, newspapers, television, and even the Web?

2. The article states that "films have long served as a barometer of American life. . ." What is meant by that statement? When they depict actual events, do films focus more on developing the film's story more than on telling the "truth," in your opinion? Do you believe films do this to a greater or lesser degree than other media?

3. In what ways does the author suggest that the September 11, 2001, terrorist attacks on New York and Washington DC have influenced filmmakers and people's interest in film? Do you agree with the author's views on this issue? Do you believe that the author is correct in asserting that for many mainstream audience members, attending movies is no longer about "a search for escape. . ." (paragraph 5)?

4. What does the author mean when he claims that documentaries are proving successful because cable and TV news, especially MSNBC, CNN, and Fox present a "highly distorted vision of contemporary reality" and are "derelict in their duty"? Do you agree that most television news is distorted; if so, does this have to do with the speed at which journalists and producers must operate, as Austerlitz suggests? What other theories might you posit about distortion in the news?

5. *Thinking rhetorically*: In several places the author uses the following phrases as rhetorical devices: *it is often said* (paragraph 2); *is often described as* (5); *it's clear that* (5); *was seen by many* (7). How would you characterize such writing, and what do you think is the author's purpose in using this technique? Do you find it effective or evasive, and why?

For Group Discussion

Among your group, discuss how many of you have personally sought out films as a way to help answer questions you have about events of major importance (the war in Iraq, corporate scandals, the presidential election, the media). Did you attend a film to order to complete your understanding or to have your already existing view reinforced by the filmmaker? If the latter, do you think that is a new role for film writers, directors, and producers? Would you make a point of seeing a film that you knew from advanced publicity was contradictory to your view on an issue?

Writing Suggestion

You've just received a commission to write a prose treatment for a new movie about your favorite, underreported political issue. Your film could focus on animal rights, prayer in schools, Third World aid, bicycle paths, or any other subject near and dear to your heart. Your 500-word treatment has to be detailed enough to convince skeptics that the issue is important and that it will be visually suited to film and win financial backing. Your text should be full of passion for your subject, factually accurate and compelling, yet should explore why you think your subject has not been given a fair airing by the media previously.

Raising the Dead: Unearthing the Nonliterary Origins of Zombie Cinema

KYLE BISHOP

The word zombie, *in everyday parlance, evokes a sense of lethargic dullness, as in, "I stayed up 'til three a.m. working on my English essay, and now I feel like a zombie." This connotation, whether we are aware of it or not, derives from its association with a particular brand of movie character: the half-decayed corpse ponderously and mindlessly walking with arms outstretched, seeking human victims to dismember and devour. Zombies shambled into mainstream American popular culture relatively recently, having first been introduced in a 1929 book about life in Haiti, including a tangential reference to a voodoo death cult that is in fact rare on Haiti. Nevertheless, that book's representation of zombies touched a popular nerve in the U.S. and inspired a string of movies featuring animated corpses with a hunger for human flesh, leading up to the definitive zombie flick: George Romero's 1968* Night of the Living Dead. *This film, with its groundbreakingly gory special effects and implied critiques of U.S. policy in the Vietnam War, became the template for the modern zombie movie, which is the subject of genre critic Kyle Bishop's analysis in the following essay.*

As **you read,** *observe the theoretical lenses through which Bishop takes an in-depth look at the rise of the zombie as an archetypal figure in contemporary culture. In particular, note the way in which he speculates about* *the complex appeals of this character, attempting to explain through several approaches, especially the Freudian psychological, the pervasiveness of zombies in modern film, video games, and so forth. Also, pay attention to your own initial preconceptions about certain theories, such as Freud's notions regarding psychosexual development in humans. Although certain readers might have acquired the notion that Freud's concepts are too simplistic in their orientation ("He thinks everything is about sex!" a student in a basic writing class exclaimed recently), in fact there is much to value within the writings of the father of modern psychology. Bishop takes care to present one of Freud's relevant subtheories—that of The Uncanny—in a palatable and comprehensible way here.*

The year 2004 saw the theatrical release of three major zombie movies: 1
Resident Evil: Apocalypse, a sequel to a movie based on a video game; *Dawn of the Dead*, a remake of a cult classic from the 1970s; and *Shaun of the Dead*, a sometimes funny, sometimes terrifying re-visioning of an established genre. In addition, dozens of low-budget zombie movies were released directly to video or appeared as made-for-television movies.[1] Zombie cinema is clearly as popular today as it was fifty years ago, but is the genre socially relevant beyond being simply a successful entertainment venture?[2] Whereas many horror films may be easily dismissed as mindless entertainment or B-reel schlock, the zombie film retains its ability to make audiences think while they shriek. But to understand this much-maligned genre, one must consider its origins and the essential nature of its visual impact.

Although creatures such as vampires and reanimated corpses   2
often have been realized by literary means, the traditional zombie story has no direct antecedent in novels or short fiction. In fact, zombies did not really see the light of day until filmmakers began to dig them out of their graves in the 1930s. The "classic" zombie horror film, which is the focus of this investigation, was pioneered by George A. Romero in the late 1960s and features a veritable plague of reanimated corpses that attack and slaughter the living. The established generic conventions of such movies are relatively simple and remarkably consistent: Ordinary characters in ordinary places are confronted with overwhelmingly extraordinary challenges, namely the unexpected appearance of an aggressive horde of flesh-eating ghouls. Zombie cinema is essentially a macabre romp—a live-action comic book brought to the big screen both to horrify and entertain.

Much has already been written concerning the more esoteric social   3
commentary offered by zombie movies, but few critics have investigated the unusual origins of these monsters and their horrific stories.[3]

Although the cinematic popularity of zombies has certainly made the move to video games and graphic novels, the zombie remains a primarily nonliterary phenomenon.[4] Establishing the folkloric origins of the zombie creature itself will explain this rather singular fact and illustrates its evolution into the more recognizable cinematic horror show developed by Romero. The zombie genre does not exist prior to the film age because of its essentially visual nature; zombies do not think or speak—they simply act, relying on purely physical manifestations of terror. This unique embodiment of horror recalls Sigmund Freud's concept of the uncanny, a phenomenon that finds itself better suited to filmic representations rather than prose renditions.

PREPARING THE POTION: EXHUMING THE VODOUN ZOMBIE[5]

Most classic monsters—from ghosts to vampires to werewolves—have   4
their origins in folklore, and the zombie is no exception. However, whereas those other creatures have cross-cultural mythologies, the zombie remains a purely American monster, born from Vodoun magic and religion. In addition, creatures such as Dracula passed through a literary tradition on their way to the silver screen, but the zombie did not. Zombie scholar Peter Dendle illustrates this point: Although possessing certain thematic characteristics that tie it to the traditions of classical horror, the zombie is "the only creature to pass directly from folklore to the screen, without first having an established literary tradition" (Dendle 2001, 2–3). This singularity makes an investigation of the anthropological roots of the zombie an essential part of understanding the film genre.

According to anthropologist Wade Davis, the modern English   5
word zombie most likely derives from the Kimbundu term nzumbe, which means "ghost" or "spirit of a dead person" (Davis 1985, xii). This concept was brought from Africa to Haiti with the slave trade and was translated into the Creole zobi, which was modernized to zombie, a word with a number of accepted meanings, from a mindless automaton to an exotic mixed drink. As far as the traditional cinematic monster is concerned, however, the designation of zombie is reserved for the cannibalistic walking dead: people brought back to life either to serve or to devour the human race. This definition is tied to the Vodoun religion, a mystical practice that supposedly harbors the magic required to strike people down to a death-like state and revive them later from the grave to become virtually mindless servants—the most subordinate of slaves (Davis 1985, 42). But, in reality, zombification is the result of pharmacology, the careful administration of powerful neurotoxins.

Davis is the world's leading authority on the zombification ritual, 6 and as a Harvard University ethnobotanist, he traveled to Haiti in 1985 in search of exotic new medicinal drugs. Davis recorded his weird experiences and botanical research in *The Serpent and the Rainbow*.[6] According to this primarily anthropological text, a limited number of powerful and unorthodox Vodoun priests, called bokors, possess a keen knowledge of natural drugs and sedatives and have created a "zombie powder"—called coup poudre—that renders its victims clinically dead (Davis 1985, 90). Davis's interest in the drug was purely scientific at first, but he soon realized that zombies are real creatures within the Vodoun religion. The method of creating such a dangerous substance is naturally a closely guarded secret, controlled by the secret societies of Haiti (Davis 1985, 260).

Those well-versed in the administration of this powder could con- 7 ceivably create the illusion of raising the dead and, thus, give the zombie legend credibility. The most potent poison included in the coup poudre comes from a specific kind of puffer fish, a nerve agent called tetradotoxin (Davis 1985, 134). This drug "induces a state of profound paralysis, marked by complete immobility during which time the border between life and death is not at all certain, even to trained physicians" (Davis 1985, 142). All major life functions are paralyzed for an extended period, and those suffering from the effects of the drug run the real risk of being buried alive.[7] If the powder is too strong or mixed incorrectly, the victim might die immediately—or suffocate slowly in the coffin (Davis 1985, 226). Unfortunately, even those victims lucky enough to be rescued from the grave inevitably suffer brain damage from the lack of oxygen; they are understandably sluggish and dimwitted (Davis 1985, 21).

575

These superstitious fears of the walking dead are not limited to 8 Haiti, however; most cultures share a strong psychological response to the concept of death. Bodies of dead friends and family are burned, buried, walled up, or even eaten, but the result is the same: The corpses are hidden from sight and mind. Although statues, portraits, and photographs are treasured as valued reminders of those now dead, no one really wants to see the face of a loved one slowly rot or be reminded of the brutal realities of mortality; such a confrontation would be frightening, to say the least. In psychoanalytical terms, Freud identifies this fear of the once familiar as the *unheimlich*, a complex term that literally means "unhomely" or "un-homey" but is usually translated as "the uncanny." This concept is key to understanding the ability of the zombie to instill fear: Those who should be dead and safely laid to rest have bucked the natural order of things and have returned from the grave.

The anthropological origins of the zombie are important to rec- 9 ognize, but what makes zombie narratives unique to cinema are not the shambling foes themselves but rather the stories they tell. Zombie folklore and Vodoun traditions clearly set the stage for the zombie horror movie as it is known and recognized today; poisoning, premature burial, loss of cognition, slavery, the return of the dead, and death itself are all key features of zombie cinema. But the classic zombie movie owes its unique existence to George A. Romero, who Dendle calls the "Shakespeare of zombie cinema" (Dendle 2001, 121). Romero took a rather insipid, two-dimensional creature, married it to an established apocalyptic storyline, and invented an entirely new genre.

ADMINISTERING THE POWDER: CREATING THE MODERN ZOMBIE

Unlike the ancient traditions of the vampire and werewolf, the zombie did not enter Western consciousness until around the turn of the twentieth century. According to Dendle, most Americans were only vaguely aware of Haitian Voudo and zombie lore from nineteenth-century Caribbean travel literature (Dendle 2001, 2). Civilized society probably dismissed such concepts as remote superstitions and pagan fantasies until the publication of William Seabrook's travel book *The Magic Island* in 1929, which brought the romantic exoticism—and possible reality— of the zombie to the attention of mainstream audiences (Dendle 2001, 2). Shortly thereafter in 1932, Kenneth Webb produced a play called *Zombie in New York City*, and "the creature fell irrevocably under the auspices of the entertainment industry" (Dendle 2001, 2). 10

Hollywood quickly recognized the marketability of the zombie, with the first true zombie movie arriving the same year as Webb's play: Victor Halperin's *White Zombie* (1932). Set in Haiti, Vodou is the central feature of the film, although the tone and style are obviously influenced by Tod Browning's *Dracula* (1931). As the white heroes travel across the countryside at night, their coach driver explains the mysterious figures they pass as "the living dead. Corpses taken from their graves and made to work in the sugar mills" (Halperin 1932). These zombies are slow, dimwitted, and lumbering—but not completely mindless; they can follow commands and perform simple tasks. They are not monsters but rather hypnotized slaves who are still alive and can be saved with the death of the Vodoun priest who enslaved them. The true villain in *White Zombie* is Bela Lugosi's mad bokor Murder Legendre, not the pitiful zombies themselves. 11

A number of similar, if unremarkable, zombie films were made over the next few years—for example, *Revolt of the Zombies* (1936), *King of the Zombies* (1941), and *I Walked with a Zombie* (1943)—but their rather prosaic view of the undead would change gradually over the next few decades with the help of EC Comics. The 1940s and '50s saw a dramatic upswing in all horror media, most notably the publication of *Tales from the Crypt* in 12

1950. According to book columnist and comic aficionado Digby Diehl, "Horror comics of the 1950s appealed to teens and young adults who were trying to cope with the aftermath of even greater terrors—Nazi death camps and the explosion of the atomic bombs at Hiroshima and Nagasaki" (Diehl 1996, 28). Terror had become a tangible part of daily life, and these early graphic novels brazenly presented images of rotting corpses, stumbling zombies, and gory violence. Film scholar Paul Wells claims the young Romero would have been directly influenced by such comics (Wells 2002, 82), for a predominately visual narrative format can be seen in his zombie movies, in which the action is presented through a series of carefully framed and largely silent images. Romero confirms this connection himself in a documentary by Roy Frumke, referring to the filming of *Dawn of the Dead* (1978) as "making a comic book."

Romero was likely influenced by popular horror films of the 1950s as well, especially those featuring end-of-the-world scenarios. According to Frumke, Romero's earliest film influence was Christian Nyby's *The Thing from Another World* (1951). This science fiction movie, based on the short story "Who Goes There?" by John W. Campbell, Jr., features a small group of isolated survivors who must fight off a mysterious foe that can take any form and exists only to kill. 13

Film scholar Robin Wood offers another connection, claiming the most obvious antecedent to Romero's zombies to be the pod-people in Don Siegel's *Invasion of the Body Snatchers* (1956), based on Jack Finney's 1955 novel (Ward 2000, 126). This unsettling story posits another view of the apocalypse, in which one's best friends and family members become threatening monsters. The film's ending departs from that of the novel, clearly illustrating the paranoia rampant in cold war America. Horror expert Stephen King writes how critics read Siegel's film as an allegory about "the witch-hunt atmosphere that accompanied the McCarthy hearings," although Siegel claimed it was really about the "Red Menace" itself (King 1981, 308). Either way, fear of the Other was clearly rampant on both sides of the political spectrum. 14

Romero established and codified the zombie horror genre in 1968 with *Night of the Living Dead*. The screenplay was based on Romero's own short story "Night of Anubis," a tale of isolation and supernatural peril that borrowed heavily from Richard Matheson's 1954 novella *I Am Legend* (Martin). Matheson's story features hordes of vampires who rampantly infect and replace the world's population. Richard Neville is essentially the last man on earth, and he must garrison himself inside his home each night to escape the hungry fangs of the vampiric infestation. During his struggle to survive, Neville must fortify his house, scavenge for food and supplies, and kill the monsters his friends and family have become. All of these fundamental plot elements are found in Romero's series of zombie movies and have become firm protocols of the genre. 15

The situation faced by Matheson's Neville is also seen in Alfred   16
Hitchcock's *The Birds* (1963), based on the 1952 short story by Daphne
du Maurier. Film scholar R. H. W. Dillard considers this film the artistic
predecessor to Romero's *Night*, pointing out how "in both films, a
group of people are besieged by an apparently harmless and ordinary
world gone berserk, struggle to defend themselves against the danger,
and struggle to maintain their rationality and their values at the same
time" (Dillard 1987, 26). *The Birds* explicitly presents the idea of the
apocalypse; in fact, the Bodega Bay town drunk warns the protagonists
that it is the "end of the world." The birds are an unstoppable collective, and the movie's heroes must board themselves up in a house
against their relentless onslaught.

The essential motifs and tropes of the classic zombie movie   17
have some thematic and stylistic roots in Haitian travel narratives
and the zombie films of the 1930s and '40s, specifically the exoticism
of Vodoun zombie folklore, and early horror and science fiction cinema, particularly the end-of-the-world scenario. In addition, the
paranoia narratives of the cold war 1950s and '60s would have given
Romero some core ideas about his general plot structure, but it was
his own imagination and invention that united the zombie legend
with these popular stories of the primal struggle for survival.
Although such movies as *White Zombie* were first, Dendle points out
that "Romero liberated the zombie from the shackles of a master, and
invested his zombies not with a function . . . but rather a drive"
(Dendle 2001, 6). With the creation of *Night of the Living Dead*,
Romero decisively established the structure of the classical zombie
movie, and many directors have since followed his lead and con-
formed to the criteria of the new genre.

578

PERFORMING THE RITUAL: EXPLAINING ZOMBIES' CINEMATIC SINGULARITY

Zombies do not exist in a vacuum, nor did they spring forth fully   18
grown from the head of Romero. In addition to being derived from
mythology, legend, and the imagination, zombies also have close ties to
other, more literary monsters. They belong to a diverse class of creatures that cross the metaphysical line between life and death, where a
strong sense of the uncanny inspires unease and fear. But whereas
ghosts, vampires, and golems have been a part of storytelling for thousands of years, the zombie is a relatively modern invention. Their lack
of emotional depth, their inability to express or act on human desires,
and their primarily visual nature make zombies ill-suited for the written word; zombies thrive best on screen.

Freud defines the abstract concept of the uncanny as "that species   19
of the frightening that goes back to what was once well-known and had
long been familiar" (Freud 2003, 124). He further points out how "this
uncanny element is actually nothing new or strange, but something . . .
estranged from [the psyche] only through being repressed" (Freud 2003,
147). The true manifestation of this fear occurs, therefore, when a
repressed familiarity (such as death) returns in a disturbing, physical
way (such as a corpse); the familiar (*heimlich*) becomes the unfamiliar or
uncanny (*unheimlich*) (Freud 2003, 148). Of course, this concept applies
to monsters other than zombies as well. As Dillard points out, "the idea
of the dead's return to a kind of life is no new idea; it is present in all the
ancient tales of vampires and ghouls and zombies, and it has been no
stranger to films. . . . All of these tales and films spring from that ancient
fear of the dead" (Dillard 1987, 20-21). Dead bodies are not only a breed-
ing ground for disease but also a reminder to the living of their own
mortality. For such reasons, creatures that apparently have overcome
the debilitating effects of the grave are treated with revulsion and fear—
especially when said creatures are hostile, violent, and ambulatory.

Freud also claims that ". . . to many people the acme of the   20
uncanny is represented by anything to do with death, dead bodies,
revenants, spirits and ghosts" (Freud 2003, 148). Therefore, it is no surprise that those supernatural creatures able to defy the powers of death
are usually at the heart of horror narratives and stories. Perhaps the
oldest campfire tale is the ghost story: What is more uncanny than
someone returning from the grave to wreak havoc on the living?
Ghosts have a firmly established tradition, both orally and literarily,
from Homer to Dante to Shakespeare to Dickens. But ghosts are merely
spirits, consciousnesses that lack physical form; zombies belong to a
much more specific phylum: the corporeal monster. Such unnatural
terrors include vampires (demons who constantly cheat death by prey-
ing on the living), golems (unnatural creatures reassembled and
brought back to life through the means of science), and zombies (mindless automatons fueled by purely animalistic passions).[8]

However, when one considers the literary origins of these beasts   21
(specifically in novels and short fiction), the zombie is virtually missing in action. Why are vampires and other supernatural creatures
prevalent in horror stories and gothic literature but not the traditional
zombie?

It is the essentially human behavior that explains the success of   22
such fiends in nineteenth-century literature, and the vampire is the
most prolific of these. Although undead, Bram Stoker's archetypical
Count acts as though still alive, using his immortality to pursue rather
carnal desires. Dracula is mysterious, cunning, and seductive, using
his piercing stare and eloquent tongue to beguile young women and

readers alike. He appears both attractive and familiar by wearing the guise of youth and vitality, but Dracula is fundamentally an uncanny symbol of mortality. Not only is he decidedly inhuman—he lacks a reflection, which is regarded as a manifestation of the soul (Stoker 1987, 31)—he also represents the reality of death itself with his drinking of innocent blood, his propensity to murder women and small children, and his habit of sleeping in the grave.

Similarly, Victor Frankenstein's intriguing monster possesses essentially human qualities that make him such a complex literary character; he thinks and feels and speaks with great passion. Contrary to most screen adaptations, Frankenstein's creature is not frightening by himself—he is in fact quite sympathetic and humane. His unnatural state makes him essentially uncanny: He is a collection of dead body parts and stitchery, a creature brought back to life through science, not the supernatural. However, although Dracula and Frankenstein's monster are both fine examples of the uncanny, neither of these classic monsters is technically a zombie; a vampire lives a conscious, basically human existence, and Frankenstein's creature is flesh made living and mortal once more. 23

In contrast to these monsters, the zombie is completely and thoroughly dead—it is essentially a walking corpse.[9] Zombies are not uncanny because of their humanistic qualities; they are uncanny because they are, in essence, a grotesque metaphor for humanity itself. Like the vampire, the zombie rises from the grave to feed off the living. Like the golem, the zombie has the form of someone familiar, yet monstrous. But the zombie is a much different creature from these established monsters: It does not think or act on reasonable motives— it is purely a creature of blind instinct. The zombie does not recognize individuals or discriminate in its quarry. Zombies have no speech or consciousness—they do not talk to their victims or speculate about their existence; they are essentially superficial, two-dimensional creatures.[10] 24

Because zombies do not speak, all of their intentions and activities are manifested solely through physical action. In other words, because of this sensual limitation, zombies must be watched. Their primary actions are visceral and violent: They claw, rend, smash, and gnaw. In addition, post-1960s zombie movies are most noteworthy not for violence or horror but for the gore (Dendle 2001, 6). Decapitations, disembowelings, and acts of cannibalism are particularly effective on the screen, especially if the audience does not have time to look away. Moreover, the recognition of former heroes as dangerous zombies realizes an uncanny effect, eliciting an instantaneous shock on the part of the film characters and the audience members alike. 25

Of course, shocking images can be conveyed quite effectively in   26
writing as well. In Stoker's *Dracula*, the somewhat feckless Jonathan
Harker methodically documents a horrific confrontation with the Count:

> I raised the lid, and laid it back against the well; and then I saw something
> which filled my very soul with horror. There lay the Count, but looking as if
> his youth had been half renewed, for the white hair and moustache were
> changed to dark iron-grey; the cheeks were fuller, and the white skin
> seemed ruby-red underneath; the mouth was redder than ever, for on the
> lips were gouts of fresh blood, which trickled from the corners of the mouth
> and ran over the chin and neck. Even the deep, burning eyes seemed set
> amongst swollen flesh, for the lids and pouches underneath were bloated.
> It seemed as if the whole awful creature were simply gorged with blood; he
> lay like a filthy leech, exhausted with his repletion. (Stoker, 1987, 53)

Stoker presents quite a visage, but the diachronic nature of prose   27
forces him to describe one aspect of the Count at a time. This gradual,
paratactic unfolding of visual detail must necessarily diminish the ultimate shock; it takes time for the audience to read it. Because humans
process visual images synchronically, literary texts present an unrealistic form of perception. The cinematic representation is much closer to
reality, showing the entire view simultaneously.

581

Aspects of the film zombie may be recognizable in other classic   28
monsters, but no traditionally literary tale conforms to the genre as it has
been so firmly established by Romero. Although they were once human,
zombies have no real connection to humanity aside from their physical
form; they are the ultimate foreign Other. They do not think, speak, or act
on passionate or conscious desires as do the monsters found in novels or
short fiction—a zombie's essentially silent and shallow nature makes it a
fundamentally visual creature instead. The primitive characteristics of
these ghouls make them ideal cinematic monsters.

RAISING THE DEAD: UNDERSTANDING THE ROMERO FORMULA

The classic zombie story pioneered by Romero, and recognized in so   29
many horror movies since, has a number of specific characteristics
that distinguish it from other tales of the supernatural. Zombie
movies are always set at the apparent end of the world, where devastating events have rendered the human race all but helpless. Yet, the
primary details in Romero's films are in essence bland and ordinary,
implying that such extraordinary events could happen to anyone,
anywhere, at any time. Zombies confront audiences with stark horror

and graphic violence, using the seemingly familiar to present the most unnatural and frightening. A detailed look at the prototypical zombie film—*Night of the Living Dead*—will best illustrate these defining cinematic features and help show the limitations of print.

Night of the Living Dead is presented on a very pessimistic stage: 30 that of the apocalypse. A strange phenomenon overcomes society, resulting in a literal hell on earth where the dead walk and no one is safe. A space probe has returned from Venus, bearing some kind of unknown radiation. For some unexplained reason, this extraterrestrial fallout causes all recently dead humans to rise and attack the living— no Vodoun rituals here. The ghouls feed on human flesh in blatant disregard of society's cannibalism taboo, and those thus killed are infected as if by a blood-borne virus and soon rise themselves, assuming there is enough flesh remaining for the corpse to become mobile. The dead are mechanical juggernauts, and those left struggling to survive are forced to adopt a much more primordial stance—it is kill or be killed, and average folks are quickly transformed into desperate vigilantes.

Society's infrastructure begins to break down, especially those 31 systems associated with the government and technology. Law enforcement is depicted as incompetent and backwater (the local sheriff is a stereotyped yokel with a "shoot first" attitude), so people must fend for themselves instead. The media do what they can, broadcasting tidbits of helpful information and advice by way of radio and television, but the outlook is fundamentally grim: Hide if you can, fight if you have to. In the end, the rigid structure of society proves little help; human survivors are left to their own devices with no real hope of rescue or support. Motley groups are forced into hiding, holing up in safe houses of some kind where they barricade themselves and wait in vain for the trouble to pass.

Of course, such a scenario is not necessarily limited to zombie 32 movies: Slasher films and alien-invasion pics often have a similar modus operandi. However, whereas those movies feature either an unrealistic cast of vivacious eye candy, computer-savvy geniuses, or stylized superheroes, zombie cinema pursues the hapless adventures of bland, ordinary (*heimlich*) citizens.[11] As *Night* opens, a rather plain, average young woman and her equally pedestrian brother are traveling to visit the grave of their father in rural Pennsylvania. While they are paying their respects and praying at the gravesite, an innocuous gentleman can be seen shuffling across the background of the frame. Johnny begins to tease his sister about her childish fear of cemeteries, and he uses the passing stranger to feed the fire: "They're coming to get you, Barbara!" he taunts, forcing his sister's disgusted retreat. As Barbara embarrassingly approaches the man to apologize, the unthinkable happens—he is out to get her! Although the zombie looks like a normal human being (albeit a bit pasty), he attacks Barbara with wanton savagery and kills her ill-fated brother when Johnny tries to intervene.

In the grand tradition of most horror films, Barbara runs away, 33 stumbling and tripping her way to the car. The zombie begins its methodical, if rather slow, pursuit, its every movement highlighted by lightning flashes and dramatic camera angles. Although she makes it to the car, Barbara is thwarted in her escape: The keys are still in Johnny's pocket. Another footrace ensues, and Barbara makes it to the relative safety of a farmhouse. Granted, the former occupants are already dead and partially eaten, but at least her friend from the cemetery is locked outside. Enter Ben, another survivor who has come to the farmhouse in search of refuge and hopefully some gasoline for his truck. At this point, the zombie film establishes another of its defining characteristics: hiding out.

The literal *heimlich* nature of the house quickly becomes something 34 far more *unheimlich*. The farmhouse symbolizes the comforting idea that one's home is a place of security, but this place does not belong to either Barbara or Ben—it is a foreign, unfamiliar environment, and they are indeed strangers in a strange land. Barbara unsettlingly discovers the masticated corpses of the house's former occupants, and Ben must defend her from some zombies that have likewise broken in. Out of desperate necessity, Ben immediately begins a radical home renovation, quickly converting the farmhouse into a fortress. He incapacitates the zombies, tosses the bodies outside, and starts boarding up the doors and windows. Barbara can do little more than sit and stare, bemoaning the loss of her brother in a catatonic state. Although the home continues to possess its physical sense of security, it has lost its power to provide any psychological comfort.

583

That the seemingly harmless and ordinary would prove to be 35 so life threatening is one of the fundamental precepts of the zombie formula. In addition to the slow-moving ghouls and the common farmhouse, the film's protagonists never become anything spectacular— Barbara is a simple girl, traumatized by the brutal slaying of her brother; Ben is a workaday "everyman"; and the Coopers, soon found hiding in the cellar, are an average middle-class family. This link to normalcy is emphasized by Dillard, who describes the essentially mundane nature of *Night* as "the story of everyday people in an ordinary landscape, played by everyday people who are, for the most part, from that ordinary locale" (Dillard 1987, 20). In his afterword to the graphic novel *Miles Behind Us*, a zombie story told in another primarily visual medium, Simon Pegg points out that the protagonists of zombie movies are not superheroes or professional monster slayers such as Van Helsing—they are common, average folk forced to "step up" and defend themselves.

However, the ordinary by itself is not threatening—it also needs 36
to be rendered as the fundamentally unfamiliar. In his introduction to
Horror Film Reader, James Ursini writes, "Horror is based on recognizing in the unfamiliar something familiar, something attractive even as
it is repulsive . . . . The best horror films are those that evoke that feeling of the uncanny in us most strongly" (Ursini 2000, 5). Ursini refers
here to Freud's sense of the uncanny as something that has been
repressed (Ursini 2000, 148). This makes the "familiar unfamiliar" (the
heimlich unheimlich) even more terrifying, for the familiar and recognizable are wrought into the foreign and uncanny. This perspective on the
monster is most apropos the zombie movie, in which the threat is not
only manifested as a hostile undead human but likely a hostile undead
human the victim recognizes as a former intimate.

The physical form of the zombie is its most striking and frighten- 37
ing aspect: It was once—quite recently—a living person. The one-time
protagonists of the movie become its eventual antagonists; thus, the
characters cannot fully trust each other. As Dillard points out, "The living people are dangerous to each other . . . because they are potentially
living dead should they die" (Dillard 1987, 22). Night introduces its
audience to a number of diverse characters, but these so-called heroes,
when infected, rapidly become the most savage and threatening of villains. This stark manifestation of the uncanny is chillingly illustrated
when poor Johnny returns near the end of the picture as a zombie, "still
wearing his driving gloves and clutching for his sister with the idiotic,
implacable single-mindedness of the hungry dead" (King 1981, 134).
His deceptive familiarity is what ultimately leads Barbara to her
doom—she hesitates at the sight of her brother, failing to recognize the
dangers of his zombification until it is too late.

This terrifying prospect is shown even more graphically when the 38
young Karen Cooper feasts on her own parents. As the battle with the
swarming zombies rages upstairs, Karen dies from a zombie bite and
succumbs to the effects of the radiation. She then gnaws hungrily on
her dead father's arm and brutally attacks her mother with a trowel.
Helen Cooper does little more than allow herself to be butchered;
shock at seeing her daughter turned into a zombie and a binding sense
of love and compassion render her impotent. When Ben eventually
retreats to the perceived safety of the cellar, he is forced to kill the
zombie versions of the entire Cooper family. Such a visceral shock
works so well in a cinematic medium because the audience instantly
recognizes the former protagonists in their zombified forms and can
intimately relate to the horrified reactions of the survivors.

Finally, the zombie monster is ultimately terrifying because in it 39
one sees one's self. Pegg discusses the essential function of the zombie:
"Metaphorically, this classic creature embodies a number of our greatest

fears. Most obviously, it is our own death, personified: the physical manifestation of that thing we fear the most. More subtly, the zombie represents a number of our deeper insecurities. The fear that deep down, we may be little more than animals, concerned only with appetite." In a very real sense, Night is the story about humanity's struggle to retain its sense of humanity. Ben and the others fight the zombies just to stay alive, but they also clash among themselves. Although he remains uninfected by the zombie plague, Ben's civility suffers and crumbles under the stress of the siege: He strikes Barbara for being hysterical, beats Mr. Cooper for disagreeing with his plans, and eventually shoots and kills Mr. Cooper. Ben is almost as violent and irrational as the zombies themselves, although he is the closest thing the movie has to a real hero.

Because anyone can potentially become a zombie, these films deal 40 unabashedly with human taboos, murder, and cannibalism, which Dillard proposes have much to do with the genre's success (Dillard 1987, 15). The dead are not allowed to rest in peace: Barbara's attempt to honor the resting place of one relative turns into a nightmare in which she vainly combats the remains of another dead relative. Ben becomes a kind of avenging angel, bashing, chopping, and shooting people—he is not only forced to disrespect the sanctity of the dead, but he also becomes a type of mass murderer. The cannibalism taboo is the one broached most blatantly. After dying in an explosion, the bodies of Tom and Judy are mercilessly devoured by the gathered zombies, and Romero pulls no punches in showing charred flesh, ropy intestines, and closely gnawed bones. Karen's cannibalistic act even borders on incest, consuming the very flesh that originally gave her life.

585

Night, as with the zombie movies to follow, fulfills its generic 41 promises with a great deal of gore and violence. This is a major reason film is so successful in telling the zombie story—blood, guts, and gore can be shown instantly with graphic detail. Humans have their intestines ripped out, zombies are cheerfully hunted and butchered, and mad doctors perform unspeakable acts on the reanimated corpses of their former associates. The synchronic nature of cinema allows these shocking images to be suddenly and thoroughly unleashed on the viewing public, resulting in the expected gleeful revulsion.

The horror of the zombie movie comes from recognizing the 42 human in the monster; the terror of the zombie movie comes from knowing there is nothing to do about it but destroy what is left; the fun comes from watching the genre continue to develop. Although zombies are technically dead, their cinematic genre is a living, breathing entity that continues to grow and evolve. Zombie-themed video games have spawned such films as *Resident Evil* (2002), and the genre's popularity and longevity have resulted in remakes of both *Dawn of the Dead* and the forthcoming *Day of the Dead* (2006). But the genre is also constantly reinventing itself with revisionist films such as *Shaun of the Dead* and Romero's own *Land of the Dead* (2005).[12] Such overwhelming contemporary evidence firmly establishes zombie cinema as a valued member of genre studies.

NOTES

[1]Some lesser known 2004 titles include *Return of the Living Dead 4* and *5, Zombie Honeymoon, Dead and Breakfast, Zombie Planet, Hide and Creep*, and *Zombie Xtreme*, just to name a few of the more provocative titles.

[2]According to the Internet Movie Database, *Resident Evil: Apocalypse* grossed $50 million domestically (with an estimated $50 million budget), *Dawn of the Dead* grossed $59 million (with a $28 million budget), and *Shaun of the Dead* grossed $13 million (with a $4 million budget). Like most horror films, zombie movies are considered safe commodities and are usually quite profitable.

[3]Romero's zombie films are rife with symbolism and social commentary: *Night of the Living Dead* is often read as a metaphor for both the horrors of the Vietnam War and the civil inequality and unrest of the 1960s, *Dawn of the Dead* is seen as a critique of consumer culture, and *Day of the Dead* is viewed as a pessimistic look at the cold war. See Dillard's "Night of the Living Dead: It's Not Like Just a Wind That's Passing Through" and Wells's *The Horror Genre: From Beelzebub to Blair Witch* for discussions on the political and social statements in *Night of the Living Dead;* see Wood's "Neglected Nightmares" and Skal's *The Monster Show* for discussions on the role of consumerism in *Dawn of the Dead.*

[4]Zombies are featured prominently in horror video games series such as *Doom, Resident Evil,* and *Silent Hill;* a number of popular zombie graphic novels also exist, particularly *The Walking Dead* series by Robert Kirkman, *George A. Romero's Dawn of the Dead* by Steve Niles, and *Remains*, also by Niles. It is curious to note that aside from some occasional cameos on Joss Whedon's *Buffy the Vampire Slayer* (1997–2003) and *Angel* (1999–2004), the "zombie story" has never been produced as a television series.

[5]According to Wade Davis, although the term voodoo is more common and familiar to Westerners, Vodoun (also rendered Vodun or Voudou) is more accurately used by anthropologists when referring to the actual religion of Africa and Haiti (xi).

[6]Davis's scientific text was quickly adapted by Wes Craven into a more mainstream horror movie in 1988. Although the first half of the film is somewhat loyal to Davis's actual experiences, Craven quickly departs from the anthropological sphere and presents a much more supernatural, violent, and spectacular version of Haiti.

[7]Premature burial does have an established tradition in both fact and fiction. Edgar Allan Poe was particularly enamored with the subject, and Freud suggests that the idea of being buried alive would be the ultimate realization of the *unheimlich* (150)—a conscious confrontation with the inevitability of death.

[8]The mummy might be considered a subclass of zombie; however, unlike its mindless cousins, a mummy is usually brought back to life by a curse, operates

by itself, does not infect its victims or reproduce, single-mindedly pursues a specific task, shows some intelligence and possibly even speech, and eventually returns to its slumber.

[9]It should be noted that many so-called zombie films fail to feature true zombies at all. Sam Raimi's *Evil Dead* films (1981 and 1987) deal with demonic possession, and the much-lauded *28 Days Later* (2002) from Danny Boyle is about living, breathing humans who have been infected by a deadly virus.

[10]Zombie comedy movies (zombedies?) blatantly disregard Romero's model, attempting to negotiate the protocols of the genre to emphasize the corny over the uncanny. In such films as *Return of the Living Dead* (1985), *I Was a Teenage Zombie* (1987), and *Braindead* (1992), the zombies speak with surprising loquaciousness and have clear memories of their former lives and relationships, and infected protagonists are eerily aware of their slow transition to the undead.

Romero's *Day of the Dead* (1985) could also be considered somewhat problematic because of the introduction of a quasi-domesticated zombie named Bub. A crazed scientist attempts to train Bub like a caged animal, using a reward system to encourage good behavior. However, even though Bub seems to recall some of his former life—he can answer a phone, flash a salute, and even brandish a pistol—his actions never escalate beyond primitive imitation. Furthermore, Bub never regains the power of speech; like other zombies, he is limited to grunts and occasional roars of outrage. In the end, Bub's supply of "zombie treats" runs out, and he quickly joins the rampaging masses of his less-sympathetic kin. The experiment is a total failure, and Bub remains what he is: a mindless zombie.

[11]Stephen Spielberg's 2005 version of *War of the Worlds* is a notable exception. Although it embraces the spectacular conventions of the alien-invasion picture, it tells the story in a decidedly mundane way, focusing on average citizens in rural locations—exactly like the classic zombie movie.

[12]Romero departs completely from this established genre staple in his 2005 *Land of the Dead*, a revisionist film that is more an indication of Romero selling out than it is a milestone of the genre's development. He proposes the possible evolution of zombies over time, showing the development of rudimentary vocal communication (still grunts only, no speech), the ability to handle firearms, and a primitive form of compassion for their own kind. Unfortunately, a zombie's brain would actually gel worse as it rots over time, so such cerebral evolution makes no sense, even in a fantastic horror film.

WORKS CITED

Davis, Wade. *The Serpent and the Rainbow*. New York: Werner, 1985.

Dendle, Peter. *The Zombie Movie Encyclopedia*. Jefferson, NC: McFarland, 2001.

Diehl, Digby. *Tales from the Crypt: The Official Archives*. New York: St. Martin's, 1996.

Dillard, R. H. W. "Night of the Living Dead: It's Not Like Just a Wind That's Passing Through." *American Horrors*. Ed. Gregory A. Waller. Chicago: U of Illinois P, 1987. 14–29.

Freud, Sigmund. *The Uncanny*. New York: Penguin, 2003.

Frumke, Roy, dir. *Roy Frumke's Document of the Dead*. Synapse Films, 1989. DVD. *Dawn of the Dead Ultimate Edition*. Anchor Bay Entertainment, 2004.

Halperin, Victor, dir. *White Zombie*. Perf. Bela Lugosi. 1932. DVD. The Roan Group, 1999.

Hitchcock, Alfred, dir. *The Birds*. Universal City Studios, 1963. VHS. *The Alfred Hitchcock Collection*. MCA Universal Home Video, 1995.

King, Stephen. *Danse Macabre*. New York: Berkley, 1981.

Martin, Perry, dir. *The Dead Will Walk*. DVD. *Dawn of the Dead Ultimate Edition*. Anchor Bay Entertainment, 2004.

Matheson, Richard. *I Am Legend*. New York: Tom Doherty, 1995.

Nyby, Christian, dir. *The Thing from Another World*. Winchester Pictures Corporation, 1951. DVD. Warner Home Video, 2005.

Pegg, Simon. Afterword. *Miles Behind Us. The Walking Dead 2*. Image Comics, 2004.

Romero, George A., dir. *Dawn of the Dead*. The MKR Group, 1978. DVD. Ultimate Edition. Anchor Bay Entertainment, 2004.

———, dir. *Day of the Dead*. United Film Distribution Company, 1985. DVD. Anchor Bay Entertainment, 2003.

———, dir. *Land of the Dead*. Universal Pictures, 2005.

———, dir. *Night of the Living Dead*. Image Ten, 1968. DVD. Millennium Edition. Elite Entertainment, 1994.

Siegel, Don, dir. *Invasion of the Body Snatchers*. Walter Wanger Productions, 1956. DVD. Republic Studios, 2002.

Skal, David J. *The Monster Show*. New York: Faber, 1993.

Stoker, Bram. *Dracula*. 1897. Ed. Nina Auerbach and David J. Skal. Norton Critical Edition. New York: Norton, 1997.

Ursini, James. Introduction. *Horror Film Reader*. Ed. Alain Silver and James Ursini. New York: Limelight, 2000. 3–7.

Wells, Paul. *The Horror Genre: From Beelzebub to Blair Witch*. *Short Cuts: Introductions to Film Studies 1*. New York: Wallflower, 2002.

Wood, Robin. "Neglected Nightmares." *Horror Film Reader*. Ed. Alain Silver and James Ursini. New York: Limelight, 2000. 111–27.

Examining the Text

1. By the author's account, the zombie is a "purely American monster." What are the "nonliterary" origins of zombies in contemporary film? What is a zombie, as it appears in non-American and early American folkloric traditions and subsequently in movies, and what are the early stages, both folk-cultural and contemporary-creative, that paved the way for the development of the zombie character we know and love in modern cinema?

2. When did zombies first appear on the "big screen"—i.e. in movies? After that point, how did zombie movies evolve into the 1950s, when they became a mainstay of the burgeoning B-movie horror film genre? What was George A. Romero's contribution to the development of zombie movies . . . not only in the '50s, but in modern cinema as well?

3. In his "Performing the Ritual" section of this essay, Bishop introduces the Freudian concept of "the uncanny" as a potential means of entry into understanding zombie films' subconscious appeal to a vast audience. Briefly explain the meaning of "the uncanny" from the Freudian theorist's perspective. How does this concept help explain movie fans' fascination with and/or attraction to zombie films?

4. Bishop argues that the zombie film, as pioneered by Romero and represented by any number of worthy successors, has several specific characteristics that distinguish it from slasher flicks, monster movies, and other supernatural cinematic renderings. What are the four distinguishing appeals of zombie movies, as enumerated by the author of this essay?

5. *Thinking rhetorically:* This essay's author, a genre theorist by profession, concludes his discussion by stating, "The horror of the zombie movie comes from recognizing the human in the monster; the terror of the zombie movie comes from knowing there is nothing to do about it but destroy what is left; the fun comes from watching the genre continue to develop." By what means does he attempt to convince readers that studying zombie films is a worthy pursuit for academics . . . as well as for students such as yourself?

589

For Group Discussion

In the fictional world of the zombie film, anyone can potentially become a zombified monster, and many people do, over the course of the typical onscreen narrative. Because of this fact, argues Bishop, zombie movies deal "unabashedly with human taboos, murder, and cannibalism, which Dillard proposes have much to do with the genre's success." In group discussion, first consider the validity of this proposition, and list several other reasons why zombie movies may be popular among persons of your generation in particular. Next, consider Bishop's "taboo theory" as manifest in other films: what other specific films, or discrete genres of film, might confront taboo subjects to reach audiences at the basest primal and archetypal levels?

Writing Suggestion

The author concludes this essay by arguing that zombie films are particularly successful because "blood, guts, and gore can be shown instantly with graphic detail. Humans have their intestines ripped out, zombies are cheerfully hunted and butchered, and mad doctors perform unspeakable acts on the reanimated corpses of their former associates. The synchronic nature of cinema allows these shocking images to be suddenly and thoroughly unleashed on the viewing public, resulting in the expected gleeful revulsion." In an essay, discuss your own relationship to the horror film and attempt to propose a psychological theory to explain your particular experience with zombie movies, chainsaw massacre flicks, monster epics such as *Cloverfield* or *War of the Worlds,* and so forth. If you experience the "gleeful revulsion" to which Bishop refers, what might this reveal about your character, your upbringing, your hard-wired excitement threshold, your fears and anxieties, and your concerns about death that is the eventual and unavoidable end for us all? If, conversely, you find yourself not in the least interested in coming face-to-face, gleefully or otherwise, with blood, gore, and unspeakably brutal practices on the big screen, what does this reveal about you and your complex personality dynamics?

Apatow and Tarantino: Two Contemporary Filmmakers

A Fine Romance

DAVID DENBY

Here's a quick quiz on English diction: What does the word Apatovian *mean? No clue? Don't bother looking it up in a dictionary, because you won't find it. Yet, in constructing this section of the* Common Culture *movie chapter we have run across the word no less than seventeen times in various movie reviews, cinema Web sites, and blogs. Since it does not yet appear officially in dictionaries, let us hereby put forth our own working definition, which goes something like,* Apatovian: adj. *of or pertaining to the film comedies of writer/director Judd Apatow. We introduce this contemporary neologism (i.e., made-up word) because this section of the movie chapter introduces two pairs of articles pertaining to modern filmmakers who are having significant impacts on movies specifically, and on broader issues of art and culture as well: Judd Apatow and Quentin Tarantino. More on Tarantino at the end of the chapter; meanwhile, turning to Apatow . . . if his name isn't immediately familiar to you, his films certainly are, because you've no doubt seen one—if not all—of his very long list of movie accomplishments, including:* Forgetting Sarah Marshall *(2008) (producer);* Walk Hard: The Dewey Cox Story *(2007) (writer/producer);* Superbad *(2007) (producer);* Knocked Up *(2007) (director/writer/producer);* Talladega Nights: The Ballad of Ricky Bobby *(2006) (producer);* The 40-Year-Old Virgin *(2005) (director/writer/producer);* Anchorman: The Legend of Ron Burgundy *(2004) (producer). In the following essay, film critic David Denby discusses the evolution of the romantic comedy, leading from movies starring Katherine Hepburn and Spencer Tracy, through Woody Allen and Diane Keaton, and finally up to what has—sometimes lovingly, sometimes dismissively—been called slacker romantic comedy . . . Apatow's* Knocked Up *being the prime example.*

*As **you** read, notice the judicious tone of distance and open-mindedness that Denby, the consummately literate film critic, brings to his subject. While clearly an avid fan of the earlier "screwball" comedies and, later, the films of Woody Allen, the author nevertheless acknowledges that Apatovian comedy is "fascinating and funny," even as he offers up some pointed critique of this contemporary form.*

591

His beard is haphazard and unintentional, and he dresses in sweats, or 1
in shorts and a T-shirt, or with his shirt hanging out like the tongue of a
Labrador retriever. He's about thirty, though he may be younger, and
he spends a lot of time with friends who are like him, only more so—
sweet-natured young men of foul mouth, odd hair, and wanker-mag
reading habits. When he's with them, punched beer cans and bongs of
various sizes lie around like spent shells; alone, and walrus-heavy on
his couch, he watches football, basketball, or baseball on television, or
spends time memorializing his youth—archiving old movies, games,
and jokes. Like his ancestors in the sixties, he's anti-corporate, but he's
not bohemian (his culture is pop). He's more like a sullen back-of-the-
classroom guy, who breaks into brilliant tirades only when he feels like
it. He may run a used-record store, or conduct sightseeing tours with a
nonstop line of patter, or feed animals who then high-five him with
their flippers, or teach in a school where he can be friends with all the
kids, or design an Internet site that no one needs. Whatever he does, he
hardly breaks a sweat, and sometimes he does nothing at all.

He may not have a girlfriend, but he certainly likes girls—he's 2
even, in some cases, a hetero blade, scoring with tourists or love-hungry
single mothers. But if he does have a girlfriend, she works hard.
Usually, she's the same age as he is but seems older, as if the disparity
between boys and girls in ninth grade had been recapitulated fifteen
years later. She dresses in Donna Karan or Ralph Lauren or the like;
she's a corporate executive, or a lawyer, or works in TV, public relations,
or an art gallery. She's good-tempered, honest, great-looking, and serious. She wants to "get to the next stage of life"—settle down, marry,
maybe have children. Apart from getting on with it, however, she does-
n't have an idea in her head, and she's not the one who makes the jokes.

When she breaks up with him, he talks his situation over with his 3
hopeless pals, who give him bits of misogynist advice. Suddenly, it's
the end of youth for him. It's a crisis for her, too, and they can get back
together only if both undertake some drastic alteration: he must act
responsibly (get a job, take care of a kid), and she has to do something
crazy (run across a baseball field during a game, tell a joke). He has to
shape up, and she has to loosen up.

There they are, the young man and young woman of the dominant 4
romantic-comedy trend of the past several years—the slovenly hipster
and the female straight arrow. The movies form a genre of sorts: the
slacker-striver romance. Stephen Frears's *High Fidelity* (2000), which
transferred Nick Hornby's novel from London to Chicago, may not have
been the first, but it set the tone and established the self-dramatizing
underachiever as hero. Hornby's guy-centered material also inspired
About a Boy and *Fever Pitch*. Others in this group include *Old School, Big
Daddy, 50 First Dates, Shallow Hal, School of Rock, Failure to Launch, You, Me*

and Dupree, *Wedding Crashers*, *The Break-Up*, and—this summer's hit—
Knocked Up. In these movies, the men are played by Vince Vaughn, Owen
Wilson, Adam Sandler, John Cusack, Jimmy Fallon, Matthew
McConaughey, Jack Black, Hugh Grant, and Seth Rogen; the women by
Drew Barrymore, Jennifer Aniston, Kate Hudson, Sarah Jessica Parker,
and Katherine Heigl. For almost a decade, Hollywood has pulled jokes
and romance out of the struggle between male infantilism and female
ambition.

Knocked Up, written and directed by Judd Apatow, is the culmi-   5
nating version of this story, and it feels like one of the key movies of
the era—a raw, discordant equivalent of *The Graduate* forty years ago.
I've seen it with audiences in their twenties and thirties, and the
excitement in the theatres is palpable—the audience is with the movie
all the way, and, afterward, many of the young men (though not
always the young women) say that it's not only funny but true. They
feel that way, I think, because the picture is unruly and surprising; it's
filled with the messes and rages of life in 2007. The woman, Alison
(Katherine Heigl), an ambitious TV interviewer in Los Angeles, gets
pregnant after a sozzled one-night stand with Ben (Seth Rogen), a
nowhere guy she meets at a disco. Cells divide, sickness arrives in the
morning—the movie's time scheme is plotted against a series of puls-
ing sonograms. Yet these two, to put it mildly, find themselves in an
awkward situation. They don't much like each other; they don't seem
to match up. Heigl has golden skin, blond hair, a great laugh. She's so
attractive a person that, at the beginning of the movie, you wince
every time Rogen touches her. Chubby, with curling hair and an oro-
tund voice, he has the round face and sottish grin of a Jewish Bacchus,
though grape appeals to him less than weed. At first, he makes one
crass remark after another; he seems like a professional comic who
will do anything to get a laugh. It's not at all clear that these two
should stay together.

593

Authentic as Ben and Alison seem to younger audiences, they are,   6
like all the slacker-striver couples, strangers to anyone with a long
memory of romantic comedy. Buster Keaton certainly played idle
young swells in some of his silent movies, but, first humiliated and
then challenged, he would exert himself to heroic effort to win the girl.
In the end, he proved himself a lover. In the nineteen-thirties, the
young, lean James Stewart projected a vulnerability that was
immensely appealing. So did Jack Lemmon, in his frenetic way, in the
fifties. In succeeding decades, Elliott Gould, George Segal, Alan Alda,
and other actors played soulful types. Yet all these men wanted something. It's hard to think of earlier heroes who were absolutely free of
the desire to make an impression on the world and still got the girl.
And the women in the old romantic comedies were daffy or tough or

high-spirited or even spiritual in some way, but they were never blank. What's going on in this new genre? *Knocked Up*, a raucously funny and explicit movie, has some dark corners, some fear and anxiety festering under the jokes. Apatow takes the slacker-striver romance to a place no one thought it would go. He also makes it clear, if we hadn't noticed before, how drastically the entire genre breaks with the classic patterns of romantic comedy. Those ancient tropes fulfill certain expectations and, at their best, provide incomparable pleasure. But *Knocked Up* is heading off into a brave and uncertain new direction.

Shakespeare knew the Roman farces—by Plautus, Terence, and 7 others—in which a scrambling boy chases after a girl and lands her. He varied the pattern. His comedies were rarely a simple chase, and the best American romantic comedies have drawn on the forms that he devised—not so much, perhaps, in the coarse-grained *Taming of the Shrew* but in *Much Ado About Nothing*, with its pair of battling lovers, Beatrice and Benedick. Why is the contact between those two so barbed? Because they are meant for each other, and are too proud and frightened to admit it. We can see the attraction, even if they can't. They have a closely meshed rhythm of speech, a quickness to rise and retort, that no one else shares. Benedick, announcing the end of the warfare, puts the issue squarely: "Shall quips and sentences and these paper bullets of the brain awe a man from the career of his humor? No, the world must be peopled."

Romantic comedy is entertainment in the service of the biological 8 imperative. The world must be peopled. Even if the lovers are past child-rearing age or, as in recent years, don't want children, the biological imperative survives, as any evolutionary psychologist will tell you, in the flourishes of courtship behavior. Romantic comedy civilizes desire, transforms lust into play and ritual—the celebration of union in marriage. The lovers are fated by temperament and physical attraction to join together, or stay together, and the audience longs for that ending with an urgency that is as much moral as sentimental. For its amusement, however, the audience doesn't want the resolution to come too quickly. The lovers misunderstand each other; they get pixie dust thrown in their faces. Befuddled, the woman thinks she's in love with a gas-station attendant, who turns out to be a millionaire; an unsuitable suitor becomes a proper suitor; and so on. It's always the right guy in the end. Romantic drama may revel in suffering, even in anguish and death, but romantic comedy merely nods at the destructive energies of passion. The confused lovers torment each other and, for a while, us. Then they stop.

The best directors of romantic comedy in the 1930s and 40s— 9 Frank Capra, Gregory La Cava, Leo McCarey, Howard Hawks, Mitchell Leisen, and Preston Sturges—knew that the story would be not only funnier but much more romantic if the fight was waged between equals. The man and woman may not enjoy parity of social standing or money, but they are equals in spirit, will, and body. As everyone agrees, this kind of romantic comedy—and particularly the variant called "screwball comedy"—lifted off in February, 1934, with Frank Capra's charming *It Happened One Night*, in which a hard-drinking reporter out of a job (Clark Gable) and an heiress who has jumped off her father's yacht (Claudette Colbert) meet on the road somewhere between Florida and New York. Tough and self-sufficient, Gable contemptuously looks after the spoiled rich girl. He's rude and overbearing, and she's miffed, but it helps their acquaintance a little that they are both supremely attractive—Gable quick-moving but large and, in his famous undressing scene, meaty, and Colbert tiny, with a slightly pointed chin, round eyes, and round breasts beneath the fitted striped jacket she buys on the road. When she develops pride, they become equals.

The cinema added something invaluable to the romantic comedy: the camera's ability to place lovers in an enchanted, expanding envelope of setting and atmosphere. It moves with them at will, enlarging their command of streets, fields, sitting rooms, and night clubs; rapid cutting then doubles the speed of their quarrels. Out on the road, in the middle of the Depression, Gable and Colbert join the poor, the hungry, the shysters and the hustlers; they spend a night among haystacks, get fleeced, practice their hitchhiking skills. In screwball comedy, the characters have to dive below their social roles for their true selves to come out: they get drunk and wind up in the slammer; they turn a couch in an upstairs room of a mansion into a trampoline; they run around the woods at a country estate—the American plutocrats' version of Shakespeare's magical forest in *A Midsummer Night's Dream*, where young people, first confused and then enlightened, discover whom they should marry.

In many of the screwball classics, including *Twentieth Century, My Man Godfrey, The Awful Truth, Easy Living, Midnight, Bringing Up Baby, Holiday, The Philadelphia Story, The Lady Eve*—all made between 1934 and 1941—the characters dress for dinner and make cocktails, and the atmosphere is gilded and swank. The enormous New York apartments, the country houses with porticoes, the white-on-white night clubs in which swells listen to a warbling singer—all this establishes a facade of propriety and manners, a place to misbehave. Except for the Fred Astaire–Ginger Rogers dance musicals, in which evening clothes are integral to the lyric transformation of life into movement, the lovers are no more than playing at formality. The characters need to be wealthy in order to exercise their will openly and make their choices. The screwball comedies are less about possessions than about a

10

595

11

certain style of freedom in love, a way of vaulting above the dullness and petty-mindedness of the sticks. (In these films, no matter how rich you may be, you are out of the question if you hail from Oklahoma or Albany—you are Ralph Bellamy.)

Many of the heroines were heiresses, who, in those days, were 12 prized for their burbling eccentricities—Carole Lombard's howl, Irene Dunne's giggle, Katharine Hepburn's Bryn Mawr drawl. Pampered and dizzy, they favored spontaneity over security when it came to choosing a man. As for the men, they came in two varieties. Some owned a factory or a mine, or were in finance—worldly fellows who knew how to float a debenture or hand a woman into a taxi—and others were gently cartooned intellectuals. Innocents preoccupied with some intricate corner of knowledge, they gathered old bones (Cary Grant, in *Bringing Up Baby*), or new words (Gary Cooper, in *Ball of Fire*), or went up the Amazon and discovered unspeakable snakes (Henry Fonda, in *The Lady Eve*). The man is the love object here—passive, dreamy, and gentle, a kind of Sleeping Beauty in spectacles—and the woman is the relentless pursuer. Katharine Hepburn in *Baby* nearly drives Cary Grant crazy with her intrusions into his work, her way of scattering his life about like pieces of lawn furniture. She's attracted by his good looks but also by what's unaroused in him, and she will do anything to awaken him. Equality in these comedies takes a new shape. The man is serious about his work (and no one says he shouldn't be), but he's confused about women, and his confusion has neutered him. He thinks he wants a conventional marriage with a compliant wife, but what he really wants is to be overwhelmed by the female life force. In the screwball comedies, the woman doesn't ask her man to "grow up." She wants to pull him into some sort of ridiculous adventure. She has to grow up, and he has to get loose—the opposite of the current pattern.

The screwball comedies were not devoted to sex, exactly—you 13 could hardly describe any of the characters as sensualists. The Production Code limited openness on such matters, and the filmmakers turned sex into a courtship game that was so deliriously convoluted precisely because couples could go to bed only when they were married. The screwball movies, at their peak, defined certain ideal qualities of insouciance, a fineness of romantic temper in which men and women could be aggressive but not coarse, angry but not rancorous, silly but not shamed, melancholy but not ravaged. It was the temper of American happiness.

Sometimes the couple in a romantic comedy are already married, 14 or were formerly married, but husband and wife go at each other anyway because they enjoy wrangling too much to stop. Who else is there to talk to? In a case like that, romance becomes less a dazed encounter in an enchanted garden than a duel with slingshots at close quarters—exciting but a little risky. The most volatile of these comedies was *His Girl Friday,* Howard Hawks's 1940 version of the 1928 Ben Hecht–Charles MacArthur play *The Front Page.* In the original, the star reporter Hildy Johnson is a man. In Hawks's version, Hildy (Rosalind Russell) is a woman who has fled the barbarous city desk and plans to marry a timid businessman (Ralph Bellamy). Her former husband and editor, Walter Burns (Cary Grant), will do anything to get her back to the paper. He doesn't seem drawn to her as a woman, yet he woos her in his way, with scams, lies, and one important truth—that she's the only person good enough to cover the hottest story in town. She knows him as an indifferent and absent husband, yet she's attracted, once again, by the outrageous way this man fans his tail. And, despite her misgivings, she's caught, too, by the great time they have together toiling in the yellow journalism that they both love. Vince Vaughn, in some of his recent roles, has displayed a dazzling motormouth velocity, but he has never worked with an actress who can keep up with him. Rosalind Russell keeps up with Grant. These two seize each other's words and throw them back so quickly that their dialogue seems almost syncopated. Balance between the sexes here becomes a kind of matched virtuosity more intense than sex.

597

15

  If Russell and Grant were exactly alike in that movie, Spencer Tracy, slow-talking, even adamantine, with a thick trunk and massive head, and Katharine Hepburn, slender, angular, and unnervingly speedy and direct, were opposites that attracted with mysterious force. In the classic comedy *Adam's Rib* (1949), their sixth movie together (they made nine), they were an established onscreen married couple, rising, drinking coffee, and getting dressed for work. How can you have romantic comedy in a setting of such domestic complacency? *Adam's Rib,* which was written by a married couple, Garson Kanin and Ruth Gordon, and directed by George Cukor, takes these two through combat so fierce that it can be ended only with a new and very desperate courtship. They become opposing lawyers in a murder case. He prosecutes, and she defends, a woman (Judy Holliday) who put a couple of slugs in her husband when she caught him in the arms of his mistress. As the two lawyers compete in court, and Tracy gets upstaged by Hepburn, the traditional sparring at the center of romantic comedy intensifies, turns a little ugly, and then comes to an abrupt stop with a loud slap—Tracy smacking Hepburn's bottom in a proprietary way during a late-night rubdown session. The slap is nothing, yet it's everything. The husband has violated the prime rule of mating behavior by asserting a right over his wife physically. The drive for equality in movies can lead to bruising competitions, and in *Adam's Rib* the partnership of equals nearly dissolves. Suddenly anguished, the movie uneasily rights itself as husband and wife make concessions and find their way back to marriage again.

Achieving balance between a man and a woman in a romantic comedy can be elusive. Marilyn Monroe, her tactile flesh spilling everywhere, was either lusted after or mocked, but only Tony Curtis, appearing in Cary Grant drag in *Some Like It Hot,* knew how to talk to her. Rock Hudson and Doris Day, in their films together, were exclusively preoccupied with, respectively, assaulting and defending Day's virtue, and they both seemed a little demented. Tom Hanks matched up nicely with Daryl Hannah and with Meg Ryan, as did Richard Gere and Hugh Grant with Julia Roberts, whose eyes and smile and restless, long-waisted body charged up several romantic comedies in the nineties. 16

In recent decades, however, Woody Allen and Diane Keaton have come closest to restoring the miraculous ease of the older movies. Short and narrow-jawed, with black-framed specs that give him the aspect of a quizzical Eastern European police inspector, Allen turned his worried but demanding gaze on Keaton, the tall, willowy Californian. In their early films together, they seemed the most eccentric and singular of all movie couples; it was the presence of New York City, in *Annie Hall* (1977) and *Manhattan* (1979), that sealed their immortality as a team. Allen, narrating, presented himself as the embodied spirit of the place, sharp and appreciative, but also didactic, overexplicit, cranky, and frightened of lobsters off the leash and everything else in the natural world. The idea was that beauty and brains would match up, although, early in *Annie Hall,* the balance isn't quite there—Keaton has to rise to his level. Initially, she's nervously apologetic—all floppy hats, tail-out shirts, and tremulous opinions—and she agrees to be tutored by Allen, who gives her books to read and takes her repeatedly to *The Sorrow and the Pity.* For a while, they click as teacher and student. If Tracy and Hepburn were like a rock and a current mysteriously joined together, these two neurotics were like agitated hummingbirds meeting in midair. 17

Working with the cinematographer Gordon Willis, Woody Allen created the atmosphere of a marriage plot in conversations set in his beloved leafy East Side streets—his version of Shakespeare's magical forest. But *Annie Hall,* surprisingly, shifts away from marriage. The quintessential New Yorker turns out to be a driven pain in the neck, so insistent and adolescent in his demands that no woman can put up with him for long. And the specific New York elements that Allen added to romantic comedy—the cult of psychoanalysis and the endless opinions about writers, musicians, and artists—also threaten the stability of the couple. Psychoanalysis yields "relationships" and "living together," not marriage, as the central ritual, and living together, especially in the time 18 of the Pill and the easy real-estate market of the seventies, is always provisional. Opinions about art—the way the soul defines itself in time—are provisional, too. In *Annie Hall,* Keaton outgrows Allen's curriculum for her and moves on, and in *Manhattan,* perhaps the best American comedy about selfishness ever made, she returns to the married man she was having an affair with. Allen loses her both times; the biological imperative goes nowhere. *Annie Hall* and *Manhattan* now seem like fragile and melancholy love lyrics; they took romantic comedy to a level of rueful sophistication never seen before or since.

19   The louts in the slacker-striver comedies should probably lose the girl, too, but most of them don't. Yet what, exactly, are they getting, and why should the women want them? That is not a question that romantic comedy has posed before.

20   The slacker has certain charms. He doesn't want to compete in business, he refuses to cultivate macho attitudes, and, for some women, he may be attractive. He's still a boy—he's gentler than other men. Having a child with such a guy, however, is another matter, and plenty of women have complained about the way *Knocked Up* handles the issue of pregnancy. Alison has a good job, some growing public fame, and she hardly knows the unappealing father—there's even some muttering about "bad genes." Why have a baby with him? Well, a filmmaker's answer would have to be that if there's an abortion, or if Alison has the child on her own, there's no movie—or, at least, nothing like this movie. And this movie, just as it is, has considerable interest and complication as fiction.

599

21   What's striking about *Knocked Up* is the way the romance is placed within the relations between the sexes. The picture is a drastic revision of classic romantic-comedy patterns. Ben doesn't chase Alison, and she doesn't chase him. The movie is not about the civilizing of desire, and it offers a marriage plot that couldn't be more wary of marriage. *Knocked Up,* like Apatow's earlier *40-Year-Old Virgin,* is devoted to the dissolution of a male pack, the ending of the juvenile male bond. Ben and his friends sit around in their San Fernando Valley tract house whamming each other on the head with rubber bats and watching naked actresses in movies. The way Ben lives with his friends is tremendous fun; it's also as close to paralysis as you can get and continue breathing. Apatow, of course, has it both ways. He squeezes the pink-eyed doofuses for every laugh he can get out of them, but at the same time he suggests that the very thing he's celebrating is sick, crazy, and dysfunctional. The situation has to end. Boys have to grow up or life ceases.

22   Ben and Alison's one-night stand forces the issue. Willy-nilly, the world gets peopled. Yet the slowly developing love between Ben and the pregnant Alison comes off as halfhearted and unconvincing—it's the weakest element in the movie. There are some terrifically noisy

arguments, a scene of Rogen's making love to the enormous Heigl ("I'm not making love to you like a dog. It's doggy style. It's a style"), but we never really see the moment in which they warm up and begin to like each other. That part of the movie is unpersuasive, I would guess, because it's not terribly important to Apatow. What's important is the male bond—the way it flourishes, in all its unhealthiness, and then its wrenching end. Alison lives with her sister, Debbie (Leslie Mann), and brother-in-law, Pete (Paul Rudd), and Ben begins to hang out with Alison at the house of the married couple, who are classically mismatched in temperament. Pete is restless, disappointed, and remorselessly funny, and Ben links up with him. Whooping with joy, they go off to Las Vegas, but they don't gamble or get laid. Instead, they hang out and eat "shrooms." They merely want to be together: it's as if Romeo and Mercutio had left the women and all that mess in Verona behind and gone off to practice their swordsmanship. When Ben and Pete get high, crash, and then return, chastened, to the women, the male bond is severed at last, the baby can be born, and life continues. In generic terms, *Knocked Up* puts the cart before the horse—the accidental baby, rather than desire, pulls the young man, who has to leave his male friends behind, into civilization.

600

As fascinating and as funny as *Knocked Up* is, it represents what can only be called the disenchantment of romantic comedy, the end point of a progression from Fifth Avenue to the Valley, from tuxedos to tube socks, from a popped champagne cork to a baby crowning. There's nothing in it that is comparable to the style of the classics—no magic in its settings, no reverberant sense of place, no shared or competitive work for the couple to do. Ben does come through in the end, yet, if his promise and Alison's beauty make them equal as a pair, one still wants more out of Alison than the filmmakers are willing to provide. She has a fine fit of hormonal rage, but, like the other heroines in the slacker-striver romances, she isn't given an idea or a snappy remark or even a sharp perception. All the movies in this genre have been written and directed by men, and it's as if the filmmakers were saying, "Yes, young men are children now, and women bring home the bacon, but men bring home the soul." 23

The perilous new direction of the slacker-striver genre reduces the role of women to vehicles. Their only real function is to make the men grow up. That's why they're all so earnest and bland—so nice, so good. Leslie Mann (who's married to Apatow) has some great bitchy lines as the angry Debbie, but she's not a lover; she represents disillusion. As Anthony Lane pointed out in these pages, Apatow's subject is not so much sex as age, and age in his movies is a malediction. If you're young, you have to grow up. If you grow up, you turn into Debbie—you fear that the years are overtaking you fast. Either way, you're in trouble. 24

Apatow has a genius for candor that goes way beyond dirty talk— 25
that's why *Knocked Up* is a cultural event. But I wonder if Apatow, like
his fumy youths, shouldn't move on. It seems strange to complain of
repetition when a director does something particularly well, and
Apatow does the infantilism of the male bond better than anyone, but
I'd be quite happy if I never saw another bong-gurgling slacker or male
pack again. The society that produced the Katharine Hepburn and
Carole Lombard movies has vanished; manners, in the sense of ele-
gance, have disappeared. But manners as spiritual style are more
important than ever, and Apatow has demonstrated that he knows this
as well as anyone. So how can he not know that the key to making a
great romantic comedy is to create heroines equal in wit to men? They
don't have to dress for dinner, but they should challenge the men intellectually and spiritually, rather than simply offering their bodies as a
way of dragging the clods out of their adolescent stupor. "Paper bullets
of the brain," as Benedick called the taunting exchanges with Beatrice,
slay the audience every time if they are aimed at the right place.

Examining the Text

1. After the general introduction mentioned in Question 5, Denby goes on to
provide a brief survey of romantic comedy through history. As the first stop in
this comedic time-travel trip, how did playwright William Shakespeare craft
his comedies, and what themes and narrative structures emerged from them?
What important social function has romantic comedy traditionally served, as
discussed in this section of Denby's essay?

2. What social-psychological function did romantic comedies serve in economic Depression-era and post-Depression-era America, according to Denby?
How did the visual nature of cinematography contribute to the role played by
motion picture comedy—especially that of the "screwball" variety—in early-
to mid-twentieth century America?

3. Denby says that the male and female protagonists of the screwball comedy
era interact in a way that is exactly "opposite of the current pattern" as exem-
plified in Judd Apatow's films. What were the specific characteristics of
women and men in the earlier romantic comedies, and how might this have
contributed to a portrayal of "equality between the sexes" during this earlier
period?

4. How did the Academy Award-winning romantic comedies of Woody
Allen—especially *Annie Hall* (1977) update the themes and portrayals of the
"screwball" romantic comedies? In what ways did Woody Allen's comedies
echo the sentiments evoked by the earlier comedies, and in what ways were his
portrayals significantly different, representing a change in the social fabric of
America?

5. *Thinking rhetorically*: Denby begins this piece by generally contrasting the
male and female protagonists of today's "slacker comedies" with the comedic

heroes and heroines of romantic comedies in bygone eras. Denby says that, although the main characters of *Knocked Up* may seem authentic to younger audiences, "they are, like all the slacker-striver couples, strangers to anyone with a long memory of romantic comedy." In what ways do the characters and situations—and implied themes—in contemporary romantic comedy differ from those of earlier romantic comedies, by Denby's account? In terms of structure and rhetorical design, how does this opening paragraph prefigure the discussion that follows in this essay?

For Group Discussion

Denby compares the comedies of Judd Apatow to the earlier romantic comedies this way: ". . . it represents what can only be called the disenchantment of romantic comedy, the end point of a progression from Fifth Avenue to the Valley, from tuxedos to tube socks, from a popped champagne cork to a baby crowning." In what ways does *Knocked Up,* and films like it, represent a de-evolution of the romantic genre, in Denby's opinion? In the whole-class setting, discuss the accuracy of the author's critique: do you agree with Denby that in the new romances, "There's nothing in it that is comparable to the style of the classics— no magic in its settings, no reverberant sense of place, no shared or competitive work for the couple to do"? On the other hand do you find in these movies a shared "magic" that reverberates for individuals of your generation—some set of qualities that Denby, who is older, might be missing? If the latter, what specific qualities might make Apatovian comedy qualify as "enchanting"?

Writing Suggestion

At the beginning of this article, Denby documents a certain kind of character that appears in Judd Apatow's romantic comedies: the contemporary young male. This description includes: "His beard is haphazard and unintentional, and he dresses in sweats, or in shorts and a T-shirt . . . he spends a lot of time with friends who are like him, only more so—sweet-natured young men of foul mouth, odd hair, and wanker-mag reading habits. When he's with them, punched beer cans and bongs of various sizes lie around like spent shells; alone, and walrus-heavy on his couch, he watches football, basketball, or baseball on television, or spends time memorializing his youth—archiving old movies, games, and jokes . . . he's anti-corporate, but he's not bohemian (his culture is pop). He's more like a sullen back-of-the-classroom guy who breaks into brilliant tirades only when he feels like it. . . . He may not have a girlfriend, but he certainly likes girls . . . " Using the rhetorical form of comparison-contrast, write an essay of five pages in which you discuss the real-life accuracy of this depiction in your experience: if you're a guy, how does this character resemble you and/or your buds, and in what ways does it completely miss the mark? If you're *not* a guy, in what ways does this characterization resemble guys you know (and love?), and in what ways do the males of your acquaintance differ from the Apatovian stereotype?

Freaks, Geeks, and Mensches: Judd Apatow's Comedies of the Mature

ALEX WAINER

If you happen to have been raised in a home with one or more Jewish parents (as was Judd Apatow, the subject of this article by film critic Alex Wainer), then you probably heard the phrase, "Be a mensch," at some point (or many points) in your development. While the word derives literally from the German, meaning simply "man," in Yiddish the phrase takes on a deep cultural resonance, along with a more moral tone: it refers specifically to a person (usually a male, but occasionally female as well, despite the literal male definition) who does good deeds, and/or is an upright or rigorously decent human being. For example, in the home of this headnote's writer, the phrase, "Be a mensch!" could be heard any time my behavior strayed from the above-given definition, as when I failed to clean my room or made fun of my sister's saddle shoes or shoplifted a ball-point pen from a local supermarket. Likewise, the term mensch *appears in the title of the following reading, because Judd Apatow's comedies often involve a male protagonist who undergoes a change from a shlub (look it up) to a mensch. As you have read in the previous David Denby article, male protagonists in Apatovian comedies tend—at the beginning of movies such as* Knocked Up—*not to be mensches: they are aimless, stoned-out, video-game addicted, and don't clean their rooms . . . and as such are kind of grown-up college freshmen. However, by the end of Apatow's films, the boys shape up and become men—and mensches, in the view of Wainer—taking on responsibilities of job and family. This is both the charm and the redeeming thematic quality of Apatovian comedies, in Wainer's opinion: the movies ultimately deliver a message that support traditional family values.*

As you read, note the way in which two intelligent, well-respected movie critics can have different—if not altogether opposite—"takes" on a movie's value. While David Denby, in the previous reading in this text, takes a mildly critical position regarding the protagonists' shift from slackers to mensches, suggesting that this represents a conformist capitulation to bourgeois middle-class expectations, Wainer seems to praise these resolutions and their moral implications. Each critic brings credible evidence to bear on his thematic conclusions, leading readers to realize that a good work of art allows for a multiplicity of "correct" interpretations, depending on one's philosophical orientation. It's up to you, the reader, to situate yourself within this dialog, and to decide ultimately which is the interpretation that rings true for you.

We are currently in the era of the boy-man (or mook). 1

Male character types in popular culture run in cycles: The 1950s 2
square jawed hero, the '60s rebel, the '70s swinger and the '80s action
hero. The early 21st-century male type is shaping up to be the hapless
20-something who is developmentally arrested. Manhood is forestalled
by indecision, partying and smoking marijuana from bongs, spending
long hours mastering video games, and living in plain fear of growing
up. A culture of boy-men characterizes numerous movie types—Adam
Sandler, Jack Black, characters in Kevin Smith films, etc.

But two recent exceptions take an ethnographic look at the 3
slacker lifestyle and discover characters searching for their escape out
of a boy's life and into manhood. Judd Apatow's raucous and insightful film comedies understand that world and these guys, but challenge
his characters to act their age.

R-RATED MORALITY TALES

The first thing to know: these films aren't made for your church youth 4
group (although I'll bet a few have watched them.). They're R-rated
and for a reason. Characters talk the way people in this subculture
speak—except probably wittier. But like all good dramas and charac-
ter-based comedies, the screenplay forces them to painfully confront
their problems. They have behavior that they must grow out of, but
first the audience has to see and hear it to understand the lives the characters live and the challenges they face.

In the last two years, Apatow has directed and co-written two 5
films, *The 40-Year-Old Virgin* and *Knocked Up* where the need to put
away childish things and belatedly face responsibilities sets these films
apart from other R-rated comedies. Here are brief plot synopses (with
spoilers) of these very raunchy films, so you won't need to watch them
to understand just how their themes run counter to the cultural flow.

BOYS TO MEN

In *The 40-Year-Old Virgin,* Andy Stillzer works at an electronics super- 6
store where his male co-workers engage in the usual masculine sexual
braggadocio. One night during a card game, as the guys are swapping
their bawdy tales of female conquest, real or imagined, it becomes
quite obvious that the nice but dorky Andy doesn't know what he's
talking about and soon has to admit that he is a virgin. When as a youth
he'd tried to fornicate—though the flesh was willing—his heart just
wasn't in it, and awkwardness led to embarrassing disaster and

decades of romantic and sexual solitude. The other guys now make it their mission to initiate Andy into sexual activity.

What follows is a hilarious commentary on the misplaced priori- 7 ties of young males who are mostly still little boys on the inside. In fact, the men in Apatow's stories are terrified of women and can only relate to them as sexual playthings, but though Andy is the most scared of all, he doesn't see women as sex objects, but as individuals. He respects the idea of sexual love with one woman so much that he has never had sex. When he tries to play the swinger, he fails horribly and hilariously.

He feels much safer immersed in his house full of hobbies and 8 hundreds of valuable mint-condition (never opened) action figures. Obviously, Andy's had to learn a lot about sublimation. In a scene charged with insightful dual meanings, taking his action figures out of its original packaging becomes a metaphor for the sexual activity everyone is urging on Andy. Unconsciously referring to more than the action figure, Andy says, "It loses its value if you take it out of its packaging."

Eventually he meets an attractive woman older than him, Trish, who is already a youthful grandmother. There's good chemistry but, 9 though they date, Andy's virginity is a secret whose revelation he thinks would scare off any woman who learned the truth. Andy finally "confesses" his sexual purity motivated by his desire to commit himself to one woman for life. "For so long I thought that there was something wrong with me . . . because it had never happened, but . . . I realize now that it was just because I was waiting for you."

In the biggest surprise of the movie, rather than finally having 10 sex, the two middle-aged sweethearts are married and after the minister tells him he may kiss the bride, he adds to Andy, "And for God's sake, consummate the thing." In a profane and obscene sex comedy, the title character endures decades of abstinence before matrimony allows him to lose his virgin status. A better advertisement for the "True Love Waits" campaign in the real world is hard to imagine.

A SECOND TAKE

Last summer saw Apatow's second directorial effort, *Knocked Up*, win 11 similar critical and box office success. Ben Stone, another layabout living off a now-dwindling insurance settlement, spends his days with his stoner buddies planning to create a Web site that chronicles the nude scenes of Hollywood stars. When he meets a beautiful blonde, Alison, at a club, the two awkwardly drink their way into her apartment and have intoxicated sex that Ben scarcely remembers in the morning.

The mismatched couple goes their separate ways until eight 12 weeks later, Alison begins to suspect she is pregnant. Contacting Ben to

605

bring him into the loop, they go to the doctor's office where they view an early sonogram with awe and dismay—indeed, there is an obviously visible tiny life growing inside her. This new and unplanned development has interrupted their lives and they are completely unprepared. Alison's mother gives her this chilling advice:

"I cannot be supportive of this. This is a mistake. This is a big, big 13 mistake. Now think about your stepsister. Now, you remember what happened with her? She had the same situation as you and she had it taken care of. And you know what? Now she has a real baby. Honey, this is not the time."

Alison refuses to "have it taken care of." Ben's father tells Ben the 14 child is a blessing and he should welcome it. When Alison tells Ben she's keeping the baby, Ben gamely agrees that he should be a part of the child's life and the two begin to work on their relationship. They go shopping for baby clothes and Ben tells her he'll read a stack of child-rearing books to prepare. But it won't be that easy for Ben to change. His friends are his support group and they are arrested adolescents. Ben doesn't really know how to be an adult, and as the months pass, Alison begins to question whether he will be a fit partner in rearing their child. When she discovers that Ben has never even taken those child-rearing books out of the bag, she breaks up with him.

Hitting rock bottom, Ben turns to his father, Harris, a thrice-married 15 man, for advice. The only thing Harris can tell his son is, "You can go around blaming everyone else, but in the end, until you take responsibility for yourself, none of this is going to work out."

Ben leaves his druggie pals, moves into his own apartment, and 16 finds a real job. He stays home in the evenings and reads the baby books. He grows up. When Alison goes into labor alone, she calls him and a new side of Ben emerges. He manages to get Alison to the hospital and stand with her through a difficult (but hilariously graphic) birth process. The gestation period has resulted in two births—one of a baby, and the other of an adult male. Ben's whole demeanor has changed from that of a man-child to someone who acts like a husband. The hard-won maturity raises the hope that the couple, once so wildly different, has been transformed by the process into good parents for their baby daughter.

Critics were struck at finding such traditional values in an R-rated 17 sex comedy. In the New York *Times*, A. O. Scott remarked, "While this movie's barrage of gynecology-inspired jokes would have driven the prudes at the old Hays Office mad, its story, about a young man trying to do what used to be the very definition of the Right Thing, might equally have brought a smile of approval to the lips of the starchiest old-Hollywood censor." *Time*'s film critic Richard Schickel wrote that Apatow "clearly believes in marriage, family, bourgeois dutifulness."

A *New York Times Magazine* profile of Apatow describes his films   18
as having "conservative morals the Family Research Council might
embrace—if the humor weren't so filthy." The reporter accompanied
the director/writer/producer, his wife, and the *Knocked Up* stars to a
chic club on the rooftop of a Las Vegas hotel and noted how uncomfortable Apatow was amidst the glitz and girls. In the same article, a friend
reports that Apatow doesn't even like it when he points out attractive
women to him. The director confirms this unease: "He's right . . . I'm
the guy who gets uncomfortable. That's why I was able to write *The
40-Year-Old Virgin* and *Knocked Up*. I believe in those guys. There's
something honorable about holding out for love and not breaking up
for the sake of the baby. I see people get divorced, and there is a part of
me that thinks, I wonder how hard they tried?"

What's striking is finding such morals in what are truly R-worthy   19
comedies. The F-word and other such language flow freely because
that is the social world of these nerds and geeks, although, as the *New
York Times* review notes, "for all its rowdy obscenity it rarely feels
coarse or crude." Although Apatow has a clear affection for his male
losers and bong-smoking boys, they serve as a sharp contrast when his
protagonists start to break away from their boys club, leaving them
looking somewhat pathetic in their immaturity. They will probably
never know the joy and satisfaction of Andy and Ben, who traded their
action figures and porn sites for commitment and fidelity.

607

This is not to advocate that readers should rush out and rent an   20
Apatow film, but I find their critical and commercial success interesting
cultural indicators that even in the midst of an age long past the restraint
and taste of yesteryear, there is an underlying attraction to the stability
and joy that can come from taking responsibility to act one's age.

Can a couple of subversively moral sex comedies reverse the   21
results of the sexual revolution? Media effects theorists argue it takes
many exposures to a given message over an extended period of time
before attitudes change and behavior is altered. Cultural transformation
is a mysterious and complex phenomenon so only the presumptuous
would read these films as harbingers of moral regeneration. But we can
still marvel when someone like Judd Apatow can make people laugh at
themselves while pondering his challenge to be a mensch.

Examining the Text

1. Describing his feelings toward the protagonists he created for *40-Year-Old
Virgin* and *Knocked Up*, writer/director Judd Apatow says, "I believe in those
guys." What personality traits and behavioral patterns make the male leads of
those two movies sympathetic in the eyes of their creator?

2. The author comments that, although "these films aren't made for your
church youth group," they do contain some implicit suggestions for correct

moral/ethical behavior within a civilized society. What qualities of Judd Apatow's comedies render them unfit for the stereotypical "church youth group," and what suggestions for upright citizenship emerge from Apatovian romantic comedy, despite their raunchiness?

3. The author of this article devotes most of his attention to two of Judd Apatow's comedies, *The 40-Year-Old Virgin* and *Knocked Up.* Briefly summarize the author's plot summary of the first of those movies, and explain the themes that emerge from the narrative of *The 40-Year-Old Virgin,* in the opinion of Wainer.

4. Wainer next turns his attention to *Knocked Up,* giving it a similar summary/analysis treatment that he gave to *The 40-Year-Old Virgin.* Report on the significant plot details of *Knocked Up,* as provided by Wainer, and discuss the ways in which the author of this article sees "traditional values" emerging from *Knocked Up:* a movie that contains, once again, a relatively "raunchy" set of circumstances and character portrayals.

5. *Thinking rhetorically*: The author of this article gives a quick rundown of "male character types" in popular movies through several decades. He then goes on to update this list, discussing personality traits of leading men in current romantic comedies. Summarize Wainer's points about male protagonists over the past several decades and then—drawing upon your own history as a movie watcher—test the critic's persuasive points: do his generalizations about these male leads hold up, or do your examples contradict the evidence he provides here, perhaps casting doubt upon his conclusions?

For Group Discussion

At the beginning of this article, author Wainer attempts to set the comedies of Judd Apatow apart from other contemporary R-rated comedies, stating that Apatovian films have a certain moral dimension that the other productions do not. In all cases, Wainer says, "a culture of boy-men characterizes numerous movie types" cast as leads in these films . . . but the non-Apatow-like comedies—films starring Adam Sandler, Jack Black, and characters in Kevin Smith films, for example—do not have the redeeming (at least in Wainer's and Apatow's minds) quality of elevating marriage and societal conformity through their narrative resolutions. In class discussion, and from your own extensive knowledge of films of this type, bring up specific examples of recent romantic comedies, both of the Apatovian and the non-Apatovian variety, in order to test the validity of Wainer's hypothesis here.

Writing Suggestion

Using the comparison/contrast rhetorical form, write an essay discussing this chapter's paired readings on the comedies of Judd Apatow. Each author—David Denby and Alex Wainer—has a unique perspective on these films, both in terms of their quality as satisfying viewing fare, and as indicators of broader societal trends and moral/ethical currents. Each critic finds much to admire in Apatovian film, and yet each arrives at significantly different conclusions about the merits and meanings of the movies under scrutiny. To construct your essay, first make an outline of the specific issues of similarity between the two reviewers' points of view, and then outline the reviewers' issues of difference. Next, employing the "point-by-point" method of comparison/contrast, follow your outline in discussing the reviewers' specific areas of likeness and dissimilarity in their "takes" on Apatow's films and their wider implications. Finally, as you move toward your conclusion, attempt to situate yourself within this discussion: what is *your* "take" on the artistic merit of Judd Apatow's movies, and how do *you* believe those movies indicate—and perhaps even construct—societal tastes, ethics, and mores?

Pulp Fiction

ALAN A. STONE

Quentin Tarantino assembles films the way radical Bauhaus architects design homes: both toss aside the conventions of their peers to produce original—and sometimes highly controversial—approaches to their craft. This section of the Movies chapter explores the controversy surrounding Tarantino's moviemaking aesthetic. In both of the subsequent readings, excessive filmic violence serves as a focal point for the authors' reactions and subsequent discussions.

In evaluating Quentin Tarantino's films, critics frequently focus on the movies Pulp Fiction *and* Kill Bill, *which—in the opinion of some commentators—put an emphasis not just on depicting the gore of violent acts, but also on suggesting the pervasiveness of violence in modern society. In the following article, originally published in the* Boston Review, *Alan Stone writes that Tarantino includes violence as an essential element of the visual experience in* Pulp Fiction. *Stone compares* Pulp Fiction *to Van Gogh's famous sunflowers painting: an artifact that, in its way, also challenged artistic expression in its time. Stone describes Tarantino's depiction of violence as "stylized" and the film as both a celebration and a satire of popular culture. Indeed, Stone notes, even the title is borrowed from popular culture, pulp fiction being a somewhat derisory description of cheap, monthly short story magazines produced in the thirties and later.*

The Boston Review *article also examines how Tarantino seeks to explore, exploit, and expand on the ordinary, juxtaposing seemingly innocuous conversation in unconventional settings, or unexpected characters in conventional settings. His use of both dialog and dramatic situations are highly individualistic; one such example is his use of a British couple, complete with seemingly out-of-place accents, as armed robbers in Los Angeles. In another situation, he has two unsentimental killers talking about differences between American fast-food in Europe and how that compares to the home-grown version in the States.*

*Is Tarantino merely out to shock audiences with his new approach to vio-
lence? Certainly, other filmmakers have used special effects to creating scenes of
carnage caused by bullets, explosions, knives, death rays, chainsaws, samurai
swords, piano wire, and bare human hands. But, says Stone, Tarantino is
mindful that some, especially European critics, have called violence in
American films a form of pornography. Stone doubts that Tarantino seeks to
cross the threshold of good taste merely to exploit some of the public's taste for
unabashed violence. Instead he sees in Tarantino a filmmaker who deliberately
blurs the line between appeasing a societal depiction of violence and mocking it
at the same time. Furthermore, he finds in* Pulp Fiction *no violence against
women and no nudity. In the end, Stone suggests there is much more to value
in* Pulp Fiction, *beneath the visual surface of blood and gore.*

*As you read, notice how Stone mentions the murder of the young man
in the second paragraph and then returns to this scene in the film toward the
end of the article. Why do you think the author chooses to do this rather than
deal with that particular scene in successive paragraphs? What effect do you
think the author was seeking in emphasizing that particular scene?*

610

If you take no pleasure in popular culture, with all its manic excesses,   1
then you are likely to be bewildered, even offended, by Quentin
Tarantino's extraordinary film, *Pulp Fiction*. Tarantino unapologetically
enjoys popular culture at the same time that he satirizes it. Unfortunately,
he also seems to specialize in violence. Still, taken on its own terms, *Pulp
Fiction* is a rare accomplishment; it opens a new aesthetic horizon in film.
Like Van Gogh's sunflowers, the ordinary suddenly takes on a striking
vibrancy; from the dazzling title colors on, it is easy to recognize the artist,
but almost impossible to imagine how one could imitate him. Tarantino, a
one-time video store clerk, now the hottest director in Hollywood, has
memory banks packed with movies and he draws on some of the most
ordinary to create something brilliantly original. This is no experimental
film of intellectual pretensions and high-brow obscurantism. *Pulp Fiction*
is already building a cult following, even as its mother-fucker language
and graphic violence offends others.

Violence in film is a serious matter, and for some people an inex-   2
cusable offense. They can see no justification for the scene in which
John Travolta's character accidentally blows a young man's brains out.
Even worse for those concerned about film violence, most of the audience laughed despite the spatter of blood and brain tissue—and with
spontaneous amusement, not the nervous hysteria often heard at horror films. The violence of *Pulp Fiction* is essential to its aesthetic;
though he knew that many would complain, Tarantino meant the
audience to laugh.

Deliberately violating the conventions of action-violence films,   3
Tarantino reimagines stylized moments of violence and exaggerates
them until they are almost surrealistic. Then he creates dialogue that
leads up to the violence and then away from it. When most directors
would be building tension and suspense, Tarantino has his killers chatting. When most directors would cut away from the violence, Tarantino
stays with the aftermath. And he has achieved something I would have
thought impossible; he has made violence humorous by doing it
tongue-in-cheek—and the tongue has a stud in it.

Tarantino's film garnered top honors at the Cannes Film Festival   4
but will probably pay for its "punkness" at the Oscars. Its box office success, however, should comfort the many aspiring Hollywood directors
who dream of doing something different. But they will not find it easy
to follow in Tarantino's tracks. His film is put together with touch, spin,
and nuance, and then goes off in your face like a letter bomb.

What Tarantino has crafted in this film can be best appreciated in   5
the performance he has extracted from John Travolta. In 1977, Travolta
gave his unforgettable portrayal of the cock-of-the-walk dancer in
Saturday Night Fever. Far from a natural dancer, he nonetheless gave a
heart-winning performance. Ever since then, he has been fighting the
battle of the bulge and trying with less and less success to prove that he
can act. One might have concluded that he was too old, too fat, and too
far over the hill for *Pulp Fiction.* But it turns out that he is brilliantly cast
in the film; everything wrong about him is right for this part. In his
early-forties he still has a teenager's winning vulnerability. His broad
mouth and high cheek bones are now bejowled but there is still a
promise of sensuality in that ruined face. His appealing and familiar
presence brings just the feel of movie nostalgia Tarantino wanted.

Travolta plays a laid back, get-along kind of guy who is living a   6
depraved and drug-addicted life as a paid killer, but has an astonish-
ingly innocent soul, as do most of Tarantino's low-life characters. This
innocence in depravity is *Pulp Fiction*'s central theme. It keeps the film
from being an exercise in sado-masochistic perversity; it is the source of
its humor and its creative energy.

The film title *Pulp Fiction* harks back to the '30s and '40s when   7
newsstands featured an array of monthly short story magazines.
Among the most popular were those about hard-nosed private investigators. Written by such authors as Dashiell Hammet, Raymond
Chandler, and James M. Cain, these stories were the forerunners of
dark, city crime movies that became *film noir.* Pulp fiction stories typically began in the front of the magazine, competing for the reader's
attention, and were then continued in the back. Tarantino, though not
old enough to remember this genre of pulp fiction, has put his film
together as if he had that structure in mind.

611

We begin with one short story: a hopped-up British couple 8
(Amanda Plummer and Tim Roth) deciding to rob the coffee shop
where they are having breakfast. Before they do, we turn the page—a
dark screen—to the next story of Travolta and Jackson going off to
retrieve a mysterious briefcase and to kill some drug dealers who
didn't pay off their boss. Then another dark screen—to the childhood
of the Bruce Willis character who grows up to be the boxer who refuses
to throw the fight. Unlike the old pulp fiction magazines, the triptych
of stories eventually comes together as the seemingly disparate plots
are interwoven by coincidence and by Tarantino's central theme.
Because the film is set in Los Angeles, its anthology structure may of
course owe much more to Robert Altman's *Shortcuts* or to his brilliant
Nashville than to pulp fiction magazines.

But Tarantino's borrowings are no defect. He is winking at his 9
audience; he wants them to be aware of his references. The more they
recognize, the more they will enjoy the texture of his tapestry. It is
because John Travolta carries so much baggage that he is so wonderful
in this film. Moreover, everything Tarantino borrows is a cliché that has
been given an original spin. *Pulp Fiction* takes the dead genre of *film
noir* and gives it new life. Finally, Tarantino's startling humor takes his
film beyond anything he has drawn from others.

Tarantino's interweaving of his three stories complicates the lin- 10
ear time structure of each plot. The most surprising result is that the
Travolta character is killed only to reappear in the final scene of the
movie, which took place earlier and is presented out of sequence. Once
you figure out the puzzle, it becomes clear that Tarantino is playing
with convention rather than rejecting or deconstructing it. Tarantino's
entire film is playful, but he is playing with the imaginary world of
film, not with reality itself.

There can be no doubt that the self-taught Tarantino intends to 11
shock his audience. The many scenes of graphic violence testify to
that. European filmmakers are concerned that violence in American
film is pornography that appeals to the lowest common denominator
and, like American fast food, is destroying the taste for better things.
Some psychologists believe that film and TV violence teach America's
young people to be violent, or at the very least, inure them to real-life
violence. Perhaps most troubling is the idea that graphic violence, like
pornography, exploits an appetite in our basest instincts that degrades
rather than edifies. Many people are refusing to see this film and a surprising number of my middle-aged friends report that their teenage
children love it but have warned them they will hate the film. These
reactions to the violence are too important to be dismissed, but I
do not believe that Tarantino has dismissed them. His film exploits
violence, but as the jury at Cannes recognized, he is neither lacking in

moral sensibility nor, even though he wallows in popular culture, is he a Philistine.

If violence is a form of pornography, then, like pornography, it presents the same problem of line-drawing between exploiting our passions and edifying them. But as our modern courts have recognized, it is necessary to go beyond that simple categorical distinction and ask whether an admittedly exploitive work of art has redeeming social value. 12

When Shakespeare wrote *Hamlet* and *King Lear*, he intended to exploit his audiences' violent passions as well as to edify them. There is, after all, a great deal of violence, even graphic violence, in *Lear*—remember "out vile jelly" as Cornwall gouges out Gloucester's eyes on stage. The greatest works of Western Civilization mock those who count graphic violence as *ipso facto* unredeemable exploitation. 13

This is not to say that Tarantino intends to redeem the violence; if anything, he seems to be mocking the arbiters of good taste with his "wicked" humor. This is most blatant, not in the scenes of violence, but in the quirky introduction to the Bruce Willis/boxer story. Christopher Walken, an actor who will be remembered for his Oscar-winning performance in *Deer Hunter* (a Vietnam war-film), makes a brief appearance in *Pulp Fiction* as a former Vietnam POW. He has come to deliver his dead cellmate's gold watch to the young boy who never knew his father. The Walken character begins to tell the boy what happened to his father in standard heroic pulp fiction rhetoric, but then veers perversely into a description of the intestinal orifice where the father hid the watch, and the intestinal disorders that complicated its concealment. 14

It is an account that no sane adult would give a child and a scene right out of a graffiti imagination. Other directors are capable of imagining such graffiti, but Tarantino was brash enough to keep it in his film. Like all toilet graffiti it can be understood as an example of adolescent bad taste and Tarantino knows that. It is "gross," it is inappropriate, it is irreverent, and one can understand why the younger generation would be warning off their fuddy-duddy parents. Yet even this heavy-handed moment belongs in the film. The scene begins as a patriotic-die-for-your-country cliché in which the reality of how the gold watch survived would have been unimagined. Tarantino's script takes up the challenge of an explanation and as he veers into scatology, he gives the finger to the false norm of noble death in all such war clichés. But Tarantino is interested less in making an anti-war gesture than in doing a send-up of a movie cliché. Similarly, this is not an anti-violence film. It is a send up of movie violence. 15

One astute teenage critic remarked that Tarantino learned something from his first film, *Reservoir Dogs*. All the guys in her high school loved the macho violence but there was not much in this male-oriented 16 film for her and her female friends. Despite its violence and male orientation, *Pulp Fiction* has something for the female gender, particularly the scenes between Travolta and Uma Thurman.

This teenage critic and her girl friends especially enjoyed the 17 episode in which the Travolta character is required to entertain the black crime boss's white wife (Uma Thurman). The previous man charged with this task had given her a foot massage; the boss took umbrage and had the massager thrown out of a four-story window. The Travolta–Thurman episode quickly turns into an over-the-top parody of a blind date. Travolta prepares himself by going to his drug dealer for a batch of the ultimate hit—a mixture of cocaine and heroin that only a seasoned addict could tolerate. Travolta mainlines the stuff the way a nervous guy might take a drink to boost his confidence before a date. Meanwhile, Uma Thurman is sniffing cocaine, not because she's uneasy, but because she is a man-eater whetting her appetite.

Thurman takes Travolta to a dance contest where they do the twist, 18 to the delight of *Saturday Night Fever* fans. Tarantino's elaborate set features vintage '50s convertibles as booths, pop culture look-alikes as servers, top-of-the-charts music, all of it so extravagant in its evocation of nostalgia as to be unreal. The scene is somehow true to the spirit of *Pulp Fiction*, a film that parodies popular culture without ever condescending to those who take pleasure in it.

The Travolta/Thurman blind date has clever dialogue, the twist 19 is a trip, and the sexual tension escalates as they tango back into her home at the end of the evening. But while Travolta is in the toilet (it turns out he is always in the toilet at critical moments) Thurman finds his drug stash, snorts it, and overdoses. Instead of a sexual conclusion, the evening ends with a slapstick resuscitation involving a huge syringe stuck in her sternum. In this funny and surreal scene it becomes clear that Travolta and his low-life friends are playing over-aged adolescents. Indeed the whole film has the spirit, energy, and sensibility of adolescence. No wonder teenagers love it.

Although Tarantino wants to shock us with violence, his film is 20 politically correct. There is no nudity and no violence directed against women; in fact a man, the crime boss, gets raped and the only essentially evil people in the film are two sadistic honkies straight out of *Deliverance* who do the raping. The film celebrates interracial friendship and cultural diversity; there are strong women and strong black men, and the director swims against the current of class stereotype.

It is the British couple who, out of place in Los Angeles in the 21 very first scene, fill the sound track with British-accented "mother fuckers." Amanda Plummer, who was born to play Ophelia, does a crazed "Honey Bunny" to Tim Roth's "Pumpkin." They are two waifs holding hands in the storm of their strung-outness on drugs and their hare-brained career of sticking up liquor stores. The juxtaposition of their lost teddy bear attachment to each other with their nervous trigger-finger desperation establishes Tarantino's tone of innocence in depravity. Samuel Jackson, who will best be remembered as the drug-addicted older brother in Spike Lee's *Jungle Fever*, sustains that tone as Travolta's hit-man partner. His presence on the screen is a match for Travolta; he has a face that looks different in every camera angle and he radiates strength. These professional killers engage first in an earnest discussion about the European nomenclature of American fast foods and then a subtle analysis of the sexual significance of the foot massage as they make their way to the apartment where they will kill three men. The Jackson character miraculously eludes a point-blank fusillade of bullets. As they leave, they debate whether he was saved by divine intervention or simple luck. Jackson, who quotes from Ezekiel to spellbinding effect when he kills people, suddenly understands his Biblical text in a quite different way. As it turns out, his life and perhaps—if it is possible for a killer—his soul will be saved by this epiphany.

This theme of redemption is present in each of the three stories. Willis as Butch the boxer rescues his would-be killer, the black crime boss, from the honkey rapists. Butch, who was to be their next victim, has the opportunity to escape, but goes back. Redeemed by this act of solidarity, he is forgiven by the crime boss for not throwing the fight and is sent on his way. 22

The British couple are also saved. They try to rob Jackson who has ended up in the restaurant where the film began. He has drawn his gun under the table and could easily blow them both away. Instead, in the spirit of justice and honor that prevails among the low-lifes in this film, Jackson does the right thing. He stares the amateur criminals down, letting them take his own money but not the mysterious briefcase that he is dutifully returning to the crime boss. We believe that the strung-out British couple are capable of a killing rampage in the restaurant—Amanda Plummer is a remarkable sight standing on a restaurant table screaming obscenities and waving a Saturday-night special. We also know that the day before Jackson would have killed them without blinking an eye, and that he will have to kill them today if they try to take the boss's briefcase. Instead Jackson sends the couple peacefully out of the restaurant clutching each other and a trash bag filled with stolen money. 23

But the best scenes involve Jackson and Travolta. When they are not killing, they are like college sophomores, one black, one white—both amateur philosophers eager to share their ideas and experiences. Tarantino's ingenious dialogue humanizes their homicidal partnership. The improbable juxtaposition of their earnest dialogue and the violence is the stylistic twist that allows us to laugh at the spatter of brains and blood in the backseat of their car. Travolta reacts like a 24 teenager unjustly blamed by his buddy for accidentally spilling the beer. And like children of over-indulgent parents, they have no idea how to clean up the mess.

Yes, they seem oblivious to the fact that a person has been killed. In that light their conversation is ludicrous. But this absurd dialogue unexpectedly transforms the meaning of the violence cliché. If Tarantino wanted to defend his film, this is where he could make his strongest arguments. *Pulp Fiction* unmasks the macho myth by making it laughable and deheroicizes the power trip glorified by standard Hollywood violence. But Tarantino is irreverent, not didactic. He goes from Road-Runner cartoon-violence humor in the Bruce Willis segment to whips and chain homosexual rape that silences the laughter. Tarantino will stop at nothing and yet never loses control. He dives into a nightmare and comes up with something funny, taking his audience up and down with him. Though Tarantino thinks his screenplay is funny, and would be disappointed if no one laughed, he doesn't consider *Pulp Fiction* a comedy. He is quite right; but if you don't get the studded tongue-in-cheek humor, you may not like this extraordinary movie.

Examining the Text

1. What do you think the author means when he writes (paragraph 3), "Deliberately violating the conventions of action-violence films, Tarantino reimagines stylized moments of violence and exaggerates them until they are almost surrealistic"? Can you think of instances in which an action movie might have followed these so-called conventions, creating nonstylized depictions of violence? What distinguishes a "stylized" depiction of violence versus a mere straightforward depiction, and what might be the desired effect in creating stylized images of violence?

2. Based on your reading of this article, how do you think the author views Tarantino's use of violence in *Pulp Fiction*? Find sections of the article that support your interpretation of the author's position.

3. The author writes that Tarantino seeks to "shock his audience." By what specific means does the filmmaker achieve this end, in the opinion of Stone? Might Tarantino have other, non-shocking intentions in his depictions of violence? Finally, since film is a visual medium, do you think that violence has to be depicted with blood and gore, or are there other effective ways to portray it?

4. *Thinking rhetorically*: What is the author's thematic intention in the following sentence: "*Pulp Fiction* unmasks the macho myth by making it laughable and deheroicizes the power glorified by standard Hollywood violence"? What textual evidence does the author provide to support his position of how Tarantino seeks to "deheroicize" *Pulp Fiction*? Is this assertion logically consistent with the author's contention (in the last paragraph) that Tarantino "delves into a nightmare and comes up with something funny"? In your opinion, does the author succeed in this article's rhetorical purpose: namely to make a strong

25

case that *Pulp Fiction* seeks to demythologize Hollywood violence by making audiences laugh?

For Group Discussion
Some research studies suggest a causal relationship between fictional violence depicted in films and actual violence in American streets and homes. In groups of four or five, discuss whether you think that violence in movies promotes real violence, or whether film violence might have a redeeming role as social commentary or as a healthy outlet for people's natural aggressive impulses. Select one member from your group to represent the "film violence is healthy" position, and one member to represent the antiviolence position. When you reassemble as a full class, have each of those group representatives engage in a debate, attempting to arrive at some consensus regarding the role of film violence in contemporary culture.

Writing Suggestion
Rent the movies *Pulp Fiction* and *A Clockwork Orange*: both films whose violence is not merely gratuitous but rather serves a larger thematic purpose as social commentary. . . at least in the eyes of many critics. Take notes on how violence is depicted in each film, and as you watch, comment also on how the violence affects you personally. Did you look away, especially at first? Did you become immune after a while? After viewing both films, write a comparison/contrast essay in which you examine the thematic role of violence in each film. To substantiate your points, include some research material: film criticism on Tarantino and Kubrick, and/or primary sources in which the filmmakers discuss their own approaches to filmmaking and attitudes toward violence in film.

She'll Kill Bill While You Chill

THOMAS DE ZENGOTITA

His biographical details are the stuff of legend. Movie-obsessed kid gets job at video store frequented by movie-industry insiders. Kid impresses many with his savvy, energy, and wit. Kid writes script, which finds its way to the right people in Hollywood. Film script gets the nod. Kid (OK, now he's a young adult) makes movie in which he draws on his encyclopedic knowledge of the movies . . . and in many ways seeks to satirize the society in which Hollywood was created. The film is a huge success and vaults our former Kid to filmmaking mega-stardom. That kid, of course, is Quentin Tarantino. In the following article, author Thomas de Zengotita examines the young filmmaker's background, his approach to writing and directing, and his two recent films, Kill Bill *and* Kill Bill II.

*De Zengotita states starkly that these two films don't contain any significant content but are, instead, more of a commentary (and a gory one at that) on American society and culture. He says Tarantino movies are full of allusions to society and, more especially, references to popular culture. Everything from pop music to TV to fast food to television sitcoms to street slang to earlier movies is blended in the filmic smoothie that has become Tarantino's hallmark. Through this process he seeks to entertain but at the same time to reach a deeper level, to make an offbeat, acerbic, and wise commentary on contemporary American culture. **As you read**, notice how the author seeks to qualify his own credentials for dissecting Tarantino's movies. What does he mean when he says, ". . . I am just a visiting participant-observer, not even close to being a native Tarantinian"? Watch out for other, similar references. What is the author's goal in using this distancing device? What's your reaction to this?*

"One of the most brilliant visual storytelling movies I've seen since the talkies. . . . It is pretty violent, I must say. At a certain point, it was like a Takashi Miike film. It got so fucked up it was funny. At one point, my friend and I, we just started laughing. I was into the seriousness of the story, of course, but in the crucifixion scene, when they turned the cross over, you had to laugh."

Quentin Tarantino on *The Passion of the Christ*

Someone should take charge of the word "sensationalism," refer it to 1 an articulated system of beliefs and practices, and put it on the list that includes, say, "socialism" and "Islamic fundamentalism." The implicated ideas and activities are out there, just waiting be formalized. Millions of people dedicate their lives to media-induced sensations, to their pursuit and their creation. Why not make it official?

The sensationalist movement is vast and varied and getting more 2 so with every innovation in representational technology. But movies are primal. And when it comes to creating sensations through cinematic depictions of violence, nobody can match Quentin Tarantino. That makes his work an ideal object of reflection for anyone concerned about the psychosocial effects of mediated violence—and I don't mean its influence on sociopaths already on the verge of mayhem, but the much subtler question of what it says about our culture. It's easy to condemn graphic gore when it's schlocky, but what are we to make of depictions that are, on their own terms, masterworks?

"Their own terms" means movie terms. It means the history of 3 movies, all kinds of movies, but especially violent movies—a self-referential world of movies within which Tarantinians dwell.

The Tarantino origin myth (that's not too strong a description) 4 puts this tenth-grade dropout and pop culture addict behind the counter of Video Archives in Manhattan Beach, California, in the late eighties. There he held court for five years, dispensing freely of analysis and opinion to a widening circle of steady customers, some of them with Hollywood connections, many of them in thrall to his astonishing mastery of movie lore—an omnivorous authority that ranged indiscriminately across genres and periods, from early Hitchcock and fifties noir to the French avant-garde and obscure Hong Kong martial arts splatter flicks. Tarantino had seen it all, and remembered it all; that was the incredible thing—credits, music, dialogue, cinematography, editing, sets, plots—everything. And he wove it all into a single hyperenergetic discourse, a comparative tapestry that seemed to render, upon the screen of a single consciousness, the entirety of cinematic experience. No wonder Hollywood players whose acquaintance he made took him seriously when he asked them to consider his early screenplays. This was no schmuck with a script; this was a living library, a walking tribute to all they held dear.

Tarantino became a mythic entity, a cult figure, because he actualized a transformation to which his followers aspire. In him, the Ultimate Fan became the Ultimate Auteur. Through *this* video store clerk, the slacker media geek was vindicated, his obsessions justified—his tastes, his slang, his values, his vast comic book collection, his online gaming, his fantasy quests—his whole investment in virtual living was redeemed.

And Tarantino understands this. He remains true to his origins. He may now be acclaimed by the establishment, honored with the chair of the jury at Cannes, but he represents a virtual way of life that postmodern media have made possible in more marginal precincts—though no true Tarantinian would get caught talking seriously about anything as ponderous as postmodernism. Sensationalists are allergic to such abstractions. They are dogmatically anti-intellectual and apolitical. They draw that line around themselves in order to protect their way of life from the uncomprehending disdain they have come to expect from society's grown-ups. And Tarantino makes it easy to defend that line. The intricacy of his plots and the density of his allusions make for a genuine complexity in his work—if not what you could call (perish the thought) depth. That complexity, so richly apparent to the cognoscenti, is more or less invisible otherwise, and so it supplies sensationalists with a trump. When it comes to Tarantino, they can truly say that their critics just don't get it.

The complexity of a Tarantino movie is all the more alluring because it lurks beneath a fabulous surface, a sensual pleasure package for the puzzles and the lore. The riveting cinematography, the blend of editing and scoring, the pacing, the way the whole composition radiates hyperreal clarity, that distinctive look and feel we also find in David Lynch

619

movies. This hyper-realism alerts the knowing viewer to a subversive intent that will lend heft to this feast of surfaces. It addresses those with the keys to the kingdom, flattering them with a wink and a nod that only they can detect. It invites them to pore indefinitely over intricacies of plot and timeline, to recline on a web of allusions so extended that even the most knowledgeable fans will never know if they have reached its end.

And it allows for inexhaustible discussion on Web sites and blogs. 8

In Tarantino movies the postmodern aesthetic of pastiche, of mix- 9 ing and citing and recycling, reaches its logical limit. His movies are literally about movies (and TV shows and ads and pop music). And not just indexically. Tarantino resurrects and manipulates tonalities and styles; entire moods, entire genres are evoked, and the playing never ends. The spaghetti western score accompanies a chicks-about-to-kick-butt buildup to a frenetic ninja blowout scene, and there is David Carradine (echoing his seventies kung fu TV show) as Bill, a villainous inversion of the original character, but deploying the same affect, flavored with (and undercut by) a hint of sadism that, in turn, contrasts (in the first [John Ford inspired] scene of Volume II) so ludicrously with (yet another Carradine echo) the oh-so-authentic flute he still carries.

Even I could go on listing allusions, and I am just a visiting 10 participant-observer, not even close to being a native Tarantinian.

Nor would I want to be. I have better things to do with my time. 11

But of that, more anon. 12

Back to the undercutting contrasts. They are importantly typical 13 of Tarantino's allusive style. He doesn't just cite, this isn't mere homage; he plays havoc with citations. He can make them fit, even when they don't—and that's his extraordinary gift, which also conveys the essential message: *It's all in fun.*

Sensationalism is the ideology of fun in general, but this particular 14 kind of fun is far from innocent. It is designed to put the Tarantinian one up, always, and to expose those who recoil from the graphic violence as congenitally out of it. If Pai Mei (the martial arts SuperMaster to whom Bill takes members of his Deadly Viper Assassination Squad for training) turns out to be the very opposite of the serene sensei we expect in this role, shouldn't that tell you something? If he turns out to be a spoiled prima donna, irascible, vain, and spiteful, the Tarantinian asks: Don't you see how funny that is? Deadly Viper Assassination Squad? Hello? Shouldn't that tell you something about the attitude here?

Then there are the plot twists and the temporality games. Chapter 15 1 of *Kill Bill I* is called "2," with a little handwritten circle around it. That refers to Uma's to do list, which names the four members of the Deadly Viper Assassination Squad she is out to slaughter—item number five being "Kill Bill," of course. As I recall (I may be wrong), you don't see that list actually being made out until the middle of Vol. II (a whole separate movie, released months later), and *that* movie begins with the massacre that precipitates the whole two-volume story, temporally speaking. I can't detect aesthetic motivation for this juggling. To me it seems designed to keep the Web sites buzzing with Tarantinians puzzling out the timeline. But I may be missing something. I probably am.

But the plot twists have effects I can follow. Their shock value is 16 strangely akin to the shock value of the goriest images—like Uma crushing Daryl's fresh plucked eyeball between her bare toes (Uma's feet deserve separate billing in this movie) on the linoleum floor of Budd's trailer (he's dead in the kitchen area, surprised by a black mamba in a suitcase full of money) while Daryl (now minus both eyes, Pai Mei having deftly extracted the first one in a fit of pique during her training year with him, but that's OK because, after it was over, Daryl poisoned Pai Mei's rice bowl and watched him die) thrashes around in the bathroom screaming in agony, bleeding from the hole in her face, ripping down the shower curtain, tearing fixtures from the walls, and, in general, giving new meaning to the expression "blind fury" as the whole scene dissolves into another case of things getting so fucked up that, as a Tarantinian, you just have to laugh—as (refer back to the dash at the top of this paragraph) when Uma finally makes it (at the end of Volume II) to Bill's luxurious Caribbean hideaway and does one of those stealth entry sequences, her priceless Hattori Hanzo sword slung across her back in that cool ninja way, her silver nine millimeter held out from her body in the official two-handed grip, and she pivoting to cover every angle as she springs into one room after the other (having crept suspensefully up to each), intent as a leopard (or a viper) on one thing only (killing Bill, remember?) and then, as she rounds the last doorframe, what does she find but her four-year-old daughter, whom she has never seen because she was born after Uma went into a coma when Bill shot her in the head (and she in a bridal gown, eight months pregnant) at her wedding (rehearsal), where he and the rest of the Deadly Viper Assassination Squad slaughtered the entire wedding party (Samuel Jackson barely recognizable in a cameo as the piano player) because Uma (code name: Black Mamba) had not only abandoned the Assassination Squad lifestyle, but had abandoned Bill, the father of the very same child, which pissed Bill off big time, but didn't stop him from taking their daughter into his keeping and, lo and behold, there he is now, playing with her, as Uma springs into that last room, and not just playing any old game, by golly, but playing a bang-bang game with a toy plastic space gun (no doubt a very specific one, recognizable to multitudes of Tarantinians), and Bill, all mock innocence, urging Uma, who is beginning to weep at the sight of her child, to join the game, and getting the little girl to bang-bang Uma, then cajoling Uma into doing one of those grip-your-stomach-and-groan-and-pretend-to-die things, because that's what the game requires, and Uma, her deadly purpose melted away (but only temporarily), complies, and after that Uma and Bill put their little girl to bed—and the upshot is: now, *that's* a plot twist.

If you followed all this, you have a sense of how recursively 17 embedded, how freewheeling and precise, a Tarantino movie is. Sort of like Proust—except for one thing.

There is no significant content of any kind. 18

And the question arises: What kind of culture invests so much in 19 something so hollow, hollow by design, hollow as a matter of principle?

A sensationalist culture devoted to fun. 20

But such a culture inevitably runs up against certain limits. There 21 are only so many ways you can produce these shocks and thrills. Tarantino is Tarantino because he found a whole new level of possibility, thanks to his reflexivity. Naïve viewers focus on the gore, but the initiated are accustomed to gore. For them, the violence and the plot twists aren't that different. Both are designed to elicit that I-can't-believe-I'm-seeing-*this* reaction, which is what you get when a how-can-he-top-*that* moment is successfully resolved.

Topping that is what Tarantino does. 22

Finally, there's the dialogue. Actor talk in movie promos is even 23 more hackneyed and formulaic than other forms of puffery, but when actors talk about being in a Tarantino movie, there is a tone of genuine admiration, mixed with bemusement, perhaps, but tinged with awe as well. They know these are not just movies starring them, but movies *about* them, about the world of their concerns, and they feel that world being transformed by this alchemist into something weighty and thick, something that achieves the standing of art without ever leaving the realm of the popular. For these actors, working with Tarantino isn't like starring in a revival of some classic play—that involves the implicit admission that what you normally do is less worthy. No, working with Tarantino means elevating what you normally do. The Ultimate Fan as Ultimate Auteur serves his actors in the same way he serves his followers. He turns total immersion in movies into a kind of wisdom.

But the actors don't seem conscious of this in so many words. What 24 they dwell on is Tarantino's dialogue, which provides the ultimate in comic contrast, a relentlessly prosaic and naturalistic verbal counterpoint to his cinematic virtuosity. Actors love the dialogue, not only for that contrast but also because it reflects their training—years of method acting, years of improvs. Most representative and most renowned is the discussion in *Pulp Fiction* between John Travolta and Samuel Jackson about how Quarter Pounders have to be called Le Royale in France because of the metric system. The kicker is that they are hit men on their way to massacre a room full of college kids while they are having this conversation. They even pause in the hall to clarify some point about fast food before busting down the door and blazing away.

How do you top *that?*   25

It was typical of Tarantino to praise Gibson's bloody movie while   26 sophisticated people everywhere were condemning it. But it was even more typical of him to find comedy in what the simple-minded Gibson meant to be transcendentally serious. The image of Tarantino and his friend chortling in their seats at the crucifixion is irresistible because it distills the issue to its essence. When I first read that description, I was reminded of Abu Ghraib guards, laughing as they tormented their prisoners, and I wondered, for a moment, what's the difference? But no sooner was the question framed than the Tarantinian reply came to me. I could imagine Quentin's face and voice:

> *The Passion of the Christ* is a *movie*, you idiot!

Ah, well, yes, of course.   27

The Tarantinian is always a step ahead, the Tarantinian is never   28 taken in, the Tarantinian can experience sadomasochistic sensations as intense and various as the master's prodigious talent can contrive— and find forgiveness in the last laugh as well.

623

The Tarantinian way guarantees immunity for the perpetually   29 entertained.

Examining the Text

1. The author comments that any deeper meanings to be found in Tarantino movies "lurk beneath a fabulous surface, a sensual pleasure package . . ." What does the author mean by this assertion, and do you agree with it or not?

2. What is meant by the statement: "In Tarantino movies the postmodern aesthetic of pastiche, of mixing and citing and recycling, reaches its logical limit"? Can you find examples in the text where the author cites particular scenes to which his statement would seem to apply? Given the desire of a filmmaker like Tarantino to push boundaries, can there really be a logical limit? Are there limits to what the public will find acceptable in a Hollywood movie?

3. Why do you think actors seem to see participation in a Tarantino film as elevating their craft? Is this a comment on "mainstream" Hollywood films, or the quality of Tarantino's films, or both? Why would actors be "bemused" by working on a Tarantino film?

4. *Thinking rhetorically*: What do you think the author means by "sensationalism" or "sensationalist" in the context of this article's arguments? What is the author's rhetorical intention—in this case, his intended persuasive purpose— in proposing that "sensationalism" belongs in the same category as "socialism" or "Islamic fundamentalism"? Do you feel that his strategy is effective here or that he's taking a position that's too extreme to be plausible?

For Group Discussion

Consider again the sentiment, ". . . I am just a visiting participant-observer, not even close to being a native Tarantinian." Discuss the qualities that potentially give a person the authority or entitlement to write a film criticism article, or to do any form of art criticism. Must you be a graduate of a university? Should you have a certain amount of experience viewing films, discussing films, reading other people's critiques? Reflecting on various art and film criticism that you've encountered, discuss what has been valuable to you, what hasn't been valuable . . . and what has been downright annoying.

Writing Suggestion

View either or both of the *Kill Bill* films and take notes, then write your own critique of the film(s). In writing critique, keep in mind that film critics routinely refer to other reviewers' articles on the same films (for example, the two Tarantino articles in this reader), and that they draw on any additional knowledge they might have about the writer/director, such as biographical information. Furthermore, since a critique is a personal assessment of a film, feel free to take a very opinionated tone in your own piece. However, if you take this tack, make sure that you support your strong opinions with evidence from research and from the film's text itself.

ADDITIONAL SUGGESTIONS FOR WRITING ABOUT MOVIES

1. In this chapter, we presented several articles that focus on a central filmic theme, namely violence. In your own interpretative essay, compare and contrast several movies dealing with a different central theme or issue. For instance, you might compare several films about the Vietnam War, or about the lives of the current generation of "twentysomethings," or about inner-city gangs, or about parent–child relationships. Choose movies that interest you and, ideally, that you can see again. You might want to structure your essay as an argument aimed at convincing your readers that one movie is in some way "better" than the others. Or you might use your comparison of the movies to draw some larger point about popular culture and the images it presents to us.

2. In a research or "I-search" essay, consider the complex relationship between film and social morality. Do you believe that films such as *Fight Club* and *Pulp Fiction* tend to encourage audience identification with the villain and help sanction violent behavior . . . or is there a more "sublime" dimension to film violence, as suggested by some of the authors in this chapter? In your research, explore what other experts say about the relationship between real and fictional violence. Can you find specific current events that support your arguments?

3. In a speculative essay that uses Kyle Bishop's article on zombie flicks as a model, explore why audiences crave movies of a certain genre: futuristic techno-thrillers, movies based on television sitcoms and cartoons, chase movies, menaced-female dramas, psychotic-killer stories, romantic comedies, supernatural comedies, and so forth. Choose a type of movie familiar to you so that you can offer as many specific examples as possible. In approaching this assignment, try to answer some of these questions: What is the "fun" of seeing this type of movie? What sort of "psychic relief" does it deliver? Are there specific types of people who are likely to enjoy the genre more than others? Does the genre serve any function for society? In what ways do movies in this genre affect us, changing our thoughts or feelings after we've seen them?

Internet Activities

1. These days, anyone with a Web site has the power to post a movie review. Choose several online reviews—written by both professional movie critics and "regular" moviegoers such as yourself—for a movie you've seen (some options are available on the *Common Culture* Web site). Write an essay in which you note the primary differences between the reviews done by professionals and those done by the regular fan(s). What aspects of the film do the professionals focus on? Are they the same as those of the regular fan or do they vary? Does one group emphasize certain elements, such as the emotions encouraged by the film, the acting, or the cinematography? Which of the reviews most closely reflects your opinion of the movie? Why do you think these reviews are the ones with which you best identify?

2. Visit a Web site for a new film you're interested in seeing and write a review of the site (some options are available on the *Common Culture* Web site). What is offered on the Web site that a potential audience wouldn't get from any other form of media? What do you like best about the Web site? What would you change? Describe the advantages of having a Web site for a new film. Are there any disadvantages? How do you feel movie Web sites will influence which movies we want to watch?

Reading Images

The image on page 626 encapsulates the dramatic (and comedic) tension in Judd Apatow's film *Knocked Up*. As you can see, it depicts actors Seth Rogen and Katherine Heigl stressing about their mutual predicament, i.e. her pregnancy. After rereading the section in Chapter 1 about how to analyze images, take notes about the particular features of this image—expressions, body composition, the text on Rogen's t-shirt, Heigl's gold earrings—and come to a conclusion about the narrative subthemes it conveys. Then, in an essay, discuss the ways in which this single frame from the movie encapsulates concepts that are raised in Denby's and Wainer's discussions of Apatovian comedy. You might conclude your essay by discussing what effect the image has on you as a reader/viewer, and whether the image—along with situations portrayed within the narrative arc of the film—leads you to conceptualize additional themes within the text of *Knocked Up:* ideas that were not raised by Denby or Wainer but that you find provocative and worth considering.

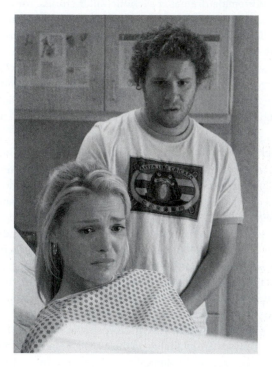

"Knocked Up," 2007. Starring Katherine Heigl and Seth Rogen. Directed by Judd Apatow.

For Further Reading:
A Common Culture
Bibliography

CHAPTER 2: ADVERTISING

Barthel, Diane. *Putting on Appearances: Gender and Advertising*. Philadelphia, PA: Temple University Press, 1988.

Berger, Arthur Asa. *Ads, Fads, and Consumer Culture: Advertising's Impact on American Character and Society*. Lanham, MD: Rowman & Littlefield, 2000, 2007.

Cortese, Anthony Joseph Paul. *Provocateur: Images of Women and Minorities in Advertising*. Lanham, MD: Rowman & Littlefield Publishers, 1999, 2008.

Ewen, Stuart and Elizabeth Ewen. *Channels of Desire: Mass Images and the Shaping of American Consciousness*. 2nd edition. Minneapolis, MN: University of Minnesota Press, 1992.

Fowles, Jib. *Advertising and Popular Culture*. Thousand Oaks, CA: Sage, 1996.

Fox, Roy. *Mediaspeak: Three American Voices*. Westport, CT: Praeger, 2001.

Kilbourne, Jean, director. *Still Killing Us Softly*. Cambridge, MA: Cambridge Documentary Films, 1992 Videocassette.

———. *Deadly Persuasion: Why Women and Girls Must Fight the Addictive Power of Advertising*. New York: Free Press, 1999.

Jones, John Philip. *When Ads Work: New Proof that Advertising Triggers Sales*. Armonk, NY: M.E. Sharpe, 2007.

Klein, Naomi. *No Logo: No Space, No Choice, No Jobs*. New York: Picador, 2002.

Lasn, Kalle. *Culture Jam: The Uncooling of America*. New York: Eagle Brook, 1999.

McQuarrie, Edward F. and Barbara J. Phillips (Eds.). *Go Figure! New Directions in Advertising Rhetoric*. Armonk, NY: M.E. Sharpe, 2008.

Mitchell, Arthur. *The Nine American Lifestyles: Who We Are and Where We're Going*. New York: Warner Books, 1983.

Parkin, Katherine. *Food Is Love: Advertising and Gender Roles in Modern America*. Pennsylvania: University of Pennsylvania Press, 2006.

Quart, Alissa. *Branded: The Buying and Selling of Teenagers*. New York: Basic Books, 2004.

Schor, Juliet. *Born to Buy: The Commercialized Child and the New Consumer Culture*. New York: Scribner, 2004.

Sivulka, Juliann. *Soap, Sex, and Cigarettes: A Cultural History of American Advertising*. Belmont, CA: Wadsworth, 1998.

Twitchell, James. *Twenty Ads That Shook the World: The Century's Most Groundbreaking Advertising and How it Changed Us All*. New York: Crown Publishers, 2000.

CHAPTER 3: TELEVISION

Andrejevic, Mark. *Reality TV: The Work of Being Watched*. Lanham, MD: Rowman & Littlefield Publishers, 2003.

Batten, Frank with Jeffrey L. Cruikshank. *The Weather Channel: The Improbable Rise of a Media Phenomenon*. Boston, MA: Harvard Business School Press, 2002.

Cantor, Paul A. *Gilligan Unbound: Pop Culture in the Age of Globalization*. Lanham, MD: Rowman & Littlefield, 2001.

Gitlin, Todd. *Inside Prime Time*. 2nd edition. New York: Pantheon, 1994.

Hartley, John. *Uses of Television*. London: Routledge, 1999.

Heller, Dana (Ed.). *Makeover Television: Realities Remodelled*. London: I.B. Taurus, 2007.

Holt, Jason (Ed.). *The Daily Show and Philosophy: Moments of Zen in the Art of Fake News*. Malden, MA: Blackwell, 2007.

Johnson, Steven. *Everything Bad Is Good For You: How Today's Popular Culture Is Actually Making Us Smarter*. New York: Riverhead, 2005.

Mander, Jerry. *Four Arguments for the Elimination of Television*. New York: Morrow, 1978.

Miller, Mark Crispin. *Boxed In: The Culture of TV*. Evanston, IL: Northwestern University Press, 1988.

Murray, Susan and Laurie Ouellette (Eds.). *Reality TV: Remaking Television Culture*. New York: New York University Press, 2004.

Newcomb, Horace. *Television: The Critical View*. New York: Oxford University Press, 2000.

O'Neill, John. *Plato's Cave: Television and Its Discontents*. Cresskill, NJ: Hampton Press, 2002.

Palmer, Shelly. *Television Disrupted: The Transition from Network to Networked TV*. Boston, MA: Focal Press, 2006.

Peterson, Russell L. *Strange Bedfellows: How Late-Night Comedy Turns Democracy into a Joke*. New Brunswick, NJ: Rutgers University Press, 2008.

Postman, Neil. *Amusing Ourselves to Death*. New York: Penguin Books, 1985.

Riegert, Kristina (Ed.). *Politicotainment: Television's Take on the Real*. New York: Peter Lang, 2007.

Spiegel, Lynn and Jan Olsson (Eds.). *Television After TV: Essays on a Medium in Transition*. Durham, NC: Duke University Press, 2004.

Verklin, David and Bernice Kanner. *Watch This, Listen Up, Click Here: Inside the 300 Billion Dollar Business Behind the Media You Constantly Consume*. New York: John Wiley & Sons, 2007.

Watson, Mary Ann. *Defining Visions: Television and the American Experience in the 20th Century*. Malden, MA: Blackwell, 2008.

Williams, Raymond. *Television: Technology and Cultural Form*. New York: Schocken Books, 1975.

CHAPTER 4: POPULAR MUSIC

Appell, Glenn and David F. Hemphill. *American Popular Music: A Multicultural History*. New York: Wadsworth Publishing, 2005.

Cloonan, Martin and Reebee Garofalo. *Policing Pop*. Philadelphia: Temple University Press, 2003.

Colegrave, Stephen and Chris Sullivan. *Punk: The Definitive Record of a Revolution*. Boston: Thunder's Mouth Press, 2001.

Forman, Murray. *The 'Hood Comes First: Race, Space, and Place in Rap and Hip-Hop*. Middletown: Wesleyan University Press, 2002.

Goodman, Fred. "La explosion pop Latino." *Rolling Stone*, n812 (May 13, 1999): 21.

Greene, Bob. *When We Get to Surf City: A Journey through America in Pursuit of Rock and Roll, Friendship, and Dreams*. New York: St. Martin's Press, 2008.

Holt, Fabian. *Genre in Popular Music*. Chicago: University of Chicago Press, 2007.

Joyner, David Lee. *American Popular Music*. New York: McGraw-Hill, 2002.

Krasilovsky, M. William, Sidney Shemel and John M. Gross. *This Business of Music: The Definitive Guide to the Music Industry*. New York: Billboard Books, 2003.

Krims, Adam. *Rap Music and the Poetics of Identity*. Cambridge University Press, 2003.

Marcus, Greil. *Mystery Train: Images of America in Rock 'N' Roll Music*. New York: Plume, 1997.

———. *In the Fascist Bathroom: Punk in Pop Music, 1977–1992*. Cambridge, MA: Harvard University Press, 1999.

McNeil, Legs and Gillian McCain. *Please Kill Me: The Uncensored Oral History of Punk*. New York: Penguin, 1997.

Moore, Allan F. *Analyzing Popular Music*. Boston: Cambridge University Press, 2003.

Neal, Mark Anthony. *Soul Babies: Black Popular Culture and the Post-Soul Aesthetic*. New York: Routledge, 2002.

Perkins, William Eric. *Droppin' Science: Critical Essays on Rap Music and Hip Hop Culture*. Philadelphia: Temple University Press, 1996.

Posner, Gerald L. *Motown: Money, Power, Sex, and Music*. New York: Random House, 2002.

Potter, Russell A. *Spectacular Vernaculars: Hip-Hop and the Politics of Postmodernism*. New York: State University of New York Press, 1995.

Queen Latifah. *Ladies First: Revelations from a Strong Woman*. New York: William Morrow & Company, 1999.

Savage, Jon. *England's Dreaming: Anarchy, Sex Pistols, Punk Rock, and Beyond*. New York: St. Martin's Press, 2002.

Strong, Martin C. and Brendon Griffin. *Lights, Camera, Soundtracks: The Ultimate Guide to Popular Music in the Movies*. New York: Canongate, 2008.

Webb, Peter. *Exploring the Networked Worlds of Popular Music: Milieu Cultures*. London: Taylor & Francis, Inc., 2007.

Weisbard, Eric (Editor). *Listen Again: A Momentary History of Pop Music*. Durham: Duke University Press, 2007.

CHAPTER 5: TECHNOLOGY

Beck, John and Mitchell Wade. *Got Game: How the Gamer Generation is Reshaping Business Forever*. Boston, MA: Harvard Business School Press, 2004.

Blood, Rebecca. *We've Got Blog: How Weblogs are Changing Our Culture*. New York: Perseus Books, 2002.

Castronova, Edward. *Synthetic Worlds: The Business and Culture of Online Games*. Chicago, IL: University of Chicago Press, 2005.

Chayko, Mary. *Connecting: How We Form Social Bonds and Communities in the Internet Age*. Albany, NY: State University of New York Press, 2002.

Fornas, Johan (Ed.) *Digital Borderlands: Cultural Studies of Identity and Interactivity on the Internet*. New York: Peter Lang, 2002.

Garrelts, Nate (Ed.). *The Meaning and Culture of Grand Theft Auto: Critical Essays*. New York: McFarland, 2006.

Gee, James Paul. *What Video Games Have to Teach Us About Learning and Literacy*. New York: Palgrave Macmillan, 2003.

———. *Good Video Games + Good Learning: Collected Essays on Video Games, Learning and Literacy*. New York: Peter Lang, 2007.

Gergen, Kenneth. *The Saturated Self: Dilemmas of Identity in Contemporary Life*. New York: Basic Books, 2000.

Holloway, Sarah L. and Gill Valentine. *Cyberkids: Children in the Information Age.* London: Routledge, 2003.

Poole, Steven. *Trigger Happy: Videogames and the Entertainment Revolution.* New York: Arcade Publishing, 2000.

Postman, Neil. *Technopoly: The Surrender of Culture to Technology.* New York: Vintage Books, 1993.

Rosen, Christine. "The Age of Egocasting." *The New Atlantis* n. 7 (Fall 2004/Winter 2005): http://www.thenewatlantis.com/publications/the-age-of-egocasting.

Shirky, Clay. *Here Comes Everybody: The Power of Organizing Without Organizations.* New York: Penguin, 2008.

Smolan, Rick and Jennifer Erwitt (Eds.). *24 Hours in Cyberspace: Photographed on One Day by 150 of the World's Leading Photojournalists.* QUE Macmillan: Against All Odds Productions, 1996.

Wolf, Mark and Bernard Perron. *The Video Game Theory Reader.* London: Routledge, 2003.

CHAPTER 6: SPORTS

Austin, Michael W. *Football and Philosophy.* Lexington: University Press of Kentucky, 2008.

Bellin, Andy. *Poker Nation: A High-Stakes, Low-Life Adventure into the Heart of a Gambling Country.* New York: Harper, 2003.

Boyle, Raymond and Richard Haynes. *Power Play: Sport, the Media and Popular Culture.* New York: Longman, 2000.

Bloom, John and Michael Nevin Willard. *Sports Matters: Race, Recreation, and Culture.* New York: NYU Press, 2002.

Brisick, Jamie and J. H. Behar. *Have Board, Will Travel: The Definitive History of Surf, Skate, and Snow.* New York: HarperCollins Publishers, 2008.

Crawford, Garry. *Consuming Sport; Fans, Sport and Culture.* New York: Routledge, 2004.

David, Paulo. *Human Rights in Youth Sport.* New York: Routledge, 2004.

Eitzen, D. Stanley. *Fair and Foul: Beyond the Myths and Paradoxes of Sport.* New York: Rowman & Littlefield, 2006.

Gerdy, John R. *Sports: The All-American Addiction.* Mississippi: University Press of Mississippi, 2002.

McLaughlin, Thomas. *Give and Go: Basketball as a Cultural Practice.* New York: State University of New York Press, 2008.

Miller, Toby. *Sportsex.* Philadelphia: Temple University Press, 2002.

Munslow, Alun (Foreword) and Murray G. Phillips (Editor). *Deconstructing Sport History: A Postmodern Analysis.* New York: State University of New York Press, 2006.

Platt, Larry. *New Jack Jocks: Rebels, Race, and the American Athlete.* Philadelphia: Temple University Press, 2002.

Rinehart, Robert E. and Synthia Sydnor. *To the Extreme: Alternative Sports, Inside and Out.* New York: State University of New York Press, 2003.

Sugden, John and Alan Tomlinson. *A Critical Sociology of Sport.* New York: Routledge, 2002.

Vlasich. James A. (Editor). *Horsehide, Pigskin, Oval Tracks and Apple Pie: Essays on Sport and American Culture.* McFarland & Company, 2005.

Walker, James R. and Robert V. Bellamy. *Center Field Shot: A History of Baseball on Television.* Lincoln: University of Nebraska Press, 2008.

Weyland, Jocko. *The Answer Is Never: A Skateboarder's History of the World*. New York: Grove Press, 2002.

Whitaker, Matthew C. *African American Icons of Sport: Triumph, Courage, and Excellence*. Westport: Greenwood Publishing Group, 2008.

Wilcox, Ralph C. et al. *Sporting Dystopias: The Making and Meaning of Urban Sport Cultures*. New York: State University of New York Press, 2003.

CHAPTER 7: MOVIES

Beltran, Mary and Camilla Fojas. *Mixed Race Hollywood*. New York: New York University Press, 2008.

Benshoff, Harry M. and Sean Griffin. *America on Film: Representing Race, Class, Gender, and Sexuality at the Movies*. New York: Blackwell, 2003.

Briley, Ron and Deborah A. Carmichael. *All-Stars and Movie Stars*. Fredricksburg: University Press of Kentucky, 2008.

Charyn, Jerome. *Raised by Wolves: The Turbulent Art and Times of Quentin Tarantino*. New York: Thunder's Mouth Press, 2006.

Denzin, Norman K. *Images of Postmodern Society: Social Theory and Contemporary Cinema*. New York: Sage Publications, 2001.

Dixon, Wheeler Winston. *Straight: Constructions of Heterosexuality in the Cinema*. New York: State University of New York Press, 2003.

Dunne, Michael. *Intertextual Encounters in American Fiction, Film, and Popular Culture*. Bowling Green, KY: Popular Press, 2001.

Fredriksen, Paula (Editor). *On* The Passion of the Christ: *Exploring the Issues Raised by the Controversial Movie*. Berkeley: University of California Press, 2006.

Fuller-Seeley, Kathryn H. *Hollywood in the Neighborhood: Historical Case Studies of Local Moviegoing*. Berkeley: University of California Press, 2008.

Griffiths, Alison. *Shivers down Your Spine: Cinema and the History of the Immersive View*. New York: Columbia University Press, 2008.

Grundmann, Roy. *Andy Warhol's Blow Job: Culture and the Moving Image*. Philadelphia: Temple University Press, 2003.

Iton, Richard. *In Search of the Black Fantastic: Politics and Popular Culture in the Post-Civil Rights Era*. New York: Oxford University Press, 2008.

Lindlof, Thomas R. *Hollywood Under Siege: Martin Scorsese, the Religious Right, and the Culture Wars*. Fredricksburg: University Press of Kentucky, 2008.

May, Larry. *The Big Tomorrow: Hollywood and the Politics of the American Way*. Chicago: University of Chicago Press, 2002.

McGowan, Todd. *Real Gaze: Film Theory after Lacan*. New York: State University of New York Press, 2008.

Phillips, Kendall R. *Controversial Cinema: The Films That Outraged America*. Westport: Greenwood Publishing, 2008.

Rodriguez, Clara. *Heroes, Lovers, and Others: The Story of Latinos in Hollywood*. New York: Oxford University Press, 2008.

Rueschmann, Eva. *Moving Pictures, Migrating Identities*. Mississippi: University Press of Mississippi, 2003.

Skal, David. *The Monster Show: A Cultural History of Horror*. Boston: Faber & Faber, 2001.

Trice, Ashton D. and Samuel A. Holland. *Heroes, Antiheroes and Dolts: Portrayals of Masculinity in American Popular Films 1921–1999*. New York: McFarland & Company, 2001.

Acknowledgments

TEXT CREDITS

p. 10 Tham, Hilary, "Barbie's Shoes," from *Men And Other Strange Myths*. Copyright © 1994 by Hilary Tham Goldberg. Reprinted by permission of Lynne Rienner Publishers, Inc.

p. 12 Leo, John, "The Indignation of Barbie," by John Leo from *U.S. News and World Report*. Copyright © October 12, 1992 *U.S. News and World Report*. Reprinted by permission.

p. 15 Motz, Marilyn Ferris, "'Seen Through Rose-Tinted Glasses': The Barbie Doll in American History" from Jack Nachbar and Kevin Lause, eds., *Popular Culture: An Introductory Text*. Copyright © 1992. Reprinted with the permission of Popular Press, an imprint of The University of Wisconsin Press.

p. 43 Muhlstein, Carolyn, "Role-Model Barbie: Now and Forever?" Reprinted with the permission of the author.

p. 49 Kalle Lasn, "The Cult You're In." Reprinted with the permission of the author.

p. 54 Roy Fox, "Salespeak" from Mediaspeak. Copyright © 2001 by Roy F. Fox. Reprinted with the permission of Greenwood Publishing Group, Westport, CT.

p. 71 Jib Fowles, "Advertising's Fifteen Basic Appeals" from *Advertising and Popular Culture*. © 1996 Sage Publications. Reprinted with permission.

p. 89 John E. Calfee, "How Advertising Informs to Our Benefit." Reprinted with the permission of the author.

p. 102 Jennifer L. Pozner, "You're Soaking In It" from Salon.com (January 30, 2001). Copyright © 2001. Reprinted with the permission of Salon.com.

p. 112 "Marilyn Y. Jones, Andrea J.S. Stanaland, and Betsy D. Gelb "Beefcake and Cheesecake: Insights for Advertisers," from *Journal of Advertising* 27, n. 2 (Summer 1998): pp. 33–52. Copyright © 1998 by American Academy of Advertising. Reprinted with permission of M.E. Sharpe, Inc. All rights reserved. Not for reproduction.

p. 137 Harry Waters, "Life According to TV" from *Newsweek* (December 6, 1982). Copyright © 1982 by Newsweek, Inc. All rights reserved. Reprinted with permission.

p. 147 Robert Kubey and Mihaly Csikszentmihaly, "Television Addiction Is No Mere Metaphor" from *Scientific American* 286 (February 2002). Copyright © 2002 by Scientific American, Inc. Reprinted by permission. All rights reserved.

p. 156 Steven Johnson, "Watching TV Makes You Smarter" from *The New York Times*, April 25, 2005. Copyright © 2005 by The New York Times Company. Reprinted with permission. All rights reserved.

p. 168 Clay Shirkey, "Gin, Television, and Social Surplus" from http://www.shirky.com/herecomeseverybody/2008/04/looking-for-the-mouse.html.

p. 175 Russell L. Peterson, "Losing Our Religion," from *Strange Bedfellows: How Late Night Comedy Turns Democracy into a Joke*, pp. 5–20. Copyright © 2008 by Russell L. Peterson. Reprinted by permission of Rutgers University Press.

p. 191 Gerald J. Erion, "Amusing Ourselves to Death with Television News: Jon Stewart, Neil Postman, and the Huxleyan Warning," in The Daily Show and Philosophy. Jason Holt, Ed. (Malden, MA: Blackwell, 2007): pp. 5–15.

p. 201 Jeffrey P. Jones , "'Fake' News versus 'Real' News as Sources of Political Information: The Daily Show and Postmodern Political Reality," in Politicotainment: Television's Take on the Real. Kristina Riegert, Ed. (New York: Peter Lang, 2007): 129-149.

p. 229 Rachel E. Sullivan, "Rap and Race: It's Got a Nice Beat, But What About the Message?" from *Journal of Black Studies* 33, no. 5 (May 2003). Copyright © 2003 by Sage Publications, Inc. Reprinted with the permission of the publisher.

p. 244 Evelyn Jamilah, "The Miseducation of Hip-Hop" from *Black Issues in Higher Education* 17 (December 7, 2000).

p. 253 "5 Things that Killed Hip-Hop," J-Zone. Republished from HipHopDX.com and .myspace.com/jzoneoldmaid.

p. 263 John Seabrook, "The Money Note: Can the Record Business Be Saved?" from *The New Yorker* 79:18 (July 2003). Copyright © 2003 by John Seabrook. Reprinted with the permission of the author.

p. 288 David Hayes, "Take Those Old Records Off the Shelf: Youth and Music Consumption in the Postmodern Age," from *Popular Music and Society*, Feb., 2006. Reprinted by permission of the publisher (Taylor & Francis Ltd. http://www.informaworld.com).

p. 310 Ian Inglis, "Sex and Drugs and Rock 'n' Roll: Urban Legends and Popular Music" from *Popular Music and Society*, Volume 30, Issue 5 Dec. 2007, pages 591-603. Reprinted by permission of the publisher (Taylor & Francis Ltd. http://www.informaworld.com).

p. 328 Bethany Klein, "In Perfect Harmony: Popular Music and Cola Advertising," from *Popular Music and Society*, Volume 31, Issue 1 February 2008, pages 1–20. Reprinted by permission of the publisher (Taylor & Francis Ltd. http://www.informaworld.com).

p. 359 Robert Samuels, "Beyond Borders," Reprinted by permission of the author.

p. 363 Neil Postman, "The Judgment of Thamus," from *Technopoly: The Surrender of Culture to Technology*. Copyright © 1992 by Neil Postman. Used by permission of Alfred A. Knopf, a division of Random House, Inc.

p. 377 Nick Yee, "The Labor of Fun: How Video Games Blur the Boundaries of Work and Play," from *Games and Culture* v1, n1 (January 2006): 68–71.

p. 383 James Paul Gee, "Good Video Games, the Human Mind, and Good Learning," in *Good Video Games + Good Learning* (New York; Peter Lang, 2007): pp. 22–44.

p. 408 Bret A. Bumgarner, "You Have Been Poked: Exploring the Uses and Gratifications of Facebook Among Emerging Adults," from *First Monday* v.12,

n. 11 (November 2007): http://www.uic.edu/htbin/cgiwrap/bin/ojs/index.php/fm/article/viewArticle/2026/1897.

p. 422 Danah Boyd, "Why Youth (Heart) Social Network Sites: The Role of Networked Publics in Teenage Social Life." MacArthur Foundation Series on Digital Learning—Youth, Identity, and Digital Media Volume (ed. David Buckingham). 2007. Cambridge, MA: MIT Press.

p. 455 William Dowell and the Editors of *Time Magazine*, "Life on the Edge" from *Time* 154, no. 10 (September 6, 1999). Copyright © 1999 by Time, Inc. Reprinted with permission.

p. 464 Maya Angelou, "Champion of the World" from *I Know Why the Caged Bird Sings*. Copyright © 1969 by Maya Angelou. Reprinted with the permission of Random House, Inc.

p. 468 Adam Gopnik, "The Unbeautiful Game," from *The New Yorker*, January 8, 2007. Copyright © 2007 Conde Naste Publications. All rights reserved.

p. 480 Jaime Schultz, "Discipline and Push-Up: Female Bodies, Feminism, and Sexuality in Popular Representations of Sports Bras" from *Sociology of Sport Journal* 1 (June 2004). Copyright © 2004 by Human Kinetics Publishers, Inc. Reprinted with the permission of the author and Human Kinetics (Champaign, IL).

p. 508 Justin Peters, "Jack of Smarts: Why the Internet Generation Loves to Play Poker," from *Washington Monthly*, May, 2004.

p. 513 John McPhee, "The Search for Marvin Garden," from *The Fourth Genre: Contemporary Writers of/on Creative Nonfiction*, 4/E. Robert L. Root, Jr., Central Michigan University, and Michael J. Steinberg, Michigan State University. ISBN-10: 0321434846, ISBN-13: 9780321434845. Publisher: Longman/Prentice Hall. Copyright: 2007, Published: 07/11/2006.

p. 524 Jill Lepore, "The Meaning of Life." Jill Lepore, from *The New Yorker*, May 21, 2007. Copyright © 2007. Reprinted by permission of the author.

p. 537 Peter Cary, Randy Dotinga, and Avery Comarow, "Fixing Kids' Sports," in *U.S. News & World Report*, May 30, 2004. Copyright © 2004 U.S. News & World Report, L.P. Reprinted with permission.

p. 552 Sydney Pollack, "The Way We Are" from *Film Comment*, September/October 1975.

p. 562 Saul Austerlitz, "The Politics of Moviemaking" from *MovieMaker* (Fall 2004). Copyright © 2004 by Saul Austerlitz. Reprinted with the permission of the author.

p. 572 Kyle Bishop, "Raising the Dead," from *Journal of Popular Film and Television* v. 33 no. 4 (Winter 2006) p. 196-205. Reprinted with permission of the Helen Dwight Reid Educational Foundation. Published by Heldref Publications, 1319 Eighteenth Street, NW, Washington, DC 20036-1802. Copyright © 2006.

p. 591 David Denby, "A Fine Romance," David Denby from *The New Yorker*, July 23, 2007. Copyright © 2007 Conde Nast Publications. All rights reserved.

p. 603 Alex Wainer, "Freaks, Geeks, and Mensches," from http://www.breakpoint.org/listingarticle.asp?ID=7282. Reprinted by permission of the author.

p. 609 Alan Stone with foreword by Joshua Cohen, from *Movies and the Moral Adventure of Life*, pp. 53–66, © 2007 Massachusetts Institute of Technology, by permission of The MIT Press.

p. 617 Thomas de Zengotita, "She'll Kill Bill While You Chill." Reprinted with the permission of the author.

PHOTOGRAPH AND ILLUSTRATION CREDITS

Chapter 1:   p. 1 Dan Krauss/AP Wide World Photos

Chapter 2:   p. 46 Timex Corporation; p. 54 Adbusters, Inc.; p. 111 The Mary Boone Gallery, New York

Chapter 3:   p. 135 The New Yorker Collection. 1991. Glen Baxter from cartoonbank.com. All Rights Reserved; p. 146 Santa Barbara News-Press

Chapter 4:   p. 227 Lou Dematteis\Corbis/Reuters America LLC

Chapter 5:   p. 357 Victor Habbick Visions/Photo Researchers, Inc.

Chapter 6:   p. 453 Mark J. Terrill/AP Wide World Photos; p. 457 AP Wide World Photos; p. 459 John Storey/Getty Images/Time Life Pictures; p. 466 AP Wide World Photos

Chapter 7:   p. 550 Universal City Studios, Inc./Photofest; p. 558 Getty Images, Inc./Hulton Archive Photos; p. 626 Suzanne Hanover/Universal\Picture Desk, Inc./Kobal Collection

Color insert: p. CI-1 (top) Aaron Goodman; (bottom) Kimmy McCann; p. CI-2 (top) Adbusters, Inc.; (bottom) Tom Allison and Chris Gomien/Carl Solway Gallery; p. CI-3 Andrew Haagen\Corbis/Outline; p. CI-4 Getty Images/Time Life Pictures; p. CI-5 Picture Desk, Inc./Kobal Collection; p. CI-6 Picture Desk, Inc./Kobal Collection; p. CI-7 Mike Blake/Corbis/Reuters America LLC; p. CI-8 Suzanne Hanover/Universal\Picture Desk, Inc./Kobal Collection

Index by Author and Title

Index by Rhetorical Mode